American, African, and Old European Mythologies

American, African, and Old European Mythologies

Compiled by

YVES BONNEFOY

Translated under the direction of

WENDY DONIGER

by Gerald Honigsblum,
Danielle Beauvais, Teresa Lavender Fagan, Dorothy Figuiera,
Barry Friedman, Louise Guiney, John Leavitt,
Michael Sells, Bruce Sullivan, and David White

The University of Chicago Press • *Chicago and London*

YVES BONNEFOY,
a scholar and poet of world renown, is
professor of comparative poetics, Collège de France.
Among his many works to have appeared in English, two
have been published by the University of Chicago Press—a
volume of poetry, *In the Shadow's Light* (1991), and a work
of criticism, *The Act and Place of Poetry* (1989), both
translated by John T. Naughton.

WENDY DONIGER
is the Mircea Eliade Professor in the
Divinity School, and professor in the Department of South
Asian Languages and Civilizations, the Committee on Social
Thought, and the College, at the University of Chicago.
Under the name of Wendy Doniger O'Flaherty she has written,
among other books, *Women, Androgynes, and Other Mythical
Beasts* (1980), *Dreams, Illusion, and Other Realities* (1984),
and *Tales of Sex and Violence: Folklore, Sacrifice, and
Danger in the Jaiminīya Brāhmaṇa* (1985), all published
by the University of Chicago Press.

The University of Chicago Press, Chicago 60637
The University of Chicago Press, Ltd., London

This paperback is drawn from *Mythologies*, compiled by
Yves Bonnefoy, translated under the direction of Wendy Doniger,
and published by the University of Chicago Press in 1991.
That work was originally published as *Dictionnaire
des mythologies et des religions des sociétés traditionnelles et
du monde antique*, sous la direction de Yves Bonnefoy
publié avec le concours du Centre National
des Lettres, © 1981, Flammarion, Paris.

The preparation of the complete English edition was
supported by grants from the French Ministry of Culture,
the Andrew W. Mellon Foundation, and the
National Endowment for the Humanities.

This book is printed on acid-free paper.

Paperback ISBN: 0-226-06457-3

Library of Congress Cataloging-in-Publication Data

Dictionnaire des mythologies et des religions des sociétés
traditionnelles et du monde antique. English. Selections.
    American, African, and Old European mythologies / compiled by Yves
Bonnefoy ; translated under the direction of Wendy Doniger by Gerald
Honigsblum . . . [et al.].
        p.   cm.
    Translation of selections from: Dictionnaire des mythologies et
des religions des sociétiés traditionnelles et du monde antique.
    Includes bibliographical references and index.
    1. Religion, Primitive—Encyclopedias.   2. Indians—Religion and
mythology—Encyclopedias.   3. Mythology, West African—
Encyclopedias.   4. Mythology, European—Encyclopedias.
I. Bonnefoy, Yves.   II. Title.
BL430.D5313   1993
291.1'3—dc20   92-39231
                                                                    CIP

Contents

PART 3 AFRICA

PART 4 CELTS, NORSE, SLAVS, CAUCASIANS, AND THEIR NEIGHBORS

Preface to the Paperback Edition

This is one of four paperback volumes drawn from the full, clothbound, two-volume English-language edition of Yves Bonnefoy's *Mythologies*. These paperback volumes are not an afterthought but were part of the publication plan from the beginning. Indeed, one of the reasons why we restructured the original French edition as we did was to make these separate volumes ultimately available. For although there is a sweep and majesty in the full edition, both in French and in English, a breathtaking scope that is the true raison d'être of the work as a whole, there is also, in the English version, a pattern that allows readers to focus on one culture at a time. And it is with such readers in mind that the University of Chicago Press has issued these paperbacks. Together, they cover almost all of the full edition: along with the present volume, the series includes *Roman and European Mythologies*, *Asian Mythologies*, and *Greek and Egyptian Mythologies*. Each contains, in addition to the culturally specific material, the prefaces and the general introductory section of the full work, which deal with methodological issues relevant to any part of it.

Since each culture poses different problems, and each section of essays embodies the work of a different group of French scholars, each section has its own methodological flavor and makes its own contribution to the more culturally specific study of mythology. This volume, combining three cultural groupings (African, American, and Old European), presents three different sorts of challenges to our conceptual frameworks of categorization, two of them diametrically opposed to one another.

To begin with, the adjective "American" may be misleading, for it refers not to what citizens of the United States tend to regard as American (that which pertains to "America the Beautiful," the fifty states), but to what citizens of other countries (including Canadians, who are sometimes justly disgruntled at our onomastic imperialism) regard as American, that which pertains to all three parts of the Americas—North, South, and Meso (or Central). American mythology in the first sense does exist of course; it is the Swedish-American mythology of Paul Bunyan and the African-American mythology of Br'er Fox and Br'er Rabbit, the mythology of Europeans and Africans who planted in the New World the seeds that they brought with them from the ancient traditions of their original homelands. American mythology of this sort would also include stories about cowboys and Indians, about

George Washington and Abraham Lincoln, about Mike Fink and John Henry and Joe Hill, perhaps even stories about Jack Kennedy. Many scholars would regard this sort of American mythology as legend or folklore rather than as mythology in the narrower sense of religious narrative. In any case, it is not a part of this collection.

But American mythology in the sense in which this collection was conceived is a body of narrative that traces its roots back to a time long before Europeans or Africans reached the shores of the New World. It is the mythology of the people we used to call "pre-Columbian" (as if they had been waiting around all those centuries for Columbus to appear so that they could at last enter the story of civilization) but now call Native Americans. It is a mythology that stretches from the Inuit on the northernmost tip of the New World, the Central Arctic, to the Tupi Guarani of Tierra del Fuego, at the bottom of the New World. This body of stories survived, adapted, changed, and appeared in new transformations even when most of the storytellers, and most of their civilizations, had been destroyed by the invaders from the Old World.

So much for the first group. But is it, in fact, a group at all? I think it is. Geographically there are undeniable links, and the perceptive reader of this volume will see other sorts of links as well, common tropes and images that form a bridge between cultures that share little else, neither language nor ecology, neither political/economic systems nor religious worldviews. Can we go beyond this group of American myths to include African myths? Here we encounter our second major problem of categorization. African mythologies have a geographical contiguity that might justify some sort of grouping, despite the great variety in linguistic and other cultural forms among Dogon and Dinka, Bantu speakers and Kabyles. This variety makes it essential at least to distinguish sub-Saharan from Northern, and East African from Western, as our subgroupings imply and allow. Indeed, the mythologies represented here are almost entirely from sub-Saharan, Western Africa, which is hardly surprising since this is also Francophone Africa, the Africa that the French know best both politically and academically.

But how useful is it to group African and American mythologies together? It has long been the habit of Western scholars to group African and American and Oceanic mythologies together, usually (at least since Lévy-Bruhl) under some pejorative term such as "primitive" or "savage." In recent decades, more politically sensitive scholars have tried to use less value-laden words, like "tribal" or "preindustrial" or "third world," but these attempts hardly provide a solution, since the problem resides not in the choice of a word for a group but in the decision to look for *any* word at all to group together peoples so disparate as Inuit and Papuan. Treating them as a single group implies that their individual differences are relatively unimportant in comparison with the really important fact that, unlike us, they have no written texts, or no internal combustion engines, or no "rationality."

To avoid such false identification of American and African mythologies, we decided to add a third group to this volume, the group that we are calling "Old European"—Celts, Norse, Slavs, Caucasians, Teutons, and what for want of a more precise term we have called "their neighbors." Indeed, "Old European" is hardly a laser-sharp focus in the first place, even if we assume that readers will not think that the term designates octogenarian Frenchmen. And here we encounter a problem of categorization that is the mirror image of the problem presented by grouping Africans or Americans, let alone Africans-and-Americans, culturally diverse peoples for

whom we have widely used though inappropriate terms. For the peoples that we have called "Old Europeans" are in fact closely linked historically, linguistically, and geographically, but we have no adequate word for them as a group. We cannot call them "Indo-Europeans" without including the other members of that group, such as the ancient Greeks and Romans (who have two volumes of their own in this paperback series), and no other term has any recognizable currency. But since we do believe that it is useful to read their mythologies as a group, we have settled for the slightly awkward "Old European," given that these cultures are all geographically circumscribed by what we now call Europe, and that they are rooted in an ancient time in which the links between them were even closer than they are now.

Here, then, are three groups of mythologies that bear far stronger ties within each group than between any one group and another. The reader who reads through each of them in turn will come away, I believe, with a rich sense of the cultural diversity of mythologies.

Wendy Doniger

Preface to the English Edition of the Complete Work

Yves Bonnefoy in his preface (which follows this preface) explains why he organized his book—and after all, this is his book—as he did. He had good reasons, and he is eloquent in their defense. But it remains for me to explain the ways in which the English edition differs from the French in more than the language in which it is expressed, since some of what M. Bonnefoy will say does not in fact apply to this edition at all, particularly in what concerns the arrangement of the articles.

M. Bonnefoy graciously if reluctantly allowed me to re-structure his work. As he put it, "Of course I will miss the formula of the dictionary, for the reasons that I indicate in my preface (the rupture with all the apriority of classification, the possibility of surprising juxtapositions, in short, the irony), *but I absolutely do not oppose* your choice, which is in response to very good reasons, and which is better adapted to the English-speaking world in which your edition will appear. I therefore give you carte blanche, with the understanding that you will publish my preface as is. For it is a good idea to point out that the book was originally what I indicate in that preface—this will bring in a supplementary point for reflection."[1] On another occasion,[2] he remarked that there was another consideration (one that, I must confess, had not occurred to me) that had persuaded him to organize his original version of the book in what he termed "the random way," while we might be able to rearrange our version in "the more organized way": French students, he pointed out, have only limited access to open stacks in the French libraries (since there is not enough room to accommodate them) and few of the bookstores are quiet enough to read in. French students therefore have apparently not formed the habit of browsing—except in a dictionary.

Without denying the validity of his arguments, let me state my reasons for the reorganization. And in order to justify the changes, I shall first state my conception of the strengths and weaknesses of the French work itself.

The Strengths and Weaknesses of the French Edition

To begin with, even in its French form, with all the articles arranged alphabetically, it is not a dictionary, nor even an encyclopedia, nor a dispassionate fact-book even for those topics that it covers (and many major items are omitted). It is a quirky and idiosyncratic set of essays, long and short, by a particular group of mythologists, most of whom are French and all of whom participate in the French school of mythology in its broadest sense. The patent omissions and biases have prompted a certain amount of criticism leveled at the French edition,[3] criticism of imbalances, of inconsistencies (in the selection of topics, in the manner of their treatment, in the style, in the methodologies, etc.), and of the choice of illustrations, as well as more substantive criticisms of the interpretations.

Some of these criticisms are just; some are not. The arguments about what *is* there (what is said about the mythologies that are discussed) are interesting; the arguments about what is *not* there are, I think, beside the point. Many of the scholars involved in the project chose not to write about what other people (including certain reviewers) regarded as "central" or "basic" themes of the mythologies they treated; they wrote long essays on the subjects they cared about personally, and gave short shrift to subjects to which other scholars might have given pride of place. The reader who continues perversely to look for ways in which the glass is half empty rather than half full will notice immediately, for instance, that there is almost nothing about Islam or Judaism in the book. This is primarily because Yves Bonnefoy had originally intended to save this material for another volume, on the mythologies of monotheistic religions—a volume that has not yet materialized. It might be argued that this justification is disingenuous, for some of the very best material in the extant volume is on Christianity, which is by most standards monotheistic. But on closer inspection it is quite clear that while the book does treat the appropriation of classical mythology by Christianity, and the incorporation of "pagan mythologies" into what might be called "rural Catholicism," it rightly does not treat main-stream, monotheistic Christianity as a mythology. Moreover, to have dealt with the central traditions of Islam and Judaism in this way would certainly have been tantamount to a betrayal of what the adherents of those religions regard as their basic tenets. Yet this Jewish and Islamic silence is also in part accounted for by the simple fact that the authors who were assembled to prepare this book did not choose to write articles on these subjects. Similarly, the African articles deal almost exclusively (though hardly surprisingly) with Francophone Africa; yet these articles constitute superb paradigms for the study of other African mythologies. So, too, there are only two articles on Buddhism per se, and there is virtually nothing about Buddhism (or Islam, for that matter) in Southeast Asia (though there is a great deal of wonderful material about indigenous Southeast Asian religions, and those two articles on Buddhism are fascinating). On the other hand, there is extensive coverage of the Turks and Mongols, whose mythologies are relatively unknown to Western readers. This sort of imbalance might be regarded as a kind of mythological affirmative action.

This is, therefore, certainly not an encyclopedia. In a famous painting by the surrealist René Magritte, a caption in his neat script, under a painting of what is clearly a pipe, declares, "This is not a pipe." I would have liked to write on the cover of this book, "This is not a dictionary of mythologies." Rather like the ugly duckling that turned out to be a terrific swan, as a dictionary this book leaves much to be desired, but as a book of mythologies it is superb, indeed peerless. If it is not a dictionary, what *is* it, then? It is a most exciting (far more exciting than an encyclopedia ought to be) collection of essays on *some* aspects of *some* mythologies, written by a group of brilliant and philosophically complex French scholars. It is highly opinionated and original, and should inspire hot, not cold, reactions. Like all multiauthored works, it is a mixed bag; there is some jargon, some wild theorizing, some boring surveys, some overclever interpretation, and some of what I would regard as simple errors of fact, but there is also an overwhelming proportion of very sound and/or brilliant articles about mythology in general and about a number of mythologies in particular. This is not primarily a book, for instance, to consult for all the stories about Apollo; one has Robert Graves for that (though this is a far better book with which to begin to formulate some ideas about the meaning of Apollo). It is, however, a book in which to discover the delightful and useful fact that in the ritual celebration of the Brazilian god Omolu, who is of Yoruba origin but came to be syncretized with Saint Lazarus, people dance to a beat called "he kills someone and eats him." I was thrilled to come upon a hauntingly sad and beautiful Inuit myth about the cycle of transmigration of a mistreated woman, a myth that agrees, in astonishing detail, with certain complex myths of transmigration that I know from medieval Sanskrit philosophical texts. Other readers will undoubtedly stumble upon strange stories that are curiously familiar to them—stumble upon them quite by chance, just as Yves Bonnefoy intended them to do.

But if the selection is not as complete as a dictionary should ideally be, neither is it as arbitrary as a nondictionary can be. Most of the great mythological traditions are covered, and within those areas most of the important myths are treated. But this is not the point. What is treated very thoroughly indeed is the problem of *how to understand a mythology*, what questions to ask, what patterns to look for. More precisely, this is a book that demonstrates what happens when a combination of two particular methodologies, those of Georges Dumézil and Claude Lévi-Strauss, is applied to *any* mythology. It is, as its title claims (in English as in French), not so much a book about myths (sacred narratives) as a book about mythologies (whole systems of myths, or even systems of ideas about myths). It is that rare and wonderful fusion, a book about methodology that simultaneously puts the methodology to work and shows you just what it can and cannot do. It is a mythodology.

Many of these articles tell the reader how to study mythology in general and, more important, how to study each particular body of mythology, how to solve (or, more often, to approach) the particular problems that each mythology presents. Some tell the reader why it is not possible to write an article about that particular mythology at all (a consideration that does not, however, prevent the author from writing the article in which this assertion is made). The most hilarious example of this (I will leave the reader to decide which article it is) is almost an unconscious satire on the pusillanimity of scholars in certain fields; in it, the author goes on for pages and pages (it is one of the longest articles in the book) telling us, over and over, why there are insufficient data, why the data that we have are skewed, why the extant interpretations of the data are skewed, why all hypotheses and generalizations about the data are worthless, why in fact it is impossible to make any valid statement about the mythology at all. This is in its way a masterpiece, a kind of Zen nonarticle on a nonsubject, a surreal piece of nonscholarship worthy of Samuel Beckett. And yet even this article has its value here as a striking example of one particular methodology, one approach to the subject, that argues in great detail, and rightly, the obstacles that oppose any truly responsible survey of the subject.

But this is the exception, not the rule. The book teems with marvelous primary material, both myths and rituals (with which many myths are inextricably linked), using the materials and the methodological considerations to animate one another, the soul of data within the body of theory, and the soul of theory within the body of data. Sometimes the methodology is in the foreground, sometimes the data; usually they are in a fine balance. In the Greek and European sections, for instance, there are startling reinterpretations of well-known stories, or new emphases on previously overlooked details in well-known stories; many of the articles on the Greeks demonstrate the cutting edge of French structuralism. As Arthur Adkins has remarked, "The dictionary in its French version is a truly remarkable work. The Greek section in particular is quite unlike any other dictionary known to me. [It] for the most part presents the views of the Paris school, and the writers come out fighting. The Paris school is undoubtedly producing the most interesting work in the field at present. . . . [The work] represents more of a *parti pris* than the title 'Dictionary' may suggest."[4] The Vietnamese section, by contrast, abundantly documents a fascinating mythology that is virtually unknown to the English-speaking world, and presents it, moreover, in the context of an enlightened political awareness that is almost unprecedented in scholarly treatments of mythology anywhere (but that is also a notable virtue of the articles in this volume that deal with the Americas and Oceania).

If this is a book as much about method as it is about myths, what is the method? It is a masterpiece of what might be called trifunctional structuralism, a joint festschrift for Claude Lévi-Strauss and Georges Dumézil, a vision of the world of mythology seen through their eyes, *la vie en* Lévi-Strauss and Dumézil. To combine the methodologies of these two scholars is in itself a most extraordinary and fruitful achievement. If I may oversimplify both approaches for a moment, Lévi-Strauss's basic method, a variant of Hegelian dialectic, is to seek the intellectual or logical framework of the myth in binary oppositions that are mediated by a third term; the Dumézilian approach is to gloss the main figures of a myth in terms of three functions that have social referents: religion and government, defense, and material production. These two theories are in no way contradictory, especially if one resolves the potential conflict between Dumézilian tripartition and Lévi-Straussian bipolarization by taking into account the mediating third term and thus making Lévi-Strauss, too, tripartite. In this sense, both of them operate with triads, though very different triads. Furthermore, they complement rather than contradict one another because they focus on different levels (Lévi-Strauss on abstract intellectual concepts, Dumézil on social functions). Combined as they are in this volume, they are startlingly innovative.

Indeed, the beauty of the book is that it is not doctrinaire in its application of the theories of these two great scholars, but rather creative and imaginative. Dumézil's trifunctional analysis of Indo-European mythology is applied, quite loosely to be sure, even beyond the bounds of the Indo-European world (where it is, properly speaking, no longer trifunctional but tripartite), and a general way of thinking in terms of oppositions and inversions forms the armature of many analyses in which the name of Lévi-Strauss is not actually invoked. The search for tripartitions of both sorts is the driving force behind many of the analyses in this book.

The book is so very French that I thought seriously of putting the word "French" in the title of the English edition: *Mythologies According to the Contemporary French School*, or *The View from France*, or *Essays in the French Style, A French Collection, A Paris Collection, The French Connection*, and so forth. Yves Bonnefoy's remarks, in his preface, explaining why he chose primarily French scholars are delightfully, if unconsciously, Francophile. He has maintained elsewhere that the preponderance of French scholars was simply a natural outcome of choosing to organize the scholarship from the geographical center of the project, Paris, rather than to range over the world at random. But as anyone who has ever had the privilege of working at the Sorbonne will immediately realize, most French scholars think that the only people who know anything are other French scholars. In this instance, at least, they would be right: such is the hegemony of French scholarship in the field of mythology right now that a well-read American or British mythologist would probably draw on precisely these same "French" approaches.

This is one of the great values of the book: it represents, as few other works in any field do, the achievements of the *crème de la crème* of an entire generation of French scholarship in a large and important field. Yves Bonnefoy himself has remarked that he loves the book because it freezes a moment in time, in history, and in space; it is the embodiment of the beauty of the Ecole Pratique.

But in a way, the guiding spirit of the book is not just that of the twin gods, Dumézil and Lévi-Strauss. It is the spirit of Yves Bonnefoy himself. This is, after all, a book put together by a poet, not by a philologist. The editor of this nondictionary is also, let me hasten to say, a scholar of the first rank, but he is at heart a poet. The reader who keeps this in mind is more likely to get from the book what it has to give than the reader who picks it up hoping that it will be a kind of mythological Guinness book of records.

The Restructuring of the English Edition

We decided to restructure the book in order to minimize its weaknesses, emphasize its sometimes hidden strengths, and make it useful to the English-speaking reader in new ways. Its primary weakness is, as I have admitted, that it is not a true encyclopedia. If the English edition were arranged alphabetically, as the French edition is, readers might look for things and not find them and get mad, as some of the French reviewers did; and, on the other hand, readers might

overlook a lot of strange and beautiful essays that no one would ever dream of looking up on purpose at all.

Bonnefoy in his preface explains why he wanted to use a dictionary format: to avoid all prearranged categories, to let the reader find things by chance, to allow accidental juxtapositions to give rise to unexpected ideas. But to some extent this argues for a false naïveté on the part of the reader and even, perhaps, on the part of the editor, for both of them *are looking for something*. In choosing the arbitrariness of alphabetical order, Bonnefoy is indeed shuffling the deck; but he does still have a deck, which, like all decks, is highly structured. The alphabetical shuffle conceals the true order but does not destroy it. Thus, for instance, all the articles on a certain subject are written by a single author, an expert on that subject. Clearly the articles were originally commissioned in this way, and they are still listed this way in the front of the French edition. And each author does have his methodological presuppositions, which the reader encounters every time he or she wanders (arbitrarily, accidentally) into that territory. Bonnefoy chose to conceal the patterns that he saw in the material in order to let readers discover them by chance; I have chosen to set out in the open the patterns that I see, and to let readers decide whether or not they want to follow those patterns. The difference lies in what sort of browsing is encouraged, cross-cultural (through the French edition's physical juxtaposition of the major articles on creation or on sacrifice) or intracultural (through the English edition's grouping of all the Siberian or Celtic articles).

Several of the translators, the Honigsblums in particular, arranged the work according to geographic areas or cultures, which made it easier to check the consistent use of technical terms. Gradually it occurred to us that this arrangement would also be useful to readers. Bonnefoy chose to mix the cultures together to encourage cross-cultural *aperçus*; I chose to separate out each culture to encourage consecutive reading in each tradition. (Another, related advantage of the present arrangement lies in the fact that this arrangement will make it possible in the future to publish sections of the work as individual books, making them available to specialists in particular cultural fields.) For the overall structure I decided to use a kind of geographical swing: beginning with Africa, then traveling up through the Near East, the ancient Mediterranean, the Indo-European world; remaining in place geographically but moving forward in time to later European culture, then back in time to South Asia; on in both space and time to Southeast Asia, East Asia, Inner Asia; across the Bering Strait to North America, South America; and finishing the journey paradisiacally in the South Pacific. Within each category of culture (Greek, Celtic, etc.), I have put the long, meditative, general essays first, and the shorter, more straightforward dictionary entries second. Several pathbreaking essays that are not tied to a particular culture, and that immediately establish the Dumézilian and structuralist stance of the book, form an introductory sequence.

Of course, since both the French and the English editions have detailed indexes, and the French edition has an outline listing the articles according to cultures, it comes down to a matter of emphasis, for in either edition the reader can find materials that are arranged alphabetically (both in the index and in the body of the work in the French edition, and in the index in the English edition) as well as materials that are grouped according to the culture (in the outline of the French edition, and in the body of the work in the English edition). In the restructured English edition, the reader can still use the index as Bonnefoy suggests the French index might be used, to find his or her favorite Naiad or Norse god, and also to find all the articles on, say, creation, or sacrifice, which cut across methodological lines. This is, after all, the same book, and can ultimately be used in all the same ways.

New problems arise out of this rearrangement, however, for some cultures don't really fit into any of the large categories—Turks and Mongols, Armenians and Albanians, Ossets and Georgians, Siberians, Malagasy, Maghreb—and so I had to settle for putting them where they seemed least out of place. Another disadvantage of my rearrangement is the fact that it exposes repetitions, necessary in an encyclopedia (where the author of any one article, who cannot assume that the reader will have read any other article, may therefore have to resupply a certain amount of basic material), but rather jarring in a book such as this (where the reader may well find it annoying to read the same story, or the same theory, almost verbatim in consecutive articles). A good example of this recycling is provided by the very first part, on West Africa, with its recurrent motifs of twinning and sexual mutilation; another occurs in the South Asian section, which pivots around the sacrificial pole and the avatar.

I decided not to cut any of these repetitions, however, for several reasons. First of all, I decided not to abridge or revise (a decision I will attempt to justify below). Second, some readers may only pick up isolated articles and will therefore need the basic information that also appears in other articles. And, finally, these repetitions demonstrate how certain scholars always think in terms of a limited number of particular myths, dragging them into whatever other subject they are supposed to be discussing. For scholars, like their native informants, do just what Lévi-Strauss says they do: they continually rework the same themes in a kind of academic bricolage, and no two variants are ever *quite* alike.

For the most part, I think the rearrangement is a positive move. For one thing, it makes it possible to *read* the book, instead of merely browsing in it or looking things up in it (though, as I have said, readers can still engage in both of these activities in the English edition). For another, it may prove more useful in this form not only to mythophiles and area specialists, but to people interested in French anthropology and philosophy.

The book is therefore *re*structured, because of course it was originally highly structured, ideologically if not organizationally. Its English title, *Mythologies,* to me echoes the wonderful books by Roland Barthes and William Butler Yeats, both with the same title, and further resonates with the French title of the great Lévi-Strauss trilogy, *Mythologiques* (treacherously translated in one English edition as *A Science of Mythology*). *Mythologies* has, finally, the advantage of being simultaneously an English and a French word, a last attempt at bilinguality before the Fall into the English version.

The English Translation

This edition was prepared "under my direction" in not nearly so important a sense as the original was "sous la direction de Yves Bonnefoy." Certain parallel procedures probably exacerbated rather than minimized the inevitable slip twixt French cup and English lip, and one of these was the employment of a team of English scholars to translate the text that was originally composed by a team of French scholars.

Gerald Honigsblum translated the entire second volume of the French edition, with the editorial assistance of Bonnie Birtwistle Honigsblum. The first volume was translated by a group of professional translators (Danielle Beauvais, Teresa Lavender Fagan, Louise Guiney, Louise Root, Michael Sells) and another group consisting of some of my students in the history of religions (Dorothy Figueira, Barry Friedman, Daniel Gold, John Leavitt, and David White). Their initials follow those of the original authors of the French articles. Bruce Sullivan did the bibliographies.

The translated articles were then checked for accuracy (in the transliteration of names, technical terms, and so forth) by specialists in each of the particular fields. Arthur Adkins did by far the most difficult task, working painstakingly and courageously through the enormous and often very tricky articles on the Greeks and Romans. Lawrence Sullivan vetted Africa and the Americas for us; Robert Ritner, Egypt; Walter Farber, Mesopotamia; Dennis Pardee, Semites; Richard Beal, Hittites; Laurie Patton, Celts; Ann Hoffman, Norse; Zbigniew Golab, Slavs; Frank Paul Bowman, Richard Luman, and David Tracy, early Christianity; Anthony Grafton, medieval and renaissance Europe; Françoise Meltzer, modern Europe; Charles Keyes, Southeast Asia; Anthony Yu and Jane Geaney, China; Gary Ebersole, Japan; Bruce Cummings, Korea; Matthew Kapstein and Per Kvaerne, Tibet; Robert Dankoff, Turks and Mongols. I did the South Asian and Indo-Iranian sections.

There are thus several levels at which inconsistencies—in style, in format (citations of texts, abbreviations), in transliteration, in ways of dealing with specific untranslatable concepts—could have slipped in: differences between the technical languages (not to say jargons) and the methodologies employed by the various academic guilds that regard themselves as the proprietors of each culture (anthropologists in Africa, Sanskritists in India, archaeologists in Sumer, and so forth); differences between the approaches of individual French authors, between our several translators, between our experts; and, over the long haul, differences in my own decisions at particular stages of the final supervision, and in the decisions of our copyeditors at the Press. We have tried to minimize the inconsistencies, but we know that many remain.

We left the bibliographies basically in their original form, with the following exceptions: in some cases we have substituted English editions for French editions, or extended the dates of continuing series, and in several cases we have added supplementary bibliographies (clearly designated as such and distinguished from the original French text). But many bibliographies and articles still cite the French editions of texts that have subsequently appeared in English.

We did not follow the usual practice of citing standard English translations of Greek or Latin or Sanskrit works that the French, naturally enough, cited in French. Instead, we translated the French translation of the classical text into English. At first glance this procedure may seem unwise, but we found it necessary because the French version of the classical text (and the subsequent analysis, which depended upon that version) often differed so dramatically from any extant English translation that the sense of the discussion would be totally obscured by the introduction of such a translation. We made an occasional exception, using a standard English translation where there were long quotations not directly analyzed in the French text, or where the available English translation was very close to what the French author had made of the original. (We were also, unfortunately, forced to translate back into English a few citations from English primary and secondary sources that time and other constraints prevented us from obtaining in the original form, and to retranslate several entire French articles that we know were originally written in English, because the English originals were for one reason or another no longer available to us.)

We decided to give Greek and Roman names, wherever possible, in the form used by the *Oxford Classical Dictionary*, which unfortunately is inherently inconsistent. The *OCD* has the advantage of avoiding pedantry by spelling most names in the way that people in English-speaking countries are used to seeing them. This means Latinizing most of the familiar Greek names (not, of course, substituting Roman names: thus we have Heracles, not Herakles, for the Greek god, but Hercules only for the Roman god), but not Latinizing the unfamiliar Greek names, and not Romanizing any of the Greek words when they are not names. All words, including proper names, that are printed in the Greek alphabet in the French edition have here been transliterated. No accents are indicated, and macrons are used not to distinguish long and short *a*, *i*, and *u*, but only on *e* and *o*, to distinguish epsilon from eta and omicron from omega.[5]

We also sought to standardize the transliteration of non-Greek names and terms, such as Gilgameš (vs. Gilgamesh) and Śiva (vs. Shiva), and we used the Pinyin system for most Chinese names.[6] But this general policy was sometimes overruled by the demands of a particular article. We strove for consistency within each article—using English titles for Greek works where the meaning was needed and traditional Latinized titles where it was not, full citations or abbreviations as appropriate, and so forth. Assuming, perhaps snobbishly, that anyone who couldn't read French couldn't read Greek or Latin, I have translated many titles and quotations that my sanguine French colleague, Yves Bonnefoy, had left in their classical splendor. Except for the titles of certain works generally known to English speakers in their original form, and terms that either are familiar to readers or have no English equivalent, I have translated everything, even terms like *polis* (for the most part), and *savoir faire*, and, sometimes, *par excellence*. I fear that this may insult some readers, but I suspect that it will be a welcome (and in any case probably invisible) crutch to *hoi polloi*.

Despite everything, the book remains idiosyncratic, but the idiosyncrasies are in large part a true reflection of the original French edition. In general, we have not *corrected* the original text at all, since, as I noted above, the work is valuable not only for the information and ideas that it contains but for being *what it is*, a moment frozen in time, a fly in amber, an incarnation of the École Pratique as it was in 1981, warts and all. The warts include matters of style and politics, such as sexist and occasionally racist language in the original text. These problems were sometimes ameliorated and sometimes exacerbated by the transition from French to English. Thus, to ameliorate, we often chose to translate *homme* as "human" rather than "man"; but the English "savage" (often more apt than "wild" or "primitive") exacerbates the negative connotations of *sauvage*, which the French often use in a positive sense.

Our respect for the integrity of the French text made us resist the temptation to correct what we regarded as errors in that text. (Of course, we made our own errors, and unfortunately the reader who does not have the French edition will not know, if he or she finds a mistake, which side of the

Atlantic it originated on.) We certainly made no attempt to correct such major problems as wrongheaded (in my opinion) opinions, nor to decipher the impenetrable semioticisms in one or two articles or to excise the unreadable lists in others. At the other end of the spectrum, however, we did correct typographic errors and a few outright howlers (such as a reference to the *Iliad* when the *Odyssey* was clearly intended). It was trickier to decide what to do about the middle ground: infelicities of expression, repetitions, and so forth. Of course we tried to clarify unclear thoughts, though we certainly did not always succeed. But for the most part, we respected our French colleagues' right to live with their own sins.

At first we made no attempt to smooth out the English, striving only to make the French thought accessible in English, leaving it awkward when it was awkward. We did try, however, to say well in English what was well said in French. In the end, however, our collective gorge rising again and again in response to such massive proportions of translatorese and the fatal attraction of the *cliché juste*, we did try to relax the translation a bit.

By and large, I opted for fidelity over beauty. This is rather a shame, for the original French text is, on the whole, very beautiful. Not for the first time I take comfort in Claude Lévi-Strauss's famous dictum that, whereas poetry may be lost in translation, "the mythical value of myth remains preserved through the worst translation."[7] I fear that we have lost much of Yves Bonnefoy's poetry; I can only hope that we have found, for the English reader, most of Yves Bonnefoy's mythology.

Wendy Doniger

NOTES

1. YVES BONNEFOY, personal communication, 28 June 1984.
2. Notes on a meeting with Yves Bonnefoy, 6 June 1988.
3. As, for example, by ROBERT TURCAN, in "Mythologies et religions: Notes Critiques, à propos du *Dictionnaire des Mythologies . . . ,*" in *Revue de l'Histoire des Religions* 200, no. 2 (April–June 1983): 189–98.
4. ARTHUR ADKINS, personal communication, 2 March 1988.
5. Our attempt to follow, consistently, the above rule resulted in the following apparent inconsistencies. A distinction is made between the treatment of two forms of the same word when it is used both as a name and as a noun: thus we have Eros (the god) and *erōs* (the emotion), Cyclops (plural: Cyclopes) for the individual and *kuklops* for the class of creature. Exceptions to the general Latinization occur in certain familiar spellings particularly with regard to *clk* (Clytemnestra, following the regular policy, but Kronos, following general usage); to -*osl-us* (Pontus, following the rule, but Helios, following general usage); and to certain plurals (Kronides, but Oceanids and Atreidae; Melissae, but Moirai). In general, upsilon is transliterated as *y* in Latinized names, such as Polyphemus, but as *u* in nouns, such as *polumētis*. And so forth.
6. For the Yoruba names, we chose to follow the French edition in using a simplified transliteration, for the system that is technically, and politically, correct is extremely cumbersome and incompatible with the methods used in other parts of the work.
7. CLAUDE LÉVI-STRAUSS, *Structural Anthropology* (New York 1963), 210.

used, to find his or her favorite Naiad or Norse god, and also to find all the articles on, say, creation, or sacrifice, which cut across methodological lines. This is, after all, the same book, and can ultimately be used in all the same ways.

New problems arise out of this rearrangement, however, for some cultures don't really fit into any of the large categories—Turks and Mongols, Armenians and Albanians, Ossets and Georgians, Siberians, Malagasy, Maghreb—and so I had to settle for putting them where they seemed least out of place. Another disadvantage of my rearrangement is the fact that it exposes repetitions, necessary in an encyclopedia (where the author of any one article, who cannot assume that the reader will have read any other article, may therefore have to resupply a certain amount of basic material), but rather jarring in a book such as this (where the reader may well find it annoying to read the same story, or the same theory, almost verbatim in consecutive articles). A good example of this recycling is provided by the very first part, on West Africa, with its recurrent motifs of twinning and sexual mutilation; another occurs in the South Asian section, which pivots around the sacrificial pole and the avatar.

I decided not to cut any of these repetitions, however, for several reasons. First of all, I decided not to abridge or revise (a decision I will attempt to justify below). Second, some readers may only pick up isolated articles and will therefore need the basic information that also appears in other articles. And, finally, these repetitions demonstrate how certain scholars always think in terms of a limited number of particular myths, dragging them into whatever other subject they are supposed to be discussing. For scholars, like their native informants, do just what Lévi-Strauss says they do: they continually rework the same themes in a kind of academic bricolage, and no two variants are ever *quite* alike.

For the most part, I think the rearrangement is a positive move. For one thing, it makes it possible to *read* the book, instead of merely browsing in it or looking things up in it (though, as I have said, readers can still engage in both of these activities in the English edition). For another, it may prove more useful in this form not only to mythophiles and area specialists, but to people interested in French anthropology and philosophy.

The book is therefore *re*structured, because of course it was originally highly structured, ideologically if not organizationally. Its English title, *Mythologies*, to me echoes the wonderful books by Roland Barthes and William Butler Yeats, both with the same title, and further resonates with the French title of the great Lévi-Strauss trilogy, *Mythologiques* (treacherously translated in one English edition as *A Science of Mythology*). *Mythologies* has, finally, the advantage of being simultaneously an English and a French word, a last attempt at bilinguality before the Fall into the English version.

The English Translation

This edition was prepared "under my direction" in not nearly so important a sense as the original was "sous la direction de Yves Bonnefoy." Certain parallel procedures probably exacerbated rather than minimized the inevitable slip twixt French cup and English lip, and one of these was the employment of a team of English scholars to translate the text that was originally composed by a team of French scholars.

Gerald Honigsblum translated the entire second volume of the French edition, with the editorial assistance of Bonnie Birtwistle Honigsblum. The first volume was translated by a group of professional translators (Danielle Beauvais, Teresa Lavender Fagan, Louise Guiney, Louise Root, Michael Sells) and another group consisting of some of my students in the history of religions (Dorothy Figueira, Barry Friedman, Daniel Gold, John Leavitt, and David White). Their initials follow those of the original authors of the French articles. Bruce Sullivan did the bibliographies.

The translated articles were then checked for accuracy (in the transliteration of names, technical terms, and so forth) by specialists in each of the particular fields. Arthur Adkins did by far the most difficult task, working painstakingly and courageously through the enormous and often very tricky articles on the Greeks and Romans. Lawrence Sullivan vetted Africa and the Americas for us; Robert Ritner, Egypt; Walter Farber, Mesopotamia; Dennis Pardee, Semites; Richard Beal, Hittites; Laurie Patton, Celts; Ann Hoffman, Norse; Zbigniew Golab, Slavs; Frank Paul Bowman, Richard Luman, and David Tracy, early Christianity; Anthony Grafton, medieval and renaissance Europe; Françoise Meltzer, modern Europe; Charles Keyes, Southeast Asia; Anthony Yu and Jane Geaney, China; Gary Ebersole, Japan; Bruce Cummings, Korea; Matthew Kapstein and Per Kvaerne, Tibet; Robert Dankoff, Turks and Mongols. I did the South Asian and Indo-Iranian sections.

There are thus several levels at which inconsistencies—in style, in format (citations of texts, abbreviations), in transliteration, in ways of dealing with specific untranslatable concepts—could have slipped in: differences between the technical languages (not to say jargons) and the methodologies employed by the various academic guilds that regard themselves as the proprietors of each culture (anthropologists in Africa, Sanskritists in India, archaeologists in Sumer, and so forth); differences between the approaches of individual French authors, between our several translators, between our experts; and, over the long haul, differences in my own decisions at particular stages of the final supervision, and in the decisions of our copyeditors at the Press. We have tried to minimize the inconsistencies, but we know that many remain.

We left the bibliographies basically in their original form, with the following exceptions: in some cases we have substituted English editions for French editions, or extended the dates of continuing series, and in several cases we have added supplementary bibliographies (clearly designated as such and distinguished from the original French text). But many bibliographies and articles still cite the French editions of texts that have subsequently appeared in English.

We did not follow the usual practice of citing standard English translations of Greek or Latin or Sanskrit works that the French, naturally enough, cited in French. Instead, we translated the French translation of the classical text into English. At first glance this procedure may seem unwise, but we found it necessary because the French version of the classical text (and the subsequent analysis, which depended upon that version) often differed so dramatically from any extant English translation that the sense of the discussion would be totally obscured by the introduction of such a translation. We made an occasional exception, using a standard English translation where there were long quotations not directly analyzed in the French text, or where the available English translation was very close to what the French author had made of the original. (We were also, unfortunately, forced to translate back into English a few citations from English primary and secondary sources that time and other constraints prevented us from obtaining in the original form, and to retranslate several entire French

Preface to the French Edition
of the Complete Work

I

A few words of introduction, not in justification of the enterprise, but in order to clarify certain of its intentions and various points of method.

One of our primary convictions was of the need to adopt the dictionary format. Encyclopedias, invariably too lengthy to be read in a single sitting, are usually approached through the index, thereby functioning like dictionaries but with certain disadvantages that dictionaries do not have. For one thing, readers of encyclopedias are deprived of those sudden juxtapositions that alphabetical order can effect between two topics that may have something in common but occur in different contexts: chance encounters from which fresh insights can emerge. And for another thing, an encyclopedia, no matter how rationally intended the order of its contents, cannot but reflect the preconceptions of the time when it was written; it thus rapidly becomes dated and, even, from the very moment of its conception, imposes certain constraints on its readers. We have only to think of the treatises of the not very distant past and their way of drawing distinctions between the Mediterranean world and what is loosely referred to as the Orient, as if western Europeans lived at the center of the world! Progress has been made in this respect, but potentially dangerous prejudices are undeniably still at work in our thinking today. "Any classification of religions . . . will always in some way be factitious or one-sided; none is susceptible to proof," wrote Henri-Charles Puech.[1] Only alphabetical order, arbitrary by definition, can eliminate hidden dogmatism or prevent the consolidation of an error as yet unperceived as such.

Furthermore, and as a corollary to its primary task of rational organization, an encyclopedia also tends toward a kind of unity—if not homogeneity—of discourse; and because any work of this kind attempts to say the most in the least possible number of pages, there will be—in order to achieve coherent exposition of the most important material—an attenuation of what, in a monograph, would remain undiminished or would even be enhanced: diversity of viewpoint, the clash of ideas and methods, to say nothing of the irreconcilability of different scholars' feelings, aspirations, and temperaments. Even when there is consensus on some point, we cannot believe that this disparity, the nutri-

ent on which all scholarship thrives, will have lost its seminal value. The advantage of a dictionary, which allows free rein to a greater number of authors, and which facilitates the juxtaposition of both detailed analysis and broad synthesis, is that it can more comfortably, or more immediately, accommodate a living science whose very contradictions and even lapses into confusion serve as a lesson that can inspire, and on which we can reflect. We might say that a dictionary can aspire to a totalization which, because it is still only potential, is less subject to the perils of dogmatic deviation. Within a dictionary's open-ended structure, every aspect of scientific research—classification or comparison, hypothesis or explanation, discovery of a law or conjecture as to its significance—will be allowed to reveal its specificity and find its own level. We may, therefore, regard the dictionary format as the most adequate expression of today's scholarship, which is suspicious of all systems, instinctively realizing the complexity and pluralities inherent in its objects of study as well as the interaction between these objects and its own methods.

There is, in short, a kind of spirit or "genius" in what might simply appear to be the way the subject matter is arranged; and in direct consequence of this conception came the following decision: that in making the choices rendered necessary by the limited space, preference would be given to the process of discovery rather than to what has already been discovered; to new challenges, new departures, and new divergences rather than to the syntheses of the past, even those still found acceptable today. In deciding what to include in the dictionary, our preference has been, in other words, for new problems rather than old (and hence overfamiliar) solutions, even major ones. *Research*, the only endeavor, today, to which we habitually apply the word "pure," has been our true objective. In this book the reader will find what are at this very moment the pivotal points being debated in regard to this or that myth or religious festival, and not a mere enumeration—the comprehensiveness of which would in any case be difficult to establish—of points already settled in the past. And let us remark in passing that, by so doing, we are merely making public, for the sake of a more general reflection, a practice that has already proved itself in certain scientific circles, but only to a privileged few. The introduction to the *Annuaire* of the École des Hautes Études (section V, religions), states that the teaching dispensed by the professors of this institution is a science "in process" and that "those responsible for teaching others will find no better way to exercise their function as the initiating and motivating force behind their students' research than by sharing . . . the results of their own, even if this means admitting to failures." In this dictionary we have not always been quite so radical as these admirable words advise, but we, too, have attempted not to "transmit what is already known, but to demonstrate as concretely as possible how knowledge is acquired, and how it grows."[2]

It should therefore come as no surprise to the reader that some of the assignments normally charged to works on mythology were eliminated from our project at the outset, notably those detailed accounts of demigods, nymphs, demons, genies, and heroes that occupy the forefront of less recent or more conventional studies. Insofar as these figures do not appear prominently among those chosen by contemporary scholars for reevaluation, merely to have listed them and added a few perfunctory remarks about each one— which, as there are thousands of them, is the best we could have done—would have been once again, and once too often, to present only the chaff instead of getting at the grain deep within, to rethrash the oversimplifications of yesteryear with an outward show of scientific objectivity. Apart from a few minor protagonists of Greek myth—retained because of their artistic or literary importance, through centuries of survival or revival or nostalgia for the gods of antiquity—we have chosen to deal, rather, with the innumerable minor characters in the drama of creation and the cosmos within the context of broader-based articles concerned primarily with *structures:* creation, cosmos, sacrifice, the divinity of the waters, divine animals or ancestors, etc.—the structures that modern science has taught us better to discern beneath the apparent disorder of myths. For only through these more active concepts, these more all-encompassing frameworks, can we realize the ultimate meaning of something that has always been only an element in the symbolic totality arising from man's desire to know; only in this way will we be able to perceive the differences, similarities, resonances, and, what is more, the perhaps hidden truth, the quality of mystery, even the power to terrify, that underlies figures who became, in the mirror of classical paintings or in the *Mythologies* of our grandparents, elegant Marsyas or lovable Flora. The reader will, however, be able to find the information that our articles do dispense about many of these tiny sparks from the larger fire, by referring to the index, where many names that he may have regretted not finding more prominently displayed in the columns of the text have been assembled.

We have, on the other hand, been generous in allotting space—and sometimes a great deal of space—to what at first glance might appear to be an excessively specific or technical development on a minor point in a remote religion, or an almost unknown tribe. We have done so because some important aspect of the most recent research in the field is thereby revealed, is therein at work, and the essay is therefore being offered, indirectly, as a concrete example of today's practical methods. In a situation of overwhelming possibility, the guiding principle presiding over the choices we did in fact make was consistently to prefer the illuminating example over the supposedly exhaustive enumeration; except on those occasions when a truly extensive, minutely scrupulous coverage of a field narrow enough to be included in the book in its entirety could also be made to serve as one of our major exemplary cases. This dictionary is in large measure a *network of examples,* each with some bearing on a particular level or category of religious experience or scien-

tific method; if we have included a study of sacrifice in a religion in which sacrifice is especially important, we have deliberately omitted an article on sacrifice for another region of the world in which, by the same token, animals or the presence of the dead have been selected from a mythic narrative in which they are felt to be essential. The advantage of this principle is that it allows us to plumb the depths, which is one way to achieve universality and thus to speak of everything, despite the occasional appearance of superficiality. The reader will note that our articles are seldom very short; allowing for the stylistic terseness characteristic of dictionaries, we strove for an average length that would permit us to publish what are actually brief monographs; I am pleased to note that the present enterprise has served as the occasion for much research, some of it completely new, either in subject matter or in approach. The reader will thus be a witness to the creative process in action.

And if he should be annoyed because he cannot find in our table of contents or even our index some name or subject to which several lines have been devoted in the *Oxford Classical Dictionary* or the *Real-Encyclopädie,* he should also bear in mind the intellectual character of our endeavor, and should listen in the depths of our pages for the stirrings of research in process, that catalyst through which, from the womb of needs as yet unsatisfied, hypotheses as yet unproved, oppositions and even conflicts, are born the research projects, innovations, and ideas that tomorrow will provide the material for new articles in the still open dictionary and, later, for a whole new volume. Any dictionary worthy of the name must affirm, with real fervor, that it will continue thus; that is, that it will turn into a serial appearing twelve times a century, an institution whose past becomes future, a rallying ground that will help keep a discipline alive.

II

What is this discipline, exactly, in our own case? And how did we define or, rather, how were we able to recognize the subjects appropriate to our dictionary?

It is entitled *Dictionary of Mythologies and Religions in Traditional Societies and in the Ancient World*—thus, apparently, introducing two distinct subjects. What really is the subject, and what, in terms of specific content, will the reader find in the book?

Let us state at the outset that what our French publisher wanted was a "Dictionary of Mythologies," explanation enough in itself, because it refers to a specific area and one abundantly rich in problems of great scientific interest today. To quote again from section V of the *Annuaire:* the current tendency for the science of religion to assume a central place in anthropological studies is due to "the increasing importance being accorded to 'myth' for the interpretation and comprehension of the human phenomenon. On this point, the most diametrically opposed schools of contemporary thought are undivided. Religious myths have attained highest priority as objects of study by the most disparate scientific disciplines and schools of philosophy, whether they are regarded as images or projections of a system of communications among men; as manifestations of archetypes of the psyche; or as the special objects of a phenomenology of human consciousness . . ."[3] Certainly we no longer believe, as did the Socrates of Plato's *Phaedrus,* that there is no need to study myth because the important thing is to know ourselves—rather the reverse. Mythology appears to us ever more clearly as one of the great aspects of our relationship with ourselves, as well as being a conception of the world and the terrestrial environment that has been undoubtedly useful; we therefore ought to draw up a balance sheet—however provisional—of the discoveries made by the present century in the various chapters of man's reflection on myth. That there is still not complete agreement among scholars as to how myth should be defined matters little; that the problem of definition may even be premature also matters little, precisely because the plurality inherent in the enterprise of a dictionary as defined above actually makes the juxtaposition of contradictory propositions seem natural and allows them to be compared with one another. Neither in this introduction nor in the body of the book, where the actual choices have been made, will the reader find a definition of myth decreed as law, as if the die were cast. Our only methodological limitation, one that in our view safeguards the rights both of the study of myths as archetypes and of the methods appropriate to myths approached as systems of communication, is to apprehend myth on the level of collective representations, where, as one of our contributors writes, myth is "the form in which the essential truths of a particular society are articulated and communicated." Despite what may be the apparent freedom of the narrative, our task must be to seek within it a body of collective knowledge in contradistinction to the ephemeral creations of the individual consciousness, no matter how impressive these may be in great novels or poems. Apart from a few fleeting insights, included solely that we might better understand and recognize the limitations we have set for ourselves, there are in our dictionary none of the "personal myths" that come from art and the free play of imagination and that perhaps belong to a dialectic entirely different from those that unite human beings under the sign of their communications in the real world, of their confrontation with real necessities, and that are accompanied and made possible by rituals and beliefs. We have similarly omitted from the book what are sometimes referred to as "modern myths," representations that are circulated by popular literature or the media, myths that do indeed touch many spirits but that differ from the great majority of mythic narratives in that they are not so much the expressions of a society as they are the expressions of a yearning for a different society, or of the fear of forces that the structures of our societies have not integrated. In our view, the place for the study of these is, rather, in a dictionary devoted to the basic categories of religious experience as such, in particular, transcendence, eschatology, and salvation.

In short, the myths in this book have been culled only from the mouths of societies or groups. This does not indicate a refusal to study the connection between myth and the deep structures of the human psyche; it merely delimits, in order to avoid any confusion, an object of thought that could then be connected with others, or analyzed in other ways than has been done here. The one form of individual creativity we did consider appropriate to include, at least through a few major examples, is the reflection of those who, although they may have relied on highly subjective spiritual or philosophical preconceptions, nevertheless attempted—as did Plato, for example, or Cicero—to understand myths as society produces them or assumes them. Objective as contemporary scholarship aspires to be, there are a few preconceptions similar to theirs still at work today, perhaps; so who can tell if in these ancient interpretations of myth there is not some lesson that could be of use to future investigations either of myth as the expression of social relationships, or of mythological figures as spearheads cutting through local custom and belief toward more universal spiritual forms?

But assuming nothing about the essence or function of myth except its relationship to a society does not necessarily mean that erecting the boundaries for a dictionary of mythologies presents no further problems. For no myth exists in isolation; none is a narrative drawing only on itself for its terms and its conventions. We still had to decide what, precisely, from a given society or culture, and from among all its conscious or unconscious communal acts, ought to be included in the book so that none of the discussion or information would be elliptical or too allusive. In other words, what complementary studies must be integrated into a dictionary of mythologies to ensure that the overall statement that it makes will not be hobbled, giving only an impoverished and therefore dangerous idea of the field?

Here is where we can justify the ambiguous precision of our title, in which the word "religion" appears next to the word "mythology." Proceeding empirically, at no great philosophical risk, we may hold as evident that in every human society mythical narrative and religious practice are closely related; and thus, that everywhere, or almost everywhere, it is the historian or analyst of religions who also studies mythologies. As a corollary to this, surely we can affirm that it makes little sense to classify and analyze myths without reference to those aspects of religion that have determined them and will certainly clarify them. And, further, if we do so, in order to make room for this additional material we should also be prepared to sacrifice some of the data about myths properly speaking: what is lost in comprehensiveness will largely be regained in the comprehension of the place and the meaning of myth. This book deals with religions as well as with myths; or, rather, it stands at the intersection where the two roads meet—always with the proviso, however, that each of our contributors has been left free to decide for himself how to apportion the two concerns in practice, taking account of the vastly different forms that the same scientific goal can assume in areas as diverse as Indonesia, for example—that huge complex of societies, languages, and religious influences, where current research is still at the stage of amassing data that must subsequently be put in order—or Vedic India, or Greece, which we know plenty about.

We do not mean that all things religious are therefore in a relationship of complicity, or even of continuity, with the production of myths and the sometimes evanescent, sometimes enduring, figures of myth; there is a dividing point at which one must take sides; the consequences are bound to be great and it is important to justify them. It may come as a surprise to the reader that the religions of Sumeria, Egypt, and Persia are included in the book, while Judaism, Christianity, and Islam are not; that the divinities—if that is the right word—of Buddhism are included, but that no reference is made to the spiritual essence of this major religious experience as it occurs in China, Japan, or elsewhere. It may also cause surprise that, more specifically, the studies of the religions which have been included do not mention what has often made them forms of transcendental experience, mysteries, quests for the Absolute, arenas of soteriological ambition for the yearnings or the nostalgia of individuals or of sects. This is because, during such phases in a religion's development, the religious principle—in its essence, perhaps, a contradictory one—turns against the mythic narrative by which it is at other times nourished. When this happens, the spirit is no longer content to rest at the level of the gods but aspires to a transcendence that it senses as amounting to something more than the representations of it provided by myth; it rejects myth or creates in place of it a gnostic system to uncover its secret meaning. And the effort thus made by the religious spirit to reach the divine within mythical manifestations that it regards as paradoxical or imperfect consequently determines that this aspect of the religious experience has no place in a dictionary of myth and of the rituals and beliefs associated with myth. We have not taken into consideration here the aspect of religion that fights the gods, the mediating powers, that holds them to be paganisms; this aspect in itself is so complex and so rich that it would take another book at least the size of this one to do it justice. The reader will therefore not find among the religions introduced in this volume those whose essential vocation is—let us try to be succinct—the direct experience of transcendent divinity; nor those which tend to have a universal message, addressed to all people everywhere, no matter what their culture or where they live; not even those religions whose moorings in the history of a specific society or a specific people have enabled them, through a founder, a theophany, a prophet, or their reform of a previous paganism, to attach to themselves legends or histories closely resembling myths. In practice, we have excluded from this book the great religions of a Word, a Promise; and especially the mystery religions, Judaism, Christianity, Islam, Gnosticism, Taoism, and the legacies of the Buddha. The one exception to this rule consists of certain incursions justified by the "pagan" nature of some of their minor aspects, such as the cult of the saints in our own churches or the gods and demons of Buddhism.

Let us hope that these religions will one day form the subject of another dictionary, one dealing, as it were, with divinity, as opposed to gods; with universal theologies and experiences of unity, in contrast to the rivulets of myths, rituals, and holy places. Upon further reflection, we ought also to reserve for another volume certain problems of boundaries, such as the way in which past and present evangelistic missionaries have regarded the myths of societies they set out to convert, not without repercussions on Christian doctrine; or—to come closer to home—the way in which at certain moments Christianity itself has played the role of a myth: a myth of truth, or progress, even at the price of relinquishing a good part of its aptitude for genuine communion. As one of our authors writes, myths are never recognized for what they are except when they belong to others; it is therefore our duty to apply to our own behavior as people of the Western world the same methods that our science reserved only yesterday for so-called primitive societies. But a great religious experience must first be described before we can go beyond it and begin the task of distinguishing its ambiguities.

And yet certain religions which might be said to represent a quest for the Absolute as obvious as any other—those of India, for instance, and perhaps also of Egypt—have been included; but this is because in their search for unity they involve myth in a very intimate, almost ultimate, manner, if only in an initial stage and as one more form of illusion. We have not used the word "polytheism" to designate the religions whose myths are dealt with in this dictionary, despite its apparent reference to the differentiation, the polymorphy, of the divine. For although there are resolutely polytheistic religions, such as those of ancient Greece or Rome, in other cultures and other lands there are religions based on more complex intuitions, in which the multiplicity of representations at once clear-cut and diffuse exist in a sort of breathing of the spirit that seems to refute our own exaggerated distinctions between entity and nonentity, between the one and the many. Might we not, perhaps, call these religions "poetic" or "figurative," since an artist knows well the imaginary nature of the figures that, nevertheless, alone can express, in the artist's vision, the essential reality? In any case, such religions belong in this dictionary by virtue of their massive and continuing recourse to the logic of myth.

III

And now for a few words of clarification concerning the geographical and historical area covered by our enterprise. Or rather—since this dictionary by definition covers all terrestrial space and every era of terrestrial history—concerning the relative proportions we decided upon for the various parts of our inquiry.

First, one remark that may be useful: if we have designated and defined myth in the context of an inquiry that by rights extends to the farthermost regions of the globe, this in no way means that we wish to affirm, by emphasizing the most powerful of these mythologies—whose links with the languages in which they are expressed are obviously close—that there is any uniformity on earth in this mode of consciousness. As has frequently been pointed out, the word *myth* itself comes from the Greek, and the concept that we project into this word, although adjusted to accommodate overlappings and overflowings, also has a logic, a coherence, and still bears the mark of its origin; there is therefore no foundation for believing that what some other ethnic group has experienced under the forms that we call myth corresponds to the same laws with which we are familiar. Perhaps there are societies that do not tend to integrate their myths into some meaningful whole but leave them as fragments that flare up and then are extinguished without, in passing, casting any light on what we ourselves are tempted to look for or to find everywhere: the outline, if only a rough one, of the vault of a universe. If in these cases we can often see nothing but an incoherent babble opening the way to higher forms of consciousness, might it not also be possible for us to sense in them an entirely different mode of consciousness, one in which the discontinuous, the partial, the forever incomplete would themselves be perceived as the very being of human meaning? Could we not see them as an ontology of the superficiality of our inscription on the world—an ontology that the planet's recent history would tend rather to confirm than to deny—somewhere beyond the ruin of our own aspirations? The representation of the divine can obey laws as diverse as those of artistic representation, which extends from the controlled irrationality of a Poussin, who was, in fact, an heir to the Greeks, to the fugitive traces on the gray wall of some works of art of our time.

This should remind us if need be that a dictionary like ours, if it is to fulfill its task of describing the variety of mythologies, must supplement its descriptions of the religious data with additional material on the cultures, mental structures, languages, and functionings of the social collectivity. To the extent that myth is one of the forms of asking questions about mystery, it represents a relationship between the human consciousness—in its cognitive functions, its praxis, its historical memory, or its exploration of the outside environment—and the culture as a whole. Recent research has clearly demonstrated that myth's manifest complexity makes it one of the most useful tools for an archaeology of the imagination, of philosophy, or of science. It was therefore essential to the present undertaking that myth appear not only as an act of speech about the divine, but as a text in which the divine is infinitely embedded in signifiers; and it is the task of the ethnologist, the sociologist, and the linguist to decipher and analyze these signifiers. A background in the social sciences is much more than an imperative for this book; it is its natural and inevitable locus, and one from which many of our contributors, either explicitly or implicitly, have strayed but little. But this consideration even further restricts the space available for the purely mythological material within the finite number of pages at our disposal. When the whole world demands to be heard, the time for each part to speak must be allotted sparingly.

How to mitigate this disadvantage? It would have been tempting to reverse ethnocentric custom and to eliminate at a stroke every trace of exclusiveness, every hierarchy; to relinquish forever the specious charm of the old Greco-Roman monopoly, and its belated acceptance of Egypt and the Near East; and thus to have offered to each separate part of the world an equal number of pages. But rational and fair as this was in principle, we knew that in practice it could never be other than a utopian ideal, at least for the foreseeable future. The first and major reason is that the analysis of myths that is most familiar to us is the work of scholars who write or read in French, English, Italian, German, and more rarely in other languages, still mostly Western ones. With all of its virtues and all of its limitations, this linguistic given constitutes an intangible fact that we must first examine before our own consciousness can be raised, before it can be made to apprehend from within how to circumscribe its own difference so as to be more receptive to categories other than its own. If the mythology of Africa or of ancient Japan is an object of study for our language, the myths and divinities of Greece and Rome, not to mention those of the Celtic and Germanic worlds, survive through hidden symbolisms, overt conditionings, artistic or philosophical references, even—and above all—through concepts, in the most intimate being of mythology, that operate on the very level on which our language apprehends and analyzes the object. And these components, all too familiar but never sufficiently explored, never sufficiently distanced, therefore demand an almost excessive attention if we in the West are ever to achieve a valid understanding of the other civilizations of the world.

This invaluable opportunity to psychoanalyze our methods, we felt, should not be sacrificed by unduly abbreviating that portion of the book dealing with our own origins; so, an important place, even though in a most attenuated manner, should once again be given to the cults and mythologies of more or less classical antiquity and to their later effects on the religious, artistic, and intellectual life of Europe, of which we, of course, are a product. And because for other parts of the world we have also had to take into account the very variable degree of progress in the field, so that it would have been unfortunate to weigh each contribution equally, we have resigned ourselves without compunction to being biased in our allocation of space, believing that to define where we stand does not—or at least so we may hope—imply a valorization of what lies nearest to us or any dogmatism. We have reserved almost half the work for the Mediterranean world, the Near and Far East, and for the historical relations between their mythologies and the European consciousness, as demonstrated by such phenomena as the survival of the classical gods or the fascination with Egypt after the Italian Renaissance. The other half of the book is for the rest of the world, here again, however, taking into account the actual importance that one region or another may have today assumed in a field that naturally is not static and that will have fresh insights to contribute to future supplements to the present volume. It is unfortunately only too true that the vast societies of Africa and Asia have in our columns once again been given less space than the tiny population of Greece. But a particular problem concerning a particular, vanishing society in Vietnam has, on the other hand, merited more of our attention than many perhaps expected aspects of our classical world. We can only hope that the reader will not find our distribution of the materials too misinformed.

IV

Here now is some practical information to help the reader find his way through the labyrinth of the dictionary. [The rearrangement of articles in the English-language edition obviates the problems discussed in this paragraph, which we have therefore abridged.] Certain religions or cultures to which, regretfully, we could only allot a few pages are represented by a single article that can easily be found under the name of the country or geographical area, thus, *Albania* or *Crete*. Generally speaking, however, our contributors had more space at their disposal and were able to address various questions that they considered not only basic but exemplary, in articles spread throughout the book. A list of the names of all the authors, in alphabetical order of their initials, allows the reader to go from the initials at the end of each article to the complete name of the author.

This same list also indicates the academic affiliations of the hundred or so scholars who were willing to contribute to the dictionary; it will be noted that most of them teach at the Collège de France, the École Pratique des Hautes Études, or in French universities. Why this preference for the French, in a century when intellectual exchange is so abundant, between some countries at least, and in which we see so many publications—of, for example, papers delivered at colloquia—that mix together in their abstracts the names of professors from Tübingen or Yale with those from Tokyo or Nairobi? It may at once be pointed out that contributions to this type of publication are usually printed in the language in which the original paper was delivered, obviously requiring of the reader that he be made aware of the linguistic and conceptual apparatus presiding at their conception. French scholars know that, in dealing with ideas originally conceived in German, or in English, they must undertake the task of recognizing schools of thought, cultural or religious conditionings or customs, the influence exerted by the words themselves—since every language has its own semantic nodes, as complex as they are uncompromising; and they also know this task may take a long time, demanding further reading or travel abroad. They further understand that it is only in connection with these vast extratextual areas that they will be able to identify and appreciate the meaning of the text itself. It is of course always possible to translate, and to read a translation. But we must not forget that it takes more than a mere rendering of sentences into a new language for these backgrounds to be revealed and for the underlying meaning to be made clear.

This is precisely the risk that prevails when an enterprise such as ours is opened to authors who think and write in different languages—which would have to be many in number for all the major trends in international scholarship to be represented as they deserve. We believed that scholars who thus had to express themselves through translation would find their work deprived of a part of its significance at the very moment when we would seem to be listening to it. Moreover, the converse is also true: problems can best be differentiated, and even antagonistic methods best be revealed, through the widest possible deployment of the unity and diversity—the cluster of potentialities simultaneously contiguous and concurrent—that is embodied in a single language at a precise moment in its history. We therefore deemed it preferable to call primarily on French scholars and, since those responding to our call number among the most eminent and the most representative, thus to offer to the reader, as an adjunct to our panorama of mythologies and religions, a matching panorama of the contemporary French schools of history, sociology, and religious studies, all of which are of the first rank and deserve to be known as such. To sum up: while a few of the original contributions to the *Dictionary of Mythologies* were translated from languages other than French, for the most part the material can be viewed as a whole, produced by a single society—an ever evolving one, to be sure, and one not inattentive to other cultures—at a crucial juncture in the development of a scientific discipline that is still young. This dictionary is French, the expression of a group of scholars all working within reach of one another, as sensitive to their areas of disagreement as they are gratified by their points of convergence. It is our hope that, if it should be translated, the translator will find it vast enough to allow for the emergence, here and there within its mass, of the unstated concept of implied bias not readily discernible in briefer texts; and that these underlying elements will be revealed in a translation offering the reader, and serving as the basis for future debate, an intellectual effort seen whole: not just the visible tip of the iceberg, but its hidden, submerged bulk as well.

V

Such were the guiding principles determining how our work should be organized. It is only proper to add, however, that despite the great trust which it was the present editor's pleasure to encounter in his authors—who sometimes produced material for him equivalent in volume to a small book—the above principles are primarily the expression of his own concept of what scholarship is, and what it is that scholars are attempting to do. Only he can be held directly responsible for them.

I have just used the word "trust." Going back to the source from which all trust springs, however, I should rather have said "generosity," because this word, glossing "trust," better characterizes both the reception that I as editor was given by specialists in their fields who could so easily have refused to credit any but one of their own, and the quality of their contributions, which to me seems patent. I see this now that the enterprise has been achieved. Most of these scholars, all of them with many tasks competing for their time, have been with our project from the beginning, when, responding to my appeal, they consented to represent their respective disciplines in a dictionary that was still just an idea—an idea to which they themselves had to give meaning. Most of them also agreed to oversee the illustration of their articles, thereby enriching the text with a variety of often rare, sometimes previously unpublished, documents directly rel-

evant to the text. Whenever minor vicissitudes befell the project thereafter, decisions were always made in a spirit of mutual understanding and cooperation. I am extremely grateful to all the authors of this book, and to those eminent individuals who were kind enough to advise me when initial decisions had to be made. Indeed, my only great regret is that I am unable to express this gratitude today to two men who are no longer with us, two men who possessed consummate wisdom, foresight, and discipline, and whose example will stand as an enduring one. Historian Eugène Vinaver's masterly command of Arthurian Romance, a borderline topic standing between myth and literature, is well known. So, too, is Pierre Clastres's intense involvement with the Indian civilizations of South America; the articles by him that we are publishing here were the last pages he ever wrote.

I now have the pleasure of thanking Henri Flammarion and Charles-Henri Flammarion, who wanted this dictionary to exist, and who showed such keen interest in the questions with which it deals. My thanks also to those who transformed typescripts, photographs, and graphics into the reality of the present book. First on the list of these is Francis Bouvet, a man attached to the project from the moment of its inception and now, regrettably, only a memory, but a cherished one. My thanks to Adam Biro, who took over the same functions and brought to them the same understanding and the same invaluable support. Thanks to Claire Lagarde, who from start to finish, and with intuitive devotion and unfailing good humor, sent out requests, acknowledged receipts, sent out requests again, read, filed, saved, and expedited contracts, typescripts, documents, and proofs, even at times when her other duties were pressing. And, finally, thanks to Pierre Deligny, who, simply because he was asked, since we had no legitimate claim to his assistance, unhesitatingly accepted in his own name as well as in that of Denise Deligny and Danielle Bornazzini the crushing responsibility for correcting three successive sets of proofs, with their intricate web of unfamiliar names, cross-references, rearrangements, accent marks, and emendations, and who brought the job to a successful conclusion, with Mesdames Deligny and Bornazzini specifically undertaking responsibility for compiling the index. Yes, to these other authors of the *Dictionary of Mythologies*, many thanks, in the name of the authors of the text.

Yves Bonnefoy/l.g.

NOTES

1. Preface, *Histoire des religions*, vol. 1 (Paris 1970) (Encyclopédie de la Pléiade).
2. *Annuaire* of the École des Hautes Études, Paris, vol. 83, no. 1 (1975–76), p. 4.
3. Ibid., p. 3.

Contributors

A.L.-G André Leroi-Gourhan, professor, Collège de France.

A.P. Arshi Pipa, professor, University of Minnesota.

B.R. Brinley Rees (retired), reader, University College of North Wales.

B.S.A. Bernard Saladin d'Anglure, professor, Laval University, Quebec.

C.L.-D. Camille Lacoste-Dujardin, directeur de recherche, Centre national de la recherche scientifique; chargé de conférences, École des hautes etudes en sciences sociales.

F.-R.P. François-René Picon, maître de conférences, University of Paris V.

G.C. Georges Charachidzé, professor, University of Paris III and École pratique des hautes études, IVe section (sciences historiques et philologiques).

G.D. Germaine Dieterlen, directeur honoraire de recherche, Centre national de la recherche scientifique; directeur d'études, École pratique des hautes études, Ve section (sciences religieuses).

G.L. Godfrey Lienhardt, reader emeritus, Oxford University.

J.G. Jean Guiart, professor, Muséum national d'histoire naturelle; director, Laboratoire d'ethnologie, Musée de l'homme; directeur d'études, École pratique des hautes études, Ve section (sciences religieuses).

J.La. Jean Laude, professeur titulaire, University of Paris I.

J.V. Jean Varenne, professor, University of Lyon.

L.deH. Luc de Heusch, professor, Free University of Brussels.

M.A.E.F.M. Mission archéologique et ethnologique française au Mexique (now CEMCA): Jacques Galinier, chargé de recherche, centre national de la recherche scientifique; Dominique Michelet, chargé de recherche, Centre national de la recherche scientifique; Anne-Marie Vié, member, M.A.E.F.M.: under the direction of Guy Stresser-Péan, formerly directeur d'études, École pratique des hautes études, Ve section (sciences religieuses).

M.Ba. Monique Ballini.

M.D. Marcel Detienne, directeur d'études, École pratique des hautes études, Ve section (sciences religieuses).

M.El. Mircea Eliade, professor in the Divinity School, University of Chicago.

P.C. Pierre Clastres, directeur d'études, École pratique des hautes études, Ve section (sciences religieuses).

P.D. Pierrette Désy, professor, directeur d'études avancées, University of Quebec at Montreal.

P.-M.D. Paul-Marie Duval, member of the Institut de France; professeur honoraire, Collège de France.

P.S. Pierre Smith, chargé de recherche, Centre national de la recherche scientifique.

P.V. Pierre Verger, corresponding member, Muséum d'histoire naturelle de Paris; formerly directeur de recherche, Centre national de la recherche scientifique, and visiting professor, University of Ife (Nigeria) and University of Bahia (Brazil).

R.B. Régis Boyer, professor, University of Paris VI.

Introduction:
The Interpretation of Mythology

Toward a Definition of Myth

From Plato and Fontenelle to Schelling and Bultmann, philosophers and theologians have proposed numerous definitions of myth. But all the definitions have one thing in common: they are based on Greek mythology. For a historian of religions, this choice is not the happiest one. It is true that myth, in Greece, inspired epic poetry and theater as well as the plastic arts; yet it was only in Greek culture that myth was subjected to prolonged and penetrating analysis, from which it emerged radically "demythologized." If the word "myth," in all European languages, denotes "fiction," it is because the Greeks declared it to be so twenty-five centuries ago.

An even more serious mistake in the eyes of the historian of religions is that the mythology that Homer, Hesiod, and the tragic poets tell us about is the result of a selective process and represents an interpretation of an archaic subject which has at times become unintelligible. Our best chance of understanding the structure of mythical thought is to study cultures in which myth is a "living thing," constituting the very support of religious life—cultures in which myth, far from portraying *fiction*, expresses the *supreme truth*, since it speaks only of realities.

This is how anthropologists have proceeded for more than half a century, concentrating on "primitive" societies. Reacting, however, against an improper comparative analysis, most authors have neglected to complement their anthropological research with a rigorous study of other mythologies, notably those of the ancient Near East, primarily Mesopotamia and Egypt; those of the Indo-Europeans, especially the grandiose and exuberant mythology of ancient and medieval India; and finally that of the Turco-Mongols, the Tibetans, and the Hinduized or Buddhist peoples of Southeast Asia. In limiting research to primitive mythologies, one risks giving the impression that there is a gap between archaic thought and that of peoples considered "of history." This gap doesn't exist; indeed, by restricting investigation to primitive societies, one is deprived of the means of measuring the role of myth in complex religions, such as those of the ancient Near East or of India. For example, it is impossible to understand the religion and, more generally, the style of Mesopotamian culture if one ignores the cosmogonic myths and the myths of origin that are preserved in the *Enūma Eliš* or in the epic of Gilgameš. Indeed, at the beginning of each new year, the fabulous events recounted in the *Enūma Eliš* were ritually reenacted; at each new year the world had to be re-created—and this requirement reveals to us a profound dimension of Mesopotamian thought. The myth of the origin of man explains, at least in part, the characteristic vision and pessimism of Mesopotamian culture: Marduk drew man out of the earth, that is, out of the flesh of the primordial monster Tiamat, and out of the blood of the archdemon Kingu. And the text specifies that man was created by Marduk in order to work the land and to ensure the sustenance of the gods. The epic of Gilgameš presents an equally pessimistic vision by explaining why man does not (and must not) have access to immortality.

Historians of religions therefore prefer to work on *all categories* of mythological creations, both those of the "primitives" and those of historic peoples. Nor do the divergences that result from too narrow a documentation constitute the only obstacle to the dialogue between historians of religions and their colleagues in other disciplines. It is the approach itself that separates them from, for example, anthropologists and psychologists. Historians of religions are too conscious of the axiological differences in their documents to put them all on the same level. Attentive to nuances and distinctions, they cannot be unaware that there are important myths and myths of lesser importance, myths that dominate and characterize a religion, and secondary, repetitive, or parasitic myths. The *Enūma Eliš*, for example, could not be placed on the same level as the mythology of the female demon Lamashtu; the Polynesian cosmogonic myth has a completely different weight from the myth of the origin of a plant, since it precedes it and serves as its model. Such differences in value do not necessarily command the attention of the anthropologist or the psychologist. Thus, a sociological study of the nineteenth-century French novel or a psychology of the literary imagination can make equal use of Balzac and Eugène Sue, Stendhal and Jules Sandeau. But for the historian of the French novel or for the literary critic, such mixing is unthinkable, for it destroys their own hermeneutic principles.

In the next generation or two, perhaps earlier, when we have historians of religions born of Australian or Melanesian tribal societies, I have no doubt that they, among other critics, will reproach Western scholars for their indifference to the scales of *indigenous* values. Let us imagine a history of Greek culture in which Homer, the tragic poets, and Plato were passed over in silence, while the *Interpretation of Dreams* by Artemidorus of Ephesus and the novel by Heliodorus of Emesa were laboriously analyzed under the pretext that they better clarified the specific characteristics of the Greek spirit, or helped us understand its destiny. To return to our subject, I do not believe it possible to understand the structure and function of mythic thought in a society in which myth still serves as a foundation without taking into account both the *body of mythology* of that culture and the *scale of values* that it implies or declares.

Indeed, wherever we have access to a still living tradition that is neither strongly acculturated nor in danger of disappearing, one thing immediately strikes us: not only does mythology constitute a kind of "sacred history" of the tribe in question, not only does it explain the totality of reality and justify its contradictions, but it also reveals a hierarchy in the sequence of the fabulous events it relates. Every myth tells how something came into existence—the world, man, an animal species, a social institution, etc. Because the creation of the world precedes all others, cosmogony enjoys particular prestige. As I have tried to show elsewhere (see, for example, *The Myth of the Eternal Return*, New York, 1954; *Aspects du mythe*, Paris 1963), the cosmogonic myth serves as a model for all myths of origin. The creation of animals, plants, or man presupposes the existence of a world.

Of course, the myth of the origin of the world is not always cosmogonic in the technical application of the term, like Indian and Polynesian myths, or the myth told in the *Enūma Eliš*. In a large part of Australia, for example, the cosmogonic myth in a strict sense is unknown. But there is still a central myth which tells of the beginnings of the world, of what happened before the world became as it is today. Thus one always finds a *primordial history*, and this history has a *beginning*—the cosmogonic myth properly so called, or a myth that introduces the first, larval, or germinal state of the world. This beginning is always implicit in the series of myths that tell of fabulous events that took place after the creation or the appearance of the world, myths of the origin of plants, animals, and man, or of death, marriage, and the family. Together these myths of origin form a coherent history, for they reveal how the world has been transformed, how man became what he is today—mortal, sexual, and obliged to work to sustain himself. They also reveal what the Supernatural Beings, the enculturating Heroes, the mythical Ancestors, did and how and why they moved away from the Earth, or disappeared. All the mythology that is accessible to us in a sufficient state of conservation contains not only a beginning but also an end, bounded by the final manifestations of the Supernatural Beings, the Heroes or the Ancestors.

So this primordial sacred history, formed by the body of significant myths, is fundamental, for it explains and justifies at the same time the existence of the world, of man, and of society. This is why myth is considered both a *true story*—because it tells how real things have come to be—and the exemplary model of and justification for the activities of man. One understands what one is—mortal and sexual—and one assumes this condition because myths tell how death and sexuality made their appearance in the world. One engages in a certain type of hunting or agriculture because myths tell how the enculturating Heroes revealed these techniques to one's ancestors.

When the ethnologist Strehlow asked the Australian

Arunta why they celebrated certain ceremonies, they invariably replied: "Because the [mythical] Ancestors prescribed it." The Kai of New Guinea refused to modify their way of living and working and explained themselves thus: "This is how the Nemu [the mythical Ancestors] did it, and we do it the same way." Questioned about the reason for a certain ritual detail, a Navajo shaman replied: "Because the Sacred People did it this way the first time." We find exactly the same justification in the prayer that accompanies an ancient Tibetan ritual: "As has been passed down since the beginning of the creation of the earth, thus we must sacrifice. . . . As our ancestors did in ancient times, so we do today" (cf. *Aspects du mythe*, pp 16ff.). This is also the justification invoked by Hindu ritualists: "We must do what the gods did in the beginning" (*Śatapatha Brāhmaṇa*, 8.2.1.4). "Thus did the gods; thus do men" (*Taittirīya Brāhmaṇa*, 1.5.9.4). In sum, the governing function of myth is to reveal exemplary models for all rites and all meaningful human activities: no less for food production and marriage than for work, education, art, or wisdom.

In societies where myth is still living, the natives carefully distinguish myths—"true stories"—from fables or tales, which they call "false stories." This is why myths cannot be told indiscriminately; they are not told in front of women or children, that is, before the uninitiated. Whereas "false stories" may be told anytime and anywhere, myths must be told only *during a span of sacred time* (generally during autumn or winter, and only at night).

The distinction made between "true stories" and "false stories" is significant. For all that is told in myths *concerns the listeners directly*, whereas tales and fables refer to events which, even when they have caused changes in the world (for example, anatomical or physiological peculiarities in certain animals), have not modified the human condition as such. Indeed, myths relate not only the origin of the world and that of animals, plants, and humans, but also all the primordial events that have resulted in humans becoming what they are today, i.e., mortal, sexual, and societal beings, obliged to work for a living, and working according to certain rules. To recall only one example: humans are mortal because something happened in the beginning; if this event hadn't occurred, humans wouldn't be mortal, they could have existed indefinitely, like rocks, or could have changed their skin periodically, like snakes, and consequently would have been able to renew their life, that is, begin it again. But the myth of the origin of death tells what happened *in illo tempore*, and in recounting this incident it explains *why* humans are mortal.

In archaic societies, the knowledge of myths has an existential function. Not only because myths offer people an explanation of the world and of their own way of existing in the world, but above all because in remembering myths, in reenacting them, humans are able to repeat what the Gods, the Heroes, or the Ancestors did *ab origine*. To know myths is to learn not only how things have come into existence, but also where to find them and how to make them reappear when they disappear. One manages to capture certain beasts because one knows the secret of their creation. One is able to hold a red-hot iron in one's hand, or to pick up venomous snakes, provided one knows the origin of fire and of snakes. In Timor, when a rice field is growing, someone goes to the field at night and recites the myth of the origin of rice. This ritual recitation forces the rice to grow beautiful, vigorous, and dense, just as it was when it *appeared for the first time*. It is *magically forced to return to its origins*, to repeat its exemplary creation. Knowing the myth of origin is often not enough; it must be recited; knowledge of it is proclaimed, it is *shown*. By reciting myths, one reintegrates the fabulous time of origins, becomes in a certain way "contemporary" with the events that are evoked, shares in the presence of the Gods or Heroes.

In general one may say:

—that myth, such as it is lived by archaic societies, constitutes the story of the deeds of Supernatural Beings;

—that the story is considered absolutely *true* (because it refers to realities) and *sacred* (because it is the work of Supernatural Beings);

—that myth always concerns a "creation"; it tells how something has come into existence, or how a way of behaving, an institution, a way of working, were established; this is why myths constitute paradigms for every meaningful human act;

—that in knowing the myth one knows the "origin" of things and is thus able to master things and manipulate them at will; this is not an "external," "abstract" knowledge, but a knowledge that one "lives" ritually, either by reciting the myth ceremonially, or by carrying out the ritual for which it serves as justification;

—that in one way or another one "lives" the myth, gripped by the sacred, exalting power of the events one is rememorializing and reactualizing.

To "live" myths thus implies a truly "religious" experience, for it is distinct from the ordinary experience of daily life. This experience is "religious" because it is a reenactment of fabulous, exalting, meaningful events; one is present once again at the creative works of the Supernatural Beings. Mythical events are not commemorated; they are repeated, reiterated. The characters in myth are brought forth and made present; one becomes their contemporary. One no longer lives in chronological time but in primordial Time, the Time when the event *took place for the first time*. This is why we can speak of the "strong time" of myth: it is the prodigious, "sacred" Time, when something *new*, something *strong*, and something *meaningful* was made fully manifest. To relive that time, to reintegrate it as often as possible, to be present once again at the spectacle of divine works, to rediscover the Supernatural Beings and relearn their lesson of creation—such is the desire that can be read implicitly in all ritual repetitions of myths. In sum, myths reveal that the world, man, and life have a supernatural origin and history, and that this history is meaningful, precious, and exemplary.

M.El./t.l.f.

The Interpretation of Myths: Nineteenth- and Twentieth-Century Theories

If we fail to trace its outline clearly at the outset, the subject we discuss here risks either being merely a collection of rather curious interpretations accepted in their own periods, or else getting lost in the underbrush of the most varied hermeneutic enterprises. There are two indispensable points of reference. We must, first of all, distinguish interpretation from exegesis. We will define the latter as a culture's incessant but immediate commentary on its own symbolism and practices, its most familiar stories. There is no living tradition without the accompanying murmur of its exegesis of itself. Interpretation, on the other hand, begins when there is some distance and perspective on the discourse of a tradition based on memory. Its starting point is probably, as Todorov suggests, the inadequacy of the immediate meaning, but there is also the discrepancy between one text and another, from which the strangeness of the first can become evident. For, in the work of interpretation, it is the prefix *inter* of the Latin word *interpretatio* that designates the space of deployment of hermeneutic activity. In the Western tradition, from the Greeks to ourselves by way of the Romans and the Renaissance, the first hermeneutics appears in the gap opened up by what a new form of thought decided to call *muthos,* thus inaugurating a new form of otherness which makes one text the mythologist of the next. But this interpretive path required one more marker to give it its definitive orientation. From Xenophanes and Theagenes in the sixth century B.C. to Philo and Augustine, hermeneutics took as its privileged object the body of histories that a society entrusts to its memory, what today we call a mythology. But the play of allegory often based itself on nothing more than a name, a word, or a fragment of a text, on which it could graft the bourgeoning symbolism whose discourse became all the more triumphant when, with the affirmation of Christian doctrine, the certainty of possessing the truth unleashed the audacities of a hermeneutics like that of the *City of God.* It is only with Spinoza—as Todorov has recently stated—that a theory of interpretation takes shape on which our modern readings still largely depend. It was he who formulated rules whose mere application was enough to uncover the truth of a meaning, inside the text and within the bounds of a work. But before it could become philology in the nineteenth century, this theory of interpretation, which Spinoza applied to Scripture, still needed the presence of a cultural object with a clearly defined shape—mythology—understood as a discourse that is other, with its own distinctive traits.

Within these limits and for both of these reasons, an archaeology of theories of the interpretation of myth can restrict itself to the nineteenth and twentieth centuries. Travel accounts since Jean de Léry have traced an axis of otherness whose two poles are the savage and the civilized, between which the Greeks serve as mediator. It is the exemplary values of Greece that are evoked, in good Renaissance style, and Lafitau (1724)—while orienting it toward a deciphering of the present by the past—was merely to systematize the path already beaten, throughout the seventeenth century, by Yves d'Évreaux, Du Tertre, Lescarbot, and Brébeuf. One of the best understood differences—the importance of which has been shown by Michel de Certeau—is that between nakedness and clothing. The detour via the Greeks allows the naked body, which a purely and simply Christian education leads one to reject as belonging to paganism and noncivilization, to be made an object of pleasure, and it may also allow the surprise of a return to oneself. Savages are so handsome that they can only be virtuous. And men's stature, the proportion of their limbs, their nakedness in the midst of the forests, in the beauty of a nature not yet offended by civilization, remind most of these voyagers of the lineaments of Greek statues and the natural privilege which distinguished, in their eyes, the heroes of Homer and Plutarch. As a Jesuit father wrote in 1694, "We see in savages the beautiful remains of a human nature that is completely corrupted in civilized peoples." Nothing could be more like an American savage than a Greek of Homeric times. But this splendid animal, whose development has known no obstacles, whose body is not deformed by labor, evokes the citizen of Sparta or the contemporary of the Trojan war only on the moral and physical level. There is no meeting on an intellectual level; all that the travelers of the seventeenth century expected from savages was that they bear witness to a natural religion of which they were the last trustees. Never, it seems, is the mythology of Homer or Plutarch compared with the stories of these first peoples of nature. One reason is probably that classical mythology, thoroughly moralized, had by then been integrated into a culture dominated by belles lettres. Myths would remain masked as long as they were not assigned their own space.

The nineteenth century saw the discovery of language as the object of a comparative grammar and a renewed philology. In this linguistic space, which is to the highest degree that of the sounds of language, mythical discourse suddenly appeared. It did so in the modality of scandal, which would feed the passionate discussions and theories of two rival schools of the second half of the nineteenth century: the school of comparative mythology, and the anthropological school. As the Sanskritist and comparative grammarian Max Müller wrote, "The Greeks attribute to their gods things that would make the most savage of the Redskins shudder." Comparison defines the nature of the scandal. It is as if it were suddenly discovered that the mythology of Homer and Plutarch was full of adultery, incest, murder, cruelty, and even cannibalism. The violence of these stories, which seemed to reveal themselves brutally as "savage and absurd," appeared all the more unbearable since they were being read at the same time as the stories of distant lands, lands that colonial ethnography was both inventorying and beginning to exploit. The scandal was not that the people of nature told savage stories, but rather that the Greeks could have spoken this same savage language. For in the nineteenth century all that was Greek was privileged. The romantics and then Hegel affirmed this enthusiastically. It was in Greece, they said, that Man began to be himself; it was Greek thought that opened up the path leading from natural consciousness to philosophical consciousness; the Greek people were believed to have been the first to have attained "the uttermost limits of civilization," in the words of a contemporary of Max Müller, the anthropologist Andrew Lang. From the moment that the mythology of Greece could resemble the language spoken by "a mind struck temporarily insane" (Lang), neither our reason nor our thought is definitively safe from an unforeseeable return of the irrational element which, the voice of the savages teaches us, is buried at the very heart of those stories that once seemed so familiar.

The mythology that is subjected to the trial of interpretation is, primarily, nothing but an absurd, crazy form of speech which must be gotten rid of as quickly as possible by assigning it an origin or finding an explanation to justify its oddness. On this point, Max Müller and Andrew Lang are in full agreement. Their divergence appears from the time when the presence of those insane statements at the heart of language and in mythic discourse has to be justified. For Max Müller, a contemporary of the discovery of comparative grammar, the only possible explanation was a linguistic one. And his *Science of Language* argues that a stratigraphy of human speech reveals a mythopoeic phase in the history of language. Since 1816, when Franz Bopp published the first comparative grammar, language had been understood as a set of sounds independent of the letters that allow them to be transcribed; a system of sonorities, animated with its own life, endowed with continual activity and traversed by the dynamism of *inflection*. In the history of language, after what is called a thematic stage, in which terms expressing the most necessary ideas are forged, and what is called a dialectal stage, in which grammar definitively receives its specific

traits, an age begins that Max Müller designates as mythopoeic, in which myths make their appearance in very specific circumstances.

At the beginning of its history, humanity possessed the faculty of uttering words directly expressing part of the substance of objects perceived by the senses. In other words, things awakened sounds in humans which became roots and engendered phonetic types. Humans "resonated" at the world, and thus had the privilege of "giving articulated expression to the conceptions of reason." As soon as the individual lost the privilege of emitting sounds at the spectacle of the world, a strange disease fell upon language: words like "night, day, morning, evening" produced strange illusions to which the human mind immediately fell victim. For as long as humans remain sensitive to the meanings of words, these first sonic beings are conceived of as powers, endowed with will, and marked by sexual traits, though the physical character of the natural phenomena designated by the words is not forgotten. As soon as the double meaning becomes confused, the names of the forces of nature break free: they become proper names, and from a spontaneous expression like "the sky rains," a myth abruptly emerges based on "Zeus makes the rain fall." There is an excess of meaning at the source of mythopoeic creation, an uncontrolled surplus of signification, which tricks the speaker, prey to the illusions of a language within which the play of these "substantive verbs" produces, in a burgeoning of images, the strange and often scandalous discourse of myths.

To this theory, which based the metaphors of language on natural phenomena and declared that a good mythologist should possess a "deep feeling for nature," without which linguistic knowledge is futile, the anthropological school immediately objected that comparative grammarians seemed to have forgotten somewhere along the way that "the Redskins, the Australians, and the lower races of South America" continued even today, in the forests and savannas, to tell the same savage tales, which can hardly be explained as the unwonted result of a few misunderstood phrases. The road the anthropological school would follow led in the opposite direction from that of the grammarians. It was no longer the past or origins that were to explain the present, but rather the mythology of contemporary savages that could account for the "savage" stories of the past. And Lang attempted to show that what shocks us in the mythology of civilized peoples is the residue of a state of thought once prevailing in all humanity. In contemporary primitives we can see the power of this state of thought as well as its coherence. At the same time, anthropologists began to investigate these gross products of the primitive human mind and to discover that things which to our eyes seem monstrous and irrational were accepted as ordinary events in everyday life. They soon came to the conclusion that whatever seems irrational in civilized mythologies (the Greco-Roman world, or India) forms part of an order of things that is accepted and considered rational by contemporary savages.

This position led to two orientations, which anthropology attempted to explore in parallel. For the first, which leads from Frazer to Lévy-Bruhl, mythology remains the discourse of madness or mental deficiency. In 1909, before he published the thousands of pages of *The Golden Bough*, the prolegomena to a history of the tragic errors of a humanity led astray by magic, James George Frazer wrote a small book (*Psyche's Task*) in which he asked how folly could turn to wisdom, how a false opinion could lead to "good conduct." And at the center of his reflection Frazer places a paradox:

primitive superstitions were the foundation of what now seems desirable to us in society: order, property, family, respect for life. Prejudice and superstition in fact served to strengthen respect for authority and thus contributed to the rule of order, the condition of all social progress. Frazer had given hundreds of examples in his already published works, and in this slim volume he is no less enthusiastic an admirer of the conduct of the son-in-law in a primitive society who avoids speaking to or being alone with his mother-in-law, surrounding her with taboos, as if these people, not yet capable of elaborating a thought-out set of laws, still had a sense that an intimate conversation between these two people could easily degenerate into something worse, and that the best way to prevent this from happening was to raise a solid wall of etiquette between them. Without knowing it, and almost reluctantly, primitive thought, even in its most obstinate errors, prepared the way for the triumphs of morality and civilization.

For Lucien Lévy-Bruhl, who published *Les fonctions mentales dans les sociétés inférieures* in 1910, primitive societies differed from ours in their mental organization: their thought, constituted differently from our own, is mystical in nature; it is ruled by a "law of participation" that makes it indifferent to the logic of noncontradiction on which our own system of thought is based. Lévy-Bruhl finds the characteristics of primitive thought, which surrenders itself to affectivity and to what he calls "mysticism," among both schizophrenics and children, who also think in an affective way and establish commonalities between things and beings whose mutual distinctiveness is obvious to the intelligence of a civilized adult. Lévy-Bruhl would increasingly identify this "prelogical" stage with "mystic experience," and Van der Leeuw, who extended his analysis, would try to show that primitive thought survives in every human mind, that it is a component of all forms of reason, an indispensable element whose symbolic load and image-making power help to balance the conceptual development of our thought. In the *Notebooks*, which were published after his death, Lévy-Bruhl found it necessary to revise his position on the mental and intellectual gap between ourselves and "savages." But his work, in profound accord with that of Frazer, seems to us today to be part of a fencing in of savage thought (*la pensée sauvage*), confining it in the prelogical and thus avoiding any contamination which might threaten our own reason.

At the very moment when these armchair anthropologists were interning primitive thought, others were setting out on voyages of discovery to Africa and Oceania, and so were discovering, alive and functioning, the rationality of a form of thought that operates through and in myth—a rationality different from our own, but no less impressive for that. The great living mythologies of the Pacific or the Sudan fulfill an indispensable function in these simpler cultures. Revealing a distinctive reality, guaranteeing the effectiveness of worship, myths codify the beliefs, found the moral rules, and determine every practice of daily life. When Marcel Griaule brought back the Dogon cosmology, with its astonishing architectures of symbolic correspondences, there could no longer be any doubt that mythology was indeed the keystone of archaic societies, the indispensable horizon of all cultural phenomena and of the whole pattern in which society is organized. Myths not only constitute the spiritual armature of human lives; they are bearers of a real "theoretical metaphysics." For the first time, then, myths came to be studied in their entirety, a study in which every detail, even the most insignificant, found its place in a holistic interpretation, an interpretation so rich, so exhaustive, that the

ethnographer, once introduced into this polysymbolic world, is in serious danger of "having nothing more to say about Dogon society than the Dogon say themselves" (Pierre Smith, 1973).

In 1903, before Frazer and Lévy-Bruhl had begun their investigations, Marcel Mauss, following the French sociological school, set forth in a few pages a program of which Georges Dumézil would one day prove to be the master craftsman. Three points seem essential. 1. To determine the mechanism of the formation of myths means to seek some of the laws of the mental activity of man in society. 2. Mythology can be reduced to a small number of myths, and each type is made up of a certain number of combinations. 3. The apparent illogicality of a mythic narrative is itself the sign of its distinctive logic. For Mauss, Durkheim's nephew and collaborator, myths are social institutions, that is, ways of acting and thinking which individuals find already established and, as it were, ready to hand; they form a fully organized pattern of ideas and behaviors which imposes itself more or less forcefully on the individuals inscribed in a society. Myth is above all *obligatory* in nature; it does not exist unless there is a sort of necessity to reach agreement on the themes that are its raw material and on the way these themes are patterned. But the constraint comes solely from the group itself, which tells the myth because it finds its own total expression in it.

A symbol through which society thinks itself, mythology informs experience, orders ritual and the economy, and gives archaic societies their categories and classificatory frameworks. For the Durkheimian school, myths—which, incidentally, are hardly mentioned in the *Année sociologique*—are of the same order as language, "a property of which the proprietor is unconscious"; and, inseparable from this, just as a language continues to bear centuries-old vocabulary and syntax, mythology implies a certain traditional way of perceiving, analyzing, coordinating. The analogy is even more precise: like language, mythology is tradition itself, it is the symbolic system that permits communication beyond words; it is the historical unconscious of the society. In this perspective, the importance of myths derives from the common nature that links them to the most archaic element of language, in that domain where sociology hoped to discover some of the fundamental laws of the mind's activity in society.

It was Mauss once again who, against Lévy-Bruhl, in 1923 defended the thesis that considerable parts of our own mentality are still identical to those of a large number of societies called primitive. But it was first Marcel Granet, then Louis Gernet, who developed a sociological analysis of religion with its legends and myths. For the Sinologist Granet, attempting to proceed from language to the fundamental frames of thought, the mythology of the Chinese provided material in which the emotions characteristic of ancient festivals were recorded. Behind the legendary and mythic tales were ritual dances and dramas from which imaginative schemas emerged that imposed themselves on the mind and on action. Farther along, social contexts and great technical feats that crystallize the productions of the imaginary order could be glimpsed. For the Hellenist Gernet, in a break with the established positivist history that was content to note the gratuitous play of the imaginary, myths reveal a social unconscious. Just as semantic analysis gives access to the great social fact of language, the study of legends and of certain mythic themes allows one to go back to transparent or explicit social practices. The mythic image thus offers the most convenient means of access, not to a timeless memory, but to archaic behaviors and social actions and—going far beyond the social data that have, as Gernet puts it, "a direct relation to myth"—to fundamental phenomena of mental life, those that determine the most general forms of thought.

The specificity of the Greeks pointed Gernet in yet another direction. Myths, in their fragments, shining splinters, offer not only the prehistoric behaviors that were their reason for being; they are at the same time part of a global way of thinking, whose categories, classifications, preconceptual models exert a major influence on positive thought and its various advances. Thus Gernet, starting from a series of traditions about types of precious objects, attempts to show how money and the economy emerge from a set of behaviors linked to the mythical notion of value—a notion that involves domains which, though separate nowadays, used to overlap or merge together: the religious, the political, the aesthetic, the juridical. Mythology is thus part of a global religious system that is symbolic in character, with a web of multicorrespondences from which law, philosophy, history, and political thought will emerge and become progressively distinct. But since Gernet thought of myths as raw material for the thought that arose with and in the Greek city, in the space of the polis, he examined the mythic element only in terms of what was beyond it, in a break with its own nature and its functioning. By failing to separate mythology either from language or from the institutional system, the sociological model of myth culminated in the paradox of sometimes losing sight of the very object that seemed finally to have been recognized and legitimated.

More serious, certainly, was the misunderstanding between Freudian psychoanalysis and the anthropological problematic, which seems to give access to a form of the unconscious inscribed in myth. In his self-analysis, as recounted in his letter to Fliess of October 15, 1897, Freud discovers that his libido awoke between the ages of two and two and a half, and turned toward *matrem* (confessors' Latin for the name of the mother). Freud refers this desire for the mother to a Greek tragedy, *Oedipus the King*, a reference both cultural and paradigmatic. The first thing that Sophocles' Oedipus gives Freud is a better understanding of himself—but the choice of a Greek paradigm already announces the universal character of Freud's discovery of the heart of the matter. The early hypothesis, that little Sigmund is *like Oedipus*, shifts toward the Freudian thesis that Oedipus marrying his mother *must have been the same as ourselves*. While Freud's enterprise, by showing that there is no essential difference between the mentally ill person and the healthy person, seems to invert the separation marked by Lévy-Bruhl, it does assume, from the beginning, a segregation of Greek myths from those of other peoples. For Freud, *Oedipus the King* still excites us and exerts a profound effect on us because every man, always and everywhere, feels love for his mother and jealousy of his father; and from the day Freud first adopted this view, the Greek myth was invested with a new privilege: that of translating better than any other "an instinctual attraction which everyone recognizes because everyone has experienced it."

It was to Greek mythology that Freud would continue to turn in his quest for successive proofs of the reality of the unconscious, comparing the discourse of dreams and fantasies with the legends of Olympus, which his successors, stubbornly but not without fidelity, were to proclaim as the language in which we can most easily read the drives and works of desire. In asking for an admission of guilt within the Oedipal configuration, psychoanalysis indeed marks a

return to myth and the religious; but in seeing both of these as merely the visible tip of the iceberg of the "Unconscious," forgetting that analytical space is that of free association, it has condemned mythology to being nothing but the symbolic and obsessive repetition of a few unconscious representations centered on sexuality.

It was in the direction opened up by Maussian sociology that theoretical work on myth became involved in the first structural analyses. Resuming the project of comparative mythology that had been wrecked by the excesses of Max Müller and his disciples, Georges Dumézil, thanks to a decisive discovery, founded the comparative study of Indo-European religions by ceasing to rely on purely linguistic concordances between divine names and adopting instead the more solid base of articulated sets of concepts. A factual discovery—in Rome, the three *flamines majores* corresponding to the Jupiter-Mars-Quirinus triad; in Iran, the tripartition of social classes—opened the way to structural analysis of the Indo-European world: the tripartite schema was an essential structure in the thought of the Indo-Europeans. Every organized society is based on the collaboration of three distinct but complementary functions: sovereignty, martial power, fecundity. Parallel to this, the gods form a functionally weighted triad, within which the Sovereign, the Warrior, and the group of divinities who preside over fecundity mutually define one another. Since there was never any question of reproducing a definitely Indo-European myth or ritual, Dumézil had to use precise and systematic correspondences to trace a ground plan of the chosen myth or ritual, indicating its articulations, its intentions, its logical significations, and then, on the basis of this schematic figure, projected into prehistory, to try to characterize the divergent evolutions which have led to analogous and diverse results in different places: Indian myth, Roman myth, Scandinavian myth, or Vedic ritual in relation to the Latin rite. For Dumézil, religions are whole patterns in which concepts, images, and actions are articulated and whose interconnections make a sort of net in which, by rights, the entire material of human experience should find its distribution.

By focusing his examination on the concept and on organized patterns, Dumézil radically parts company with a history of religions that thought in terms of genesis and affectivity. For historians like H. J. Rose and H. Wagenvoort, all religion is rooted in the sense of the "numinous" that the human race experiences spontaneously when confronting the phenomena of nature: there is no divine power who was not first one of these *numina*, in which magico-religious force, diffused in the natural world, is concentrated. For Dumézil, by contrast, the observer never reaches isolated facts, and religion is not a form of thought soaked in emotionality. It is in their mutual relations that the various elements can be apprehended, and there always remains, virtually or in action, a representation of the world or of human action that functions on different levels, under a particular type on each level. The religious system of a human group is expressed "first of all in a more or less explicit conceptual structure, which is always present, if sometimes almost unconscious, providing the field of forces upon which everything else comes to be arranged and oriented; then in myths, which represent and dramatize these fundamental intellectual relationships; and then, in turn, in rituals, which actualize, mobilize, and use the same relations." Independently of these gains in the Indo-European domain, Dumézil's method affirmed the virtues of the concept that can equally inform a myth or underlie a ritual. From this point on, "the surest definition of a god is differential, classificatory," and the object of analysis becomes the articulations, the balances, the types of oppositions that the god represents. Against the historians of genesis, Dumézil affirms the primacy of structure: the essential problem is not to determine the precise origin of the various elements that have been fitted together but to accept the *fact* of the structure. The important thing, Dumézil declares, is to bring the structure itself to light, with its signification. It would seem to follow that structures are there, that it is enough to be attentive to them, to avoid forcing them, and to show a little skill in disengaging them. Thus it is not necessary to construct structures as one would elaborate a model of the set of properties accounting for a group of objects. In a sense, structuralism is still in the age of hunting and gathering. Myths, for Dumézil, are the privileged theater that makes visible fundamental conceptual relations. But in the spirit of Mauss's sociology, to which he owes a curiosity for "total social facts" that causes him to explore simultaneously all the works produced by the human mind, myths cannot be deciphered until they have been put back into the totality of the religious, social, and philosophical life of the peoples who have practiced them. The mythology posited by the earlier comparativism of Frazerian inspiration as separate from language, as a more or less autonomous object, endowed with permanence and chosen to locate the common themes elaborated by the Indo-Europeans, was referred back to the language of which it formed a part and, through this language, to the ideology that grounds it and runs through it.

The structural analysis developed by Lévi-Strauss was established under the same kind of conditions as the comparative and philological analysis of the nineteenth century. The gratuitous and insane character of mythic discourse was again the point of departure. For Max Müller this was shocking; for Lévi-Strauss it was a challenge. He took up the challenge after he had shown that kinship relations, in appearance contingent and incoherent, can be reduced to a small number of significant propositions. If mythology is the domain in which the mind seems to have the most freedom to abandon itself to its own creative spontaneity, then, says Lévi-Strauss, to prove that, on the contrary, in mythology the mind is fixed and determined in all of its operations is to prove that it must be so everywhere. The structural analysis of myths thus finds its place in a wider project, which aims at an inventory of mental constraints and postulates a structural analogy between various orders of social facts and language.

This whole approach to myth applies to a new domain the methods of analysis and principles of division developed for linguistic materials in the methods theorized by the Prague school and more particularly by Roman Jakobson. But while myth is assimilated to a language from the outset, it is not identical either to the words of a text or to the sentence of communicative discourse. Mythology is a use of language in the second degree; it is not only a narrative with an ordinary linguistic meaning: myth is in language and at the same time beyond natural language. In the first stage of an ongoing investigation ("The Structural Study of Myth," 1955), Lévi-Strauss tries to define the constituent units of myth in relation to those of structural linguistics. Mythemes are both in the sentence and beyond it. In this perspective, the constituent unit is a very short sentence, which summarizes the essential part of a sequence and denotes a relation: "a predicate assigned to a subject." But this sentence is not part of the explicit narrative; it is already on the order of interpretation, the product of an analytical technique. These sentence relations, then, are distributed on two axes: one horizontal, following the thread of the narrative, the other vertical, in columns, grouping together relations belonging to the same "bundle." It is on the level of these bundles of relations that the real mythemes are located. At the same time, structural analysis poses two principles as essential to its practice: there is no authentic version of a myth in relation to others that are false; correlatively, every myth must be defined by the whole set of its versions. There thus takes shape the project of ordering all the known variants of a myth in a series forming a group of permutations.

The next stage of his investigation ("The Story of Asdiwal," 1958) led Lévi-Strauss to propose that myth makes full use of discourse, but at the same time situates its own meaningful oppositions at a higher degree of complexity than that required by natural language. In other words, myth is a metalanguage and, more precisely, a linked sequence of concepts. Attention will be turned, therefore, to registering the various levels on which myth can be distributed. The cutting up of the mythic narrative which in the first phase (1955) seemed to be entrusted to the whim or ingenuity of the model-builder, is now subject to testing—indispensable to all formal analysis—in terms of the *referent*: "the ethnographic context," which the later transformational orientation of the *Mythologiques* would cease to pursue. The surveying of pertinent oppositions in a mythic sequence thus finds the fundamental guarantee of its legitimacy in previous knowledge of an organized semantic context, without which the myth is in principle incomprehensible. Ritual practices, religious beliefs, kinship structures: the whole of social life and social thought is called upon to define the logical relations functioning within a myth, and at the same time to establish the different types of liaison between two or more myths. In the four-volume *Mythologiques* (1964–1971), the progressive analysis continues to show relations between myths, the social life of those who tell them, and the geographical and technological infrastructure, but it does not restrict itself to this back-and-forth between levels of signification and an ethnographic context that reveals the philosophy of a society. The meaning of a myth is no longer inscribed in its structures' reference to a social infrastructure; rather, the position the myth occupies in relation to other myths within a transformation group is henceforth the vector of an analysis that reveals the autonomy of a mythic thought in which every narrative refers back in the first instance to another, picking up and organizing its elements in a different way. Just as each term, itself without intrinsic signification, has no meaning other than a positional one in the context in which it appears to us, in the same way each myth acquires a signifying function through the combinations in which it is called upon both to figure and to be transformed. It is these transformations which, in the last analysis, define the nature of mythic thought.

It has been objected that this practice of mythological analysis makes a choice for syntax against semantics; and, likewise, that while it has been possible to apply the practice successfully to the mythologies of so-called totemic societies, since these are rich in classificatory structures, it excludes Semitic, Hellenic, and Indo-European societies from its field of interest, societies whose mythological thought is marked by renewals of meaning and by a semantic richness that exceeds the powers of structural analysis. One can reply, on the one hand, that for this type of analysis, which gets at the meanings of myths by multiplying the formal operations that allow us to uncover the logical framework of several narratives, the semantics of myths is necessarily enriched through the inventorying of the syntax. On the other hand, the practice of structural analysis is hardly alien to our familiar mythologies, such as that of the Greeks; one may, indeed, be surprised at the remarkable similarities between the way the Greeks themselves thought their mythology and the method used by ethnologists in approaching myths told by nonliterate peoples. More pertinent objections have come from anthropologists such as Dan Sperber, who denounces the semiological illusion of structuralism as well as the distance between the linguistic models invoked and an intuitive practice whose specific procedures, unlimited in number and nature, offer knowledge of the intellectual operations from which the stories we call "myths" are woven.

M.D./j.l.

BIBLIOGRAPHY

The titles listed are in the order and within the limits of the problems formulated by this article.
T. TODOROV, *Symbolisme et interprétation* (Paris 1978). M. DE CERTEAU, "Ethno-graphie: L'oralité, ou l'espace de l'autre," in Léry, *L'écriture de l'histoire* (Paris 1975), 215–48. G. CHINARD, *L'Amérique et le rêve exotique dans la littérature française du XVIIe au XVIIIe siècle* (Paris 1934). M. DETIENNE, "Mito e Linguaggio: Da Max Müller a Claude Lévi-Strauss," in *Il Mito: Guida storica e critica* (2d ed., Bari and Rome 1976), 3–21 and 229–31, with bibliography. H. PINARD DE LA BOULLAYE, *L'étude comparée des religions*, 1 and 2 (Paris 1925). J. DE VRIES, *Forschungsgeschichte der Mythologie*, Orbis Academicus, 1, 7 (Munich 1961). K. KÉRÉNYI, *Die Eröffnung des Zugangs zum Mythos* (Darmstadt 1967). G. VAN DER LEEUW, *L'homme primitif et la religion*, Étude anthropologique (Paris 1940). P. SMITH, "L'analyse des mythes," *Diogène* 82 (1973): 91–108. M. MAUSS, *Œuvres*, V. Karady, ed., 3 vols. (Paris 1968–69). L. GERNET, *Anthropologie de la Grèce antique* (Paris 1968). S. C. HUMPHREYS, "The Work of Louis Gernet," *History and Theory* 10, 2 (1971). J. STAROBINSKI, "Hamlet et Freud," preface to French trans. by E. Jones, *Hamlet et Œdipe* (Paris 1967), IX–XL. S. VIDERMAN, *La construction de l'espace analytique* (Paris 1970). S. FREUD, "Zur Gewinnung des Feuers," in *Gesammelte Werke* (London 1932–39), also in English. G. DELEUZE and F. GUATTARI, *L'anti-Œdipe* (Paris 1972), "Psychanalyse et familiarisme: La sainte famille," 60–162. H. FUGIER, "Quarante ans de recherches dans l'idéologie indo-européenne: La méthode de Georges Dumézil," *Revue d'histoire et de philosophie religieuse* 45 (1965): 358–74. M. MESLIN, *Pour une science des religions* (Paris 1973), "Psychanalyse et religion," 113–38. P. SMITH and D. SPERBER, "Mythologiques de Georges Dumézil," *Annales E.S.C.*, 1971, 559–86. J.-P. VERNANT, "Raisons du mythe," in *Mythe et société en Grèce ancienne* (Paris 1974), 195–250. P. RICŒUR, s.v. "Mythe (3. L'interprétation philosophique)," in *Encyclopædia Universalis* (Paris 1968), 11:530–37. CL. LÉVI-STRAUSS, *Structural Anthropology*, 2 vols. (New York 1963, 1976), originals in French; *Mythologiques*, 4 vols. (Paris 1964–71), = Introduction to a Science of Mythology, 4 vols., entitled *The Raw and the Cooked* (New York 1969), *From Honey to Ashes* (London 1973), *The Origin of Table Manners* (New York 1978), and *The Naked Man* (New York 1981).

MYTH AND WRITING: THE MYTHOGRAPHERS

The word *mytho-logy* is but one instance of many in which the proximity of myth and writing inevitably results in a kind of violence, its victim an original word, sacred in nature and condemned to fixity by a profane order. Beyond the words which by their very texture bear witness to this phenomenon (such as *mythography*), Greek privilege has held fast. When strange and unforgettable stories, which sounded very independent and yet bore obvious resemblances to the mythology of antiquity, were brought to us from all continents, early anthropologists turned instinctively to Greece, where a few centuries earlier great minds from Xenophanes to Aristotle had faced the problem of limiting the dominion of myths and had resolved it within their own intellectual activity by drawing a boundary at which mythical thought fades away before the rationality of scientists and philosophers. The split between the land of myth and the kingdom of *logos* served as a precedent for the decision made by Tylor and his disciples to impose a historical limit on the reign of mythology over the human mind. This opposition between two forms of thought and two stages of human intelligence, the latter canceling the former, took the form of a sharp contrast between reason, which used all the resources of the written, and a mythological activity tuned to the fantasy of an incessant babbling.

Henceforth, never the twain shall meet. For those practicing historians who tend to favor written traces, oral discourse has become so totally inaudible that it is quite illegible whenever it manifests itself as writing—a contrived writing, which masks the incoherence of traditions sustained through memory by imposing a factitious order of mythographical classifications. For others, the Greeks so thoroughly ensured the triumph of reason and *logos* that they ruined their former system of thought for good, allowing only frail remains to survive as witnesses of a lost state to which only two possible roads of access still remain: one is the discovery, by an ancient traveler in a forgotten village, of a tale saved from the contamination of writing thanks to a few natives unaware of the progress of culture; the other is the less hazardous road of historical and geographical investigation through which one gains access to a long-deferred vision of a landscape that authenticates the narrative or the myths of which it is the guarantor, the recovered witness.

Within this framework, the truth of the myth is enclosed in a speechlike nature, which writing more or less obliterates, at times by shackling the freedom of a self-expressive memory with the constraints of an interpretation subject to foreign rules; and at other times, more often than not, by reducing the myth's own speech to silence in order to speak on its behalf and to condemn it to an absolute otherness. In an attempt to rectify this division, structural analysis introduced a summary separation between cold and warm societies, the former deprived of a temporal dimension, the latter open to history and to the continual renewals of meaning that writing facilitates. The border thus drawn appeared all the more definite as it seemed to reiterate the distinction between oral and written literature, a distinction reinforced, if not justified, by the decision made by this type of analysis to look for the essential of the "myth" not in the narration but in the story transmitted by memory, a story whose narrative form was left to the discretion and talent of each narrator.

Yet another issue arises, for which the Greek model inspires a formulation that suggests the progressive emergence of writing in a traditional society. Since the time E. A. Havelock first published his studies, the Homeric epic, which Milman Parry had recognized as belonging to oral practice, can no longer be considered an enclave of a living tradition that made room for a culture of the written. The introduction of an alphabetical writing technique caused no immediate changes, nor did it produce any profound up-heaval. Greece experienced not a revolution of writing but, rather, a slow movement with uneven advances depending on the areas of activity; by the turn of the fourth century, writing prevailed mentally and socially. Until the end of the fifth century, Greek culture had been essentially of the oral type. It entrusted to its memory all traditional information and knowledge, as do all societies unacquainted with written archives. And it is here that we must revise the notion of *mythology*, with which the Greeks encumbered us as a consequence of their entanglement with *logos*. For the unified concept "myth," which nowhere seems to be defined as a discrete literary genre, must fade away in favor of a set of intellectual operations fundamental to the memorizing of narratives that together make up a tradition. Claude Lévi-Strauss suggests the term *mythism* for the process by which a story, initially personal and entrusted to the oral tradition, becomes adopted by the collective mode, which will distin-guish between the crystal clear parts of the narrative—that is, the levels that are structured and stable because they rest on common foundations—and the conjectural parts—details or episodes amplified or neglected at each telling, before being doomed to oblivion and falling outside the bounds of mem-ory. Every traditional society develops, with varying success, a widely shared creative memory, which is neither the memory of specialists nor that of technicians. The narratives we agree to call myths are the products of an intellectual activity that invents what is memorable.

When writing appears, it neither banishes traditional memory to a state of decay nor sustains an oral practice in imminent danger of becoming extinct. Writing occurs at different levels and in different orders, but always at the encounter between an act of remembering and the works that memory creates. Writing was to introduce a new mem-ory, word-for-word memory, which comes with the book and with education through the study of written texts. Compet-ing ever so slowly with the former kind of memory, mechan-ical memory alone is capable of engendering the idea, familiar to us, of the *correct* version, a version which must be copied or learned exactly, word for word. In Greece between the sixth and fifth centuries, the first historians, those whom the Greeks call "logographers," selected writing as the in-strument of a new kind of memory that would become an integral part of thought and political action. This new way of remembering was constructed on the boundary between a type of oral tradition with its remembrances, spoken narra-tives, and stories circulating by word of mouth, and, on the other side, the dominant obsession of the new investigators, who respected as knowledge only what had been seen, and who would ultimately condemn, without appeal, those who accepted traditions of the past that were transmitted without precise terminology or rigorous proof. This was the battle-ground, the wide open space of writing, for the confronta-tion between variants that became different versions of the same myth, usually examined from within the confines of a city in quest of self-image or political identity.

Elsewhere, other routes were taken that linked writing to the production of myths whose successive variations were inseparable from the hermeneutic activity of scribes and interpreters devoted to textual exegesis. From the moment the traditional narratives of the Bible, the Book of the Hebraic world, were committed to writing, they were swept away by the inner workings of a system of writing which, though initially consonantal, in its hollows called for a vocalic complement to bear its meaning, since one cannot read a consonantal text unless one understands it, that is, unless

one attributes to it a meaning set apart from other possible meanings. In the continuity of interpretation thus opened up, the hermeneutics that was focused on the mythical accounts of Israel claimed a privileged place, which made it more sensitive to the permanence of fundamental themes endlessly revived and reevaluated, but also forced it to be the infinite exegesis, forever interned within its own symbolic wealth.

M.D./g.h.

BIBLIOGRAPHY

R. FINNEGAN, *Oral Poetry: Its Nature, Significance and Social Context* (Cambridge 1977). J. GOODY and J. WATT, "The Consequences of Literacy," *Comparative Studies in Society and History*, 1963, 304–45. J. GOODY, "Mémoire et apprentissage dans les sociétés avec et sans écriture: La transmission du Bagre," *L'homme*, 1977, 29–52. E. A. HAVELOCK, *Preface to Plato* (Cambridge, MA, 1963). R. KOENIG, "L'activité herméneutique des scribes dans la transmission du texte de l'Ancien Testament," *Revue de l'Histoire des Religions*, 1962, 141–74. CL. LÉVI-STRAUSS, *Mythologiques* 4 (Paris 1971): 560 (translated as *Introduction to a Science of Mythology*, New York 1969–). L. SEBAG, *L'invention du monde chez les Indiens Pueblos* (Paris 1971), 472–85. J. VANSINA, *De la tradition orale: Essai de méthode historique*, Musée royal de l'Afrique centrale (Tervuren 1961).

Some mythographic texts of ancient Greece: APOLLODORUS, *The Library*, J. G. Frazer, ed. (London 1921). DIODORUS OF SICILY, *The Library*, vol. 4, C. H. Oldfather, ed. (London 1935). ANTONINUS LIBERALIS, *Metamorphoses*. HYGINUS, *Astronomica*, B. Bunte, ed. (Leipzig 1875). HYGINUS, *Fabulae*, H. I. Rose, ed. (Leiden 1933). *Mythographi graeci*, 5 vols., R. Wagner, Martini, A. Olivier, and N. Festo, eds., Bibl. Script. graec. Teubneriana (Leipzig 1896–1926). *Mythographi Vaticani*, G. H. Bode, ed., vols. 1–2 (1834; reprinted Olms 1968). ACUSILAUS OF ARGOS, PHERECYDES OF ATHENS, and HELLANIKOS OF LESBOS, in *Fragmente der griechischen Historiker*, F. Jacoby, ed., I: *Genealogie und Mythographie* (Leiden 1922; 2d ed., 1957).

PREHISTORIC RELIGION

To speak of "prehistoric religion" without specifying time and place is tantamount to assimilating under modern thought facts and contexts that came to light at very different times and places, tantamount to creating a kind of average image that can only be validated by the judgment of our own way of thinking projected onto some arbitrarily chosen facts. Prehistoric religion no longer occasions a debate in which either pro- or anticlerical convictions are at stake. The science of prehistory has been enriched by much new data and major changes in methodological approaches. Rather than arguing about whether the atheist brute evolved first into the magi-cian and then into the priest, scientists have given priority to inquiries that bring out the deep connections among play, aesthetics, social behavior, economic realities, and practices that rest on a metaphysical framework. The proofs that can be proliferated from a so-called religious approach are largely derived from the realm of the unprecedented, from the presence of peculiar facts found in a context where they are least expected, such as the discovery, on a Mousterian site inhabited by Neanderthal man, of fossil shells, which he collected and brought back to his dwelling place, or the discovery that he gathered red ocher or buried his dead. These diverse elements do not fit in with our vision of Neanderthal man. Yet how could there not be a striking contrast between this primal brute with his bulky brow ridges and the subtle quality of a religiosity polished by two millennia of Christianity and all of ancient philosophy? Neanderthal man was not, in the final analysis, as short of gray matter as was long believed, though the metaphysical level of his cultic activities was certainly very different from ours (at least, as we imagine ours to be).

What matters is the existence of practices within a psychological realm not directly tied to techniques of acquisition, manufacture, or consumption, even if these practices do flow back into material life. Man acquired religious behavior when he developed the whole system of symbolic thought, which cannot be separated from language and gesture as it works out a network of symbols that present a counterimage of the outside world. That Neanderthals had already developed this network of symbols is beyond doubt, but whether one can go on to distinguish evidence of a primordial religion or an extremely diffuse symbolic complex remains questionable. The gathering of magical shells and ocher supports the view that the pump had been primed for the simultaneous evolution of the fields of art, play, and religion, three fields which to this day cannot be separated.

Homo sapiens picked up where Neanderthal man left off, with regard to the gathering of "curios" (shells, fossils, crystals, iron pyrites, stalactite fragments, etc.) sometimes found together in the same pile. Ocher became much more plentiful. The first use of manganese dioxide, a black dye, coincided with the production of a greater number of drawings engraved on bone or stone surfaces. By the Aurignacian period, these drawings took the form of rhythmic incisions and figurative tracings. By 30,000 B.C., figurative art had developed to the point at which subjects could be divided into the following groups: female sexual symbols (sometimes also male), figures of animals, and regularly spaced incisions or punctuations. These themes predominated throughout the development of Paleolithic art, a subject to which we shall return.

Burial Grounds and the Cult of Bone Remains

Neanderthals buried their dead. The practice of inhumation is attested by several obvious tombs and, statistically, by the numerous finds of skeleton fragments. Shanidar in Iraq is the site of the only discovery of a Neanderthal laid out on a bed of flowers, from which a great number of fossilized pollens were found. In Monte Circeo (Italy), in a similarly convincing find, a skull was placed in the center of a cave chamber. In the face of such striking testimony, it is difficult not to ascribe to the immediate predecessors of humankind as we know it today sentiments analogous to our own regarding the afterlife in a parallel universe, a universe which may have been as inexplicit as that of the average subject of any of today's major religions. Difficult as it may be, given the available evidence, to describe Neanderthal man's attitude toward the supernatural, it is even more difficult to demonstrate the meaning of what falls into the category of the "cult of bone remains." Because bone is the only physical element (human or animal) that survives decomposition, any bones found as evidence in an unusual situation could have played a part in a cult. Whether with respect to Neanderthal man or to *Homo sapiens*, we have some evidence that can be explained in terms that are not at variance with an interpretation based on the supernatural. Separated by several scores of millennia, the skulls of Monte Circeo (Mousterian) and the skull from Mas-d'Azil (Magdalenian) attest the special character of the head (the whole head

or merely the skull). Although the idea of "graves" of animals has been advanced repeatedly, it seems that natural phenomena were more often at issue than man himself, especially in the case of the remains of cave bears.

The burial graves of fossil *Homo sapiens* are rare, and hardly a single grave dating from the Upper Paleolithic Age (30,000–9000) has been excavated either with care or with all the technical means that would have assured its documentary value. We do, however, have a certain number of facts at our disposal (graves; bodies, either curled up or stretched out; a head protected by a stone; ocher dusting; and funereal household objects, including, at the least, clothing and ornaments worn by the dead person). In addition, the double children's tomb at Sungir, north of Moscow, where hundreds of ornamental elements adorn the bodies and large spears made of mammoth ivory were found in the grave, bears witness to the development of the concern to equip the dead, a development that occurred at a remote phase of the Upper Paleolithic Age. Obviously, graves do not all reflect identical religious intentions, nor can we be certain what kind of sentiments led to these emotional displays. Mortuary furniture is ordinarily less sumptuous. In several cases we might even speculate that the presence of certain vestiges was connected with accidental conditions surrounding the filling of the grave. But a rather constant factor is the presence of ocher, which varied according to the population's wealth in dyes. Ocher gave the soil and the skeleton that it covered a reddish coloration. This practice, common during the Upper Paleolithic Age, is the indisputable sign of acts whose meaning goes beyond a simple natural emotion. If the use of ocher supports various interpretations according to habitat, the sheer fact of its being brought into a grave where a body had been laid constitutes the most distinct feature of the belief in an afterlife, since the dead person was considered still capable of using what he was offered.

Personal Adornments

Jewelry appeared in the West around 35,000 B.C. Its prior origin is unknown. Throughout Europe, its appearance coincided with the first manifestations of the Upper Paleolithic Age. During the Châtelperronian epoch (35,000–30,000), it appears already quite diversified: at that same time we find annular pendants carved out of bone, as well as teeth from various animal species (fox, wolf, marmot, aurochs, etc.), made so that they could be hung by means of a perforation of the root or a slit. Fossil shells were treated in the same way. It may seem far-fetched to regard ornamental pendants as anything other than purely aesthetic objects, and, in fact, some may have had exclusively decorative functions. However, among the hundreds of pendants acquired from European sites, the majority reveal a preoccupation with magic at one level or another. Those that unambiguously represent male and female sexual organs must surely have had some sort of symbolic value (fig. 1). The cylindrical fragments of stalactite and points of belemnites designed to hang may have a meaning of the same order. This symbolic function of sexual images may have been extended to include fragments of shattered assegai spears that were perforated but otherwise untreated (see the symbolism of the assegai below). The role of teeth designed to hang must have been rather complex, at least in the early stages, for the teeth of some animals, the marmot for example, do not seem to have the characteristics of a trophy or a talisman. This is not true of the atrophied canines of reindeer, which even today are symbols of masculinity and

Pendants with genital designs. Left: series of female symbols; right: phalloid symbol. 7.5 cm. Isturitz (Pyrénées district). (Fig. 1)

were imitated in bone or soft stone when pendants first appeared.

The same applies to shells. For the most part they seem to have a purely aesthetic function, but the rather frequent discovery of porcelain (Cyprea), universally attested in prehistoric and historic times as a protective female symbol, makes it highly probable that the collection of shells served as talismans. In short, having gone beyond a strictly decorative function, long and oval pendants encompassed both the aesthetic and the religious realms, and probably the social realm as well, although we still have too little data to clarify the matter.

The Occurrence of Wall Painting

The development of personal adornments does not diminish the importance of the collections of natural curiosities; rather, it was an added feature that prevailed until the end of the Upper Paleolithic Age, ca. 9000. Adornments evolved throughout this period. But in the Aurignacian and the Perigordian Ages, the main event was the spread of pictorial

works. Between 30,000 and 20,000, certain forms began to appear in engravings. These first forms were executed on blocks and probably on the walls of rock shelters as well. Despite their crudeness, they shed light on the concerns of their creators. The repertoire of these works is very limited; representation of the female genitalia, highly stylized, is the most widespread. A few representations of the male genitalia can be found, but they were apparently replaced quite early by abstract symbolic figures: dotted lines or bar lines that seem to accompany explicitly female figures. There are also highly geometrical figures of animals, parallel to one another and often juxtaposed or superimposed on one another. The Aurignacian-Gravettian bestiary includes the horse, the bison, the ibex, and other imprecise figures indicating that from the very beginning art made use of two clearly defined registers: human figures symbolically rendered, starting with the representation of the entire body and progressing, by way of genital figures and animals, to geometric figures. During the ensuing 20,000 years, the details may have varied but the basic figures, human and animal, remained in the same relationships. These relationships cannot easily be established on the basis of the engraved blocks alone; displacement in the course of time and, especially, following excavations has destroyed the spatial ties that might have guided us to their meaning. But something happened, perhaps by the Gravettian Age but certainly around 15,000: penetration deep into caves and the execution of paintings or engravings, sometimes more than a kilometer from the opening. This boldness on the part of Paleolithic men is of immediate interest to us because the works produced at such locations preserved their positions with respect to one another and with respect to the wall itself. We can therefore raise questions about the possible religious ideology of the creators of these figures. What motives could have inspired the Magdalenians of Niaux or Pech-Merle to their speleological adventure? It is hard to believe that it was just a matter of curiosity, and one is inclined to think that in their eyes the cave must have seemed a mysterious amalgam of female forms. Direct evidence is furnished by the numerous oval cavities or cleft lips painted on the inside in red ocher (Gargas, Font-de-Gaume, Niaux). The execution of numerous genital symbols in deep side passages indirectly reinforces the hypothesis of the woman-cave. To date, explicit male symbols are rare but one may find, on Aurignacian blocks, for instance, signs made up of series of dots or rods accompanying oval or triangular figures depicted with different degrees of realism. All stages of development come together, with regional nuances, from the whole female figure to the pubic triangle rendered as an empty rectangle. This tendency of male and female signs to conceal themselves behind abstract graphics may well have been a response to taboos of a socioreligious character. This hypothesis becomes all the more plausible as other figurative anomalies give evidence of the same meaning. Not only is there no known instance of human or animal mating anywhere in Paleolithic art, but sexual organs are explicitly represented on relatively few figures. At Lascaux (where, however, the bulls have obvious sexual characteristics), two figures appear (fig. 6): the "jumping cow" in the Axial Diverticulum and an engraved horse in the Passage, both of which have their hooves turned in such a way that the underbelly on both animals is visible and completely empty. This strange mannerism in figure drawing is not easily explained, but it does show the complexity of Paleolithic thought. Curiously, secondary sexual characteristics (the antlers of the cervidae, the thick withers of the bovidae, and

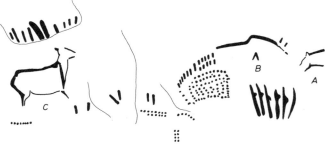

Middle part of the first great panel of the Cave of Pindal (Asturias). Animals A and B (horse and bison) are reduced to the minimal identifiable size: dorsal line and horns for the bison, which also bears a scar from a wound in the shape of an inverted V; central portion of the head and the neck and withers for the horse. Above the bison and the horse, S^2 line of the so-called claviform type (see fig. 5). The photograph includes only the right side of a series of red and black paintings. Between group A-B and the doe (C), there are several groups of S^1 and S^3 signs. The doe is 85 cm long. (Fig. 2)

the horns of the ibex) are rendered very exactly; and, moreover, the animals are frequently depicted in couples, the female in front and the male behind. It is certain that the figures basically connote what might be thought of as a "fertility cult," a generally banal statement that takes on a subtlety in the present instance by virtue of the apparent contradiction of the representation.

Animals

Paleolithic materials yield other peculiar data. The hundreds of figures that cover the walls of caves seem at first glance to defy any kind of order. Even though the idea of a coherent whole emerges from the way the figures are arranged, few prehistorians have used this possible organization to delve further into the ideology of the artists. One rather surprising fact stands out: the fauna that are represented display variations that seem to reflect the environment. In some caves the bison, together with the horse, is the principal subject (Font-de-Gaume, Niaux, Altamira), whereas in others the aurochs plays the main role (Lascaux, Ebbon). But in all the cases cited above, the complementary bovid (bison or aurochs depending on the site) is represented by one or more figures separated from the rest. Another point should also be mentioned: the reindeer that figure in

great numbers among the food wastes of the hunters at the time of these works occupy little space in the iconography of certain grottoes such as Lascaux, Niaux, or Altamira. At Lascaux, rather paradoxically, though the bony remains of reindeer make up almost all the animal wastes, only one figure can be attributed to the reindeer, and even that is somewhat doubtful. Thus the fauna depicted do not always correspond to what Paleolithic man hunted. This fact is important because, if it were confirmed, it would lead us to conclude that at least some of the animals represented played a role unconnected with the food that people then lived on. The number of sites for which it was possible to draw up a list of the animals depicted and a parallel list of the animals consumed as meat is unfortunately too limited to verify this hypothesis.

Groupings

We referred above to groupings of animal figures and signs, starting with the Aurignacian Age (30,000). The most frequent, almost exclusive animal grouping is of horses (100%) and of bison (56%) (or of aurochs, 39%, in other words, 95% for bovidae). This initial dyad, moreover, occupies the center of all surfaces used, and may be repeated several times in the same cave. The groupings in wall paintings have a complexity that derives from the diversity of the caves in which the decorations appear. So, too, geographical location and chronological evolution are reflected in various applications of the initial figurative formula and in the more or less pronounced use of natural forms. In any case, it is likely that the cave or the surface of the shelter wall was the object of a deliberate choice, and that the figures were not piled one on top of another haphazardly.

The horse(A)-bovid(B) twosome appears at all sites (fig. 7.1). Although we must allow for the possibility of caves or shelters that might not fit the basic AB formula, practically speaking the AB group is always present and dominates the groupings both numerically and topographically. But rarely does the AB group appear alone. Another category of animals intervenes, namely, group C (stag, mammoth, and occasionally chamois and reindeer). Among the wall painting groups, the ibex is most often the accompanying animal, but the stag, hind, mammoth, and reindeer also play the same role, most often on the sidelines, on the outer perimeter of the central panel groupings, or in the intermediary sections. The most frequent formula is thus AB + C, making up a triad with one interchangeable element: the ibex at Niaux, the mammoth at Rouffignac, the stag at Las Chimeneas. In the same cave, we can also see "moving" animals, or the following: at Niaux, the stag marks the deepest part of

the large painted surface, the rather numerous ibexes framing the AB figures; at Lascaux, the situation is similar—ibexes appear three or four times immediately to the side of a group of animals, stags being equal in number but farther to the side. In a cave like the Combarelles, in which the figures number into the hundreds, the "third animal" is represented by the reindeer, the ibex, and the mammoth, which are concentrated in the general area of the side panel of each decorated gallery.

Finally, there is also a D category to which fierce animals belong: the rhinoceros, the bear, and the big cats. The bear is a relatively rare animal in Paleolithic iconography and has no clearly defined place, but the rhinoceros and the big cats are marginal animals, most often situated in the deepest or most peripheral parts of the figured group. At Lascaux, Font-de-Gaume, the Combarelles, to cite only a few, the big cats are in this position. In these three places, the rhinoceros occupies an analogous position: at Lascaux, at the bottom of the Well; at Font-de-Gaume, at the end of the main gallery next to the big cat; and at the Combarelles, superimposed over the "lioness" from the end of the second gallery. The complete formula for the grouping is C + AB + C (+ D) in the case of a cave with a single composition, one that forms part of a series. In extreme cases, as in Lascaux or Combarelles, one may encounter a series of groupings with the basic formula repeated time and again.

Cave of Pech-Merle (Lot). Middle and left of the great frieze painted in black. Two groups of animals can be seen: the group on the left and the group on the right each include a horse (A) and two bison on the right, two aurochs on the left. The mammoths present in both groupings make up group C. Between the two groupings, there are also three animals marked by signs: (1) a bull (B²) bearing a sign (S¹) with a male connotation on his side (see fig. 5); (2) a cow (B²) marked by wounds (S²); (3) diagonally across from both animals, a mammoth bearing three rows of thick red dashes. The figures are between 60 and 120 cm long. (Fig. 3)

Signs

Signs seem to follow the same general patterns as animal figures. They fall into three categories (fig. 5). The first is made up of male symbols (S^1) ranging from the human body depicted in its entirety to a simple little stick. In between are sometimes very abstract transitions (lines branching out with two extensions at the base, as in Lascaux). The signs of the second group (S^2) correspond to female symbols. Like the signs of the first group, they range from a complete female representation to an empty or partitioned rectangle. The third group (S^3), in comparison with the other two, is homologous to the animals of group C or CD. It is made up of aligned dots or a series of little sticks aligned or clustered. In several cases, the S^3 signs are repeated at the beginning and the end of the figurative series. This phenomenon is quite evident at Lascaux, where the aligned dots are found at the entrance and at the far end of the Axial Diverticulum, between the Passage and the Nave, at the bottom of the Well, and at the end of the Diverticulum of the Big Cats. The signs of the third group, therefore, occupy a position rather set back, most often in the background, as at Font-de-Gaume, Pech-Merle, and El Castillo.

The relationship between signs and animals corresponds to the following broad lines: the S^1S^2 group is found juxtaposed with the animals of groups A and B (fig. 2), as in the case of the Diverticulum of the Big Cats at Lascaux (fig. 6), in which the S^1S^2 signs are in the central panel, right across from an AB group (horse-bison). But the signs may be independent of the animal figures, grouped in a separate diverticulum. Good examples can be found at Niaux (Black Room), at El Castillo, at La Pasiega, and, notably, at Cougnac. The relationship between animals and signs may thus be defined by the following formula:

$$C + AB + C + D$$
$$S^3 + S^1S^2 + S^3$$
$$\text{or}$$
$$C + AB + C + D/S^1S^2,$$
$$S^3 \qquad S^3$$

Both formulas can even be found in the same cave (La Pasiega).

This complex arrangement must have encompassed an ideology whose elaborate character may be perceived through the arrangement. The situation is further complicated, however, by the role played by the cave itself. Natural caves have many accidental features that evoked, for Paleolithic man, sexual forms, generally female. These natural structures, fissures or stalagmitic formations, sometimes underscored in red (Gargas, Niaux), are also frequently completed with an S^1 sign (little sticks or dots: Gargas, Combel de Pech-Merle, Niaux), proving that the natural phenomenon was considered equivalent to S^2. This is particularly clear in Niaux, where two fissures in the inner gallery were marked at the entrance by a sign of male connotation (branching sign) accompanied in one of the two cases by a horse with its head extended in the direction of the fissure.

In the course of millennia and in a territory as vast as that of Paleolithic cave art, figurative traditions must have undergone numerous variations, and it is remarkable that we should come across an ideographic system that is so well constructed. Yet two rather important questions, concerning the role of wounds on animals and the role of hands, remain largely unresolved.

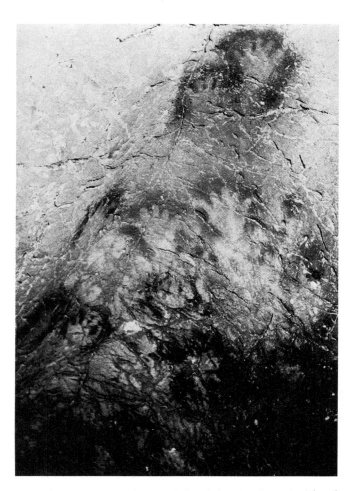

Cave of Gargas (Hautes-Pyrénées). Panel showing "negative" hands with "mutilated" fingers. Most such hands, colored red or black, are grouped in twos by subject, and appear to have been executed by folding in the fingers or by applying a stencil. (Fig. 4)

Wounds

In art objects as well as mural art, we find animals with wounds. Ever since research on prehistoric religion began, this detail has been thought to reveal the practice of magic spells. This explanation is not altogether impossible, but certain elements lead us to believe that it does not resolve the problem entirely. In fact, 96% of the animal figures on file (between 2,500 and 3,000) show no wounds. We might ask ourselves if the two series, animal and sign, really belong to the same symbolic system, or if two lines of symbols might have existed without any organic ties between them. Signs do seem to have played their role at the same times and in the same places as animals. What is more, both evolved synchronically, and both underwent parallel stylistic transformations. It is very unlikely that signs were slipped in among animals, with no connection to them, in the course of various rituals; too many signs are connected to animals by their position for the relationship not to be a close one, as the Pech-Merle paintings show (fig. 3). This does not preclude the claim that signs are sometimes independent, as at Altamira, where the signs and the animals of the Great Ceiling make up two distinct clusters; or as at El Castillo or La Pasiega, where, for one important portion, the painted

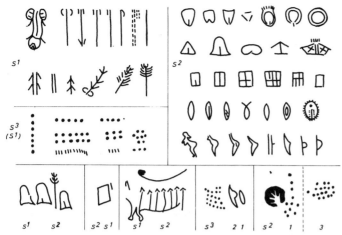

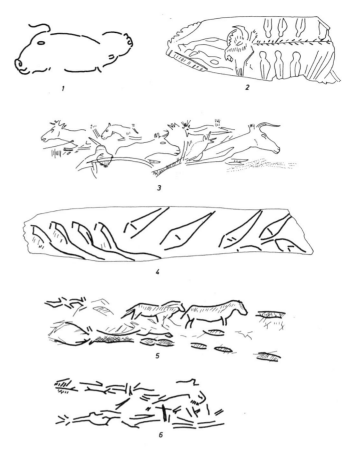

Geometrization of male and female symbols. S¹: phalloid derivatives. S²: principal series of vulvar derivatives. S³: rows of punctuation (dotted lines) and barred lines. Below, from left to right: S¹-S² groupings. El Castillo (Santander): triangle derivatives and branching sign. Lascaux (Dordogne): maximal geometrization and abstractions (empty rectangle and bar). Lascaux: crooked bar (S¹) and seven aligned wounds (S²). S¹, S², S³ groupings. Niaux (Ariège): bar (S¹), claviform (see same S² figure), cloud of dots (S³). Pech-Merle (Lot): at the entrance of a deep side passage, three figures that appear to correspond in value to S³: dotted line with four lateral dots (see same S³ figure). The negative hand probably corresponds to S², and the cloud of dots, farther into the passage, probably corresponds to S³. (Fig. 5).

Lascaux (Dordogne): (1) Engraved horse with rump turned such that the perineal region is exposed but devoid of primary sexual characteristics. 60 cm. (2) Paintings from the axial gallery, central part of the righthand wall. Aurochs in the same posture as the horse in front. Secondary sexual characteristics (general profile) are attributable to a cow, but primary characteristics, notably the udder, are invisible. This figure is included in the grouping formula A-B S¹-S² (horse-aurochs, bars, gridlike sign; see fig. 5). 1.70 m. (Fig. 6)

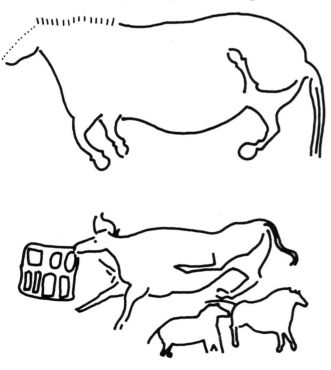

Gourdan (Haute-Garonne). The principle of association of animals A and B may also be applied to portable objects. This engraving on bone plaquette represents the aurochs-horse twosome with the heads of both animals assembled like the faces on playing cards. About 6 cm from nose to nose. (2) Raymonden (Dordogne). Partial pendant (or fish spatula). A scene of a religious nature seems to be unfolding: six or seven persons (perhaps more) are lined up on either side of a line resembling barbed wire at the end of which is the severed head of a bison and two paws with ill-defined hooves. Near the knee, one of these legs bears a "chestnut," a horny growth that is the vestige of the multifingered hoof of the ancestors of the *equidae*. It may indeed be a horse leg, and this grouping with its sacrificial look may refer to the A-B model. (3) Torre (Guipuzcoa). Roll of fine engravings around a bone tube. From left to right: stag, man, horse, chamois, two small ibex with frontal horns, and aurochs. This series of animals referring to A-B model + C is of more than purely artistic interest: between the subjects are abstract tracings (parallel or crossed strokes, beginnings of spherical figures, clouds made of fine dots, etc.) which must have ensured that Magdalenians could "read" this mythogram. (4) Mas-d'Azil (Ariège). Bone plaquette engraved with horses and fish, already strongly geometrized. Mythographic theme born out by several examples. (5) El Valle (Santander). Bone tube with engraved bird. Subject related to preceding one: two horses, one behind the other, a stag facing forward, numerous features with no apparent meaning, perhaps a snake, and some oval figures, probably fish. (6) El Pendo (Santander). Bone tube engravings, like the preceding ones, but virtually uninterpretable. There remains a part of the head and neck of a horse and a herbivore with visible horns (or antlers) and ears borne by a very long neck. Note that these two figures occupy the same situation as those of the El Valle tube. (Fig. 7)

signs are collected in a side passage; or at Cougnac (Lot), where S^1 and S^2 signs are located in a side alcove away from the animal figures, while the S^3 series occurs in the figured panels.

Whether these are two series of symbols executed simultaneously and experienced as forming the frame of a single ideological block, or whether they are two separate series with elements that were to enter one another on synchronic but distinct levels—either case presupposes a highly complex intellectual content, intimately tied to an elaborate social system. Could they be symbols of the propagation of humans and animals, a cosmogony that calls into play the complementary forces of male and female? It is difficult to reach a conclusion without going beyond the available data, but certainly we are in the presence of something quite different from what was long imagined about "the Paleolithic savages."

Of the 4% of animals showing wounds in the thoracic or the neighboring abdominal areas, if we do a percentage count by species, the greatest number goes to the bison (8%), then to the horse (2.5%), with zero or less than 1% for all other species. There is yet another striking fact. Although wounded animals are encountered throughout the Franco-Cantabrian region, most cases occur in the Ariège sector of the Pyrenees, with the greatest number represented at Niaux (25% of figured animals). The value of the wound as a testimony to magic spells for game might be merely an accessory phenomenon, but the hunting symbolism to which it refers is certain. The fact that wounds appear essentially only on the bodies of the basic twosome is perhaps connected with the AB = S^1S^2 equation, the wounds being the equivalent of S^2, that is, the female connotation. Three pieces of evidence may be invoked to support this contention: a horse at Lascaux bearing seven wounds on its body and an S^2 sign (fig. 5) on its neck and withers; a bison at Bernifal whose shoulder has an oval wound flanked by two little sticks; and a bison at Niaux engraved on clay, which has three wounds and two little sticks on its side. These parallel sticks belong to the highly varied portion of masculine symbols. One of the best examples of the relationship between signs and animals is that of the great panel of Pech-Merle (fig. 3) made up of two groupings that share the same C animal (C^2 mammoth). One is the aurochs-horse (AB^2), and the other the horse-bison (AB^1). Between the two groupings of figures are three animals: a bull, a cow, and a mammoth. Each bears different signs. The bull bears a double line of dashes with lateral extensions (S^1, of male character). The cow is riddled with wounds that seem to play the role of S^2 signs. The mammoth is covered with red spots aligned to form the equivalent of the S^3 sign. From this evidence we can hypothesize that "wounds" have the value of a female symbol. Establishing this symbolism would open a vast realm of possibilities for the symbolic system of Paleolithic art, one that involves the alternation of symbols of life and death.

Hands

While the problem of wounds allows us to do no more than hint at some kind of metaphysical solution, *positive* hand imprints (in which a hand is smeared with color and pressed flat against the wall) and *negative* hand imprints (in which a hand is laid flat against the wall and outlined in color) raise questions equally resistant to clear answers. Positive hands are substantially rarer than negative hands and show up infrequently in groupings, but the Bayol cave in the Ardèche region has a good example. It shows six positive hands in a grouping that includes an aurochs, two horses, and one big cat, all treated in a very particular style.

There are several types of negative hands, probably corresponding to several different traditions. The first category is made up of hands integrated in a grouping that includes, notably, dottings; this is the case in Pech-Merle, where in six instances hands are associated with dotted lines in close proximity to the two crisscrossed horses and once with eleven dotted lines above the opening of a very low side passage (fig. 5). The same arrangement of animal figures and dottings is found in El Castillo. In the Périgord, negative hands appear in isolation (one at Font-de-Gaume, one at Combarelles, several grouped at Bernifal, etc.). At Roucadour (Lot), the hands are superposed over the animals, and they have long pointed fingers incised on a black background. The Pech-Merle hands give the impression of being inserted in an arrangement where they play an important role, surely as important as the S^2 signs with their female connotation.

The hands in the cave of Gargas (Hautes-Pyrénées), like those in the neighboring grotto at Tibiran, are very different in nature (fig. 4). Repeated scores of times in different panels and hollows of the cave, they have the special feature of cut-off or, more likely, bent-in fingers. The various combinations of fingers might have been part of a kind of symbolic code of the animals most commonly represented in figurative art (horse, bison, ibex, etc.). The same digital formula appears again in side-by-side hands repeated twice and alternating between red and black (fig. 4). Examples can also be found at the openings of niches or fissures, in the position normally occupied by animals or signs of CD and S^1 groups. As strange as it may seem, the "mutilated hands" of Gargas, which include many children's hands, are not missing all five fingers. They seem to correspond to a fairly rational application of signals involving variably bent fingers, gestures that can still be observed today among certain groups of hunters, notably the Bushmen. Aside from the monumental aspect of the connections between the groups of hands and their natural support, the ideographic aspect is extremely impressive.

Animal and human figures make up the ground on which our tentative explanation of wall painting rests. This explanation calls on data which, in the way they are assembled, suggest a complex ideological construct. To what extent can objects that are found not on walls but on sites of living quarters corroborate this claim?

Objects

Caves contain particularly precious data, if only because the images have preserved their location on walls. A no less precious source of information, however, may be found on the surfaces of Paleolithic floors strewn with objects that bear human and animal figures. Some of these objects are fairly soft fragments of stone or fragments of bone on which figures have been incised or sculpted. No practical function can be attributed to them, and we are struck by their resemblance to the figures on walls. Given their iconographic content, we ask whether they could have played the same role in living quarters as the figures played in the cave, and whether they were used to reproduce the same combinations. These questions are difficult to answer decisively, for the possibilities of iconographic combinations are extremely varied. The figures (statuettes, plaquettes or blocks, weapons or tools, personal adornments) may have been assembled in a meaningful way (according to the C-A-B-C + D model), a configuration that may presuppose, for example, either several plaquettes each bearing one figure, or several plaquettes each bearing several animal figures. Unfortunately rare are the cases where portable objects are found in their functional places, and even rarer are sites where the excavators took the trouble to record the exact position of the relics. Yet we can begin by assuming that, since caves existed only in a limited number of areas while vast territories lent themselves only to open-air settlements, the plaquettes of stone, ivory, or bone or the statuettes which sometimes abound at such sites fulfilled the role that otherwise devolved upon cave walls.

We may also assume that the other decorated objects reflect, in whole or in part, the same ideological scheme that is displayed by the grouping of the figures on the walls.

Statuettes

Statuettes of animals are relatively rare in the Paleolithic art of western Europe. The cave of Isturitz (Basses-Pyrénées) stands out as an exception with its numerous animals (bison, horses, bears) incised in soft rock. The true domain of animal figures in round relief is central and eastern Europe. The pictorial repertory of Europe east of the Rhine is mostly made up of statuettes molded in clay mixed with powdered bone (Moravia), incised in bone or in mammoth ivory; and figurines of mammoth, horse, bison, and big cats. The functions of these statuettes are as yet unclear, but since they must have assumed the same role as that played by the engravings and paintings in the caves, they must have the same symbolic ranges.

One category of figures is made up of female statuettes, inaccurately called "Venus" figures, that appear in various forms depending on the stages of the Paleolithic epoch and the regions in which they were executed. The items discovered at Kostienki (on the Don River), on Ukranian sites, at Predmost in Moravia, Willendorf in Austria, and at Brassempouy and Lespugue in southwestern France show in the details of their execution that they belong to the same pictorial traditions. Were the religious traditions that they were supposed to illustrate of the same nature? That is hard to answer, for the good reason that female statuettes can only symbolize a limited number of functions, generally relating to fertility. Based on what we know today, it would be difficult to say any more about them, except perhaps that the statuettes discovered in living quarters may have played an identical role to that of the signs in the groupings of figures on the walls. Male figures by their very scarcity seem to have occupied a much more modest place.

In brief, plaquettes, which are far more numerous in the West than statuettes, and statuettes, which are more numerous than plaquettes in central and eastern Europe, seem to have had the same functions. Given the resemblances between portable art (on plaquettes and statuettes) and mural art, we can ascribe identical functions to them and assimilate them to the same religious process. Unfortunately, this does not entirely clarify the details of the process that we know to have borrowed the same basic symbols throughout all of Europe for twenty thousand years. The formula A-B, C, D + S^1, S^2, S^3 did not necessarily have the same ideological implications in the Urals as it did on the banks of the Vézère. The hundreds of plaquettes of engraved schist from Gönnersdorf (dating from the Magdalenian epoch ca. 10,000) left lying on the ground may not have had the same function as the heavy engraved blocks of the Aurignacian epoch around 30,000.

It seems possible nevertheless to discern in the groupings of art objects and mural art alike the systematic presence of two animals A-B, often associated with one or two animals from group C. Human figures and male and female symbols are also present, as they are in wall paintings. The specialized use of certain objects may have influenced the choice of the figures that were drawn on them. There were relatively few decorated objects during the first millennia; realistic figures, at least, were rare. It is not until the middle and late Magdalenian Age, from 12,000 to 9000, that objects made of reindeer horn and bone begin to be covered with figures. Propelling devices—hooked pieces probably designed to hurl assegais at game—most often depict a single animal, close to the hook. On objects in this category the most eclectic assortment can be found: horse, bison, mammoth, ibex, reindeer, big cat, fish, bird. The propelling devices (their real use is still unknown) thus fall in the same iconographic category as plaquettes and statuettes.

Perforated Sticks

Perforated sticks are a different story. A kind of lever made of reindeer horns, the stick consists of a cylindrical handle with a bifurcation at one end in which a hole three centimeters in diameter has been pierced at the thickest point. Its real use was to straighten out, while hot or cold, the long assegai spears that had kept the curvature of the horns from which they had been made. The class of perforated sticks includes a large number of carefully decorated objects. In a significant proportion of them, the handle is sculpted in the shape of a phallus. Sometimes both extensions of the head of the object have this decoration. There are also many perforated sticks that bear the A-B grouping (horse-bison) or the third animal, in the form of a stag, a reindeer, or an ibex. A whole series of perforated sticks are decorated on their lateral extensions with two heads of bison, highly geometrized and often reduced to two sets of parallel bars. This decorative element can be found from the Asturias to Switzerland. Some perforated sticks feature realistic scenes, such as the one at Dordogne in Laugerie-Basse, which on one side shows a man knocked over by a bison and on the other side a horse; or the one in La Madeleine, which has a man, a snake, and two horses on one side, and two bison on the other. Certainly these animals were not grouped in a fortuitous manner: the H-B + A formula (Human-bison + horse) is the same formula as in the famous scene on the Well at Lascaux (a man knocked over by a bison, with a horse on the opposite wall). The second scene, however, must refer to another mythic content, for its formula, H-A + B (+ S) (Human-horse + bison [and snake]), has no known equivalent, but it does highlight the imperative character of the representation of the complementary animal: in the first case, the horse; in the second, the bison. We should also note that, as at Lascaux, the second animal is on the side opposite to the one with the scene.

Assegais

Assegais make up a category of particularly expressive decorated items. The ornamentation on these spears appears relatively early, around 20,000, and consists of geometric patterns, sometimes of a highly simplified animal figure. These markings may correspond to different hunters in the same group. But as time went by, the animal figures multiplied on some of these assegais. During the late Magdalenian era, some were covered with rows of horses on a raised field, which suggests that they served as instruments for parades or rituals rather than as effective weapons. The ends of assegais are often perforated to make them into pendants. Such pieces may have been part of a particular assegai that was lucky in its hunting and thereby served as a "talisman." The numerous pendants found in the Upper Paleolithic Age are largely inspired by sexual symbolism (cowrie shell, oval pendants, stag canines, etc.). It is thus likely that the assegai played a dual symbolic role. A few indices seem to support this contention, namely, the probable assimilation in mural art of male symbols with the assegai and female symbols with the wound. Many details from the natural relief of walls, such as oval niches painted red and the wounds on certain animals, support such a hypothesis. But it is difficult to consolidate the ideological aspects of this symbolic frame of reference.

Other decorated objects that might shed light on the religious thought of Paleolithic man require an even more sensitive interpretation. Harpoon points with realistic decoration are extremely rare. Conversely, we do have a considerable number of spatulas in the shape of fish, often highly geometrized. They may bear symbolic meaning, but at what level? The scale of values may range from a representation of a primarily aesthetic character to an instrument indispensable for the execution of a ritual. The same may be said of the rings of bone, three or four centimeters in diameter, with a very eclectic range of animal engravings on both sides. The fish spatula with its inevitable iconographic base (usually a species of *Salmonidae*), and the rings of bone on which all species are represented (including the human species) provide us only with a basic assumption and certainly not with evidence for an entire superstructure of beliefs. It is therefore by reference to the figures on walls and plaquettes that the iconography of portable objects can be analyzed. We may also want to view in the same spirit the so-called silhouette outlines, small pendants carved out of a hyoid bone, of which there are many known examples showing heads of horses as well as a group of eighteen ibex heads and one bison head, which may remind us of the triad horse-bison-ibex, the model of wall depiction.

One last category of materials is made up of groupings of figures engraved mostly on cylindrical objects (tubes of bird bone, assegai shafts, etc.), similar to the perforated sticks referred to above. Some of these objects bear explicit figures, like the bone tube of Torre (Spain), which in the space of fifteen centimeters depicts a series of busts including a stag, man, horse, chamois, ibex, and aurochs (fig. 7.1). This grouping, which may also incorporate signs in parallel or converging lines cross-hatched inside with ladders, is not far removed from certain wall groupings, such as the diver of Portel (Ariège), whose middle part is occupied by a horse, a bison, and male and female signs, while the periphery is occupied by the third sign (S^3), an ibex, and a stag. It would be hard not to regard these various assembled animals as the protagonists of a mythical story, a mythogram rather than a catalogue of the presumed victims of a spell of hunting magic. But whatever the figures may designate precisely, we cannot yet afford to go outside the realm of fact to venture an explanation. Thus we have a whole series of groupings on cylinders or plaquettes, graphically explicit but just as mysterious as ever, such as the strange object found in Les Eyzies on which eight hunters carrying assegais on their shoulders

seem to be parading in front of a bison, or another item from Chancelade (fig. 7.2) on which seven human silhouettes appear to surround a bison's head and severed front hooves. These two examples, probably variants of the same theme, show how the discovery of new versions might help us to decipher an increasingly important part of the Paleolithic message.

A significant number of specimens (figs. 7.4, 7.5, 7.6) bear an ornamentation that is very difficult to identify: a row of curves and ovoid figures including a recognizable horse here and there or a highly simplified stag, or sometimes a fish. Given the constancy with which geometric motifs replace explicit figures, we could almost speak of ideograms, though we need not see in these semigeometric figures the elements of "writing." We can assume that the geometrized symbols preserved their meaning, so that a grouping like "chevrons-broken lines" could be equivalent to, for instance, "horse-snake," chevrons being the tail end of a row of horses, and the broken line being the geometrization of the snake's body: both cases exist in an explicit form.

It might seem surprising to hear so little said about "prehistoric religion." As far as practices are concerned, our knowledge consists mainly of gaps. We may imagine that the caves were shrines in which highly elaborate rituals took place, but all we *have* is wall decorations. The fact that the dead were buried with ocher and, at least in some cases, with funerary personal effects, leads us to ascribe to Upper Paleolithic man some notion of an afterlife, but we know nothing about its modalities in any detail. The tablets or engraved blocks tell us about iconographic activities that must have had a religious purpose, but we are far from being able to assert what kind of purpose it was. The same applies to decorated objects (perforated sticks, propelling devices, spatulas, etc.) of which we cannot even claim to know the exact usage. Nevertheless, the wealth of the iconography and the constancy of certain relationships between figures and between figures and the surfaces on which they appear make it possible for us to sketch the bare outlines of a system of religious thought, though its background is still very murky. The complexity and quality of these groupings express feelings (with nuances tied to places and times) that reflect simultaneously the aesthetic and religious life of Paleolithic man.

A.L.-G./g.h.

BIBLIOGRAPHY

H. BREUIL, *Quatre cents siècles d'art pariétal* (Montignac 1952). P. GRAZIOSI, *L'arte dell'antica età della pietra* (Florence 1956). A. LAMING-EMPERAIRE, *La signification de l'art rupestre paléolithique* (Paris 1962). ANDRÉ LEROI-GOURHAN, *Préhistoire de l'art occidental* (Paris 1965); *Les religions de la préhistoire* (Paris 1971); "Les signes pariétaux de Paléolithique supérieur franco-cantabrique," *Simposio intern. de arte rupestre* (Barcelona 1968), 67–77, fig.; "Considérations sur l'organisation spatiale des figures animales dans l'art pariétal paléolithique," *Actes del Symposium intern. de arte prehis.* (Santander 1972), 281–308; "Iconographie et interprétation," *Val Camonica symposium 72* (Capo di Ponte 1975), 49–55. ARLETTE LEROI-GOURHAN, "The Flowers Found with Shanidar IV, a Neanderthal Burial in Iraq," *Science* 190 (1975): 562–64. L. MEROC, "Informations archéologiques, Circonscription de Toulouse, Mas d'Azil," *Gallia Préhistoire* 4 (1961):256–57.

"NOMADIC THOUGHT" AND RELIGIOUS ACTION

When the rainy season comes, the mendicant monk stops wandering and heads back to his monastery.[1]

For some years now, nomadic societies have awakened strong and renewed interest among ethnologists. On an intuitive level, these societies scattered over the globe seem to be mutually comparable, and attempts have been made to construct models of such societies, that is, to go beyond the empirical diversity that science seeks to overcome. These attempts at synthesis, notably the collective work published under the direction of Lee and De Vore[2] on hunter-gatherers, and the works of B. Spooner[3] on pastoral nomads, are evidence of the special position that nomadic societies occupy today in ethnology.

The term "nomadism" covers quite diverse phenomena: hunter-gatherers and pastoral nomads move over greater or lesser distances, more or less frequently; hunter-gatherers make use of wild objects, and pastoral nomads domestic objects, to mediate their relation with the natural environment. Although nomadic societies differ among themselves in their type of economy and in the breadth and frequency of their movements, as a group they contrast with societies that do not move, settled societies, and it is in this light that we shall consider them for the purposes of this study, setting aside the ways in which the group could be subdivided. Dissimilar in many ways, both social and economic, these societies share not only itinerant behavior but also certain characteristics, which we will examine in order to determine whether they are reflected at the level of thought and worldview. Starting with a limited amount of work done on this subject, we can but suggest a direction of study and posit some hypotheses for research. To find pantheons common to nomads, if such a thing were possible, would require far more concerted and exhaustive studies. But it may already be possible to isolate from its various contexts an attitude to the supernatural world and religion that is common to nomads, and to define a framework within which we might study their mythology.

"Free, individualistic, subject to no state nor to any tyranny," such is the "traditional stereotype" of the pastoral nomad.[4] But it is also an objective piece of information to the extent that it is derived from the image that the nomad has of himself. When this self-image comes into close contact with settled societies, it may even be more pronounced, thus affirming in a deliberate way the difference between nomadic and settled ideologies. Pastoral nomads have a realistic vision of the world and a rather meager ceremonial life. They practice a great deal of divination but little witchcraft. Religion is centered on the individual rather than on the group; indeed, a pantheon comprising a great number of divine figures seems to be more common among farmers. If nomads show little interest in religion, and if they refer to manifestations of the supernatural in "stoic terms," this does not mean that they are any more "secular"[5] than any other group. The cosmology of pastoral nomads in the Middle East, for example, tends to be expressed in Islamic terms. Through this filter, as Spooner points out, it should be possible to see those elements of cosmology that antedate Islam or are not integral to it. When these are compared with other cosmologies from nomadic populations in regions lacking such a culturally dominant ideology, it may be possible to isolate the elements that derive from the nomadic adaptation.[6]

The mythology of hunter-gatherer societies presents notable similarities. The myths that retrace the origins of a society are apparently universal and come out of the same mold. In these myths, the culture hero creates mankind and its customs; he domesticates fire, teaches arts and crafts, and shapes the landscape and animals. In the cosmology, spirits are not gods: culture heroes or creator spirits no longer intervene in the affairs of men, and that is why they are not worshiped. They have to do with existential ideology and not with normative ideology. Just as the accent is placed on the person in nomadic society, so the world of spirits is strongly individualized; egalitarianism within the group is reflected in the absence of any hierarchy among the spirits. The individual deals directly with the world of the supernatural. Except for the shaman/doctor, there is no reliable mediation by specialized individuals.[7] The culture hero who offers the world to humans after he has created them is not totally absent from nomadic societies; but probably more characteristic of such societies is the strongly existential aspect of the ideology as well as egalitarianism. The absence of authoritarian chiefs and of a certain type of power excludes certain types of divine figures. Moreover, nomadic hunters pay little attention to what does not involve them directly. Accordingly, the Mbuti are more concerned with the present than with the past or the future. They are practical people. They eschew all speculation about the future or the hereafter on the grounds that not having been there they do not know what it is like and not knowing what it is like they cannot predict what their behavior will be. They say that to try to look into the future is to "walk blindly."[8] Knowledge is considered a way of living rather than a rule. And it is precisely in their behavior in the face of—rather than by the content of—myth or the supernatural that the clear outlines of a way of thinking peculiar to nomads begin to emerge. We see in hunter-gatherers certain features already observed in the pastoral nomads, and profoundly different from the religious attitudes of settled societies. Before we describe nomadic societies as nonreligious or hardly religious, we might first ask whether ethnologists hold too narrow a conception of ritual and symbolic behavior, and whether their analytic tools may be too closely tied to the categories of settled societies, which would hamper their perception of religious phenomena among nomads.

Among the Basseri, pastoral nomads of Iran, the paucity of ritual activity is striking;[9] they are indifferent to metaphysical problems and to religion. But is this really a lack, or are the descriptive categories that are being used incapable of describing the reality of the situation? The central rite of the society is migration itself. For the Basseri, migration is laden with meaning, though not expressed by means of technically unnecessary symbolic acts or exotic paraphernalia. The Basseri respond not to the utilitarian aspects of activities but to movement and its dramatic forms, to the meanings implicit in the sequence of their activities.[10] Is it not rather ethnocentric to assume that an activity that is important from an economic point of view cannot also be important from a ritualistic or symbolic point of view? The migrations of nomads are more than mere business trips; they are also ritually motivated and determined, and our difficulties in observation seem to be due to our conflation of these two domains.

In this discussion of the relationship between religious attitude (taken in a rather broad sense) and nomadism, societies with seasonal variations are both exceptional and typical because they are alternately nomadic and settled. The gathered habitat of the winter season contrasts with the scattered habitat of the summer season, with its mobility and the splintering of the group into families in the narrowest sense of the word. There are two ways of occupying land, but there are also two ways of thinking: "This contrast between life in winter and life in summer is reflected not only in rituals, festivals, and religious ceremonies of all sorts. It also profoundly affects ideas, collective representations, in a word, the whole mentality of the group.[11] . . . In summer, life is somewhat secularized."[12] The ecological constraints to which the group is subject make nomadism necessary, and the group's requirements come to restrict religious thought and practice. But just as we must consider the role of adaptation to the environment, we must also refine our categories of analysis, and when appearances evoke secularization, we must understand that the foundation has yet to be deciphered. The mobility that characterizes nomadic societies is indeed the central feature of their organization, but it is also the main obstacle to our understanding.

"We must beware of any tendency to treat fixed and permanent ties linking together aggregates of people as normal, and loose, impermanent bonds as abnormal and requiring special explanation."[13] The migrations of hunters or pastoral nomads by far exceed those that would be required by the demands of the natural environment and of access to natural resources. The fluidity and the constant coming and going, both of groups and of individuals within the groups, have a political function: they make it possible to ensure order, the resolution of conflicts, and, paradoxically, cohesion, because the lines of fusion and fission of groups and individuals do not necessarily follow the lines of kinship. Among nomads, social relations become activated through changes of place: proximity or distance are not relevant, and space is in a sense negated. Finally—and, in our view, this is an essential point—the changes of place have a religious function: they are highly valued, so highly that Barth sees them as the central rite among the Basseri. It is movement that leads nomads "into closer recognition of the one constant in their lives, the environment and its life-giving qualities. Under such conditions of flux where band and even family relations are often brittle and fragmentary, the environment in general, and one's own hunting territory in particular, become for each individual the one reliable and rewarding focus of his attention, his loyalty, and his devotion."[14] In other words, the nomad "does not have the impression of inhabiting a man-made world. . . . He is controlled by objects, not persons. . . . There is not an anthropomorphic cosmos. Hence there is no call for articulate forms of social intercourse with nonhuman beings and no need for a set of symbols with which to send and receive special communication."[15] The nomad does not seek to improve the environment in which he lives. In this sense, he is controlled by objects and a world that are *wild*, and he is in direct touch with nature. The domestic animals through whose intervention he exploits the wild objects, if he is pastoral, serve only to mediate this relationship with nature. Whether he is a hunter-gatherer or a shepherd, he does not impose his Culture on Nature as do settled peoples. Mobility and fluidity of groups and within groups; decentralized societies, or rather societies with multiple centers; egalitarianism; direct contact with nature—such are the poles that may affect the ideology of nomads and that may be reflected in collective representations and in rituals.

With a few examples, we have sought to come to terms with nomadism and its underlying ideology as a "certain type of behavior,"[16] rather than as a mode of economic production or as a variable determined by environment. This particular attitude, in the face of the supernatural and the symbolic world, is governed by what we might call a nomadic way of thinking that participates in the "primitive/wild/*sauvage*" way of thinking but preserves its own characteristics within it. The analysis of the content of the myths of various nomadic societies may indeed highlight the lines of force around which "nomadic thought" is organized, and will finally allow us to spell out the specificity of a way of thinking in which what is normal is not what is fixed, and the fluid and the moving are order and not chaos.

F.-R.P./g.h.

NOTES

1. M. MAUSS, "Étude de morphologie sociale," in *Sociologie et anthropologie* (Paris 1966), 472.

2. R.-B. LEE and I. DEVORE, eds., *Man the Hunter* (Chicago 1968).

3. B. SPOONER, "Towards a Generative Model of Nomadism," *Anthropological Quarterly* 44, no. 3 (1971): 198–210; "The Cultural Ecology of Pastoral Nomads," in *Addison-Wesley Module in Anthropology*, no. 45 (Reading, MA, 1973).

4. B. SPOONER, "Cultural Ecology of Pastoral Nomads," 35.

5. Ibid., 39.

6. Ibid.

7. E. R. SERVICE, *The Hunters* (Englewood Cliffs, NJ, 1966).

8. C. M. TURNBULL, *Wayward Servants* (Garden City, NY, 1965), 247.

9. F. BARTH, *Nomads of South Persia* (Boston 1961), 135.

10. Ibid.

11. M. MAUSS, "Étude de morphologie sociale," 447–48.

12. Ibid., 444.

13. J. WOODBURN, "Stability and Flexibility in Hadza Residential Groupings," in *Man the Hunter*, Lee and DeVore, eds., 107.

14. C. M. TURNBULL, "The Importance of Flux in Two Hunting Societies," in *Man the Hunter*, Lee and DeVore, eds., 137.

15. M. DOUGLAS, *Natural Symbols* (London 1970), 60–61; cited in Spooner, "Cultural Ecology of Pastoral Nomads," 40.

16. CL. LÉVI-STRAUSS, "Hunting and Human Evolution: Discussion," in *Man the Hunter*, Lee and DeVore, eds., 344.

2

The Americas and the South Pacific

The Mythology of the Inuit of the Central Arctic

In the mid-1970s, the population of the Inuit—spread over more than twelve thousand miles of coastline from eastern Siberia to the lands lying east of Greenland—was approximately one hundred thousand. Inuit, "the human beings" (or its variants Yuit and Suit), is the term by which they refer to themselves; but better known, since the end of the seventeenth century, is the term "Eskimo," which the French borrowed from the Algonquians; it means "eater of raw meat."[1] Those who live in Greenland, after two and a half centuries of Danish colonial presence, refer to themselves as Kālādlit.

The Inuit are distributed as follows: approximately two thousand in Siberia, thirty thousand in Alaska, twenty thousand in Canada, and fifty thousand in Greenland.

The ancestors of the Inuit (or the Proto-Eskimos) came from Asia some ten thousand years ago, crossing over the Bering Strait, which at that time connected Siberia with Alaska. Then, after they had lived in Alaska for five thousand years, their descendants (called Paleo-Eskimos) began to emigrate eastward, eventually reaching Greenland as well as the Quebec-Labrador peninsula, where the pre-Dorset and Dorset cultures would develop.

Four thousand years later (barely a thousand years ago), a new culture called the Thule developed in northern Alaska. This was characterized by its skin boats and its dogsleds. In less than four centuries, the Thule culture extended its influence to encompass all of the Arctic regions of North America, from Alaska to Greenland.

These ancestors of the Inuit were remarkably well equipped for hunting marine mammals (including the right whale), but they also hunted land mammals (especially the caribou).

This final great wave of migration which prehistory reveals to us may be viewed in connection with the great linguistic and cultural homogeneity observable from Greenland to north Alaska, though the southern Alaskan groups are different from the northern group both culturally and linguistically. Other differences appear in certain regions of the Inuit territory: the best known are those which have been observed among certain island groups (such as the Sagdlirmiut of Southampton Island) or continental groups (such as the Caribou Inuit, west of Hudson Bay), as well as among the Ammassalimmiut of Greenland, on the western edge of the Inuit zone.

I. Inuit Mythology

Inuit mythology, in anthropomorphizing the natural environment and in establishing divisions between that environment and the social milieu, reflects and serves as the foundation for social order and customs. Most beliefs and individual and collective rites, in the everyday organization of life, refer everything to that mythology.

This mythology of hunters follows an unpredictable course in which connection counts for more than explanation. A mythology of small groups, it treats social relationships at their most basic level. As a vast system of relationships and symbols, the mythology is often compared by the Inuit themselves with oneiric productions, as dreams and myths are based on the same order for them. When we realize, moreover, that death and sleep are states of the same nature for the Inuit (which explains the appearance of the dead in dreams), a panorama of mental activities and productions opens up before us.

II. Mythic History and the Emergence of Culture

It was thought for a long time that Inuit mythology contained no coherent and detailed explanation of mythic history or the emergence of culture and was essentially composed of fables about animals, heroic epics, and accounts of accidental events of no general interest.[2] We shall attempt to show that this notion does not stand up to meticulous examination and, indeed, that it arises from the fact that our Western societies are used to treating their history in a very explicit and linear fashion, while the Inuit, on the other hand, are a hunting society with an oral tradition that speaks in its own nonlinear and often indirect fashion through a mass of myths, rites, and prescriptions. Theirs is a history in which many developments are merely implied or simply defined by their absence in accounts which apparently say nothing about them.

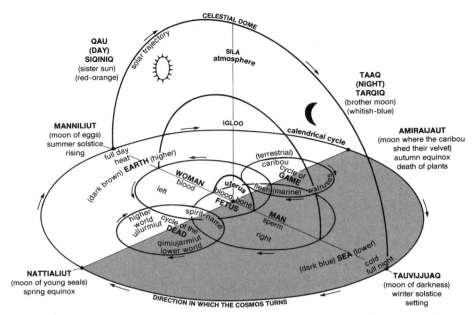

Differentiation, complementarity, and analogical construction in Inuit thought. Three-dimensional representation.

I will attempt to reconstitute their mythic history from data collected principally by K. Rasmussen in the central Arctic in 1921–24, and completed by data that I collected in the same region between 1971 and 1978.[3] A scientific analysis of this remains to be done, but the pioneering work accomplished by C. Lévi-Strauss for Native American mythologies reveals the benefits that may be derived from a systematic application of the structural method to the mythology of the Inuit.

1. The Conception of the Universe and of Its "Prehistory"

For the Inuit of the central Arctic, the universe in the primordial period included the earth which was, properly speaking, a sort of round disk washed by the sea. It was populated by animals and by humans who were not Inuit. It upheld, with the help of four pillars, the celestial vault which constituted another world populated with animals after the image of the earth. Just below the terrestrial disk was a cramped world in which it was impossible to stand up straight, below which was a final lower world which also replicated the earth and was populated with animals.

It then came to pass that the pillars that held up the celestial vault became dislocated and caused the earth to pitch, along with its inhabitants, which explains the presence of so many spirits beneath the terrestrial mound. A diluvian rain fell from the sky and drowned all other life.

2. The Life-Giving Earth in the Time of the Great Blackness

"In the time that followed there appeared two small mounds of earth from which were born two men, two adults, the first Inuit. They soon wished to reproduce, and one of them took the other to be his wife. The wife-man became pregnant and when his time came, his companion, anxious to bring the fetus out, composed a magic song:

Here is a man
Here is a penis
May he form a passage there
A great passage
Passage, passage, passage.

This song split the penis of his partner, who was transformed into a woman. All of the Inuit descend from them" (Rasmussen 1929, 252).

The first man was named Uumarnituq and the first woman Aakuluujjusi. They brought forth animals either by creating them or by bringing them back from other worlds (Saladin d'Anglure 1974).

In these earliest times it was always dark on earth. All was somber, and neither places nor animals could be made out. There were no heavenly bodies in the sky, there was no ice on the sea, neither tempest nor storm nor lightning nor winds. At the bottom of the sea, trees grew, which would sometimes wash up on the shore.

At that time the Inuit were poor and ignorant, with few hunting instruments and no knowledge of game: the only animals they hunted were the lagopus and the Arctic hare. In order to see their prey, they wet their fingertip with saliva to make it luminous, and pointed it in the air. But they often had to be content with scratching the ground and eating the earth, which at that time was their primary food. For clothing, they had only the sparse and fragile skins of birds and white foxes.

Among the first animals of this age were the crow, the white fox, the wolf, and the bear. But there was confusion between the world of animals and the world of humans. Humans could easily transform themselves into animals and animals could metamorphose into humans—to whom they thus became very close, speaking the same language, living in similar habitations, and hunting in the same way in spite of the differences between their respective habits.

There were no marine mammals, no big game, and thus no taboos. Life was without great danger but also without the real joy that follows effort and exertion.

There were no shamans in that time: people were afraid of disease and were unaware of the rules of life and of ways of arming themselves against danger and wickedness. They nevertheless discovered the protective power of amulets. First among these was the shell of the Itiq (anus) sea urchin, which one person would point toward the diseased area of the patient while farting, at the same time as another person was blowing on the diseased organ: these two acts combined all of the vital force emanating from the human body.

Among the first humans, it was not rare for women to be sterile; thus they would go out in search of "children of the earth," babies that were to be found in the ground. They had to go far away and to search for a long time to find boys, whereas there was an abundance of girls. Death did not exist, and the number of Inuit increased progressively. (After Rasmussen, 1929, 1931)

These narratives show us the essential place occupied by the earth (*nuna*) in Inuit mythological thought—not only as the generator of the human race, but also as regulator of Inuit social reproduction in the first times of humanity. On the demographic level it furnished babies to sterile women, and on the economic level it afforded essential food in a time when game was rare and difficult of access. These accounts also show us the importance of the new humanity's discovery of the magical effectiveness of breath and of the spoken word. Sexual difference is created by a song, and the first case of healing is by means of the vital breath (associated with the sea urchin).

Many natural constraints remain, however, to be overcome: the creation of woman indeed allows man to free himself in part from a dependence on mother earth for procreation, but feminine sterility is still great; the search for small game allows him to explore a new solution to the problem of provisionment, but the earth continues to be his principal food, and the endless darkness hinders any advance in hunting. A new danger threatens humanity, that of overpopulation, as death does not exist. Finally, the important role played by woman for the increase of human beings, either by procreating or by collecting the "babies of the earth" in the course of long journeys, creates a new dependence for man, who remains ignorant, poor, and nearly sedentary because of his inability to hunt.

3. Light, Death, and the Beginnings of Culture

The magical power of words was progressively explored and put to work by humans or by the metamorphosed animals who resembled them, in an attempt to surmount the obstacles that threatened the survival of the new humanity.

"One day the crow, meeting the white fox, said that he wanted light, the better to find his food. But the fox preferred the dark, the better to pillage the places where men hid their meat. The crow then cried 'qau qau qau' (light . . .), while the fox retorted 'taaq, taaq, taaq' (darkness . . .). The crow won out, and since that time day has alternated with night" (Saladin d'Anglure 1974).

"According to several myths of the central Arctic, the first Inuit lived on the island of Millijuaq in the Hudson Strait. They became so numerous that the island began to rock slowly in the sea under their weight. The people panicked until an old woman cried, 'May humans die, because there is no more room for us on earth; may they make war and disperse'; and humans became mortals, made war between themselves, and dispersed in every direction" (Rasmussen 1929, 92; Boas 1907, 173; Saladin d'Anglure: field notes).

With the appearance of the "short life" and the alternation between day and night, humans disengaged themselves further from the tutelage of the earth, which was characterized by darkness and endless life. Woman is again implicated in this process of differentiation and discontinuity, which simultaneously affirms her status and marks the dawn of culture while ensuring human survival. A variant of these two myths, from Greenland, further attributes to the same person the origin of day and of the short life.

Now that they had light, the Inuits could truly acquire technical knowledge and develop hunting. Qau, the radical which means light, is also found in compounds in the words "forehead" and "knowledge."

"At this time they had nothing to harness dogs with, and discovered that their houses (made of snow, stones, or peat),

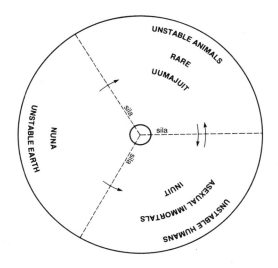

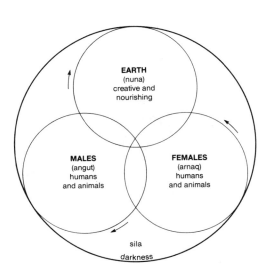

Mask, "Spirit of the Mountain." Sitka, Alaska, Sheldon Jackson College. Courtesy Amon Carter Museum, Fort Worth, Texas.

In mythic times, animals could easily turn themselves into human beings. Illustration of the myth of the woman who married an eagle and left him when she discovered his way of life. Drawing by Davidialuk Alasuaq. Povungnituk, Canada, B.S.A. collection.

which were animated by spirits and endowed with life, had the power to move about with their occupants inside by sliding over the ground when certain magic words were pronounced. They thus used them to go to places in which game was abundant. This continued until the day the Inuits complained that many children were being killed by the houses as they fell from their beds while the houses were moving—at which time the houses suddenly ceased their movement" (Rasmussen 1929; Saladin d'Anglure 1974).

Oil was not used to fuel lamps as it was possible to burn fine snow.

4. Contradictions, Human Disorders, and the Need for a Cosmic Order (Sila)

The destruction of humanity had now been averted by the appearance of death, and thus of a certain demographic equilibrium. The exploitation of game had also been rendered possible by the light of day. But no sooner were men slightly more liberated from their primary dependence on the earth than they commenced to use their new powers of antagonism and war: they brought on death and transgressed the rules they had sought to establish in order to organize their social relationships and their relationships with nature.

The sun, moon, stars, thunder, lightning, the cold wind from the north, and the warm wind from the south were all living beings, either human or animal. Their own misbehavior or the mistreatment they had suffered made them climb up into the sky, where they came to participate in the new world order, the cosmic order of Sila. Sila is at once air, ordered movement, cosmic periodicity, the rationality of the mind, and the understanding of and respect for this order.

"The sun and the moon were brother and sister. One day the brother was deceived by his mother: while he was suffering from sore eyes, she made off with his first white bear, which she ate in secret instead of sharing it in common as is the rule for the first game brought in. When his eye was healed by a dive which gave him great visual power, he caused the death of his mother by harpooning a great beluga while she was attached to the thong of his harpoon to help him in his hunt" (Rasmussen 1929).

Symbolically cutting the umbilical cord that attached him to his mother, he attached her to the beluga with the cord that was the thong of his harpoon, thus sacrificing her to his game (a social product), following the rule of the social distribution of products.

"Having become orphans, the brother and sister had many adventures until the day when, under the cover of darkness, he took advantage of her sexually. When she discovered his identity after blackening his face with soot, she reacted violently, cut off one of her breasts, and threw it at him, saying, 'If you love me so much, eat this.' Then she picked up the breast he had refused, made a torch of it, and fled into the sky, where she became the sun, Siqiniq. He pursued her with another torch—which went out—and he became the moon, Taqqiq" (Saladin d'Anglure 1974).

By her voluntary mutilation and the sacrifice of her fertility, Siqiniq established the foundation for another rule of distribution: that of exogamy or matrimonial exchange. Involuntarily incestuous, taken advantage of in a darkness which recalls the blackness—and thus the confusion and continuity—of the earliest times of the earth, Siqiniq (the sun) is now placed in a celestial position of luminosity and mobility, with an ordered trajectory and a productive seasonal periodicity.

Her severed and bloody breast, which her blood brother did not dare to consume, was never to give milk; this breast, having become a flaming torch and shining sun, would now warm humanity. Furthermore, through its symbolic representation, the oil lamp, it would illumine the microcosm constituted by the domestic family and its new rule of exogamy. By means of the cooking that it makes possible, it finally establishes a definitive separation between the bleeding woman (by virtue of her reproductive properties) and bloody meat (the game produced by the hunter). Henceforth, this separation is marked on the face of the woman in the form of a radiating facial tattoo, a sort of symbolic cooking which is effected by inserting soot from an oil lamp under a girl's skin after her first menstruation.

Her brother Taqqiq (the moon), of powerful vision and overflowing sexuality, emerges from his earthly adventure both darkened and frustrated. He nevertheless becomes a celestial instrument of this order and of its reproduction. The principal agent of the division of the calendar, he is also charged with making sterile women fertile, bringing game to unfortunate hunters, and defending orphans who have been mistreated and disfavored on earth.

"It was also a brother and a sister who were the source of thunder and lightning. They wished to avenge themselves upon the adults who had reprimanded them because of their overly noisy games. They began to produce thunder and lightning with firestones and a dried skin; when they urinate, it rains on humans" (Saladin d'Anglure 1974).

As for the winds, they are controlled by a male and a female spirit, whose attributes are described in many accounts:

> The parents of the baby giant Naarsuk were assassinated; when he was found, the people were astonished by his size and strength—he could hold up three women seated on his erect penis. He was abandoned with nothing but laced skin for clothing. He rose into the air and became the spirit-lord of the wind (the cold north wind) which rushes out when his laced swaddling clothes come unlaced. Another wind spirit, this one female, lives in a snow igloo: when the heat of her lamp makes holes in the walls, the warm southern wind blows on earth. (Rasmussen 1929, 1931; Saladin d'Anglure 1974)

All of these sidereal or atmospheric spirits, through their position and the order of their movements, constitute Sila: to move in the direction of the sun is to "act according to Sila" (Petersen 1967). Mankind progressed and began to gain control over its reproduction.

5. The Ecological Order or the Failure of Female Autonomy

The primordial couple, the ancestors of the Inuit, caused a number of animals to appear on earth.

"One day Aakuluujjusi took her trousers and transformed them into a caribou whose fur resembles, by its coloration, the trousers of a woman. She gave the animal sharp teeth and long tusks. Then, taking off her jacket, she made a walrus with horns on its head. But the Inuit took fright before these animals that attacked them on land and in the water: she therefore decided to interchange their horns and tusks, and kicking the forehead of the caribou she broke some of its teeth to render it inoffensive, and caused its eye sockets to bulge out to weaken its vision. She then said, 'Stay far away, like true game.' But the caribou were now too quick for the hunters, so she reversed the direction of the hair on their bellies to slow them down" (Rasmussen 1929; Saladin d'Anglure 1974).

These were the first big game animals of the Inuit, terrestrial and marine game around which they would organize their new socioeconomic life. New relationships began to be established among humans and between animals and humans, replacing the primordial confusion. It still remained to circumscribe the limits of humanity and of animality and to establish the nature of their connections. The myth of Uinigumasuittuq contributes to the resolution of these problems:

> Uinigumasuittuq ("she who did not wish to marry") lived with her parents and their dog Siarnaq. She refused all suitors. Nevertheless, one day she accorded her favors to a handsome visitor. It was their dog, metamorphosed, whom no one had recognized; he returned often and she became pregnant. The father then discovered the identity of their guest and in fury he placed the couple on an island. The girl made the dog swim back and bring food from her father's house. The father supplied them many times, but then one day he loaded the dog with rocks, causing him to drown. The girl soon gave birth to beings who were half human and half dog. On the advice of their mother, they tore their grandfather's kayak apart when he came to bring them meat; then, overwhelmed, Uinigumasuittuq sent her children away so that they might survive. The first puppies were set adrift in a southerly direction in the sole and upper leather of a boot; they disappeared in the fog amid a metallic din and became the ancestors of the white man. She sent others toward the continent to the south, and these became the ancestors of the Indians. Another group became the ancestors of the Tunit, a prehistoric people; and the final pup, sent toward the north, became the ancestor of the Ijirait, invisible beings who live on caribou.

> After the dispersal of those who were the originators of the human races, she returned to her father's home. But twice more she refused her suitors (a metamorphosed caribou and wolf) before she finally agreed to follow a third, a petrel who had taken a human form. He took her in his kayak, but too late she discovered his ugliness and his sarcastic laugh, which disgusted her. She then succeeded in escaping, with the complicity of her father, in a boat made of skins. But the petrel discovered her flight and stirred up a terrible storm; in panic the father threw his daughter into the water, and when she tried to hold on to the boat's sides he cut off the fingers of both of her hands and poked out her eyes. She sank into the sea, but bearded seals and ringed seals were born from her severed hands. In despair, the father let himself be covered by the tide and joined his daughter and his dog at the bottom of the sea, where they have lived ever since. They control the movements of marine game animals and punish after death all persons guilty of sexual infractions—of bestiality in particular. (Saladin d'Anglure 1974)

Several observations may be made about this new episode in the slow emergence of culture as it is conceived by the Inuit.

The first of these concerns what may be called Uinigumasuittuq's attempt at female autonomy. Since the incest taboo gave woman her trade value, it was tempting for her to take advantage of this new power, which is what she attempted to do in striving to keep control of her sexual life—first by refusing her suitors, and then by offering herself to the dog or the petrel. These two unhappy experiences culminate in a double mutilation, the first a moral one, with the loss of her children, who could survive only through dispersal and cultural division, and the second a physical one, with the loss of her hands and eyes, which separated her from culture and from her productive-reproductive functions.

Her banishment to nature brought on by her blindness, her inability to produce, and her immobilization at the bottom of the sea cannot help but recall the primordial time. Her human origin nevertheless gives her a very important role as an intermediary between humans and the new extension of nature constituted by marine animals, her creatures, as well as an intermediary between the Inuit and the new extension of humanity constituted by the new human races, her children.

The resources she brings to men give her a status which balances that of the earth: they establish her as regulator of the ecological order, but only with a heavy counterpart—the final submission of women to social rules of matrimonial exchange as established by men. Men would henceforth have free access to the women of the group, within the limits of the incest prohibition.

The differentiation between hunters and game animals leads to the exclusion of animals who have become game, both from matrimonial alliances and from sexual relationships (bestiality), and this differentiation founds the new order.

But parallel to this differentiation and to the woman's banishment to nature, there is a symmetrical and inverse rapprochement of nature toward man through the promotion of the dog. The dog is promoted to the rank of a means of production in hunting and transportation, is promoted to a personal name in addition to a species designation (a privilege which it alone shares with humans), and is finally promoted to domesticity and even a certain commensality, which confers almost magical powers upon it. When a man is seriously ill, his life may be saved by sacrificing the life of his dog, who thus carries away the ailment with him.

The acquisition of the dog as a means of production corresponds in mythic history to the acquisition of the kayak. Both are very explicit symbols of productive virility, of the social expansion of masculine sexuality. In several regions of the central Arctic, a man's right to marry depends upon the acquisition of a kayak whose prow is metaphorically designated by the name of *usuujaq* ("that which resembles a penis").

Man's access to productive mobility coincides exactly with the loss of mobility on the part of houses (and thus of women, which they symbolize), which now must fulfill their destinies as containers.

It is interesting to note further that, in a rebellious leap against her father after he had killed her dog/lover, Uinigumasuittuq attempts to destroy this male supremacy by sending her canine children out to attack the paternal kayak.

6. The End of Metamorphoses and the Recovery of Continuity

The appearance of the great distinctions—of man/woman, life/death, darkness/light, humans/game animals, and terrestrial game/marine game—beyond resolving certain crucial problems faced by the first Inuit, allows mythic thought to become conscious of the realities of the universe and to elaborate new principles which could simultaneously consolidate the cultural order and guarantee its reproduction.

With death, the short life (*inuusiq*) became the rule. It was thus believed that every living being was allotted at birth a determined time of life on earth. By means of light, shadows (*tarraq*)—doubles or reflections of living beings, without

Shaman's drum. Sitka, Alaska, Sheldon Jackson Museum collection. Photo Ernest Manewal.

An Inuit (Inuk) is seized with fear on discovering a tattooed "flying head" in an old igloo. Such flying heads, half-bird and half-human, taught the Inuit the panting songs that are their language. Drawing by Davidialuk Alasuaq. Povungnituk, Canada, B.S.A. collection.

weight or materiality—were discovered, and it was supposed that these survived the body in the afterlife, in the form of souls (*tarniq*).

Finally, the differentiation between game animals and humans and between living and dead humans made possible and necessitated the classification of living beings and of their living spaces. This was done by naming: at the level of species for game animals and at the personal level for humans.

With specific names for game animals, each species was thought of as a multiple and renewable ensemble of potential resources for man.

The personal names given to humans made it possible to think of each individual as the sum of all the productive capacities and qualities of his deceased homonyms; these names also, by their absence of gender, made it possible to obliterate sexual differentiation, thus helping women to surmount the contradictions of their dependence.

So it was that the double-soul (*tarniq*) and the name-soul (*atiq*) gave a new continuity to life, beyond the limits of the present moment. Since life on earth had become short in order to make possible the continuity of human society, it once again became continuous on the level of Sila, the universal order. Culture could now reproduce itself through the reproduction of the factors and relationships of production. All that remained was to begin the appropriation of terrestrial and marine regions, the sole portions of the present that were to remain continuous and permanent. A double naming process was applied to this end, the first in order to situate the resources and activities of production and the second to preserve the memory of past people and events.

Another myth, that of Arnakpaktuq, illustrates the search for the continuity of life; it shows us how a female soul that was unsatisfied in its conjugal life decided—after a fruitless search for a better life in the womb of animals of diverse species—to live again as the son of her brother:

A woman suffered constant ill treatment at the hands of her husband. She wanted to die, and one day while he was beating her she slipped under the blankets of her bed; the whining of a dog was heard . . . she had transformed herself into a dog. He harnessed her to his sled, but she was completely ignorant of canine hauling and was thus beaten again until she learned from the other dogs how to behave.

All went well until she made a mistake; and when she was thrashed, she let out a human cry. He killed her and threw out her corpse to be devoured by wolves: she became a wolf, and, completely ignorant of the life of the wolf, she had to learn from them how to hunt. Then, as a wolf, she died, and when a caribou stepped on her corpse, she penetrated his body and became a caribou. A new and long apprenticeship thus began for her.

She was harpooned by a hunter while she was crossing a lake. She was butchered and hidden in a cache for the winter, after which she was eaten and her bones thrown onto the shore next to the bones of a walrus. When the tide covered them up she passed into a walrus bone that came back to life and became a walrus. She learned to dive and to eat like a walrus, but she did not like the way they rubbed their muzzles.

She died yet another time, passed into a crow that had come to rest on the corpse of the walrus, was killed by a polar bear, and fell onto the remains of a ringed seal

which she entered to become a seal. She learned how to breathe through breathing holes cut into the ice in the winter, and it was at such a hole that she felt the point of a harpoon run through her head. She had been harpooned by a hunter who was none other than her brother.

When her brother's wife butchered her, she entered her body and became a fetus, although up to that time her future mother (her sister-in-law) had had only miscarriages. The fetus found itself in a little house which quickly became too narrow. The time came to come out. When she was almost out, she perceived a woman's knife (*ulu*) and the point of a man's harpoon (*savik*); she first wanted to take the woman's knife, but she changed her mind, seized the point of the harpoon, and came out in the form of a baby boy. The choice she had just made changed her sex. Later the boy became a great hunter and told his story. (Saladin d'Anglure 1974)

Arnakpaktuq's tale in a sense constitutes the myth of the origins of hunting. By explaining the acquisition of the knowledge of hunting by the Inuit, it justifies the new hunter-game relationship, which excludes metamorphoses between humans and animals. It also serves as a basis for beliefs concerning the connection of identity with name, and the reincarnation or transmigration of souls. Finally, it alienates woman into a status subordinate to man, by leading her to believe either that she might have access to masculinity in a future life or that she has been a man in a past life—which allows her to see herself as transsexual, to live as a transvestite, as a boy, in her youth, and to bear the identity of a male eponym during her life (Saladin d'Anglure 1977a).

Order and continuity were thus restored in the universe, but the fragility of their balance soon necessitated the elaboration of a complex system of prescriptions and prohibitions that applied principally to the junctures in the great productive-reproductive cycles: the cycle of human life (pregnancy, childbirth, childhood, and adolescence), of souls (entering and leaving the body), and of game animals (production and consumption).

This new order was now governed by the great master-spirits of Sila (time), Taqqiq (the moon), Siqiniq (the sun), and Kannaaluk (the girl at the bottom of the sea), the dominant figures of Inuit myth and religious beliefs.

In everyday life, however, respect for this order had become too complex for the laity and too important to the socioeconomic survival of the Inuit, in which women still occupied a dominant role in the reproduction of life. It was necessary to transpose into practical life the male domination that had been established at the mythic level; it was necessary to entrust to specialists the interpretation of myths and of empirical reality; it was necessary to establish intermediaries between the visible and the invisible, between the dead and the living, between game and hunter, between men and women. This would be the function of the Angakkuq (shaman), a mainly masculine function (Meyer 1932: 422) to which women could gain access only with difficulty, except in old age. The great shamans were always men.

III. Shamanism, New Light, and Political Power

With the development of shamanism and of its practices, knowledge and power became essentially masculine privileges. An Iglulik myth tells how the first shaman, a man, came into being: A period of famine and trouble befell the Iglulik region one day. Many Inuit died of hunger and all were anxious and confused because they did not know how

31

to face the situation. At this time a man, taking advantage of a meeting in one of their houses, asked to go behind the curtain of skins, at the front of the platform, and announced his intention to descend to the place of the mother of marine animals. No one was to watch. He dived down under the earth with the help of auxiliary spirits that had become associated with him at the time of a solitary retreat he had taken. He visited Kannaaluk and brought abundance back to men, along with game. This is how the first shaman appeared. He was later followed in this by others who gradually extended their knowledge of hidden things and elaborated a sacred language to communicate with the spirits, thus helping humanity in many ways (Rasmussen 1929).

The principal attribute of the shaman was *qaumaniq*, light, vision, the profound knowledge of things and beings; his agent was *tuurngaq*, an auxiliary spirit which could be acquired through a solitary experience of communication with the earth mother, through a visit to a cave or a stay in a deserted place. A progressive diminution of knowledge and power followed among the uninitiated, a sort of return to the chthonic origins of humanity, to the primal night of the maternal womb—to the benefit of the shaman who, substituting himself for the woman as she substituted herself for the earth, succeeded in taking control of social reproduction, thanks to his imaginary operations, and thus in ensuring male domination even as he metaphorically took over the principal female processes and characteristics of the reproduction of life.

Shamanic seances, especially those that are designed to renew communication with game, seem always to stem from scenes of pregnancy and childbirth, borrowed either from myths, like the primordial darkness relived through the extinguishing of lamps, or from reality, like the untying of the belts and laces of spectators at childbirths, the crouching posture taken on the platform of a house (a posture close to that of a woman in childbirth), or the staccato and panting cries that the shaman emits before his soul succeeds in passing through the narrow way that leads to the beyond.

In a primary phase, the shaman attempts to bring his auxiliary spirit into himself. Then, when he has succeeded, he applies himself to making his soul leave his body and to guiding it through a narrow tunnel to the light, the knowledge that allows him to repair cosmic, ecological, social, or psychological disorders provoked by humans. All shamanic rites are carried out with the left hand, the inverse of reality, in which the right hand takes priority. When laterality is used in Inuit culture to differentiate between the sexes, right is male and left is female.

As the ally and protector of men, the shaman became a public confessor, particularly of women, to whom the majority of ills were attributed and who were therefore subjected to strict prohibitions. He also had the privilege of treating the sterility of couples by intervening as sexual partner in reproduction.

The cosmic order was now controllable through the shaman, whose knowledge and power assured its effectiveness on the level of social reality.

B.S.A./d.w.

NOTES

1. Recent research by ethnolinguists suggests another meaning for the term "Eskimo": "one who speaks the language of a foreign land" (see J. Mailhot 1978).
2. After the works of Franz Boas, in particular.
3. Our research, begun on the staff of the C.N.R.S. under the direction of Professor C. Lévi-Strauss, has been continued at Laval University, Quebec, Canada. One part of the material presented here has been published in B. Saladin d'Anglure 1977a, 1977b, and 1978.
4. The works of R. Savard are a first tentative effort on this road; we cite here only his principal work (Savard 1966). Several other works on Inuit mythology have been published, some on other regions, some on themes treated in a comparative fashion, but a great deal of work remains to be done on this subject.

BIBLIOGRAPHY

F. BOAS, "The Eskimo of Baffin Land and Hudson Bay," 2 vols. (New York 1907). J. MAILHOT, "L'étymologie de 'Esquimau' revue et corrigée," *Études/Inuit/Studies* 2, no. 2 (1978): 59–69. R. PETERSEN, "Burial Forms and Death Cult among the Eskimos," *Folk* 8–9 (1967): 259–80. K. RASMUSSEN, "Intellectual Culture of the Iglulik Eskimos," in *Report of the Fifth Thule Expedition*, vol. 7 (Copenhagen 1929); "The Netsilik Eskimos, Social Life and Spiritual Culture," in *Report of the Fifth Thule Expedition*, vol. 8 (Copenhagen 1931). B. SALADIN D'ANGLURE, *La mythologie des Inuit d'Igloolik* (Ottawa 1974), a report manuscript deposited at the National Museum of Man; "Iqallijuk ou les réminiscences d'une âme—nom Inuit," in *Études/Inuit/Studies* 1, no. 1 (1977a): 33–63; "Mythe de la femme et pouvoir de l'homme chez les Inuit de l'Arctique central (Canada)," *Anthropologie et sociétés* 1, no. 3 (1977b): 79–98; "L'homme (Angut), le fils (irniq) et la lumière (qau), ou Le cercle du pouvoir masculin chez les Inuit de l'Arctique central," *Anthropologica*, n.s., 20, nos. 1–2 (1978): 101–44. R. SAVARD, *Mythologie esquimaude, analyse de textes nord-groenlandais*, Centre d'études nordiques, Travaux divers no. 14 (Quebec 1966). E. M. WEYER, *The Eskimos, Their Environment and Folkways* (New Haven 1932).

NATIVE AMERICAN MYTHS AND RITUALS OF NORTH AMERICA

The eminent mythographer Stith Thompson was right to emphasize the fact that "outside of Western civilization, few ethnic groups have been studied as much as the Indians of North America" (1946, 297). Thus, at the outset the researcher is confronted with a mass of documents, some of which date back to the conquest and even earlier if one does not contest the authenticity of the *walam olum*, for example, which recounts the origin of the Delaware people (Rafinesque 1832; Brinton, vol. 5, 1882–85).

The study of North American mythology constitutes a project all the more ambitious in that the themes that compose it are abundant and prodigiously diverse. In addition, it should be noted that no anthropologist before Claude Levi-Strauss achieved a grand synthesis of the ethnic myths of the two Americas; the difficulties involved in such an attempt seemed insurmountable. Until then some researchers were content to record tales without attaching to them any specific analysis, unless it were classical, while others, like Franz Boas, Elsie Clews Parsons, and Paul Radin, to name only a few, set about introducing a more comprehensive analysis of specific groups, specifically the Kwakiutl, the Pueblo, and the Winnebago. One might also add that North American mythology belongs to peoples whose sociological characteristics (ethnohistory, language, and culture) are sometimes totally different from and unconnected with one another. Take, for example, the Naskapi of Labrador, the Pomo of California, the Nez Percé of Idaho, and the Hopi of Arizona; at most, these tribes are united only by spatial and temporal links, that is, on the one hand the continent upon which they have lived since prehistoric times, and on the other hand the facts of conquest, which have come to transform the initial basic data in a manner both insidious and brutal.

In this regard, since Clark Wissler, anthropologists have devoted themselves to defining cultural and geographical areas which do not necessarily take into consideration the principal linguistic families. Nevertheless, these unities of an ecological type make it more possible to discern the ethnographic reality of the peoples who have lived or still live in these territories. One might define these geographical areas as cultural spaces occupied by one or more Native American groups (bands or tribes) whose activities and special characteristics are so similar that they form a kind of ethnic homogeneity in the general sense of the term. This is a purely formal definition, since notable differences may be encountered within a single ecocultural space.

I. Myth and Society

Just as certain themes recur in universal mythology, one can observe comparable subjects reflecting preoccupations common to the Native American peoples. Aside from myths that deal with sequences specific to each group and thus are original by definition, a similar way of thinking recurs continually, though the structure of the myth may be posed in a different manner. The rituals that may eventually be attached to it present a dramatization characteristic of each tribe.

In this ideological order, Native American thinkers have long reflected upon cosmogonic myths, reinventing the creation of the world and the emergence of humanity. Visionaries, they integrated cosmic space and terrestrial space into the everyday world. The original source of the myths resides in the attempt to interpret the very essence of nature and society. Moreover, the myths establish schemata which often represent opposing forces. At the beginning of a subject or in the course of its development, a myth will pose an a priori idea, such as, for example, the division of humanity into nomads and sedentary peoples, which is often founded upon historical reality. The emergence myth of the Acoma (Pueblo) shows clearly the division between hunters and agrarian peoples (Sebag 1971, 469).

Likewise, in the *walam olum*, the Delaware say that in the beginning they formed a single nation:

> And as they traveled they found that certain of them were prosperous and others vigorous. Thus, they separated, the first group becoming builders of huts, and the second hunters. The bravest, the most unified, the purest, were the hunters (Brinton 1882–85, 183).

This dualism between humans may reflect what happens among the gods. The cosmogonic myth of the Skidi Pawnee develops this antagonism in the very heart of the cosmos. This suggests that the gods are at times strangely similar to humans.

In their version of the creation of the world, there is a dichotomy between men and women. The myth relates how Tirawa, the Creator, made the stars and delegated to them a great power, giving pride of place to the Star-of-Morning. The latter, in turn, helped his younger brother, the Sun, to make the light. Tirawa chose them as the "chiefs of stars situated in the village in the East," while Star-of-Evening and Moon were named the "chief of stars situated in the village in the West." In the East were the men, and in the West, the women. After a time, the stars in the East began to desire the stars of the West. One after another the star-men went to the village of the star-women. They said that they were coming to get married. Moon, who received them, invariably responded to each one: "Very well, that is exactly what we desire. Come and follow me." But she drew them into a trap, pushing them into an abyss. Finally, Star-of-Morning fulfilled the role of mediator by marrying Star-of-Evening, while Sun married Moon. The children born of the union of these stars peopled the earth (Linton 1922, 3–5). It is on this myth that the sacrificial rite of the young captive woman is based. She was immolated in homage to Star-of-Morning. This ritual would follow upon the vision of a warrior, who then had to find his victim among an enemy tribe. Among the Pawnee, only the Skidi (Wolves) observed this practice. The last ceremony took place around 1828 (ibid., 5–16).

II. Culture Heroes and Tricksters

Once the problem of the origin of the world was resolved, it was necessary to introduce heroes into the world with the mission of guiding human beings. Indeed, it is never easy for humanity to be born after previous stays in chaotic locations, as is attested by the Zuñi myth of emergence, nor to break with the illusion of a "paradise lost," as the Navajo myth of emergence sometimes leads one to believe.

The perspicacious sages thus placed on the scene the hero, the bearer of the benefits of civilization: fire, light, water, plants, animals (sometimes including humans), language, etc. The hero is also the founder of rituals and secret societies. For one reason or another, it is often difficult to distinguish him from another demiurge, the trickster.

The culture hero often has a younger twin brother (Iroquois, Algonquin, Hopi, Apache, Navajo, Kiowa, Winnebago) with whom he quarrels to the death, like Gluskap and Malsum (Micmac, Passamaquody, Malecite), Silex and Bourgeon (Iroquois), Manabozo and Wolf (Central Algonquin).

This architect of the world belongs as much to the natural order as to the supernatural. He has a body, he lives, suffers, and can marry. Manabozo marries a muskrat, just like the Messou of the Montagnais, who, after "repairing" the world, which has been destroyed by a deluge, undertakes to repopulate the earth by means of this marriage (Le Jeune [1634] 1972, 16). The hero can have a human or an animal form, and can be man or woman, young or old, according to his disguise.

The twins represent respectively the malevolent and benevolent forces (Algonquin, Iroquois). In other cases, it is the warrior twins whose common task it is to rid the world of enemies and monsters before initiating the social order.

The parents and the grandmother of the demiurge twins usually belong to the supernatural universe. Masewi and Oyoyewi, the Hopi twins, are the sons of the sun. One of them faces north, the other south, guarantors of the equilibrium of the earth. The Great Hare of the Winnebago has for his father the west wind or the north wind, in different instances. The Kiowan culture hero, taken in by grandmother spider after the death of her mother, is himself a descendant of the sun. He is called Half-boy because he makes a double by cutting his body in two by means of a solar ring (Momaday 1974, 38 and passim). Among the Huron Iroquois and the Algonquin, the mother is a virgin who dies in childbirth, and the children are taken in by the grandmother, who has previously fallen from the sky.

The trickster often appears to be a close relative of the culture hero by elective affinity. He is one of the most popular characters in North American mythology. Portrayed with the traits of the coyote, crow, mink, jay, or magpie, this antihero takes on the mission of traversing the wide world,

Ethnic Distribution of Native American Tribes
(Canada and the United States)

Ecological Areas	Geopolitical Distribution*	Principal Ethnic Groups**	Linguistic Division***
1. Western Subarctic	a) Inner Alaska, Yukon, Mackenzie	Tanana, Kutchin, Tutchone, Hare Kaska, Slave, Dogrib, Yellowknife, Carrier	Athapaskan
	b) British Columbia, Alberta, Saskatchewan, Manitoba		Sekani, Beaver, Sarsi, Chippewyan
2. Eastern Subarctic	Quebec, Ontario	Montagnais, Naskapi, Cree, Ojibwa, Algonquin	Algonkin
3. Forests on the Atlantic	New Brunswick, Quebec, Newfoundland, Prince Edward Island, Nova Scotia, Maine, New Hampshire, Vermont, Massachusetts, Connecticut, Rhode Island, New Jersey, Delaware, New York	Beothuk Micmac, Malecite, Abenaki, Penobscot, Pennacook, Mohican, Delaware, Algonquin, Powhatan, Nanticoke, Narragansett	(?) Algonkin
4. Forests on the Great Lakes	Ontario, Michigan, Indiana, Illinois, Wisconsin, Minnesota, New York	Ottawa, Ojibwa (Chippewa), Potawatomi, Miami, Menominee, Sauk, Fox, Kickapoo, Illini	Algonkin
		Wyandot (Huron), Susquehannah, Erie, Mohawk, Oneida, Onondaga, Cayuga, Seneca	Iroquoian
		Winnebago	Siouan
5. Southeast	Florida, Georgia, Alabama, Missouri, Louisiana, Carolinas, Virginia, Kentucky, Tennessee	Creek, Choctaw, Chickasaw, Seminole	Muskogean
		Natchez Cherokee, Tuscarora	Muskogean (?) Iroquoian
		Catawba, Biloxi	Siouan
		Shawnee	Algonkin
6. Plains and Prairies	a) north: Alberta, Saskatchewan, Montana, Wyoming, Colorado, Dakotas, Nebraska, Kansas	Cree, Blackfoot, Cheyenne, Arapaho	Algonkin
		Yankton, Santee and Teton Sioux, Crow, Hidatsa, Mandan, Osage, Ponca, Omaha	Siouan
	b) south: Oklahoma, Texas	Pawnee, Arikara	Caddo
		Kiowa, Comanche	Tanoan
		Mescalero and Lipan Apache Kiowa-Apache	Athapaskan

Ecological Areas	Geopolitical Distribution*	Principal Ethnic Groups**	Linguistic Division***
7. Southwest	Arizona, New Mexico	*Circumpueblo:* Chiricahua and Jicarilla Apache	Athapaskan
		Interpueblo: Navajo	Athapaskan
		Pueblo: Tiwa, Tewa, Towa, Hopi Keresan Zuñi	Tanoan Keresan Zuñian
		Subpueblo: Pima, Papago, Yuma Havasupai, Yavapai	Tanoan Yuman (Hokan) Hokan
8. Great Basin	Nevada, Utah, California, Oregon, Idaho, Wyoming, Colorado	Paiute (south), Paiute (north)	Uto-Tanoan
		Shoshone, Bannock, Ute	(Shoshonean)
		Mohave	Hokan
9. California	California	Maidu, Miwok, Yokuts, Wintun, Costanoan	Penutian
		Pomo, Yana, Chumash, Shasta	Hokan
		Yuki	Yukian
		Wiyot	Algonkin
10. Plateau	British Columbia, Alberta, Washington, Idaho, Oregon, Montana	Salish, Puget Sound, Okanagan, Shuswap, Thompson, Sanpoil, Kalispel, Coeur d'Alene	Salish-Wakashan
		Flathead, Pend d'Oreille, Klamath, Modoc	Penutian
		Nez-Percé	Sahaptin
11. Northwest Coast	Alaska, British Columbia, Oregon, Washington, California	Yurok	Algonkin
		Hupa, Tlingit, Haida, Eyak	Athapaskan
		Chinook	Penutian (?)
		Niska, Gitskan, Tsimshian	Tsimshian (Penutian)
		Haisla, Heiltsuk, Kwakiutl, Nootka, Bella Bella	Wakashan-Kwakiutl
		Bella Coola, Salish, Tillamook	Salish

*States or provinces, in whole or in part.

** This table does not reflect the following: (1) extinct tribes (e.g., Natchez,. Beothuk, Biloxi, Catawba); (2) exile forced by governmental policy (e.g., Dakota [19th century, to Canada], Tuscarora [18th century, New York State], and Osage, Ponca, Pawnee, Arapaho, Cheyenne, Kickapoo, Delaware, Shawnee, Wichita, Chickasaw, Choctaw, Creek, Cherokee [19th century, Oklahoma]; groups from the latter three tribes are also found in the Southeast).

*** These classifications are offered merely as signposts and do not claim to be definitive.

Sources:

H. DRIVER, *Indians of North America* (5th ed., Chicago 1965).

P. DRUCKER, *Indians of the Northwest Coast* (New York 1963).

R. F. HEIZER and M. A. WHIPPLE, *The California Indians* (2d ed., Berkeley 1973).

A. L. KROEBER, *Cultural and Natural Areas of Native North America* (Berkeley 1963).

C. WISSLER, *Indians of the United States* (New York 1967).

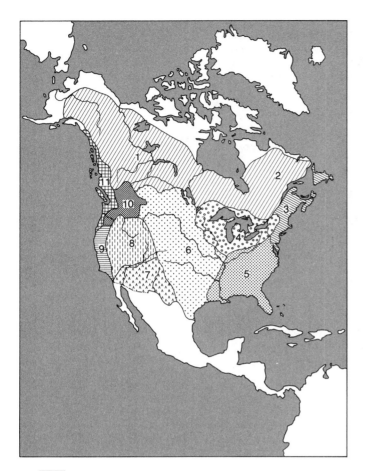

////	1 Western Subarctic
////	2 Eastern Subarctic
▨	3 Atlantic
⊙	4 Great Lakes
░	5 Southeast
░	6 Plains and Prairies
⋀	7 Southwest
▥	8 Great Basin
▤	9 California
▨	10 Plateau
▦	11 Northwest Coast

where he has numerous adventures, often crazy and erotic. He is an ambiguous character. He is both dupe and trickster, humble and pretentious, altruistic and selfish, creator and destroyer.

If it is true that people project their fantasies upon him, what should we make of this enigmatic character who joyfully violates taboos, enters forbidden places, disguises himself as woman or man according to his desires? Nevertheless, this imposter has as a double a humorist-philosopher who is under no illusions about his condition. In an episode taken from one of his extravagant pranks, the

trickster (Winnebago in this case) lets himself be fooled by the branch of a tree, which he believes to be a man's arm. After conversing for a long time with the branch in question, he realizes his stupidity and makes this reflection: "In truth, it is just for this reason that people call me *wakundkaga*, the eccentric fool, and they are quite right" (Radin 1976, 14).

From an anthropological perspective, the trickster integrates himself into the reality of Native American societies. Indeed, these societies often have ceremonial institutions which do not fear the intrusion of a clown during the most serious activities. Take the case of the Navajo clown who had the "privilege of ridiculing, defying, and parodying the most important and most sacred ceremonies, characters, and costumes" (Steward 1930, 189).

We relate this example only to show that the clown of the above citation is nothing less than a public trickster who introduces into the course of the ritual elements that are used by the other, the demiurge, to contradict the natural course of events.

Nevertheless, in his grand moments the trickster brings aid and support—this is especially the case with all the heroes who have this ambivalence within them, such as Manabozo (central forest), Iktome, "The Old Man" (Plains), the Crow (Northwest Coast)—in case of famine, for example, although he himself is most often afflicted with this problem.

Alas, though the trickster is a magician-hero, he can do nothing against death. He even goes so far as to avenge himself against those who request immortality by transforming them into stone statues. He is caught in his own trap when, after he has cheerfully voted for a death without resurrection, he witnesses the death of his son.

III. The Order of the World

In another conceptual order, certain Native American tribes developed the idea of a supreme creator whose functions vary considerably according to the region. Some myths can leave the impression that the Creator whom they depict acts in a rather singular manner, in that he delegates most of his tasks to two secondary gods. He seems to do nothing or, at most, to be in a state of prodigious boredom in an eternal void. Maheo or Heammawhio, the "great chief from on high" of the Cheyenne, gives this impression somewhat: "In the beginning there was nothingness, and Maheo, Spirit from among the Spirits, lived in the void. There was nothing but Maheo, alone, in the infinitude of the void" (Marriott and Rachlin 1972, 22; Grinnell 1972, 2.88).

Olelbis, the Wintun (California) Creator, lives with two wives, to whom he delegates the creative tasks. However, this is not the case with Old Man, the Blackfoot Creator. Old Man is quite busy; he travels the earth from north to south and discusses with Old Woman the question: "Should one give humans eternity?" He forms, constructs, and prepares the terrestrial scene, neglecting neither to rest nor to amuse himself, sliding along the hillsides (Feldmann 1971, 74–79). But Old Man is more than just a debonair Creator; he also appears as a trickster from time to time. He is found with variants among the Kiowa, the Crow, and the Arapaho (Thompson 1946, 319).

Certainly, this notion of a languid and hieratic creator is purely subjective. Everything that exists bears a sacred potential. Sun and moon, planets and stars, as well as all the astronomical phenomena associated with them (eclipses, solstices, equinoxes), though the importance varies according to the tribe, have always inspired the aboriginal mythol-

An Offering of tobacco to the Bear Spirit. Cree painting. Private collection.

ogers. Prolonged contact with the earth (often identified with the mother) by means of fasting in a hole in order to provoke a vision, repeated exposure to the sun (often identified with the father), by means of dance or prayer, are so many religious ways of entering into relation with the spiritual forces of which the Creator, whatever he might be like, is an integral part.

Similarly, winds, rains, clouds, thunder, and lightning are means of communication between the terrestrial and supra terrestrial forces. A few examples will suffice to illustrate this aspect: among the Oglala, thunder could decide the career of the *heyoka* (the "contrary"). As his name indicates, the "contrary" had to interpret his thought and his acts in an inverse way. The *heyoka* would go nude in winter on the plain, pretending that it was warm; in summer, he would cover himself in a bison skin under the pretext of great cold. When he prepared his meals he would throw drops of boiling water on his legs, pretending that the water was ice cold. He would mount his horse back to front, reversing the normal position of the rider, and ride backwards—in brief, he would act against every apparent logic. Among the Cheyenne, the Society of Contraries (which had nothing to do with the *heyoka*) was composed of women and elderly men who would become part of it after they had dreamed of thunder and lightning. Among the Oglala, Hehaka Sapa (Black Elk) still relates how, during his grand vision, two men armed with lances came out of the clouds (Neihardt

1961, 22). Among the Omaha, *mixuga*, that is, the moon (considered in many myths to be a hermaphrodite) would determine the sexual future of the young adolescent who, through her instruction, could become a *berdache*. During the quest for the vision, the adolescent might see the moon appearing with a bow and arrow in one hand and a basket belt in the other. If the boy was not quick enough to seize the bow, he would then become a *berdache*, that is, a homosexual. Just like the *heyoka*, he was regarded by his tribe as a sacred being (Desy 1978).

Lakes and rivers, mountains and valleys, plants and animals are enrolled in the realm of the sacred, since they are part of the universe. Invested with a power, they may have different significations, so that men, animals, plants, or places become *poha* for the Shoshones, *wakan* for the Dakota, *xupa* for the Hidatsa, *maxpe* for the Crow, *orenda* for the Iroquois, *manitu* for the Algonquin, that is, sacred. But these terms contain, in addition, a qualitative connotation which places them in the realm of the exceptional. For all these categories, as Marcel Mauss writes, "although all the gods are *manitus*, not all the *manitus* are gods" (Mauss 1966, 112).

From another perspective, there are motifs in the myths common to Native Americans which reflect a universal mode of thought, like the myths of Orpheus or Prometheus, for example. A communal or individual mythology attempts to explain the flood, the end of the world, the universal conflagration, the sojourn of the dead, or the existence of a world beyond, except that the Navajo have no belief in a glorious immortality and have a horror of the dead. This explains why the Ghost Dance was not successful among the Navajo. It was Wovoka, along with Tavibo, a Paiute prophet, who was the instigator of this dance. The ritual, which spread like a powder trail throughout the West in 1890, is of a messianic character: "A day will come when all Indians, dead and alive, will be reunited on a purified earth in order to live in happiness, free from death, disease, and misery" (Mooney 1965, 19).

The Kiowa had a rather original conception of the afterlife (a conception quickly transformed by the missionaries): they believed that only the souls of those who had committed evil on earth would transmigrate into the abode of the owl; the others would disappear into nothingness (Marriott and Rachlin 1972, 17).

The Native American sages also reflected upon the myths that recounted the gifts of nature. These often have corollary rituals, such as the sacred pipe of the Oglala and the ceremony that is attached to it, taught by the woman "White Bison" (Brown 1972, chapter 1). Later, the sun dance will be instituted to support the ritual of the sacred pipe (ibid., chapter 5).

The acquisition of fire, corn, tobacco, and techniques of hunting and fishing are often central themes of myths. Among all the agrarian peoples, corn is the occasion for elaborate ceremonies. There are numerous myths referring to Corn Silk, goddess of the plant in question. Among peoples of the far north, tobacco served as a propitiatory offering. The Cree, the Montagnais, and the Naskapi continued to place pinches of tobacco in the skull of the bear in order to appease his spirit, which is great and benevolent. He is called, in addition, grandfather or grandmother.

The Native American sages had a final task to accomplish in order to establish the order of the world: to designate in terrestrial space signs symbolic of what had occurred in cosmogonical space; to consecrate the territory through the mediation of priests, medicine men, or shamans; in a word, to see to it that each territory would be the center of the world. Thus it is that "in the perspective of archaic societies, everything that is not 'our world' is not yet 'a world.' One makes a territory 'one's own' only by 'creating' it again, that is, by consecrating it" (Eliade 1965, 30).

But in the course of the ages, it came about that this hierophanic space branched out. The ancients knew the importance of this center and knew how far they had searched for it before it was established. The Zuñi creation myth teaches this to us very well. In a passage of this myth, the Rain Chiefs settle with their people in the Kachina village. But after a while, they begin to ask themselves if the placement of their village is in fact the center of the world. And so they gather together each night to discuss the matter and to build the altar that will confirm for them the location of the center (Parsons 1.230 and passim).

In the *hako* ceremony of the Pawnee, the circle designated by the medicine man represents the territory given by Tirawa to his people. Similarly, when one climbs to the top of a hill, the horizon one sees, where the earth and sky meet, delimits a circle of which one is the center (Alexander 1916, 97). And it is in this perspective of "sacred" territory that we are able to interpret the anger and hysteria of the Cree to the west of James Bay upon the government's decision to exploit their ancestral hunting territories for hydroelectric projects.

The religious quest for the center of the world also supports another interpretation: the constancy with which all the Native American tribes call themselves the "first men," the "human beings," the "real people." Hehaka Sapa did not err, he who ended the account of the secret rites of the Oglala with this incantation, still recited as a prayer by the Indians of today. He knows that the center of the world has been profaned among his people and that the ball—which symbolizes the earth in some way—is lost:

> In this unhappy time into which our people are plunged, we desperately seek the ball. Some no longer even attempt to capture it. Just thinking of that makes me weep. But a day will come when someone will seize it, for the end is rapidly approaching. Only then will it be returned to the center, and our people with it. (Brown 1972, 138)

IV. Problems of Our Times

It would be a serious misunderstanding to believe that the myths and rituals of the Native American peoples belong to a finished past. Certainly, some nations famous for their sociological complexity have disappeared: the Natchez and the Mandan, to cite only two. (Following smallpox epidemics, the Mandan survivors joined the Hidatsa. Today they live on the Fort Berthold reservation in North Dakota.) On the other hand, other tribes were able to safeguard their institutions jealously, for example, the following groups: Pueblo, Lakota, Iroquois, Algonquin, Kwakiutl, and Athapaskan. In addition, the "pan-Indianism" of the last few years has made possible a revival of rituals practiced by Native Americans of various tribes, such as the creation of small spiritual communities where a mythographic erudition is held in common. The medicine men do not hesitate to travel throughout the territory just as the prophets and political visionaries of old used to do (Tecumseh [Shawnee], Pontiac [Ottawa], Cornplanter [Seneca]), as well as all the unknowns who took on the mission of bringing the "good word" to scattered groups.

For this reason, though it cannot be claimed that mythological erudition has remained the same since the conquest,

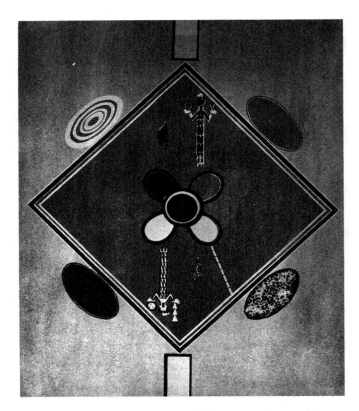

Navajo sand painting. Paris, Musée de l'Homme collection. Museum photo.

or that it has not been the victim of cultural erosion, its actual power cannot be denied. Anything is possible if one keeps in mind the fact that neither the rituals nor the myths are static. As Franz Boas wrote: "Mythological universes seem destined to be annihilated when they are barely formed, so that new universes might be born from their debris" (in Lévi-Strauss 1958, 227).

Although some peoples have been able to preserve up to the present day rituals which for the most part take place far from prying eyes, we have no right to say that their function is to entertain the tourist by producing "folklore." Folklore exists, no doubt, and there are many powwows to remind us of it, but despite the fact that nothing stops it from eventually gaining respectability, it exists on a lower level, proof of a savoir faire which bears witness to the wisdom of the ancients.

We conclude this too brief analysis by turning to the museums which have acquired ethnographic collections, including certain objects invested with a sacred value centuries old.

Don Talayesva related in his book the surprise of Hopi visitors upon visiting a museum in Chicago. To their great fright and consternation, they discovered behind the display cases ceremonial masks reserved for the sole use of officials during festivals in the pueblo (Simmons 1942). What can one say to a member of the secret society of the "Black Eyes" searching desperately in the museums for the original mask that presided over the foundation of the society? (Parsons 1939). The Iroquois have also taken steps to gain possession of all the wampum (a kind of belt that related the heroic deeds of the tribe), some of which had been entrusted in 1898 to the State University of New York.

Nearer to our time, in 1973, after the events at Wounded Knee, Wallace Black Elk (grandson of Hehaka Sapa), the guardian of the sacred pipe that had belonged to Crazy Horse, his grandfather's cousin, found that the pipe had been stolen. When he spoke of it, he did so with an indescribable emotion, but he also showed great concern for the thief, whose life seemed to him to be in danger.

The descriptive function of museums gives little incentive to the amateur to gain a proper perspective of objects which, deprived of their initial function, have been transformed into "things." However much attention is given to their presentation, these objects have passed irrevocably into another world. Hans G. Gadamer writes in this regard: "One should admit, for example, that the image of an ancient deity, which was not exposed in the temple as a work of art intended for a reflective appreciation of an aesthetic kind, and which is today on display in a modern museum, contains in itself, under the form in which this image appears to us today, the world of religious experience in which it originated. The conclusion to be drawn is important: that world which is its own still becomes part of the world which is ours" (1975, 11).

We need to reestablish the tenuous bond that tied these objects—which are the bearers of signs coded in space and time—to another cultural universe. For, despite a museographic destiny, the Tlingit masks, the Mandan altars, the Navajo sand paintings, the Crow sacred pipes, the Montagnais curative beads are all intrinsically part of a mythological "becoming." In their way, these objects always carry the charge of spiritual emotion with which they were endowed at the time they were used ritually.

P.D./m.s.

BIBLIOGRAPHY

1. References in This Article

H. B. ALEXANDER, North American, in The Mythology of All Races 10 (Boston 1916). D. G. BRINTON, The Lénâpé and Their Legends (Philadelphia 1882–85). P. DÉSY, "L'homme-femme" (the berdaches in North America), Libre 3 (1978). DON TALAYESVA (see Simmons, ed., below). M. ELIADE, The Sacred and the Profane (New York 1959). S. FELDMANN, ed., The Storytelling Stone (New York 1971). H. G. GADAMER, Truth and Method (New York 1975); original in German. G. B. GRINNELL, The Cheyenne Indians, 2 vols. (Lincoln, NE, 1972). P. LE JEUNE, "Relations de ce qui s'est passé en la Nouvelle-France en l'année 1634," in Relations des Jésuites (Montreal 1972). C. LÉVI-STRAUSS, Structural Anthropology (New York 1963). R. LINTON, The Sacrifice of the Morning Star by the Skidi Pawnee (Chicago 1922). A. MARRIOTT and C. RACHLIN, American Indian Mythology (New York 1972). M. MAUSS, Sociologie et anthropologie (Paris 1966). N. MOMADAY and J. MOONEY, The Ghost Dance Religion (Chicago 1965). J. G. NEIHARDT, ed., Black Elk Speaks (Lincoln, NE, 1961). P. RADIN, The Trickster (New York 1976). N. SCOTT MOMADAY, The Way to Rainy Mountain (4th ed., New York 1974). L. SEBAG, L'invention du monde chez les Indiens pueblos (Paris 1971). L. W. SIMMONS, ed., Sun Chief (New Haven 1942). J. H. STEWARD, "The Ceremonial Buffoon of the American Indian," Michigan Ac. of Science (1930). S. THOMPSON, The Folktale (New York 1946), 297–363.

2. General Sources

H. B. ALEXANDER, The World's Rim (Lincoln, NE, 1953). J. DE ANGULO, Indian Tales (New York 1953). D. G. BRINTON, The Myths of the New World (New York 1876). J. CURTIN, Creation Myths of Primitive America (London 1899). C. HAYWOOD, A Bibliography of North America Folklore and Folksong, 2 vols. (2d ed., New York 1961). Å. HULTKRANTZ, Conception of the Soul among North American Indians (Stockholm 1953); The North American Indian Orpheus (Stockholm 1957). C. LÉVI-STRAUSS,

The Savage Mind (Chicago 1966); L'homme nu (Paris 1971). R. H. LOWIE, "The Test Theme in North American Mythology," Journal of American Folklore 21 (1908). J. W. POWELL, "Sketch of the Mythology of the North American Indians," U.S. Bureau of American Ethnology (Washington 1879–80). C. S. RAFINESQUE SCHMALTZ, The American Nations, 2 vols. (Philadelphia 1832). S. THOMPSON, Tales of the North American Indians (Cambridge, MA, 1929). R. G. THWAITES, ed., The Jesuit Relations and Allied Documents: Travels and Explorations of the Jesuit Missionaries in New France, 1610–1791, 73 vols. (Cleveland 1896–1901). R. UNDERHILL, Red Man's Religion (3d ed., Chicago 1974).

3. Regional Sources
Northwest Coast, Plateau

M. BARBEAU, Haida Myths (Ottawa 1953). F. BOAS, "Ethnology of the Kwakiutl," U.S. Bureau of American Ethnology (Washington 1913–14); The Religion of the Kwakiutl Indians, 2 vols. (New York 1930). E. E. CLARK, Indian Legends of the Pacific Northwest (Berkeley 1933). A. H. ERNST, The Wolf Ritual of the Northwest Coast (Eugene 1952). T. MCILWRAITH, The Bella Coola Indians (Toronto 1948). E. SAPIR and M. SWADESH, Nootka Texts (Philadelphia 1939). J. R. SWANTON, "Tlingit Myths and Other Texts," U.S. Bureau of American Ethnology (Washington 1909). J. TEIT, Traditions of the Thompson River Indians (Boston 1898).

California

L. J. BEAN, Mukat's People (Berkeley 1972). J. CURTIN, Myths of the Modocs (Boston 1912). E. W. GIFFORD, Central Miwok Ceremonies (Berkeley 1955). A. L. KROEBER, World Renewal: A Cult System of Native Northern California (Berkeley 1926). E. M. LOEB, Pomo Folkways (Berkeley 1926). H. SEILER, Cahuilla Texts (Bloomington, IN, 1970).

Southeast

A. S. GATSCHET, A Migration Legend of the Creek Indians, 2 vols. (Philadelphia 1882–85). J. H. HOWARD, The Southeastern Ceremonial Complex and Its Interpretation (Columbia, MO, 1968). J. F. KILPATRICK and A. G. KILPATRICK, Notebook on a Cherokee Shaman (Washington 1970). J. MOONEY, "The Sacred Formulas of the Cherokee," U.S. Bureau of American Ethnology, 7th annual report (Washington 1885–86); "Myths of the Cherokee," U.S. Bureau of American Ethnology, 19th annual report (Washington 1897–98). J. R. SWANTON, "Religion Beliefs and Medicinal Practices of the Creek Indians," U.S. Bureau of American Ethnology, 42d annual report (Washington 1928); "Social and Religious Beliefs and Usages of the Chickasaw Indians," U.S. Bureau of American Ethnology, 44th annual report (Washington 1928).

Southwest, Great Basin, Southern Plains

A. F. BANDELIER, The Delight Makers (New York 1946). R. L. BUNZEL, "Introduction to Zuni Ceremonialism," U.S. Bureau of American Ethnology (Washington 1932). F. H. CUSHING, Zuni Folk Tales (New York 1901). G. GOODWIN, "Tales of the White Mountain Apaches," Memoirs of the American Folk-Lore Society 33 (1939). C. KLUCKHOHN, Navaho Witchcraft (Cambridge, MA, 1944; Boston 1967). A. MARRIOTT, The Ten Grand Mothers (Norman, OK, 1945). A. ORTIZ, The Tewa World (Chicago 1969). M. SCHEVIL LINK, The Pollen Path (Stanford 1956). C. L. SMITHSON, "Havasupai Religion and Mythology," Anthropological Papers, no. 68 (Salt Lake City 1964). H. A. TYLER, Pueblo God and Myths (Norman, OK, 1964). B. B. WHITING, Paiute Sorcery (New York 1950).

Subarctic and Forest Regions

M. BARBEAU, Huron and Wyandot Mythology (Ottawa 1915). REV. W. M. BEAUCHAMP, "Iroquois Folk-Lore," Empire State Historical Publications, 31 (Port Washington, NY, 1922). J. M. COOPER, "The Northern Algonquian Supreme Being," Catholic University of America, Anthropological series 2 (Washington 1934). J. N. B. HEWITT, "Iroquoian Cosmology," part 1, U.S. Bureau of American Ethnology (Washington 1903); part 2, ibid. (1925–26). W. J. HOFFMAN, "The Midewiwin," U.S. Bureau of American Ethnology, 7th annual report (Washington 1891). D. JENNESS, "The Ojibwa Indians of Parry Island," Bull. of the Dept. of Mines 78 (Ottawa 1935). P. RADIN, Some Myths and Tales of the Ojibwa of Southeastern Ontario (Ottawa 1914); Winnebago Hero Cycles (Baltimore 1948). R. SAVARD, Carcajou ou le Sens du Monde, ministère des Affaires culturelles (Quebec 1972). F. G. SPECK, Naskapi (Norman, OK, 1935). L. TURNER, "Ethnology of the Ungava District, Hudson Bay Territory,"

U.S. Bureau of American Ethnology (Washington 1889–90). M. L. WILLIAMS, ed., *Schoolcraft's Indian Legends* (East Lansing, MI, 1956).

Plains, Prairies

A. W. BOWERS, *Mandan Social and Ceremonial Organization* (Chicago 1950). L. BLOOMFIELD, "Sacred Stories of the Sweet Grass Cree," *Bull. of the National Museum of Canada*, no. 60 (1930). G. A. DORSEY, *The Pawnee: Mythology* (Washington 1906); *The Mythology of the Wichita*

(Washington 1904). V. DUSENBERRY, *The Montana Cree: A Study in Religious Persistences* (Göteborg 1962). A. C. FLETCHER, "The Hako: A Pawnee Ceremony," *U.S. Bureau of American Ethnology*, 22d annual report (Washington 1900–1901). F. LA FLESCHE, "The Osage Tribe, Rite of the Wa-xo-be," *U.S. Bureau of American Ethnology* (Washington 1930). R. H. LOWIE, The Crow Indians (New York 1966). P. J. POWELL, *Sweet Medicine*, 2 vols. (Norman, OK, 1969). C. WISSLER, ed., *Sun Dance of the Plains Indians* (New York 1921).

THE CREATION OF THE WORLD IN NATIVE AMERICAN MYTHOLOGY

I. The Woman Who Fell from the Sky

They recognize as chief of their nation a certain woman whom they call Ataentsic, who they say fell to them from the sky. (Père Paul Le Jeune, "De la Créance, des Moeurs et Costumes des Hurons," 1636)

Ataentsic[1] lived happily above the vaults of the sky, in a land which resembled Earth. One day, when she was cultivating a field, her dog, which accompanied her, saw a bear and followed it. In order to escape from the dog's fangs, the bear, cornered at the edge of an abyss, jumped in. The dog jumped in after it, and Ataentsic, impelled by curiosity and despair, leapt in as well. Although she was pregnant, her fall into the water did her no harm.

In another version, Ataentsic, wishing to cure a very ill husband, set about cutting down a tree with curative powers. But the tree fell over a precipice and Ataentsic jumped after it. Her fall, however, was noticed by the tortoise, which "had its head out of the water; seeing her and not knowing what to do, amazed at what it saw, the tortoise called the other aquatic animals to get their advice. And behold, they all assembled forthwith. The tortoise showed them what it had seen and asked what they thought should be done. The majority brought the matter to the beaver, which through decorum took the entire question to the tortoise, which was finally of the opinion that they should set to work immediately, dive to the bottom of the water, bring up some soil, and put it onto the tortoise's back. No sooner said than done, and the woman fell very gently onto this island" (Le Jeune [1636] 1972, 101).

Soon Ataentsic gave birth to a daughter who, although she was a virgin, gave birth to the twins Taiscaron and Iskeha.[2] The two had a violent quarrel. While Iskeha armed himself with the horns of a deer, Taiscaron, convinced that a blow with a wild rose bush would take care of his brother, struck the first blow. But Iskeha mortally wounded his brother and came out the victor in the battle (ibid. 102).

It was thanks to Iskeha, their culture hero, that the Hurons learned the techniques of making fire, fishing, hunting, and navigation, as well as how to cultivate wheat and gather maple syrup (ibid. 103).

A more elaborate version of this myth is found among the Iroquois. The Seneca version tells how the daughter of the Chief of the Sky fell ill. Her father had her carried close to a nutritious tree, the only one that the celestial people possessed. He ordered that the tree be uprooted. A man who was very dissatisfied with this decision kicked the girl, knocking her into a hole. Some aquatic birds that noticed her fall placed her gently on the back of the tortoise. The

sequences that follow resemble the version of the Huron. The fistful of mud brought back finally by the toad was spread out carefully upon the shell of the tortoise, and as it spread out it formed an island.

The woman who fell from the sky gave birth to a daughter. Later, when both were busy gathering potatoes, the daughter disobeyed her mother by facing the east wind. Her mother had warned her about this, saying that, if she did this, she would become impregnated by the west wind (Feldmann 1971, 56–70).

Just before giving birth, the young woman heard the twins quarreling in her womb. While the first came forward to be born through the normal channels, the second pushed out and was born through his mother's armpit. The firstborn was Juskana (Little Bud) and the second Othagwenda (Flint). The grandmother held Othagwenda responsible for the death of her daughter and bestowed all her affection upon Juskana.

These accounts contain the essentials of the themes that recur in the nations to the east and west of the Great Lakes. The special relationship of the grandmother with her grandson is an image widespread in North America (Grandmother Spider in the Southwest and Grandmother Bat in the Great Plains, for example). The grandson is the culture hero. When the grandmother falls from the sky, the earth is always covered with antediluvian waters (the deluge occurs later because of the clumsiness of some demiurge or the misdeeds of a marine monster). It is also the tortoise that serves as the support for the earth, an idea which is also found among the Mandan, according to whom the earth is carried by four tortoises.

The twins who dispute in the womb of their mother are a common figure. However, among the Ojibwa, the hero Manabozo speaks in a friendly way with his brother Wolf. They love each other so much that when Wolf accidentally drowns, Manabozo remains inconsolable. In another version, he is so furious at this death that he attempts to take on Manitu. Nevertheless, another version says that he ends up killing his brother. And Gluskap, the culture hero of the Micmac, also quarrels with his brother. The two plan to kill one another. Gluskap (called the liar or the deceiving one) emerges the victor in a combat with his brother Malsum by eliminating him in the same way that Iskeha killed Taiscaron (Mechling 1914, 44).

From this perspective, it seems clear that the legend of Dekanawida borrows freely from the myth of the origin of creation. This account—of which there are many versions—also constitutes a political attempt to explain the laws and responsibilities of the new constitutions of the League of the Iroquois (which is thought to have originated in the middle of the fifteenth century, a time which would correspond with the total solar eclipse of 1451).

According to the version of Newhouse (Fenton, *The Constitution of the Five Nations* 1971, 14 and passim, 65 and passim), the account begins with a woman of great goodness who was living alone with her daughter. Now the daughter found that she was pregnant without ever having known a man.[3] After the birth of the infant, the grandmother tried on numerous occasions to rid herself of it, but the baby always came out the victor in these trials. The old woman was astounded and adopted it. The infant was named Dekanawida. A little later, he left the two women and undertook finally to visit the neighboring peoples who were always at war. Another version says that Dekanawida undertook his circuit in a craft of white stone. It was to the people of the flint (the Hurons, or "forked tongues," according to the Iroquois) that he directed the first stage of his voyage. He overcame a trial there—a most common thing for all culture heroes—by clambering to the top of a tree situated at the edge of a ravine, which they cut down at the base. In this way he proved to the people of the flint his loyal intention to establish peace.

He continued along his path and arrived among the Ongweowe (the "true men," that is, the Iroquois). He overcame another trial by helping Ayonwatha (Hiawatha)[4] to conquer Adodaro, a kind of cannibal despot who had imposed his evil law upon the "true men" (Fenton 1971, 17).

The references to the myth of the woman who fell from the sky are rather obvious. Dekanawida is the messiah who proposes to remake the world by delivering it from chaos. Like the culture heroes, he travels magically, overcomes a whole series of trials, and battles monsters. These references are there to indicate that the legend of Dekanawida serves to support an organization of the fifteenth century (the League of the Iroquois) and originates in a historical reality: the tribes' incessant wars with one another. The myth of origin, like the legend, tells that the hero's task is to structure the world and society. It is in this sense that the myths are the reflection of society.

II. The Magpie That Came from the Earth

"My friend," asked Masauwu, "but where do you come from? You seek something, perhaps? To tell the truth, I have never heard of you. I live here alone."

"I have come out of the earth," answered the magpie.

"Is this possible?"

"Yes, I have come out of the earth."

"Oh! I have indeed heard of certain folk who live underground."

"It is from there that I come."

"But what goes on there down below?"

"Oh! You know, we have a lot of problems. . . ."

(Elsie Clews Parsons, *Pueblo Indian Religion* vol. 1, 1939, 238)

In the first world, the Hopi were like ants. In the second world, they metaphormose into new animal creatures. In the third world, they begin to resemble men a little, but they still have a long tail of which they are deeply ashamed. (The Zuñi had sticky bodies and webbed hands; they walked on one another and spat on one another.) They acted in a bizarre fashion. The young men made love to old women and the old men to young girls. The women did not want their husbands. They beat each other, cast spells upon each other, killed each other. Some people fell ill, others went mad. The chiefs expressed great dissatisfaction with this impossible situation.

As they were traveling, they arrived at a river. They decided to separate, the women to one side, the men to the other. Each group planted corn and watermelons. It seems that the men succeeded better at this task. But the deluge came. The women constructed a tower which collapsed. The men planted reeds (another version states that it was the spider woman who did this) which pierced the terrestrial crust.

Badger was the first to venture forth, but he was not able to see anything because of the dark (elsewhere it is said that the badger was too tired and had to give up his exploration). Finally the magpie flew off. In the distance she saw a house and a field of corn. A man, who had his back to the bird, did not hear her coming. When he saw the magpie, he tried to put on his mask, but it was too late. It was Masauwu,[5] (Parsons 1939, 1.236 and passim).

Among the Navajo, the present world represents the fifth level of a laborious ascension. (It is impossible to give a comprehensive account of all the sequences of this emergence myth, one of the most complete in existence. We refer the reader to the study by Gladys A. Reichard, 1950.) Three beings shared the first world, which was plunged in darkness: First Man, First Woman, and Coyote, but the place was too constricted, so that all three agreed to climb up. Two men lived in the second world, which was feebly illuminated: Sun and Moon. However, each of the four cardinal points (east = black; south = blue; west = yellow; north = white) hid a person.

Discord was established among the inhabitants of the second world after Sun attempted to seduce First Woman. Of course, Coyote, who knew everything, had the occupants of the cardinal points intervene. They decided they had to clamber up again to the higher level, where the space would be large enough to separate Sun from First Woman.

The third world resembled Earth. There were four oceans and four beautiful mountains.[6] The new arrivals were welcomed by the inhabitants of the mountain, who warned them that all would go well as long as the marine monster was left in peace. But Coyote, strong in skill, transgressed the warning. Unable to resist the incomparable beauty of the two children of the monster, he carried them off. The marine monster, furious, avenged himself by pouring the waters of the oceans (or of the great sea) into the third world. The inhabitants began to pile up the four mountains, but since that was not enough, they planted a giant reed. They were thus able to continue their climb into the fourth world. This world, though more vast than the one which preceded it, was not yet the good world. Thanks to First Woman and First Man, the "people" (as the Navajo call themselves) were able to emerge onto the Earth.

While the Huron and the Iroquois explicate the genesis of creation upon a sky-earth axis, at the other extreme, the Pueblos and the Navajo emerge laboriously from the bowels of the earth, after they have undergone physical transformations, have been put to flight by the deluge, and have successively traversed several subterranean worlds.

Between the celestial origin of the peoples of the west and the subterranean origin of the peoples of the southwest, the Creek of the southwest, the peoples of California, and the Kwakiutl of the Northwest Coast give other versions. It is Esaugetu-Emissi (the "master of breath") who has the power of creation for the Creek. These used to live in a celestial kingdom as pure spirits before they took human form. Elsewhere one finds the idea, which is quite widespread among the Californian peoples, of a creator who models from mud, or from the union of the earth (sister) and the sky (brother), in order to people the planet (Spence 1975, 122, 348 and passim).

A typical theme of the Kwakiutl, by contrast, recounts the arrival of the ancestor of the Numayma (or Nemema: the inhabitants of each village who have this ancestor in common), under the guise of an animal (bird) or a human. He might also come forth from the ocean, taking on the traits of an aquatic mammal, or emerge from the subterranean world in the form of a spirit. The ancestor immediately sets about the task of sculpting human figures from earth or wood, or bringing back to shore people who have drifted astray. As soon as he has finished his work, he shouts all around him to hear himself answered by another ancestor who is just as busy as he (Boas 1975, 304–5).

Although there is no real creation myth among the Kwakiutl, the theme of the ancestor-sculptor sets out rather nicely the synthesis of the subjects that compose the emergence of humanity and the creation of the world.

Nevertheless, there are peoples who hesitate between the high and the low and who opt for solutions different from those that we have considered. These include, for example, the Mandan, the Hidatsa, and the Arikara, all three neighboring tribes of the upper Missouri.

As Claude Lévi-Strauss has written: ". . . the myths seem troubled by the choice between a terrestrial or celestial origin. They marry the two theses, and the Hidatsa sages schematize their system by tracing a kind of Y: the two arms of the fork represent the emergence of one part of the ancestors, who lived in the bowels of the earth, and the descent from the sky of the other part; the common trunk evokes the adventures of the two groups after they came together and were associated with each other" (Lévi-Strauss 1968, 378).

In the Arikara creation myth, Nesaru was the guardian of the universe. Through a window, he was able to see a lake where two ducks swam incessantly. Then came Wolf Man and Lucky Man who sent the ducks to look for mud. With this mud, Wolf Man modeled the prairies and Lucky Man designed the valleys and the hills. Then both made an incursion underground where two spiders lived, female and male. They were hideous and dirty. The two visitors undertook to clean them. They instructed them in sexual matters, of which they were entirely ignorant. Very quickly, they set about procreating. The female spider gave birth to animals and to a race of giants. Nesaru expressed his irritation at all this. Consequently, he made the corn grow, and its grains penetrated the earth and gave birth to a race of normal people. Then he provoked the deluge which destroyed the giants but spared the others.

The survivors were unhappy in this world, for they walked upon one another. They too sought a pathway up, but did not find one. Nesaru delegated the goddess Corn to go underground with the mission of bringing them back. The people clung about her so that she was unable to find the path back. Badger began boring a tunnel. He stopped before he reached the surface because of the light; the mole relieved him, but she too was afraid of being dazzled. Finally the long-nosed mouse arrived at the surface, an achievement which was balanced by the loss of the end of her nose. Even so, the tunnel was still too narrow and the people were pushing and shoving each other at the entrance. But the thunder roared and the tunnel was enlarged. Finally all were able to emerge (Burland 1965, 84–86).

We conclude with the Arikara myth, which makes it possible to put in place the last links that compose the genesis of humanity. For the Arikara, humanity, in the final analysis, comes from grains of corn. But such ultimate

recourses to solutions of replacement are usual. Among the Mandan (the bison clan), humanity takes its origin from the transformation of the prairie dog (*Cynomys sp.*). This is because neither human nor animal—nor, in some cases, plants—should be distinguished. For the Sioux sages discussed the question of who, bison or human, should eat the other.

These myths teach us a lesson about the wisdom and also the boldness of Native American thought. Whether they belong to the celestial, subterranean, or terrestrial order, these myths always keep a visual power and a spectacular dynamic which fascinates through the beauty of the word and the image that they inspire. For whatever reason, the myths of creation do not lack an acute sense of drama, humor, and passion.

P.D./m.s.

NOTES

1. Ataentsic means "old woman." She is also called Awehai (fertile Earth) or Moon. Ataentsic is not entirely devoid of the characteristics of the trickster. In certain cases she may make herself young or old. She is at once creator and seducer. In another variant she may be seduced by her grandson.

2. Taiscaron means "flint" (the blood that escapes from a wound on his flank was transformed into "firestone"), "frozen to the second degree," or "black." Iskeha means "sun," "the good," "white," "the dear little sprout," or "the young bud" (Le Jeune [1636] 1972, 102; Tooker 1962, 151).

3. Compare this story with that of the Winnebago demiurge the Great Hare, which begins in exactly the same way. See Radin 1976, 63.

4. Not to be confused with the Hiawatha of Longfellow. The author drew his inspiration from the adventures of the demiurge Manabozo (or Manabush, Chibiabo, Wenobojo).

5. Masauwu in this case is the guardian of the chthonic universe. He is also an agricultural god. He wears his mask in order to frighten the magpie. If he had been able to do it, the people of the third world would not have been able to emerge. But since he was not fast enough, Masauwu must cede the Earth and what is cultivated on it: corn, watermelon, cantaloupe, and gourds.

6. It is interesting to note that the Navajo, who are Athapaskan speakers who had emigrated from northern Canada to New Mexico and Colorado, identify the four mountains in question, situated in Arizona, as follows: Big Sheep (north), Taylor (south), Humphrey (west), and Pelado or Sierra Blanca (east). Note: among the Pueblos, the Grand Canyon of the Colorado River is often regarded as the topographic place of emergence.

BIBLIOGRAPHY

F. BOAS, *Kwakiutl Ethnography,* H. Codere, ed. (2d ed., Chicago 1975). C. BURLAND, *North American Indian Mythology* (London 1965). W. N. FENTON, ed., *Parker on the Iroquois* (Syracuse 1971). P. LE JEUNE, *Relation de ce qui s'est passé en Nouvelle-France en l'année 1636* (Montreal 1972). C. LÉVI-STRAUSS, *The Origin of Table Manners* (New York 1978). W. H. MECHLING, "Malecite Tales," *Mem.* 49, Dept. of Mines (Ottawa 1914). E. C. PARSONS, *Pueblo Indian Religion,* 2 vols. (Berkeley 1939). G. A. REICHARD, *Navaho Religion,* 2 vols. (New York 1950). L. SPENCE, *Myths and Legends of the North American Indians* (New York 1975). E. TOOKER, "An Ethnography of the Huron Indians, 1615–1649," *B.A.E.* (Washington 1964).

THE SUN DANCE AMONG THE NATIVE AMERICANS: THE REVIVAL OF 1973

The founding myths of the sun dance show clearly that this ritual was introduced in order to celebrate the creation of the world or to commemorate the revival of the earth (Dorsey 1905, 46–55; Brown 1972, 3–9 and 67–100; Lévi-Strauss 1968, 163–84). As this ceremony came to be celebrated more and more, tribes added sequential features that signaled its importance from the point of view of time and space. Though the sun dance has taken on a syncretic appearance and may be performed for revolutionary ends,[1] it is important to emphasize that at the same time it embodies a strictly mythological way of thinking.[2]

While the sun dance was most elaborate among the Arapaho, Cheyenne, and Dakota, tribes such as the Comanche copied it from the Kiowa in 1874, and the Ute adopted it as late as 1890, a time that corresponds with the ghost dance of messianic inspiration, which was based in part on a myth like the myth of Orpheus.

The sun dance goes by different names: the "dance without drinking" (Cree), "the ceremony of the renewal of life" (Cheyenne, among others); the "sacred or mysterious dance" (Poncas); "to dance gazing at the sun" and sometimes "the sun gazes at the dance" (Dakota). This ritual was performed by twenty odd tribes of the Plains: Kiowa, Ute, Wind River Shoshones, Crow, Blackfeet, Sarsi, Gros Ventre, Arapaho, Cheyenne (Northern and Southern), Oglala, Ponca, Arikara, Hidatsa, Assiniboin, Sisseton, Dakota, Ojibwa, and Plains Cree (Spier 1921, 473). Conversely, the Pawnee, Wichita, Omaha, Mandan, and a few tribes of the Siouan linguistic group did not observe it. The Mandan celebrated the *O-kee-pa* (Catlin 1967 and 1973, 1.155–84), a ritual commemorating the flood, highly elaborate and complex, which, like the sun dance, lasted four days with its attending privations, fasting, and mortifications.

We must hasten to add that not all tribes practiced torture. Among those mentioned above, the Kiowa, Wind River Shoshones, and Northern Cheyenne did not use torture or used very little. Writers do not agree on this question (Spier 1921, 473; Mayhall 1971, 150).

At the time when the horse was introduced into the Plains, many tribes turned this vast territory into their permanent habitat. The Cheyenne, Gros Ventre, and Lakota groups that lived farther east in the regions bordering on the Prairies, the forests, and the Great Lakes, adapted very quickly to the Plains. The Minnesota Sioux who went to the Dakotas are the best example of this.

A ceremony like the sun dance could not help but become enriched by the new cultural and ecological circumstances. In any case, the progressive change of territory made it possible for these groups further to develop warring societies,[3] and with them there opened up a ceremonial upon which the immediate history of the tribes in question was to be inscribed.

Unlike other ceremonies reserved for specifically female or male societies,[4] the sun dance was above all tribal in character. In fact, the entire tribe—with the exception of a few "impure" individuals—was invited to participate in this grand ceremonial that took place in June or July, and sometimes in August as it does today, after the collective hunting parties which had dispersed during the winter had regrouped in a large meeting place.

Among the Dakota Sioux, the sun dance took place yearly, although it could also be performed in response to an individual wish. Such was the case with the Crow, who performed it after a warrior had expressed a desire for it when a relative had been murdered by an enemy tribe (which explains its sporadic character) (Lowie 1963, 198). This analogy between the ceremony and affairs of war was indeed clearly established, for it was customary before the ceremony began for warriors to recount their exploits.

Despite its elliptical name—given to it by European observers—and the impressive spectacle made by the dancer in his intoxicating connection with the sun (for the spectator can no longer tell with certainty who gazes at whom, the sun or the dancer), the sun dance is above all a celebration of renewal. To be sure, the sun is a prestigious and highly emblematic component in the eyes of the performer, since that performer dances for four days, bare-chested, his body exposed to the burning rays of the sun. In addition, he does this without eating and in principle without drinking, so that the pain-racked body uses the sun as its instrument of torture in order that it may touch the one called the Great Spirit.

Viewed from this perspective, the sun is above all an intermediary between Wakan Tanka (Sioux) and the dancer, as are also the thunderbird (the performer blows almost continually into a whistle shaped like the wing of an eagle), the bison (which is one of the objects of the sacred altar), the medicine man, and the dancing woman who symbolizes "the female white bison" who came to bring the sacred pipe to the Sioux. The moon serves as a counterpart to the sun; for the ceremony takes place at the time of year when the sun is at its highest point, which is also when the moon is full in June and July. This being so, although there is a special relationship between the dancer guided by the celebrant and what takes place on the spiritual level, since the vision remains the ultimate step, the performance of the sun dance is a popular event of a highly religious nature.

There are several descriptions of this ritual performed by the Indians of the Plains. We refer the reader who is interested in a step-by-step account to the works of J. O. Dorsey (1889–90), J. E. Brown (1972), G. B. Grinnell (vol. 2, 1972), J. G. Jorgensen (1972), R. H. Lowie (1915 and 1919), Skinner (1919), L. Spier (1921), J. R. Walter (1917), W. D. Wallis (1919), and C. Wissler (1918).

For our part, we were able to attend the renewal of this ceremony in 1973, an exceptional opportunity, since white men are excluded from the territory. The celebration took place on the camping grounds of a celebrated medicine man, Henry Crow Dog, at a spot called "Crow Dog's Paradise" on the Rosebud Sioux reservation in South Dakota.

We can attest to the great religious atmosphere that prevailed in the camp, in which all recording and photographic equipment had been strictly forbidden. Many very old people, who came from all the corners of South Dakota, were barely able to contain their intense emotion. The same was true of the singers seated around the ceremonial drum at the entrance of the bower. The campgrounds were heavily guarded by young "warriors" (militants who had for the most part participated in the siege of Wounded Knee). They also kept order among the spectators seated around the bower where the dance was taking place.

As in the time of the great celebration at the end of spring, the ceremony was prepared four days in advance and lasted four days straight, the last day being reserved for the corporeal offering. On this occasion, the celebrants stuck skewers under the chest muscles of the participants; the skewers were tied to a central pole by a rope (in this case, the pole was the trunk of a young poplar). Each of the approx-

Member of the Crazy Dog Society. North America. Paris, Musée de l'Homme collection. Photo P. Coze.

imately thirty participants danced until he was freed. At the end of the day, just before sunset, at the same time as the sacrifice of the dancers was taking place, the medicine man cut a piece of flesh from the shoulder or arm of those among the spectators who wished this to be done. In return, they received a small bag symbolizing the sacred altar that belongs to the sun dance.

As in times past, the bower, covered with branches, encircled the sacred space reserved for the dancers and kept the spectators cool while the sun's rays were beating down in the center where the four cardinal points were indicated: north, south, east, west. To the west of this bower, a forbidden zone was marked off in which a ceremonial tepee and a sweat tent had been erected. A little to the south was the area set aside for profane festivals and also a place where all the spectators could get food free of charge that was prepared by a group of young women.

Without wishing to claim that since 1904, when the U.S. government banned the sun dance as "immoral and barbarian," this ceremony had never been performed in its entirety, we can affirm that the ritual procedure was respected as it seldom had been since the nineteenth century. In fact, whereas the official ban goes back to 1904, local agents of the Bureau of Indian Affairs were known well before that date to have been ordered to break down the religious culture on the spot. The dance had been authorized once more in 1934, the

year of the Indian Reorganization Act, which was passed in order to correct a government policy that had prevailed for one hundred years. As early as 1883, for example, orders came from Washington giving agents full power to imprison participants. So the last time the sun dance was performed was in 1883, on the Sioux reservation of the Cheyenne River in South Dakota (R. M. Utley 1972, 33). This reservation is at present a place where the ritual is once again performed.

We must unfortunately confess that quite often the sun dance is a pale copy of what it must have been in the last century. To be convinced of this, one need only see a film like *Lost Sun,* which was produced in 1961 by the Canadian Film Board. This film, shot among the Blood (Blackfoot) Indians in Alberta, far from giving the impression of being an ethnographic document, rather seeks to convince the viewer that this is an obsolete and moribund bit of "folklore." Similarly, modern descriptions in certain books leave the reader disappointed or perplexed (for instance, the chapter entitled "The Defeat of the Rodeo" in E. Schorris 1972, 137–54).

It is useful to note these facts in order to understand that the authentic revival of this ritual in our time is much more than a visual representation. The sun dance takes place on two levels simultaneously: the mythical and the real. This is the source of the symbolic and expressionistic power of such an institution.

P.D./g.h.

NOTES

1. The medicine man (*hunkpapa*) Sitting Bull had the following vision during the sun dance before the attack at the Little Big Horn: he saw dozens of white soldiers fall on the battlefield; this was the famous defeat of Custer in 1876.

2. In this regard, compare this ritual to that of the Ojibwa *midewiwin* (Landes 1968, 71–237).

3. One of the last (end of the nineteenth century) would be that of the Crazy Dogs of the Cheyenne. This society was composed of a few warriors who took an oath to die in battle; see Grinnell 1972, 2:48.

4. One of the Sioux women's societies was dedicated to the "Holy Woman Above." Among the Cheyenne women there were warriors called "Manly Hearted Women."

BIBLIOGRAPHY

See also the general bibliography.
J. E. BROWN, ed., *The Sacred Pipe* (Baltimore 1972). G. CATLIN, *O-kee-pa: A Religious Ceremony and Other Customs of the Mandans,* edited by John C. Ewers (New Haven 1967); *North American Indians,* 2 vols. (New York 1973). J. O. DORSEY, "A Study of Siouan Cults," *U.S. Bureau of American Ethnology,* 11th Annual Report (1889–90): 351–544; *The Cheyenne,* Field Columbian Museum, "Anthropological Series" 9, 1905. G. B. GRINNELL, *The Cheyenne Indians* 2 (Lincoln, NE, 1972). J. G. JORGENSEN, *The Sun Dance Religion* (Chicago 1972). R. H. LOWIE, "The Sun Dance of the Crow Indians," *A.M.N.H.* 16, part 1 (New York 1963): 1–50; *Indians of the Plains* (New York 1963). R. LANDES, *Ojibwa Religion* (Madison, WI, 1968). C. LÉVI-STRAUSS, *The Origin of Table Manners* (New York 1978) (trans. from French). M. P. MAYHALL, *The Kiowas* (2d ed., Norman, OK, 1971). E. SHORRIS, *The Death of the Great Spirit* (2d ed., New York 1972). L. SPIER, "The Sun Dance of the Plains Indians: Its Development and Diffusion," *A.M.N.H.* 16, part 7 (New York 1921). R. M. UTLEY, *The Last Days of the Sioux Nation* (7th ed., New Haven 1972). J. R. WALKER, "The Sun Dance and Other Ceremonies of the Oglala Division of the Teton Dakota," *A.M.N.H.* 16, part 2 (New York 1917): 51–221. W. D. WALLIS, "The Sun Dance of the Canadian Dakota," *A.M.N.H.* 16, part 4 (New York 1919): 317–80. C. WISSLER, "The Sun Dance of the Blackfoot Indians," *A.M.N.H.* 16, part 3 (New York 1918): 225–70.

MESOAMERICAN RELIGION

The name "Mesoamerica" refers synchronically to an area of civilization and diachronically to a collection of neighboring cultural traditions that arose in central and southern Mexico and in Guatemala, a group whose borders have varied in the course of the centuries. The term was first used in the first sense; it attempted to define the complex of "superior" civilizations that, at the beginning of the sixteenth century, stretched from north to south, starting roughly with the Rio Panuco and the Rio Sinaloa, passing through the Rio Lerma, stretching west to what is now Honduras and to the Gulf of Nicoya. Despite tremendous geographic, linguistic, and ethnic differences, this vast zone presented a cultural unity in which, among other common elements, the convergence of religious systems occupied an important position. Research into the historical depth of such a unity has made it possible to broaden the meaning of the term "Mesoamerica."

Among the developmental phases of the diverse cultures that have made up Mesoamerica, one period has traditionally been given a special rank: the period that witnessed the rise and apogee of the great metropolis of Teotihuacan on the central Mexican plateau and the vigorous growth of the great Mayan cities, a growth marked for six centuries by the uninterrupted erection of stelae bearing dates and inscriptions. The term "Classic" used for this period has produced as its consequence a system of reference for the naming of periods that preceded and followed it. The millennia that have separated the appearance of the first tribes on what was to become the territory of Mesoamerica and the beginning of the Classic Period make for a slowly evolving spectacle. But it is above all starting with the Early Preclassic Period that numerous distinctive elements of the Mesoamerican tradition appear, especially in the religious realm. The dynamics of the Olmec world may not have resulted in the standardization of the zones that came under its influence, but it does indicate without a doubt the beginnings of Mesoamerica as a reality. At the other end of the historical spectrum, the Spanish Conquest interrupted the autonomous development of the native civilizations. Isolation or contact, resistance to the invader or acceptance of him, all created disparate situations that are revealed in the study of present-day Indian societies.

Our knowledge of religious phenomena in the oldest periods comes mainly from the interpretation of archaeological vestiges. The results obtained in this way are still embryonic and often speculative. The uneven development of archaeological research has resulted in significant disproportions of space and time in the order of our understanding. The second group of sources available to the historian of religions is made up of the collection of indigenous pictographic documents that have been preserved, almost all dated in the Late Preclassic Period or in the early period of colonization. In many cases, the subject matter is mythical and ritualistic. To this set of documents one could add the numerous eyewitness accounts of the conquistadores and missionaries, the first and last ethnographers of the pre-Columbian world. Modern ethnology, finally, enables us to examine the road traveled by native cultures and to rediscover the traces of ancient visions of the world, in spite of the mutations imposed by contemporary societies.

This presentation of Mesoamerican religious thought has been sketched in the shape of eight articles: mythic and ritual order, creation, space and time, sky, earth, fire, the human being, and cosmic disorder.

Such an essay must rest on three constraints:

—the need to point out correspondences and invariables, even at the admitted risk of minimizing divergences and transformations,

—the thematic classification of phenomena that makes it possible to emphasize the birth, the development, and the result of great concepts but that can also offer an illuminating and simplified religious reality,

—finally, the preeminence given to speculative religious thought over practice, an attitude that incurs the danger of obscuring the fundamental relationships between religion and socioeconomic systems.

These initial choices, compounded by the imperfection of our knowledge, have resulted in a series of limitations and lacunae. The earliest periods and the least-known regions, western Mexico in particular, often remain in shadow. Finally, though it has been possible to deal with a maximum number of themes, it has not been possible to give certain aspects the space that they deserve. For example, the most sophisticated speculations of the philosopher-priests of Tenochtitlan have been barely touched upon.

The religious history of pre-Columbian Mesoamerica, which is known to have lasted for more than twenty centuries, challenges anyone confronting it with the fundamental problem of the unity or plurality of the religions throughout the different cultures that have been grouped together under the rubric of Mesoamerica. It also raises the equally important question of the levels of religion within each culture. Moreover, the analysis of contemporary visions of the world cannot draw any conclusions without ascertaining the impact of Catholicism on the old traditional base.

It is difficult to understand Mesoamerican religions as a unique whole without first taking into account the originality and multiplicity of the works produced by the civilization that nourished them (ceramics, statues, codices, and so forth) and the richness of the vernacular languages, of which some thirty are spoken today, each translating its own vision of the world.

The evolution of Mesoamerican social formations certainly did not follow the same paths everywhere. State societies with very strong social stratification coexisted with peasant communities with little hierarchy. Starting with the Preclassic

Structure 6 of San José Mogote (Oaxaca), one of the first stone public buildings in Mesoamerica (1350 B.C.). Photo M.A.E.F.M.

and moving from one culture to another, marked sociological differences appeared, particularly between the social complex of the high plateau and that of the Gulf Coast, and it is likely that the religious superstructures, of which we know far too little, reflect such contrasts. The phenomena of spreading and diffusion, especially evident beginning with the Olmec horizon, had only a limited impact. Indeed, they could not prevent the creation of scores of local religions, whose development was largely autonomous. But in spite of the multiplicity of processes in the construction of religious systems, common characteristics swept such multiplicity away into areas of shadow. On the eve of the Conquest, Aztec society had a caste of priests who were developing an esoteric knowledge very clearly distinguished from popular religious practice, a situation similar to that of the Mayan region during the Classic Period. Extremely strong similarities unite the ideology of the Mayan and Aztec elite on the one hand, and the simpler religion of peasant groups of these two cultures, on the other, the social stratification engendering a stratification of systems of knowledge. Furthermore, it seems that with the cult of *Itzam Na* among the Maya of the Classic Period and with the reflection of the poet-sovereign Netzahualcoyotl of Texcoco in the fifteenth century, we witness the rise of a way of thinking that opens up the possibility of monotheism. These are isolated experiences to be sure, but they indicate the potentialities attained by religious thought in Mesoamerica before the Conquest.

Because the first missionaries who arrived followed in the steps of Cortés, military order in New Spain was immediately intermingled with the moral order of Christianity.

Evangelical politics initially took the direction of an open fight against "idolatry," namely, the veneration of ancient deities and the celebration of ceremonies whose motivation profoundly baffled Christian sensibilities, such as rituals of flaying symbolizing the renewal of vegetation, or tearing out the heart in order to feed the solar deity.

But two elements were to modify permanently the ideology of the pastoral mission: on the one hand, the brutal methods of imposition of colonial power, and on the other, the shortage of manpower among the priesthood. Very rapidly, part of the clergy, who included in their ranks remarkable humanists like the Franciscan Bernardino de Sahagún or the Dominican Bartolomé de las Casas, took up the cause of the Indians against the military and the colonizers. Without losing sight of the integration of the Indians into the Christian nation, this faction of the clergy managed effectively to guarantee their defense within the missionary regions. In the central plateau, in the zone formerly occupied by the Aztecs, the collapse of the old religion was so sudden that Indian religiosity had no other recourse than to express itself through the Gospel, mixing it with bits and pieces of ancestral beliefs. The same did not hold true everywhere, and among the Maya in the south of Yucatan, fierce resistance to the invaders and their religion was sustained until the end of the seventeenth century and left scars still visible today. The superficial character of the evangelization, which spread rapidly throughout the Americas, led to inevitable rearrangements. Most often deprived of their clerics and their dogma, native groups set out to recreate their religious universe in light of the Christian religion. Each group reacted according to its own conceptual system. Some offered substantial zones of permeability, such as the multiple correspondences between the solar deity and Christ among the Huichol. Others, on the contrary, offered only resistance: the cycle of the rain gods has been largely preserved among the

The Carnival at Huehuetla (Tepehua Indians). Among many present-day native groups, the Carnival serves as a refuge for traditional beliefs. Photo M.A.E.F.M.

Maya right up to our time. The open confrontation between the two religions is still at issue, resulting in situations of rejection, as was recently the case among the Lacandon, or, more generally, in a situation of precarious equilibrium.

The flexibility of Christian concepts and the absence of orthodoxy greatly facilitated the absorption of a large part of the native spiritual heritage. Thus, the idea of "diablo" or of "demonio," heavily laden with the residues of various origins and constituted in the course of the Middle Ages in the West, would allow the survival of certain native concepts of evil and human nature.

This is why the lines between the religion of the Indians and the popular faith of the mestizos (whose worship of the Virgin of Guadalupe is a living symbol of syncretism) are very often difficult to recognize. Mexican Catholicism is an institution impregnated with Indian religious feeling, and its effects can be felt even in the urban world.

Today, Catholicism is firmly rooted in Mesoamerica. Originally a symbol of domination, it has now become an instrument of the defense of the Indian faith against mestizo mercantilism and serves as a refuge for the marginal communities that are dominated by the global society.

Despite all of this, the continual shrinking of the ancient religious patrimony follows its inexorable course. Among the younger generations, contact with the Indian worldview has been broken. With the few remaining native priests and old men, a universe is in the final stage of burning out.

M.A.E.F.M./g.h.

BIBLIOGRAPHY

There are many studies of religious phenomena in Mesoamerica, and it is not possible to mention all of them here. A choice has therefore been made despite the difficulties and imperfections that such an operation entails. A detailed bibliography appears below. The publications cited are arranged in four large sections according to their nature:

I. Codices: pictographic manuscripts with their principal interpretations
II. Ancient written sources
III. Archaeology and ethnohistory: syntheses and monographs
IV. Contemporary ethnological studies

Within each section, titles are preceded by numbers. At the end of each article on Mesoamerica, numbered bibliographic citations refer to these numbers. For the present article, see, in particular, for section II: 9, 16 (22 or 44), 23, 25, 26, 27, 29, 38; section III: 6, 8, 12, 17, 19, 25, 29, 35, 38, 39, 46, 50, 51, 54, 55, 57, 62, 63, 64, 69, 72, 73, 74, 75; section IV: 21.

I. Codices: Pictographic Manuscripts with Their Principal Interpretations

(1) F. ANDERS, *Codex Tro-Cortesianus* . . . , Introduction and Summary (Graz 1967); (2) *Codex Peresianus* (codex Paris) . . . , Introduction and Summary (Graz 1968). (3) C. BURLAND, *The Selden Roll*, an ancient Mexican picture manuscript in the Bodleian Library at Oxford (Berlin 1955); (4) *Codex Laud*, Bodleian Library, Oxford (Graz 1966). (5) *Códice Ramírez*, Manuscrito del Siglo XVI entitulado "Relación del origen de los indios que habitan esta Nueva España según sus historias" (Mexico City 1944). (6) J. COOPER CLARK, *Codex Mendoza*, the Mexican manuscript known as the collection of Mendoza and preserved in the Bodleian Library, Oxford, 3 vols. (London 1938). (7) J. CORONA NUNEZ, *Antiguedades de México, basadas en la recopilación de Lord Kingsborough*, 4 vols. (Mexico City 1964–67). (8) E. FÖRSTEMAN, *Commentary on the Maya Manuscript in the Royal Public Library of Dresden*, Papers of the Peabody Museum, Harvard University, vol. 4, no. 1 (Cambridge, MA, 1906). (9) W. E. GATES, *Commentary upon the Maya-Tzeltal Perez Codex*, Papers of the Peabody Museum, Harvard University, vol. 6, no. 1 (Cambridge, MA, 1910). (10) E. T. HAMY, *Codex Telleriano Remensis*, Mexican manuscript at the Bibliothèque nationale (Paris 1899); (11) *Codex Borbonicus*, Mexican manuscript at the bibliothèque du Palais-Bourbon (Paris 1899). (12) G. KUBLER and C. GIBSON, *The Tovar Calendar*, an illustrated Mexican manuscript ca. 1858 (New Haven 1951). (13) W. LEHMANN, "Die fünf im Kindbett gestorbenen Frauen des Westens und die fünf Götter des Südens in der mexicanischen Mythologie," *Zeitschrift für Ethnologie* 37 (1905): 858–71. (14) J. F. LOUBAT, *Il manoscritto messicano-vaticano 3773*, Codex Vaticanus B (Rome 1896); (15) *Il manoscritto messicano Borgiano del Museo Etnografico della S. Congregazione di Propaganda Fide* (Rome 1898; 2d ed., Mexico City and Buenos Aires, 1963, 4 vols.); (16) *Il manoscritto messicano vaticano 3738, detto il Codice Rios* (Rome 1900) = Codex Vaticanus A or Codex Rios; (17) *Codex Fejervary-Mayer*, pre-Columbian Mexican manuscript of the Free Public Museums, Liverpool (Paris 1901). (18) *Codex Magliabecchiano XIII-3*, post-Columbian Mexican manuscript of the National Library of Florence (Rome 1904). (19) C. MARTINEZ MARIN, *Códice Laud*, Instituto National de Antropología e Historia (Mexico City 1961). (20) Z. NUTTAL, *Codex Nuttal, Facsimile of an Ancient Mexican Codex*, Peabody Museum of American Archaeology and Ethnology (Cambridge, MA, 1902). (21) F. DEL PASO Y TRONCOSO, *Descripción del Códice Cospiano*, manuscrito pictórico de los antiguos Nauas, que se conserva en la Universidad de Bolonia (Rome 1898; 2d ed. by K. A. Nowotny, Graz 1968); (22) *Descripción, historia y exposición del códice pictórico de los antiguos Nauas, que se conserva en la biblioteca de la Cámara de los Diputados de Paris* (Florence 1898). (23) E. SELER, *Das Tonalamatl der Aubinschen Sammlung*, eine altmexikanische Bilderhandschrift der Bibliothèque nationale de Paris (Berlin 1900; English trans., Berlin and London 1900–1901); (24) *Codex Fejervary-Mayer*, eine altmexikanische Bilderhandschrift der Free Public Museums in Liverpool (Berlin 1901; English trans., Berlin and London 1901–2); (25) *Codex Vaticanus no. 3773*, Codex Vaticanus B, eine altmexikanische Bilderschrift der Vatikanischen Bibliothek (Berlin 1902, 2 vols.; English trans., Berlin and London 1902–3); (26) *Codex Borgia*, eine altmexikanische Bilderschrift der Bibliothek der Congregatio de Propaganda Fide (Berlin 1904–9, 3 vols.; Spanish trans., Mexico City and Buenos Aires 1963, 4 vols.). (27) J. E. S. THOMPSON, *A Commentary on the Dresden Codex, a Maya Hieroglyphic Book* (Philadelphia 1972).

II. Ancient Written Sources

(1) F. DE ALVA IXTLILXOCHITL, *Obras históricas* (Mexico City 1891–92; 2d ed., Mexico City 1952, 2 vols.). (2) H. ALVARADO TEZOZOMOC, *Crónica mexicana escrita por D. Hernando Alvarado Tezozomoc . . . precedida del Códice Ramírez* (Mexico City 1878; 2d ed., Mexico City 1944). (3) A. BARRERA VASQUEZ, *El libro de los cantares de Dzitbalché*, una traducción con notas y una introducción (Mexico City 1965). (4) A. BARRERA VASQUEZ and S. RENDON, *El libro de los libros de Chilam Balam* (Mexico City 1948). (5) G. DE CHAVEZ, "Relación de la provincia de Meztitlán," *Boletin del Museo Nacional*, época 4, 2 (1925): 109–20. (6) *Códice Chimalpopoca, Anales de Cuauhtitlán y Leyenda de los soles*, P. F. Velazquez, trans. (Mexico City 1945). (7) CONQUISTADOR ANONIMO, *Relación de algunas cosas de la Nueva España y de la gran ciudad de Temestitán México, escrita por un compañero de Hernán Cortés*, in *Colección de documentos para la historia de México* (Mexico City 1858), 1:368–98. (8) *Costumbres, fiestas, enterramientos y diversas formas de proceder de los indios de Nueva España*, publicado por F. Gómez de Orozco, *Tlalocan* 2 (1945): 37–63. (9) F. D. DURAN, *Historia de las Indias de Nueva España y islas de Tierra Firme*, critical ed. by A. Garibay, 3 vols. (Mexico City 1967). (10) M. S. EDMONSON, *The Book of the Counsel: The Popol Vuh of the Quiche Maya of Guatemala* (New Orleans 1971). (11) G. FERNANDEZ DE OVIEDO Y VALDES, *Historia general y natural de las Indias, islas y tierra firme del mar oceano*, 4 vols. (Madrid 1851–55). (12) F. A. DE FUENTES Y GUZMAN, *Recordación Florida*, discurso historial y demostración . . . del Reyno de Guatemala, 3 vols. (Guatemala City 1932–33). (13) A. M. GARIBAY, "Relación breve de las fiestas de los dioses: Fray Bernardino de Sahagún," *Tlalocan* 2 (1948): 289–320; (14) *Veinte himnos sacros de los Nahuas*, los recogió de los nativos F. Bernardino de Sahagún (Mexico City 1958); (15) *Poesía nahuatl*, 3 vols. (Mexico City 1964–68). (16) J. GENET, *Relation des choses du Yucatan*, Spanish text and French trans., 2 vols. (Paris 1928–29), French edition incomplete. (17) *Historia de los Mexicanos por sus pinturas*, in *Nueva colección de documentos para la historia de México* (Mexico City 1891; new ed., Mexico City 1941), 3:228–63. (18) *Idolatrias y supersticiones de los Indios*, Anales del Museo Nacional de México, vol. 6 (Mexico City 1892; 2d ed., Mexico City 1953). (19) W. JIMENEZ MORENO and S. MATEOS, *Códice de Yanhuitlán* (Mexico City 1940). (20) E. DE JONGHE, *Histoyre du Méchique*, unedited French manuscript of the sixteenth century, published by de Jonghe, *Journal de la Société des Américanistes*, n.s., 2 (1905): 1–41, French trans. by A. Thevet. (21) J. LAFAYE, *Manuscrit Tovar: Origines et croyances des Indiens du Mexique*, edition based on the manuscript in the John Carter Brown Library (Graz 1972). (22) F. D. DE LANDA, *Relación de las cosas de Yucatán* (8th ed., Mexico City 1959), many editions, of which two have French translations by Brasseur de Bourbourg (Paris 1864) and by Genet (Paris 1928–29). (23) F. B. DE LAS CASAS, *Apologética historia sumaria . . .* , Edmondo O'Gorman, ed., 2 vols. (Mexico City 1967). (24) M. LEON PORTILLA, *Ritos, sacerdotes y atavios de los dioses*, texts of the informants of Sahagún I (Mexico City 1958). (25) F. J. DE MENDIETA, *Historia eclesiástica indiana* (Mexico City 1870; 2d ed., Mexico City 1945, 4 vols.). (26) F. T. DE BENAVENTE MOTOLINIA, *Historia de los Indios de la Nueva España*, in *Colección de documentos para la historia de México* (Mexico City 1858; 2d ed., Mexico City 1941), 1:1–249. (27) *Memoriales o libro de las cosas de la Nueva España y de los naturales de ella*, E. O'Gorman, ed. (Mexico City 1971). (28) D. MUÑOZ CAMARGO, *Historia de Tlaxcala* (Mexico City 1892; facsimile ed., Guadalajara 1966). (29) F. DEL PASO Y TRONCOSO, *Papeles de la Nueva España . . .* , 6 vols. (Madrid 1905–6). (30) *Fray Bernardino de Sahagún: Historia de las cosas de Nueva España*, vols. 5, 6, 7, and 8 (Madrid 1905–7). (31) J. B. POMAR, *Relación de Tezcoco*, in *Nueva colección de documentos para la historia de México* (Mexico City 1891), 3:1–69. (32) K. T. PREUSS and E. MENGIN, *Die mexikanische Bilderhandschrift tolteca-chichimeca* (Berlin 1937–38). (33) *Procesos de indios idolatras y hechiceros*, Publicaciones del Archivo General de la Nacion, vol. 3 (Mexico City 1912). (34) G. RAYNAUD, *Les dieux, les héros et les hommes de l'ancien Guatemala d'après le livre du Conseil* (Paris 1925; 2d ed., Paris 1975). (35) A. RECINOS, *Memorial de Solola, anales de los Cakchiqueles, Título de los señores de Totonicapan* (Mexico City 1950). (36) *Relación de las ceremonias y ritos y población y gobernación de los Indios de la provincia de Mechuacán* (Morelia 1903; 2d ed., Madrid 1956). (37) R. L. ROYS, *The Book of Chilam Balam of Chumayel* (Washington 1933). (38) F. B. DE SAHAGÚN, *Historia general de las cosas de Nueva España*, anotaciones y apendices de A. M. Garibay, 4 vols. (Mexico City

1956), numerous earlier editions, including a French translation by D. Jourdanet and R. Simeon (Paris 1880); (39) *Florentine Codex*, Nahuatl text and translation into English by J. O. Anderson and C. E. Dibble, 12 vols. (Santa Fe 1950–69). (40) L. SCHULTZE-JENA, *Popol Vuh, das heilige Buch der Quiche-Indianer von Guatemala* (Berlin 1944). (41) E. SELER, *Einige Kapitel aus dem Geschichtswerke des Fray Bernardino de Sahagún aus den Aztekischen übersetzt* (Stuttgart 1927). (42) A. THEVET, see E. DE JONGHE. (43) F. J. DE TORQUEMADA, *Los veinte i un libros rituales y monarchia indiana . . .* , 3 vols. (3d ed. facsimile, Mexico City 1943–44). (44) A. M. TOZZER, *Landa's Relación de las cosas de Yucatán*, a translation cited with notes (Cambridge, MA, 1941).

III. Archaeology and Ethnohistory: Syntheses and Monographs

(1) F. ANDERS, *Das Pantheon der Maya* (Graz 1963). (2) *Wort- und Sachregister zu Eduard Seler, Gesammelte Abhandlungen* (Graz 1967). (3) P. ARMILLAS, "Los dioses de Teotihuacán," in *Anales del Instituto de Etnografía Americana* 6 (1945): 35–61. (4) A. BARRERA VASQUEZ, "La ceiba-cocodrilo," in *Anales del Instituto Nacional de Antropología e Historia* 7 (1974–75): 187–208. (5) T. S. BARTHEL, "Die Morgensternkult in den Darstellungen der Dresdener Maya Handschrift," *Ethnos* 17 (1952): 73–112. (6) E. BENSON, ed., *Dumbarton Oaks Conference on the Olmecs* (Washington 1967). (7) H. BERLIN, *Las antiguas creencias en San Miguel Sola, Oaxaca, México* (Hamburg 1957). (8) I. BERNAL, *El mundo olmeca* (Mexico City 1968). (9) H. BEYER, *El llamado "calendario azteca"* (Mexico City 1921). (10) "Mito y simbología del México antiguo," *México Antiguo*, vol. 10 (1965). (11) C. BOWDITCH, *The Numeration, Calendar Systems and Astronomical Knowledge of the Mayas* (Cambridge, MA, 1910). (12) C. BURLAND, *The Gods of Mexico* (London 1967). (13) P. CARRASCO, *Los Otomíes: Cultura e historia de los pueblos mesoamericanos de habla otomiana* (Mexico City 1950). (14) A. CASO, *El teocalli de la guerre sagrada* (Mexico City 1927); (15) *Las estelas zapotecas* (Mexico City 1928); (16) "El paraíso terrenal en Teotihuacán," in *Cuadernos Americanos* 6 (1942): 127–36; (17) *El pueblo del Sol* (Mexico City 1953); (18) *Los Calendarios Prehispánicos* (Mexico City 1967); (19) "Religión o Religiones mesoamericanas," in *Verhandlungen der XXXVIII Internationalen Amerikanisten Kongresses* (Munich 1971). (20) A. CASO and I. BERNAL, *Urnas de Oaxaca*, memorias del Instituto Nacional de Antropología e Historia (Mexico City 1952). (21) J. CORONA NUNEZ, *Mitología tarasca* (Mexico City 1957). (22) M. COVARRUBIAS, *Indian Art of Mexico and Central America* (New York 1957). (23) B. DAHLGREN DE JORDAN, *La Mixteca: Su cultura e historia prehispánicas* (Mexico City 1954). (24) J. FERNANDEZ, *Coatlicue: Estética del arte indígena* (Mexico City 1954). (25) K. FLANNERY, "Formative Oaxaca and the Zapotec Cosmos," *American Scientist* 64 (1976): 374–83. (26) G. FOSTER, "Nagualism in Mexico and Guatemala," *Acta Americana* 2 (1944): 85–103. (27) J. GARCIA PAYON, "Interpretación de la vida de los pueblos Matlatzincas," *México Antiguo* 6 (1942–43): 72–90, 93–119. (28) A. M. GARIBAY, *Historia de la Literatura Nahuatl*, 2 vols. (Mexico City 1953–54). (29) C. GIBSON, *The Aztecs under the Spanish Rule: A History of the Indians of the Valley of Mexico, 1519–1810* (Palo Alto, CA, 1964). (30) O. GONÇALVES DE LIMA, *El maguey y el pulque en los códices mexicanos* (Mexico City 1956). (31) Y. GONZALEZ TORRES, *El culto a los astros entre los Mexicas* (Mexico City 1975). (32) N. HAMMOND, ed., *Mesoamerican Archaeology: New Approaches* (London 1974). (33) R. HEIM and G. WASSON, *Les champignons hallucinogènes du Mexique* (Paris 1958). (34) A. HVIDTFELDT, *Teotl and Ixiptlatli: Some Central Conceptions in Ancient Mexican Religion* (Copenhagen 1958). (35) P. KIRCHHOFF, "Mesoamérica," in *Acta Americana* 1 (1943): 92–107. (36) W. KRICKEBERG, "Das mittelamerikanische Ballspiel und seine religiöse Symbolik," *Paideuma* 3 (1948): 118–98. (37) P. JORALEMON, *A Study of Olmec Iconography*, Studies in Precolumbian Arts and Archaeology (Washington 1971). (38) W. JIMENEZ MORENO, "Religión o Religiones Mesoamericanas," in *Verhandlungen des XXX-VIII Internationalen Amerikanisten Kongresses* (Munich 1971). (39) J. LAFAYE, *Quetzalcoatl et Guadalupe* (Paris 1974). (40) M. LEON PORTILLA, *La Filosofía Nahuatl estudiada en sus fuentes* (2d ed., Mexico City 1959); (41) *Tiempo y Realidad en el pensamiento maya* (Mexico City 1968). (42) A. LOPEZ AUSTIN, *Augurios y abusiones*, texts of the informants of Sahagún (Mexico City 1967); (43) "Cuarenta clases de magos del mundo Nahuatl," *Estudios de cultura Nahuatl* 7 (1967): 87–117; (44) *Juegos rituales Aztecas* (Mexico City 1967); (45) *Hombre-dios: Religión y política en el mundo nahuatl* (Mexico City 1973). (46) R. MACNEISH, "Ancient Mesoamerican Civilization," *Science* 143 (1964): 531–37. (47) I. MARQUINA, *Arquitectura prehispánica* (Mexico City 1951). (48) S. W. MILES,

"The Sixteenth Century Pokom-Maya," *Transactions of the American Philosophical Society*, n.s., 57 (1957): 731–81. (49) C. NAVARRETE, *The Chiapanec: History and Culture* (Provo 1966). (50) H. B. NICHOLSON, "Religion in Pre-Hispanic Central Mexico," in *Handbook of Middle American Indians* (Austin 1971), 10:395–446. (51) J. PADDOCK, *Ancient Oaxaca* (Stanford 1966). (52) K. PREUSS, "Phallishe Fruchtbarkeits-Dämonen als Träger des altmexikanischen mimischen Weltdramas," *Archiv für Anthropologie* 29 (1903): 129–88; (53) "Die Feuergötter als Ausgangpunkt zum Verständnis der mexicanischen Religion, in ihrem Zusammenhänge," *Mitteilungen der Anthropologischen Gesellschaft in Wien* 33 (1903): 129–233. (54) R. RICARD, *La conquête spirituelle du Mexique* (Paris 1933). (55) C. ROBELO, *Diccionario de mitología nahoa* (Mexico City 1951; 1st ed., Mexico City 1905–8). (56) A. RUZ LHUILLIER, *Costumbres funerarias de los antiguos mayas* (Mexico City 1968). (57) W. SANDERS and B. PRICE, *Mesoamerica: The Evolution of a Civilization* (New York 1968). (58) P. SCHELLHAS, *Representation of Deities of the Maya Manuscripts* (Cambridge, MA, 1904). (59) O. SCHONDUBE BAUMBACH, "Deidades prehispánicas en el área de Tamazula-Tuxpan-Zapotlán en el Estado de Jalisco," in *The Archaeology of West Mexico* (Ajijic 1974). (60) L. SÉJOURNÉ, *Burning Water: Thought and Religion in Ancient Mexico* (New York 1956). (61) E. SELER, *Gesammelte Abhandlungen zur Amerikanischen Sprach und Altertumskunde*, 5 vols. (Berlin 1902–23). (62) SOCIEDAD MEXICANA DE ANTROPOLOGIA, *Teotihuacan* (Mexico City 1966–72); (63) *Religión en Mesoamerica* (Mexico City 1972). (64) J. SOUSTELLE, *La penseé cosmologique des anciens Mexicains* (Paris 1940). (65) L. SPENCE, *The Gods of Mexico* (London 1923). (66) B. SPRANZ, "Göttergestalten in den mexikanischen Bilderhandschriften der Codex Borgia Gruppe: Eine ikonographische Untersuchung," *Acta Humboldtiana* (Wiesbaden 1964). (67) G. STRESSER-PEAN, "Les origines du Volador et du Comelagatoazte," in *28ᵉ Congrès International des Américanistes* (Paris 1947); (68) "La légende aztèque de la naissance du soleil et de la lune," *Annuaire de l'École pratique des Hautes Études*, 1962, 3–32. (69) S. TAX, ed., *Heritage of Conquest: The Ethnology of Middle America* (Glencoe, IL, 1952). (70) J. E. S. THOMPSON, "Sky Bearers, Colors and Directions in Maya and Mexican Religion," in *Contributions to American Archaeology* (Washington 1934); (71) "The Moon Goddess in Middle America with Notes on Related Deities," in *Contributions to American Archaeology* (Washington 1939); (72) *Maya History and Religion* (Norman 1970). (73) R. WAUCHOPE, general ed., *Handbook of Middle American Indians*, 15 vols. (Austin 1964–75). (74) G. WILLEY, *An Introduction to American Archaeology 1: North and Middle America* (Englewood Cliffs 1966). (75) E. WOLF, *Sons of the Shaking Earth* (Chicago 1952).

IV. Contemporary Ethnological Studies

(1) G. AGUIRRE BELTRAN, *Medicina y Magia* (Mexico City 1963). (2) R. BEALS, *Cherán, a Sierra Tarascan Village* (Washington 1946). (3) V. BRICKER, "El hombre, la carga y el camino: Antiguos conceptos mayas sobre tiempo y espacio, y el sistema zinacanteco de carbos," in *Los Zinacantecos* (Mexico City 1966), 355–72. (4) R. BUNZEL, *Chichicastenango, a Guatemalan Village* (Seattle 1959). (5) R. BURKITT, *The Hills and the Corn: A Legend of the Kekchi Indians of Guatemala* (Philadelphia: 1920). (6) P. CARRASCO, *Tarascan Folk Religion: An Analysis of Economic, Social and Religious Interactions* (New Orleans 1952). (7) H. FABREGA and D. SILVER, *Illness and Curing in Zinacantan: An Ethnomedical Analysis* (Stanford 1973). (8) G. FOSTER, "Sierra Popoloca Folklore and Beliefs," *University of California Publications in American Archaeology and Ethnology* 42 (1945): 177–250; (9) *Empire's Children: The People of Tzintzuntzan* (Washington 1948). (10) R. GIRARD, *Los Chortis ante el problema maya*, 5 vols. (Mexico City 1949). (11) C. GUITERAS HOLMES, *Perils of the Soul: The World View of a Tzotzil Indian* (Glencoe, IL, 1961). (12) E. HERMITTE, *Poder sobrenatural y control social en un pueblo maya contemporáneo* (Mexico City 1970). (13) W. R. HOLLAND, *Medicina Maya en los Altos de Chiapas* (Mexico City 1963). (14) A. ICHON, *La religion des Totonaques de la Sierra* (Paris 1969). (15) I. S. KELLY, "World View of a Highland Totonac Pueblo," in *Summa antropológica en homenaje a Roberto Weitlaner* (Mexico City 1966), 395–411. (16) O. LA FARGE, *The Year-Bearer's People* (New Orleans 1931). (17) O. LEWIS, *Life in a Mexican Village: Tepoztlán Restudied* (Urbana 1951). (18) J. S. LINCOLN, "The Maya Calendar of the Ixil of Guatemala," in *Carnegie Institution, Contributions to American Anthropology and History*, 7, vol. 38 (1942), pp. 97–128. (19) C. LUMHOLTZ, *Symbolism of the Huichol Indians* (New York 1900); (20) *Unknown Mexico*, 2 vols. (New York 1902). (21) W. MADSEN,

Christo-Paganism: A Study of Mexican Religious Syncretism (New Orleans 1957). (22) M. OAKES, *The Two Crosses of Todos Santos: Survivals of Mayan Religious Beliefs* (New York 1951). (23) E. C. PARSONS, *Mitla, Town of the Souls* (Chicago 1936). (24) T. PREUSS, *Die Nayarit-expedition*, Die Religion der Cora Indianer (Leipzig 1912). (25) R. S. RAVICZ, *Organización Social de los Mixtecos* (Mexico City 1965). (26) R. REDFIELD, *Tepoztlán, a Mexican Village* (Chicago 1930); (27) *Folk Culture of Yucatán* (Chicago 1941). (28) R. REDFIELD and A. VILLA, *Chan Kom, a Maya Village* (Washington 1934). (29) L. REYES GARCIA, *Pasión y Muerte del Cristo Sol, Carnaval y cuaresma en Ichcatepec* (Xalapa 1960). (30) A. ROUHIER, *Monographie du peyotl* (Paris 1926). (31) A. J. RUBEL, "Ritual Relationships in Ojitlan," *American Anthropologist*, vol. 56 (1955). (32) L. SCHULTZE-JENA, *Indiana I. Leben, Glaube und Sprache der Quiche von Guatemala* (Jena 1933); (33) *Indiana II: Mythen in der Muttersprache der Pipil von Izalco in El Salvador* (Jena 1935); (34) *Indiana III: Bei den Azteken, Mixteken und Tlapaneken der Sierra Madre del Sur von Mexico* (Jena 1938). (35) J. SOUSTELLE, *La famille Otomí-Pame du Mexique Central* (Paris 1937). (36) G. STRESSER-PEAN, "Montagnes calcaires et sources vauclusiennes dans la religion des Indiens Huastèques," in *Revue d'histoire des religions*, vol. 141 (1952). (37) N. D. THOMAS, *Envidia, Brujería y Organización ceremonial en un pueblo zoque* (Mexico City 1974). (38) J. E. S. THOMPSON, *Ethnology of the Mayas of Southern and Central British Honduras* (Chicago 1930). (39) A. M. TOZZER, *A Comparative Study of the Maya and the Lacandones* (London 1907). (40) A. VILLA, *The Maya of East Central Quintana Roo* (Washington 1945); (41) "Los conceptos de espacio y tiempo entre los grupos mayences contemporáneos," in *Tiempo y Realidad en el pensamiento maya*, L. Portilla, ed. (Mexico City 1968). (42) E. Z. VOGT, *Zinacantan, a Maya Community in the Highlands of Chiapas* (Cambridge 1968). (43) G. WASSON, "Ololiuhqui and the Other Hallucinogens of Mexico," in *Summa antropológica en homenaje a Roberto Weitlaner* (Mexico City 1966), 329–57. (44) R. WILLIAMS GARCIA, *Los Tepehuas* (Xalapa 1963). (45) C. WISDOM, *Los Chortis de Guatemala* (Guatemala City 1961).

MESOAMERICAN MYTHIC AND RITUAL ORDER

I. The Myths

The Mesoamerican mythology of the pre-Cortés period is known primarily through the Aztec texts of central Mexico and through the cosmogonic narrative of the Quiche transcribed in the *Popol Vuh*. For the other peoples, we have only fragmentary data which, in the case of the Maya of Yucatan, are scant indeed. Collected during the sixteenth century, these narratives are complex, often contradictory compilations abounding in details about the natural environment, the plant and animal worlds, and so forth. They have made possible the understanding or interpretation of numerous sculptures, frescoes, and various pictographs. For example, one can cite the case of a great human head sculpted in stone that was found at the site of the great temple Tenochtitlán in Mexico City. The lower edge of the neck bears bas-reliefs and thus indicates that this head was not broken off from a larger piece. The closed eyes indicate death. The face bears glyphs in the shape of small bells. Thanks to this last detail, it has been possible to identify the piece as a representation of Coyolxauhqui ("she who is painted with small bells"), a moon goddess, who according to one myth was decapitated by the sun god Huitzilopochtli.

Mythological texts from the sixteenth century have been supplemented by those that are currently being collected by ethnologists and linguists in certain regions of Mexico and Guatemala that have remained Indian. Conservation of the language is generally a precondition for maintaining the mythological tradition, but this alone is not sufficient. Relatively few myths have been preserved in the Mexican central plateau, northern Yucatan, and the highlands of Chiapas and Guatemala. On the other hand, the mountains of Nayarit, the eastern side of Mexico, and the tropical forest of eastern Chiapas and of southern Belize have provided Cora, Huichol, Huastec, Nahuatl, Tepehua, Totonac, Mize, Popoloca, and Mayan myths.

Myths tended to die out in Mesoamerica. Not only were they driven back into the farthest reaches of the region, but they often survived only in the memories of old men, healers, or musicians, the last trustees of ancestral knowledge. They suffered the same oblivion into which certain elements of the ancient civilization have fallen: war, human sacrifice, the ritual ball game, the social hierarchy with its nobles and chiefs, and so forth. On the other hand, certain myths have annexed elements that were Spanish or biblical in origin.

Wherever they survive, myths occasionally still preserve their sacred force. They explain natural phenomena. They guarantee the bases of native morality, imposing rules of behavior and warning against the transgression of social, familial, and community norms. They provide the ideological basis for ceremonies, songs, dances, and games. They may inspire certain elements of costume. They bestow a grandeur upon the humble acts of traditional techniques like ceramics, spinning, weaving, and agriculture.

Pre-Columbian cosmogonic myths with their successive creations and destructions of the universe have become progressively impoverished. The story of a great flood, reinforced by the teaching of Christianity, is often well preserved. It has still been possible to collect myths of the birth of the sun and moon in different forms and in many regions. The myths of the morning star survive especially among the Huichol and the Cora of the Nayarit Sierra. Elsewhere, these myths are often replaced by the exploits of a young culture hero. The gods of lightning, mountains, and caves often provide important themes. Masters of animals or plants, animal guardian spirits, the dead, and ghosts still have their place in legends today.

The fusion of native beliefs and the European legacy is very common. The assimilation of Christ to the sun has concretized a whole set of ancient beliefs about presolar times and about the struggle that marked their end. This has resulted in the presence, in certain places, of representatives of pagan deities of long ago in the dance of the Moors and Christians that has become for the Indians an evocation of the birth of the sun.

Similarly, Carnival and Holy Week are often the occasion for the presentation of dramas about the ancient gods of war or the rebirth of vegetation. The dance of the Volador reenacts the journey of the souls to heaven. A whole mythic cycle comments on the return of the dead and threatens terrible punishment for those who fail to welcome them with the appropriate munificence.

II. Rituals: Elements of the Ceremonial and Typology

Rituals play an essential role in every religion. In Mesoamerica, ritual has preoccupied generations of specialists,

Coyolxauhqui, "she who is painted with small bells," Aztec goddess of the moon. Mexico City, Museum of Anthropology. Museum photo.

The dance of the Volador. Nahua Indians (Pueblo de Atla, Pahuatlan, Puebla). Photo M.A.E.F.M.

from the priestly governors of the great Olmec centers to the alcaldes of certain communities today in the highlands of Guatemala, including the thousands of religious professionals of Tenochtitlan, who were divided into thirty-eight categories according to the census of Sahagún. But ritual activity was also, and perhaps even more, the business of each individual, who not only participated in or had to attend official ceremonies organized by the hierarchy, but who was constantly compelled to perform acts or to utter words that were regarded as duties to the sacred. For the sacred pervaded the totality of the universe, and human beings experienced it at every moment of their lives. In addition, ritual obligation in Mesoamerica rested on yet another premise, that humans and gods have a common stake in the perpetuation of the world, as was articulated by the myths; and it was the celebration of this vital relationship that the rituals assured.

In Mesoamerica, the ceremonies always included a period of time and rituals of preparation that culminated in a vigil, whether it was a major or minor festival, current or pre-Columbian. Continence and fasting were the two traditional observances of these preparatory periods, the duration of which varied according to the importance of the ceremony. Sometimes reduced to a few days, they could also last an entire year, as in the case of the *teocuac* at Tenochtitlan, young men, "eaters of god," who were the incarnations of the elder brothers of Huitzilopochtli. Fasting and continence were the first two steps toward purification that had to precede any celebration. Breaking the fast or the continence was fatal,

because this destroyed the force of the ritual. Purity was a prerequisite not only for the participants but also for places and objects. For purity (called *zuhuy* by the Maya) was one of the great obsessions that prevailed in Mesoamerican rituals. In certain cases, the lustration of the officiating priests by water or by incense, together with confession, was the crowning touch for the preparations.

The ritual per se was composed of at least two, often simultaneous elements: the offering and the prayer. The nature of the offering was highly variable, beginning with the ornamenting of idols and altars (notably with paper cutouts) and gifts of food or burning incense, and ending with sacrifices. The sacrifice of an animal or a human was a fundamental act of homage to the gods. For blood was the primary divine element, as is witnessed not only by the myths and their pictographic translations in the codex, but also by the ancient Mexicans' custom of annointing the mouths of idols with the "precious liquid," and perhaps by the etymology of the Yucatec term for the sacrifice: *p'a chi* ("open the mouth"). In Aztec mythology, which provides the most insistent legitimizations of sacrifice, the sun must be revitalized each morning upon emerging from his nocturnal journey in the realm of the dead. The considerable escalation of the number of human sacrifices during the Postclassic Period should not, however, lead us to forget that we are dealing with a very ancient type of offering, which was undoubtedly practiced since Preclassic times (Izapa-Monte Alban) and had taken on multiple forms (tearing out the heart, decapitation, piercing with arrows, drowning, and so forth). Self-sacrifice, in which the celebrants extracted the blood from a part of their bodies with various types of needles, appeared in a remote period; it was, alternately or at the same time, a penitential practice or a ritual of offering. The prayers that accompanied the offerings could be prayers of petition, of thanksgiving, or of propitiation. All the prayers were geared to a material end, which was either wished for or had already been obtained. Finally, the liturgy, depending on circumstances, could be enhanced with additional activities (songs, dances, processions), which in certain cases today are the only surviving elements of ancient rituals practiced on the margins of Catholic ceremonies.

In Mesoamerica, ritual took its place in the dual framework of the community and the nuclear family. Despite numerous correspondences and sometimes actual overlapping, the public ceremony can be contrasted with the private ritual. In ancient Mexico, the organization of community rituals was the realm reserved for professional priests. Today, it is almost always the domain of the majordomos, a religious elite periodically renewed and primarily charged with the responsibility of carrying the economic burden of the cult (see below, section III). The collective ritual life in pre-Columbian and contemporary societies follows the precise rhythm of the calendar. Among the Aztecs, two great series of festivals would correspond respectively to the unfolding of the solar and ceremonial calendars; the end of each of the eighteen twenty-day periods of the solar year was marked by a specific ceremony, the nature of which was for the most part directly related to the phases of the agricultural cycle. The festivals, fixed according to the *tonalpohualli*, were the means of specific celebrations of the gods (somewhat like the cult of the saints), on the days that were associated with them. But it was the ends of the cycles, the due dates, that haunted the imagination and that certainly gave rise to the most impressive ceremonies: the festival of the *toxiuhmolpilia*, "the binding of the years," celebrated every fifty-two years during the Postclassic Period on the central high plateau, the ritual of the death and resurrection of the *baktun* among the Maya of the Classic Period. Added to this entire fixed liturgical complex were numerous episodic celebrations that concerned either a part or the whole of the community. Droughts and dearths, the inauguration of sanctuaries and departures for war, every exceptional event was and sometimes still is ritualistically treated in a spectacular manner. For theatricality is one of the peculiarities of the public rituals, a great number of which consisted in the representation of genuine religious dramas; almost every festival of the Aztec solar calendar included the reenactment of a fragment of myth such as the defeat of the moon during the month of Tititl. The dance of the Volador and the ritual ball game were great "classics" in the liturgical repertory.

But religious fervor in Mesoamerica can perhaps best be measured by the importance of individual and familial rituals. The fabric of daily life is dotted with ritual practices, whether they be domestic rituals at the altar of a home or more solemn ceremonies that accompany the great moments of an individual's life: birth, baptism, the giving of the name, marriage, death. For at every moment, the Mesoamericans turn to their gods, as we are reminded in this prayer to the "heart of the sky," taken from the *Popol Vuh*:

> Grant life and prosperity to my children, to my servants; cause to be fruitful and multiply those whose duty it is to feed you and to assure your survival and those who invoke your name on the roads, in the fields, on the banks of rivers, in the shade of trees and creepers.

The Festival of Ochpaniztli (Borbonicus Codex, p. 30). Paris, Library of the Palais-Bourbon. Library photo.

III. Rituals: Practice and Social Function

In the indigenous conceptual system, the social order was lived as a replication of the general order of the world, the latter serving to justify the former. Ritual was the means by which one periodically brought to life the profile of the social and sacred hierarchies and by which one gathered the community around the idea that the world existed only through the action of the gods. And this action was possible only as a result of the worship and the compensatory offerings made by humans in conformity with ancestral models.

Where did the ritual begin? Among today's Indians, daily life is punctuated by a series of rigid actions just as much in the relationships between relatives and in economic transactions as in the way of addressing ancient deities or pious images on the Christian home altar. This applied effort to regard life as a somewhat obsolete attachment to austere norms of behavior still rather accurately characterizes the most conservative native societies of Mesoamerica. But increasingly, as a function of the growing integration of communities into the national society, young generations disengage themselves from such constraints.

Certain essential rituals remain nonetheless, for they are necessary to the cohesion of diverse communities. Among the Otomi and the Mazahua, oratories, small chapels designed for the worship of ancestors, constitute the basic framework for the social structure of a village. The Tzeltal and the Tzotzil of Chiapas have a ceremonial organization that is notably apparent on certain festival days and that

Ball game field at Copan (Honduras). Photo M.A.E.F.M.

affirms that each individual belongs to his or her own neighborhood or barrio. As a basic subdivision of the village, this neighborhood plays multiple political and religious roles.

Similarly, in ancient Aztec society, the *calpulli* were territorial units that encompassed groups of relatives and were characterized by an eponymous deity as well as by particular rituals. Territorial subdivisions like the *calpulli* survive today among the Maya of the highlands of Chiapas, in Chinantla, and even in certain zones of central Mexico. Sometimes even a neighborhood that has become mestizo will oppose a neighborhood that has remained indigenous, each one thus maintaining its different types of religious practices.

The performance of rituals tended and still tends to reinforce the establishment. Although ancient Indian society had priestly groups distinct from other groups of leaders, the civil and religious powers were not strictly separated, because both were supposed to have originated from the same sacred source. By the tenth century, the famous Toltec sovereign Ce Acatl Topiltzin was regarded as an incarnation of the god Quetzalcoatl. Later, the Aztec during their migration would receive orders from their god Huitzilopochtli, orders that were naturally transmitted by the priests. Aztec sovereigns were sacred characters, and their names would evoke the gods. The last of them, Cuauhtemoc, actually bore the mystical name of the setting sun, "falling eagle."

After the Conquest, the Spanish administration gradually deprived the kings, chiefs, and native nobles of their powers, replacing them with dignitaries elected or appointed for limited periods of time. Thus, with the consent of the

Sunday meeting of the *governadores* of Teguerichic (Carichic). Tarahumara Indians. Photo M.A.E.F.M.

authorities, a system of political and religious responsibilities, sometimes tied to organizations of Catholic brotherhoods, was progressively developed. This system of responsibilities, which organized and regulated the munificence of individuals for the benefit of the community, enjoyed tremendous success among the Indians. It corresponded to their ideal of individual wealth that should be used for the profit of everyone. Moreover, it had antecedents in the socioreligious organization of pre-Cortés times.

Throughout the colonial period, and to this day, the same system of responsibilities, straddling both the political and the religious sectors, has played the role of a coercive instrument in local affairs, imposing the observance of festivals and exercising political authority. In the course of his life, each person must fulfill a large number of functions that will lead him progressively to take more prestigious responsibilities. Among the Maya of Chiapas and Guatemala, the system has had its most far-reaching application. Sometimes it even forces a civil servant to leave his home during his entire term of office and to reside in a ceremonial center made up of functional dwellings belonging to the community.

At the basis of this system is a multitude of minor support roles with less responsibility. These are reserved for young people, who are brought in to play the roles of police officers, deputies, and jacks-of-all-trades. They supply a permanent source of free labor that complements the periodic forced labor of the group of adult men. In this way, the system functions as a framework for socialization. But at a higher level, it also becomes the locus in which political strategies are exercised, for the highest posts, which correspond to roles in upper-level management, are few. In the past, these posts were the object of stiff competition, and this is often still the case, even though the system has entered a period of crisis.

One of the functions of the system is, therefore, economic. It tends to level out individual resources through a redistribution of wealth and through a destruction of monetary surpluses. But today the weight of the responsibilities tends to accentuate rather than even out economic inequities, for it heavily increases the indebtedness of the poor without decreasing the wealth of the rich. In addition, wealthy Indians seek to divest themselves of community responsibilities. One way to do this is to convert to Protestantism, which affirms a break with ancient religious traditions, pagan and Catholic alike. This weakening of commitment to the collective enterprise leads above all to the decline of festivals, a relatively recent phenomenon that has nevertheless spread rapidly. Lately, as in pre-Columbian times, the costs of the cult have weighed most heavily on the Indian communities. The festivals had, and still have, an essentially ostentatious character: the distribution of food and beverages, the cost of equipment, and support for dancers, fireworks, and choral societies.

Although the ancient pagan calendar still survives in a more or less altered form in certain sectors of Guatemala and southern Mexico, it no longer marks time for the succession of grandiose and often bloody festivals that the sixteenth-century chronicles describe for us. A curious exception is the important movable feast that the Quiche of Momostenango still celebrate on the day of the "eight monkeys." However, in many places, ceremonies, indeed veritable festivals, continue to be celebrated in honor of the ancient gods, but these are generally unpretentious demonstrations tied to seasons or to weather forecasting. Certain communities maintain for

such use a small non-Christian temple in the form of a modest-looking house situated in an out-of-the-way place and called in Nahuatl xochicalli ("flower house" or "precious house"). More generally, the festivals have today become an integral part of the cycle of solemn days of the Roman Catholic church. In each village, the most important festival is generally the feast of the local patron saint. Here one almost always sees dances, some of which are indigenous in origin, such as the Volador, while others have been instituted by the missionaries, such as the dance of the shepherdesses, the dance of the Conquest, or the dance of the Moors and Christians. The festival of the patron saint is sometimes overshadowed by the festival of Holy Week, Christmas, or the Virgin of Guadalupe.

All Saints' Day, now fixed on the first of November, and the movable feast of Carnival have often preserved a large measure of native characteristics and continue to be immensely popular. When the festival reaches its final stage of decadence, its religious aspect is reduced to a simple Mass that attracts only a few of the faithful, whereas the general public crowd the square where groups of Indian dancers have been replaced by the street stalls of mestizo merchants.

In ancient Mesoamerican religion, there were pilgrimages. Some of these have been Christianized through the efforts of missionaries and continue to attract considerable crowds of Indians. The best known is that of the Virgin of Guadalupe on the site of the ancient shrine of the mother goddess. The Sacromonte and Chalma are also substitute pilgrimages. But there are still traditional pilgrimages in the most conservative regions.

M.A.E.F.M./g.h.

BIBLIOGRAPHY

See the bibliography at the end of the article "Mesoamerican Religion," and especially section I: 7, 11, 22; section II: 3, 8, 9, 13, 15, 24, 31, 35, 36, 38, 43; section III: 10, 21, 36, 45, 62, 67; section IV: 4, 6, 19, 23, 25, 26, 29, 31, 32, 33, 36, 39, 42, 44.

MESOAMERICAN CREATION MYTHS

I. Creation Myths in Pre-Columbian Societies

Creation myths must have appeared at a very early period in the Mesoamerican area. One of the first pieces of evidence of their existence may be revealed in the Olmec or Olmecoid representations in the Preclassical style which show the union of a jaguar and an anthropomorphic being.

The interpretation of the symbolic content of these bas-reliefs and paintings still remains, in part, to be done. In addition, these archaic manifestations are too isolated to permit even a summary reconstruction of the oldest theogony-cosmogonies. On the other hand, the elements known from the decades before and after the Conquest present a large series of images of genesis, from which, despite the divergences in detail, it is possible to extract some important invariables. On the high plateau of central Mexico, the principal versions of the creation myths are expressed in

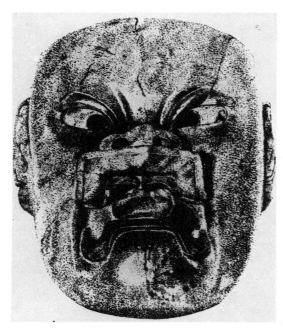

Jade mask of a jaguar-man (drawing by Eugenia Joyce). A major theme in Olmec art, it may illustrate one of the most ancient myths of creation in Mesoamerica. Washington, D.C., Dumbarton Oaks Collection.

titles of "prince" and "princess of our flesh" and in the *Popol Vuh* as "Father" and "Mother of the Son," the generative cell of all life. Even the other gods descend from them: they are the firstfruits of the carnal union sometimes evoked in the codices. In the work of universal creation, certain gods of the first generation (notably Quetzalcoatl and Tezcatlipoca) played the role of special assistants, according to the tradition of central Mexico. Nevertheless, nothing that exists escapes the attention of the primitive god and his mate, who reign over the first and last sign of the days of the Aztec calendar, respectively.

The creation of the world—all the myths agree on this point—was neither an immediate reality nor the result of an evolutionary process. Rather, the history of the universe, from its very beginning, presents a succession of creations and destructions whose number and nature vary according to the sources (see table), but which have common implications. It seems, therefore, that instability is inherent in the heart of the world, either by reason of the struggle among the contradictory elements of the universe (earth, wind, fire, and water) which, in the Aztec tradition, led to the overthrow of the four previous suns and which can bring about the annihilation of the fifth, or as a result of the interventions of the gods who are concerned to improve the human race (*Popol Vuh*). Hemmed in between the past flood and the future cataclysm, the indigenous world of the sixteenth century is eminently precarious. For this reason many of the rites have as a goal a reduction of the risk of rupture, the search for preservation, for the maintenance of the cosmos. The succession of cycles has, in addition, established the union of life and death which impregnates the entire universe.

Schematic Table of the Cycles of Creation according to the Aztec and the Quiche (16th century)

Leyenda de los Soles (1558)	*Popol Vuh*
First Sun (Ocelotonatiuh) Sun of the Jaguar (with a duration of 676 years). The Universe devoured by jaguars.	*First Creation* Humanity created out of mud but without stability. Race endowed with speech but without intelligence. Impossibility of resisting the action of the water. Destruction by the gods, discontent with their work.
Second Sun (Ehecatonatiuh) Sun of the Wind (364 years). Universe destroyed by a hurricane. Survivors transformed into monkeys.	*Second Creation* Man created out of the wood of a tree (*tzite*) and woman out of a reed. Race endowed with speech, with the faculty of multiplying itself, but without soul and forgetful of the gods. Black rain of resin and rebellion of animals and domestic objects. Flood and transformation of survivors into monkeys.
Third Sun (Quiahuitonatiuh) Sun of Rain (364 years). Universe consumed by a rain of fire. Survivors transformed into turkeys.	
Fourth Sun (Atonatiuh) Sun of Water (676 years). Universe drowned by a flood. Survivors changed into fish.	*Third Creation* Man created out of corn. Humanity intelligent and careful about the sacred. After the destruction of the Spanish, a new world will be born.
Fifth Sun (Ollintonatiuh) Sun of Movement. The Universe will perish in an earthquake. (Annals of Cuauhtitlan).	

Aztec sculpture (Stone of the Sun) as well as in pictographic manuscripts and texts of the sixteenth century (*Codex Vaticanus A, Historia de los Mexicanos por sus pinturas, Leyenda de los Soles, Anales de Cuauhtitlan, Codex Florentino*). These documents are relatively late but seem to be based on older, perhaps less structured, versions. A first indication of this antiquity may be the presence in the codices of fragments of myths that are clearly pre-Columbian, representative of beliefs not only of the Valley of Mexico but of all of central Mexico. Likewise, the convergence of myths collected on the high plateau in the sixteenth century and of those preserved by the Nicaraos (whose migration from central Mexico toward Nicaragua goes back to the ninth century) argues in favor of their antiquity. The second group of documents which have come down to us, and which express, in part, the ancient pre-Columbian origin, originate in the Maya region, particularly in the highlands of Guatemala (*Popol Vuh, Anales de los Cakchiqueles*). The information collected in the central and southern Maya zones is much more sparse or belongs to periods too far removed from the conquest.

In the corpus as a whole, certain common traits stand out which could have constituted a Central American mythic kernel, perhaps dating from the end of the Classical Period.

All creation proceeds from a primitive divine couple (Hunab Itzam Na and Ix Chebel Yax of the lowlands of Yucatan) or from a double principle, man and woman, sometimes incarnated in two deities, sometimes intermingled in a single deity. The latter is the case among the Aztec, who invoke Ometecuhtli, the "lord of duality," and Omecihuatl, the "lady of duality," or sometimes Ometeotl, the "deity of duality." It is from this primordial pair that all living beings have issued; it is this couple which, fundamentally, presides over the creation of the world. For this reason these original deities are designated in certain Aztec texts by the

Cut paper work representing the old sun, predecessor of the present sun. San Lorenzo Achiotepec (Otomi Indians).

Finally, all the creation accounts pose, in an almost identical fashion, the problem of the relations between humans and the gods, between creatures and their creator. At the origin of humanity, a contract was established. First of all, humans owe their existence to the gods: they were created through the sacrifice of the deity. According to Leon Portilla, this is what is implied in the Aztec term *macehualli*, "that which has been merited." In the myth of central Mexico, Quetzalcoatl descends to the kingdom of the dead to seek the bones, pulverized and sprinkled with the blood of the gods, from which the human race is born. But humankind also owes to the gods the creation and the gift of the elements necessary for their survival: the creation of the sun and the moon at the cost of a collective sacrifice of the pantheon, the gift of water and plants, in the first rank of which is corn. Therefore, the beginnings of humanity are marked by a major liability to the gods. An initial debt has been contracted. The gods demand payment. They need the attentions of humans, their prayers, their offerings. "Precious water," the *chalchihuatl*, the blood of victims, is their nourishment, without which the universe goes quickly to perdition.

II. Myths of Creation in Contemporary Indigenous Societies

In the traditions of the Indians of today, the ancient conception of a series of universal cataclysms is reduced, in general, to the idea that the present world was preceded by a flood and will be destroyed in turn in the future. Nevertheless there are exceptions, especially in the Maya regions. The myth of the flood is often enriched with various details of biblical origin, among the Totonac, for example, who say that the chest that plays the role of an ark came back down to earth after forty days. Among the Maya Mopan of Belize, the son of Adam and Eve, a solar numen, provoked a deluge of water which chilled him. Among the Otomi, it is believed

that the end of the present world will be caused by a rain of fire.

Here is an example of a present-day flood myth, collected by H. Lemley among the Tlapanec Indians:

> A vulture addressing a man who was working on the mountain said: "Do not work any more, for now the world is coming to its end." The vulture then said to a tree: "Get up," and to a rock, "Get up." The tree rose but not the rock. Then the vulture said to the man, "Construct a box without telling anyone, not even those in your family, or else they will begin to cry. Therefore, it is better if you say nothing." When the man had finished constructing the box, the vulture put him inside, along with a dog and a hen. A little later, the man saw through a crack in the box that it was raining and he also heard the animals that lived in the water shaking the box, with the desire, it seemed, to eat the man. He also saw that the world was filled with water. Then he noticed that the earth was so swampy that it was impossible to walk. So he put his head back inside. Later, he abandoned the box when he saw that vegetation was growing and he went to work the land. The hen changed into a vulture and flew above the land. Wherever the vulture went, mountains and valleys formed behind him.

> Every day the man went to work, and every afternoon when he returned from his work, he would see tortillas which had been prepared for his dinner, but he did not know who had made them.

> The man went to a mountaintop every day. He sat down to see who was coming to prepare the tortillas, but the dog remained in the house each time. Finally, he saw that the dog was taking off its skin, and he entered the house immediately. When he was inside, he saw a woman grinding the corn, and saw the skin of the dog in a pile on the bed. So the man took the skin of the dog and threw it into the flames to burn it, but the woman said, "Do not burn my clothes, for if the skin is burned, my children will not grow." For this reason the woman stayed, without ever taking off her skin again.

Among the Pocomam, the flood is the founding act of civilization. Before the cataclysm, the world was peopled by a cannibalistic humanity with neither faith nor law. Afterwards, it was to be the humanity of the men of the present, the progeny of a couple who escaped from the flood and were banished by God for having sinned.

In the abundance of creation themes certain preoccupations seem to impose themselves with special force, such as the cycle of corn deities, covering the area from the civilizations of the central plateau to those of Yucatan and the Guatemalan highlands with their individual variants. The culture hero (Quetzalcoatl among the Aztec) discovers corn hidden behind a crag which he penetrates through a fissure, disguised as an ant. This mountain or Tonacatepetl reappears in a Kekchi version in the form of Sakletch. In the Cakchiquel tradition, it is split apart by lightning. It is interesting to note that, among the Tepehua, the sun hidden in the mountain takes the place of the corn in the mythical account:

> The sun was sought. A lizard that was a *topil* (policeman) went to inform the authorities that, under a stone that was impossible to move, there was a strong light. A woodpecker was brought, and it opened the rock by striking it once with its beak. There, the sun was found

squatting down. All the dancers ran up. The sun said that it was going to come out and it wanted the dances always to be like this. The sun came out and it seems that a kind of glass was put in its heart so that it would not shine so much. Such is the sun now.

In this story there is an identification of corn and sun that underlies various present-day accounts without being clearly expressed.

Among the Quiche, man, a divine creation, is fashioned from corn paste. Among the Aztec, corn was rather the "Lord of our Flesh," the vital principle indispensable for survival.

In the present-day indigenous cosmologies, the vision of the sun/moon duality is an extension of the tradition of a couple with antagonistic and complementary principles, characterized as Grandfather and Grandmother (Quiche), Father and Mother (Tarascan), Son and Mother (Tzotzil) or more conventionally Husband and Wife (Yucatan, Oaxaca, central high plateau).

In a mixed version of the creation myth of the sun and the moon collected by P. Carrasco, a young boy and his sister assassinate their grandfather. Pursued by their grandmother, they reach a river, the boy first.

In order not to be held back by his sister, he took off his sandals and struck her in the face with them, smearing her face with mud so that she would not be seen and followed. They were close to the place where the earth ends, and it was then that the boy climbed first into the sky where his grandmother could not follow him. His sister took time to recover a part of her sight, after she had washed her face a bit, and it was only at the moment when the little man was about to hide on the horizon that the girl could rise into space. The spot that is seen on the moon is the mud that her brother threw. It is for that reason that it shines less than the sun.

The allegory which used to explain the appearance of the celestial bodies has more or less resisted time. In central Mexico today it takes the form of a Manichaean combat between God and the Devil, Christ and the Jews, Good and Evil. The characters change, but the structure of the account remains unchanged.

M.A.E.F.M./m.s.

BIBLIOGRAPHY

See the bibliography at the end of the article "Mesoamerican Religion," especially section II: 1, 2, 6, 17, 20, 26, 32, 34, 35, 37, 38; section III: 8, 37, 60, 61, 68; section IV: 9, 14, 44.

MESOAMERICAN RELIGIOUS CONCEPTIONS OF SPACE AND TIME

The vision of the world and the procedures of ritual life in Mesoamerica were submitted, from an early time, to a twofold principle of organization, the spatial and the temporal. Classificatory schemata (the orientation of the world and the establishment of durations of time) served, at least from the time of the recent Preclassical Period, as a framework for the religious universe. Questions and observations about space and time, far from constituting distinct preoccupations, were always closely intermingled. There are numerous proofs of the fundamental unity of these categories, be it a question, for example, of the quadripolar distribution of the signs of the days in the Aztec ceremonial calendar, of the location of the five "year bearers of the Venus cycle" between the four cardinal points and the center, or of the semantic confusion, which still exists in several Indian languages, between terms simultaneously expressing location in space and in time.

The observation of the celestial bodies and, in particular, of the apparent movement of the sun constitutes the common starting point of spatiotemporal considerations. Perhaps having an essentially economic character in the beginning (the rhythm of agricultural cycles), these become the prerogative of priestly specialists among the Olmec and the first occupants of Monte Alban. Astronomy, established as a science, is supported by an arithmetic put to religious use, and its earliest archaeological traces are dated B.C. It nevertheless remains inseparable from its astrological applications and would form the basis for the authority of the elites of the Classical Period. The collapse of the Classical civilizations (especially in the Mayan area) and then the Spanish conquest brought about the nearly total abandonment of the ancient systems of reference and of their sacred content. Though certain elements remained, they were, for the most part, transposed, and are sometimes difficult to recognize.

I. Time

From a very early date, the process of time had fascinated the peoples of Mesoamerica. Though no group seems to have arrived at a conceptualization of time in itself, abstract and undefined (as there are both multiple and singular spaces in the Indian conceptual system, so time is perceived under the form of both particular time and heterogeneous times), the flow of duration gave rise to a series of speculations and efforts to quantify it. It is even possible that certain Mayan astronomer-priests came to the conclusion that time had no beginning. Three great systems of the comprehension of time were used: two of these, the ceremonial calendar and the solar calendar, seem to have been quite widespread. The use of the third, after its invention by the Olmec, is limited to the Mayan area: it too is founded on the tropical year, but it situates each event in relationship to a date of origins (the "long count" or the computation of long durations).

The fundamental idea that seems to have governed the elaboration of these different modes of counting is the cyclic repetition of increasing units, each one submitted to the influence of one or several deities and associated with one of the directions. It is likely that the formation of these classificatory schemata was progressive (something that archaeology does not easily take account of) and that in the last centuries B.C. it caused the sudden proliferation of different calendrical systems. The computation of the long count is attested from the first century B.C. (stela 2 of Abaj Takalik, 2 of Chiapa de Corzo, C of Tres Zapotes, and 1 of El Baúl), while certain glyphs for days of the ceremonial year, as well as others representing the months of the solar year, were in use at Monte Alban from the time of the first phase of the occupation of the site, around 600 B.C.

The various modes of recording time have units and counting operations in common from one zone to another (even with their differences): twenty days follow one another without changing, designated by signs, of which two series are given as examples in the accompanying table.

Aztec (Central Mexico)	Quiche (Guatemala)
cipactli, aquatic monster	*imox* (earth)*
ehecatl, wind	*ikh*, wind
calli, house	*akhbal*, darkness, night
cuetzpallin, lizard	*kat* ?
coatl, serpent	*can*, serpent
miquiztli, death	*ceme*, death
mazatl, deer	*ceh*, deer
tochtli, rabbit	*khanil* ?
atl, water	*toh* (rain storm)*
itzcuintli, dog	*tzih*, dog
ozomatli, monkey	*batz*, monkey
malinalli, grass	*ee*, teeth
acatl, reed	*ah*, reed
ocelotl, jaguar	*balam* (jaguar)*
cuauhtli, eagle	*tzikin*, bird
cozcacuauhtli, vulture	*ahmac*, insect incarnating
ollin, earthquake	the spirits of the dead
tecpatl, flint	*noh* (earthquake)*
quiahuitl, rain	*tihax* (obsidian knife)*
xochitl, flower	*canac* (rain)*
	hunahpu, god who hunts with a blowpipe

*Obsolete.

—The ceremonial calendar (*tonalpohualli* of the Aztec, *tzolkin* of the Maya) is the result of the combination of the twenty signs for the days and the series of numbers from 1 to 13, coupled with the names of the days and repeated without interruption until the repetition of the initial day, at the end of 260 days: thus, the first day is 1 *cipactli*; the fourteenth day is named 1 *ocelotl*, the twenty-first day 8 *cipactli*, and so on, until the cycle comes back to the beginning, at the end of the $20 \times 13 = 260$ days.

—The solar year is composed of eighteen "months" of twenty days, to which are added five days which are considered to be inauspicious and which are designated, among the Aztec, by the general term *nemontemi*. Each year receives, as its name, the name of the initial day or the "year bearer." As a result of the time lag introduced by the five *nemontemi* in the succession of twenties, four different signs can inaugurate the year.

—The *xuihmolpilli* or Aztec "century" is the period of fifty-two years, at the end of which one day—doubly designated by its place in the ceremonial calendar and its position in the solar year—is repeated (on the conjunction of the two calendars, see the explanatory diagram).

—The Maya computation of the long count in which each date is calculated with reference to a starting point (the year 3113 B.C. according to Goodman-Martinez-Thompson) essentially uses the following units: *kin* (day), *uinal* (20 days), *tun* (360 days), *katun* (7,200 days, 20 *tuns*), *baktun* (144,000 days, 20 *katuns*).

—Two other counting cycles, although secondary, were known and often used: the lunar cycle and the Venusian year.

Time, as measured by these different systems, is never perceived as an objective and neutral element; calendars, much more than instruments for counting, always have particular religious functions. Thus there is a connection

"Monument" 3 from San José Mogote (Oaxaca). Dating from the sixth century B.C., this representation includes, between the legs of the figure, one of the oldest known calendric notations from Mesoamerica.

between the long count and the myths of creation, the end of the world, the primordial role of the *tonalpohualli-tzolkin* in divination, and the use of the solar calendar to mark the rhythm of the religious life of the communities. Several traditions attribute the invention of calendrical measurements to one of the gods (especially to Quetzalcoatl in his role as civilizing hero). Beyond this original bond, each part of each system is invested with one or several divinities and is affected by their combined qualities. The Maya as well as the Aztec identify the actual elements of time designation with the gods. A given day is influenced not only by one of the thirteen diurnal Lords and the nine Lords of the night, but also by the god associated with the sign itself, by the master of the group of thirteen, by the god that rules over the "month," and by the "year bearers." Furthermore, the spatial distribution of time culminates in a new play of influences, which engages directions and their properties. To clear up this tangle of connections and oppositions, there is nowhere to turn but to the knowledge of the astrologer-priests, who are the only individuals who possess the keys to this complex arithmetic. In the most complex pre-Columbian societies, in a manner parallel to that of the social hierarchies, there was a kind of dichotomy in the perception of time

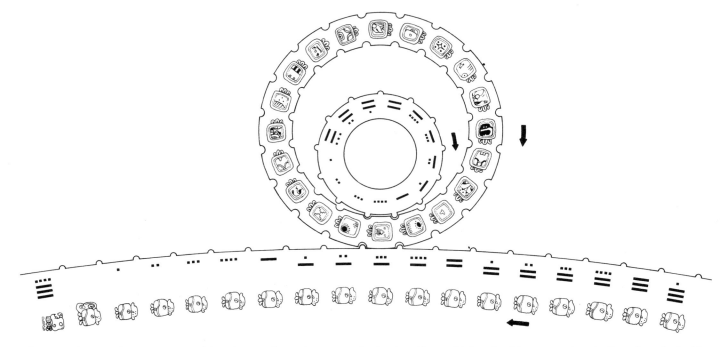

Diagram showing the conjunction of the Mayan solar and ceremonial calenders. By combining the thirteen numbers indicated on the inside circle (a dot stands for one, and a line for five) with the twenty daily glyphs in the outer circle with which they line up, 260 days can be counted. The association of each of these days with one of the 365 days of the solar year (represented on the circle of which only an arc is shown) expresses complete dates. The one indicated in the center of the diagram (reading from top to bottom) is 4 ahau 8 cumku. Adapted from *National Geographic* 148, no. 6 (December 1975).

between the elite holders of sophisticated knowledge and the members of the communities who shared a more practical knowledge (time concretized in rituals) and a blurrier knowledge (the time of myths and of the ancestors, the time of the flood or earthquake that would annihilate the world).

With the Spanish conquest, most of the ancient systems of the apprehension of time disappeared throughout nearly the whole of the Mesoamerican region. Some groups, particularly those of the Maya highlands of Mexico and of Guatemala, preserved the knowledge and practice of a few pre-Columbian elements: the Jacaltec diviners of Guatemala still deal with year bearers, groups of thirteen, groups of twenty, and inauspicious days (*hō-pic*, the "five women").

In the same way, among the Tzeltal of Oxchuc (Chiapas), the solar year, the only one known until about thirty years ago, still followed the ancient division into eighteen months of twenty days, completed by the period of the *Xma-Kaba-Kin*, the "days without name." In most cases, however, the Christian calendar is the only one used and simply co-opts certain of the functions of the ancient calendars: the five *uayeb* days were transferred to Holy Week by the Zutuhils of Santiago Atitlan and the Kekchis of Upper Verapaz, and were accompanied, as was previously the case in the Yucatan, by a cluster of rites to Mam, the god of evil. The "santos," like the festivals of the months of the old solar year, have not only acquired a privileged place in ritual life, but, in the same fashion, serve as reference points in the seasonal organization of agricultural labors. The adoption of European beliefs has often been supported by resemblances to earlier traditions (for example, the recognition of inauspicious days—Tuesday and Friday). But the presence of these disparate and disguised elements cannot mask the almost total loss of the ancient magic of time.

II. Space

The idea of a space assimilated to a stratification of layers is very ancient. The traditional view of the Maya defines the universe as a superposition of infraterrestrial and celestial worlds of unequal sizes, contained in a cubical volume and cut by a second plane, the surface of the earth. In observing the course of the sun and its displacement in the course of the year, during intersolstitial periods, the Maya took the east-west axis as the basis for their cardinal orientation of the world, discriminating between qualitatively distinct and sacralized portions of space. This religious geometry seems to have been familiar to the whole Mesoamerican world and to have served as the basis for the construction of a veritable symbolization of space.

Horizontally, space is broken up into regions endowed with specific properties, which encompass the reference points of the system of orientation: east, west, north, south, and center. In the Aztec and Maya traditions, which are the best known, each direction has a series of particularities, qualities, and powers. Among the Aztec, the east is the favorable region par excellence, as the land of the rising sun and of the rain gods; the west is the land of flowers, but also the entrance to the dark house which the setting sun and the evening star enter; the north is the endless arid plain, swept by the freezing wind that comes down from the world of the dead; the south is the land of spiny things, which forms a sort of replica of the north, but where the drought may be corrected by irrigation.

These characteristics were concretized in a personified vision of each space, with which one or several divinities were associated. Certain of these were regarded as kinds of atlantes who supported the sky—the Bacabs, for example, who were so important in ancient Mayan religion. For the Aztec, Tlaloc, the storm god, was present at the four cardinal points, but his power was especially located to the east, where Tlahuizcalpantecuhtli, the god of the morning star, and Tonatiuh, the solar god, also reigned. To the north are situated the black *Tezcatlipoca,* also named *Itztli* ("obsidian"), the white god Mixcoatl, and the goddess Itzpapalotl ("obsidian butterfly"). Quetzalcoatl was the god of the west. Huitzilopochtli and Mictlantecuhtli dominated the south. Xuihtecuhtli, the god of fire, seems to have been assigned to the center of the world.

For the ancient Maya the cardinal points were clearly associated with certain essential colors, as some of their descendants still recall. Among the Aztec, the ancient data are either poorly known or contradictory, and the modern data are faulty. The table presents the Maya data and an Aztec version. To these have been added, following Ichon, the colors of the gods of thunderbolts of the four directions among the modern Totonac.

Dominant Colors of the Directions according to Diverse Mesoamerican Traditions

Direction	Maya (Yucatan)	Tzotzil	Aztec (16th century)	Totonac
East	red	red	blue	red
West	black	black	red	blue
North	white	white	white	yellow
South	yellow	yellow	yellow	green

It is at the center that all of the properties of the directions are fused. In Mesoamerica the ceremonial space of the village is generally the middle, the point of impact of all the directions, the sacred space or "half of the world," according to present-day Indians (Chiapas, central Mexico). The village, as religious microcosm, separated clans and lineages, starting from its center, and served as a point of fusion of the community in its ritual experience. Today, the church serves as symbol of this *omphalos* at which successive levels of the celestial and infraterrestrial universe are united. Before Cortés, every religious act invoked a reference to the cardinal directions. Even today one need only observe ceremonial cycles to understand this need to orient human actions: the sacralization of the four entrances to the village and the offerings to the four directions in the cornfields of the Maya of Yucatan, and the placing of ritual material in a particular direction, generally toward the east.

The perception of the universe on the vertical plane generally contrasts, in its imprecision, with the view of horizontal spaces. These two systems of coordinates were not perceived independently of each other. They were thought to intersect at many points of contact, these being the directions. Celestial space was divided into thirteen superimposed layers, and the netherworld into nine. This conception, still held today by the Tzeltal, was shared by the Aztec, but with certain nuances (thirteen or seven heavens, according to different traditions). Though the layering of the levels of the Maya pyramid was related to a scalar conception of the universe, the characteristics proper to each of the levels would appear to have been of interest only to esoteric thought. The collections of myths offer an image of the universe whose contours are more exact for the infraterrestrial portion (the place of genesis and of dissolution) than for the celestial levels. This complex symbolism is clearly connected, at least among the Maya, to the idea of two sexually distinct worlds: a male and diurnal sky and a female and nocturnal earth, which fuse in the act of creation.

The symbolism of ascent implies the symbolism of stages, of degrees, projected in the striated vision of the mountain. These planes of the pyramid allow for a cadenced progression toward the sacred. This was also the case with the mast in the dance of the volador. The Maya and Aztec traditions speak of five cosmic trees, one at the center and four on the periphery. Descent is related to notions of regression and of an entrance into the world of the dead (tomb of the Pyramid of Inscriptions at Palenque).

III. Space and Time

In Mesoamerican civilizations, the categories of space and time are in such mutual correspondence that they constitute a single corpus of ideas. The linearity of time was, for the Maya, an idea assimilated to the diurnal course of the sun. In this primary form of computation, each unit of time represented a "burden" that was carried the length of the solar trajectory. The signs of duration are still visualized, in surviving indigenous societies, in the form of topographic elements (the past time of the ancestors entirely included in the mountain, the journey of the dead on different paths leading to another world that depends on the nature of the death, the crossing of a river, the Aztec's *Chiconauhapan,* etc.).

In Aztec religion, the *tonalpohaulli* calendar and its rhythms clearly evoked this overlapping of concepts, with the four signs of days (*acatl, tecpatl, calli, tochtli*) associated with the four cardinal directions. The day and its thirteen divinities were to coincide with the thirteen levels of the diurnal sky, and the nine divinities evoke the nine levels of the netherworld.

The successive cosmic cataclysms are directly related to the temporal idea of the cycle, since they are in essence connected with regular repetition. Furthermore, they express the total pervasion of space and the annihilation of creation.

The study of the morphological and syntactic categories of Mesoamerican languages makes it possible to emphasize this

Spatial Sense		Temporal Sense
TZOTZIL:		
1. *nopol*	"near"	"soon, quickly"
2. *klal*	"as far as"	"until"
3. *ts'sk'al*	"behind"	"after"
4. *b'u*	"where"	"always"
5. *yo?*	"place where"	"time when"
6. *hva'leh k'ak'al*	"when the sun is at the height of a man on the horizon"	
7. *cha'va'leh k'ak'al*	"when the sun is twice as high as a man on the horizon"	
OTOMI:		
1. *bę'fa*	"behind"	"next, following"
2. *bę'to*	"before"	"at the beginning of time"
3. *yatho*	"far"	"a long time ago"
4. *īgayatho*	"near"	"a short time ago"
5. *pwö*	"very far"	"a very long time ago"
6. *getā*	"near"	"at all times"
7. *nubwü pwös ra hyadi* "at the place of the sunrise; east"		"when the sun rises"
8. *nubwü yü ra hyadi* "at the place of the sunset; west"		"when the sun sets"

unity. The terminology of space and time can, in certain cases, delimit a single semantic field, as is highlighted by the two brief examples which are borrowed, respectively, from the Tzotzil (Zinacantán) and Otomi (south of Huasteca) languages.

M.A.E.F.M./d.w.

BIBLIOGRAPHY

See the bibliography at the end of the article "Mesoamerican Religion," especially section I: 8, 11, 12, 13, 17, 22, 23, 24, 27; section II: 16 (22 or 44), 38; section III: 4, 9, 11, 18, 25, 41, 64, 65, 70; section IV: 3, 15, 16, 18, 41.

THE SKY: SUN, MOON, STARS, AND METEOROLOGICAL PHENOMENA IN MESOAMERICAN RELIGIONS

I. The Sky

In Mesoamerican traditions, the sky is presented under many aspects and does not appear as a unity of substances or qualities. The division of space into seven or thirteen strata seems to be the fruit of distinctly esoteric speculations, at least in the attribution of properties to each level. The sky, more simply, is conceived as a horizontal colored band or a superimposition of bands (traditional representations from the codices), a roof (the upper part of *Itzam Na*, the "house of iguanas," an ophidian monster whose body is covered with planetary symbols), or a vault that encloses the universe. Having collapsed on the earth at the end of the last cosmic catastrophe that destroyed the world, the sky has been restored and remains supported by objects (generally trees, an ax among the Mixtec) or caryatid hero-divinities (the Bacabs of the Maya, a group of four men controlled by Quetzalcoatl and Tezcatlipoca among the Aztec). These supports maintain a permanent contact between sky and earth, but the essential connection is established at the center of the world, at the heart of the ceremonial enclosure, where the pyramid rises, where the *yaxche* tree (the sacred Mayan ceiba) grows, where the ladder ends, where the cord is suspended.

The celestial substance is never described but is perhaps evoked, in part, in the Nahuatl term *ilhuicatl* with a double semantic content ("sky" and "sea"). Like the sea, the sky is an immutable element, beyond human reach, the enclosure of the world. At the western and eastern horizons, the sky and sea meet: the setting sun plunges into the ocean infra-world, from which it reemerges when it rises. Though, among the Maya, the idea of a coupling, the source of all life, between the male sky and the female earth dominates, other traditions present an inverted image of this cosmic sexual act; for the Otomi, the celestial uterine cavity is penetrated by the mountain. The origin of this divergence lies in a dualism which is supported by both the sky and the earth. The diurnal sky, the realm of the fertilizing sun, is globally opposed to the darkness of the night dominated by the lunar star, associated with water, earth, fertility. The sun-moon antagonism gives the sky its fundamental ambivalence.

The celestial vault draws its importance from the bodies and divinities that inhabit it. It is the place of origin of atmospheric phenomena and the home of the stars, although a whole current of thought seems to have situated the clouds, the stars, and even the sun-moon pair immediately beneath the first celestial layer; but the sky is above all the residence of the major gods, even those who are non-Ouranian in appearance (Mictlantecuhtli rules over the subterranean realm of the dead but also lives in the sky: in the night of death, sky and earth are intermingled). At the top of the celestial pantheon, in the most distant spheres, the primordial divinity of duality or the creator couple reigns.

II. The Sun-Moon Pair in Pre-Columbian Religions

In creation myths, the sun and moon play an essential role among the peoples of Mesoamerica. However, while these two major luminaries seem to have occupied a preeminent place in the classical pantheon, the Postclassical Period relegated the divine beings who incarnate them to a secondary rank. This relative deposition was accompanied by the promotion of multiple divinities who were endowed with properties that were solar, lunar, or both solar and lunar. The ancient importance of the sun and moon is attested by numerous indices. At Teotihuacan, in the Tzacualli phase (A.D. 1–150), the ceremonial center was organized around pyramids dedicated, according to Aztec tradition, to the sun and to the moon. In the following period, while new elements of the pantheon were progressively set in place, the central point of the city was displaced toward the south and coincided with the temple of Quetzalcoatl. In the Mayan area, during the Classical Period, the gods of the sun and the moon occupied an important position. The solar god, invoked as Ah Kin ("the one of the sun") or Kinich Ahau ("face of the sun"), was the master of the day, fire, energy, by turns a young man and an old one, the object of veneration and fear. Ix Chel, the Yucatecan lunar goddess, presided over childbirth and procreation and ruled over diseases and medicine, but her ancient role seems to go beyond these few functions; she was also, originally, a divinity of water and earth; *caban* ("earth") was the day associated with her, and her titles of "Mistress of the Sea" and "Mistress from the Midst of the Cenote" clearly connect her with the aquatic element. In Aztec religion, the same moon-earth-water connection also held for the goddess Tlazolteotl, of Huastec origin, best known for her earthly specialization. Among the Cora and the Huichol, until our own time, the moon was a divinity of the earth and vegetation. This totalizing aspect of the two divinities makes the couple that they form an incarnation of the primary duality, an image of the old primordial couple from whom all life has sprung, a celestial transposition of the two vital principles which have been the object of the oldest religious manifestations, the Earth-Mother and the fertilizing Fire.

Not all the traditions agree in presenting the sun and moon as husband and wife. In certain cases, they are only brother and sister, but even when the lunar body appears with the traits of a male god (Tecciztecatl of the Aztec), the principle that he incarnates remains distinctly feminine: the symbol of the moon, Tecciztli, the "shellfish of the sea," also represents the woman's sexual organ. Whatever their relationship may be, therefore, the two luminaries, conceived as antithetical and complementary, serve as poles of the universe. It is on their opposition that one of the most popular schemata of distribution of the categories of thought is based, between hot and cold, light and dark, dry and wet, pure and impure. Metaphorically, eclipses result from the antagonism between the two luminaries (a marital dispute

Quetzalcoatl, feathered serpent. Paris, Musée de l'Homme collection. Photo Oster.

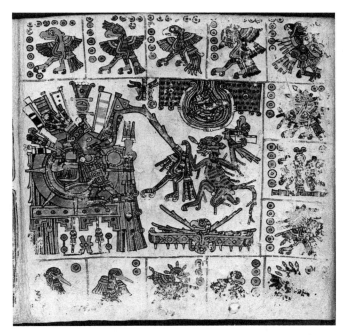

The sun and the moon in the Borgia Codex (p. 71). Vatican Library. Library Photo.

Schematic Table of Aztec Solar-Lunar Divinities

Sun	Moon
Tonatiuh, "sun."	Metzli, "moon."
Original name: Nanahuatl, "the scurfy"; later became Teotl, "the preeminent god," or Xipilli, "the prince of turquoise."	Also called by his original name: Tecciztecatl, "he of the land of marine conchs" (the great marine gastropod shellfish).
Calendrical name: Naui Olin, "four-movement" or "four quakes of the earth."	Calendrical name: Naui Tecpatl, "four knife of stone."
Usual representation: a radiant disk.	Usual representation: a vase full of water, depicted in profile, containing a stone knife or a rabbit.
Associated animals: eagle, jaguar, wolf.	Associated animals: shellfish, rabbit.
Patron divinity: Tonacatecuhtli and Xiuhtecuhtli.	Patron divinity: Tlaloc.
Piltzintecuhtli, "chief of princes." The sun as patron of nobles dedicated to war.	Coyolxauhqui, "she whose face painting represents little bells." A lunar goddess decapitated by the sun in the myth of the birth of Huitzilpochtli.
Huitzilopochtli, "hummingbird of the left." Solar warrior, conqueror of the moon and the stars. God of the blue sky and more especially of the southern sky.	
	Also associated with the moon:
Also associated with the sun: Xiuhtecuhtli, "lord of turquoise" or "lord of the year," god of fire.	Tlazolteotl, "goddess of impurity." Earth goddess whose nose ornament was in the form of the lunar crescent.
	Chalchihuitlicue, "she who has a green jadeite skirt."
	Ome tochtli, "two rabbits." God of intoxication and of the renewal of vegetation. His nose ornament was in the form of the crescent moon.
Formerly, the gods Tezcatlipoca, Quetzalcoatl, and Tlaloc and the goddess Chalchihuitlicue were transformed into suns (before the present sun).	

III. The Sun-Moon Pair in Contemporary Religions

The diversity of mythical projections about the sun and moon of the Postclassical Period was succeeded, after the Conquest, by a partial assimilation of the image of Christ to the sun and of the Virgin Mary to the moon, in the framework of Christian "dualism." This reequilibration, bipolarization, and condensation of images is common in Mesoamerica. Installed at the head of the old pantheon of former times, God hereafter governed the mass of minor divinities. However, in several indigenous traditions, Christ occupied a position subordinate to the image of the Father, and was relegated to the rank of a secondary culture hero. But on the whole, the Christ-Sun-God fusion has been complete. Certain images have had an exceptional impact on the indigenous and mestizo sensibility, such as the Virgin of Guadalupe, a receptacle of pre-Columbian beliefs about fertility, rain, and the mountains, except in the Mayan area.

The cult of the saints succeeded the polytheism of earlier times, but it consolidated the religion that came from the encounter of the two cultures, the host of male saints gravitating around the solar divinity, the female saints accompanying the lunar numen. Quite often the position of the

for the Indians of Yucatan). Similarly, one of the symbolic contents of the ball game (*ollamaliztli*) seems to have been the struggle of the powers included in the sun and the moon.

In the Postclassical Period, all the energy of which the two primordial stars were carriers was portioned out, distributed in several series of new gods. In the Mayan lowlands, the effacement of the lunar goddess was paralleled by the development of the role of the corn god. Among the Aztec, Tonatiuh and Tecciztecatl still personified the sun and the moon but were placed in the background. The ancient divinities were replaced by a divine company of gods, but the fascination that the old astral pair exercised was not altered. Every day, nine times a day, the priests of Tenochtitlan continued to offer their homage to the great luminary.

Terra-cotta sculpture of Tlaloc. El Zapoltal, Veracruz. Xalapa Museum. Photo M.A.E.F.M.

of the primordial divinity, they are encountered wherever the mark of the sacred is asserted: fountains, tombs, mountains, etc. Thus, the symbol of the cross, known since pre-Columbian times and associated at that time with divinities of the water, participated, after the Conquest, in solar imagery, without, however, losing its old connection with the aquatic element: around the festival of the Holy Cross, in the month of May, the anticipation of the rains culminates.

Solar and Lunar Divinities in the Present-Day Religions of Mesoamerica

Peoples	Sun	Moon
Pame	*Kunhu* sun, *dyus kunhu,* "sun god," the name by which one invokes Christ.	(Virgin of Guadalupe?)
Otomi	*Hyadi* sun, often invoked by the name of *tsidada jesu,* "our father Jesus."	*Zāna,* moon, often invoked by the name of *tsinana gwalupe,* "our mother Guadalupe."
Matlalzinca	*Insutata,* "our revered father," the name given both to the sun and to God.	*Insunene,* "our revered mother," the name given both to the moon and to the Virgin Mary.
Huastec of Ixcatepec	*Totiotsi,* "our god," the name given to Christ, assimilated to the sun.	?
Totonac	*Chichini,* sun, assimilated to Jesus Christ. He is addressed by the name of Dios. Often conflated with Saint Dominic, Saint Francis of Assisi, or Saint Lazarus.	(The Totonac considered the moon to be *malkuyu* like an evil and harmful god. They honor a mother goddess *natsi itni* who is assimilated to the Virgin Mary but who is not a lunar divinity.)
Huastec	*Ak'icha,* sun, assimilated to Dios, Christ.	*Its',* moon, assimilated, to a certain degree, to the Virgin of Guadalupe and to the Immaculate Conception.
Tzotzil of Zinacantan	*Totik k'akal,* "our father the sun," assimilated to *riosh kahval,* "God our Lord."	*Chul metik,* "divine mother," is the name given to the moon, the mother of the sun, assimilated to the Virgin Mary.

IV. The Stars and Planets

In ancient Mesoamerica, the nocturnal sky was compared poetically to the mottled fur of a jaguar or to the spangled star skirt of the goddess of primordial times. The sky also inspired astronomical observations and beliefs that remain, to a great extent, unknown.

Certain authors believe that the ancient Mexicans recognized a series of zodiacal constellations, but this remains imperfectly demonstrated. It is known that the Aztec ac-

saints appears to be in some way intermediary between the world of humans and the world of the great divinities, with whom they are, however, occasionally conflated. Closer to the religious existence, they facilitate relations with the sacred. The Indians appeal to them, through prayer, in order to obtain an echo to their unhappiness. In Chiapas the "talking saints," veritable oracles, amplify this type of belief.

When they do not accomplish their task, the saints deserve to be punished. A special role has devolved upon the local patron saints, eponymous divinities of towns or villages whose protection they assure. This custom is proper to all of Indian and mestizo Mexico, with the possible exception of Yucatan, where the saints do not seem to have received specific worship; they were grafted onto the traditional pantheon and cohabit with other divinities. Crosses, symbols of the center of the world, are invested with a sacred power throughout the Mayan area. They are authentic divinities with whom people may communicate through the mediation of traditional priests. Substitutes or complements corded importance to the Pleiades, Orion, the Big Dipper, Scorpio, and perhaps the Southern Cross. A text of Torquemada relates that the festival of the new fire, celebrated every fifty-two years, took place on the night when the Pleiades appeared on the eastern horizon at the moment of the sun's setting, and at the hour when that constellation reached the center of the sky. The Milky Way is mentioned in the myths and appears to have been connected with the pair of primordial divinities.

It is probable that the Indians of ancient Mesoamerica had observed the planets, but the surviving texts explicitly mention only Venus, and the data drawn from the interpretation of myths and pictographic manuscripts are unreliable. It is possible that the protean god Xolotl, one of the last victims of the rising sun, represented the planet Mercury.

The importance of the planet Venus was nearly as great as the importance of the sun and the moon. The Maya had precisely calculated the cycle of its appearances. The Aztec century of 104 years, called *huehuetiliztli* ("one old age"), was equivalent to the calendrical period of correspondence between 65 Venusian years and 104 solar years.

The god of the planet Venus, Tlahuizcalpantecuhtli ("lord of the house of the dawn"), was described as an infallible archer, whose arrows of light were particularly formidable at the moment of the heliacal rising of the planet. The fact is that this god (like Xolotl, moreover) had ties with the world of the dead, from which he emerged. But he was also a beneficent god and an auxiliary of the sun. As the double star of morning and evening, Venus occupied an important place in the speculations of the ancient sacerdotal body and contributed to the complex personality of the god Quetzalcoatl.

The Indians of today have, in general, little memory of the ancient constellations, but accord importance to Venus and continue, like their ancestors, to fear the inauspicious omens announced by comets and meteorites.

V. Rain, Clouds, and Lightning

Nearly all the Mesoamerican peoples had in common the belief in a great god, the master of lightning and dispenser of rainstorms, whose residence was generally situated in the eastern ocean. This god was called Tlaloc by the Aztec, Aktsin by the Totonac, Tzahui by the Mixtec, Cocijo by the Zapotec, Nohotsyumchac by the Maya. His most ancient representations may have been those of the jaguar divinity of the Olmec at the beginning of the first millennium B.C., a half-feline, half-human figure, recognizable by his fleshy lips with drooping corners. This may have been the source of later representations of this divinity among the various Mesoamerican peoples.

All water was thought to proceed from the *teoatl* sea, "the divine water." Water was the precious element, the essential condition of plant life and agriculture. Its symbols were the green jadeite stone and the green feathers of the quetzal bird. Among the Aztec, the goddess whose skirts were adorned with jadeite, Chalchihuitlicue, associated with the moon, was the very essence of the water of the sea, lakes, rivers. The Gulf of Mexico was designated as Metztli Apan, "the place of the water of the moon." According to the Cakchiquel of Guatemala, the moon was the mistress of Lake Atitlan and ruled the sea. Everywhere, water was placed under the patronage of female divinities. A colossal statue of Teotihuacan is generally interpreted as representing the goddess of the waters.

The great god of the storm lived, according to several traditions, in the middle of the ocean, in a paradise of abundance and fertility that the Aztec called Tlalocan. He rarely stirred, and manifested himself chiefly at the beginning of the rainy season, by distant thunderclaps which seemed to fill the atmosphere and were compared to the roars of a jaguar. He had near him, at least in the dry season, his messengers, Tlalocs for the Aztec, Chacs for the Maya, who were like reductions of his own person. It was sometimes said that these were the divinized souls of men who had died by drowning, by being struck by lightning, or from dropsy. These little gods were also thought to have their residences at the four cardinal points, whence the ancient symbolism of the cosmic cross. When they came to the land of men, they took shelter in the interior of the mountains, which were thought to be filled with water, or in the chasms of the Yucatecan limestone plateau.

Chacs or Tlalocs brandished lightning in the form of resplendent arms, stone or bronze axes, and transported rainwater in pitchers or gourds, even in cloth. They were the benefactors of humanity, but if they were angry with it, they might inflict disastrous droughts or send only inauspicious rains, fogs, and mildew, entailing the loss of crops.

Children and young virgin girls were the designated victims of these divinities of the water, to whom they were assimilated after the sacrificial apotheosis. These practices were suppressed by evangelization and are now replaced by simple offerings of food and drink, which are still very common, especially when there is a drought. Indeed, beliefs concerning the divinities of rain, lightning, and water have been preserved to our time in numerous native Mesoamerican groups, not without being occasionally colored by European elements. In this way the water goddess has often become "the Siren." In Yucatan, the Maya now conceive of the Chacs as horsemen, armed with blazing swords or machetes, and their chief is Saint Michael the archangel.

Another aspect of the cult of the water is presented by its ritual and purifying role, which was often connected with "the virgin water," the *zuhuy ha* of the Maya, which issued from a spring or cavern that had not been polluted by frequent contact with humans. From its birth, the native child was (and often still is) bathed, in the company of its mother, in the steam bath commonly called Temascal. Later, water was to cleanse his body and contribute to the removal of his sins. Sometimes, in Yucatan, the corpse of the dead man was washed immediately after death and this water, mixed with a maize paste, was consumed by the parents of the dead man, who thus took on a part of his sins.

Water is the principle of life, death, and resurrection. It can temper the heat of the sun or bring forth a deluge. It is truly fruitful only when united with fire, as in the storm or the steam bath. This union of opposites was expressed by the sign *atlachinolli*, the glyph of the ritual strife that was regarded as redeeming humanity.

VI. The Winds

In Mesoamerica, the winds draw upon a complex and little-known ideology. They are, first of all, connected with the cardinal points. The present-day Maya situate their gods of the winds in the second sky and their gods of lightning in the sixth. The ancient texts about the Maya do not clearly distinguish between the *pauahtuns*, wind gods, the *bacabs*, supporters of the sky, and the *chacs*, storm gods. The present-day Totonac make the winds the companions of thunder. The Aztec and Otomi said that the wind was charged with sweeping the path of the water gods so that the latter might make rain.

Aztec tradition attributed quite diverse peculiarities to the winds, corresponding to the directions of space from which they blew. The only favorable wind was the east wind, which came from the Tlalocan. The west wind was cold, but rather benign. The north and south winds were inauspicious and destructive.

The connection between the wind and the vital breath suffices to explain why Quetzalcoatl-Ehecatl, the Aztec wind god, is depicted in the Borgia Codex as a god of life in opposition to Tezcatlipoca, who is represented with the attributes of the dead. The personality of Quetzalcoatl was extremely complex but presented aspects which were above all favorable.

But the wind might bring evil spells, introduce thorns into the human body, and contribute to the loss of the soul. These malevolent properties attributed to the wind combined with popular Spanish beliefs about "bad air" which have been assimilated everywhere without difficulty.

M.A.E.F.M./b.f.

BIBLIOGRAPHY

See the bibliography at the end of the article "Mesoamerican Religion," above, especially section I: 6, 10, 14, 15, 16, 20, 25, 26, 27; section II: 6, 9, 16 (22 or 44), 35, 37, 38; section III: 3, 5, 12, 16, 22, 31, 59, 60, 63, 64, 65, 71; section IV: 13, 14, 29, 38, 44, 45.

THE EARTH IN MESOAMERICAN RELIGIONS

I. The Earth Monster or Mother Earth

Mesoamerican mythical thought imagines the surface of the earth as having the characteristics of an animal, sometimes a monstrous animal, whose sex and nature vary according to the traditions. In the Classical Period, a creature half-cat, half-frog (depicted, notably, on numerous yokes), seems to constitute one of the first representations of the earth monster. Earlier, the jaguar, a favorite theme in Olmec iconography, also had a chthonic aspect. For the Maya of the Classical Period, the earth was the lower part (the ground floor) of the "house of the iguanas": Itzam Cab or Itzam Cab Ain ("iguana-earth," or "iguana-earth-crocodile"). The Aztec "lord of the earth," Tlaltecuhtli, appears in the form of a monstrous creature with gaping jaws, inspired by the *cipactli*, or giant crocodile, that swims in the waters created by the gods at the beginning of the world. This zoomorphic vision of the earth is still alive today: Totonac myths associate the earth, whose master is simultaneously a man and a woman, with a turtle or a caiman, whereas for their Huastec neighbors it is the great female crocodile. But all such representations generally deal only with the surface of the earth. Its deeper, essential role is only partially evoked in the images of animals through which it appears. That role is expressed, in all periods and places, in the form of multiple deities.

The cults of the earth, in its basic dual aspect, are very old. The locus of genesis and dissolution, provider of food and eater of corpses, the earth fuses the principles of life and death. The dynamic of the world is founded on this union of opposites that takes place within her womb: for all new life is born out of a previous death. Mankind was created out of bones which Quetzalcoatl went to fetch in the heart of the earth, in the realm of the dead. For the Otomi of today, sperm is a product of bone. This sense of the deeply ambiguous character of the earth is part of the most archaic expressions of religious life. During the early Preclassic Period (1300–900 B.C.), on the central plateau, an abundance of female figurines may be interpreted as a sign of a predominant fertility cult: Mother Woman and Mother Earth are thus among the first deities of whom evidence has been preserved. The cult of the dead and of the ancestors seems to be

even older. The primitive and embryonic pantheon seems to be documented by the couple made up of Fire and Earth, but the Earth is associated with the night sky and the element of water. During the Aztec period, earth goddesses were for the most part still assimilated to Tonacaciuhatl, the primordial female deity. Overall, the earth remains the great feminine principle of the world, despite the existence of earthly elements of the opposite sex (male) and the presence of divine male representatives of fertility within the pantheons.

Since the Conquest, two series of beliefs and rituals have especially persisted in the cults of the earth, one connected with topographical irregularities (mountains, caves, springs, rivers), and the other with wild and cultivated plants.

II. Mountains

In the Mesoamerican world, the mountain is endowed with a remarkable accumulation of symbols.

In Tenochtitlan, one of the monthly festivals was dedicated to mountains. Each of these was modeled in miniature with amaranth paste and topped with a human head made of the same substance. The gods represented in this way were called Tepictoton ("dwarfs of the mountains") or Ehecatotontin ("dwarfs of the wind"). They were assimilated to the souls of dead people who had been drowned or struck by lightning and had then become gods of lightning or rain.

Mountains were thought to be full of water and were thus closely connected with water deities. But in Mexico and Guatemala, many mountains are active or extinct volcanoes, from which they derive their connection with divinities of fire. This is illustrated by the traditional representations of the old god of fire, the Aztec Huehueteotl, who has a brazier on his head. In the eyes of the Otomi of today, the mountain is an erect penis pointed at the sky. But the same Otomi also note that on the sides of mountains there are caves, cavities with a uterine symbolism, which often serve as cult sites. In Yucatan, there are practically no mountains, but the Maya of Guatemala also practice a cult of mountains with a frequently analogous ideology.

Thought to be hollow, the mountain is also an image of the underground world. Corn was hidden inside a mountain before it was brought to mankind. This "house of corn," Cincalco, was a dark place located to the west, as was the gate of hell. There was a god of the inside of mountains, whom the Aztec called Oztoteotl ("the god of caves") or

Coatlicue, Aztec earth goddess. Mexico City, National Museum of Anthropology. Museum photo.

Tepeyollotl ("the heart of the mountains"). His idol, once venerated in a cave near Ocuila, was replaced in popular worship by the Christ on the cross of the shrine of Chalma.

By the Preclassical Period, each town or village was mystically connected with a mountain. This is witnessed by the architecture of the pyramid, built in the middle of an agglomeration of stones and designed to attract rain like the real mountains with their surrounding agglomerations of clouds.

The great pyramid of Cholula, called Tlachihualtepetl ("the artificial mountain"), was said to have been built before the birth of the present sun, by mythical giants who sought to reach the sky. For the mountain is the special locus of communication with both the celestial world and the netherworld. The myths of the Pipils of El Salvador describe the world as a huge, hollow, cosmic mountain within which men live.

The Tzotzil of the Chiapas highlands, studied by W. Holland, venerate the sacred mountains in which the souls of the ancestors of their lineage dwell. Each of these mountains has thirteen levels, in the image of the thirteen levels of the sky and the thirteen degrees of the social hierarchy of the village. The animals that guard the highest dignitaries live near the top of the mountain, just as the principal deities live at the top of the sky. The mountain and the sky are thus in the image of human society.

III. Vegetation

In Mesoamerican religious thought, vegetation is intimately connected with water and rainstorms. The "four hundred rabbits" (Centzon Totochtin), degenerate forms of the gods of thunder, are typical vegetation deities. It is not through pure chance that, in the legends of the flood, it is a rabbit who orders the fallen trees to stand up. The "four hundred rabbits" each wore a nose ornament in the form of a crescent moon, evidence of the universal belief that certain activities connected with vegetation are dependent on the phases of the moon.

The gods of lightning are also the gods of the four cardinal points. The Maya and the Aztec share the idea that each cardinal point marked the site of a tree that supported the sky. In Mayan texts, each tree is the same color as its point on the compass. The Maya also locate in the center of the world a cosmic tree with a straight trunk, whose horizontal branches spread out over the various levels of the sky. This was a ceiba tree, known in Mayan as *yaxche* ("green tree"), indicating, among other things, the color assigned to the center of the world.

The locus of plant fertility par excellence is the eastern paradise of the great god of lightning, a paradise called Tlalocan by the Aztecs, and represented by a famous Teotihuacan fresco. This mythical place, apparently inspired by the spectacle of warm, humid lands, owed its fertility essentially to the abundance of water, whose symbolic color was the green of vegetation. Clay female figurines, which are the oldest religious representations of the Preclassical Period, are supposed to evoke the human fertility that is associated with the fertility of earth and water, the producers of vegetation.

Since its origins, corn has been the most sacred plant species in the Mesoamerican world. Mankind owes its survival to it, and the Quiche myths of the *Popol Vuh* go so far as to say that the first men worthy of the name were fashioned by the gods out of a dough made of corn. The young god of corn is often described in the myths as a civilizing hero whose birth was miraculous. This god was called Cinteotl by the Aztec, who regarded him as the son of the goddess of the earth. His calendar name was *ce xochitl* ("a flower"). But the texts sometimes speak of a female Cinteotl, and other Aztec deities of corn, Xilonen ("the ear of still green corn") and Chicomecoatl ("seven snakes"), were also goddesses, one young and the other mature. Corn joins the two sexes and passes through all the ages of life, and then through death and resurrection.

The corn deities, always exposed to many dangers, were then and still are hedged by a genuine affection. Their cult did not directly implicate human sacrifices; such sacrifices were rather addressed to the deities of earth and water, on whom the life of the plant depended. Corn was furthermore mystically associated with the sun and the planet Venus, both of whom were summoned to pass the test of the netherworld themselves.

Flowers symbolized beauty, youth, pleasure, lust, and sometimes blood. The deities of flowers among the Aztec, Xochipilli ("the prince of flowers") and Xochiquetzal, a goddess whose name may be translated "precious flower" or "precious feather," were also connected with corn, the sun, and the morning star.

The agave, a plant found in the semiarid plateaus, held a

Pyramid of the sun at Teotihuacan. Photo Guy Stresser-Pean.

"The Lord of the Forest." Otomi paper cutout. Photo M.A.E.F.M.

major place in the religion of one part of Mesoamerica. Its sweet-tasting sap had intoxicating properties when fermented, which made it the beverage of immortality in ancient Mexico. The whiteness of its sap made people compare it to milk, which is why the Aztec goddess of the agave plants, Mayauel, was said to have countless breasts like Artemis of Ephesus. But the gods of intoxication were strictly speaking the "four hundred rabbits," the gods of the vital power of plants. The principal god among these, Ome tochtli ("two-rabbit"), had become young again after a drunken sleep, which may explain why the Aztec reserved the drinking of agave wine (pulque or *octli*) for old men, at least theoretically. The Huastec sometimes absorbed the pulque in the form of an enema to bring about ritual intoxication. The Aztec poured it out in libations, notably as offerings to the god of fire.

The Mayan peoples did not use pulque. Their fermented ritual drink was a kind of mead, the efficacy of which they augmented by soaking in it a piece of bark from a tree called *balche*. The Lacandons of the Chiapas forests and some northeastern Maya still use *balche* in their ceremonies. In northwestern Mexico, the Huichol and Cora continue to use corn beer, commonly called *tesguino*.

But the Indians especially resorted to other sacred plants in order to communicate with the supernatural world. In the arid or semiarid regions of central and northern Mexico, they used peyote, a small cactus whose pulp contains mescal. The Cora and Huichol still revere this cactus as a god and surround its use with a whole ritual. In central and southern Mexico to the Isthmus of Tehuantepec, the use of hallucinogenic mushrooms was extremely widespread. The Aztec name for these mushrooms was *teonanacatl* or "divine flesh." The fact that they appeared at the moment of the rainy season evidently associated them with the gods of lightning. They are still used today, notably by Mazatec diviners, and are sometimes the occasion for veritable communion meals. But in many other regions, diviners and healers resort to modern alcoholic beverages when they commune with the gods.

Tobacco was also a ritual plant in ancient Mexico and may have served to communicate with the world of the sacred. But it was primarily used in the area of religious prophylaxis. Moreover, its smoke, like that of indigenous incense or copal (Nahuatl *copalli*), was supposed to attract clouds through sympathetic magic.

It was in connection with a vegetation cult that human sacrifice by flaying took place, a practice that goes back to the Preclassical Period. The victims of these sacrifices, men or women, were first killed by having their hearts ripped out. Then they were flayed , and a priest or devotee put on the skin of the victim in order to perform various rites. People suffering from skin diseases could treat themselves in this way on condition that they wore this funeral vestment for a full twenty days. The Aztec god of these sacrifices was called Xipe Totec, "our flayed lord." A hymn sung to him has come down to us. It refers to young corn and the new crop stimulated by the coming of the rainy season. Exegetes have thereby interpreted these rites of flaying as having been, above all, symbols of the renewal of vegetation following the sterile months of the winter dry season.

M.A.E.F.M./g.h.

BIBLIOGRAPHY

See the bibliography at the end of the article "Mesoamerican Religion," especially section I: 20, 26; section II: 6, 9. 14, 28, 34, 35, 38; section III: 4, 6, 12, 24, 30, 33, 52, 63, 65; section IV: 5, 13, 24, 30, 39, 43, 45.

FIRE IN MESOAMERICAN MYTHOLOGY

In the Aztec pantheon, the god of fire, Xiuhtecuhtli, or Huehueteotl, was known as "the Lord of the Otomi," a people fascinated by the nocturnal forms of creation. This god was the one who came closest in nature to Tonacatecuhtli, the supreme masculine divinity enthroned in the summit of the sky. One of the names given to Xiuhtecuhtli designates him as living in "the turquoise pyramid," i.e., in the blue daylight sky. It was said that this was the oldest of the gods, and he was generally represented, from Preclassical times, in the form of a bent-over, wrinkled, toothless old man. But this old man carried a brazier on his head, since the god of fire was also the god of volcanoes, and most particularly of the volcano of Colima, in western Mexico.

As god of the zenith, Xiuhtecuhtli had, along with Tonacatecuhtli, chosen the hero who had become the present sun after throwing himself into a brazier. In a festival especially consecrated to him, people placed the effigy of Huehueteotl on top of a ritual greased pole. In this elevated position, the effigy of the god bore the attributes of the *cuecuex*, the divinized souls of warriors, whose deaths had rendered them worthy of inhabiting the celestial dwelling of the sun. But as the god of volcanos, fire also had a subterranean aspect which was connected with the idea of the evening sun swinging down into the chasm of night and death, to be reborn the following dawn.

As a god of ancient times, the sun was "the lord of the year." Even today, certain Otomi groups of the eastern Sierra Madre annually perform a ritual of renewing the fire. Fur-

thermore, it was formerly through a grandiose festival of the new fire that the Aztec celebrated "the binding of the years," at the end of their "centuries" of fifty-two years, and after hours of nocturnal anguish during which the destruction of the world was feared.

As the very expression of heat, fire was associated with hot chili pepper, the symbol of masculine vital strength. Its sacred tree was the pine, whose wood supplied torches which made lighting at night possible. It was said to have the changing colors of flame, being red, yellow, or bluish. But it was also fire that produced the soot and charcoal used by

The old god of fire and volcanoes, Huehueteotl. Totonac ceramic. Mexico City, National Museum of Anthropology. Museum photo.

certain dancers to coat their faces in evocation of ghosts risen from the land of the dead. In striking contrast, Xiuhtecuhtli was the patron of the days of *atl* ("water") in the Aztec divinatory calendar. A beautiful text collected by Sahagún describes this god in his mythic home, surrounded by water and mist. This is because its vital strength, both creative and fertilizing, was one that acted upon its opposites, like light in darkness, heat in the midst of cold, the male principle in the midst of female elements, and finally death, which gives rise to apotheosis.

Fire has a purificatory power. It makes possible the elimination of all stains, which explains why its bird is the vulture—eater of impurities and charged with cleaning the world—among present-day Otomi. Smoke was used in lustration rites. The ancient Maya purified themselves by walking on live coals, a rite which still survives among the Tzotzil of the highlands of Chiapas.

The vivifying and purificatory activity of fire in combination with that of water appear clearly in the multiplicity of ritual uses formerly made of the steam bath or *temascal* (Nahuatl *temascalli*) throughout the Mesoamerican culture region. Vestiges of this still remain, and in quite a few native villages the rites of birth and childbirth entail the passage of the mother and newborn child through its salvific and vivifying steam.

Finally, by virtue of its essential role in agricultural, culinary, and mechanical techniques, fire is regarded as the condition for and origin of all civilization. In every dwelling, the fireplace, which constitutes a domestic instrument and a tutelary power, must be present. It was maintained by women, but fed and fueled by men, who even today may, from time to time, offer a few drops of pulque or brandy into it as a libation.

M.A.E.F.M./d.w.

BIBLIOGRAPHY

See the bibliography at the end of the article "Mesoamerican Religion," and especially section I: 26; section II: 6, 17, 38; section III: 12, 13, 53, 65; section IV: 14, 24, 35.

Huehuetla nurse-midwife's dance. Tepehua Indians. Photo M.A.E.F.M.

The human person and its constituent parts, from San Pedro Chenalo, Chiapas. Tzotzil Indians. Drawing M.A.E.F.M.

THE MESOAMERICAN IMAGE OF THE HUMAN PERSON

Every religious system includes a set of beliefs about the human person, beliefs which determine specific types of relationships between humans and society, and between humans and the world. In the Mesoamerican domain, these beliefs and their multiple implications are really known only from the period just before the Conquest and thereafter. Our knowledge of pre-Conquest material comes from collections of oral traditions made by the first European witnesses of the indigenous world. Information for earlier periods is sporadic in nature, consisting mainly of hypothetical deductions.

The ethnohistorical and ethnological data show the individual as an assemblage of several elements. In its most highly elaborated form, for example, among the Tzotzil of Chiapas, the image of the person includes five component parts, although two or three of these are often confused. At the center of the body (1) is found the life principle, the element of dynamism and movement (2). The soul (3), an immaterial element which exists before birth and survives after death, is a kind of reflection of the life principle (the breath, the *ch'ulel* of the Tzotzil, the *listakna* of the Totonac), and dwells in all of the organs simultaneously. The concept of *yollotl* used by the ancient Nahua seems to refer both to the seat of dynamism and to its manifestations (moral values, virility, etc.). The mind (4), center of intelligence and knowledge, often constitutes a second soul, which the Aztec call *ixtli* or face. The animal double (*tonal* or *nahual*) is the last element of the structure of the individual (5). While the animal double is external to the individual, the two still have a truly consubstantial relationship. The life of a person depends on the interaction of the above components.

The funeral rituals suggest that people have long been thought to possess an element which survives the dissolution of the body. The custom of burying furniture, and sometimes sacrificed animals or people, with the dead has existed since the Preclassical Period. This custom should probably be interpreted as providing aid to whatever remains of the dead person in the world beyond. The frequent presence of miniature objects in Classical and Postclassical burials of several regions may be related to a belief in the persistence of the soul in the form of a dwarf, a belief still held by the Tzotzil and the Totonac. The notion of an animal double may also be an ancient one. In the myth of the creation of humankind, Quetzalcoatl himself calls his double, his *nahual*, to his aid.

The religious thought of Mesoamerica locks human beings into a narrow determinism from birth until after death. The individual's earthly fate depends directly on his birthday and the combined forces acting on this day. The position of Venus on this day plays a particular role in the fate of the newborn child. The nature of the animal double, which every person has, is also a function of his birthday. Finally, certain peculiarities of the newborn child are signs of his future destiny: in several traditions, for example, a tuft of hair on the head indicates a future sorcerer. Similarly, the umbilical cord is always an object of special attention, since it is endowed with magical properties. Thus inequality among people is established from the beginning; it is outside the control of individuals. To attenuate the blind and sovereign influence of the *tonalpohualli* (the calendar of divination), the Aztec had no option but to choose favorable days for naming children— but their intervention was limited to this. The attempts of the *tlamatinime* (or philosopher-sages) to influence the course of fate could only give certain people a provisional illusion of freedom. In this conception humans are merely playthings in the hands of the gods. Their appearance on earth is necessary for the perpetuation of creation, whose origin is marked by a fundamental debt to the gods. At every moment of his life, man is faced with duties which he must perform for the world of the sacred, because of the initial permanent contract which made the gods the creators of humankind and men the servants of the gods.

Even though people are subject to the law of their destiny, they move back and forth in the course of their lives between two poles which wage a constant struggle with the universe as its stake: order and disorder. For disorder is everywhere, on the cosmic level with destructive earthquakes, floods in the rainy season, volcanic eruptions; on the social level with wars and other conflicts; on the mental level with personality disorders and deviance. People on earth thus live in a precarious situation. At any moment the equilibrium of the elements which constitute the person can be shattered: the result is "espanto" (terror which can bring on loss of the soul), sickness, or death. Established in inequality by a primordial decree, people are also vulnerable to "envidia" (jealousy). But disorder is also the permanent obsession of entropy, of the fate of the world that becomes progressively degraded to end in a cosmic cataclysm. It is the struggle of antagonistic principles, the solar divinities against the lunar divinities, the "combat" between man and woman, which must nevertheless result in re-creation.

In the arsenal of myths and rites are to be found the means of taming and controlling the forces of destruction and the dangers of the deterioration of the world.

M.A.E.F.M./j.l.

BIBLIOGRAPHY

See the bibliography at the end of the article "Mesoamerican Religion," especially section II: 14; section III: 26, 28, 40, 60; section IV: 11, 12, 13, 14, 17.

COSMIC DISORDER, ILLNESS, DEATH, AND MAGIC IN MESOAMERICAN TRADITIONS

I. Illness

To the Indians of Mesoamerica, illness was never a random occurrence; it was the sign of a disturbance of the relationship between man and the cosmos ruled by supernatural forces. Indigenous medicine therefore had two aspects: its religious nature, considered essential, which attempted to reestablish normal relationships between the patient and the gods, and its profane side, which tended to treat the simple material symptoms of the disorder.

Illness was due mainly to the punitive action of the gods, sanctioning lapses in the social or sacred order or in the rules for moral conduct or rituals. The stain of sin brought punishment sooner or later, whether it was for theft, adultery, improper use of sacred objects, failure to make offerings to the dead or to the gods, etc. Punishment could be inflicted by spirits of the earth, of the water, and especially of the air. These last were thought to transport impalpable noxious substances, often represented as tiny thorns, which could enter the body. But the action of the gods or the forces of nature might also be unleashed or directed by evil witchcraft and even by the more or less unconscious power emanating from certain individuals. One of the fatal consequences of this action is the loss of the soul, which escapes the body and is then held captive in unknown regions. This belief in the loss of the soul is still extremely widespread among the common people in Mexico and Guatemala. It is referred to in Spanish as "espanto," since it is believed to be easily triggered by emotion or shock.

The active or passive reactions of individuals to these fearful occurrences vary greatly. Individuals with strong personalities, notably those who have a strong animal as a double, easily resist supernatural aggression and are, in addition, gifted with a contingent malevolent power. Pregnant women and individuals who have the evil eye are formidable, sometimes without wanting to be. On the other hand, children have a natural weakness which makes them easy victims; they need to be surrounded with ritual precautions. Certain conditions such as bitterness (*mohina*) or apathy (*chipil*) are equally debilitating.

To the natives, the real treatment for illness is essentially a matter of religion and ritual. It consists above all in offerings and prayers to appease the wrath of supernatural beings. The cure for a disease sometimes includes sucking to extract the thorns of the disease. The reintegration of the soul into the body requires that it be sought at a great distance, brought back, and persuaded to return to its place. These are quasi-shamanistic activities which sometimes involve the use of hallucinogens.

The religious aspect of medicine, strongly linked to pagan beliefs, was evidently condemned by the Spanish authorities during the colonial period and was considered diabolic by the missionaries. It nevertheless survived, in the hands of the healers ("curanderos") who are priests, diviners, and magicians combined. Despite the reputation for witchcraft that is attached to their profession, some of them find clients not only among the rural Indians but often among the bourgeois mestizos of the city.

The other, more profane aspect of native medicine was advanced enough to merit the esteem and sometimes the admiration of the conquering Europeans. The Aztec were expert in the use of medicinal plants and knew how to let blood, set fractures, handle difficult births, etc. The Maya

Mixtec funerary vase. Zaachila, Oaxaca. Mexico City, National Anthropological Museum. Museum photo.

Even though the Indians admit that a fault of the patient must have been at the origin of his illness, they believe no less that the onset of the pathological process is generally caused by the practice of malevolent magic. So the healer is engaged in a battle, and he will not triumph unless he is stronger than the one who cast the spells. He can then be content with curing the patient, but he may also be asked to send the malevolence back to its author, and thereby engage in an act of sorcery properly so-called. The power of the healer is thus ambivalent. It restores a person's balance but may also destroy it. In the same way, despite his protestations, the healer is often taken for a sorcerer, which at times exposes him to reprisals.

Of course, there are specialists in malevolent magic, although they do not advertise themselves as such and they exercise their activities in the strictest secrecy. The indigenous society creates a favorable atmosphere for sympathetic magic. Sorcery offers an answer to the disorder caused by natural or economic constraints and to the obligations imposed by political and religious structures. It catalyzes, amplifies, and in a way resolves the anxiety and the social tensions created by jealousy, the true instrument of coercion against individuals who transgress the communal norm of poverty. Sorcerers are sometimes considered to exercise the law of justice. On the other hand, formidable magic powers are often attributed to native dignitaries. The accusation of sorcery is readily made against neighboring villages or neighboring peoples.

Sixteenth-century texts demonstrate that the Aztec had different sorts of sorcerers and necromancers. Some could change themselves into animals. Some claimed to engage in nocturnal activities as bloodsucking vampires. Others were thieves who put their victims to sleep, using an image of the god Quetzalcoatl and the left arm of a woman who died in her first childbirth. Still others used poisons or narcotics. There was also a love magic, which used aphrodisiac plants or symbolic birds. Indians and mestizos still believe that a man who wears a dead and dried hummingbird on his person will have a greater chance of success in amorous pursuits. Another form of magic was attributed to the Huastec, who were reported to be great conjurers. Finally, let us add that the sorcery indigenous to Mexico has been enriched by numerous European borrowings since the sixteenth century. Sometimes, as among the Tarascans, Indian sorcery was completely engulfed by the sorcery of the Spanish tradition.

In modern times, the rites of the Christian religion or European recipes for countermagic are often resorted to as protection against sorcery. But the traditional native practices still have followers.

III. Death

Ancient Mesoamerican civilization had two principal types of funeral practices: burial, which seems to have been the rule in the earliest periods, and incineration, which predominated among the Aztec and Otomi at the time of the Conquest. The latter custom seems to have been connected with fire cults and celestial gods; and clearly, among the Aztec and the Otomi, the dead who had been called by the gods of lightning and rain were buried.

For Mesoamerican Indians, death represents the final rupture of the balance between the components of the self, an irreversible separation of the elements from themselves. Drunkenness, dreams, and sexual activity provided anticipatory experiences of this state. Yet this explosion of the

were no less capable. Spanish medicine, with Francisco Hernandez and others, was enriched by its contact with Indian medicine, while at the same time communicating certain new ideas in return, such as the Hippocratic opposition of hot and cold.

But the "scientific" aspect of the indigenous medicine should not allow us to forget its religious foundation, which is seen even in the properties attributed to various remedies. Indian beliefs about illness are connected with the expiatory and painful aspects of the pre-Columbian ritual, aspects which survive to this day in certain flagellations during Holy Week.

II. Magic and Sorcery

The indigenous conception of illness made traditional medicine into an activity situated at the boundaries of religion, magic, and herbalism. The healer is, above all, a magician. Even while he is addressing the gods to ask for a cure, it is faith in his personal power that creates the belief that his prayer will be answered. When he uses hallucinogenic plants to go into a trance, he is straddling the boundary between magic and religion.

unity constituting a human being does not seem ever to have been viewed as leading to annihilation. Even the cremated dead were given a green stone that took the place of their "heart," that is, their soul or vital element. Buried corpses were thought to conserve a part of their energy. It was said that humanity had been created from bones taken from the world of the dead, crushed, and watered with blood by Quetzalcoatl. Death is therefore the source of life, as is illustrated in the famous bas-relief of the tomb of Palenque. Furthermore, death permits the element which survives it to enter into the sacred, but under variable conditions.

The idea of free will was foreign to the Mesoamerican mentality. The destiny of each individual in existence was essentially determined by the day of his birth, according to whether it was favorable or unfavorable. In the same way, the manner of his death was decided by the gods, and his destiny in the hereafter depended on his manner of death. We have details on Aztec traditions on this subject.

Most of the dead, for example, those who died of old age or of some illness, went to the subterranean world of the gods of death, the Mictlan. In order to get there, they had to complete a long journey fraught with terrible perils: mountains that collide, winds that cut like blades, serpents, etc. Finally, they had to swim across a terrible river, which could not be done without the help of a dog. A dog was therefore sacrificed or represented in effigy during the funeral rites. This concept of a subterranean world of the dead is certainly very old and was common to the entire Mesoamerican region.

Those called by Tlaloc, the god of lightning and rain, died from lightning, drowning, and edema. They joined him in a paradise of freshness and fertility called Tlalocan. They were buried with a stick of dry wood, which, in this delightful place, would immediately become covered with flowers and leaves. The idea of this paradise is attested in a famous fresco of Teotihuacan, dating from the middle of the first millennium A.D. The idea is still held today among certain native peoples, notably the Totonac.

Children who died young, before being weaned, went to the thirteenth heaven. There they found a tree whose fruits were shaped like breasts, from which they hung. This belief was shared by the Maya. As for the Nicaraos, Nahuas who emigrated to Central America toward the middle of the ninth century A.D., we know only that they believed that the souls of these little children were destined to be reincarnated, which does not seem incompatible with certain Central American beliefs. The tree of breasts, according to many traditions, was situated in the Aztec Tlalocan or its eastern Mayan equivalent.

A final celestial apotheosis was reserved for warriors killed in combat or on the sacrificial stone, as well as for women who died in childbirth. The women were considered to have fought with courage and to have taken a prisoner when they succumbed. All of these souls were thought to take part daily in the procession of the sun, men in the eastern sky, women in the night sky. The idea of a celestial abode reserved for the souls of warriors and women who died in childbirth may have developed most during the militaristic centuries of the Postclassical Period. The Nicaraos, however, ancient emigrants to Central America, also believed that the souls of warriors became companions of the sun, in the eastern sky.

A fundamental opposition seems therefore to have existed between men who died of more or less natural causes and

others. It may at first have been believed that these others had gone to a western paradise, from which they could climb up to the sky.

Whatever it was, the role of predestination in the ancient Mesoamerican beliefs about the afterlife left no room for metaphysical doubts. The almost obsessional question asked by the Aztec philosophical poets therefore seems all the more original:

Where are we going, alas, where are we going?

Is it death or life that awaits us there?
In the hereafter, will we be given the power to live again?
Will we again know the pleasure given by god, the giver of life?

Four centuries of Christianity have not yet brought an end to the old pre-Columbian foundation of beliefs about death. There are still Indians who create an effigy of a dog and bury it with the dead person to help him cross the underground river. In certain villages, people who die from drowning or lightning are still buried apart from the other dead because their final destinations are thought to be different.

Abodes in the Afterlife

Types of Death	Aztec	Nacaraos	Maya	Contemporary Totonac
Ordinary death	Subterranean world (after a long voyage)	Subterranean world	Subterranean world	Subterranean world (with retributional justice)
Drowned, struck by thunder, edema, etc.	Tlalocan, paradise of fertility	?	?	Aquatic realm of the God of Thunder and the Eastern Sea
Children who died young	Tree of milk in the thirteenth heaven or in Tlalocan	Possibility of reincarnation	Tree of milk in heaven	Western paradise (possibility of reincarnation)
Warriors killed in combat or in sacrifice	Celestial paradise of the rising sun	Celestial paradise of the rising sun	Celestial paradise	(Not known at present)
Women who died in childbirth	Celestial paradise of the setting sun	?	Celestial paradise	Celestial paradise

M. A. E. F. M./d.b.

BIBLIOGRAPHY

See the bibliography at the end of the article "Mesoamerican Religion," especially section II: 7, 15, 29, 33, 38; section III: 14, 16, 26, 33, 43, 56; section IV: 1, 6, 7, 13, 20, 21, 31, 37, 45.

MYTHS AND RITUALS OF THE SOUTH AMERICAN INDIANS

A serious attempt to report on the Indian religions of South America would not be possible without first mentioning, however briefly, certain general facts about the cultural terrain. Evident to the specialist, they should nevertheless be included here in order to help the general reader to approach the religion: can one understand the practices and beliefs of the South American Indians without first knowing how these people live and how their societies function? Let us recall what is only apparently a truism: South America is a continent whose immense area, with rare exceptions (such as the Atacama Desert in the extreme north of Chile), was entirely populated by people at the time of the discovery of America at the end of the fifteenth century. Moreover, this population was very old, going back almost thirty millennia, as the work of prehistorians attests. And it is important to observe that, contrary to recent widespread assumptions, the density of the indigenous population was relatively high. Demographic research, notably that carried out at the University of California at Berkeley, radically undercuts the "classical" point of view according to which South America, except for its Andean part, was nearly deserted. The antiquity of the population, its size (several tens of millions), and the size of its territory gave South America suitable conditions for a very large cultural and, therefore, religious differentiation.

What are the principal sociocultural characteristics, the essential ethnological determinants of the South American peoples? The territorial extension and consequent climatic variation established a succession of ecological environments and landscapes, from the humid equatorial forest in the north (the Amazonian basin) to the Patagonian savannas and the harsh climate of Tierra del Fuego. The differences in the natural environment demand specific human adaptations and create widely contrasting cultural models: settled farmers of the Andes, migratory slash-and-burn farmers, and nomadic hunter-gatherers. But it should be noted that the cultures of hunters are, in South America, very much in the minority. Their territory corresponds, essentially, to the zones where agriculture was impossible either because of the climate (Tierra del Fuego) or because of the nature of the vegetation (the Argentinian pampas, which have no forest). But everywhere else, wherever agriculture is possible with the indigenous technology (use of fire, the stone ax, the dibble, etc.), it exists, and has existed for several millennia, as the discoveries of archaeologists and ethnobotanists demonstrate. Agriculture, therefore, embraced the greater part of the South American continent. As for the few islets of societies of hunters which capriciously interrupt the monotony of the cultural landscape, it can be shown that the absence of agriculture results not from the persistence through time of a preagricultural mode of life, but rather from a loss. The Guayaki of Paraguay and the Siriono of Bolivia practiced slash-and-burn farming, like their neighbors. But as the result of various historical circumstances, they lost it in very early periods and therefore became hunter-gatherers once again. In other words, instead of an infinite variety of cultures, there is rather an enormous homogeneous block of societies with a similar mode of production.

But on the other hand, we know that to mark a principle of order in the diversity of peoples who inhabit a given region,

Araucanian shaman. Paris, Musée de l'Homme collection. Photo Mostuy.

to subject the multiplicity of their cultures to a primary classification, one would by preference call upon linguistic criteria. And then the image of a nearly perfect cultural unity disappears, that image suggested by the almost continental recurrence of nearly identical material bases. What is, in fact, the broad linguistic picture of South America? In perhaps no other region of the world is the parceling out of languages so extreme.

The great linguistic families are counted by tens, each of them consisting of a number of dialects that are so far removed from the mother language that the people who speak them cannot understand one another. Furthermore, a considerable number of languages have been recorded that are called "isolates" because they are impossible to integrate into the principal linguistic stocks. From this extraordinary linguistic differentiation a kind of cultural atomization results. The unity of language establishes, most often, the cultural unity of a people, the "style" of its civilization, the spirit of its culture. Here or there, doubtless, there are exceptions to this "rule." Thus the Guayaki, nomadic hunters, belong, from the point of view of their language, to the Tupi-Guarani linguistic branch, which encompasses farming tribes. Such aberrant cases are very rare and arise out of historic connections which are fairly easy to establish. One essential point should be borne in mind: the millions of Tupi-Guarani, for example, occupy an immense territory and speak the same language, with variations in dialect too slight to prevent communication. Despite the great distances that separate the most far-flung groups, cultural homogeneity is remarkable in socioeconomic life as much as in ritual activities or the structure of myths. Cultural unity in no way signifies political unity: the Tupi-Guarani tribes participate in the same cultural model without constituting a "nation," since they are in a permanent state of war among themselves.

But in recognizing this affinity between language and culture and in discovering in language the principle of unity of culture, one finds oneself by that same logic constrained to accept the immediate consequences of this relationship, i.e., that there should be as many cultural configurations, and therefore systems of beliefs, as languages. Each ethnic group has a particular ensemble of beliefs, rites, and myths. The problem then is methodological: one cannot simply adopt the illusory solution of a "dictionary" which would make the interminable list of known tribes and the teeming variety of their beliefs and practices fall into order. The difficulty of choosing a method of presenting religious data comes, in large part, from the contradiction between the cultural homogeneity on the socioeconomic plane and the irreducible heterogeneity on the cultural plane. For each ethnic group has and cultivates its particular personality, between the material bases and the "point of honor." Could one not discover, nevertheless, some lines of force capable of making decisions in an identity that is too abstract, some transversalities able to regroup differences that are too specific? Precisely such a partition among the Amerindian peoples is what struck the first Europeans landing in the New World: on the one hand, the societies of the Andes subjected to the imperial powers of the mighty machine of the Inca state and, on the other hand, the tribes that populate the remainder of the continent, forest Indians, Indians of the savanna and of the pampas, "people without faith, without law, without king," as the chroniclers of the sixteenth century called them. It is not surprising to learn that this European point of view, largely founded on the ethnocentrism of those who formulated it, echoed exactly the opinion that the Incas expressed about the populations which thronged the borders of the empire: these people were to them nothing but despicable savages, just good enough, if they were successfully subdued, to pay tribute to the king. And it is hardly surprising to find that the repugnance of the Incas for these forest people had much to do with customs that the Incas thought barbarous. It was, quite often, a question of ritual practices.

It is really this line that separates the indigenous peoples of South America: the peoples of the Andes and the others, the civilized and the savages or, in terms of traditional classification, the high cultures on the one hand, the forest civilizations on the other. The cultural (and beyond that, religious) difference is rooted as much in the mode of political functioning as in the mode of economic production. In other words, there is no substantial difference—from the point of view of rituals and myths—between hunters and farmers, who together form a homogeneous cultural block in contrast with the Andean world. This opposition, otherwise stated as that of societies without states (or primitive societies) and societies with states, at least makes it possible to structure the religious space of pre-Columbian South America and at the same time to ensure an economical arrangement of the account of that space. Thus, the first part of this account will be devoted to the religious world of primitive societies, where farmers and hunters are mixed. The presentation of Andean religion will occupy the second part: this will involve distinguishing two autonomous planes, one inherent in the very old tradition of peasant communities in this region, the other much more recent, resulting from the formation and expansion of the Inca state.

This will assure the "covering" of the two domains where the spirituality of the South American Indians is developed. However, though it is consistent with the general sociocultural dimensions of these societies, the bipartition of the

Village kraho in Brazil. Paris, Musée de l'Homme collection. Photo Arhex.

religious field does not offer a sufficiently exact image of its object. A number of ethnic groups that conform to the classical "primitive" model both in their mode of production and in their political institutions nevertheless deviate from this model precisely in the unusual, even puzzling, forms of their thought and religious practices. Such a deviation is pushed to its extreme by the Tupi-Guarani tribes, whose religious ethnography demands a special development which will constitute the third part of this account.

All the documents about Indian South America should be regarded as ethnographic source material. The available information is therefore quite abundant, since it began to be established at the time of the discovery. But it is at the same time incomplete: some tribes which have disappeared survive in name only. Even so, this lack is largely compensated for by the results of two decades of research in the field among populations that are hardly or not at all destroyed. Documents about primitive societies extending from the sixteenth-century chroniclers to the most recent work are at our disposal. As for the Andean religions, which were almost annihilated by the Spanish by the middle of the seventeenth century, they are known to us from the descriptions left by the companions of Pizarro and the first colonizers, to say nothing of the testimony gathered directly, soon after the Conquest, from the survivors of the Incan aristocracy.

P.C./d.f.

BIBLIOGRAPHY

The diversity of South American religions requires that the bibliographic citations be divided among the three major subjects treated in this work. See the articles "Indians of the South American Forest," "Religions and Cults of the Societies of the Andes," and "Religious Thought and Prophetism among the Tupi-Guarani Indians of South America," below.

INDIANS OF THE SOUTH AMERICAN FOREST

Travelers, missionaries, and ethnologists have often noted, either to their joy or to their dismay, the strong attachment of "primitive" people to their customs and traditions, or, to put it another way, their deep religiosity. Spending some time among an Amazonian society, for example, allows one to experience not only the piety of the Indians, but the way in which religious concerns so thoroughly pervade social life that the distinction between the secular and the religious seems to dissolve, and the boundary between the realm of the sacred and the domain of the profane disappears: nature, like society, is permeated with the supernatural. Thus, animals and plants may be both natural beings and supernatural agents: a falling tree that causes injury, or a snakebite, or the attack of a wild animal, or a shooting star will all be interpreted not as accidents but as the effects of deliberate aggression by supernatural powers such as forest spirits, souls of the dead, and enemy shamans. This resolute denial of both the role of chance and the discontinuity between the profane and the sacred should logically lead to the abolishment of the autonomy of the religious field, which is evident in all the individual and collective events of the ordinary life of the group. In fact, though it is never totally absent from the many facets of primitive culture, the religious dimension is affirmed as such in certain specific ritual circumstances. These will be more easily determined if we first isolate both the place and the function of the various divine figures.

I. The Gods

The European idea of religion defines the relationships between humans and gods, and more precisely, between men and God, in such a way that European evangelists and seekers were haunted, sometimes without their knowledge, by the conviction that there are no authentic religious occurrences outside monotheism. They therefore tried to discover either local versions of a great single god or the embryonic germ of the unity of the divine among the South American Indians. But ethnography shows us the vanity of this enterprise. The ritual practices of these peoples almost always take place, as we will see, without any implicit or explicit reference to a unique or central divine figure. In other words, the religious life, understood through its ritual realization, functions in a space exterior to what Western thought is accustomed to calling the realm of the divine: the "gods" are missing from the cults and rites which men celebrate because they are not intended for those celebrations. But does the absence of worship signify the absence of the gods? It used to be thought possible to discern some dominant divine figures here or there in the myths of various tribes. But who determines this dominance, who evaluates the hierarchy of these representations of the divine? Precisely those ethnologists, and more often those missionaries, who, steeped in the monotheistic illusion, imagine that their goal is achieved by the discovery of such and such a named divinity. Who are these "gods" which no cult comes to worship? Their names designate the visible celestial bodies: the sun, moon, stars, constellations metamorphosed from human beings to stars according to numerous myths; they are also named for "violent" natural phenomena: thunder, tempests, lightning. Very often the names of these gods refer not to nature but to culture: mythical founders of civilization, inventors of agriculture, culture heroes who are sometimes destined, once

their earthly mission is accomplished, to become celestial bodies or animals—the Twins, the mythic heroes of the Tupi-Guarani tribes, abandon the earth in order to transform themselves into the Sun and Moon. While the Sun, "our older brother," plays a very important part in the religious thought of the modern-day Guarani, he is not the object of any special cult. In other words, all of these gods are for the most part only names, more common than personal, and as such, indicators and designators of something beyond society, the Other of culture: the cosmic alterity of the skies and the celestial bodies; the earthly alterity of nearby nature. Above all, the original alterity of culture itself, the order of law as a social (or cultural) institution, is contemporaneous not with humans but with a time before humans. It has its origin in mythic prehuman time, and society finds its foundation outside itself, in the set of rules and instructions left to them by the great ancestors or culture heroes, who were often called Father, Grandfather, or Our Father. The name of this distant and abstract god, indifferent to the destiny of humans, this god without worship, that is, deprived of the usual relationship which unites gods to humans, is the name of the law. Inscribed in the heart of the society, this law guarantees to maintain its order and asks only that men respect the tradition. This is clearly what we learn from the example of the tribes of Tierra del Fuego, among whom Americanists have sometimes been tempted to recognize the most clearly developed figures of "savage" monotheism. In fact, Temaukel of the Ona or Watahinewa of the Yahgan gather under their names the intangible norms of social life left to men by these gods and taught to adolescents during the rites of initiation. In contrast to Andean societies, the other South American peoples never depict the gods. The only noteworthy exceptions are the *zemi*, or idols of the Taino-Arawak of the Antilles, and the divine images which were housed in the temples of certain tribes of Colombia and Venezuela. But historians of religions point to influences coming from Mesoamerica, in the first case, and the Andes, in the second case: or what are called the high cultures.

A religion without gods, like that of the South American Indians, is strange: the absence is so irritating that more than one missionary has proclaimed these people to be veritable atheists. Yet they are extremely religious people: but their religious sense, rather than being individual and private, is social and collective in that it is primarily concerned with the connections between society as the world of the living and that Other, the world of the dead.

II. The Rituals of Death

From the very start, we must avoid the confusion between the cult of ancestors and the cult of the dead. Native thought distinguishes clearly between the ancient dead and the recently dead, and each of these two categories of the nonliving calls for different treatment. Between the community of the living and the community of the ancestors there has been established a diachronic relationship marked by a break in temporal continuity and a synchronic relationship marked by the desire for cultural continuity. In other words, Indian thought situates the ancestors in a time before time, a time in which the events told in the myths took place—a primordial time in which the various moments of the foundation of the culture and the institution of the society took place, the veritable time of the ancestors with whom the souls of the ancient dead mingle, anonymous and separated from the living by a great genealogical depth. In addition, the society, instituted as such in the founding act of its mythic

Departure of a family into the forest (Kayapo). Brazil. Musée de l'Homme collection. Photo Caron.

ancestors, constantly reaffirms through the voice of its leaders and shamans and by means of ritual practices its desire to persevere in its cultural identity, that is, to conform to the norms and rules which were the legacy of the ancestors and transmitted by the myths. For this reason, the ancestors are often honored with rituals in circumstances which are determined. There it is revealed that, far from being assimilated to the dead, the ancestors and their mythic acts are thought to be the very life of the society.

The relationship with the dead is quite different. They are first of all the contemporaries of the living, those who are torn from the community by age or disease, the relatives and allies of the survivors. But though death extinguishes the body, it also brings into being, into autonomous existence, that which, for lack of a better term, we call the soul. According to the particular beliefs of each culture under consideration, the number of souls may vary: sometimes a single soul, sometimes two, occasionally more. But even when there are more than one, one of them becomes the spirit of the deceased person, a kind of living dead. The funeral rites properly so-called, insofar as they concern the dead body, are essentially designed to separate the souls of the dead definitively from the living: death liberates with it a flux of evil, aggressive powers against which the living must protect themselves. Since the souls do not wish to leave the village or camp, they wander, especially at night, near relatives and friends, for whom they become sources of danger, illness, and death. Just as the ancestors, as the

mythic founders of society, are marked with a positive sign and are therefore close to the community of their descendants, so the dead, as potential destroyers of this same society, are marked with a negative sign, so that the living wonder how to get rid of them.

It follows that one cannot speak of a cult of the dead among the peoples of South America: far from worshiping the dead, they are much more concerned with erasing all traces of their memory. This is why ceremonies like the "festival of the souls of the dead" of the Shipaya or the rites at which the Bororo call forth the dead (*aroe*) seem to refer more to the attempt to gain the goodwill of the ancient dead, or ancestors, than to any desire to celebrate the recent dead: with the ancestors, the community of the living tries to contract and reinforce an alliance which will guarantee its survival; against the dead, it puts various mechanisms of defense into effect as protection against their attacks.

What is done with the dead? Generally, their bodies are buried. Almost everywhere, in the area under consideration, the grave is a cylindrical hole, sometimes covered with a small roof of palms. There the body is left to decompose, usually in the fetal position, its face turned in the direction of the supposed dwelling place of souls. The almost total absence of cemeteries is due not to the periodic shifting of village sites, when the gardens become unproductive, but to the fundamental relationship of exclusion which separates the living and the dead. A cemetery is a fixed space reserved for the dead, whom one can therefore visit and who are in this way maintained permanently and in close proximity to the space of the living. But the principal concern of the Indians is to banish even the memory of the dead: how therefore could they reserve a special area, a cemetery, for them? This desire to break with the dead leads a number of these societies simply to abandon their village when someone dies, in order to put the greatest possible distance between the grave of the dead person and the space of the living. All the possessions of the deceased are burned or destroyed and a taboo cast against his name, which can never again be spoken. In short, the dead person is completely annihilated.

The belief that the dead are able to haunt the living to the point of anguish does not, however, imply a lack of emotion among the living: the various signs of mourning (shaved heads for women, for example, black paintings, prohibitions of sex or food, etc.) are not merely social, for the pain expressed is genuine. Nor is the burial of the dead perfunctory; it is done not in haste but according to the rules. For this reason, in a number of societies, the funeral rites take place in two stages. A most complex ceremonial cycle follows the burial of the dead among the Bororo: a ritual hunt, dances (among others the dance called the *mariddo*, performed by men who wear enormous rolls of leaves on their heads), and

chanting for a period of approximately two weeks. The skeleton, stripped of all flesh, is then exhumed, painted with *urucu*, and decorated with feathers. Placed in a basket, it is finally carried on parade to a nearby river and thrown in. The ancient Tupi-Guarani generally buried their dead in great funeral urns buried in the ground. Like the Bororo, they then exhumed the skeletons of famous chiefs or powerful shamans. Among the Guarani, the skeleton of a great shaman became the object of a cult. In Paraguay, the Guarani still retain the custom of occasionally keeping a child's skeleton: invoked in certain circumstances, it assures mediation with the gods and thus facilitates communication between humans and divinities.

III. Cannibalism

Certain societies, however, do not bury their dead; they eat them. This type of cannibalism must be distinguished from the more widespread practice reserved by several tribes for their prisoners of war, as when the Tupi-Guarani and the Carib executed and ritually consumed their captives. The act of eating one's own dead rather than the dead of the enemy is called endocannibalism. It can take many forms. The Yanomami of the Venezuelan Amazon region burn the

Tupinamba warriors. Engraving. Paris, Musée de l'Homme collection. Museum photo.

corpse on a pyre; they collect the bony fragments that are not consumed by the fire and grind them to powder. This will later be consumed, mixed with mashed bananas, by the relatives of the deceased. The Guayaki of Paraguay, on the other hand, roast the dismembered corpse over a wood grill. The flesh, accompanied by the pith of the *pindo* palm, is eaten by the entire tribe, with the exception of the family of the dead person. The bones are broken and burned or abandoned. The apparent effect of endocannibalism is a total integration of the dead with the living, since the one absorbs the other. We might therefore think that this funeral rite is diametrically opposed to the usual attitude of the Indians, which seeks to widen the distance between the living and dead to the fullest extent possible. But the contrast is merely apparent. In fact, endocannibalism pushes the separation of the living and the dead to the limit, in that the living, by eating the dead, go so far as to deprive them of a tomb, their final attachment to space: there is no longer any possibility of contact between the two groups. Endocannibalism therefore accomplishes in the most radical manner possible the mission assigned to funeral rites.

We see therefore how mistaken is the confusion between a cult of ancestors and a cult of the dead. Among the South American tribes, not only do no cults of the dead exist, since the dead are destined for complete oblivion, but, in addition, native thinking tends to regard its relationship with the world of mythic ancestors as positively as its relationship with the world of the actual dead is negative. Society seeks union, alliance, and inclusion with its ancestors and founders, while the community of the living keeps the community of the dead in a state of separation, rupture, and exclusion. The result is that any event that threatens to change a living person for the worse is logically seen as connected to the supreme change, death viewed as the division of the person into a corpse and a hostile spirit. Illness, as it involves a risk of death, concerns not only the individual destiny of the person but also the future of the community. For this reason, therapeutic undertakings are intended, beyond the cure of the sick person, for the protection of society. This is also why the medical act, because of the theory of illness that it embodies and by which it functions, is an essentially religious practice.

IV. Shamanism and Illness

As a physician, the shaman takes his place at the center of the religious life of the group which commissions him to ensure the good health of its members. How does one become sick? What is illness? The cause is related not to a natural agent but to a supernatural origin: aggression from such and such a spirit of nature, or from the soul of a person recently dead, the attack of a shaman from an enemy group, the transgression (voluntary or involuntary) of a food or sex taboo, etc. The Indian etiology immediately associates illness, as a corporeal problem, with the world of invisible forces: the shaman's task is to determine which of these forces is responsible for the illness. But, whatever the cause of the illness, whatever the perceivable symptoms, the form of the illness is almost always the same: it consists of the provisional anticipation of what death realizes definitively: the separation of the body and soul. Good health is maintained by the coexistence of body and soul unified in the person. Illness is therefore the loss of this unity through the departure of the soul. Treating the illness and restoring the health of the person is a matter of restoring the body-soul unity of the individual: as a physician, the shaman must

Shaman wearing a cap with small bells and holding a maraca. Musée de l'Homme collection. Photo Perrin.

discover where the soul is being held prisoner, free it from the captivity in which it is being held, and bring it back to the body of the patient.

The shaman. We must first resolutely discard the widespread conviction, unfortunately disseminated by certain ethnologists, that the shaman, who is essential to the life of every tribal society, is a kind of mentally ill person whom society takes charge of and saves from illness and a marginal existence by making him responsible for communication between this world and the world beyond, between the community and the supernatural. By transforming the psychopath into the physician, society is supposed to be able to integrate him while at the same time profiting from his gifts and thereby to block the probable development of his psychosis: the shaman, in this view, is no longer the physician of his tribe but a very sick person cared for by his society. Those who proffer such an absurd theory have obviously never seen a shaman.

In reality, the shaman is no different from his patients in any way save in having knowledge which he puts at their disposal. Gaining this knowledge does not depend on the personality of the shaman but on a long period of study and patient initiation. In other words, people are rarely predisposed to become shamans, so that at the outset, anyone who wishes can become a shaman. Some have this wish, some do not. Why might someone wish to become a shaman? An incident (dream, vision, strange encounter, etc.) might be interpreted as a sign that this is the path to follow, and the shaman's vocation is thereby revealed. The desire for prestige may also determine this professional choice: the reputation of a successful shaman may greatly exceed the confines of the group in which he exercises his talents. The warrior component of the shaman's activities seems to be a much greater determining factor, however; the wish to have the power of a shaman, a power which will be exerted not on humans but on the enemies of humans—the innumerable hosts of invisible powers, spirits, souls, and demons. The shaman confronts these as a warrior, and as such he hopes both to conquer them and to restore the health of the patient.

Certain tribes (for example in the Chaco) repay the shaman for his medical practices with gifts of food, fabric, feathers, ornaments, etc. Though the shaman has considerable status throughout the South American tribes, the exercise of his profession is not without its risks. As master of the life to which his powers may restore the sick, he is also master of death: these same powers are thought to confer upon him the power to attract death to others, and he is believed to be able to kill as well as cure, although not through personal malevolence or perversity. The figure of the wicked sorcerer who casts spells is rare in South America. But if a shaman suffers several successive failures in his cures, or if inexplicable events begin to occur in his society, the guilty party is quickly discovered to be the shaman himself. If he fails to cure his patients, it is said to be because he did not want to cure them. If an epidemic breaks out or a curious death takes place, the shaman has no doubt entered into an alliance with evil spirits in order to terrorize the community. He is therefore a character of uncertain fate: at times having great prestige, but at the same time responsible in advance for the ills of the group, an official scapegoat for guilt. And let us not underestimate the risk the shaman runs—the usual penalty is death.

As a general rule, shamans are men. Certain exceptions are known, however: among the tribes of the Chaco (Abipon, Mocovi, Toba, etc.), for example, or among the Mapuche of Chile, or the Guajiro of Venezuela, this function is often filled by women, who distinguish themselves no less than their male counterparts. Once the candidate is assured of a shamanic vocation, the young person undertakes his professional training. The training is of variable duration (from several weeks to several years) and is generally acquired under the direction of another shaman who has been established for a long time, although it may be the soul of a dead shaman who undertakes the teaching of the novice (as among the Campa of Peru). Among the Carib of Suriname, there are schools for shamans. The instruction of shaman apprentices takes the form of an initiation: since the illnesses which they plan to treat are due to the effects of supernatural powers upon the body, they must acquire the various means to deal with these forces in order to control, manipulate, and neutralize them. The shaman's preparation is thus designed to help him acquire the protection of one or more spirit guardians who will be his auxiliaries in his therapeutic endeavors. The goal of the apprenticeship is to put the soul of the novice in direct contact with the world of the spirits. This often leads to what is called a trance: the moment when the young person knows that the invisible forces have recognized him as a shaman, knows the identity of his spirit guardian, and receives the chant which will thereafter accompany all his cures. To allow the soul initiatory access to the supernatural world, the body must be abolished in some way. For this reason the shaman's training includes asceticism of the body: through prolonged fasting, continual sleep deprivation, isolation in the forest or the brush, massive absorption of smoke or tobacco juice (Tupi-Guarani, Chaco tribes, etc.) or hallucinogenic drugs (Amazonian northwest),

the apprentice reaches such a state of physical exhaustion and bodily ruin that he seems almost to experience death. At that time, the soul, freed from its earthly weight, its bodily burden lightened, at last finds itself on the same footing with the supernatural: at the ultimate moment of the trance, in the vision sent to him from the invisible world, the young apprentice is initiated into the knowledge which will henceforth make him a shaman.

V. Therapies, Travel, Drugs

As we have seen, native thought states that illness (with the exclusion of all the diseases introduced into the Americas from Europe) is a rupture of the soul-body unity of the individual, and the cure is the restoration of this unity. It follows that the shaman, as a physician, is a traveler: he must go out in search of the soul which is being held captive by the evil spirits. Aided by his auxiliary spirit, he undertakes a long voyage of exploration in the invisible world, fights the keepers of the soul, and restores it to the body of his patient. For each cure, therefore, the initiatory voyage which first helped the shaman to acquire his powers must be repeated: the shaman must put himself in a trance state, exalting his spirit and lightening his body. Moreover, the treatment or the preparation for this voyage hardly ever takes place without the consumption of large quantities of tobacco, either smoked or drunk as juice, or of various drugs, cultivated above all in the west and northwest Amazon regions where the Indians use them extensively. For certain groups, such as the Guarani, the soul, as a principle of individuation which makes the living body a person, is identified with the proper name: the soul is the name. A particularly serious illness may be diagnosed as an inadequacy in the name of the sick person: the error in naming is therefore the cause of the illness, as the patient does not possess the soul name which is right for him. The shaman must therefore undertake a voyage to discover the true name of the patient. When the gods have communicated it to him, he tells it to the patient and his relatives. The patient's recovery is proof that he has succeeded in finding the right name.

While his spirit is searching for the lost soul (sometimes traveling a great distance, even to the sun), the shaman dances and sings around the patient, who is either seated in a chair or stretched out on the ground. In many societies, the shaman marks the rhythm of his dancing and chanting with a rattle (maraca), which is both a musical instrument and the voice of the spirits with whom he is conversing. Depending on the nature of the problem diagnosed (the identity of the spirit who has captured the soul), the shaman may also need to metamorphose himself in order to effect a cure: sometimes he transforms himself into a jaguar, serpent, or bird. From time to time, he interrupts his movement to blow on the patient (often tobacco smoke), massage him, or suck the painful area. Everywhere the breath and the saliva of the shaman are reputed to have great power. When the lost soul has been reintegrated into the sick body, the patient is healed and the cure is ended. The shaman often proves his success by exhibiting, at the end of the cure, a foreign substance which he has succeeded in extracting from the patient's body: a thorn, small stone, feather, etc., which he has kept in his mouth. The absence of the soul and the presence of a foreign body are not two different causes of the illness. Much more often, it seems, in the place vacated by the capture of the soul the evil spirits leave an object which, by its very presence, attests to the absence of the soul. The reinsertion

Sacred hut where provisions for feast days are kept. Orinoco Guaraúnos region (Venezuela). Paris, Musée de l'Homme collection. Museum photo.

of the soul is therefore, by the same logic, publicly indicated by the extraction of a perceptible, palpable object which guarantees the reality of his cure to the patient and proves the competence of the shaman.

Although essential, the therapeutic role is not the only function of the shaman. We have already indicated the difficulty in drawing a clear line between the social and the religious, the profane and the sacred, the ordinary and the supernatural among Indian cultures. This means that the shaman's intervention is constantly called for by the different events which punctuate both individual lives and the life of the community. He is called upon to interpret dreams and visions, to decide whether a sign is favorable or not (for example when a war expedition is being planned against an enemy tribe). In this last case, the shaman may act as a sorcerer or caster of spells: he is capable of sending maladies down upon the enemies which will weaken or even kill them. In short, there is no ritual activity of importance in which the shaman does not play a decisive role.

VI. Rites and Ceremonies

The religious life of the societies under consideration cannot be reduced to the ritualization of their relationship to the dead or to illness. Of equal importance is the celebration of life, not only in its natural manifestations (the birth of a child), but also in its more properly social aspects (rites of passage). In accordance with the profound religious sense of these peoples, the religious sphere takes into account and pervades the great stages of individual destiny in order to deploy them in socioritual events.

Birth. The birth of a child is much more than a biological matter. It concerns not only the father and mother of the newborn child but the entire community, precisely because of its implications and its religious effects. The coming into existence of an additional member of the group upsets the cosmic order. The surplus life, through the imbalance it creates, provokes the awakening of all sorts of powers from which the group must protect the child, as they are the powers of death and hostile to all new life. This attempt at protection is expressed (before and after the birth) in numerous rites of purification, food taboos, sexual prohibitions, ritual hunts, songs, dances, etc., all of which are performed in the certainty that the infant's life would be threatened by death if they were not done. The couvade, practiced by all the Tupi-Guarani tribes, has particularly attracted the attention of observers: the father of the child, from the time of childbirth, lies in his hammock and fasts there until the umbilical cord falls off; unless he does so, the mother and the child risk serious danger. Among the Guayaki, a birth, through the cosmic disorder it causes, threatens not only the child but his father: under penalty of being devoured by a jaguar, he must go into the forest and kill a wild animal. The death of the child is, of course, attributed to man's defeat by these evil powers.

Initiation. It is not surprising that there is a structural analogy between the rites associated with birth and those which sanction the passage of boys and girls to adulthood. The passage is immediately comprehensible on two levels: first it marks the social recognition of the biological maturity of individuals who can no longer be considered children; then it expresses the group's acceptance of the entrance of the new adults into its midst and of the full and complete participation of these young people in society. But the break with the world of childhood is recognized in native thought and expressed in the ritual as a death and rebirth: to become an adult means to die to childhood and to be born to social life, since from that moment on, girls and boys may freely express their sexuality. This is why the rites of passage, like the rites of birth, take place in an extremely dramatic atmosphere. The community of adults at first pretends to withhold recognition of the new members, resists accepting them as equals, making as if to see them as rivals or enemies. But the community also wishes, through the ritual practice, to show the young people that their pride in attaining the age of adulthood is at the cost of an irremedial loss, the loss of the carefree, happy world of childhood. In a great many South American societies, therefore, the rites of passage include a component of very painful physical testing, a dimension of cruelty and pain which makes this passage an unforgettable event: tattooing, scarification, whippings, stinging by wasps or ants, etc., which the young initiates must endure in the strictest silence: they faint, but without a sound. This pseudodeath, this provisional death (unconsciousness deliberately induced by the masters of the ritual), shows clearly the structural identity which Indian belief establishes between birth and passage: that of a rebirth, a repetition of the first birth which must therefore be preceded by a symbolic death.

VII. Myth and Society

We know, on the other hand, that the rites of passage are also identified as rituals of initiation. Every initiatory step is

Mask worn during the banana festival. Tapirare. Paris, Musée de l'Homme collection. Museum photo.

designed to bring the postulant from a state of ignorance to a state of knowledge; its goal is to conduct him to the revelation of a truth, to the communication of knowledge. What knowledge do the rituals of the South American Indians communicate to the young people, which truth do they reveal, to what understanding do they initiate them? The teaching involved in the initiatory rites does not concern the interpersonal relationship which unites master and disciple, nor is it a matter of an individual adventure. What is involved is the social per se, society in itself, on the one hand, and the young people who will belong fully to this same society, on the other. In other words, the rites of passage, as initiatory rites, are intended to communicate to the young people a knowledge of the society that is preparing to welcome them. This says little: the knowledge acquired through initiation is not, in fact, knowledge *about* the society, and therefore knowledge exterior to it. It is necessarily the knowledge *of* the society itself, a knowledge that is immanent to it and, as such, constitutes the very substance of the society, its substantial Self, that which it is in itself. In the initiatory rite, the young people receive from society—represented by the organizers of the ritual—the knowledge of what is, in its being, society, what constitutes it, institutes it as itself: the universe of its laws and standards, the

ethico-political universe of its law. The teaching of this law, and, consequently, the requirement of fidelity to this law, will assure the continuity and permanence of the very being of society.

VIII. Myth and Foundation

But what is the origin of the law as a foundation for society, who promulgated it, who was its legislator? Native belief, we have already seen, saw the relationship between society and its foundation (that is, between society and native belief itself) as a relationship of exteriority. Or, in other words, society, though perhaps self-reproducing, is not self-founding. The function of assuring the self-reproduction of society, the repetition of its Self, in accordance with the rules and standards traditionally in force, has particularly devolved upon the rites of initiation. But the founding act of the social, the institution of the society, comes from the presocial or metasocial: this is the work of those who preceded men, in a time before human time, the work of the ancestors. And myth, as a story of the great deed that founded society, the deed of the ancestors, constitutes the foundation of society, the storehouse of its maxims, standards, and laws, the very sum of knowledge transmitted to the young people during the ritual of initiation.

In summary, then, the initiatory dimension of rites of passage lies in the truth toward which the initiates are led; this truth acknowledges the foundation of society, under the auspices of its organic law, and this self-knowledge of the society affirms its own origin in the founding deed of its ancestors, who are chronicled in its myths. This is why the ancestors are necessarily, implicitly or explicitly, involved and present on the level of the concrete process of the moments of the ritual. They are the ones from whom the young people are preparing to receive their instruction. Major figures in every rite of initiation, the ancestors are the real object of worship in the rites of passage: the true worship of the mythic ancestors or culture heroes consists in the rites of initiation which have for so long held a central importance in the religious life of the Amerindian peoples.

Among the Yahgan of Tierra del Fuego, the special moment in religious life was the initiation rite of girls and boys: it consisted essentially of teaching the initiates the traditional rules of the society, instituted in mythic times by Watahinewa, the culture hero and great ancestor. Among the Bororo, the souls (*aroe*) are invited by a particular group of shamans (*aroettaware*) to participate in certain ceremonies, including the initiation of the young, whose passage to adulthood and entrance into the social world is thus supervised under the aegis of the founding ancestors. In the same way, the Cubeo of Brazil link the initiation of boys to the invocation of the ancestors, represented on this occasion by great trumpets, elsewhere by calabash maracas. It is also most probable that among the tribes of the northwest Amazon (Tucano, Witoto, Yagua, Tucuno, etc.) or the Upper Xingu (Kamayura, Aweto, Bacairi, etc.) or the Araguaia (Caraja, Javae) who represent their gods in the form of masks worn by male dancers, these masks, like the musical instruments, symbolize not only the spirits of the forest or the rivers, but also the ancestors.

The tribal societies of South America are completely absorbed in their religious and ritual lives which function as an unceasing affirmation of the community Self. Each ceremony is a new occasion to remember that if society is good, viable, it is by virtue of the respect for standards established long ago by the ancestors. We therefore understand why the reference to the ancestors is logically implied in the initiatory rites: the mythic discourse, the word of the ancestors and the ancestors alone, guarantees the perpetuity of society and its eternal repetition.

P.C./d.b.

BIBLIOGRAPHY

E. BIOCCA, *Yanoama* (London 1969), in several languages. A. BUTT, "Réalité et idéal dans la pratique chamanique," *L'homme*, 2, no. 3 (1962). P. CLASTRES, *Chronique des Indiens Guayaki* (Paris 1972). A. COLBACCHINI and C. ALBISETTI, *Os Bororos Orientais* (São Paulo 1942). M. DOBRIZHOFER, *An Account of the Abipones* (London 1822), in several languages, originally in Latin. R. GIRARD, *Les Indiens de l'Amazonie péruvienne* (Paris 1963), originally in Spanish. J. GUMILLA, *El Orinoco Ilustrado y Defendido* (Caracas 1963). M. GUSINDE, *Die Feuerland-Indianer*, 3 vols. (Vienna 1931–39). *Handbook of South American Indians*, Smithsonian Institution, vols. 1, 3, 4 (Washington 1946). F. HUXLEY, *Affable Savages* (London 1956). C. LÉVI-STRAUSS, *Mythologiques*, 4 vols. (Paris 1966–71). J. LIZOT, *Le cercle des feux* (Paris 1976). P. LOZANO, *Descripcion corografica del Gran Chaco Gualamba* (Tucuman 1941). A. METRAUX, *Religions et magies indiennes d'Amérique du Sud* (Paris 1967). M. PERRIN, *Le chemin des Indiens morts* (Paris 1976). G. REICHEL-DOLMATOFF, *Amazonian Cosmos* (Chicago 1971). L. SEBAG, "Le Chamanisme ayoreo," *L'homme*, 5, nos. 1 and 2.

RELIGIONS AND CULTS OF THE SOCIETIES OF THE ANDES

In entering the Andean world, one reaches a cultural horizon, a religious space which is very different from that of the inhabitants of the forests. For these people, although in large part farmers, the specific importance of the natural food resources remains very considerable: hunting, fishing, gathering. Nature as such is not abolished by gardens, and the forest tribes rely as much on wild fauna and plants as on cultivated plants. Their technology is by no means deficient—it would suffice for them to increase the surface of the cultivated land; but less effort is required for the "predatory" exploitation of the ecological environment, which is often very generous (game, fish, roots, berries, and fruits). The techno-ecological relationship that the Andean peoples maintain with their natural environment follows another line altogether: they are all farmers and almost exclusively farmers, in the sense that wild resources count very little for them. That is, the Indians of the Andes establish a relationship with the earth which is infinitely more intense than that of the Amazonian Indians. For them the earth is really the nourishing mother, and naturally that has a profound effect upon religious life and ritual practice. From the point of view of the real and symbolic occupation of space, the forest Indians are people of territory, while those of the Andes are people of the land: they are, in other words, peasants.

This rooting in the land is very ancient in the Andes, where agriculture is attested from the third millennium B.C. Its exceptional development is exemplified by the very advanced specialization of its cultural techniques, the abundance of irrigation works, and the astonishing variety of vegetable species. These species were obtained by selection and adapted to different ecological levels, which are tiered from sea level to the high central plain. Andean societies are distinguished on the South American horizon by a characteristic that is elsewhere absent: they are hierarchical, stratified, divided along a vertical axis of political power. Aristocracies or religious and military castes reign over a mass of peasants who have to pay them tribute. This division of the social body into dominators and dominated is very old in the Andes, as archaeological research has established. The Chavín civilization, dating from the beginning of the first millennium B.C., shows that the habitat had already become urban and that social life was organized around temples, ritual sites, and places of pilgrimage, under the aegis of priests. The history of the Andes appears to be, from this epoch, a succession of empires strongly tinged by theocratism, of which the last and best known was that of the Incas. For the pre-Incan Andean religions, only fragmentary information remains, furnished by the funerary contents of tombs, the surviving monuments, the textiles and the ceramics, etc. The Inca period, which extended from the thirteenth century to the arrival of the Spanish, is naturally better known, thanks to abundant archaeological documents but also from the descriptions of chroniclers and the reports of missionaries who systematically undertook to wipe out the idolatry and convert the Indians to Christianity.

The establishment and the expansion of the Inca empire, as could be expected, modified the religious face of the Andes without, however, profoundly altering it. In fact, the political imperialism of the Incas was at the same time cultural and particularly religious, since the subjected peoples were forced not only to recognize the authority of the emperor but to accept the religion of their conquerors. Yet the Incas tried hardly at all to substitute their own body of beliefs for that of the populations which were integrated into the empire: they never tried to wipe out local cults or rites. That is why two great religious systems are found in the Andes at this period: the religion of the Incas, properly speaking, whose diffusion kept pace with political expansion, and the local religions, which thrived long before the rise of the Inca state.

I. The Popular Religion

The popular religion clearly expresses the relationship of the Andean Indians to the world: it is essentially a religion of peasants, an agrarian religion, whether it belongs to the people of the seacoast or the inhabitants of the plateau. The principal preoccupation of the Andean Indians was to reconcile all the forces which presided over the regular repetition of the cycle of seasons and assured the abundance of harvests and the fertility of herds of llamas. This is surely why, beyond local peculiarities, pan-Andean cults and beliefs encompass the seacoast and the plateau, or the Quechua and the Aymara and the Mochica.

II. The Gods

The natural elements that rule over the daily life of these peasant peoples (the sun and the moon, often thought of as brother and sister and simultaneously as spouses; the evening and morning stars; the rainbow; the Pacha-Mama, mother earth . . .) are exalted to the status of divine powers. All these divine figures were the objects of cults and of imposing ceremonies, as we will see. The essential Andean agricultural plant, corn, is represented by numerous images of gold, silver, or stone: they are the *sara-mama*, corn mothers, from whom the abundance of the harvest is expected. These divinities are honored with offerings, libations (drinks of fermented corn), or sacrifices (particularly the immolation of llamas, whose blood is sprinkled on the cornfields and anoints the faces of the participants in the ritual).

III. The Cults of Ancestors and of the Dead

The cults of the ancestors and of the dead show the distance which separates the forest tribes from the Andean peoples. Among the former, as has been noted, the ancestors are not the dead who are the contemporaries of the living, but mythical founders of society. In the Andes, by contrast, the socioreligious life of the community rests in large part on the cult of both the ancestors and the dead: the latter were the descendants of the former, and Andean thought, in contrast with Amazonian thought, strives to mark the continuity between the world of the living and the world of the dead, a continuity of the peasant community which occupies the same soil under the protection of its gods and of its dead. The mythical ancestor was frequently represented by a rock, *markayok*, venerated as much as the place, *pakarina*, through which the ancestor came out from the subterranean world. Each community or *ayllu* thus had its ancestor and worshiped him: *markayok* and *pakarina*, attesting to the permanence and the identity, through time, of the *ayllu*, established the solidarity of the families that comprised the community.

While the funerary rites of the forest Indians tend to abolish the dead, to cast them into oblivion, the Andean Indians, by contrast, place them in cemeteries: the tombs were grouped in the shelter of caverns, or in a kind of cave built in the form of a tower, or in holes dug into cliffs. They continued to participate in the collective life, because relatives came to visit them to consult them, regular offerings maintained their well-being, and sacrifices were offered to them. Far from forgetting their dead, the Indians of the Andes did everything possible so that the dead would not forget the living but would guard their prosperity: a relationship of alliance and of inclusion, not one of exclusion and hostility as in the forest. This is why, as the Spanish priests charged with wiping out idolatry said, the real dead, in the form of skeletons or of mummies (*malqui*), were, like the mythical dead, the objects of cults and veneration: in certain ceremonial circumstances, they were ornamented with precious feathers and textiles.

The Huaca

Huaca is the name that the Indians gave to every being or natural object supposed to contain a supernatural force. The sacred stones representing the ancestors were *huaca*, as were the mummified dead. But *huaca* were also the idols and the sites where they were found, a mountain or a plant, a spring or a grotto, a child born malformed, a temple, a constellation, or a tomb. On a journey, the special sites, such as a mountain pass or a stopping point, were marked by piles of stones, *apacheta*, which travelers also regarded as *huaca*: they added their own rock to it and offered a quid of coca in sacrifice. Space was thus entirely quartered off by the supernatural, and the system of the *huaca* constituted a kind of sacred coding of the world.

To the group of the *huaca* belong not only the points of contact between spatial expanse and the sphere of the

Mochican vase with a representation of a human sacrifice. Paris, Musée de l'Homme collection. Museum photo.

sacred, but also objects, figurines, and amulets which represent the tutelary powers of each family. These are the *conopa:* sometimes rocks in strange forms or colors, sometimes carved or molded statuettes in the form of a llama or an ear of corn. The familial *conopa* remain under cover in houses whose occupants they protect from disease, or they are buried in fields, guaranteeing their fertility. The communal *conopa* (those of the *ayllu*) were, at certain times of the year, taken out of their hiding places: homage was given, sacrifices of llamas or coca were offered, and prayers were addressed to them.

There was in each community at least one curer or shaman. He was often designated by the thunder god, who struck him with the thunderbolt. Besides his therapeutic functions, he fulfilled the office of diviner. But, unlike the forest tribes, shamanism in the Andes was not the center of religious life. That was developed in a set of ritual practices all of which tended to ask the gods, the ancestors, the dead (all the forces that were called *huaca*) to assure the well-being of the *ayllu* by guaranteeing the prosperity of mother earth. This eminently agrarian religion expresses the profound investment of the peasant in his soil, which it is the mission of the diviners to guard.

IV. Inca Religion

In its origin and its substance, Inca religion does not differ profoundly from the so-called popular religion. In the thirteenth century A.D., the Incas were a small tribe of the region of Cuzco. Farmers and herders, their religious and ritual life was rooted, like those of all the peasant communities of the coast or the plateau, in a desire for the repetition of cosmic order, for the eternal return of this order, and in the hope that through the rituals that celebrated them and the sacrifices that were offered to them, the divine forces, the ancestors, and the dead would guarantee to humans the fertility of the earth and the permanence of society. For reasons which remain mysterious, the Inca tribe inaugurated in the thirteenth century a march of conquest which was stopped only by the arrival of the Spanish. But during this relatively short period, the Incas greatly expanded the boundaries of their empire (which numbered between twelve and fifteen million inhabitants in 1530) and built an astonishing power machine, a state apparatus which still amazes us by the "modernity" of its institutions.

The imperial society, inscribed in a rigorously hierarchical pyramid, expresses first the radical division between the triumphant aristocracy of the Incas and the masses of people, ethnic groups, and tribes integrated into the empire whose power they recognized by the tribute they paid. At the summit of this hierarchy the monarch reigned, the Inca, simultaneously the chief of his ethnic group, the master of the empire, and the representative on earth of the principal divine power. It would be a mistake to believe that the politico-military expansionism of the Incas was accompanied by religious proselytism, so that they imposed their own system upon the peoples whom they subjugated, by eliminating the traditional beliefs and rituals of the conquered people. First of all, in its essential outlines the religion of the Incas scarcely differed from that of their tributaries: moreover, their enterprise of domination aimed only to obtain the obedience of their subjects and not, as did the Spanish, to wipe out their "idolatry." In fact, they let the traditional religious "code" survive, in order to superimpose upon it a "supercode" consisting of their own religion: freedom of religion was left to the vassals of the Incas, on condition that, in addition, they recognize and honor the gods of their conquerors.

The conquerors, as their power gradually increased, proceeded to renovate their old system of beliefs by exalting certain figures of their pantheon, by giving a grandiose character to their festivals and traditional ceremonies, by conferring a considerable sociopolitical weight upon the religion through the institution of a numerous and highly hierarchical clergy, through the construction of temples and multiple sites of cults, and through the allocation to the clergy of an important part of the tribute paid to the Incas by their subjects.

V. The Cult of the Sun

The solar star, Inti, stands out as a major figure of the Inca pantheon by virtue of a double logic: that of the tradition which for a long time had made the sun a pan-Peruvian divinity; and that of the sociopolitical innovation which, through the institution of an imperial system, incorporated practically all the archaic despotisms and led to the identification of the master of the empire with the sun. This is why the sun became the principal Inca god, as the great founding

ancestor of the royal lineage: the emperors were the children of the sun. Also, the worship of the sun had the value of both a dynastic ancestor cult and an official religion imposed on everyone: it was through the cult of the sun that Inca religion became a state religion.

When the Incas obtained the submission of an ethnic group, they immediately took a number of administrative measures (a census of the population, of resources, etc.) and religious measures: the conquered people had to integrate the cult of Inti into their religious system. This involved setting up a ritual infrastructure consisting of the temples that had to be built, the clergy destined to officiate at them, and, of course, the gift of important resources to the clergy which would ensure their subsistence and allow them to perform the sacrifices required for the worship of the sun. We know that for each subjugated community the Incas established a tripartition of the lands: one part remained at the disposition of the *ayllu*, another was allocated to the state, and the third was consecrated to the sun. The construction of numerous temples of the sun built in the provinces followed the model of the most famous among them, that of the imperial capital, Coricancha, the true religious and political center of the empire and the site of the cult and pilgrimage, where the mummies of past emperors were found. The wall enclosing Coricancha had a rectangular plan and was four hundred meters long. All along the carefully executed masonry ran a band of fine golden plates thirty to forty centimeters high. Coricancha sheltered diverse sanctuaries filled with golden or silver offerings and the lodgings of the numerous personnel designated for the service of the temple. There was also a garden planted with stalks of golden corn. By working ritually in this garden, the Inca himself opened the season of sowing in the empire.

Besides the hierarchical group of priests, diviners, and servants, the personnel of each sun temple included a group of women, the virgins of the sun, the *Aclla*, chosen from the entire empire by royal functionaries, who selected them for their grace and beauty. Assembled and educated in convent-like institutions (*aclla-huasi*), they learned to make luxurious fabrics of vicuña or alpaca, offered in enormous quantities during sacrifices; they prepared the *chicha*, a drink of fermented corn which was required for all ceremonies. Though they were, like the vestal virgins, pledged to absolute chastity, the Inca nevertheless chose from among them his concubines or women whom he gave as gifts to great men of the empire whom he wished to recompense. A certain number of them were sacrificed in times of crisis: the succession of a new emperor, the serious illness or death of the Inca, an earthquake, etc. Four thousand persons, it is said, composed the personnel of Coricancha, of whom more than fifteen hundred were virgins of the sun. In each temple, the virgins were subject to the authority of a matron, Mama Cuna, regarded as the wife of the sun. At the summit of the religious hierarchy of the empire was the great priest of the sun, the Vilca Oma, the uncle or brother of the emperor, who lived ascetically in Coricancha where he directed the religious life of the empire.

VI. The Cult of Viracocha

Viracocha was an anthropomorphic divine figure, both very ancient and pan-Peruvian, since he was known and honored both by the Aymara and by the Quechua. Throughout the often obscure myths that are dedicated to Viracocha, one can make out the image of the eternal god, creator of all

Kenko ceremonial hemicycle. Paris, Musée de l'Homme collection. Photo Metais.

Cuzco. On the right, the Accla Huasi (Convent of the Virgins), and on the left, the Amaru Kancha (Temple of Huayna Capac). Paris, Musée de l'Homme collection. Museum photo.

things (sky and earth, sun and moon, day and night), and of the civilizing hero. When he had created and destroyed several successive humanities, he engendered the people of the present day, to whom he assigned their respective territories, and taught the arts which would make it possible for them to live and the norms whose observance would assure social and cosmic good order. Once his duty was accomplished, Viracocha, on arriving at the seacoast, trans-

formed his coat into a boat and disappeared forever, heading west. From the time of their first contacts with the Spanish, the Indians called them *viracochas*.

The Incas imposed the cult of their ethnic god, the sun, upon their entire empire. By an inverse course, they transformed Viracocha, a pan-Andean figure, into a tribal god. It was under the reign of the great emperor Pachacuti (who reigned from 1438 to 1471) that this alteration in the hierarchy of the Inca pantheon can be precisely fixed, at the end of which Inti ceded the central position to Viracocha, although the emperor remained the descendant of the sun. The preeminence accorded to Viracocha may have been the cumulative effect of several factors: the theological work of priests seeking a more fundamental religious presence than that of anything visible, even the sun; the personal belief of Pachacuti himself, whom Viracocha, in a dream, helped to win an essential military victory over the Chanca; and, the final factor, the logic immanent, perhaps, in every despotic system, such that its theocratic vocation tends occasionally to be realized in the affirmation and institution of monotheism.

In any case, this was the course Pachacuti followed when he built a temple at Cuzco to Viracocha, where the god was represented in the form of a solid gold statue, "the size of a ten-year-old child." In each provincial capital, a sanctuary was built to Viracocha, tended by a clergy consecrated to his exclusive service and with resources destined to assure the maintenance of the temple and the priests. The cult of Viracocha—ancient Lord, distant Lord, very excellent Lord—never became a popular cult, like that of the sun. Perhaps the Incas did not maintain it because, among other things, they were anxious to institute a more abstract, more esoteric cult, a cult less rooted in the perceptible world than were the popular cults, in order to mark, even on a religious plane, the specific feature of their dominant caste. This is why the cult of Viracocha, unlike the popular cults, did not survive for a single instant the fall of the empire.

VII. The Cult of Thunder and the *Huaca*

Illapa, thunder, was also a pan-Andean figure of the Inca pantheon. Master of the storm, of hail, of lightning, and of rain, he produced his rumbling in the sky by snapping his sling. The Andean peoples, as farmers, were very attentive to the activities of Illapa, whom they begged to grant them sufficient rain and to whom they offered large sacrifices in the event of drought. The agrarian character of Andean societies explains the superior position, after Viracocha and Inti, of Illapa in the Inca pantheon.

For the caste of the Incas, as for the peasant masses, the *huaca* constituted a sacred "grid" of space. To the popular network of the *huaca*, the Incas added their own system, defined in sanctified places by a real or imaginary bond between the person of the emperor and any place through which he passed or of which he dreamed. Whatever they were, the *huaca* were venerated and honored by sacrifices (corn beer, coca, llamas, and chosen children and women, whose hearts were offered to the divinity). The city of Cuzco alone, it is said, contained five hundred of them. The *huaca* of the empire were dispersed along imaginary axes, the *ceque*, which started at Coricancha and reached out, like rays, to the boundaries of the empire. The proliferation of divinities, lesser and greater, is the indication, in the Andes, of an inundation of space and time by the sacred. The punctuation of time by ritual practices corresponds to the marking of space by the *huaca*.

VIII. Festivals and Ceremonies

Rare or unforeseen events were the occasion for important ceremonial demonstrations: eclipses of the moon or sun, earthquakes and droughts called for solemn sacrifices to appease the anger of the gods. Everything that affected the person of the emperor had repercussions for the well-being of the empire: as the son of the sun, he occupied the point of contact between the world of the gods and the world of humans, in such a way that the collective destiny of the people depended directly upon the personal destiny of the Inca. On the other hand, to transgress the norms of social life was to offend the emperor and therefore to incite the anger of the gods. This is why the enthronement of a new Inca, the death of the emperor, his illnesses, and his military defeats called into question the health of the empire itself and the survival of the people: numerous human sacrifices (children, prisoners of war, and virgins of the sun) attempted to reestablish the altered social and cosmic order in favor of humans.

These exceptional circumstances, in which sinister disproportions gaped in the "prose of the world," called for a ritual response improvised in some way. But there was also an annual cycle of religious ceremonies which followed the movement of social life very closely, a movement articulated principally in the agrarian cycle: sowing, harvest, solstices, and payments of tribute. Although the year was divided into twelve lunar months, it was the movement of the sun in the sky that preoccupied the Indians of the Andes. Each month was marked by a particular festival which determined the moment of planting, harvesting, dividing the fields, preparing them for sowing, etc. These festivals took place in the temples and, usually, on public grounds reserved for this purpose, notably on the public square of Cuzco, where all the figures of the Inca pantheon were then exhibited, including the mummies of past emperors. In this regular ceremonial cycle, three festivals stand out for their importance and their magnificence: two of them correspond to the solstices, while the third was originally a lunar festival.

The southern winter solstice (June 21) was dedicated to the Inti Raymi, a celebration of the sun and at the same time a glorification of her son on earth, the Inca himself. For this reason all the high functionaries and local chiefs of the country were summoned to the ceremony at Cuzco. The emperor, surrounded by all his relatives and the court, waited in the large square of his capitol for the first light of the solar star to appear. All then knelt and the Inca offered the sun a drink of *chicha* in a silver vase. Like all great festivals, the Inti Raymi was accompanied by libations, sacrifices, songs, and dances. During the period of the southern summer solstice (December 21), the Capac Raymi took place, also a solar festival but in addition dedicated to the performance of initiation rites which marked the young nobles' passage to adulthood. While among the peasant masses this passage was not ritually marked, it was, by contrast, the occasion for great ceremonies in the dominant caste: entrance into adulthood and entrance into the aristocracy of the lords. Like all initiatory rituals, the *huarachicoy* (*huara* is the loincloth given to the young people at the end of the ritual) consisted in, beyond sacrifices to the gods, physical ordeals (flagellations, contests, fasting, and races), exhortations to follow the example of the ancestors, and so

forth. With the loincloths of adults they were given weapons and their ears were pierced to be adorned with disks. In the *huarachicoy*, the accent was placed less on the passage to adulthood than on the full entrance into the aristocracy and on the necessity for absolute fidelity in service to the Inca.

The third great Incan ceremony took place in September. The *sitowa* was an undertaking of general purification of the capital from which evils were expelled. At the appearance of the new moon, the crowd, assembled in the large square, cried out, "Illnesses, disasters, misfortunes, leave this land!" On the four principal roads leading to the four regions into which the empire was divided, four groups of one hundred armed warriors rushed forth, driving back the evils before them. In the city, the inhabitants shook out their clothes at the entrance of their homes. Songs, dances, and processions cadenced the night. At dawn, everyone took a purifying bath in the rivers. The gods and the emperors participated in the *sitowa* because their statues and mummies were exhibited on the square. White llamas were offered to them in sacrifice and a dough of corn meal specially prepared for this occasion was dipped in the blood of these animals. The gods and the mummies were anointed with this dough, the *sanku*, and all the inhabitants of Cuzco ate a piece of it.

In this society, impregnated with religiosity, every enterprise, individual or collective, humble or imperial, had to be preceded by an inquiry into the will of the supernatural powers. This is the source of the very important role of the diviners, who would observe the disposition of coca leaves thrown on the ground, the trickle of saliva running between fingers, the entrails of sacrificed animals, the lungs of llamas into which one blew in order to interpret the pattern of blood vessels. Since every disorder in such a world could only arise from some transgression (voluntary or involuntary) of some interdiction, it was also incumbent on the diviners to discover the guilty and to purify them. When circumstances demanded it, collective and public sessions of confession took place, designed to reestablish the sociocosmic order which was troubled by the sins that had been committed. The temples of Pachacamac and Lima, traditional pilgrimage sites, were the homes of oracles famous throughout the empire, whom the emperors themselves did not hesitate to consult. Despite the efforts of the Church, a number of native rites, syncretically mixed with the Christian cult, survive today among the Aymara of Bolivia and the Quechua of Peru.

P.C./d.f.

BIBLIOGRAPHY

L. BAUDIN, *L'empire socialiste des Inka* (Paris 1928). G. H. S. BUSCHNELL, *Le Pérou* (Grenoble 1958), French trans. F. A. ENGEL, *Le monde précolombien des Andes* (Paris 1972). GARCILASO DE LA VEGA, *Comentarios reales de los Incas* (Buenos Aires 1943). GUAMAN POMA DE AYALA, *Nueva Coronica y Buen Gobierno* (Paris 1936). A. METRAUX, *Les Incas* (Paris 1962). J. MURRA, *Formaciones economicas y politicas del mundo andino* (Lima 1975). F. PEASE, *Los Ultimos Incas del Cuzco* (Lima 1972); in French, *Les derniers Incas du Cuzco* (Tours 1974). J. H. ROWE, "Inca Culture at the Time of the Spanish Conquest," in *Handbook of South American Indians*, 2 (Washington 1946). N. WACHTEL, *La vision des vaincus* (Paris 1971). R. T. ZUIDEMA, *The Ceque System in the Social Organization of Cuzco* (Leiden 1962).

RELIGIOUS THOUGHT AND PROPHETISM AMONG THE TUPI-GUARANI INDIANS OF SOUTH AMERICA: THE LAND WITHOUT EVIL

Despite its brevity, this essay on the religions of the societies of the forest and the Andes will nevertheless endeavor to include their essential characteristics in constructing a faithful picture of the religious beliefs and practices of the South American peoples. The religiosity of the forest societies appears to be both public and collective. It is sung, danced, and acted out; as the sacred totally permeates the social, so, inversely, the social totally penetrates the religious. To say that religious sentiment exists primarily in its public expression does not minimize in any way the intensity of individual devotion. Like all tribal peoples, the Indians of South America have shown and continue to show an exemplary steadfastness in their fidelity to their myths and rituals. Nevertheless, the personal equation of religious life tends to be dwarfed by the collective dimension, which explains the enormous importance of ritual practice. The exceptions to this general rule merely make it stand out even more. During the second half of the nineteenth century, various scholars collected from among populations now extinct, who then lived along the lower and middle courses of the Amazon, a set of texts that differ significantly from the "classical" corpus of myths. The religious, indeed the mystical, uneasiness contained in these texts suggests the existence in these societies, not of narrators of myths, but of philosophers or intellectuals dedicated to the task of personal reflection, in sharp contrast to the ritual exuberance of other forest societies. Rare as this may be in South America, this idiosyncrasy was carried to the extreme by the Tupi-Guarani.

The term Tupi-Guarani covers a great many tribes that belong to the same linguistic group and share great cultural homogeneity. These populations occupied a very large territory: in the south, the Guarani lived from the Paraguay River in the west to the Atlantic coast in the east. The Tupi inhabited the same coast up to the mouth of the Amazon in the north and extended deep inland for an indeterminate distance. These Indians numbered several million. As far as economic life and social organization are concerned, the Tupi-Guarani conformed to the model that prevailed throughout the forest area: slash-and-burn farming, hunting, fishing, villages made up of several large collective houses. A notable fact among these Indians is their population density, substantially higher than that of the neighboring populations; communities could assemble two thousand or more people. Although all of these tribes have long since disappeared, with the exception of about five thousand Guarani who survive in Paraguay, they are nevertheless among the best known on the South American continent. The coastal Tupi were the first Indians to establish contact with Europeans at the dawn of the sixteenth century. Travelers and missionaries of various nationalities have left an abundant literature about these people that is rich in observations of all sorts, especially in the area of beliefs and customs.

As with all the tribal societies of the continent, the religious life of the Tupi-Guarani centered on shamanism. The *paje*, shaman-medicine men, performed there the same tasks as elsewhere and ritual life was always conducted, in whatever the circumstances (initiation, the execution of a prisoner of war, burials, etc.), in accordance with norms that ensured social cohesion at all times. The norms and rules of life were imposed on humankind by culture heroes (Maira, Monan,

Sun, Moon, etc.) or by mythical ancestors. Up to this point, the Tupi-Guarani do not differ at all from the other forest societies. Yet the chronicles of French, Portuguese, and Spanish travelers bear witness to a difference so considerable that it gives the Tupi-Guarani an absolutely original place in the spectrum of South American indigenous tribes. Indeed, the newcomers confronted religious phenomena of such an abundance and nature that they were completely incomprehensible to the Europeans.

What did the religion involve? Besides the incessant wars among the various tribes, these people were profoundly driven by a powerful movement of strictly religious origin and intention. Of course, the Europeans could only see the pagan manifestation of the devil in all of this and viewed the makers of this movement as Satan's henchmen. Serious errors in judgment were made in response to the strange phenomenon of Tupi-Guarani prophetism. It was interpreted until recently as a kind of messianism, as the common response of many primitive peoples to a grave crisis resulting from the contact with Western civilization. Messianism was thus a reaction to culture shock. But it was a serious misunderstanding of the radically different nature of Tupi-Guarani prophetism to reduce it to the level of messianism, for the simple and incontrovertible reason that it had been an Indian practice long before the whites ever arrived, possibly toward the middle of the fifteenth century. At issue therefore is an indigenous phenomenon that owes nothing to contact with the West, and that furthermore was not even directed at the whites. We are dealing with a prophetism for which ethnology has discovered no equivalent anywhere else.

I. Prophets

Ill-equipped to understand the phenomenon of prophetism, the first chroniclers were, however, careful enough not to confuse the shamans with certain enigmatic individuals who were prominent in that society, the *karai*. These had nothing to do with therapy, which was reserved for *paje* only. Nor did they fulfill any specialized ritual function. They were neither priests of a traditional cult nor founders of a new cult. Neither shamans, nor priests, who then were the *karai*? These men were exclusively devoted to the spoken word. Speaking was their sole activity. Men of discourse (the content of whose discourse will be discussed below), they were committed to giving speeches everywhere they went, and not just in their own community. The *karai* moved about all the time from village to village, haranguing the Indians who would listen. This nomadic vocation of the prophets was all the more astonishing because the local groups, sometimes allied into federations of several villages, waged war on one another mercilessly. But the *karai* were allowed to circulate with impunity from one camp to another. They ran no risks, and were fervently welcomed everywhere. The people went so far as to clear the foliage from the roads to the village, and they would run ahead to meet them and escort them into the village in a procession. No matter where they came from, the *karai* were never regarded as enemies.

How was this possible? In tribal society, the individual is first defined as belonging to a kin group and a local community. A person is thus put in a genealogical chain of relatives and in a network of allies. Among the Tupi-Guarani, where descent is patrilineal, one belonged to the lineage of one's father. Yet this is the strange statement that the *karai* made about themselves: they asserted that they had no father but were the sons of a woman and a deity. Here the megalomaniac fantasy by which the prophets made themselves divine

Guarani shaman's pipe. Paris, Musée de l'Homme collection. Photo J. Oster.

Guarani calabash. Paris, Musée de l'Homme collection. Photo J. Oster.

is less significant than their denial and refusal of a father. Proclaiming the absence of a father was tantamount to denying that one belonged to a lineage, and by extension, to society. To make such a statement in this type of society is to incur a charge of incomparable subversion, because it denies the very framework of primitive society, the bonds of blood.

It is obvious that the nomadism of the *karai* stemmed from their not belonging to any community whatsoever, and not from some fantasy on their part or a lust for travel. They were from nowhere and by definition could not settle anywhere, since they were not members of any lineage. This explains why they could not be taken for representatives of an enemy group when entering any village. To be an enemy meant to be set within a social structure, which was precisely not the case for the *karai*. And this is also why, being from nowhere, they were in a way from everywhere and at home everywhere. In other words, their semidivinity, their partial nonhumanity, removed them from human society and compelled them to live in accordance with their nature as "beings from afar." But at the same time it assured them total security during their travels from one tribe to another. The Indians felt no hostility toward them as they would toward a stranger, because they considered them to be gods and not men, which is another way of saying that far from taking the

karai to be madmen, the Indians never questioned the coherence of what the *karai* said and were ready to accept their words.

II. The Discourse of the Prophets

What did the *karai* talk about? The nature of their discourse was commensurate with their status vis-à-vis society. It was discourse beyond discourse, as they themselves were beyond society. Or to put it another way, what they uttered before the fascinated and enchanted Indian crowds was a discourse that broke with traditional discourse, a discourse that developed outside the system of ancient norms, rules, and values bequeathed and imposed by the gods and the mythical ancestors. That is why the prophetic phenomenon that stirred these people is so perplexing to us. Here we have a tribal society that tends to persevere by resolutely maintaining conservative norms that have prevailed since the dawn of human time, and from this society emerge enigmatic men who proclaim the end of such norms, the end of the world that depends on such norms and is committed to respect them.

The prophetic discourse of the *karai* may be summarized in one assertion and one promise. They relentlessly asserted the fundamentally evil character of the world, and they expressed the certainty that the conquest of a good world was possible. "The world is evil! The earth is ugly!" they said. "Let us leave it!" they concluded. Their absolutely pessimistic assessment of the world met with general approval from the Indians who listened to them. As a result, despite its complete difference from the usual discourse that holds all tribal society together—the discourse of repetition and not of difference, the discourse of faithfulness to tradition and not the discourse that is an overture to innovation—the discourse of the *karai* did not sound to the Indians like sick discourse, like a madman's delirium, since it rang out as the expression of a truth that they were fully expecting, like a new prose articulating the new form, the evil form, of the world. In summary, it was not the discourse of the prophet that was sick, but the world they were speaking about, the society in which they lived. The unhappiness of living in this world was rooted for them in the evil that was destroying society, and the novelty of their discourse was exclusively connected with the change that had gradually come to light in social life to alter it and disfigure it.

Where did this change come from and how did it take effect? We shall not attempt to give a genealogy of the difference in this society, but only to shed light on its principal effect: the appearance of prophets and of the discourse that spoke of the immanence of evil. The radicalism of the discourse was a measure of the depth of the evil that it unveiled. Tupi-Guarani society was quite simply experiencing the pressure of various forces and was in the process of ceasing to be a "primitive" society, i.e., a society that refused change and difference. The discourse of the *karai* stated the demise of the society. What sickness had corrupted the Tupi-Guarani to this point? The answer lies in a combination of factors: demographic (heavy population increase), sociological (a tendency to concentrate the population in large villages instead of the usual dispersion), and political (the emergence of powerful chiefs). As a result of all this, this society experienced the most deadly innovation: that of social division and inequality. A deep malaise was gnawing at these tribes, the sign of a grave crisis. The *karai* recognized this malaise and announced that it was the presence of evil and misfortune in society, the ugliness and mendacity of the world. The prophets were more sensitive than others to the slow transformations that were taking effect around them. They were the first to become clearly aware of these transformations, and they undertook to proclaim what everyone felt more or less confusedly, but the *karai* proclaimed it with such force that their discourse did not sound like the aberrations of madmen. There was complete agreement between the Indians and the prophets who told them that the world had to be changed.

III. The Land without Evil

The emergence of the prophets and their discourse that identified the world as a place of evil and unhappiness resulted from historical circumstances peculiar to the Tupi-Guarani: a reaction to a deep crisis, the symptom of a grave sickness of the social body, a premonition of the death of the society. By way of remedy in the face of this menace, the *karai* exhorted the Indians to abandon *ywy mba'emegua*, the evil earth, in order to join *ywy mara eÿ*, the land without evil. This is in fact the dwelling place of the gods, the place where arrows go hunting by themselves, where corn grows without human care, a territory of divine beings free of all alienation, a territory that, before the destruction of the first humanity by the universal flood, was a place shared in common by men and gods. Thus the return to the mythical past provided the prophets with the means to escape the present world. But the radicalism of their desire to rupture with evil was not limited to the promise of a world free of worry; it further empowered their discourse with a charge to destroy all norms and rules, for the total subversion of the old order. The call to abandon all rules left no exceptions. It explicitly included the ultimate basis of human society, the rule of the exchange of women, the law prohibiting incest: "Henceforth," they said, "you may give your women to whomever you please!"

Where was the Land without Evil located? Here again the unlimited mysticism of the prophets appeared in its full scope. The myth of paradise on earth is common to almost all cultures, and mankind may attain this paradise only after death. But for the *karai*, the Land without Evil was a real, concrete place, accessible here and now, i.e., without passing through the trial of death. According to the myths, it was generally situated to the east, toward the rising sun. From the end of the fifteenth century, the great religious migrations of the Tupi-Guarani were devoted to finding it. Led by their prophets, Indians by the thousands abandoned their villages and gardens, fasted and danced relentlessly, became nomads like their prophets, and proceeded to move eastward in search of the land of the gods. On reaching the seacoast, they discovered their major obstacle, the sea. Beyond it, surely, lay the Land without Evil. On the other hand, certain tribes thought that they might find it to the west, toward the setting sun. More than ten thousand Indians accordingly set out from the mouth of the Amazon at the beginning of the sixteenth century. Ten years later, the three hundred who were left reached Peru, already occupied by the Spanish. The rest had died of privation, hunger, and exhaustion. The prophetism of the *karai* was an assertion of the deadly risk that society ran, but it also expressed in its practical effect—religious migration—a will for subversion which went as far as the desire to die and even mass suicide.

Prophetism did not vanish with the coastal Tupi. It has persisted among the Guarani of Paraguay, whose last migration in quest of the Land without Evil took place in 1947, when a few score of Mbya Indians went to the region of Santos in Brazil. The migratory flux has dried up among the last remaining Guarani, but their mystical vocation continues to inspire their *karai*. The prophets, no longer able to lead their people to the Land without Evil, engage constantly in inner voyages that take them on the path of a search in thought, a task of reflecting on their own myths. It is a path of strictly metaphysical speculation, as is attested by the texts and sacred chants that can still be heard from their mouths today. Like their ancestors five centuries ago, they know that the world is evil and they wait for the end to come. They no longer seek access to the Land without Evil but expect the world to be destroyed by fire and by the great celestial jaguar, who will spare the Guarani Indians alone among contemporary humanity. Their immense, pathetic pride maintains them in the certainty that they are the Chosen and that, sooner or later, the gods will summon them to join them. In their eschatological expectation of the end of the world, the Guarani Indians know that their kingdom will come and that the Land without Evil will be their true dwelling place.

P.C./g.h.

BIBLIOGRAPHY

C. D'ABBEVILLE, *Histoire de la Mission des Pères Capucins en l'Isle de Maragnon . . .* (Graz 1963). L. CADOGAN, *Ayvu Rapyta: Textos miticos de los Mbya-Guarani del Guaira* (São Paulo 1959). F. CARDIM, *Tratados da terra e gente do Brasil* (Rio de Janeiro 1925). *Cartas dos Primeiros Jesuitas do Brasil,* 3 vols., S. Leite, ed. (São Paulo 1954). H. CLASTRES, *La terre sans mal* (Paris 1975). P. CLASTRES, *Le grand parler: Mythes et chants sacrés des Indiens Guarani* (Paris 1974). Y. D'EVREUX, *Voyage dans le Nord du Brésil, fair durant les années 1613 et 1614* (Leipzig and Paris 1864). J. DE LÉRY, *Histoire d'un voyage fait en la terre du Brésil,* 2 vols. (Paris 1880). P. LOZANO, *Historia de la conquista del Paraguay . . . ,* 5 vols. (Buenos Aires 1873). A. METRAUX, *La religion des Tupinamba et ses rapports avec celle des autres tribus tupi-guarani* (Paris 1928). R. DE MONTOYA, *Conquista espiritual . . .* (Bilbao 1892). C. NIMUENDAJU, *Leyenda de la Creacion y Juicio final del Mundo . . .* (São Paulo 1944), for the Spanish trans. A. SEPP, *Viagem as Missoes Jesuiticas . . .* (São Paulo 1972). G. SOARES DE SOUZA, *Tratado descriptivo do Brasil em 1587* (São Paulo 1971). H. STADEN, *Vera Historia . . .* (Buenos Aires 1944), for the Spanish trans. A. THEVET, "La cosmographie universelle: Histoire de deux voyages," in *Les Français en Amérique,* vol. 2 (Paris 1953).

RELIGIONS AND MYTHOLOGIES OF OCEANIA

During the last century, Oceania has been a popular field of ethnological inquiry because of the variability of its social and symbolic systems. This variability has justified the great amount of theoretical reflection devoted to Oceania in preference to the continental civilizations with their large populations. Each Oceanian culture is of such complexity that an observer may convince himself that he is a specialist in it after a few years, only to discover twenty years later that he has yet to uncover the greater part of its secrets.

It is easy to yield to the temptation of classifying the elements of knowledge obtained by several generations of amateur observers and alleged specialists. This classical procedure, intellectually convenient, casts a mantle of modesty over reality, a reality that is less brilliant than it appears to be. It is thus appropriate first of all to examine it closely.

The first observers—adventurers who married locally and settled down to a bourgeois old age, or missionaries who devoted their lives to the Pacific—made up the ruling class on archipelago after archipelago, from the early part of the nineteenth century. They established the ideology of the time, which justified domination by a presupposed racial superiority. After they had consolidated their power, they assumed a protective role, very much like the love of a father for children he deems incapable of progressing intellectually beyond adolescence, since they are in the grip of primitive impulses.

Such a priori assumptions did not inspire respect for the tradition or facilitate the collection of data. The Oceanians quickly found out what the souls of their temporary masters were made of. Even if they realized that people might be interested in their tradition, they saw to it that each of their interlocutors would get only what he was capable of understanding and appreciating. The filter through which knowledge had to pass differed depending on whether they were dealing with a strict Protestant, a curious trader in exotic goods, a military man, or a civil servant who was cultivated, secular, and accessible to romanticism, and thus more likely to be respectful of what could be confided to him.

In the eighteenth century, the Polynesians were thought to be children of nature, unaware of evil. It was not until the social revolution brought about in England by the terrible conditions at the beginning of the Industrial Revolution that Protestant missionaries could introduce the notion of sin and decide to found on the islands a universe that would be free of sin. At the same time, the Romantic movement in literature, espousing the cause of ancient European paganism, had its influence on the first regiments, both military and civilian, of the nascent European colonization. Polynesian priests and sages were identified with Celtic bards and druids. Sir Walter Scott, at the height of his glory in England and continental Europe, was thus indirectly responsible for these events.

Understanding the material benefit that would result from having their culture accepted at the level where Western intellectuals would put it, the Polynesians furnished the information necessary to encourage that movement. And in application of the principle that one must avail oneself of someone inferior in order to establish oneself as superior, they participated actively in everything that at that time designated Melanesia as a locus of barbarism. This barbarism was defined by contrast with a Polynesia closely related to the classical civilizations which were, as they were known through books, the basis of Western education. Setting aside elements of spectacle—ceremonies in uncovered enclosures paved with stones called *marae*—the sociopolitical structures of eastern and western Polynesia feature nothing essentially different from what one can find in at least half of Melanesia.

Extending the idea of Polynesia's greater value than the rest of the Pacific, the first specialists eagerly studied the Polynesian migrations that brought with them a superior civilization and that could reach Melanesia only indirectly, to dominate it. That Te Rangi Hiroa, better known as Sir Peter H. Buck, was the principal proponent of this idea—in his *Vikings of the Sunrise*, the Polynesians come from Asia by way of Micronesia—shows clearly to what extent the idea had been integrated into the modern struggle for the survival and integrity of the people speaking Polynesian languages. The young generation of Polynesian university students express new feelings when they challenge that thesis in their attempt to establish a political solidarity with Melanesia. This new awareness, born of the current conditions of increased independence for their countries, comes at the end of an evolution that in the course of nearly two centuries of contact has made the Polynesians the accomplices of European colonization in Melanesia: they supplied preachers, petty officers, and even soldiers.

Thus the Polynesians, first brought from afar or taken from groups who had remained Polynesians established on the outer reaches of Melanesia (Vila in Vanuatu) and later Melanesian groups, given preference by Christian missions and then by governments, were the first informants of the Europeans. They have been for the most part men and women well trained in the white man's techniques of subtle manipulation and accustomed to telling him only what he wanted to hear.

Only a few persons who have risen above the ordinary—through the benefits of intellectual training in a university or elsewhere, a training on the average better than most get—have ever attempted to go beyond the easy way in order to bear witness to the Oceanian cultures themselves. R. M. Codrington, head of the College of the Melanesian Mission, an Anglican establishment on Norfolk Island, gave notebooks to his Melanesian students from Aoba and from the Banks Islands in the southern and central Solomons when they went away on vacation on the missionary ship *Southern Cross*. He would ask them to write about what they knew of their own cultures and to write it, at their leisure, in the language of Mota Island, the lingua franca transcribed and chosen by the mission. These written materials served as the foundation for a comprehensive work. If ever these notebooks could be found today, they would certainly be worthy of a separate publication. The same technique of obtaining information was used by Codrington's younger colleagues, the Reverend G. E. Fox and the Reverend W. G. Ivens, to establish the materials for their classical monographs on the Solomon Islands.

Maurice Leenhardt went even farther. He lived at a time when there was neither training nor teaching in ethnology in France, except for a few armchair scholars, beginning with Sir James Frazer, who were interested in the comparison of exotic institutions and beliefs. At this time, when Marcel Mauss was just barely beginning to show his genius, Maurice Leenhardt applied the classical doctrine of Protestant churches, that is, evangelizing by way of the sacred texts, and worked for many years to codify and write the language of the Valley of Huailu in east central New Caledonia. He published a printed journal in which various authors attempted to write short analyses of their own society at the same time that Leenhardt distributed a questionnaire, also printed, with questions derived from the traditional lexicon and, consequently, from vernacular concepts. The files established on the basis of these questionnaires represent true ethnological studies. This encouraged various Melanesian authors to express themselves spontaneously about what they felt was worth keeping alive in their culture, yielding texts of remarkable beauty written in a language that was archaic and sometimes difficult to understand. Half a century later, one linguistic group after another pursued the same methods of research, now modernized, under the aegis of André Haudricourt, and ensured the collection and publication of a corpus in a vernacular; this massive collection, which continues to reveal an extraordinary richness, will make possible an almost entirely new analysis of the symbolic systems of the region. All of this tends to prove that we still have almost everything left to learn and that it would be appropriate, if only for the sake of efficacy, to put the control of such research operations in the hands of the Oceanians, since in any case nothing will ever be known unless they have sanctioned it.

To this point of view can be added the results of a new mode of behavior, among the younger generation, of all those who, in increasing numbers, want to know if it is appropriate to let Europeans continue to intervene in their affairs. For some indefinite time to come, the very existence of Western specialists will be the object of a considerable and sometimes definitive dispute. We will have to adjust to this and realize that Oceania, far from being completely acculturated, has barely unlocked its secrets.

How did European analysts apprehend these symbolic universes that appeared so strange to them and that they attempted to reduce to what they knew, or what they thought they knew?

I. The Biblical Bias

The first filter was that of the teaching of the Bible, especially the Old Testament and most especially the books of Judges and Kings. The first generation of Europeans who settled in the Pacific, missionaries, officials, and traders, British for the most part, had been brought up on the scriptures. Missionary preaching at that time tended to use those parts of the Bible that were most accessible, and found the texts narrating the process of the constitution of the kingdom of David and Solomon most suitable for preaching. As the missions dreamt of Christian kingdoms, and the Oceanians dreamt of the white man's means of power, each of them saw in these texts a quasi-pedagogical model for the conquest of a power sanctified by God. The concepts that could be directly assimilated by the Oceanians were, therefore, concepts of a political power justified through religion; and they were able to find illuminating parallels in their own reinterpreted traditions. Thus, both sides simplified both the analysis of the factors that constituted European political power and the real possibilities that Oceanian societies had of rivaling that power. This situation between Europeans and Oceanians, however dialectical it may have been, was one of the greatest factors in determining, during the last century, the modalities of their contact and, during the first half of the twentieth century, the modalities of the lack of understanding by European observers of fragments of knowledge brought to them for political ends of which they were not always conscious.

We may thus be able to understand today why the description of Polynesian systems was so poor for so long and why even the classical monographs published by the Bernice Pauahi Bishop Museum in Hawaii present descriptions in the form of critical catalogs, the result of an ill-adapted questionnaire, which never make possible any understanding of how the society functions or of what is represented by the beliefs that were seemingly identified. It was not until 1930 that the Rockefeller Foundation launched an effort through the University of Sydney to put together in a matter of a few years an efficient team of researchers committed to a coherent program uncluttered by romantic a prioris, who would obtain results that were truly analytical and hence comparable, with the purpose of identifying the structure of the societies that were studied. Since 1945, this effort has been undertaken again in a more diversified way by various Australian and New Zealand universities, and particularly by the Australian National University at Canberra. In recent years, national universities have been established (the University of Papua New Guinea at Port Moresby) and also multinational universities (the University of the South Pacific at Suva, Fiji), in which the disciplines of the humanities and the social sciences take on a new aspect and students often vigorously challenge traditional British social anthropology. This is where tomorrow's synthesis will be worked out in the service of the independent nations of the Pacific. We will have to reckon with these new centers of knowledge and with these non-European colleagues who have different motivations from ours and who have greater direct access to their own societies. They are already indifferent to our favored theories, but are grateful for any means of making available to them the documents that have been collected by us or our predecessors.

II. The Classical Bias

The second filter was that of the classical education received by the European elite. All tradition was understood in the light of Greek and Latin mythology, and all rituals were appreciated on the basis of our meager understanding of the religions of antiquity. Gradually, new comparative concepts were introduced, derived from the results of Mediterranean scholarship or archaeology. This reasoning by analogy was doubly compounded, in its relative inefficiency, by the enduring idea, still held today by certain Marxists, that all civilizations can be placed in chronological sequence. Since the beliefs of antiquity had supposedly culminated in Christianity and then in modern-day unbelief, the Oceanian systems had to find their place in some linear evolution, as primitive systems. It never dawned on the least of our great forebears (and too many of our current colleagues still act in the same way) that these societies were from the very first the result of a millennia-long adaptation to their environment, that they were far from being static, and that—having become increasingly complex and refined, following a dialectic process, from crisis to crisis, in conditions that we know little about—they represent extraordinarily diversified models resulting from a constant quest that was material and especially spiritual. While the technologies, all too well adapted to their ends, remained relatively stable, and only relatively so, the spirit of invention ran riot on the intellectual plane. The Pacific represents a true experimental laboratory, one that has no equal, in which, every few kilometers, the will for autonomy found in each local group has pushed that group to constitute itself as an independent cultural unity and to play with its institutions and with the concepts peculiar to its tradition so as to arrive each time at a specific synthesis.

This assertion demands the only method suitable to the circumstances, that is, to collect all possible data meticulously, without allowing a single point to escape us, in order to create an exhaustive inventory. We are far from our goal. Such an enterprise depends entirely on the goodwill of the Oceanians and can only be envisioned today if they have full control of it.

III. The First Elements of Understanding—Maurice Leenhardt

And yet, despite all this, at every instant we must be satisfied with our knowledge such as it is and pose the problem of the functional quality of the concepts that are employed.

Of course, well-bred people quickly abandoned the demonic image that the first missionaries assigned to individuals designated by local tradition, though they allowed the term "devil" or *tepolo* to survive in the languages that

Apuema masks (*pwemwa*) made of carved wood, wicker, hair, and feathers, worn by men during festivals. New Caledonia. Paris, Musée de l'Homme collection. Museum photo.

incorporated a lingua franca lexicon received from the nineteenth century. These terms, which hold research back, are maintained in their negative formulation by the Melanesian and Polynesian clergies formed by Catholic and Protestant missions.

To avoid resorting to the term "devil," British authors adopted the term "spirit," designating a disembodied person; but the French translation of this term (*esprit*) sounds bad, and the literal French translation of the expanded term "spiritual world" sounds even worse (*monde spirituel*, a theological phrase in the French context) and is better translated by *monde des esprits* ("world of spirits").

It was necessary to define these "spirits" by qualifying the word spirit with certain terms that were meant to make it more specific and closer to perceived reality, for example, ancestral spirit, protective spirit, totemic spirit, guardian spirit, child spirit, etc. Despite attempts at precision in definitions elaborated out of local data, these terms, chosen to facilitate comparison, are somewhat of a blindman's bluff and hardly recover vernacular concepts. No satisfying theory that could stand the test of time was developed from these Western terms.

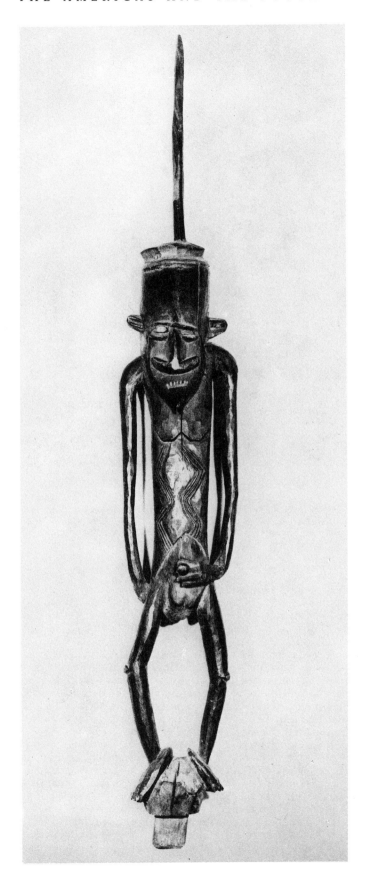

The first person to bring an element of understanding to this area, thanks to the extreme precision of his method and the quality of his data, was Maurice Leenhardt, who began by observing the identity between the corpse (*bao*) and the revered person who belonged to the invisible world (also known as *bao*). This verbal equivalence, confirmed by numerous written materials and numerous vernacular texts, gives evidence of a more generally attested institution, namely, the cult of the dead. This cult was maintained in a quasi-clandestine state throughout the period of Christianization and would suddenly reemerge during times of crisis (cargo cults and messianisms). But Christian informants did not like to discuss this practice for fear of reprisals by the church (exclusion from communion). All the recent studies, conducted in conditions in which fear of repression was much less alive, have revealed the essential existence of a daily relationship between the living and the dead, thus confirming for the rest of Oceania Maurice Leenhardt's analysis in New Caledonia. This is no small matter and deserves further discussion.

Why was the apparently simple problem of the cult of the dead in Oceania never raised? It could easily have been designated by another term, such as ancestor worship, thus connecting it with the Jesuits' case of conscience at the Court of China in the seventeenth century. The answer to this question is that there was a desire at all cost to identify the Polynesians with the megalithic civilizations of Europe and to see in Melanesians the representatives of a stage in the evolution of human societies prior to what had been attested and known about the peasant and urban societies of the Far East.

IV. Totemism

Hence the vogue for totemism. This naming system, connecting humans with a protecting animal, had been described by remote authors for the Indians of the North American plains. The overwhelming influence that the American Lewis H. Morgan had upon the thought of the first authors who dealt seriously with the Australian aborigines was to ensure the transfer of the concept of totemism so as to explain all forms of formalized relationships between humans and their natural environment. It was subsequently to be found everywhere in the world, including of course in the rest of Oceania. There is no term more ill-suited to describe the actual systems attested there, unless we simply make it into a category for the sake of reference and, unlike most authors, never attempt to use it as a definition. Such a definition either covers only one case, only one strictly localized institution from which it is elaborated, or is so general as to be a grab bag. It could not have any theoretical weight in any case, as three quarters of a century of scientific experiment have well demonstrated.

In Australia, moreover, authors no longer knew what saint to dedicate themselves to. They began to talk about totemic ancestors in order to account for the characters in myth who could pass without transition from animal form to human behavior, and in order simultaneously to attribute to them the origin of the material and spiritual forms of the culture,

Rare ridge-tile arrow, representing the god known as Kaveuren, whose footsteps cause a spring to flow. He is partial to pregnant women and has the ability to send his sexual organ to distant places. Paris, Musée national des arts africains et océaniens. Museum photo.

though no genealogy ever established any of them in the position of the origin of a line of descent.

V. The Problem of Language

The real problem is that of the universe of myth, placed in a time frame that Australian authors call the time of the dreaming. The spatial limits of this universe coexist with those of the world of the living so closely that the mythical world appropriates the celestial, underwater, and underground worlds, eventually superimposed on one another. Humans do not set foot in it except through an intermediary. The limits appear to be endowed with a certain static quality, since they are known a priori. The temporal frontiers of this same universe can stretch infinitely into the past, but this world is present at all times in close proximity to men, who enter it through each of their deeds, especially the most intimate ones, the strongest tie between the living and the myth being established on the occasions of birth, sexual union, or death.

In order to understand this, we must raise the problem of language. It has been said for so long that "primitives" are incapable of conceptual thought that we continue to claim that the languages of those we rig out in that name should be essentially descriptive. In reality, things are much simpler than the theoreticians would lead us to believe. A concept is never anything other than an abstract label given to a term in the lexicon. "Pig" designates the animal, but it is also an insult implying a series of images and a preconception about certain kinds of behavior. The term is, moreover, much more insulting to a German or to a modern American than it is to a Frenchman, who tends to laugh it off. That is because the same word, used on the same occasion, does not call forth exactly the same concept in one culture that it does in another.

Similarly, Oceanians have looked around, in many ways that were obviously or subtly different, to choose the terms of a classification or the hangers upon which to suspend ideas to express and therefore to transmit.

Since we are dealing with societies with an oral tradition, we must add that the poetic model "from evening to dawn" does not entirely apply. The symbolic universe of the Oceanians is polysemic, but in a less relentless way than that of the age classes and initiation rites of certain African systems. What a grandfather says to children around the family hearth represents one state of the tradition, different from that which comes from exchanges between adults, men and women sitting around another fire, the fire of a meeting house; different also from the one that will be created around a fire burning in a temporary shelter, in fields of yams, taros, or sweet potatoes; different still from conversations between a man and his son, or his sons, walking along the paths that mark the routes that belong to his lineage and define his portion of the habitable world, the surrounding natural world, and the invisible world that penetrates both. There has been little awareness of the value of gesture, which does more than merely punctuate spoken language. Gesture is also speech itself, according to the terms used by Melanesian authors, because its meaning is known by everyone and is integrated into the discourse of which it is a parallel form. To move a yam from one point to another, to pass it from one person to another, to grill it on the fire, or to steam it in an earthenware pot, and then to place it on a clean leaf to protect it from the soil, on a prescribed spot, before eating it ritually, alone or sharing the pieces with those who are entitled to it: all of this can dispense with discourse or at the

very least can sustain a complementary discourse, leaning on action without describing it, but throwing the cryptic recitative of all the implications of the gesture to the crowd, to the people, or saying it in a calm or low voice.

We are not dealing here with the overt possibility of recourse to countless anecdotal situations, but rather with a functional system. All rituals, all acts of private or public life, are contained within a definite space, according to a symbolic triangulation that defines each point of that space. There one grows crops, there one eats, there one sleeps, there one dances, there one defecates, there one prays; there one lies in the form of a skeleton in the fetal position, a dry skull laid on a flat stone—one does not go near it because it is forbidden—there one walks, there one hunts, there one fishes, there one has divinatory dreams, there one looks for medicinal herbs, there one deposits a stone or an offering; there one comes to transmit the myth, or the part of the myth that is one's own, because one could not do it anywhere else. No act of the symbolic life that claims to establish the link between the society of the living and the invisible world can be accomplished without a material support, a gesture or a sign, because it is proper for the spoken word to be supported and for the sign never to be equivocal. The description of the system is achieved both by speaking and by walking, and one speaks only in appropriate places or along appropriate paths, which may take years, the time it takes for an adolescent to become an adult, marry, and have his first child, the time that marks the break from his dependence on the preceding generation.

VI. The Need for an Exhaustive Corpus

This is the reason for the paucity of the texts collected by the first European observers. They were looking for a literature of the type found in the tales recorded by Grimm or Perrault and consequently accorded no importance to anything but a good story; thus they left out the toponyms and all the details of the information that the text meant to convey. Today such documents turn out to be difficult to analyze seriously. Add to that the long-standing ignorance of the importance of studying all the known variants of a theme or the confusion among several themes. Not until Claude Lévi-Strauss came along was it possible to escape from the fixed notion of all previous generations, namely, that there had been one original, authentic, and ancient text, and that it was necessary to discover that text by pushing each version through the sieve of a method of criticism designed to pick out archaisms, additions, modernisms, and contaminations. The claim was made that one could treat tradition as if it were a matter of separating pure metal from dross and retrieving the elements of a true gospel from a body of more or less apocryphal texts. This driving force was so rife in Polynesia until the fifties, and even after, that no one raised the problem of the necessity of collecting all the versions, and consequently an enormous documentation has been lost, perhaps forever. The analysis of one isolated text, however, is very difficult to do, and unless one is very familiar with local ethnography—and not just through books—such an analysis may turn out to be a highly deceptive exercise.

Similarly, no one has yet been able to undertake the study of rituals. For such a study is scientifically impossible at a given point if one does not have available an exhaustive corpus of the oral tradition in the vernacular, the only means of understanding in the culture's own terms the references that can explain each action. The enormous work accomplished by Sir Baldwin Spencer and F. J. Gillen in their attempts to describe the rituals of the aborigines of central Australia has not yet been the object of a renewed analysis, so complex and interwoven are the symbolic systems that appear in it, and the vernacular texts that would make truly productive work possible are lacking.

VII. The Contact between the Living and the Dead

The reference to modalities of contact between the living and the dead offers us a special key to the way in which this contact is experienced. One of the great themes is the descent into the land of the dead, which is found on the everyday level at least in New Caledonia and Vanuatu, and apparently to some extent everywhere else. In the first instance, who among Melanesian Catholics or Protestants would confess to having taken such a compromising journey? There are, however, some rare cases that bring to life the very rich mythology that is still widespread. They depict the chief grieving over the sudden death of his young wife; he proceeds to seek her in the underwater world of the dead, braving the perils and avatars of the route, assisted by a protecting bird or even by the guardian of the barrier that marks the entrance to the world ruled by Tein Pijopatch, whose body is spotted, covered with eyes. There dwell the dead, who in contrast with the living eat lizards instead of meat, bamboo shoots instead of cane sugar, excrement instead of root vegetables; who, unlike the living, dance clockwise and play ball by throwing a bitter orange. On the way to the underwater world, the identity of the deceased is verified by a being who feels the lobe of the left ear and pierces it, causing great pain if the lobe is not already pierced. Through trickery, some people are said to have succeeded in retrieving their wives from the state of death and have brought them back to life. The story is also told of the chief who died but remained in love and who tried in vain to deceive his wife and to make her believe that he was still alive.

Elsewhere, in Vanuatu, the voyage can be frequent; it is an exploit of seers, male or female. I say seers because simple mortals do not know how to find the way, which follows one of the deep roots of one of the gigantic banyan trees that shade the squares where people dance. The journey still takes place today. It explains missing persons and the birth of children with physical characteristics different from what they ought to be. It assures every person of the sustained protection of the dead for the benefit of the living. Messages are received from the beyond, messages which may contain instructions or merely offer the interpretation of a strange fact, the inspiration for a song, or, more rarely, a prophecy. On Tana there is an inversion of the myth of Orpheus: it is the seer who becomes infatuated with a woman from the underground land of Ipay, brings her back with him, and loses her because he does not respect the prohibition that she imposes, that he should not unite sexually with his earthly wife or eat hot food before a certain time lapses. She does, however, leave him a new cultural element, a clone of a yam, for example, as proof of her carnal existence.

There seems to be an uncrossable frontier here. The union between a dead person and a living person can only be ephemeral. In the first theme, union between spouses could be reestablished because the husband made his wife come back from beyond death. In New Caledonia, sexual union between a living person and a dead person is possible, since the dead may appear at any moment in a deceptive form. They can be recognized at night: they snore, their joints

Ceremonial headdress included in the so-called Nalawan cycle. Paris, Musée national des arts africains et océaniens. Museum photo.

become dislocated, or the body disappears, leaving only the head visible. But who are these visitors from the beyond?

VIII. The Active Dead

This problem leads to the topic of the dead who become active, who are often malevolent and anonymous, because they do not belong to one's lineage, but who may in extreme cases bear a name. And it is at this point also that the reference to the term "god" arises. The first British missionary observers did not want to use this term, not because they were troubled by their memories of Olympus, but because they had to select from within the vernacular lexicon a term that would fit well with the more recent notion of a demiurge or culture hero, so as to translate the name of Jehovah.

Once the choice was made, it was necessary to introduce a semantic extension to their customs and to reject all language habits that might have tended to favor the previous meaning of the word. Hence they chose the term "spirit."

Maurice Leenhardt proceeded from another point of view, which consisted in introducing the Greek and Hebrew terms into the written language—through the translation of the Bible—and into the spoken language, rather than looking for equivalents that might be more than approximate and perhaps spiritually dangerous. In the second phase of his career, when he was involved in research and university teaching, he was less constrained than others and adopted the term "god," which finally made it possible to pose the problem of the deification of the dead. But the Melanesian pastors that he had trained preached in their language and the choice did not embarrass them. If one takes "god" in the generally accepted sense of a personage situated beyond the sensible world, capable of appearing with human traits, endowed with a power superior to our physical norms and therefore made the object of worship involving prayers and offerings, the term is qualified to represent what happens to the dead person once the breath has left his body.

But then we are confronted by the distinction that Codrington was forced to make among the spirits: between those who had been humans and those who had never been humans. There is the crowd of anonymous dead who can be called forth on a deserted spot, among the Big Nambas on the northern end of Malekula Island in Vanuatu, that may be asked where a marauding hog might be, or a wife who has run away from her husband. This contact is established on both sides of a temporary wall made of interwoven reeds where a square opening has been arranged through which a bamboo passes, or a bundle of the central veins of coconut palm leaves, held on the side of the living by three men whose eyes are closed, while the crowd of men dances around it before stopping to ask the questions; the answer comes in a movement from top to bottom to say yes or a movement forward and backward to say no. Precautions must be taken. A dissatisfied inquirer who had discharged his gun on the other side of the line to show his anger died a few days later of an uncontrollable swelling of his stomach.

There are also the dead people in one's own lineage; a list of them is recited in a traditional order in invocations, but one prays particularly to the most recent and the closest, the one who has just died, the father or grandfather. In New Caledonia they do this while speaking into the steam of a yam cooking in a pot, after pulling out the plug of leaves; in Vanuatu they do it while continually spitting out a fine rain of kava, which they produce by chewing the kava root or drinking a beverage made from it. In north Malekula they do it while spitting continually in the direction of the skulls of dead people placed on a flat stone on the floor of the men's hut; or, on Tana, on the edge of the square for dancing, after wailing in the particular modulations that are the signature of one who drinks and prays, they address themselves to the dead, to the ones they know, the ones whose existence beside them they are not anxious to test too closely. But, as they said to me on Tana, "How can you stop the dead from talking?"

IX. The Gods

If the dead are the gods, who then are those gods who are not from among the dead because they have never been human? Are they dead people from long ago whose histo-ricity has been forgotten? This attractive hypothesis does not stand up, since the same individuals are valued over a considerable area, by dozens of lineages, even across linguistic barriers. That the facts cannot be very well reduced to our patterns of thinking is especially demonstrated by the obvious ambiguity of this category. There are, however, gods who are placed at the beginnings of certain genealogies, such as Tein Kanaké, Dui Daulo, and Bwae Bealo in the area where the Paici language is spoken in New Caledonia, but we do not know very well what they are: genuine ancestors who have been deified—though they are placed at the origin of too many lines of descent for this to be credible—or culture heroes placed in the position of ancestors in order to affirm an identity among lines of descent that may have had different origins. The problem remains wholly unresolved. José Garanger discovered the skeleton of Roy Mata in an extraordinary group burial on the island of Retoka near the southeasternmost tip of Efate in Vanuatu. We have not yet been able to find the remains of New Caledonian heroes, and no one can tell us where to look for them.

Gomawe, by contrast, in New Caledonia, exists at the origin, when the earth appeared above the water and when humans appeared on earth. On Huailu, he is said to have the technique of a potter, because he molded bodies out of a mixture of clay and water. The great myth of the Paici says that he has Bumè pull one of his teeth so that he can offer it to the rays of the moon. He places it on the rock sticking out of the water on top of the mountain Tyaumyê. From each tooth a worm emerges, which is transformed into a human being through a series of operations, implicit or explicit according to different versions.

Whether or not Gomawe is the originator of humankind, he appears in multiple forms: sea serpent, lizard, bubbles at the bottom of a waterfall, a dead log floating downstream, or in human forms, among them the god whose extensible phallus seeks out at a distance the sexual organs of pregnant women. Everywhere he places his foot is the origin of a spring, that is, of life. He is all sorts of characters who are identified with one another, and, at the end of the list, he is master of the realm of the dead and is represented both by his feathered mask and by the face carved on the heads on coins (which must not leave the "sacred basket" of the clan) or carved high on the handle of the "monstrance ax." He is accompanied by less popular characters, like Kapwangwa Kapwityalo, who watches over the game of bitter oranges during the death dances; Hway Hway, the keeper of the barrier gate; Dangginy, the bird that crosses from the living to the dead, serves as messenger, and helps widowers who are looking for their wives who died in the flower of youth. All of these beings are male. But there is also a female deity, Toririhnan, mistress of the thunderstorm and flooding, which she brings by blowing her nose with her finger, and who is known throughout the northern part of the island for having tried to substitute herself for the pregnant wife of a chief by drowning the woman and filling her own belly with pieces of pottery. The legitimate wife, carried by the current to the sea, landed on a distant island where she gave birth to two sons and raised them; and when they grew up to be strong and brave, she returned with them and was recognized. The usurper was shut up in her cabin, and the cabin was then set on fire. It is said that she perished in the flames, but that, nevertheless, she continues to reside on the mountain above Hienghene and that from the clouds she continues to regulate precipitation.

One of the criteria for the existence of a deity, in common

terms, is the presentation of gifts and prayers addressed to the deity. Generally speaking, prayers are not addressed to the gods we have just mentioned. Consequently, there is no major organized worship. But each god belongs to a well-localized group, and rarely to several groups; each god is thus the object of an adaptation, which eventually involves offerings and prayers. After a century and a half of colonial repression and Christianization, there is still no evidence that there were rituals on behalf of these beings, but this must nevertheless have been the case in a certain number of instances.

X. The Firstfruits of the Harvest and the Invisible World

This brings us to a seemingly general phenomenon: the link, which Maurice Leenhardt established at a different level, between the genesis of life, both human fertility and the fertility of the soil, and at least some of the beings that we have just discussed. Pragmatically speaking, we are referring to the firstfruits of the yam harvest, yams being everywhere the subject of public and private rituals, establishing a chain of partial or compensatory allegiances. To whom are prayers addressed in a remote spot and on the occasion of the first yam, in New Caledonia? Whom do you thank for a yam or a white chicken in Vanuatu?

Here we touch upon an essential factor in the Oceanian symbolic worlds. The relationship between the yearly harvest, which may turn out to be good, bad, or indifferent, and the invisible world that takes responsibility for it is always manifest in a precise location, nearby or distant, in an abandoned grave, in the middle of the fields, or outside the fields. This location is still respected today and is where a designated individual, usually the youngest son, who could be called a priest, will go to pray at the first symbolic sign of the harvest to come. It is of no concern to us here with whom he decides to eat this first yam. But whom does he address?

Our criteria for classification again turn out to be inoperative. The man of the firstfruits invokes all sorts of things and people. It could be the sun, a lizard, a sea serpent, as well as Tein Pijopatch or Toririhnan. The Ihuwa, from Lounakiya-mapën to Tana, make a pandanus basket called *nat pwatil* ("belly of man"), which contains smaller baskets, each one representing one of the internal organs, and place within it representative fragments of each form of food, wrapped in leaves or lianas regarded as heavy. The first basket is said to contain famine, *numus*, which one must feed in order to prevent it from coming out and spreading all over the country. Famine is thus a power held in awe, but not personified.

At Seniang, in the southwestern part of Malekula, according to information supplied by the late A. B. Deacon, which we verified in the field more than twenty years ago, the altar of the clan also serves as a charnel house—the dry skulls, cleaned out by ants, are used in the making of mannequins known as *rambaramb*. A stone there carries in it the deity to whom people pray; the priest designates it by a proper name for those deities that are represented as humans (the culture hero Ambat or one of his brothers, the ogress Nevinbumbaau, her husband Temes Malau or their son Mansip), by the term that corresponds to the symbol of the deity's power (the cycad when the being who is invoked provokes the death of a man on request), or by the term that indicates its efficacy— *namar* (famine). It also seems that the rituals known as *nerew* can take place at the onset of the agricultural season as well as at its end, especially when one can reverse the process and provoke famine among one's neighbors instead of being content with merely protecting one's own people from famine.

The rituals of the *xoro* on the Big Nambas plateau on northwest Malekula call on a mythical power, the *xoro*, of which we know nothing except that it occurs at the time of the firstfruits to sponsor the new year: the fire previously extinguished in the hearths is renewed, the old pandanus mats, women's skirts, and men's penis coverings are replaced by new ones; and, thirty days after the first of the six days of obligatory sexual abstinence, the prophets who will forecast events in the coming year are revealed. The *nal* ritual, parallel to that of the *xoro* but on behalf of neighbors, is no more specific about the individual that is invoked, except that the invocations are made to the moon and the prophets are determined on the basis of an invasion of harmless land snakes of the python family into the house of the masters of the ritual.

In Australia, the ritual sites owe their existence to a group of individuals who are regarded as the entire group of ancestors of all men, never individually as the ancestor of any one descent line. On each of these sites, people will come to pray just before the rainy season. This prayer can be a symbolic gesture with or without words, but it can also consist in the restoration of paintings that represent the gods, together with the animals, plants, or atmospheric elements that one wants to multiply or to deter, as conditions dictate. The link between the beings that are present at the origin of things and the animals, plants, or other beings is more or less clear. It is clearer for the so-called historical rituals, which trace the high deeds and wanderings of the divine beings, though still without ever making explicit the connection with the rituals of multiplication. Is this connection implicit in each case? This is quite possible, but in the absence of analyzable vernacular texts, it is difficult to decide.

XI. Mythical Cycles

The mythical cycles are not always present in an obvious way. Some have the appearance of a coherent whole. None of them seems to provide the exclusive basis for any symbolic system that is fully understood. There seems to be some sort of measured rhythm, but one that is not strictly observed.

The very notion of a mythical cycle is imprecise, however. There may be a corpus of myths that can be recited individually or in a single stretch over a period of several consecutive days and dealing with the same social group. There may also be an apparent, fleeting coherence across several groups, through the appearance of parallel versions of the same themes, or closely related themes, in different places. There may also be a coherent cycle, clearly affirmed, that seems to have spilled over the boundaries of the group that is its principal owner. Finally, there are quasi-universal themes, or those that are simply regularly attested. All of these have been the objects of more publications than anything else we have seen, because they correspond more closely to our ways of thinking. But the cycles are inscribed in a highly diversified manner within global structures that are different in each case. Since these are too numerous for us to cite them all, a few examples will suffice.

On the island of Makura, which belongs to the Shepherd Islands in Vanuatu, the story is told of Sakora, who set out in a dugout canoe in a northeasterly direction to look for the origin of the sun. He finally arrived on the island of Merig, populated exclusively by women who lived together, each receiving at night the visit of a flying fox, or fruit bat, who

Tararamanu. Drawing by Saunitiku. From C. E. Fox, *Threshold of the Pacific* (London: Kegan Paul, 1924).

Two Maam males (evil spirits) dancing with a Maam female. Namatbara painter, Crocker Island, Arnhem Land, Australia. Paris, Musée national des arts africains et océaniens (K. Kupka collection). Museum photo.

served as her husband. Sakora offered to replace the fruit bats; he killed them and introduced the women to true sexual experience, at the same time making them pregnant. At the end of several years, Sakora tired of this role and returned home, carried through the air by the Tuarere, winged women who fly from island to island to fish, swim, or comb their hair. He kept one of these as his wife by means of a trick, hiding her wings. After a quarrel between their children and the father, she found her wings again, put them on, and flew back to her sisters.

A journey to the island of Merig, the smallest and one of the most isolated of the Banks Islands, can yield many surprises. A genealogical inventory, together with a land survey, quickly shows that there is a microsociety of sixty inhabitants with a special tradition. All the husbands come from the outside, at the age when isolation becomes bearable. All the landowners are women, whose children, boys and girls, all go into exile at each generation, leaving to the mother only one or two girls who will in turn receive a husband who has come from afar. Myth and reality are virtually identical. Merig is indeed the island of women. Moreover, its inhabitants claim an origin myth that is a variant of the myth collected on the island of Makura, the theme of which turns out to be known throughout the region.

This single example touches upon one of the problems in the study of mythical cycles, namely, the problem of cross-fertilization. Should this be called a cycle? The theme of

winged women is attested all the way from Denmark to Vanuatu. What about in places beyond this constellation? It would be more unusual to find an instance where the theme did *not* occur. I know of no such negative example in New Caledonia or in Tana, in the southern part of Vanuatu.

Attempts have already been made to map the distribution of themes. The results are no more convincing than the *Kulturkreise* of the German and Austrian schools before 1930. This leads one to presuppose migration movements for which at the moment we have no possible proof. Why is the theme of the journey of food—tubers, fruit, edible leaves— found simultaneously in Tana (the route moving from the southeast to the west), in Vanuatu, and on Maré in the Loyalty Islands (the route moving from the west to the east)? Why is the theme of the chief's daughter married to the sun, which is attested on Uvea (Ciau, the daughter of Bahit), so infrequent?

The theme of the intermeshed arrows that make up a bridge is used on Pentecost Island, in the story of a husband who goes to find his wife, a winged woman who has run away from him, and on north Malekula, in the story of a man who goes looking for a fat sow of his that escapes; he finally finds her at Elephant Point, after she has given birth to a human baby boy.

The Polynesian myth of Mauitikitiki-a-Taranga, a girl who miscarries, is abandoned to the sea, and is saved by the effect of the sea foam, is the myth of the trickster, who tricks all the gods, ties up the sun and disrupts its orbit, pulls islands out of the sea by fishing them out with a mother-of-pearl hook, and succeeds (in the form of a bird) in stealing the fire in the underworld. He finally dies while attempting to steal eternal life from the goddess Hine-nui-te-po by entering her through her vagina; but one of the birds accompanying him bursts out laughing and awakens the goddess, who contracts her sphincter, thus strangling Maui and assuring that men will not escape death.

There are innumerable versions of the life and death of Mauitikitiki. The Melanesian texts, at least those that we have collected on Vanuatu, are no less literary and no less labyrinthine than those that come from classical Polynesia. But in all the literature specially devoted to Mauitikitiki in Polynesia, there is no serious implication that she was the object of a cult. By contrast, in Vanuatu, on Emae in the Shepherd Islands and on the southwesternmost tip of Tana, Mwatikitiki (Mauitikitiki) still receives offerings of yams or white hens and is addressed in prayer. Current information thus strongly confirms what the first missionaries had learned from their Polynesian evangelists. Katharine Luomala, a specialist in the mythology of Maui, thinks that the myth spread from Polynesia to central Vanuatu and from southern Vanuatu to the Santa Cruz Islands. One could reverse this argument and suggest that nothing is certain except that the myth of Mauitikitiki is common to both zones and that a secularized narrative that turned into a symbolic and literary construct, deprived of any local support, could just as well have originated in the south of the Melanesian arc. We do not have the means of solving this problem at this time. It would also seem that the emergence of a class of priests, interpreters and amplifiers of the tradition, is a phenomenon observed essentially in eastern Polynesia and on the outer perimeter of Polynesia. They may well have made use of a Maui myth and turned it into something of their own. Our inadequate knowledge of Tahiti and the Windward Islands has nonetheless given us two versions of the myth of Maui. In one, which is scholarly, Maui is full of virtues; in the other, which is popular, Maui retains the image of a trickster.

The Tangaloa cycle varies widely. In Aniwa and the east coast, facing Tana, Tangaloa is only a kindly snake, who is put to death; this results in the origin of the first coconut tree, which grows out of the burnt corpse of the snake. The Tahitian cosmographic myths make him into a demiurge, while still other variants view him only as the god of the ocean. The people of the Wallis Islands strip Maui of his role of fisherman of the islands and give this role to Tangaloa.

"Ta'aroa (the one and only) was the ancestor of all the gods. He created everything. Since time immemorial the great Ta'aroa, the original, has existed. Ta'aroa grew by himself in solitude. He was his own parent, having neither father nor mother. Ta'aroa had countless forms, but there was only one Ta'aroa up above, down below, and in the night. Ta'aroa was confined in his shell and in the night for thousands of years."

These fragments of a text on the creation of the world, dictated in 1822, give a faint idea of the imagery and ambiguity that make it possible for a theological interpretation to substitute for the myth a cosmogonic poem that sets the criteria of a literary tradition.

Statue representing the god Tangaroa. Island of Rurútu, Austral Islands, French Polynesia. London, British Museum. Museum photo.

The reigning chief Paiore of the Tuamotu island of Anaa drew a sketch that the resident administrator Caillot obtained, a sketch that laid out his conception of superimposed earths and skies. The primordial egg, in which Tangaroa had enclosed himself, according to Tahitian tradition, contained Te tumu (the foundation) and Te papa (the stratified rock). The egg broke open, giving birth to three superimposed platforms. On the lower platform, Te tumu and Te papa created humans, animals, and plants. It took three attempts to obtain a viable man and woman, whose children increased in number and took up the task of raising the platform that was above them; then they moved onto it with animals and plants by making an opening through this second platform, the first sky, which they first softened by means of a fire. They then repeated the same process with the third platform and settled upon it too, leaving above them the superimposed skies. But Tangaroa set fire to the earthly world and for this deed was banished to an underground world.

We could go on indefinitely, taking each of the figures from Polynesian mythology, relating its avatars, and demonstrating a gigantic "system of transformation," to use Lévi-Strauss's terms. The schematization of the transitions of every possible theme from one divine individual to another, or from one particular acceptance to another, would be of interest only to a few specialized readers. There has already been an attempt to put these themes into a thematic index, though no tool of any demonstrated usefulness has been derived from it. There is, nevertheless, a consensus that the collection has a coherence. This is certainly the case if we think of the last period, at least in Tahiti, during which it was attested that the cult of Oro, the god of war, replaced the cult of cosmogonic deities, divine rivalry thus masking local power struggles through the rivalries between clans of priests and theologians.

There are also other cycles that we have treated as incomplete cosmogonies, wrongly, since this term, however attractive it may be, masks a value judgment and some chronological implication: a transition from one cosmogony (the incomplete one) to the other (completed) or vice versa. In fact, the solution chosen was the wrong one. The attractive cosmogony corresponds to a social support whose function is to reproduce it or cause it to evolve, namely, a class of priests seeking independence with respect to political power. The quasi cosmogonies that are found in Melanesia can have much more diversified functions.

The Paici tradition in north central New Caledonia places the origin of men on Mount Tyaumyê and attributes it to Bumè's intervention. The different available versions of the myth end with the explanation of the origin of the regional clans and their split into two intermarrying phratries, who incidentally share between them the useful universe, including animal and plant forms, atmospheric elements, and the regional gods endowed with a civil status. The practice of exchanging sisters and circulating shell coins is instituted in the myth, with variants as to the identity of the first partners. Demographically and linguistically speaking, this mythical cycle enjoys the support of the overwhelming majority on the island, united through flexible and multiple ties designed to form a loose military confederation that at times put up successful resistance to the intruding French military forces.

The first known mythical cycle in New Caledonia is the cycle of the lizard, published in 1830 by Maurice Leenhardt. In varying versions, it tells the story of a chief who goes to bring in his snares and picks up a fabulous lizard, who settles down on the chief's back. When it falls asleep and slides off to the ground during the night, the man quickly takes flight and the lizard pursues him. The chief meets people on his flight, all of whom first offer to help the chief to victory, but then are frightened away. After covering all of New Caledonia, from east to west and from north to south, the fleeing chief finally meets the one whose function is to speak to the lizard and return his protecting animal to its kindly role at the edge of the forest. A detailed examination of the characters who appear in the course of this narrative reveals that they were not chosen indiscriminately, and that they belong to one of the networks of related individuals who share the great earth among themselves, each having their branches on the nearby Loyalty Islands.

Unlike New Caledonia, where the sea had to recede from the heights so that man could be born, Vanuatu raised the problem of the origins of the sea, which existed only in the form of a secret condiment in the food of the culture hero, Barkolkol, Tagaro, Qat, or Mwatikitiki, who appropriated it for himself. A friend or relative who solves the mystery and wants to steal the condiment lifts the stone and lets the sea pass through. A version collected in Tana depicts the biblical Noah, who was robbed of his salt water and went east in a dugout. One day he returned and brought his descendants the power that until then had been reserved for whites. This reinterpretation of the Old Testament is not new. MacDonald recorded on Efate, at the dawn of Christianization, a tradition claiming that Mauitikitiki's grandson, Tamakaia, stole the sea from his grandfather by opening the gates that enclosed it, built himself a dugout out of banana peels, and left for England, where he was known as Jehovah. Similarly, the dugout which is Noah's ark is found above a mountain pass at the north end of a mountain range culminating in Mount Panié in New Caledonia. These Christianized versions contain recognizable attempts of syncretism at the start of European contact, but they have their limits. In general, the Old and New Testaments were treated as myths to be added to the existing body of myths without ever raising the slightest questions about the actual existence of holy places or about the historicity of the individuals of the Christian pantheon. Maurice Leenhardt had noted earlier the people's surprise when soldiers wrote in 1917 that they were passing through a place close to Palestine. I myself noticed fifty years later the bewilderment of all of my wife's Melanesian relatives when she told them about her trip to Jerusalem. They had never entertained the thought that anything they were taught in church could actually exist.

A frequent theme is that of the five fingers that become real characters: Mauitikitiki-a-Taranga and her brothers in the versions of the myth of Maui in which Maui is not alone. In southeast Malekula, A. B. Deacon recorded the myth of Ambat and his brothers who were trapped one after another by the ogress Nevinbumbaau and were stuck in a ditch until Ambat came to free them. The same brothers later attempted to kill their youngest brother Ambat because they envied him his beautiful wife Lindanda, who learned of her husband's death when she saw blood on the comb he had left her. She escaped from the brothers, who thought they had won. Thus the gods and civilizing heroes can die. This does not prevent Ambat from receiving offerings and prayers at the *nembrbrkon,* a sacred place dedicated to him on the island of Tomman. There is no historicity in the death of the gods, nor do they have to be considered ancestors in the biological sense, nor are the real dead prevented from becoming gods. A very broad liberalism prevails. It is up to each local society to constitute the set of characters, myths, and symbols it deems appropriate for itself.

Other classical cycles should be mentioned, starting with

the cycle of the rainbow snake in northern Australia. Lloyd Warner has pointed out the connection between the initiation rites of young men from the northeasternmost corner of Arnhem Land and the image of the snake Yurlunggur coiled up in his water holes. The snake rises to the sky and falls back to earth because he experiences unbearable pain after he swallows the Wawilak sisters who belong to the same moiety as he does. This all happens because they danced at the edge of his water hole during their menstrual period, and their menstrual blood flowed into his shelter and awakened in him a violent incestuous desire. Interpretations that do not always fit with the myth have been given by this same author and by Lévi-Strauss, Karel Kupka, and myself. The relative artificiality of these analyses comes from their applications to texts written in English and not in the local vernacular. Throughout the region the rituals connected with the rainbow snake are designed to ensure normal rainfall and consequently the food and the survival of human society.

Another Australian cycle tells of the search for red ocher. In the myth, this quest is connected with the proliferation of fat emus. A couple of emus were hunted by dogs for several hundred miles, to Parochilna, where they dug into the ground and became deposits of red ocher. This story is the origin of the journey made by young men along the same road, where they are received by each of the local groups who share the myth. In the course of several days, the initiation of young men to the myth is accomplished by means of colorful games in which they participate and which reenact the details of the story told. The novices are received by those who have made the journey and have brought back red ocher, which on this occasion entitles them to theoretically incestuous sexual relations with women from their own exogamous moiety.

XII. Incest

Much has been written for a long time about the incest taboo. A recurrent theme of many myths is the theme of desired or consummated incest. The consequences vary. Certain lines of descent are known to have incestuous origins. They derive from this a special status at the very least, if not outright pride. Bronislaw Malinowski was one of the first to record a myth dealing with incest. There is the myth of Inuvayla'u, whose penis moved like a snake on the ground or under water and penetrated the vulva of his brother's wives, or the wives of his uterine nephews. His actions go unpunished for a long time, as the women do not dare to speak up. When the truth comes out, the hero castrates himself and goes into exile. In a myth that takes place in Kumilabwa, a sister accidentally spills on herself some drops of a coconut oil that was prepared as a love potion for her own brother. Overcome by the magic force, she sets out in search of her brother, who is swimming, takes off her skirt on the way, and forces him to have intercourse with her. The two of them hide in a cave and die there. A mint leaf grows out of their chests. Since then, this same mint is the basic ingredient for love potions, and the myth is used to justify incest, which does occur.

XIII. Myths of Origin

Myths are easily made up of models. Myths of origin are the most obvious example. They are everywhere and of all kinds. Almost every institution is based on a myth of origin. One of the simplest ones, common in initiation cycles, is the myth claiming that the techniques for making masks or musical instruments were invented by a woman. Some men took her by surprise, robbed her of her invention, killed her, and saw to it that no woman could ever again have access to such knowledge.

Local villages and groups also claim to have a myth of origin. Some of these myths represent complex sets that cover an entire region, with more or less detailed variants depending on the place of the village or group within the system. One of the most developed myths is the myth of the *lue jajiny,* the two girls at the origin of most chiefdoms in the district of Lösi, i.e., the southern part of the island of Lifou, the central island of the Loyalty Islands. According to some, they came out of the hole of Masalo; according to others, they came from the northern district, where they are supposed to have participated in an abortive attempt to set up a single political system. They were welcomed by the *wanan-athin,* the oldest inhabitants of the region, who had peculiar features: long hair, double-jointedness, and, in the women, pendulous breasts. The younger of the two shows respect for her hosts, prepares meals for them, and unites with them sexually. Of the two, she is the first to have children, who will later enjoy political preeminence in the area. The older of the two follows suit with some delay. She too has children, who spread to the interior and the east coast. They are at the origins of the elder chiefdoms, called *anga haetra,* as opposed to the others, called *angete lösi,* and they challenge the preeminence of the Bula chiefs, who were patrilineal descendants of the younger sister. The origin from a hole, i.e., in an ancient grotto with a caved-in roof, is generally thought to refer to an origin from outside of the island. Maurice Leenhardt shares this opinion. This kind of information is often regarded as the "secret" of the lineages in question, and in any case there is a corresponding prohibition against mentioning it in public. There is no graver insult in Oceania than treating someone as a stranger, which implies denying his rights to the earth, unless it happens that the person concerned has a particular status derived from his foreign origin, or unless he belongs to a clan dispersed over several islands, a clan whose members have preserved their mutual bonds, refusing to hide their origins under a veil of modesty.

Douglas Oliver has recorded, from the Siuai of Bougainville, the myth of origin of the Ta, through two sisters, Noika and Korina, who together, inside a cave, initiated some of the elements of the local culture, the making of pearls from shells and the invention of magic formulas governing growth, welfare, and prosperity rites. After their marriage, they separated because of a quarrel; one left with her people, the other one stayed. The various incidents are strictly localized: the origin of a food taboo, the birth of a nonhuman child: an arboreal rat that becomes the symbol of the matrilineal descendants of the two sisters and crops up repeatedly in the story. Douglas Oliver was the first author to recognize the value of these localities (*urinno,* sacred places) as signs of the land tenure being claimed.

The myth of Ciau, the daughter of Bahit, the northern chief of the island of Uvea (Loyalty Islands), has long been a puzzle to me. She had the habit of going with her attendants to a beach of white sand and shell called Hony and there bleaching her hair. One day as she was washing her hair with seawater, two fish came and stationed themselves, one under each armpit, and whisked her away to the tiny island of Sëunö Oüdet, the island where the sun goes to rest every evening. There she finds the sun's mother, who welcomes her and hides her lest she be burned by the rays of her son. The sun arrives, finds her, marries her, and gives her a child. One day when the brat misbehaves, the father gets angry

and insults his wife by calling her a foreigner. The next day the young woman takes her son and goes off into the sea. The two fish return, take her under the armpits, and bring her back to Hony. She is joyously welcomed at Wekiny, at the court of her father Bahit. But the sun soon arrives demanding his son (not his wife), and arrests his movement over the country. Everything in sight dries up and burns. The earth cracks and the people must seek refuge underground. They decide to reunite sun and son. One man builds a pyre of green wood, to produce a lot of smoke, in a locality called Webelu; he places the child on it and sets it on fire. The smoke then carries the child toward the sun, who then continues its course. This man's descendant in each generation receives the name of Hoi (he gives allegiance to Wasau, the younger lineage of Bahit). He is the master of rain and sun and looks after their rituals at Webelu, and the function of the myth of Ciau is to justify his worship. Twenty pages full of highly literary text to give substance to a privilege that could have been expressed in a few lines! How many Polynesian texts lost, when they were collected, the few key words that would have allowed us to understand their raison d'être? Perhaps all of them.

This last text is connected with the cycle of the Xetiwaan, as they are known on the Loyalty Islands (elsewhere they are known as Naatyuwe or Tyidopwaan, depending on the linguistic group, and on Kunié as Ketiware). These people, who are verbally abused when they are not present, claim a common place of origin, which concerted scholarship indicates might be Tonga. Such is at least the working hypothesis. Their outstanding feature is their refusal to be integrated into the existing political system unless they can hide behind assumed traditional names and unless they are regarded everywhere as the masters of the rituals that guarantee the control of rain and the sun. At the same time, the Xetiwaan take pride in their special relationship with the shark: it does not attack them and they never eat its meat. The elder of the Xetiwaan, Xetiwaan Inangoj from the southeastern coast of Lifou, boasts of a *watenge ne ea,* a magic for navigation, which is in keeping with his origin. The Xetiwaan are thought to have considerable powers when it comes to the sea. Xetawaan Dromau of Tingeting, in the Wetr region of northern Lifou, is supposed to have changed into increasingly smaller fish to seek out inside the stomach of a whale the magical hook *wageledra* lost by Zangzang, the lord of the land at Tingeting.

XIV. Ogres and Ogresses

Ogres and ogresses, already seen in connection with Nevinbumbaau and Ambat's brothers, are a recurring theme with an important connotation. The people that the Europeans thought to be cannibals do not practice cannibalism to any significant extent. Whether it is Tramsëmwas on Tana, Mutuama on Efate, or Kahwikahok in northern New Caledonia, the outline is basically the same. The country is laid waste by the cannibal and only one elderly couple remains, or a woman with one or two sons. They manage to hide so well that the sons grow up to be adults and become adept at martial skills: they carefully hide weapons along the road on which they anticipate having to retreat before the advancing enemy, whom they finally overcome. The former population

Votive picket, tied to the priest by a thin rope made of fibers from the coconut outer shell, during the invocation. Paris, Musée des arts africains et océaniens. Museum photo.

returns. It is either liberated from the enclosure that served as a food storage area, or they resume normal life as soon as the cannibal's stomach has been opened.

Raymond Mayer reports the story of the ogress Lona (from the Úvea of the Wallis Islands). The sole survivor of the land is Pikipikilauifi, a little girl hidden by her parents in a chestnut tree. She meets Mele, Lona's daughter, who plays with her without telling her mother (Lona) in order to protect her little friend. Lona sees it all from the house, takes Pikipikilauifi by surprise, and eats her, but Mele's despair and anger drives Lona to vomit the swallowed child and die.

The country is eventually said to have been divided up into localized social categories by the avengers, heroes who succeeded in killing the cannibal and in putting in place those whose lives they restored. The hero may have come from the outside, as in the case of Mwatikitiki (Mauitikitiki).

XV. Pictorial Representations

The *Adoro ni Matawa* of San Cristobal in the Solomon Islands are among those rare individuals for whom we have pictorial representations. According to Maekabia, who hails from the village of Fagani and whose interpretation was cited by C. E. Fox, Tararamanu is a god of the open sea without any home, not even on shore. He appeared to three brothers as they were fishing for bonito with a long bamboo fishing rod. As their dugout was drifting and they were catching nothing, they saw a red rainbow across the island of Ugi. The rainbow disappeared and was followed by a shower and then by a white trail crossing the horizon "like a white-barked tree in the forest," lighting up like a fire, and driving before them a shoal of leaping bonitos. The three brothers then brought back a miraculous catch. Tararamanu was in the apparition; one of the three brothers was possessed by him and Tararamanu spoke through his voice as follows: "You call your dugout Wakio. You shall not do this again, but rather name it like my own dugout Sautatare-i-roburo (pursuer of bonitos to where they live). There you shall build an altar to me and I shall give you fish. You shall offer sacrifice to me in the dugout and at the village altar." His will was done, and Tararamanu gave them all sorts of fish in abundance, but he would shoot arrows at whomever he did not like.

The lack of visual representations of heroes and gods from the Oceanian pantheon causes us much trouble. Some great Polynesian gods are exceptions to this rule, but rarely. There is a statue of Tangaroa, for instance, showing, in this case, the marks of his role as a demiurge, with creatures stuck to his body and other separable figurines inside his hollow back. This unique piece is in the British Museum.

If we take an inventory of sculpted pieces that unmistakably represent a mythical character, when all doubtful cases are eliminated, the list is short: Kalaipahoa, the Hawaian god of evil deeds, who came from Oahu, as seen in a piece in the Bernice Pauahi Bishop Museum; Tangaroa Upao Vahu, the sea god in the act of creating humans, sculpted on Rurutu; Kukailimoku, a representation of a human face made of hard wickerwork covered with a tight net, each knot tying a cluster of feathers, the Hawaiian god of war, of which there are several other known representations; Kuula, a god in the shape of a Hawaiian fish, rendered in the form of a stone fish brought along for fishing; small gods in the form of humans,

Wooden statue of the god Ku. Hawaii. London, British Museum. Museum photo.

Tjurunga. Schist plate with engravings symbolizing events of the past in the lives of ancestors and each one of their adventures. Paris, Musée national des arts africains et océaniens (Guiart). Museum photo.

figure was an idol to be destroyed or confiscated that no one took the trouble to note its exact meaning. The image of the ancestor, the only standing sculpture to have survived the Moriori culture on the Chatham Islands, gives no hints other than the fact that it was fear-inspiring, but the fear may have originated from the location of the sculpture, which was struck in the ground inside a cemetery.

Other forms of divine representation were apparently as satisfactory: fine braids on Tikopia, tapa, packets of fibers made from coconut shells (the god Oro on Tahiti), red feathers, adzes; this explains why a great number of sculptures had only ornamental or architectural functions, and why sculpted divine representations do not correspond to a systematic solution.

Melanesia is no better in this respect, with the exception of masks. In New Caledonia, masks represent the master of the land of the dead, Tein Pijopatch. In Vanuatu, in the Seniang region, southeast of Malekula, and probably on the southern coast of this same island, masks are known to represent the ogress Nevimbumbaau, her husband, and her son, but never the civilizing hero Ambat. Elsewhere human figures represent symbols of the social status of individuals or groups. In the rest of Melanesia, these instances are rather rare, unless one does what Codrington, Fox, and Father Patrick O'Reilly did, that is, give people paper and pencil and ask them to draw characters from their pantheon.

Aboriginal Australia is more open from this standpoint, whether it be the paintings on bark in Arnhem Land studied by Karel Kupka or the engraved schist plates, finished in ocher and emu grease, which represent the peregrinations of the ancestors in "the dream time."

XVI. Recent Messianic Movements

A word should be said about the messianic movements which have strewn the Pacific since the arrival of the Europeans, both in Polynesia and in Melanesia. The neopagan rebellion, called the Rebellion of the Mamaias, at the turn of the century in Tahiti, is not well documented. It had a parallel on Samoa. Fiji has experienced several such movements, of which the first is particularly well known, the Tuka, based on the worship of the dead and on the refusal to be dominated by noble Christian converts who lived on the coasts. The other movements await approval for study.

The New Guinea and Melanesian cargo cults received greater publicity in the years after the war. Also based on a return to the cult of the dead and the refusal of direct domination by whites, administrators, traders, and missionaries, they took various forms and succeeded in molding political movements in recent years (Bougainville). The common denominator was the notion that the white man's means of power arrived in cargo ships, and that the only way to gain satisfaction was by resorting to the dead and to ancient deities, since the whites did not want to share. Treated with contempt by European settlers and viewed as irrational movements, these cargo cults began very early. They have had concrete results, politically and economically, and play a part in the many forms of resistance put up by Oceanians to white domination. Only the well-known cases have been reported, and the thinking that was expressed in spectacular behaviors may have been very general, public demonstrations taking place at points of maximum tension. Moreover, if we take the example of Sumatra, where forms of messianism go back a long way, and if we see one or two instances, such as archaeological proof of the myth of Roy Mata in Vanuatu, as an initiating culture change, it seems

with erect penises, vertical with respect to the body, brought along by fishermen from Rarotonga and placed in the prow of dugouts; the "goddesses" of the island of Lifuka in the Tonga Islands; the lizard men of Easter Island. The "staff gods" of Rarotonga seem rather tempting examples but less certain: one main head dominates secondary heads, the whole enclosed in tapa cloth.

A New Zealand peg with a rope of plant fibers, topped by a human head with its tongue sticking out, served as an altar of repose offered to the particular god invoked; they had to roll out the rope held at one end by the seated priest, after they painted the whole thing in ocher and decorated it with feathers; one example found in the Auckland War Memorial Museum had been used in the worship of Maru, the god of war. The reason why the personalities and practices so many gods of war survived is because Europeans were fascinated by them: first to get them out of circulation and second to take pleasure in showing them off as their possessions in Europe. Beyond that, there was such a belief that any human possible that prophetic movements in Oceania were an accepted form of social, religious, and political change, whenever a new level of awareness was attained and no other solution was at hand.

J.G./g.h.

BIBLIOGRAPHY

Giving a bibliography has become a senseless rite, unless the bibliography is analytic and exhaustive and thus represents a useful tool for the work of other researchers. The list given below is composed of landmarks and so that the great names may not be forgotten. The bibliography of the subject treated includes many hundreds of titles, of which each ought to be the object of an analysis of contents in order to be truly useful. The Oceanians would probably prefer to maintain their oral traditions in place of such an exhausting exercise.

A. BASTIAN, *Die heilige Sage der Polynesier Kosmogonie und Theogonie* (Leipzig 1881). R. BERNDT, *Kunapipi: A Study of an Australian Aboriginal Religious Cult* (Melbourne 1951). E. BEST, *Maori Religion and Mythology* (Wellington 1924). K. O. L. BURRIDGE, *Mambu* (London 1960). E. CAILLOT, *Mythes, légendes et traditions des Polynésiens* (Paris 1914). R. H. CODRINGTON, *The Melanesians: Studies in Their Anthropology and Folklore* (Oxford 1891). A. B. DEACON, *Malekula: A Vanishing People in the New Hebrides*, Camilla Wedgwood, ed. (London 1934). A. P. ELKIN, *The Australian Aborigines: How to Understand Them* (Sydney 1945); "The Rainbow Serpent Myth in North Western Australia," *Oceania* 1 (1930): 349–52. W. ELLIS, *Polynesian Researches during a Residence of Nearly Eight Years in the Society and in the Sandwich Islands*, 2 vols. (London 1829). R. FIRTH, *The Work of the Gods in Tikopia*, 2 vols. (London 1940). R. P. M. GAGNÉRE, *Étude ethnologique sur la religion des Néo-Calédoniens* (Saint-Louis 1905). J. GUIART, *Un siècle et demi de contacts culturels à Tanna, Nouvelles-Hébrides* (Paris 1956); *Structure de la chefferie en Mélanésie du Sud*, travaux et mémoires de l'Institut d'ethnologie, vol. 66 (Paris 1963). J.-J. GUIART, M.-S. LAGRANGE, and M. RENAUD, *Système des titres dans les Nouvelles-Hébrides centrales: D'Efate aus îles Shepherds*, mémoires de l'Institut d'ethnologie, vol. 10 (Paris 1973). C. E. FOX, *The Threshold of the Pacific* (London 1924). C. HANDY, *Polynesian Religion* (Honolulu 1927). T. HENRY, *Ancient Tahiti, Compiled from Notes of J. M. Orsmond* (Honolulu 1928). H. LAVAL, *Mangareva: L'histoire ancienne d'un peuple polynésien* (Braine-le-Comte 1938). P. LAWRENCE, *Road Belong Cargo* (London 1964). P. LAWRENCE and M. J. MEGGITT, eds., *Gods, Ghosts and Men in Melanesia* (London 1965). J. W. LAYARD, *Stone Men of Malekula: Vao* (London 1942). M. LEENHARDT, *Do Kamo* (Paris 1947); *Notes d'ethnologie néo-calédonienne*, mémoires et travaux de l'Institut d'ethnologie, vol. 8 (Paris 1930).

PAPUA NEW GUINEA

Papua New Guinea appears to be a vast mosaic of different cultures teeming with different local religious phenomena. It is nonetheless possible to identify certain common cultural constants that may serve to define, at the heart of this diversity, a New Guinean model of mythological and ritual representations.

I. Mythology

Religious ideology distinguishes within the cosmic order two features that are simultaneously separate and linked together: the sensory and the intelligible, separate because they are marked by opposing characteristics, but linked together in that one (the sensory world) draws from the other (the intelligible world) the causes and principles of its coherence. The conception of empirical order integrates this contradiction, which is assumed to be a necessary contradiction between the two simultaneous instances of the thought process and which recovers the obsessional theme of the relationship between what is generated and what is becoming. The thing that is sensory shares with the thing that is intelligible the same definitional equivocation, the same ontological uncertainty. Because it is produced by a transcendental power that human beings claim they cannot control, visible reality can disappear by the same volition that caused it to appear in the first place. The transcendence that is thus liable to manifest itself positively or negatively beyond man's control is paradoxical, in that as myth it appears as a force that is self-sufficient, while as ritual it appears as a force that is instituted, the end result of a human product (Guidieri 1978).

The sensory aspect, constituted by the immanent reality of the natural environment, economic resources, and living creatures, is most often conceived as the anthropomorphized projection of the supernatural world that represents the intelligible side of the universe. This latter, intelligible aspect includes the invisible realm of supernatural creatures: mythical heroes, occult forces, demons, celestial deities, spirits of the dead, ancestors, and so forth, whose existence, attested by mythical discourse, justifies the whole body of religious beliefs and practices. The themes of these beliefs and practices can be grouped around two types of entities: independent spirits and ancestral spirits.

The independent spirits, whose existence the mythology traces back to the very founding of the universe and whose origins are strictly supernatural, have prospered (and continue to progenerate) in the human environment by exerting the regulatory powers that have been (or are now) more or less invested in them. This category of entities is the one that is involved in most myths of creation, notably the stories of the origins of the first men and of the natural or cultural laws that govern their universe. The question of the genesis of the physical world and the birth of supernatural heroes seems to have been practically banished from mythological discourse, which prefers to narrate the actions performed by the heroes of the early times and to describe those times, which is useful for justifying the current state of things.

Thus, for the most part, the myths posit the existence of the earth—flat, dry, and uninhabited—before the existence of the principal deities who created the first human beings, endowed the universe with the natural attributes it is known to have (rivers, mountains, forests, animals, etc.), and established the norms of social and cultural institutions. Consequently, the exemplary deeds of the founding spirits performed in mythical times must provide the sole referential criteria for current human behavior, for which what is traditional therefore becomes mandatory.

This ideal of conformity to what is said to have existed is reinforced by the general observation that phratries, clans, or subclans often have exclusive possession of a whole set of secret myths that evoke the bonds of linear descent that unite the group to its ancestral deities. These deities are generally said to have a power of metamorphosis that is ultimately able to accomplish their petrification into things of nature (trees, rocks, plants, and so forth). This characteristic aptitude of spirits to transform themselves by assuming the most diverse

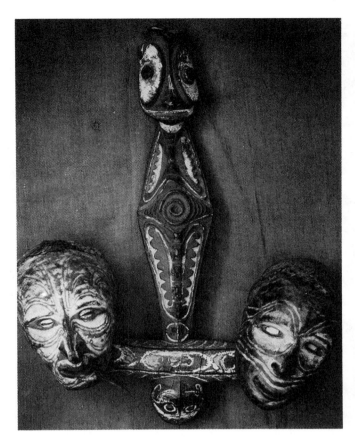

Skull rack with two skulls covered with molding showing the features of the deceased. Melanesia, New Guinea. Paris, Musée de l'Homme (Madeleine Rousseau collection). Museum photo.

Mask made of rough bark and painted black and white. Papua New Guinea (Bay of Kerewa). Paris, Musée de l'Homme collection. Museum photo.

shapes familiar to humans explains the human feeling of utter confusion between objective reality and mythical reality, which are conceived as fundamentally similar and interdependent. In New Guinea, people experience at the very core of their person this cosmogonic duality that they assimilate within themselves in terms of the dichotomy between body and soul. Every human being is endowed with a "soul" present inside the body diffusely and without form. The soul can leave the body temporarily during sleep or permanently when the person dies. Thus, dreams are seen as the manifestation of such flights of the soul and its encounters with supernatural creatures from an intangible world to which people in their state of wakefulness have no direct access.

The spirits of the dead are defined as the immaterial components of humans that survive after death and persist indefinitely in the universe in a disembodied form. Ideas about the exact destination of souls and the location of the land of the dead sometimes appear rather ill-defined, though there is a general consensus that the ancestors' place of residence is to the west or underground. The route that leads to that place is strewn with obstacles, dangers, and trials to overcome, whose description forms the substance of the myth. The fate of the soul and the things that can happen to it are tied to the earthly personality and the circumstances surrounding the death of the dead person. For instance, among the Baktaman of central New Guinea, a violent death in combat or as the result of an accident makes it impossible for the spirit to live in the land of the dead, which can be attained only through a nonviolent death. That is why in the human environment, in addition to the independent spirits that haunt the forests, the rivers, and the air, there are also souls of the dead who have no homeland, who wander about interfering in the lives of human beings. The nature of this interference, sometimes positive and sometimes (more often) negative, depends on the culture; sometimes it is connected with the wholly anthropomorphic character of the spirit, sometimes with the powers inherent in its ancestral status, and sometimes with the degree of its interest in the affairs of the living. In certain cases (the Huli of the southern highlands), the influence of the spirits increases with their antiquity and varies with their sex, malevolence apparently being a specific feature of female spirits. In other cases, by contrast (the Kyaka of the western highlands), less power is attributed to remote ancestors—even if they are founding ancestors—than to the spirits of the recent dead, whose good or evil influence is the shared lot of both sexes.

Both types of entities, the independent spirits and the spirits of the dead, share a common dimension: ancestry. Ancestry is innate in the first instance, inherently given to the spirit since the beginning of its existence; it is acquired, in the second instance, at the end of a liturgical process of transformation. The mythological and the genealogical are therefore defined in New Guinean thought as the two aspects of memory fit to ensure the intangibility and durability of representations of belief. But discourse is not the only place where memory can find its actualization, and the question of ancestry inevitably leads to a consideration of the rituals in which such subjects of representations are invoked in a dramatic mode.

II. From Myth to Cult

The independent spirits correspond to the initiation rites whose object is to reveal the mystery of such spirits. The spirits of the dead correspond to the funerary cults performed on the occasion of a death.

Initiation rites share with other rites the explicit ultimate objective of enhancing fertility, fecundity, growth, success, and efficacy; appeasing the spirits; promoting the wealth of the clan and the strength and courage of its members; ensuring success in combat and trade; protecting men from the risk of impurity through contact with women; and, notably, teaching ethical principles and social values to novices, as shown by the example of initiation among the Kamano, Usurufa, Jate, and Fore in the eastern highlands: "You must not steal another man's pig or steal his fire. You must not do these things. But you may kill men. If a man uses sorcery against another, you may kill him. You must become strong, you must be big to do these things. You must look after your gardens. You must build enclosures for them and plant crops in them. You must not eat anything from a woman's hand. If a woman offers you food, refuse; if you do not, you will lose your strength and become sickly. You must not eat anything from the hands of young men, because they have copulated with their wives; if you do so, your body will be nothing but flesh and bones . . ." (Berndt 1962).

But it is in the latent, esoteric content of the initiation rituals rather than in this manifest end that it is possible to understand their import: they aim to furnish a tangible proof of the existence of a transcendental reality, to render perceptible what is unintelligible and thereby to allow the spirit of the novice to set in motion the process of the acquisition of belief. This objective is met by means of a ritual object that serves as a simulacrum or material "double" of the entity that is its referent. Depending on the culture, such objects vary in number and nature: flutes among the Mundugumor and Iatmul south of Sepik, Kamano, Usurufa, Flore, Siane, Chimbu, Kuma, and Gahuku-Gama in the highlands; bullroarers among the Marind Anim of West Irian, Arapesh, Abelam of Sepik, Kamano, Fore, and Orokaiva, Koko, Elema of Papua New Guinea; gongs among the Arapesh, Abelam, Tchambuli; masks among the Iatmul, Tchambuli, Kerewa, Namau, Elema, Turamarubi of Papua New Guinea; stones among the Mbowang, Kyaka, Enga, Huli, and Mendi of the highlands, and so forth.

Through the simulacrum, the reification of the transcendent spirit takes place. Through the object, the invisible presence is brought forth to be seen, to be perceived in a mystical way. The mystery revealed in the initiation is that of the incarnation of the subject into the object (of the idea into the thing); the object turns out to be nothing but an illusion, the screen of an immaterial world beyond, of an idea that transcends it and for which it stands as an incarnate allusion. For the novice, who expects to encounter the supernatural creature that has been foretold and given an extravagant and terrifying representation by his naive imagination, coming face to face with the simulacra is a decisive event. Wavering between his inability to sustain the childish belief to which the initiation has just dealt a brutal blow and the commensurate impossibility of giving it up altogether (Guidieri 1977), the new initiate can find a conceivable (and livable) compromise only in a belief transformed into the mystical rather than empirical existence of the spiritual entity as it is incarnate in the ritual object. This object, through which he comes to know the spirit model, is the instrument of the process of the acquisition of belief, at the end of which the novice gains access to the higher status of adult believer and male mystifier. Endowed this time with a new and real knowledge, he is expected not only to believe but to make others believe, to comfort in their cunning and ignorance, through his own deceitful talk, the women with whom he previously shared the inferior status of the credulous uninitiated. This demonstrates the principle of hierarchical opposition of the sexes, for which the ritual process seems to be the periodic reiteration.

In most cultures where myths justify the origins of ceremonial practices, the story begins with a description of the time when women had a dominant role and possessed sacred objects that they had discovered or created; it then goes on to conclude by evoking the inversion of the situation, by which men acquire through cunning or force not just power but also a monopoly over objects. Thus, for example, the Kamano and Fore myth of the sacred flutes:

Jugumishanta and Morufonu [the ancestral founding couple] were living at Koripika. Jugumishanta built a small segregation-hut where she slept by herself, her husband having built a large house for himself. At her place Jugumishanta planted wild ginger. She cut a length of bamboo and bored a hole in its surface, making a flute, and this she hid in the ginger foliage. Later she took it out and, hiding it in her skirt, left the camp. Reaching a secluded place, she began to play the flute; and from his own hut her husband heard its cry. "What is this that cries?" he said. "I would like to see it, but perhaps it

Marind Anim actors impersonating Dema spirits and carrying their bullroarers and drums. Southern New Guinea. Amsterdam, Kon. Instituut v/d Tropen. Institute photo.

would kill and eat me.'' So he thought to himself, and was afraid. Day after day Jugumishanta played her flute, and her husband became increasingly curious. Returning one night, she plucked out some pubic hair and placed it in the barrel of the flute; this would enable it to cry out if handled by someone other than herself; she then hid it in the ginger foliage. Later, when she went out to work in her garden, Morufonu made sure she was out of sight. Then he went down to her house and following her footprints eventually found the ginger bush and the flute. He dug up the ginger and took it back to his own house, where he planted it and prepared to play the flute; but the flute was playing by itself, warning Jugumishanta. As he lifted it to his mouth, the pubic hair within the flute touched him, and he immediately began to grow facial and body hair. [This explains why men are much hairier than women.—Berndt's note.] When Jugumishanta heard her flute, she ran back to her house and finding it and her ginger gone came to Morufonu and asked him, ''Who stole my flute?'' Morufonu replied, ''I heard something playing outside your hut, and I grew angry. I came down and found it. You couldn't play it properly, but I do it well. You must not look at it now, it is something belonging to me.'' He then placed the flute in the ginger foliage; it ''turned'' [became transformed—Berndt's note] and grew into a clump of bamboos with ginger growing at its base, seen today at Koripika. . . . Now men cut branches and make flutes, playing them in the bush at night during the pig festival so that pigs will increase.

During the night, too, they enter the village, decorated with branches of foliage, playing their flutes, while women, children, and young boys fasten their doors and stay in their houses. Moon after moon the flutes are played, increasing the pigs and making them grow larger, improving and advancing the crops, until finally pigs are killed and a festival is held. If a woman looks at a flute, she is killed; if a young boy is caught looking at the players, his nose is bled. (Berndt, pp. 50–51)

The majority of the mythical narrations about the origins of ritual objects thus tell the story of a dispossession (confiscation) in which the women are the victims and the men are the winners, appropriating for themselves the Kuma flutes or the Marind and Elema bullroarers. This turn of events in mythical times explains why in the current norms of New Guinea cultures, and Melanesian culture in general, women are excluded from the sacred domain of ritual practices, the fundamental meaning of which rests on the mystery of the object. On the basis of this mystery, forever denied to the knowledge of women, males assert the legitimacy of their supremacy in the sexual order. The presence of the simulacrum, reserved exclusively for manipulation by men, signifies the concrete and indisputable proof of their superiority (a peculiar proof, entirely self-contained, since it never needs to be made to the interested parties). But such superiority, so fragile because it is artificially founded on a mystifying discourse addressed to women, is not acquired once and for all. It is a precarious virtue which needs to be reaffirmed at

"Murup" mask made of painted wood, worn by men at festivals. New Guinea, Sepik. Paris, Musée de l'Homme collection. Museum photo.

Male sculpture made of wood, seeds, and human hair; eyes and ear ornaments made of mother-of-pearl; designs in black on brown background (sacred flute ornament). New Guinea. Paris, Musée de l'Homme collection.

regular intervals. Through ritual representation, males have the means of this reaffirmation. On such occasions, the ideology of contrasts, which in these cultures makes a woman a figure of impurity and a man a container, not impure but empty—and therefore vulnerable because threatened in his integrity by an opposite identity—finds its spectacular expression in ritual. Several features of this dramatization make up the characteristic constants tied to the communal theme of male sexual anxiety. The treatment given to this obsession which is focused on the female principle of fertility and procreation is brought about through the rejection and/or imitation of this principle. In rites of initiation, rejection is the actual practice of all New Guinean society, whether it takes the form of nose bleeding (Kuma, Chimbu, Kamano, Fore, Usurufa, Jate, Siane, Gahuku-Gama), of an incision on the penis (Kamano, Fore, Siane, Kuma, Arapesh, Abelam, Wogeo), or deep scarifications (Iatmul, Tchambuli). In all cases, the practice aims at draining from the body the substance most likely to endure and convey contamination: blood. The discharge is liberating in that it allows the male to rid himself of the female impurity, notably transmitted by the mother, and at the same time to put an end to his nonadult status. Thus freed from the negative forces that were stifling the male identity inside him, the initiate can at last aspire to the revelation of the cultural attributes of masculinity (flutes, gongs, masks, bullroarers) and gain access to his new status. Yet ethnographic evidence shows that what Bettelheim calls the "envy" of femininity remains in men despite all the acts designed to widen the gap that separates men from the feminine pole. Imitation, which appeared quite explicitly in the transvestite rites of the Iatmul, Kuma, Mbowang, and Arapesh, achieves the clearest symbolism when blood is regarded not only as a substance but as a dynamic entity that has a particular function: it is the process that becomes relevant for manifesting the difference. Thus the bleeding of certain organs or, in other cultures, circumcision and subincision, express not only the desire to eliminate from oneself any trace of female impurity but also an attempt by men to reproduce fictitiously upon themselves the exemplary periodicity of the specifically female mechanism of menstruation. Alongside this theme of cyclic movement there also appears, in the rituals of Papua New Guinea, the theme of giving birth, which finds its psychoanalytic equivalent in the initiatory symbolism of the death and rebirth of the novice (Allen 1967).

In all cases, however, liturgical artifice offers the male identity anxiety only a solution of temporary compromise that must be reiterated if it is to be effective. The ritual setting is the time and place of this reiteration. Beyond that, males merely have to protect themselves individually, by acts of purification, against the dangers of daily sexual promiscuity with women.

It should be noted that the antagonistic relationship between the sexes, characteristic of Melanesia in general, reaches an unparalleled dimension in Papua New Guinea (where this opposition has not been resolved), through the generation of a striking proliferation of models that represent sexuality (Guidieri 1975).

In funerary rites, the central referent is no longer the deified mythical subject but the formerly human entity that death projects outside the world of the living, the entity to whom one resorts in order to attain a particular status. A man who dies does not immediately acquire the name (and consequently the function) of an ancestor. Being an ancestor, in other words, is not a favor from death but a virtue which is earned in the process of transformation that death sets in motion.

When an individual has stopped living, the nonsubstantial part of his being escapes from the body and undertakes the journey that will take it to the land of the dead. The route to that place is particularly perilous, according to numerous myths, strewn with a succession of obstacles to be overcome and sufferings to be endured that make the journey look like a true initiation, and only at its end does he acquire the status of a completed dead person, that is, an ancestor.

Thus, in the conceptual thought of Papua New Guinea, death is defined not as the endpoint of a process of growth leading to annihilation but rather as the starting point of a new symmetrical evolution. In this evolution, the living have a role to play, since by their liturgical action they help the dead reach the final goal of transformation. The rites surrounding the corpse constitute the earthly equivalent of the occult course traversed by the soul moving toward its destiny, and they furnish an objective representation of the dead man's trajectory. They enact this trajectory, make it visible, that is, conceivable. Thus, in the example of Marind Anim, after the funeral the tomb is opened twice. The first time, shortly after death, the substance that is exuded by the decomposing body is extracted from the exhumed corpse, in imitation of the homologous practice that is performed on the soul as it travels on its initiatory road toward becoming an ancestor. This practice, consisting of tearing out the entrails of the soul, is a torment inflicted by a deity whose name, Adak ("to make a gash," or "to press"), evokes precisely the actions performed by the celebrants in order to collect the liquids from the corpse. At the end of these operations, the tomb is closed again; the dead man has become an ancestor. About one year later, the tomb is opened for the second time, and the bones of the dead man, now free of their flesh, are washed and painted red before they are arranged at the bottom of the tomb, which this time is closed forever. This process effectively "doubles" the mythical action in the same way that the supernatural events experienced by the soul in order to achieve its accession to ancestry "double" the actual initiation imposed on the male in order for him to become a complete adult (Van Baal 1966).

The other specific element of the funerary cults consists of bringing into place among the ritual objects that are the instruments of the liturgical process not only simulacra but relics, that is, the imperishable remains of one who has definitively attained the status of individuality. The memory that is actualized in the mortuary rite is therefore a memory that does not obliterate the anthropomorphic origin of the deified transcendence that is the ancestor. Such an entity, which can only be an identity, is assured of its temporal connection with the present by means of the genealogical discourse that shores up the memory of the living by conceptualizing it.

Mortuary rites, like initiation rites, function in both the visible and the invisible dimensions, but according to inverse modalities. While the initiation process aimed to make transcendance reach deep inside the immanent, through the intervention of artificial objects, the funerary liturgy orchestrates the accession of the immanent to the transcendant, by means of natural objects. It consecrates the transfiguration of the temporary and the perishable into the idea of the immutable.

In both cases, ritual produces transcendance and plays a role in that extraordinary moment when the Papuan brings his thought to its fullest expression.

M.Ba./g.h

BIBLIOGRAPHY

ALLEN, *Male Cults and Secret Initiations in Melanesia* (Melbourne 1967). F. BARTH, *Ritual and Knowledge among the Baktaman of New-Guinea* (New Haven 1975). G. BATESON, *Naven* (Stanford 1971); "Music in New-Guinea," *The Eagle*, vol. 48 (1935). R. M. BERNDT, *Excess and Restraint* (Chicago 1962). B. BETTELHEIM, *Symbolic Wounds*, rev. ed. (New York 1962). GLASSE, SALISBURY, BERNDT, MEGGITT, and BULMER, *Gods, Ghosts and Men in Melanesia* (Oxford 1965). R. GUIDIERI, "Note sur le rapport mâle/femelle en Mélanésie," *L'Homme*, 15, 2 (1975); *Introduc-tion à l'anthropologie des croyances*, course of the Department of Ethnology at the University of Paris-X (Nanterre 1975–78). O. MAN-NONI, *Clefs pour l'imaginaire ou l'autre scène* (Paris 1969). M. MEAD, *Sex and Temperament in Three Primitive Societies* (London 1935). NEVERMANN, WORMS, and PETRI, *Les religions du Pacifique et de l'Australie* (Paris 1968). M. STRATHERN, *Women in Between: Female Role in a Male Role, Mount Hagen, New-Guinea* (London 1972). J. VAN BAAL, "The Cult of the Bull-Roarer in Australia and Southern New-Guinea," in *Bijdragen . . . .*, 119.2; *Dema: Description and Analysis of Marind-Anim Culture, South New-Guinea* (The Hague 1966). F. E. WILLIAMS, "Natives of the Purari Delta," *Anthropological Report*, no. 5 (Papua 1924); "Bull-Roarers in the Papuan Gulf," *Anthropological Report*, no. 17 (Papua 1936); *Oro-kaiva Society* (Oxford 1930); *Drama of Orokolo* (Oxford 1940).

3

Africa

Forms of the Symbolic Function in the Art and Myth of Sub-Saharan Africa

Before examining the connections between mythology and the production of what, in Western terms, is called "artistic," we must first acknowledge certain ambiguities that have been inspired and maintained by a theoretical haze attributable in part to hurried, scattered documentation, often irreparably flawed, and partly to the misuse of terminology. These ambiguities are all the more dangerous because they mask difficulties we must be aware of if we want to base our research on a more stable and better-marked foundation than has existed to date. The difficulties are of several different types, yet are tangled together. I will separate them only to facilitate discussion.

In the first place, the collection of myths governing both the behavior and the thought of the various, and very distinct, cultures of sub-Saharan Africa was undertaken quite late: hardly anyone was concerned with it before the last decade of the nineteenth century. And the work was very uneven because of the extreme disparity in research methods used to collect and analyze the myths (methods that would not be described and standardized until the second quarter of the twentieth century). The work was also uneven because of its scattered and sporadic application: in the search for myths and in their exploration, certain groups were given particular attention—such as the Mande, the Dogon, and the Bambara—while others were ignored for some time before any kind of inventory was taken. We must resign ourselves to the gaps that still exist in our documentation: they can no longer be filled. For several decades, and especially since attaining their independence, the countries of sub-Saharan Africa have embarked upon an irreversible process of transformation, whereby traditional practices and forms of behavior have fallen into disuse, and the myths that created and justified them have been forgotten. The Malian philosopher Hampate Ba noted (and deplored) the fact that with the death of each old person, the equivalent of an entire library disappeared forever.

The second difficulty arises with the constraint to rethink and question more precisely a theoretical approach to concrete phenomena that are poorly discernible from outside the culture in which they have been observed. The difficulty lies in ideas of myth that have been formed within a history, ideas that must be reconsidered. Because mythologists from the end of the nineteenth century worked exclusively from written material, they considered the myth as a text, whose meaning and authenticity they debated doggedly—in order to find its hidden meaning. The hermeneutic work was not undertaken until the correct reading of the text had been clearly established. All that was left to do then was to research the different modalities, historic or otherwise, in which this text had been elaborated, and the successive alterations that it had gone through in space (during its circulation) or in time (during its evolution). In sub-Saharan Africa, however, the transmission, conservation, and perpetuation of myths were not done in writing: these functions were carried out in the course of initiations. African wisdom holds that learning cannot be dissociated from understanding: it cannot be acquired or disposed of by those who are not ready for it—or who are imperfectly prepared; its acquisition and disposition must be based upon qualifications that should be acquired progressively, according to the physical and spiritual development of the individual. African thought is thus fundamentally opposed to the written form, which, without discernment or order, attempts to convey what should, in its continuity, embrace the maturation of the individual.

In order to distinguish between cultures that give pride of place to the written word and those that refuse to fix thought and its transmission in writing, and to distinguish them according to the types of mental processes that determine methods of intellection as well as forms of behavior for both types of cultures, we must make one observation: as a broad generalization, discursive writing, through its own rhetorical system and its various articulations, leads the reader to a conclusion, while initiation does not direct the person undergoing it to any ultimate truth to be achieved at the final level. Its truth is made up only by and in the path that it marks and that marks it in turn. Theoretically, initiation is infinite, ending only in death. Or, more precisely, initiation does not end at all: it is only interrupted. Death marks its limit. In a sense, it is *gnosis*, and continuous, impossible to complete. But it is also, and at the same time, in a very pragmatic way, the accommodation of the individual person (who progressively unravels for himself the data given by nature) to the order of the cosmos (as it was, at the beginning, conceived by an unimaginable creator). It is this intricate combination of a gnostic design with apparently pragmatic practices that produces the proper climate for initiation to take place and to reveal its meaning, in terms of both significance and purpose. It is important not to dissociate the two elements that compose it, either to give one more importance than the other or to consider one to the exclusion of the other: the unity of symbolic representations and material forms of behavior, which everything leads us to believe is central to African thought, would be seriously affected in its very meaning. It should also be noted that the instruction dispensed in schools of initiation is not exclusively verbal; it can even dispense with oral discourse. Often, it plays in several different registers: the behavior of the candidate in a critical situation (frightening, dangerous), his habituation and resistance to deprivation and physical suffering, but also the learning of dance, sign language, and even, at times, the silent presentation of a series of objects, including statuettes. This leads us to a third difficulty which, if ignored, would leave in shadow a problem whose investigation could furnish us with important methodological tools.

In 1914, the Russian painter Vladimir Matveï-Markov praised "the profound thought of Negroes . . . expressed through the plastic arts." In 1915, Carl Einstein wrote that sub-Saharan African art was a product of "formal thought." Because they worked within the formalist movement at the beginning of the century, one a defender of "futurism," the other of "cubism," these two men entered into violent conflict with the ethnology of their times in their interpretation of "Negro art." In doing so, they isolated a methodology as well as a problematic that are proving most fertile today: they force us to reconsider both classical functionalist theory and the symbolist theory that was later to derive from it.

In functionalist theory, the Westerner is not entitled to speak of groups of objects as "works of art" when in black Africa they are intended for something else entirely and when they are not considered works of art by their user, unless he is prepared to commit the sin of ethnomorphism. Thus, a mask is first and foremost designed to be worn and to be used in the midst of initiatory, agricultural, or funeral ceremonies—where it is only one element among many; a statuette is first and foremost attached to a cult, for which it is only a support or instrument. The instrumentality of a sculpture therefore becomes more important than its artistic characteristics—the study of which may even jeopardize its being understood. To the more radical aspects of this theory, several objections must be raised.

To restrict the use of the phrase "work of art" to the specific study of productions intended for disinterested contemplation, delectation, or the expression of the unique personality of their creators is to confine oneself to a single aesthetic: that of the classical and romantic West. Here we commit the sin of "Europocentrism." Furthermore, it has been demonstrated that in evaluating sculptures and objects produced by their own culture, Africans (as strictly conducted surveys have shown) *did* make distinctions regarding the level of artistic accomplishment that such objects demonstrated, confirming the judgments of Western experts on the same body of work. Finally, although these objects do not fit into certain Western categories such as "free art," "decorative art," or "court art," quite a large number of sculptures and other objects—the number varying according to the region—are fashioned in such a way as not to allow them to be reduced to their pure instrumentality within a cult: the

Left: Statuette of a woman and two children. Wood. Dogon. Paris and New York, H. Kramer collection. Photo I.P.N. *Right:* Statue of a female figure. Wood. Bambara. Paris, P. Langlois collection. Photo I.P.N.

bronze plaques at Benin, once attached to pillars supporting the canopies of the royal palaces, the sculpted pillars that supported the roofs of the houses of Bamileke chieftains (in Cameroon), or, in Zaire and Angola, the collections of delicately worked cups, makeup boxes, seats, and other objects.

The debate would be academic, however, if it bore only on the question of justifying the use of the word "art" to describe African productions. Even though its basic meaning is seldom applied precisely and without prejudice, it has a completely different connotation. Despite warnings given by Jean-Jacques Rousseau in his *Essay on the Origin of Languages*, Western thought shows some resistance to the very idea that there may be a second alternative to the transmission of thought through writing, besides that of the spoken word. In fact, the teachings dispensed during initiation are conveyed by many means that modulate what is being taught. And according to a myth common to the Dogon and Bamana, the spoken word was revealed to man in the form of three objects, each associated with a technique: a grain of millet, a loom, and a drum. The order of these three objects reveals, among other things, a genesis of space: from a point to three dimensions.

We are encouraged therefore to base the problems of African iconography on a totally different foundation, using different assumptions: first, that myth is not organized like a written text whose original version, still unaltered and *true*, must be determined and which is illustrated in some way by material productions. Second, that myth may be transmitted in some way other than through the spoken word. What is at stake here is a more refined and subtle approach to determining the relation between mythic activity and the objects that embody it, that make it visible, readable. This process is also, as Vladimir Matveï-Markov and Carl Einstein have emphasized, the working of true formal thought, insofar as formal thought not only conveys but produces meaning.

Symbolist theory should be reconsidered here, as well: according to this theory, not only masks and statuary but also architecture, music, and choreography, useful objects (from clothing to household utensils), and even body markings (tatoos, scarification, face painting) are related to a coherent system of signs that explicates the meaning of myths according to the particular level attained through initiation. Derived from functionalist theory, symbolist theory nevertheless changed functionalism substantially, especially in displacing our expectations: we are no longer in the realm of pure instrumentality; rather, we have been returned to a system. Hence its heuristic value: developed not in the abstract, but through strictly conducted research and fieldwork, in an intensive and continuous fashion, symbolist theory furnishes us—and that is all it does—with the state of a mythology located at a particular time and place. The theory forces us to break down into categories something that Western culture classifies and ranks in order (decorative arts, cosmetics, true sculpture, etc.) but that can hardly be separated in African cultures. Between all these manifestations, through the mediation of heavily weighted signs, there are exchanges which reveal their fundamental unity.

Research undertaken by Marcel Griaule and his students since 1931 among the Dogon and the Bamana (Republic of Mali), the Sonrhaï (Niger), the Kurumba (Upper Volta), and the Fali (North Cameroon) has uncovered the existence of a rich and complex metaphysical system that is shared by all the populations who consider themselves descended from the Mande. Not all of these populations produce sculpture (the Sonrhaï and Fali, for example, do not). Among the works produced by those who do, there are differences that indicate that they are unique to the population in question. There are stylistic differences, but there are also differences in the iconography, which varies widely, although to an unequal extent, depending on the center of production. It must be noted, first, that a myth can be dressed in different forms and signs, and one must try to find out whether these are not differential indicators, produced as identifying marks of a particular culture. Second, within the myth, each population stresses the themes it considers most important, or to which it attributes such and such a fact. For this second point I shall borrow from the Dogon, whose sculptural production is an important body of work, among the most diverse stylistically and iconographically, and whose mythography has been the best developed. The Dogon population itself has both wide stylistic variety and wide iconographic variety. And the connections between the stylistic and the iconographic series raise important questions. Certain well-established iconographic series—figures with raised arms (a reference to the spirit Nommo)—are treated in all the styles classified to date. But other series (depictions of dogs) exist, to my knowledge, only in one clearly defined formal system. Finally, there is one clearly categorized series, depicting groups of couples seated on the center of the *imago mundi*, which combines two different styles—one for the four

Nommo pairs with raised arms (in the lower half) and the other for the man and woman seated on the disk above.

Given the existence of such peculiarities within a single body of work, the questions that should be asked in relating stylistic and iconographic series will differ, depending on whether one chooses to proceed synchronically or diachronically. Synchronically, we must deal with the reactualization, even the unification, of elements whose disparate character (which can be imputed either to chronological stratifications or to geographical dispersion) must be reconciled, since it is not significant for the concerns at hand. Diachronically, we must consider the very history of the country and the Dogon people: a stylistically homogeneous series of statuettes with raised arms is attributed by modern-day Dogon to the Tellem—the group that preceded them on the Bandiagara cliff. But this theme was concretized in all the other stylistic series of the Dogon region. First observation: the survival of the image does not necessarily imply the survival of its original meanings. Second observation: if, from a strictly typological point of view, with no chronological interpretation, the entire series of statuettes with raised arms is placed in order, the succession thus produced shows elements of the myth of the sacrifice of Nommo, his metamorphosis into a serpent, the progressive differentiation of his limbs, and their articulation. Proliferating around a single theme, multiple meanings will in turn be preferred or devalued, and will become specialized through the play of

Songhai mask from the Lomami region. Wood, esparto, and fibers. Tervuren, Musée royal d'Afrique central. Photo I.P.N.

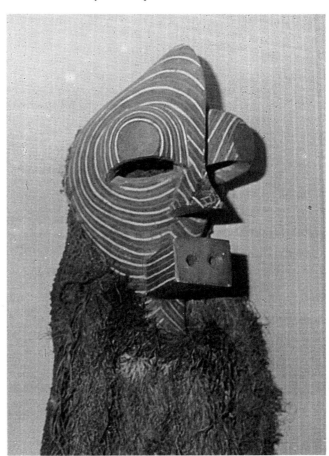

Teak mask. Gabon. Paris, Païlès collection. Photo I.P.N.

Ivory mask. Lega. Private collection. Photo I.P.N.

formal thought. This process will not break up the structural schema that produced those meanings, but by increasing the number of their combinations will further enrich them. Third observation: the stylistic transformations of a single theme seem, as they were produced, to have been integrated into a system (the system of myth, not as an unchangeable body of work, but as an activity) as significant figures: the seats of the *imago mundi*, which combine two different styles, manifest a presumably Tellem influence in the figures with raised arms, and a totally different formal composition in the seated couple; they testify that the new arrivals did dominate their predecessors, but that these predecessors still retained their identity, sometimes assimilated to the founding heroes, sometimes as "masters of the earth."

Inscribed on these objects are not only a myth of origin and a cosmogony, not only a history, but also a political structure. This is done through formal stylistic differentiations, which are then given a meaning in mythic activity. Formal activity, then, far from being subject to a symbolist function in which it would merely illustrate the sequences of the mythic narratives, appears to lead positively to questions about the study of myths. It seems to intervene directly in mythic activity, whose developments it can guide, and, finally, it appears to describe, under the veil of myth, historic occurrences considered noteworthy by the parties involved, for whom it serves as archivist. In this way, the study of sub-Saharan iconography demonstrates a highly heuristic quality, yielding a more detailed and subtle approach to African cultures through synchrony and diachrony.

More useful than "symbolist function" is the term "signifying function," since the relationship between signs or groups of signs and what they are thought to signify cannot be viewed univocally. Signs or groups of signs can create new meanings, either by transforming themselves or by redistributing themselves within the combinations with which they are associated. The capacity of formal activity to intervene directly in the course of the orientations taken by mythic activity is clearly confirmed by initiation rites: among the Tscholkwe (Angola) and Senufo (Ivory Coast), candidates are presented with a group of objects, figurines or small statues, whose different possible combinations produce the myth without any oral intervention.

It may even be possible to go further and to distinguish, through an analysis of formal structures, concepts that are not stated explicitly but could nevertheless be reformulated with reference to man's place in the cosmic order. An extended study of the ways in which mass is distributed in statuary has uncovered a certain number of figures that determine this distribution: spirals, the opposition of voids and solids, symmetry, and the opposition and counterpoint of masses. These figures demonstrate a double attitude toward rhythm: it is a matter of simultaneously channeling the energy that traverses nature in order to appropriate it for one's own use, and of controlling it, mastering it, or taking possession of nature through culture. This double attitude corresponds to a double function. On the one hand there is the vitalist function of rhythm, which has an equivalent in dances of possession as well as in beliefs about the descent of speech. Such beliefs are confirmed by statues showing two figures, one with his arms raised and his feet on the head of the Hogon (the religious leader), whose skull has been cut off at the level of his brain. The other function of the double attitude to rhythm is its power to order and classify, a power that combines and redistributes significant elements, organizes them according to a precise formal code, and, in music, manifests itself in stressed sequences.

J.La./d.b.

BIBLIOGRAPHY

Few specific studies have been devoted to the problem covered here. However, one general collective work makes a preliminary survey of the question: *African Art as Philosophy*, DOUGLAS FRAZER, ed. (New York 1974). Monographs and specialized articles abound with information that makes it possible to address the problem anew. There are bibliographies of the subject, relatively complete through 1967, in the following reference works: M. LEIRIS and J. DELANGE, *Afrique noire: La création artistique*, L'univers des formes (Paris 1967). J. DELANGE, *Les arts de l'Afrique noire* (Paris 1967). See also J. LAUDE, *Les arts de l'Afrique noire* (Paris 1966). For an interpretation of the arts of sub-Saharan Africa from a formalist perspective, see C. EINSTEIN, *Negerplastik* (Leipzig 1915), and V. MARKOV, *Iskusstovo Negros* (Saint Petersburg 1919). These two works have been translated into French, the first by Liliane Meffre and the second by Jacqueline and Jean-Louis Paudrot, in *Travaux et mémoires du Centre de recherches historiques sur les relations artistiques entre les cultures, Université de Paris*, no. 1 (Paris 1976).

On general problems concerning the role and function of art in African cultures: M. GRIAULE, *Arts de l'Afrique noire* (Paris 1947); "Le problème de la culture noire," in *Originalité des cultures* (1954). And, above all, the remarkable synthesis by A. A. GHEERBRANDTS, *Art as Element of Culture, Especially in Negro-Africa* (Leiden 1957). This work may be usefully complemented by a most erudite statement of the question by F. HERMANN, "Die afrikanische Negerplastik, als Forschungsgegenstand," in *Beiträge zur afrikanischen Kunst* (Berlin 1958). For reservations that should be maintained toward the purely functionalist theory, see J. LAUDE, "Esthétique et système de classifi-

cations: La statuaire africaine," *Sciences de l'art*, 1965; J. L. PAUDRAT, "Tradition et création: La sculpture africaine," in *Catalogue de la collection africaine Barbier-Müller* (Geneva 1978).

The intensive research that has been carried out on the correspondences between art and myth is very unequally distributed among the cultures studied. It has been particularly thorough with regard to the Dogon and the Bamana of Mali. See M. GRIAULE, *Masques dogon* (Paris 1938); "Art et symbole en Afrique noire," *Zodiaque* (October 1951), 5; "Les symboles des arts africains," *Présence africaine* 10–11 (1951); J. D. FLAM, "Some Aspects of Style Symbolism in Sudanese Sculpture," *Journal de la société des africanistes*, 1970, 40; J. LAUDE, "La statuaire du pays dogon," *Revue d'esthétique*, 1964, 17; *African Art of the Dogon: The Myths of the Cliff Dwellers* (New York 1973); D. ZAHAN, "Les couleurs chez les Bambara du Soudan français," in *Notes africaines* (Dakar 1951), 50; *Les sociétés d'initiation chez les Bambara: Le n'domo, le koré* (Paris and The Hague 1960); "Signification et fonction de l'art dans la vie d'une communauté africaine: Les Bambara," in *Actes du colloque sur l'art nègre*, 1 (Paris and Dakar 1967).

For the Senufo (Ivory Coast): G. BOCHET, "Le Poro de Dieli," in *Bulletin de l'Institut français d'Afrique noire* 21, ser. B, 1–2. R. J. GOLDWATER, *Senufo: Sculpture from West Africa* (New York 1964).

For the Akan group (Ashanti and Baoulé): R. S. RATTRAY, *Religion and Art in Ashanti* (Oxford 1927); E. MEYEROWITZ, *The Akan of Ghana: Their Ancient Beliefs* (London 1958); and, above all, H. COLE and D. ROSS, *The Arts of Ghana* (Los Angeles 1978).

For the cultures of Cameroon: R. LECOQ, "Quelques aspects de l'art bamoum," in *Présence africaine* 10–11 (1951); *Une civilisation africaine: Les Bamiléké* (Paris 1953); T. NORTHERN, *The Sign of the Leopard: Beaded Art of Cameroun* (Storrs, CT, 1975); J. P. LEBEUF, *L'habitation des Fali, montagnards du Cameroun septentrional* (Paris 1961).

For the cultures of Zaire: L. BITTREMIEUX, *La société secrète des Bakhimba, au Mayombe* (Brussels 1936), and *Symbolisme en de Negerkunst* (Brussels 1937); J. MAËS, *Aniota Kifwebe* (Antwerp 1924); R. HOTTOT, "Teke fetisches," *Journal Roy. Anthr. Institut* 86 (1956); H. BURSENS, "La fonction de la sculpture traditionnelle chez les Ngbaka," in *Brousse*, 2 (Léopoldville 1958); *Umbangu, arts du Congo au Musée royal du Congo belge*, L'art en Belgique, 3, commentary on plates by A. Maesen.

For the cultures of Angola: M. L. BASTIN, *Art décoratif Tschokwe*, 2 vols. (Lisbon 1961); M. LIMA, *Fonction sociologique des figurines du culte hamba, dans la société et la culture tschokwe de l'Angola* (Luanda 1971).

THE MYTHOLOGY OF THE MANDE AND THE CHOICE OF THE DOGON AS A SUBJECT OF STUDY

The region called the Mande or Manding reaches to the south and west of Bamako, capital of the republic of Mali. It includes the upper valley of the Niger to Kurussa in Guinea and covers the Mandingo mountains. The population is approximately 600,000.

Historically, the region was long ago occupied by Soninke and Kagoro families who came down from the Sahel after a series of droughts and wars had led to the decline and fall of the Uagadu empire. Descendants of these families still occupy most of the communities of the Mande.

In the twelfth century, after the defeat of Sumanworo Kante, who had occupied it with his troops, the Mande became the seat of the Mali empire established by the conquering Sundiata Keita. This empire spread progressively from Senegal to Kano in Nigeria. It inaugurated a system that was simultaneously religious, social, economic, and political, based on an important myth that must be understood if we are to penetrate the infrastructure of this organization, which can be termed international.

Genealogists declare that thirty allied families, who formed the original foundation of the Mali empire and are said to have had their roots in the Mande, spread over a very large area of western Africa. These families included not only all the Mandingo language groups (Malinke, Bambara, Diola, Kassonke), but a number of peoples from Mali, Senegal, the Ivory Coast, Upper Volta, Togo, and Dahomey. Delegates from some of these groups still return every seven years to Kangaba for the rebuilding of the *kama blō* sanctuary in the ancient Mandingo city; during the ceremony, the names of the families from which these populations descended are recalled.

The Mande has been the subject of many studies and publications on the geography, history, archaeology, and social and economic life of the societies that occupy it now, as well as the languages that make up the Mande group. We will make it our field of study for the principal myths of black western Africa, and particularly for the cosmogonic myth, which has been collected from the Dogon, the Bambara, the Malinke, the Bozo, the Soninke, and the Minyanka. Despite conversions to Islam beginning in the Uagadu empire and occurring in the Mande from the twelfth century on, despite those that take place today, despite education and changes in life due to present-day economic and political conditions, the tradition has remained as strong as ever.

From a geographical standpoint, the course of the Niger from its source at Lake Debo connects all the different populations of the Mande and forms the principal axis of its mythology. The mythology has many variations, which embellish certain sequences and reduce others, but the essence and design remain the same. Due to linguistic differences, the main characters have different names according to the ethnic context, but they have the same characteristics, act in the same way and serve similar functions.

In the article "Twins, a Dominant Theme in West African Mythologies" (see below), in which the cosmogonic myth is related, we chose to present the Dogon version for two reasons:

1. The Dogon are Malinke who, in about the twelfth century, left the Mande region where they lived (and where their relatives still live), in order to maintain their traditional religion. After a long migration, they took refuge among the cliffs of Bandiagara, where they have maintained their beliefs and customs without change to this day. And, as in their place of origin, they have left representations of their beliefs all over their land: their cosmology is written on many surfaces in many ways and on the altars where rituals are regularly performed.

2. Between 1967 and 1973 the Dogon celebrated the Sigui ceremonies, which take place every sixty years. These ceremonies—once celebrated in the Mande but abandoned in that region—are held, among other reasons, to commemo-rate and reactualize certain episodes fundamental to Dogon cosmology, the object of their beliefs and the central axis of their social and religious life.

G.D./d.b.

BIBLIOGRAPHY

The principal ancient authors who mention the Mali (Mande) are: SA'DI, *Tarikh Es-Soudan* (Paris 1964). KATI, *Tarikh El-Fettach* (Paris 1964). EL BEKRI, *Description de l'Afrique septentrionale* (Paris 1965). IBN BATTUTA, *Voyages* (Paris 1969). J. LÉON L'AFRICAIN, *Description de l'Afrique* (Paris 1956).

Other Publications

M. DELAFOSSE, *Haut Sénégal-Niger* (Paris 1912). G. DIETERLEN, "Mythe et organisation sociale au Soudan français," *Journal de la Société des Africanistes* 25 (1955): 39–76; "Mythe et organisation sociale en Afrique occidentale (suite)," *Journal de la Société des Africanistes* 29 (1959): 119–38; "Contribution à l'étude des relations protohistoriques entre le Mandé et l'actuel Ghana," *Actes du symposium international sur les religions de la préhistoire* (Capo di Ponte 1975), 368–77. H. LABOURET, *Les Manding et leur langue* (Paris 1934). R. MAUNY, "Tableau géographique de l'Afrique de l'Ouest au moyen âge d'après les sources écrites, les traditions et l'archéologie," *Mémoires de l'I.F.A.N.* (Dakar 1961), vol. 61. C. MONTEIL, "Les Empires du Mali," *Bulletin du Comité historique et scientifique de l'A.O.F.* (1929). J. VIDAL, "Au sujet de l'emplacement du Mali," *Bulletin du Comité historique et scientifique de l'A.O.F.* (1923).

GRAPHIC SIGNS AND THE SEED OF KNOWLEDGE: THE 266 BASIC SIGNS IN WEST AFRICA

According to J. Février's definitions in his *Histoire de l'écriture*, many graphic systems recorded in West Africa could be called "synthetic writing" (suggesting or connoting a sentence or a sentence fragment) or "idea writing"; others could be called "analytical or ideographic writing," or "word writing."

For the Malinke, Bambara, Dogon, Bozo, and Minyanka, the primary signs, numbering 266, represent "the basis of knowledge," *doni dyu* (in Bambara); "the seed of all knowledge," *doni siya wo siya*—but also, and above all, the basis of creation. The saying goes, "The origin of all creatures [i.e., all things that have existed, exist, or are going to exist] is [resides] in the signs"; "knowledge has come out of [issued from] signs." These signs themselves are thought to come from a single sign, *ti kele pe*, also called "the burning or hot sign," or "support sign," *ti kalama*, the symbol of both the unity and the multiplicity of God the creator.

This idea has much greater implications than one might at first assume, for it conditions all representations tied to the creation of the universe. For all the peoples from the Mande, the universe came out of a word, the spirit and thought of a creator God who first brought forth, out of nothing, "signs" that designated in advance all that was to make up creation. Then God created matter in the form of an initial placenta on the walls of which were engraved the first signs of beings and things (eight seeds and two pairs of mixed twins, the prototypes of future man). It follows that what are ordinarily called "spiritual principles" were at first conceived only as the essence of signs inscribed in the initial placenta, or "womb" of God.

That is why the 266 basic signs correspond to the number of days totaling the nine months required for human gestation. Here as elsewhere in black Africa, the connection between the biological plane and the cosmogonic system is self-evident; this connection also underscores the all-important time factor in the initiatory teaching structure (in the Bambara society of the Komo, classes of initiates are divided into categories corresponding to the 266 signs of creation).

The genesis of the signs immerses the initiate in the most deeply hidden mystery of creation. With the signs, he penetrates the secrets of cosmogony, for the signs have been manifest since the beginnings and even preceded the creation of the things they designate. In fact, the ideas represented by these ideograms were projected into reality in the guise of the beings, elements, and sentiments they represent, which were named at the same time (each sign has its own device). The signs are sacred, and their use is a function of this sacralization. Each sign (each "picture of the signs") is, depending on the case, traced on the ground, painted on small wooden boards or pieces of calabash, drawn in caves, woven or embroidered on fabrics, or proclaimed through its device, on completion of some act of interest to the community, at a ceremony, at a ritual in anticipation of an event, or on other occasions. The sign that plays a role in the genesis of the being or thing it promoted continues to bear witness to that being or thing until "the end of time."

Let us examine this aspect of the Malinke shrine of Kangaba (a village on the Niger River a hundred kilometers

Making signs on the Mande shrine (fourth day). Kangaba. Photo G. Dieterlen.

Paintings from the Circle of Mopti (Mali). Paris, Musée de l'Homme. Photo Griaule.

upstream from Bamako)—the *kama blō*—the "vestibule of the master of the sky," also known as the "vestibule of the Mande" (*māde blō*). This building is one of the relatively recent replicas of a shrine that all traditionalists situate at Kri Koro, "Kri the very old," in the Mandingo Mountains, both the mythical and the historical homeland of all the populations who claim to be from the Mande (Malinke, Bambara, Bozo, Dogon, Minyanka, etc.). Every seven years, the Keita families gather at the *kama blō* to celebrate the diffusion of the great families of the Mande (one such ceremony took place in 1975). After the roughcasting of the walls, the next step in the ritual is to execute the 266 sacred "signs" on the inside walls and to paint the outside walls of the hut; then a new roof is built.

Because of their extreme sacredness, it has not been possible to examine—let alone record—the signs inside the *kama blō*. But it is nevertheless useful to mention one classification of these signs that was collected from Malinke informers from Kangaba. They divide into four groups the primordial series that is reproduced every seven years inside the shrine according to a scheme closely connected to the sequences of the cosmogonic myth and the history of the Mande peoples. The groups are as follows:

1. eight signs for the eight primordial seeds and for the stage of the genesis of matter in the form of an initial seed, now materialized by the smallest of cereal grains, fonio;
2. four for the four elements and the four cardinal points;
3. nine for the eight ancestors of humanity and the Mande shrine;

4. the other signs are shared among the families originating from the Mande.

It has also been demonstrated that in every Mande village the hut of the great initiation societies (Komo, Kwore, Nya, etc.), which houses the objects of the cult, should be regarded as the replica of the shrine of the *kama blō*. In the hut or the sacred grove, each of these societies secretly keeps a small board of the signs, called the *nya ti wala ba*, "board of the great signs" that bear witness to the genesis of divine creation as they do in the Mande shrine.

In the initiation society of the Komo (in Malinke, Bambara, Minyanka, and even Senufo country), the quadrangular sign board is painted in the colors of the rainbow and fire, branded with the 266 signs of creation; for this reason, it also has "the pictures of the Sky and Earth."

The 266 sacred signs of the Komo—which are theoretically the source of other parallel series—are classified in groups of twenty-two categories associated with their genesis. It is said that "the great signs number twenty-two times twelve concrete things, plus two abstract things" promoted by God. The grouping of signs according to a genetic type of classification makes for a learned science of numbers. "The mystery of creation is to be found in numeration and numbers," says a Bambara motto recorded and interpreted by Yussuf Cissé. The signs thus represent the totality of beings, of things, and of the concrete and abstract acts of the universe itself as a whole (the past, the present, and the future; the visible and the invisible; the known, the unknown, and the unknowable, etc.); they constitute both the origin and the sum total of all knowledge.

This multiplication may be expressed by the materialization of other series of signs observed at various levels in other initiation societies (Kwore, Nya, and Nama), in the context of collective rites (circumcision, the making of masks) or of techniques. In either case, research is needed to identify the relationship between these series and that of the Komo and probably with that of the *kama blō* as well.

For the Dogon, the development of beings and things is also prefigured by 266 primordial signs inscribed within the consciousness of a single God. Dogon men of learning worked out a remarkable theory of signs. Two guide-signs and eight master-signs give life to the mobile (complete) signs that in turn bring things into existence. Amma propels the signs into space, where they go through a series of explosions before taking on material dimensions in images, figures, and drawings.

Research conducted among Dogon men of learning has revealed four levels of inscription in this mythical geography, which indicate successively the four developmental stages of a sign, the fourth one leading to the materialization of the thing or the being that it designates.

1. The first series reveals the "primary signs" of God's creation, known as the *bummo* (traces), which belong by their very essence to Amma (God) and as such are set apart. These signs, the symbol of Amma's work, accomplished in his womb, are executed ritually—and generally only once—under the foundational altars or in the interior of shrines where no one other than the priest in charge may enter.

2. After this first series, also referred to as the "abstract signs," comes the sacred series, the *yala* (marks) or images made of dotted lines. "The *yala* of a thing," say the Dogon, "is like the beginning of the thing." That is why *yala* are traced on the corners of the foundation of a house before it is built. They are also traced in caves before the making of masks.

3. The third series of signs is that of the *tonu* (figure), a sketch or sometimes an outline of things. The *tonu* is a schematic tracing in which the graphic elements are generally separate.

4. The fourth series constitutes the *toymu*, the "drawing" of the thing always represented as realistically as possible. It is also the thing itself. When one builds a house, it is as if one had made a complete drawing, *toymu*, of the house.

Among the Dogon, then, as in most of the societies of the Mande, the system of graphic signs helps to explain the genesis of a world whose components were all sketched originally in the consciousness of a single God.

We should add that such a system is also found outside the Mande area, notably among the Ewe-speakers and the Gurmanche. The works of Michel Cartry in the Gurmanche country have shown that the use of signs is the function of a sacralization, comparable in several ways to the sacralization of the signs in the Mande. In analyzing the ritual of excision in these populations, he has shown how a calabash carved with signs must be placed on the abdomen of a young girl for the operation to be fully effective. "There must be direct contact between the stomach of the girl and the signs inscribed on the calabash," he says. "The young girl must be physically impregnated with the signs of procreation, and she must incorporate them. The meaning of the ideograms is never taught to young girls during their initiation. This sign acts by virtue of its inscription in the body. . . . The inscription of a mark in the body does not merely carry the value of a message; it is also an effective instrument that acts directly upon the body itself. . . . The signs rule over the things they signify, and the artist who makes the signs, far from being a mere imitator, performs a work reminiscent of the divine work."

G.D./g.h.

BIBLIOGRAPHY

M. CARTRY, "Notes sur les signes graphiques du géomancien gourmantché," *Journ. Soc. Africanistes* 33, 2 (1963): 275–306; "La Calebasse de l'excision en pays gourmantché," *Journ. Soc. Africanistes*, 1968, 189–225. Y. CISSÉ, "Signes graphiques, représentations, concepts et tests relatifs à la personne chez les Malinké et les Bambara du Mali," in *La notion de personne en Afrique noire*, Colloques internationaux du CNRS (Paris 1973), 131–79. G. DIETERLEN, *Essai sur la religion bambara* (Paris 1951). G. DIETERLEN and Y. CISSÉ, "Les fondements de la société d'initiation du Komo," *Cahiers de l'homme*, n.s., 10 (Paris and The Hague 1972). J. FÉVRIER, *Histoire de l'écriture* (2d ed., Paris 1959). S. DE GANAY, "Aspects de mythologie et de symbolique bambara," *Journal de psychologie normale et pathologique*, 1949, 273–94. M. GRIAULE and G. DIETERLEN, "Signes graphiques soudanais," *Cahiers de l'homme* 3 (1951); "Le renard pâle," 1: "Le mythe cosmogonique," fasc. 1: "La création du monde," *Travaux et mémoires de l'Institut d'ethnologie* 72 (Paris 1965): 62–88. P. JESPERS, "Signes graphiques et mythologie des Minyanka du Mali," *Journ. Soc. Africanistes*, forthcoming.

We wish to thank M. Philippe Jespers, who contributed to the development of this article as well as to the other articles on West Africa.

TWINS, A DOMINANT THEME IN WEST AFRICAN MYTHOLOGIES

The concept of twinning is a dominant theme in the mythologies of West Africa. There is almost no society which has not developed a complex system of representations and rituals about twins.

For all the populations that consider themselves part of the Mande (Malinke, Bambara, Dogon, Bozo, etc.), twins incarnate an ideal of ontological perfection, recalling at least partially the mythic times when the first living creatures were pairs of twins of the opposite sex. Today the birth of twins "recalls this happy condition, and that is why it is celebrated everywhere with joy. Twins are thought to be invulnerable; they play a decisive role in all rituals connected with fertility" (M. Cartry).

I. The Myth of the Creation of the World

Let us examine the myth of the creation of the world (in its broad outlines). God—Amma for the Dogon, Mangala for the Malinke and the Bambara—created the universe from the infinitely small, a sort of initial atom, represented by the smallest of all seeds, the fonio. This "seed of the world" contained the strength of the four elements (fire, earth, water, and air). The image of life, it was animated by an internal and turbulent movement; as it developed, it exploded and formed "the egg of the world." Like a womb, on whose wall the first signs would be engraved, this egg contained two pairs of mixed twins, growing in the egg in the shape of fish. But from one of the halves of the egg a unique being (named Ogo by the Dogon, Pemba by the Malinke and Bambara) came forth before term. In order to possess the universe alone, Ogo stole a piece of his placenta and, using it as an ark, cast himself into the initial void. The stolen piece became the Earth, and Ogo went inside it in the hope of finding his twin, whom he thought he had brought with him. His quest was in vain and he returned to the sky; but Amma had already given his twin to the couple remaining in the other half of the egg. Incomplete and impure, Ogo was transformed into an animal, the Pale Fox, *yurugu* (*Vulpes pallidus*), and passed his impurity on to the soil of the planet. (Ogo had already sown a seed of fonio, which was made red by the blood of the stolen placenta.)

Faced with Ogo's feverish agitation, Amma wished to start his creation over again by creating new pairs of twins in the sky. In order to do this, he first sacrificed one of the male twins who remained in the egg. Gathering up the body, after he had dismembered it into sixty-six parts, he molded it into the shape of a man with the earth of his own placenta and resuscitated it, using the purest sap of the *pelu* tree (bastard mahogany). Then he sent down upon the earth of the Fox the shell of the second half of the egg. This was in the form of a rectangular ark, which carried in its center the resuscitated master of the word and of water, and four other mixed pairs, children created from his own placenta. The ancestors of all humans, the pairs of twins were placed at the corners of the ark, connected with the four elements and with the four trees symbolic of vegetable resurrection and the purification to be gained through the sacrifice of one who would henceforth be called Nommo, "to give to drink."

The ark, the second pure earth, destined to attach itself to the first, also contained all the animals, minerals, and vegetables that would populate the planet. The descent of

Wooden statuette representing the celestial twins, the *Nommo* of the heavens: the *nommo dye* (on the left) and the *nommo titiyayue* (on the right). Private collection.

this structure coincided with the appearance of solar light, while the other stars began to move.

On the fourth day, a solar eclipse took place during which the Fox's twin sister, Yasigui, descended alone and in human form. She was to put an end to twinning on earth by communicating to the ancestors her own impurity, which was the consequence of the provocation of her brother at the fetal stage of the formation of the universe. Born of the union of the ancestors of the ark, humanity should in fact have developed from mixed twins, but the Fox's twin would transmit to it, from its earliest years following the descent of the ark, the impurity of the red fonio seed.

The marriages of the eight ancestors of the ark were initially marriages of exchange called *tille ya gyi*. The four brothers exchanged their twins two by two: Amma Seru married the twin of Lebe Seru, and Binu Seru married the twin of Dyongu Seru. The first goal of these unions was to unite: (a) the four cardinal points, (b) the four elements, (c) the clavicular contents of those involved (the eight seeds). It also served to unite the four lineages according to a distribution of the primordial territory. This was the prototype of the first marriage between twins, with all its multiple implications (cosmic, social, and religious).

Enter Yasigui on the scene, descending alone upon the earth after the ancestors of the ark. The second year, Lebe Seru married Yasigui. The marriage proved fatal for humanity: the year before, Yasigui had consumed the red fonio, which had been first planted by her twin brother the Fox, and she treacherously fed it to her husband. This impure grain was the taboo attached to the family plot sown the year before by Lebe Seru. In order to purify the field, he was sacrificed on the hole of the Fox's fonio, and then his body was buried in the family field.

But as a consequence, normal twin births were no longer permitted. Because of the fonio, the wife of Lebe Seru, pregnant by him, gave birth after his death to a single child. In addition, since the harvest of Lebe's field had been divided between the three other brothers, their wives also gave birth to single children.

The third year, Dyongu Seru prepared a field of his own and married Yasigui in the hope of having the twins that he did not have with his twin sister. To this end, he used the land situated to the south of the Fox's field of fonio. He took seven seeds from the granaries of the family field and Lebe's field. In planting the seeds, he wanted "to take one of the souls," the liver, the intestine, and the kidneys of the sacrificed Nommo, and the knee and the foot of Lebe Seru (who had died the second year). The field thus prepared represented a person, replacing the twin that his wife did not have, and was called the "field of the twin." At the top of the field, he buried alive a catfish, a hypostasis of Nommo resurrected in the family clay. Yasigui became pregnant with twins. But Dyongu Seru, since he had broken a series of prohibitions, was also sacrificed above the fonio hole. These events disturbed the twin births: the first wife of the deceased gave birth to a single child, while the twins carried by Yasigui mutated within her womb into a single albino to which she gave birth.

The funeral services and the ceremony "ending the mourning" (dama) for Dyongu Seru, during which a great mask representing him was carved, were celebrated by the community. Binu Seru married Yasigui. Yasigui was at this point no longer impure, since she had been enthroned as yasigine during the dama of Dyongu Seru; she therefore gave birth to normal, although single, offspring. Such is the epilogue of the myth that marked the end of the early time, the time of twin births.

II. The Structure of the Person: Social and Religious Institutions

The end of twinning was therefore the price that man was forced to pay for the sin committed by a bold ancestor, Ogo, during the initial stage of the formation of the universe, and by his twin Yasigui during the development of the first earthly community.

But there was more, because the idea of twinning greatly exceeds the field of beliefs connected with the birth of twins per se. It is for this reason that a pair of twins of the opposite sex is undoubtedly pivotal in deciphering the structure of the person within each individual born singly. Like the eight ancestors descended from the ark, the humans who were born of them, who include nontwins, were provided, first, with a body and, second, with twin souls—the ni and the dya among the Bambara—of opposite sexes. During life, one of the souls, the ni of the same sex as its bearer, animates it, while the other, the dya, remains in the clay, in the power of the creator of humanity, Nommo (for the Dogon) or Faro (for the Bambara and the Malinke), who in this way protects the individual while at the same time controlling his actions. Humans, no matter what the generation, are the descendants of Nommo, put to death and then resurrected in the form of a human couple, male and female, and each of the beings thus formed possesses these twin souls.

But the ramifications of this myth also provide a principle for explaining the social and religious institutions of the people of the Mande. According to native scholars, in fact, all of their great institutions—marriage, cathartic alliance, commerce, and initiation—are based on the model of twinning.

1. Marriage

Dogon and Bambara myths teach that humans would always have been born as a set of mixed twins, had it not been for a dangerous ancestor—named Ogo among the Dogon, and Pemba among the Malinke and the Bambara— who interrupted this order of things. For the "intensive" law of formation of couples, humanity was forced to substitute an "extensive" rule of alliances, and thus the "female cross-cousin" was chosen as "the surrogate for the absent twin." Among the Dogon this kind of marriage is called deme ya dyi, marriage of preference: it recommends union with the daughter of the mother's brother. But it is rarely realized; another marriage is equally acceptable: each of two men is supposed to marry the other's sister, even if the women are not their twins. These two unions are thought to reproduce the mythic marriages of the ancestors of the ark. They are said to result in twin births.

The preferred marriage tries to reconstruct symbolically the couple of the first twins created by God in the beginning; it is not by chance that it is rarely realized (in historical times), because the Dogon believe that the rupture of such a union would bring grave disorders upon the community. This is also true among the Bambara, Malinke, and Bozo.

2. Cathartic Alliance

Along the same lines, it is useful to point out the particular case of the avuncular relationship that united the mother's brother with his sister's son. This relationship is maintained among the Dogon and Bambara by all kinds of actions and jokes made by the nephew toward his uncle: he regularly steals grain from his granaries; he publicly reproaches him for not marrying his sister, etc. But in this joking relationship the reproaches to which the mother's brother is subjected are definitely profitable for him. He receives benefits that are double what he might have received if his sister's son had not acted in this way: his harvest will be better in the future, his flocks more prolific. This accounts for the important role that the sister's son plays in the family rites which are intended to increase the fertility of the land.

There are also "cathartic alliances" that unite social groups at a distance from each other—alliances between villages, and even between tribes. The analysis of the reciprocal nature of the "cathartic allies" (called mangu by the Dogon, senanku by the Bambara, and dagara by the Bozo) suggests that certain aspects of the principle of twinning are also connected with these relationships. This idea was developed in a famous article in which Marcel Griaule reported that the Dogon and the Bozo were "joking relatives," or mangu, each of whom claim to have what the other is lacking. The Bozo, fishermen of the Niger and the Bani, are thought to have eight fish eggs in their clavicles, while the Dogon, cultivators of the Cliffs of Bandiagara, have eight seeds in the same place. Recent studies have shown how these supports of their spiritual elements—the eight seeds and the eight fishes—are the symbols of the eight vibrations of the "word" that Amma placed in the primordial seed. This word gave organic life to each individual, as the vibrations gave it to the first "living" seed, the fonio. The articulations of the "word of Amma" will thus be present in the articulations of the human skeleton, symbolically represented in the clavicles and their contents.

In addition, the fish eggs and seeds are the essential components of the placenta of Amma (God the Creator), components which in very early times both Bozo and Dogon shared. Twins at their origin, they swore an oath by which they recognized their complementarity: this translates today into a series of prohibitions that seal their mythic union and whose rupture involves the most serious consequences. All sexual relationships, for example, are forbidden between them; this would constitute incest, which would have the effect of completely emptying the contents of the clavicles of the two allies. This means that the Dogon involved would lose his seeds and the Bozo his fish eggs. On the other hand, in each other's company and through the exercise of their prerogatives, each multiplies his energy. The insults that they are obliged to exchange upon meeting are addressed to that part of themselves which is in the other; and the powers that they communicate to each other in this way are of mutual benefit throughout their lives. The cathartic function of the ally in relationship to his partner is seen in the case of the breaking of a prohibition; he himself undertakes purification, and his presence facilitates the reestablishment of the disturbed forces.

3. Commerce

Finally, the structure of the commercial relations that unite the *mangu* is based, as is the structure of their "cathartic kinship," on the model of twinning. The model was illuminated by the two chapters of Marcel Griaule's *The God of the Water* entitled "Twins and Commerce," in which Ogotemmeli explains that not only the things (fish, seeds, etc.) that are exchanged but also the men who do the exchanging are like twins.

G.D./d.b.

BIBLIOGRAPHY

A. ADLER and M. CARTRY, "La transgression et sa dérision," *L'homme* 11, 3 (July–September 1971): 5–63. G. CALAME-GRIAULE, *Ethnologie et langage: La parole chez les Dogon* (Paris 1965). M. CARTRY, "Le Lien à la mère et la notion de destin individuel chez les Gourmantché," in *La notion de personne en Afrique noire*, Colloques internationaux du CNRS (Paris 1973), 255–82. G. DIETERLEN, "Les âmes des Dogon," *Travaux et mémoires de l'Institut d'ethnologie* 40 (Paris 1941); "Les correspondances cosmobiologiques chez les Soudanais," *Journal de psychologie normale et pathologique*, 1950, 350–66; "Mythe et organisation sociale au Soudan français," *Journ. Soc. Africanistes* 25 (1955): 39–76; "Parenté et mariage chez les Dogon," *Africa* 27, 2 (1957): 107–48; "Mythe et organisation sociale en Afrique occidentale (suite)," *Journ. Soc. Africanistes* 29 (1959): 119–38; *Essai sur la religion bambara* (Paris 1961). M. GRIAULE, "L'alliance cathartique," *Africa*, October 1948, 242–58; "Rôle du silure *Clarias senegalensis* dans la procréation au Soudan français," *Afrikanische Studien* 26 (1955): 299–311; *Dieu d'eau: Entretiens avec Ogotemmêli* (2d ed., Paris 1975). M. GRIAULE and G. DIETERLEN, *Le renard pâle*, 1: "Le mythe cosmogonique," fasc. 1: "La création du monde" (Paris 1965). D. PAULME, *Organisation sociale des Dogon* (Paris 1940), 451–58.

THE PLACENTA IN WEST AFRICAN MYTHS AND RITUALS

Many West African populations have elaborated rigorous conceptions of the function of the placenta and continue to treat this organ with meticulous rituals. For these people, "Creation," as Michel Cartry remarked, "is conceived far more on the model of biological reproduction than on the model of skilled craftsmanship, and this surely explains the often extraordinary developments in the notion of the placenta that are found not only among the Mande but also among the Yoruba, Ewe-speakers, and the Gurmanche."

Among the Dogon, so long as a woman has not expelled the placenta she is said not yet to have delivered, the father is not advised, and the saying goes, "The child has been born, but not his little brother." Here as in many parts of West Africa, the placenta is considered to be the twin brother of the child. When it is expelled, the umbilical cord is cut with a razor or a knife by one of the attending matrons. The placenta and the umbilical cord attached to it are then placed in a piece of pottery, which is placed in the family courtyard under a compost heap of stems and stalks left there to rot. A flat rock that covers the pottery is assimilated to the pond of the begetter of humanity, Nommo. For seven weeks, the new mother performs her morning ablutions on this rock and also bathes her newborn child on it. Leaving the placenta for seven weeks in the water of the pond and abandoning it under the compost heap is tantamount to keeping it alive indefinitely. (Seven is also the number used for the multiplication of the divine "word.") Since it has watched over the maintenance and growth of the fetus during its nine months of gestation, it is considered to be "always alive, intangible and not subject to the risks of impurity." "The placenta," say the Dogon, "is always pure," even long after the birth of the child.

This assertion, which underscores the sacralization of the placenta, can be understood only if the problem is posed in terms of what it represents. For the Dogon, every placenta on earth is the double of the placenta of the "womb of Amma" in which the creation of the universe was conceived. But this placenta was double in nature, say the Dogon scholars, and its two parts were joined by Amma himself. A figure of two V's, one inverted and placed on top of the other, recalls the shape of the double placenta. It is referred to as "Amma forming two points," i.e., developing the space of the world. This sign, which also constitutes one of the basic representations of the formation of the sky and the earth, is made ritually in the field of its function and indicated on the front of the house of the Hogon, the tribal religious chief of the Dogon and the guarantor of the earth's fertility.

This two-way split also foreshadows the two elements that emerge at the birth of a human being, namely, the child *i* and his placenta *me*. This dual representation refers to what happens biologically at the time when the fetus is formed, namely, a division between the enveloping membrane (which is also called *i guru*, "the nest of the child") and the placenta. Here more than anywhere else, the connection between the biological realm and the cosmogonic system is evident.

This idea is also prevalent among the Gurmanche geomancers of Burkina Faso, for whom, Michel Cartry reports, "the development of each individual depends on the nature of the sign inscribed in the substance that linked him to his mother, just as the development of the human species depends on the signs inscribed on the primeval placenta. . . . Here ontogeny recapitulates phylogeny."

In the beginning, say the Dogon, was Amma, and he rested on nothing. "Amma's ball of an egg" was closed into itself, but was made up of four parts called "clavicles," also ovoid in shape, that were joined together as if welded. The four clavicles contained the germs of the four elements, *kize nay,* literally, "four things" (water, air, fire, earth); similarly, the imaginary bisecting lines that separated them marked the collateral directions called *sibe nay,* literally, "four angles," i.e., space. Thus the fundamental elements and future space were present in the morphology of the primordial "egg" in the form of signs.

Among the Dogon, Amma's egg is represented in the form of an oblong board covered with signs and called the "womb of all the signs in the world"; its center is the umbilicus. The egg is divided into four sectors, each containing eight figures, each of which produced eight more. The oval thus contains $8 \times 8 \times 4$, or 256, to which are added 8 (2 per half-axis) and 2 for the center. And so the total is the 266 "signs of Amma."

Before creating the universe, Amma had carved the signs of that universe on the walls of his own placenta. The number of these signs, the theoretical 266, corresponds exactly to the number of days required for the nine-month gestation period of a human being. Cosmic matter and creative matter *par excellence,* this initial placenta is where Amma germinated the grains that were to be placed in the clavicles of the first twins, there to become the support for their spiritual elements. At this stage the twins were still fish—catfish—assimilated to the human fetuses that are immersed in the waters of the womb and attached to their placentas.

The vertiginous developments of the myths about the rupture of this membrane are also well known. Ogo, one of the male twins, before he had reached his full development came out abruptly and tore out a piece of his placenta, which he used as a support as he descended into the darkness of the primal void. This destruction of the primordial placenta was a determining factor in the history of mankind. Since Amma no longer wanted to reintegrate into a new universe the placenta stolen by Ogo—which had become impure earth—he decided to regenerate the residue of the placenta. To this end he emasculated and then sacrificed Ogo's twin brother, who was still gestating in the form of a fish. After reassembling the dismembered body of the twin, Amma cast him in the form of a man, using the earth of his own placenta, and revived him by using the sap of a very pure tree.

Many Dogon rituals use the image of a humanity in formation in the placenta of the regenerated universe. During the night before the sixtieth anniversary celebration of the Sigui—whose main purpose is to commemorate the revelation of speech to men—all the male participants go into

the bush to an isolated cave, where they abstain from food and drink. For them, this fast has a positive meaning: "Since when does one need to eat and drink when one is in the womb of one's mother?" In the morning when the ceremonies begin, their heads are shaved, an act that assimilates them to newborn children. Then they put on the traditional costume of the Sigui and dress to look like fish: a white cap representing the head of a catfish, a pair of wide black pants gathered at the ankles with its tail bifurcated, the black recalling the waters of the womb; on the chest, a kind of crossbelt decorated with cowries that are the fish's eggs, etc. They hold in their right hands a crooked staff, the symbol of the sexual organ of Nommo, the mythical begetter of humanity, and a half calabash that will be used to drink the Sigui beer. This receptacle is the image of the "womb of Amma" in which the gestation of the universe took place as in a matrix.

Present in the rites of procreation during life, the image of humanity taking shape in its placenta is also present in the funeral rites during which the dead proceed to their fate. The dead person's mouth is covered with a muzzle that symbolizes the wattles of the fish; his head is covered with a white band that encircles the top of his skull to form the top of the fish's head, etc. All the ritual dances that the women and girls perform during the funerals recall, with very supple movements of their arms and hands, which are held out in front of them, the swimming of fish. The assimilations go on, because a dead person who continues to preserve his spiritual elements (that is, his basic elements) until the afterlife is said to be like "a fish of heaven."

Though not all the populations of the Mande have always elaborated myths that explicitly narrate what might be called the history of the placental formation of humanity, this history is nevertheless present in several regions of West Africa.

Particularly relevant in this context is a complex system of graphic signs that decorate the famous portable altars on the foundations of the great initiation societies of the Bambara. The societies of the Komo, Kwore, and Nya each possess 266 altars (*boliw*) that refer to a system of 266 signs carved on a small board. Here, as with the Dogon, the 266 altars, also known as the "signs of the creation of the universe," correspond to the number of days that make up the nine months of human gestation. Collectively, parallels to the 266 signs are present in the structure of Komo society on the level of the number of initiation classes. The 33 Komo classes group $33 \times 2 \times 4$, or 264, categories corresponding to 264 of the fundamental signs, the first 2 signs being represented by the Komo chief who is the head and the masked dancer who is the base of the institution. Each of these classes has a secret name and refers to a name of God or to one of the 266 categories of the creation of the world.

According to an old tradition, each altar is the symbolic image of the placenta of the human being or the object of which it is the witness. Witnesses of the lives of beings conceived in heaven by God and foreshadowed by the signs, the *boliw* are regarded as the supports of the continued survival of those beings; they guarantee their lasting power, regularly assured and augmented by the preservative sacrifices that are performed for them.

This process is illuminated by the mythic account that relates the origin of one of the oldest *boliw* of the Bambara kingdom of Segu, the *makōgo ba,* which is considered the placenta of a hippotragus (a mythical horse-goat): "When the mythical smith killed a male hippotragus during a hunt, the female, about to deliver, begged him to spare her, which he did. She gave birth and then ejected the placenta of her offspring, which she gave to the craftsman who in turn consecrated it as an altar.'' Here as elsewhere in many initiation societies, Bambara, Malinke, or Minyanka, the placenta of an antelope is offered in the myth as a remarkable and moving demonstration of divine purity.

G.D./g.h.

BIBLIOGRAPHY

M. CARTRY, ''Le lien à la mère et la notion de destin individuel chez les Gourmantché,'' in *La notion de personne en Afrique noire*, Colloques internationaux du CNRS (Paris 1973), 277–82. G. DIETERLEN, ''L'image du corps et les composantes de la personne chez les Dogon,'' in *La notion de personne en Afrique noire* (Paris 1971), 205–30. G. DIETERLEN and Y. CISSÉ, ''Les fondements de la société d'initiation du Komo,'' *Cahiers de l'homme*, n.s., 10 (Paris and The Hague 1972). M. GRIAULE and G. DIETERLEN, *Le renard pâle*, vol. 1: *Le mythe cosmogonique*, fasc. 1: *La création du monde*, travaux et mémoires de l'Institut d'ethnologie, vol. 72 (Paris 1965), 61–174.

WEST AFRICAN MYTHS OF CIRCUMCISION

Circumcision is practiced in almost all regions of West Africa. Certain populations do not observe the custom and find thereby a means to differentiate themselves from Islam (the Kabiye of north Togo, for example). At the same time, all evidence suggests that wherever the rite was known before the spread of Islam in the ninth century, its justifying principle was already contained in a solidly supported system of thought, especially among the populations who claim descent from the Mande.

Even today circumcision is at the center of a number of speculative theories about this cultural area. Studies have been done of the Dogon, the Malinke, the Soninke, the Bambara, and the Bozo, whose cosmology and religion were established on the same principles. Among these groups, circumcision is generally associated with an endemic disorder of the universe which was originally provoked by a hero who disturbed the divine order. To define the meaning of this rite, we will here summarize in broad outline the myth that relates the story of the creation of the universe by a single God.

The Dogon, the Bambara, the Malinke, and the Bozo teach that the first creatures who were of two sexes originally took form in a primordial egg conceived by God himself. These creatures were fish—catfish—assimilated to human fetuses in the womb, still attached to their placenta. But from one half of the egg, one of the males came out prematurely, and so that he alone might possess the universe, he tore off a piece of his placenta and formed an ark, on which he descended into empty space. The torn piece of placenta became earth and then formed the planet Earth. He made his way across the Earth in an attempt to find his female twin again, without whom he felt unable to realize his unbounded desire for domination. This ancestral disturber of the divine order is named Ogo by the Dogon, and Pemba by the Malinke and the Bambara (the Yoruba, outside the influence of the Mande, call him Edshu).

According to the myths of the Dogon and the Malinke, Ogo searched the Earth, which was stained with the blood of his placenta, hoping to find his twin whom he thought he had torn away with him. His search proved futile on Earth, so he returned to the sky. But Amma (God) had already entrusted his female twin to the couple in the egg's other half to prevent Ogo from reaching her. The whole story of the circumcision is then linked to Ogo's coming and going—his bold movement between Earth and the sky.

To protect the sky from Ogo's fevered agitation, Amma transformed the rest of his celestial placenta into a burning sun so that Ogo would no longer come near. Amma then forced the sun out of his womb and toward the west. The opening made for the sun's departure recalls the actions of the rebel, which were the origin of the appearance of death on the Earth formed by his placenta.

Just before Ogo's last return to the sky, Amma attempted to repair the damage that Ogo had done by castrating one of Ogo's celestial brothers, Nommo, who spilled his blood to purify the still-forming universe. Then Ogo, no longer able to approach his own burning placenta—the sun—approached the sacrificial victim and removed the four ''souls of sex'' which were in his foreskin. Ogo tried to steal the semen from Nommo's severed sex organ, but he could obtain only a part of it, with which he ran off along the path of the flow of the blood of the castration.

When he had arrived at the end of the ''line of blood,'' Ogo wanted to leave to descend to Earth again with the object of his larceny. But one of his other brothers, Nommo the Circumciser, present in the egg in the form of a fish, already lay in wait. Without awaiting the orders of Amma, he lunged toward Ogo to block his route. Though he did not succeed in preventing Ogo's escape, Nommo nonetheless was able to grab the tip of Ogo's penis, which he then circumcised with his teeth. He thus took back the ''souls of sex'' of the victim sacrificed by Amma. Then, to take back the stolen seed, the circumciser broke Ogo's teeth, ripped out his tongue—the organ of ''speech''—and wounded his throat, depriving him of his voice. This act prefigured Ogo's loss of speech as well as his downfall into an animal of the bush, the Pale Fox. To this day, the officiant at the circumcision of young Dogon says: ''Nommo put a saddle and a bit on the Fox to go to circumcise him. His broken teeth became stars.''

Thus, the circumcision of Ogo constituted a punishment for his theft of the divine placenta. The tearing off of his foreskin was the price that Ogo had to pay for his earthly placenta. The rite would later be repeated for all men, because by circumcising the human being one repeats what (on the cosmic level) Ogo had done in an attempt to seize his twin. The rite also commemorates what was done to Ogo in order to take back the spiritual elements that he had stolen, as well as the foreskin that served as their physical support.

This violent mutilation of Ogo disturbed the order of the universe still in formation. The blood of the circumcision fell on the placenta of the sacrificed victim at the very spot where the blood of that victim's castration had stopped and where Venus had arisen. Then, next to Venus, the ''star of menstruating women,'' Mars was born in an invisible position. Made of ''soft copper,'' and red as the blood of Ogo's circumcision, the star is a witness in the sky to the removal of Ogo's foreskin, and therefore to his femininity. (Each of these events was represented graphically by signs among the Dogon.) The name of the star expresses the fact that the blood of circumcision is regarded as being of the same essence as the blood of menstruation. While he bleeds, the circumcised man is ''impure'' as though he were menstruating. The Dogon call circumcision ''the menstruation of men.'' The circumcised are isolated during their recovery, as women

Cave of circumcision. In the foreground, the male sexual organ and the smith's throne; in the background, the altar of Amma. Dogon. Bongo.

are each month in the "house of menstruating women."

Meanwhile, Ogo, after fiercely resisting the operation, hit Nommo the Circumciser with such force that he let go of the foreskin and then pushed it into the sun, where it was transformed into a kind of lizard. The lizard, who shared Ogo's agressiveness, excised the star. After the lizard's passage through the sun, the *nay na* cicada, "mother of the sun," came out as a product of the operation. The excising of the star would prefigure that of Ogo's twin, Yasigui, who later appeared on Earth after the descent of the "ancestors." But one of the most serious consequences of Ogo's circumcision was the loss of his foreskin. That loss deprived him, as an androgynous being, of the physical support for his femininity; it rendered his personality singular and masculine, making him lose the unity of his personality. Moreover, it confirmed his definitive separation from his female twin, because he would always be deprived of one part of the sexual elements that he had attempted to steal.

After his mutilation Ogo descended again to Earth, no longer capable of stealing anything; alone he pursued his fascinating destiny in the form of the Pale Fox (*Vulpes pallidus*). Humans, by contrast, would later descend from Nommo, who was sacrificed as an androgyne and revived in the form of a human couple, male and female, each of the two beings having all the spiritual elements of body and sex. Sexual union—and, therefore, marriage—became possible because it was necessary for reproduction and the multipli-

cation of the species, which corresponds to Amma's original design.

After the descent of the ark of the ancestors, however, the conduct of the Fox and his battle against the established order caused new serious incidents (adultery, theft, and so forth) to appear in the community of man, and this put an end to twin births. So it was the blacksmith, as the representative of the sacrificed Nommo, who had to circumcise the male and excise the female ancestors of humanity so that they would be capable of marriage.

In all of these developments, the experiences of the Pale Fox vividly express the obligations that weigh on humanity: a human being is really a failed set of twins. To conform to the demands of marriage, then, men will forever have to lose their female elements by having their foreskin removed, and on the other hand, women must lose their male elements by having their clitoris excised. These operations, according to the interpretation given by the Dogon, are designed to establish the person within his or her own sex.

The Bambara, who share exactly the same conceptions, believe that an evil force, the *wanzo*, takes part in the myth. This force, which is located on the foreskin and the clitoris of children when they are born, must be washed away by the blood of circumcision and excision. Originally caused by the impurity of Mouso Koroni, "the little old woman," the *wanzo* is the result of a curse put on her after she betrayed God's plans for the creation. After being mutilated while having sexual relations with her twin brother, Pemba, she was driven by jealousy to seek revenge against all women, and her madness and despair drove her to the extreme of her treachery. With her nails and teeth, she circumcised and excised the men and women whom she encountered. The *wanzo* that she carried with her thus penetrated the human race, making the operation necessary for all those who would survive.

All children, at the moment when they touch the earth on which they are born, receive the *wanzo*, the "word of Mouso Koroni," in their blood and on their skin. Among men the force is found particularly on the foreskin, and among women particularly on the clitoris. It represents the presence of disorder in the individual: "It renders a man unable to live with anyone or to support himself." To become a stable being, to marry, procreate, and make sacrifices, the child must lose his or her *wanzo*. The removal of the foreskin and the clitoris achieves that result. Most of the forces run into the earth with the blood of the mutilated organ. The rest of the force escapes with the smoke of the fire over which the children jump (three or four times, depending on their sex) before going back into their house. Their new state is confirmed when they remove their old clothes and at the same time put on new ones. But the *wanzo* does not disappear. It remains captive in the masks of the children's society of the village, the N'domo, to which the uncircumcised belong. Thus, none of the individual forces are lost. The *wanzo*, evil at its origin but now captive and directed, serves to consolidate the collective energies of the children's societies of which it is the foundation.

It is only when an adolescent boy has been freed from the forces attached to his foreskin that he is allowed to enter into the society of men. Thus the operation of circumcision is in itself an initiation which, according to the now classic interpretation, seeks to "establish the person within his or her own sex." It will later serve as the point of departure for other initiations. In all the population groups of the Mande, and most notably among the Bambara and the Malinke, circumcision is the necessary precondition for initiation into the great societies of the Komo, the Nama Koro, Kwore, and Nya, where adolescents receive their traditional instruction and where they are taught to respect the ancestral laws.

G.D./d.b.

BIBLIOGRAPHY

M. CARTRY, "La Calebasse de l'excision en pays gourmantché," *Journ. Soc. Africanistes* 2 (1968): 189–225. G. DIETERLEN, *Essai sur la religion bambara* (Paris 1951). G. DIETERLEN and Y. CISSÉ, "Les fondements de la société d'initiation du Komo," *Cahiers de l'homme*, n.s., 10 (1972). H. GRIAULE and G. DIETERLEN, *Le renard pâle* (Paris 1965), 1:244–82. M. LEIRIS and A. SCHAEFFNER, "Les rites de circoncision chez les Dogon de Sanga," *Journ. Soc. Africanistes*, 1936, 141–62. D. ZAHAN, *Sociétés d'initiation bambara: Le Ndomo, le Koré* (Paris and The Hague 1960).

WEST AFRICAN MYTHS OF BLACKSMITHS

Blacksmiths generally form socially endogamous groups in West Africa. They are independent and quasi-international—a smith is "at home" wherever there is a forge, and he can settle wherever he wishes, wherever he is invited as "master of metals and of the fire." Blacksmiths live symbiotically with the people near whom and for whom they work, people whose technology varies from fishing to herding to agriculture. All those who need tools and weapons for the hunt—as they once did for war—treat blacksmiths in particular ways, but ways with common characteristics. Each group has its own smiths who play simultaneously a social and a religious role, sometimes of primary importance.

In order to isolate the position and the status of the smith, it is necessary to take note of the details of certain sequences of the cosmogonic myth that treat the sacrifice of the instructor of humanity (among the Dogon), or of Faro (among the Bambara, Malinke, and Bozo). The smith, whom the Dogon regard as the twin of Nommo, is always associated with the stages of the sacrifice and resurrection of Nommo.

I. The Myth

In order to repair the damage caused by Ogo, the hero who disturbs the divine system, the god Amma decided to castrate and sacrifice one of the twins, the celestial Nommo, who was still being formed in the world egg:

1. Before the sacrifice, Amma "divided in half the four souls of the body of the victim (which are indicative of the presence of the four elements), in order later to fashion the four souls of the sexes." From this time on, all living beings would have these two pairs of elements, necessary for reproduction.

2. Next, he cut the umbilical cord at the same time as he castrated the victim, emptied the testicles of their contents, and set aside both the seed and the emptied sexual organ.

3. He then sacrificed Nommo and divided the body into pieces which he threw into space in order to purify the earth, the seat of Ogo, who was transformed into a Fox at that time.

4. He resuscitated Nommo in the form of a human couple, using the material of the placenta from which he had separated him when he had cut the umbilical cord.

5. He then created the eight ancestors of men, "sons" of the victim, also with the placental matter.

6. Finally, he also created other human beings, who would be regarded as being of a different biological status. For this he used the material supplied by Nommo's placenta, but only that material upon which the blood of the victim had flowed.

The medicine man (and his twin sister) were created with the part of the placenta on which the blood had flowed from Nommo's neck at the time of the sacrifice; the smith (and his twin sister) were created with the victim's umbilical cord and with the blood that had issued from his severed sexual organ and umbilical cord.

In this way the marginal and ambivalent position of men of caste—smiths and medicine men—is justified in the developments of the myth: the ancestor of the smiths, unlike the ancestors of the agriculturalists who were created solely from the placenta of the sacrificed Nommo, comes, as the myth states precisely, from the umbilical cord that remained at-

The forge of Akunga. Bandiagara area (Mali). Paris, Musée de l'Homme collection. Photo N'Diaye.

tached to the placenta of the sacrificial victim and from the blood that flowed both from the cord and from the sexual organ, which were cut off at the same time. Thus it is said that the smith is the "witness" of Nommo, the instructor of humanity.

Their twinhood is also translated in an expression that associates them through the blood of which they are made: "Nommo and the smith are made of red blood, like a shining ball." It is also said: "Nommo and smith are twins; both are red as copper." In smithery, the heat of the fire and the coals blackened the smith. This is also why smiths, according to popular belief, can transform themselves at will into any sort of living being, either animal or vegetable, as Nommo himself does.

Along with the origin and the creation of the smith, the tools, materials, and work of this craftsman are also treated in detail in the myths. It is appropriate here to refer to various sequences that underline once more the intimate association between the "works of the master of the forge" and the sacrifice for the purification and reorganization of the universe.

We learn elsewhere of the wealth of mythic developments concerning the grain of fonio sown by the Fox, the hero who disturbs the universe. This seed had germinated in the placenta of the Fox and had spread its impurity to the earth. In order to destroy the red fonio (*Digitaria exilis*), the god Amma, at the moment of resurrection, had the blood of the victim's heart thrown out in the form of "a ball," which became very hot. This constituted the anvil: like an inflamed mass, like a "hot ball of fire," it fell, upside-down, hollowing out a gigantic crater in the ground. The impure fonio was hit, but sprang back and scattered over it. The anvil, the instrument of purification, could not remain in this polluted place; it sprang out of the hole to dig itself into a place outside, to the south, where it plunged deep into the ground: the part of the anvil that remained exposed would be used by the smith when he set up his first smithy. The crater became filled with water after the first rains had fallen.

At the same time as he threw the blood of the heart-anvil, Amma also threw the blood of the spleen on the ground; this was transformed into a metallic mass called *sagala*, which the smiths subsequently used, before they began to extract iron from terrestrial ores.

After the descent to earth of an ark which supported nearly all of the beings created by Amma in the sky, including the resuscitated male Nommo and the eight ancestors of men—"his sons"—the smith in turn descended, but under special conditions. The creation of the smith with the blood of castration is recalled by the events that would follow the descent of the ark. The smith received the penis and emptied testicles of the sacrificial victim, which were held in the sky by Amma and which had contained its seed, made up of the four vital elements. He also received the amputated "arm" which, emptied of its marrow and transformed into a hammer, contained the sixteen cereal grains. After the descent of the ark, Amma would order the smith to be the last to descend—as twin—by using the elements of the sexual organ as a support: he placed his two arms in the testicles and his legs along the length of the shaft. These elements would be transformed on the ground in order that the penis and testicles once again could become the nozzle and bellows, respectively. The smith descended to earth accompanied by his twin sister. By virtue of the presence of the four elements, he was able to extract and work iron. He carried the cereal grains in his hammer in order to cultivate them: their "souls" would instantly come to place themselves in the iron hoe at the time of agricultural work.

Apart from his own twin sister, the smith was also accompanied by the twin sister of the resuscitated victim, Yasa. While descending, he stole a piece of the sun, that is, the fire that was to serve to light his forge. He landed at a spot on earth at which he gathered a piece of *sagala*, which he would use in the manufacture of the first set of iron tools. Still accompanied by the two women, he took a long journey which led him to the place where the anvil had thrown itself, at which site he set up his forge. The seed of the sacrificial victim was in part composed of water, which Amma sent down to earth in the form of rain so that seeds could germinate. The water filled the crater made by the anvil and became a "pool": when the Fox came there to drink, Amma threw down from the sky one of the mineral elements of the contents of the sacrificial victim's sexual organ, that is, an "ax of rain" to drive him away. The smith would make this celestial stone into his workbench.

From that time on, the craftsman had his basic materials, all of celestial origin: the bench and the anvil, the hammer, the ore, the bellows and the nozzle, and the fire. Helped by Yasa—the twin of Nommo—from whom he sliced an arm to make his hammer and a hand to make his tongs, he lit the fire and forged the first instruments for plowing: he did this to help men, to whom he had given the seed grains entrusted to him by Amma, which he had brought down from the sky in the hammer—the arm of Nommo.

Able to fashion the weapons and tools that men needed, the smith is also a master of "knowledge." He circumcised and excised the ancestors of humanity in order to make them fit for marriage on the one hand, and to prepare them to receive the "word," or teaching, on the other.

The conduct attributed to the Fox and his battle against the established order result in some serious incidents (of which the appearance of death on earth is the most noteworthy) which continue until the commemoration of the revelation of the "word" sixty years later: the teaching was transmitted to the young people by the smith who survived the eight primordial ancestors. The myth ends with his death and the celebration of his funerary rites sixty-six years after his descent to earth.

II. The Status of the Smith

The sequences of this "history of creation and of the world" present some themes concerning the craftsman which throw light on his positive and negative evaluations, not only among the Dogon, but also in all the Mande regions.

1. The smith is a twin in essence, as were the first living creatures brought to life by God. He has specific powers and privileges intrinsic to twinhood, notably a certain intangibility. It is on this basis that he is able to invoke God to bring rain—which is the seed of the sacrificed demiurge, his twin, whose sexual organ he manipulates at his forge.

2. Also by his essence, he is a part of the generation of the fathers: no matter what age group he may belong to, he is regarded as ontologically located at the same level as the members of the oldest generation. By virtue of his nature and his estate, the smith is seated next to the main priest of the village or region at the time of certain collective ceremonies. One of his functions consists in forging or carving in wood, the sacred material, the attributes and emblems of power for the main priest, as well as for chiefs or kings.

3. On a biological level, the blood that circulates through his veins is a mixed blood made in part of sacrificial blood, which accounts for the ambivalent status of this caste. Smiths are endogamous; no other blood is mixed with theirs through marriage. For the Dogon, however, breaking the taboo is thought to have a greater effect on the smith than on his wife, regardless of her family connections.

4. The tools and materials manipulated by the craftsman are symbols of the organs and limbs of a being who has been sacrificed—and has thus gone through the supreme stage of impurity that is death—and resuscitated, an event that constitutes a triumph over impurity and the loss of life. The smith works simultaneously in the "pure" and the "impure." His work thus remains associated—on the cosmic level—both with the rupture of a previously established order and with the organization and functioning of a new world.

5. The sacrificial blood that flows through the smith's veins first issued from the umbilical cord and sexual organ of the demiurge, which are considered to be the most "alive" parts of the body. It is on this basis that the smith alone may practice circumcision. This is another way of saying that he may cause the blood of others to flow, in this case with impunity: circumcision is on a certain level assimilated to a sacrifice in which the smith is the officiant. The results of this act are similar to the mutation that he effects upon the materials he manipulates: circumcision transforms the child in order to make him a man (vir) in the fullest sense of the word. At the same time, the craftsman simulates a second cutting of the umbilical cord (represented by a small stick placed on the penis): the circumcised boy is at that moment definitively separated from his mother to enter into the society of men. From this time on, he is qualified to receive progressively the traditional instruction that the smith who has crafted his body promotes.

6. Although he does not play any particular role in the teaching which young people receive from their elders, the smith is nevertheless a master of initiatory knowledge throughout the Mande region. This fact is emphasized in the last episodes of the Dogon myth: it was the smith "who transmitted the 'word' to the young people at the time of the second Sigui before he died." The craftsman plays an eminent role in the ceremony of "world renewal" which begins—every sixty years—at some population center in which the fall of the anvil is masterfully represented (by a rocky mass more than one hundred meters in height).

Smiths played an equally important role in the foundation of the great Mandean initiation societies of the Komo, the Nama, and the Kwore, societies that greatly expanded at the time of the Mali empire (at the beginning of the thirteenth century) and that spread with the extension of that empire's borders and influence. For example, the creation of the Komo cult, established today among the Bambara, Malinke, Minyanka, Senufo, etc., is attributed by a very old tradition to seventeen smiths called the "seventeen smiths of the initial Komo," who are still honored today during annual or septennial ceremonies. A cast-iron chain made up of seventeen links, preserved in the Komo hut, represents the chain of descent of the cult's seventeen founding smiths. On the mythic level, it also represents the piece of the long chain that held the ark that descended to the Mande region with the eight ancestors of humanity.

On another level, many Mande populations have established in the territories where they settled after their migrations—for both initiatory and ritual purposes—various installations in caves and places sheltered by rocks, menhirs, cave paintings, etc., all of which are related to various sequences of the myth that we have roughly sketched. They also interpreted irregularities in the natural terrain so as to assimilate them to a system of representation of the elements of the mythic smithy. Most of the arrangements in a given territory reproduce or repeat others which are distributed over a considerable area of West Africa—and whose character is international. They are well known to informed men and women among such diverse peoples as the Malinke, the Marka, the Sarakolle, the Bambara, and the Bozo, whose cosmologies and religions are supported by the same principles as those of the Dogon.

All of the events connected with the fall of the anvil and the descent of the smith and the "ax of rain" which would become his bench become the objects of geographic representations spanning a vast territory. At the level of the international caste of the smiths, the fall of the anvil is geographically associated with the formation of Lake Bosomtwi in Ghana. According to a very old tradition, the anvil hollowed out the crater in which the lake is found. This object is represented at Kumasi (modern Ghana) by a kind of iron peg planted in the summit of one of the hills of the city, not far from the tombs of the Ashanti kings. Certain stone replicas of this "mythic anvil" are found among the Dogon in the caves used for the preservation of traditions and for initiations. But the most spectacular representation is situated in the Yougo range, where a natural block of very great size, dominating the range to the east, represents the anvil, while the crater that it hollowed out is portrayed by a carefully delineated arrangement found below, on the slope of the mountain across from the anvil.

In a parallel fashion, the anvil is represented by a needle located on the slope of the Mandingo Mountains, not far from the village of Nyenguene. The Soninke who founded this village are in charge of this cult.

If it is possible before their installation, Dogon postulants to the priesthood go to Kumasi to make their vows before the symbol of the mythic anvil. And smiths in the course of their apprenticeship and initiation also make the pilgrimage to the anvil and visit Lake Bosomtwi.

Over the past several decades, the crater of this lake has

been the object of geological and mineralogical studies. Specialists have formulated three hypotheses: a volcanic origin, an origin from a tectonic movement, or an origin from the impact of a meteorite. The latest research has supported the last hypothesis. It is interesting to compare the results obtained through this research with the accounts of our informants who unreservedly attribute the crater to the impact of a burning metallic mass of great size that "came from the sky." This poses the question of how a similar event of such antiquity—the crater was formed over a million years ago—came to be mentioned and translated in the traditions of the peoples of West Africa.

G.D./d.w.

BIBLIOGRAPHY

G. CALAME-GRIAULE, *Ethnologie et langage: La parole chez les Dogon* (Paris 1965). G. DIETERLEN, *Essai sur la religion bambara* (Paris 1961); "Contribution à l'étude des forgerons en Afrique occidentale," in *Annuaire 1965–1968*, École pratique des hautes études, section 5, Sciences religieuses (Paris 1965), 5–28. G. DIETERLEN and Y. CISSÉ, "Les fondements de la société d'initiation du Komo," *Cahiers de l'homme*, n.s., 10 (1972). M. GRIAULE and G. DIETERLEN, "Le renard pâle," 1: "Le mythe cosmogonique," fasc. 1: "La création du monde" (Paris 1965): 306–84. D. ZAHAN, *Sociétés d'initiation bambara: Le Ndomo, le Koré* (Paris and The Hague 1960).

MYTHS AND PRACTICES OF SACRIFICE AMONG THE DOGON

In black Africa, the principal axis of almost all rituals is blood sacrifice. For the Dogon, for example, no matter what the place, the purpose, or the circumstance, every sacrifice reenacts the mythical sacrifice of the reorganization of the universe. Like its prototype, every sacrifice is both cathartic and reorganizing. It frees the life forces of the victim in order to purify anything or anyone that is weakened and thereby threatened by shortcomings, errors, and the breaking of taboos. Its purpose is a revitalization of the whole, a resurrection, that is, a total renewal of life in all of its fullness.

I. The Myth of Sacrifice

We will first recall the sequence of events in the myth of sacrifice of the Nommo (mentioned in the article on the blacksmith).

1. After a first attempt that failed, the universe as a whole emerged from something infinitely small created by the "word" of the one god, Amma. This infinitely small thing grew into a vast womb called the "egg of the world." It split up into two twin elements containing two placentas, which were to give birth to two sets of twins that would be the instructors and prototypes for mankind and would possess the creative word, while assuming the form of fish (catfish). But out of one of the halves of the egg came, prematurely, a single male creature named Ogo. In order to be the sole possessor of the universe that was in the process of formation, Ogo tore a piece out of his placenta and stole eight of the seeds created by Amma. Then he went down into empty space with the help of the piece of placenta, which had been

transformed into an ark; this ark later became the earth, whose womb he entered in an attempt to find his twin sister.

The premature intervention of Ogo, the incest that he committed by penetrating into his own placenta, i.e., his mother, and above all the theft and sowing of one of the seeds (the fonio), acts associated with the incest, created lasting trouble for the order of creation.

Though he noticed the disorder caused by Ogo, Amma nevertheless refused to go ahead with a second creation, and events followed their course in a single universe.

The atonement for the disorder was the sacrifice of the *semu* Nommo, who had the same essence as Ogo and his twin; the sacrificer chosen by Amma was the *titiyayne* Nommo, born from the other placenta. The *semu* Nommo was resurrected and then descended to earth to right the wrong caused by Ogo. This sacrifice of purification allowed Amma to continue his work of creation and to reestablish the initial order that had been disrupted by Ogo's action.

2. Amma began by dividing into two each of the four souls of the body of Nommo, thus creating four additional souls: his souls of sex. From then on, all beings formed by Amma were to be no longer androgynous but sexed.

3. Next came the emasculation of Nommo and his separation from the placenta by the cutting of the umbilical cord. From this double operation, which purified the initial double placenta, the star Sirius (*Sigi Tolo*) was born. The blood from the castration flowed from the center southward, and from there was born the planet Venus (*Yazu*). From the cord that had remained at the center came a small star said to be the "star that accompanies Venus." The first stages of sacrifice were thus at the origin of the formation of the stars and the planets.

Amma's goal was to set apart successively all of the "articulations of the word" that were crudely developed inside the initial fonio seed and that he had given to Nommo. By setting apart the content of the sex organ, he set apart the eighth word, the witness of the fonio's germination and of the fertility granted from the beginning to the victim and his twin brothers.

The sperm from the sacrificed creature contained six elements symbolically related to the six *yala* (images) of sex of the white fonio grain that Amma had created to bring about the second universe after the failure of the first, in the center of the internal spiral of the primordial egg.

The sacrifice of Nommo thus constituted a new start for the course of the universe based on principles parallel to those that had prevailed at the time of its creation. The semen of the sacrificed creature and its content were preserved in heaven by Amma, and their eventual role would be fundamental for life on earth: water from the sex organ fell in the form of rain on Ogo's soil and formed the networks of fresh water and the sea, bringing with it all the elements it contains.

4. At the time of the castration, Ogo, wanting to take possession of what he lacked, i.e., his twin sister and the rest of his placenta, went back up to heaven. But since his twin sister had been given shelter by Amma, and the rest of his placenta had become the sun, Ogo approached the victim and got hold of the four "souls of sex" that were lodged in his foreskin, grabbed a mouthful of the Nommo's semen, and fled. The sacrificer, trying to stop him, managed to catch the tip of Ogo's sex organ with his mouth. He bit it off, circumcising him with his teeth, and thus retrieved the "souls of sex."

The mutilation of Ogo constituted a punishment for his former misdeed: the theft of a piece of his placenta at the

Blood from a chicken on the facade of the house of the Binu. Mali. Paris, Musée de l'Homme collection. Photo Griaule.

Totemic shrine. At the top, traces of sacrificial millet gruel. Mali. Paris, Musée de l'Homme collection. Photo N'Diaye.

time of his premature departure. In circumcising a human being, one reenacts what Ogo did on a cosmic scale in his attempt to seize his twin sister and what was done to him to separate him from the stolen spiritual elements for which his foreskin had become the physical support.

5. When he arrived on earth, Ogo intended to continue his work, but the creator transformed him into a quadruped. He lost his name, Ogo, and took another, *yurugu*, because he had become a *Vulpes pallidus*, or Pale Fox. He reached his final form after a long and complex fate; he became the permanent element of disorder in the universe, or rather, the agent of disorganization.

6. In circumcising Ogo, the sacrificer had acted too quickly, without waiting for Amma's orders. For if he had not been circumcised, Amma would have destroyed Ogo to keep him from ever being a nuisance again. This rash act resulted in Ogo's blood soiling heaven and earth. A purification of the heavenly and earthly places became more necessary than ever. Therefore Amma proceeded to sacrifice the one he had just emasculated and to distribute pieces of his body in order to purify space and the universe that was being formed. Later he was to resurrect the victim who would be the symbol and the support of the organized world.

7. After he had tied the victim to the piece of his umbilical cord that had been detached during the emasculation and transformed into a tree (*Prosopis africana*), the sacrificer cut off his head and, at the same time, his pectoral fins. The creature sacrificed in this way represented all men and animals. The tree that was to die with him stood for all plants.

8. The blood of the sacrificial victim flowed on him, representing the whole of the "life of the world." It is compared with the menstruation that precedes procreation. It was the "menstrual blood of the earth," whose future life it ensured. The blood of the sacrificial victim fell on him and before him, on his earth-placenta, and it moved across space; a prefiguration of rain, it formed "strings of rain" along which it continues to come down to earth today.

In the plan of the construction of the universe, the emasculation of Nommo and later the circumcision of Ogo determined the creation and movement of the stars, which bore witness to the blood, or to the clavicle grains and the spiritual

elements, or to the time of the division of the body into parts, the vital organs.

9. Holding Nommo with his head hanging down to let the blood flow out, Amma walked northward; then he stopped, and Nommo lost seeds from his right clavicle, from which came white fonio. On this spot, the star of fonio was born (*pō tolo*), the first companion of Sirius and the symbol of the origin of the universe. Farther on, the sacrificial victim lost the seeds from his left clavicle, from which came female sorghum, and finally his life. From this spot arose *emme ya tolo*, the second companion of Sirius, who, along with *pō tolo*, was later to circle Sirius. The blood continued to flow, bringing with it the seeds of the other clavicles. When it stopped, the first *sa* tree (*Lannea acida*) grew as a witness of the blood of the sacrificial victim.

10. Amma then proceeded to divide all of the Nommo's body, except the arms, into sixty pieces to which were added the six elements from the contents of the semen, thus adding up to a total of sixty-six portions, a number equivalent to the number of the *yala* (images) of the egg of Amma that were the components of the image of the primordial seeds.

Amma thus stressed once more with the number of the portions the renewed movement of the essential elements that had presided at the creation of the universe. He then ordered four piles to be made of the body, opened up the sky, and had the pieces of the dismembered body thrown through the opening, in the four directions, in order to purify space, the four cardinal points, and the Earth of the Fox. The division into four piles and the throwing into space are recalled annually during the sacrifice performed at the winter solstice in the family house by giving the essential parts of the victim to the four oldest men.

11. When the cathartic dispersion had been performed, Amma gathered together the organs of the victim, molded them into the shape of a man, and gave them life again by using the bark of the *pelu* tree (*cailcedrat*), which was born of the victim's gallbladder.

With the victim's placenta, he also created four mixed pairs, the children of Nommo and the ancestors of men. He made them descend to earth with the help of the remainder of the placenta that was transformed into an ark and contained all the animals, minerals, and plants that were to multiply and sustain life on the planet.

II. Speculations and Customs of the Dogon

All the heavenly sites where these mythical events took place are the object of a detailed spatial depiction inscribed on the ground of certain villages in the Sanga region so that they stake out a "mythical territory." A series of altars placed either on the *lebe dala*, a kind of terrace symbolically representing the victim's placenta, or on the "road of blood," signify Nommo's sacrifice and resurrection. They represent the various parts of the victim's body and form a bond between the victim and the men who are considered his descendants. Such altars are used by various levels of the foundation of the social organization: the tribe, the totemic clans, and the lineages.

When examined as a whole on the level of representation, the morphology of emasculation, sacrifice, and resurrection, the operations that take place, and the mythical locale of their execution establish specific relationships between Nommo's placenta, his body and vital organs, the stars born of the sacrificial blood, the plants and animals made at the same time, and finally the men who will be created with the material of his placenta.

In general, the stages of the sacrifice of Nommo are recalled by every sacrifice today, whatever the place, the purpose, the agent, or the modalities:

—The chick or young chicken that is slaughtered before the actual sacrifice and that is significant for divination represents the emasculation.

—The libation of "millet water" that precedes the sacrifice of the main victim represents the flow of seeds from the clavicle.

—The victim's blood represents the blood of sacrifice.

—Throwing the liver on the altar represents the resurrection.

—The partitioning of the body is recalled by cutting up the victim and carefully distributing the meat to the participants.

The Dogon say that Nommo "showed men the first example of sacrifice," its value as a gift, its power, and its far-reaching effects; for it seals all human relationships.

Libation at the altar of divination by the Fox. Photo Griaule.

But Dogon speculations and explications of agrarian sacrificial rites do not stop there. The libations of "millet water" on family altars at harvest time are meant not to bring the firstfruits to the monitor of the universe, but to keep them from all risk of impurity by reintegrating the harvested grain into their own clavicles and by asking him to entrust their souls—the eight *kikinu*—to his heavenly brothers. This is done to avert any loss of vital strength in the seeds that are stored for safekeeping in special granaries until the following sowing season. The displacement of the "souls" of cultivated plants occurs in the opposite direction on the day when sacrificial activities take place under parallel conditions: those in charge of the cult ask Nommo to intervene so that the souls can be returned to the seeds with the falling rain. The seeds that have been set aside are distributed to all the farmers, who mix them with their own before sowing them. At the same time, Nommo is asked to watch over the integrity of the fields and their contents until harvest time. The cycle is thus complete.

III. Other Regions of West Africa

Research conducted in other regions of West Africa has not always revealed, as in the case of the Dogon, the theme of a "mythical hero whose sacrifice would be perpetually reenacted" by sacrificial rites, although these rites do play a major role in the customs of these peoples. Accordingly, in the great initiation societies of the Bambara, Malinke, Minyanka, etc., the creative power of God is made visible in sacred enclosures by the "coming out" of 266 altars, called *boliw* by the Bambara, which are usually preserved in cotton bags. These altars periodically receive libations and blood sacrifices. As witnesses to the everlasting nature of the 266 divine categories by being gathered together in one large bag they symbolize the original unity of the "signs rolled up in a ball," *ti kuruma*, at the time of their appearance in the womb of the initial void. On the occasion of the "coming out," they guarantee the everlasting vitality of divine categories, ensured and augmented by the sacrifices of preservation dedicated to them. At the same time, what characterizes the septennial and annual ceremonies of the initiation societies (Komo, Nama Koro, Kwore, Nya) is the frequency of blood sacrifices performed on such altars, which are arranged in jars according to a rigorously prescribed order. As in all operations of this kind, the purpose is periodically to "refresh" the "signs" and the stages of the creation of the universe for which these altars are the support. On the occasion of the rites of the Komo, the initiate recites the following Bambara maxim: "In the universe, all things have entered one into the other; the anniversary of the Komo renews all things within the universe."

G.D./g.h.

BIBLIOGRAPHY

M. CARTRY, "Le statut de l'animal dans le système sacrificiel des Gourmantché (Haute-Volta)," in *Systèmes de pensée en Afrique noire: Le sacrifice* 1, cahier 2 (1976): 142–75. G. DIETERLEN, *Essai sur la religion bambara* (Paris 1951), 23–26 and 130–33; "Introduction à de nouvelles recherches sur le sacrifice chez les Dogon," in *Systèmes de pensée en Afrique noire: Le sacrifice* 1, cahier 2 (1976): 43–50; "Analyse d'une prière dogon," in *L'autre et l'ailleurs: Hommage à Roger Bastide* (Paris 1976), 348–72. G. DIETERLEN and Y. CISSÉ, "Les fondements de la société d'initiation du Komo," *Cahiers de l'homme*, n.s., 10 (1972): 251–95. M.

GRIAULE, "Remarques sur le mécanisme du sacrifice dogon," *Journ. Soc. Africanistes* 10 (1940): 127–30; *Dieu d'Eau* (Paris, new ed., 1975). M. GRIAULE and G. DIETERLEN, "Le renard pâle," I: "Le mythe cosmogonique," fasc. 1: "La création du monde," *Travaux et mémoires de l'Institut d'ethnologie* 72 (Paris 1965): 225–384. L. DE HEUSCH, "Le sacrifice ou la violence de Dieu," in *Systèmes de pensée en Afrique noire: Le sacrifice* 1, cahier 2 (1976): 67–83.

MASKS IN WEST AFRICAN TRADITIONAL SOCIETIES

Even today, in the traditional societies of West Africa, the institution of masks is closely tied to the agrarian rituals, funeral rituals, and rites of initiation that are so significant to village communities. The ceremonies in which masks play a central role almost always have as their purpose the recalling of the mythical events that took place at the time of origins and that led to the organization of the universe in its present form.

That is why when today one tries to describe a mask within the framework of the cosmogony of which it is a part, the description cannot be limited to the part of the mask that covers the head of the person wearing it. In the great societies of initiation among the Bambara, when an initiate speaks of the "head of the Komo," he means all the elements that constitute the mask: the head that borrows its morphological elements from the swollen skull of the old hyena (associated with profound understanding), from the "mouth" of the crocodile who was the first to put the ark of creation in the pond, and from the horns of the antelope that symbolize by their pointed ends the first lightning of creation; the tunic, made of strips of cotton on which the feathers of vultures have been affixed, bearing the 266 signs of creation; the "elephant's feet" tied to the dancer's ankle and symbolizing the pillars, beams, and supports of the universe; the iron or copper whistle that evokes by its strident sound the first whistling of creation; the stiletto of thaumaturgy, the foremost instrument of ritual executions, etc. Finally, the "head of the Komo," called *komo kû*, also designates the wearer of all these objects and the dance that the wearer performs.

All of this is evidence of the highly sacred character and the deep significance of the wearing of the mask of Komo, which appears to be a microcosm, a dynamic summary of the universe. For this reason, it is called "the burden of the universe" and, by analogy with this name, "the deep knowledge of the universe." Originally, the infallible knowledge for which the mask is here the support was given to Faro, whom the Bambara and the Malinke regard as the helper of creation and the instructor of the universe. This knowledge, like all that exists, has two natures, one visible, palpable, and concrete, and the other hidden, secret, inward, and profound. Faro taught these two aspects of knowledge to two of his chosen ones, the vulture and the hyena, the future patrons of the societies of masks and the most assiduous, attentive, and respectful listeners to their instructor's commentaries on creation. Under the patronage of these two carnivorous scavengers, the vulture and the hyena, were placed the societies of the masks that represent them among the Bambara, the Malinke, and the Minyanka. As a result, these societies are regarded as the keepers of the "true values," the "true signs," and the totality of knowledge.

During the ceremonies of initiation of the Komo, the young people are assembled outside the village in a sacred grove. There, in the presence of the mask, they undergo tests designed to measure their physical and moral maturity and are given instruction that progressively reveals the knowledge of the universe. This teaching, arranged in graded levels over several years, is conceived as a succession of "words," increasingly explicit and associated with the different parts of the mask. In the initiation society among the Nama Koro, a group that are neighbors of the Komo, the young initiates crouch one by one, their hands behind their backs, in front of the *wara da*, the "mouth of the hyena," while the initiator draws three elements out of the mouth: the "belt of the village," the "foot of the *nama*," and the "thing that penetrates into the mouth." Combining gestures and words, he reveals to the initiates the names of the elements of the mask, their emblems, and their "utterances," and he inculcates in them a respect for the laws of the society of which the mask is in many ways the guarantor; for it is said that it "carries all the things of the universe."

Later, in the course of the masked dances, the meaning of the great initiations is recalled: the adolescent must suffer the death of his former state in order to be born into the state of adulthood. In the society of the Komo, the herald cries, shortly before the masks come out, "The initiates are about to die one after the other. The old hyena has called no one. Welcome to all. Make them rot! Knead them, old hyena." In the society of the Nama Koro, the masks even go so far as to simulate devouring the postulants, for it is said that the Nama Koro is a hyena that eats the initiates only to expel them later in her excrement, from which they are extracted, washed, and purified.

Altogether different uses are made of the masks that are carved inside brush enclosures (in caves or woods) and that make a public appearance in the village at funerals and the beginnings and endings of seasonal work (sowing, tilling, and harvesting). These masks generally belong to the male association of the village, sometimes even to an association of children, such as the Bambara N'domo.

Among the Dogon, each circumcised male becomes a member of the village's society of masks. He must carve (or have carved for him) and wear the mask of his choice so that he can dance during the funeral services that mark the end of the mourning period. This society, called *awa*, constitutes the male association responsible, among other things, for the worship of the first person who died—the mythical ancestor Dyongu Seru—represented by the Great Mask, which is the property of the village. The dignitaries responsible for this ritual are the *olubaru* recruited in each family of the village when it is time for it to have its turn to play the role during the ceremony of the Sigui, which every sixty years reenacts the events that led to the death of this ancestor. These dignitaries go on a three-month retreat, during which they receive instruction. They live in the bush, in a cave that has been hung with recently carved masks, where they are taught by the elders. The newly promoted dignitaries learn by heart incantations and texts in the "language of the Sigui," which relate in a summarized form the story of the creation of the world and the appearance of death on earth and among humans. Until the celebration of the rituals of the Sigui sixty years later, they will be responsible for the worship of the "first ancestor," who died through the mediation of the Great Mask, the basis of his spiritual elements.

Here, as in most of the regions of Africa, the mask marks the interface between life and death. On the cosmic level, the

Dogon mask. Paris, Musée de l'Homme collection. Museum photo.

Mask representing a hyena. Mopti region of Mali. Paris, Musée de l'Homme collection. Museum photo.

Crocodile mask. Mali. Paris, Musée de l'Homme collection. Photo Dr. Pagès.

Dana masks: hunter, white monkey, two antelopes. Mali. Paris, Musée de l'Homme collection. Photo Griaule.

construction of the mask is associated with the rupture of a cosmic order previously established by God.

This is certainly one of the reasons why women are generally excluded from everything connected with the activities in which masks are used, for through their connection with death, masks would interfere with fertility, which is the major preoccupation of all traditional African societies. Also excluded from the society of masks are the Hogon, the religious head of a tribe, and the totemic priests, whose essentially "living" character excludes them from the rituals at the conclusion of the mourning period.

Women are, however, represented in the society of masks by a dignitary, the *yasigine*, the "wife of the Sigui," who is consecrated at the sixtieth anniversary ceremony of the Sigui. On the religious level, she represents Yasigui, the twin sister of Ogo. Ogo, one of the first beings created by god, was the founder of disorder in the universe; he fell from grace and was transformed into a fox. The myth exuberantly develops the story of the responsibility of Yasigui for the events that led to the appearance of death, which came to strike all living beings. Shortly after the descent to earth of an ark carrying almost all the creatures created by god in heaven, among whom were Nommo, the instructor of humanity, and the eight ancestors, his sons, Yasigui descended, but under very special conditions. Alone and deprived of her twin brother—who had already been transformed into a Pale Fox—she quickly entered into the community of the "first

ancestors" in order to sow disorder among them.

Exactly three years after the descent of the ark, Dyongu Seru, one of the four male ancestors, fathered two single children, who were the fatal result of his consumption of fonio, an impure red grain that Yasigui had treacherously mixed in with the other grains. Dyongu Seru then had the ill-fated idea of marrying Yasigui, in the hope of obtaining the twins that he had not had with his twin sister. Later, urged on by his new wife, he sowed in his own field the seed that he had stolen from the fields of his brothers, thus reenacting on earth and on his own account the theft committed in heaven by Ogo, the hero who disturbed the divine system.

However, the establishment of this personal field, the theft in the fields of the family community, and the marriage to Yasigui constituted a series of errors and disorders that had serious consequences for the community. Dyongu Seru, after becoming impure, was sacrificed over the mouth of the pot of fonio. The funeral and the ceremony of the "conclusion of the mourning" (*dama*) of Dyongu Seru, during which the Great Mask representing him was carved, were celebrated by the community of the reunited brothers, while Yasigui, who had sown the disorder, was enthroned as *yasigine*, the woman of the masks.

Thus, after his death, the ancestor was forgiven. His brothers carved in his image a great mask on which his spiritual elements were grouped together. To that end they highlighted the wood of the mask with four colors associated with the four elements of life: black for water, red for fire, white for air, yellow for earth.

Recent research has revealed that after the sacrifice that led to his death, the ancestor was revived in the form of a snake, only to suffer then a second physical death, this time final. The account of this second death corresponds to the version recorded by Marcel Griaule, according to which the ancestor died because, after being transformed into a snake as old men were at the ends of their lives, he had violated a vow of silence and spoken in the common language to young adolescents who had provoked him on the road to the village. According to this version of the myth, the ceremony of the Sigui was instituted to seek pardon from Dyongu Seru for having forced him to break a vow of silence.

Since then, in each community and for each Sigui, a Great Mask is carved every sixty years in order to give life back to the mythical ancestor, who is thought to be present in the midst of the community, and to celebrate the consolidation of his spiritual elements and his accession to the status of ancestor. The Great Mask, called *imina na*, is hidden in a cave, beside the masks of previous Sigui. In this cave, it is as if he is at home and is served by the dignitaries of the society, his descendants, who, under the control of a chief who is responsible for him, ensure the annual sacrifices that will be offered to him. He is brought out of the cave only for the funerals of his servants or for the funerals of the chiefs of the very old lineages.

Next to the dignitaries of the society of masks, who are responsible for the worship of the first man who died, all the men qualified to wear a mask perform a parallel office for each deceased member of the lineage. During the rituals conducted at the moment of the conclusion of mourning, the *dama*, the masks dance and address themselves to the spiritual elements of the dead person, who must be accompanied, led, or directed until the funeral pottery is deposited in the altar of the family that consecrates his transition to the rank of ancestor.

Each time mourning is concluded, the Great Mask continues to lie in the cave where it receives libations of sacrificial blood at the beginning of the ceremony. As Marcel Griaule wrote: "The need to carve a large piece of wood for each Sigui can be clearly explained: it renews the support for the soul of the first dead ancestor, whom the society as a whole has an interest in honoring and in containing in a fixed shelter. On the other hand, given the current state of our knowledge, it is difficult to understand the reason for the renewal of ordinary masks." The ordinary masks have as their purpose the reenactment of the important events that have taken place since the origins of the world. The masks climb up onto the terrace of the dead person and then go to the public square, where they break into dances that are often quite spectacular.

In a state of general exaltation, under the effect of the emotion stimulated by the conclusion of mourning, the masks make their appearances one by one on the square.

Bambara masks. The masks coming out at night at Bambougou. Photo Ligers.

Wearing the *kanaga* (characteristically in the shape of the cross of Lorraine), the dancers repeat the whirling movement that originally animated all of creation by moving their heads and torsos in a circle that almost brushes the ground. The *sirige* mask, called a "house of many floors," is a mast measuring four meters or more in height, representing a succession of grids and rectangular solids that connote the steps of the descent of the ark of creation. The mask itself can be surmounted by two figures that represent the resurrected Nommo couple, the ancestors of men. Although it is extremely tall, it too is animated by a vast sweeping movement, and while the masks, which are loudly exhorted, display the entire cosmogony on the village square, the men sing to celebrate simultaneously the resurrection of the dead man and his immortality.

Among the Bobo, masks made of leaves are the heritage that was transmitted to men by the supreme god Wuro at the end of the cosmogonic period. They incarnate that part of Wuro that is still present in the world. By their origin, they are devoted to men and to society, but since they are made of vegetable matter they also participate in nature. Thus, it is their vocation to help men perpetuate in the cosmos the earthly balances that Wuro instituted between the two poles of his creation: the bush and the village. Every year these masks leave the village: they "cleanse" it and capture in their fresh leaves the human faults and mistakes that have accumulated and are charged with harmful forces that produce imbalances. Then they go off to lose themselves in the bush, thus regenerating the order that had been compromised.

The Bambara, the Bozo, and the Soninke or Marka, who live on the banks or near the Niger River, hold two annual public ceremonies in which many masks appear. One of these ceremonies takes place during the day, during the period of collective fishing that brings together all the riverside residents who use the same canal. The other ceremony takes place at night during the harvest of the fonio. The personality or mythical event that each mask evokes is expressed through its morphology, the dance that it performs, the songs that accompany it, and its place in the parade. Each entrance, as Jean Laude notes, "is a cosmogony in action that regenerates time and space, attempting thereby to free man and the values that he holds from the degradation that reaches all things in historical time."

G.D./g.h.

BIBLIOGRAPHY

G. DIETERLEN and Y. CISSÉ, "Les fondements de la société d'initiation du Komo," *Cahiers de l'homme* (Paris and The Hague 1972). M. GRIAULE, "Masques dogon," *Travaux et mémoires de l'Institut d'ethnologie* 33 (Paris 1938). M. LEIRIS, "La langue secrète des Dogon de Sanga," *Travaux et mémoires de l'Institut d'ethnologie* (Paris 1948). G. LE MOAL, *Les Bobo: Nature et fonction des masques* (Paris 1980). D. ZAHAN, *Sociétés d'initiation bambara: Le Ndomo, le Koré* (Paris and The Hague 1960).

ASTRONOMY AND CALENDARS IN WEST AFRICA

In West Africa one of the functions of cosmology, taken in its strictest sense, is to recall the remarkable events that occurred at the beginning and that have resulted in the formation of the universe as we know it. Not only to recall them, but also to imbue them with a permanent reality by fixing the dates of grand ceremonies—every sixty years, every seven years, or every year—with which the revolution of the heavenly bodies is closely associated.

I. The Astronomical Systems of the Dogon: The "Star of the Fonio"

It is from this perspective that the populations that say they are related to the Mande have often elaborated astronomical systems of considerable complexity. The spiraling world of stars that is seen by the Dogon, the Bambara, and the Malinke revolves around a theoretical axis that joins the polestar to one of the stars of the Southern Cross. These two stars, called the "eyes of Amma" (God), support and oversee this spiraling world in which a series of 266 stars or constellations called "stars of the support of the foundation of the world" represent the series of 266 signs of the creation, the first expression of the thought of God.

In this vast whole, two systems occur among the Dogon and are at the source of various calendars, punctuating the life and activities of men: (1) the one, nearest to the earth, has the sun as its axis, the burning evidence of the residue of the placenta of Ogo, the disturbing hero of the system of creation; (2) the other, farther away, Sirius, is evidence of the placenta of Nommo, who was sacrificed by Amma—in his celestial placenta—to repair the damage caused by Ogo, the "landowner."

Each stage of the sacrifice (cutting the umbilical cord, castration, draining the blood, setting aside the vital internal organs, cutting the body into pieces) is also the beginning of the formation of a star.

The two stellar systems also issue from the remains of a primordial double placenta from which, for the Dogon, the whole creation, purification, and reorganization of the universe proceed.

But, strangely, the most important star of this double system is neither the sun nor Sirius. In 1953 Marcel Griaule discovered among the Dogon the role of a small star called the "star of the fonio" that revolves around Sirius in orbits of fifty years. Invisible to the naked eye, it is the smallest but most important of all stars, the one whose role is magisterial—for the totality of all the spiraling worlds of heavenly bodies formed by Amma. The name of the star, *pō tolo*, indicates its priority: *pō*, which designates the fonio, comes from *polo*, "beginning"; *tolo* comes from *to*, "deep." Thus, *pō tolo*, according to an indigenous etymology, means "deep beginning." The star is associated with the infinitesimal, the *pō*, the "grain of the world" which at the beginning was animated by the "word" of Amma with an internal and whirling movement, a grain that exploded and formed the "egg of the world."

Because of the creative role of *pō pilu*, the white fonio, the star is regarded as the reservoir, the source of all things. The Dogon even affirm that it is the movements of *pō tolo* that keep all the other stars in their places: indeed, it is said that without this movement none of the stars would "hold." It is *pō tolo* that compels them to maintain their trajectory: it particularly regulates the trajectory of Sirius, which is the only star not to follow a regular curve and which it separates from other stars by surrounding Sirius with its own trajectory.

The movements of *pō tolo*, the heavy embryo of the world and proof of Amma's whole creation, have an active effect: by the force of its whirling its contents are ejected in the form of "infinitesimals" comparable to grains of *pō pilu*, white fonio, that grow rapidly: the star, white like *pō pilu* (*Digitaria exilis*), thus continues to distribute germs of the divine life that the grain that it represents received at the beginning.

The heliacal rising of Sirius, recalling the conjunction of the two initial placentas, and the revolution of "the star of the fonio" around Sirius are associated with the performance of sexagenary ceremonies of the Sigui that among the Dogon now commemorate both the revelation of the spoken word to men and the appearance of death on earth.

II. Dogon Calendars

The sun and the moon are the basis of the two principal calendars utilized by the Dogon. The first lunar month, the month of harvest, opens the lunar year; it recalls the conception of the first animate beings created by Amma. The solar year begins at the winter solstice, which determines the ceremony of *goru*; at this time a sacrifice is offered on the altars of the ancestors, beneath which signs of their gestation are engraved. At Sanga the apparent solstitial and equinoctial positions of the sun were formerly measured by sightings made by the use of three altars of "the union" placed to the west of the village of the Ogol. The operator placed a small staff vertically at the top of the altars and used a known landmark on the horizon to observe the rising sun. This measurement was taken four times a year by one or another of the chiefs of the joint family; it was called the "measure of the direction of the moment" (time).

The two distinct calendars—solar and lunar—are sometimes joined, sometimes dissociated, particularly for the performance of the rites that commemorate the episodes of the formation of the universe and the events resulting from the peopling of the earth.

On the level of social organization, the apparent positions of the sun are divided among the four Dogon tribes, associated with the four ancestors who came down on the ark: the rituals performed by their members take place at the two solstices and the two equinoxes. In addition, these positions recall the episodes of the myth: in the course of the successive rites of the year, the four tribes commemorate the stages of disorder caused by Ogo and the restoration of order through the sacrifice of his twin, Nommo.

In addition to the solar and lunar calendars, the positions of the planet Venus determine another calendar among the Dogon. The six positions of the planet, each called an "eye of Venus," signify in the cosmogony the flow, onto the placenta and in space, of blood from the castration and slaughter of the sacrificed Nommo and, in a parallel manner, the flow of the clavicular contents, the bases of earthly food. The luminary is represented beneath the altars by the "line of (sacrificial) blood" associated with any of the six positions that Venus occupies successively in its revolution around the sun. Each of its positions is represented under the altars by a graphic sign made from a circle flanked by external rays of numbers increasing from one to six. Moreover, these figures are at the same time used for the instruction of apprentice diviners, on a table of divination where they designate the movement of the planet in space.

The Venusian calendar, determined by six positions observable in the course of the year, is associated with various activities of men. Proof of the flowing of the blood and the clavicular contents of the progenitor of humanity, Venus in the heavens is the witness of the placenta of *pō*, the fonio. Its positions in the course of the year recall the stages of germination of the basic cereals originally contained in the first grain, that is, the annual death and resurrection of the millet. From this perspective, Venus constitutes an agricultural calendar called the "work of the winter season."

Since Venus is also associated with the castration of Nommo and the circumcision of the Fox, its positions used to determine the date of circumcision of men whose "father" is brought to life again. In various places, at the regional level, arrangements commemorate the circumcision of mythical ancestors. The calendar is no longer observed for circumcision; the Dogon declare that they only count the number of years "separating two ceremonies."

But the Dogon conceive the existence not only of the spiraling world of stars just mentioned, in which our planet is found, but also a multitude of other stellar worlds. The system is represented by one of the theoretical figures that are produced in order to explain the meaning of the *sirige* mask. The face of the mask is surmounted by a long perforated board made from a series of grills alternating with solid parts. Each of the pairs evokes the earth and the starry skies of one of these spiraling worlds: their number, seven, and their superimposition signify their infinite multiplication.

III. Malinke and Bambara

This correspondence between mythical events and the movement of the stars, firmly established among the Dogon, is also found among the Malinke and Bambara. Youssouf Cissé has described among the Bambara a table of numbers of the creation, the *sumangolo*, "which, by enumerating its constitutive elements, recovers the basic numbers of the creation and the numerical relationships common to the structure of man and to the structure of the world," which is associated with an entire stellar system.

Close correspondences are established between the anatomical composition of human beings and certain astronomical cycles: the thirty-three vertebrae, which constitute a person's ontological support and axis of gravity, correspond to the thirty-three lunar years at the end of which the lunar and solar calendars once more coincide (the Bambara and Malinke year begins at the winter solstice; if the new moon appears on that day, thirty-three lunar years will pass before there is a winter solstice on the first day of the new moon).

On the other hand, the number seventy-eight symbolizes in the "table of the numbers" the number of lunar years in the revolution of Halley's comet, which appears every seventy-six years: "Known for a very long time by the Malinke, who have made the duration of its revolution one of the bases of their calendar . . . Halley's comet is the symbol of men seventy-seven years of age, called 'burning souls.' " This "long year," as the Malinke call it, serves to fix, every seven years, the ceremonies for repairing the hut of the *kama blō*, which evoke, in the upper valley of the Niger, the descent of the ark and of the ancestors of the forty-four families who even today declare that they are descended from the Mande.

We can affirm, therefore, that among the Dogon, as among the Bambara and the Malinke, there are cosmobiological relations of great richness that are based on extremely complex astronomical observations and are connected with other myths of the creation of the world.

G.D./b.f.

BIBLIOGRAPHY

Y. CISSÉ, "Signes graphiques, représentations, concepts et tests relatifs à la personne chez les Malinké et les Bambara du Mali," in *La notion de personne en Afrique noire* (Paris 1973), 131–79. G. DIETERLEN, "Les cérémonies soixantenaires du Sigui chez les Dogon," *Africa* 41, no. 1 (1971): 1–11. M. GRIAULE and G. DIETERLEN, "Un système soudanais de Sirius," *Journ. Soc. Africanistes* 20 (1950): 273–94; *Le renard pâle* (Paris 1965), vol. 1: *Le mythe cosmogonique*," part 1: "La création du monde."

TOTEMISM AND THE INSTITUTION OF THE *BINU* AMONG THE DOGON

In West Africa one of the functions of totemism taken in its broadest sense is to manifest and promote the existence of categories and correspondences, classifications in every way comparable to those analyzed by Claude Lévi-Strauss. The example of the institution of the *binu* (the word comes from *bina*, "returned," and *viay*, "come") seems to be among the most significant.

Given its characteristic features—a clan, a name, a taboo—the institution of *binu* falls under the rubric of totemism as it was defined by Marcel Mauss. The members of a large indivisible family, a *ginna* (literally, "large house"), patrilinear and patrilocal, are grouped under the same totem. Sometimes several *ginna* share the same *binu*, but in such a case the *ginna* alone is exogamous, and there is no clan exogamy. Each *binu* is associated with one of the parts of the human body, and each part in turn has a mythical connection with a star or a constellation in space, and with certain animals, plants, or objects on earth.

It is at the level of the myth that tells of the creation of the world by a single God that these associations appear, in close connection with a sacrifice for the purification and reorganization of the universe in formation. The victim sacrificed by God is among the first living creatures he created. The sacrifice must repair the disorder caused by the rebellion and premature "birth" of one of the twin brothers, both then at the fetal stage (they are fish—silurids—in the waters of the womb and still connected to the placenta). Each step of the sacrifice (severing the umbilical cord, castration, cutting the throat, bloodletting, removal of the vital internal organs, cutting the body into pieces) lies at the origin of the formation of both a star and a species of animal or plant. The victim is then resurrected in the form of an adult human. This resurrected person, charged by God with watching over the movement of the universe, is the object of a totemic cult, each *binu* symbolically representing one of the parts of his body.

The twenty-two principal elements of the resurrected body correspond, for the Dogon people as a whole, to the twenty-two "great totems" (*binu na*); all other totems are thought to have originated from these, as "families" progressively developed. These principal totems are directly related to the twenty-two categories into which the Dogon classify the constituent elements of the universe. This aspect of totemism connects the ontology and morphology of "speech" in all senses of the term: thought, spoken word, language, etc.

In the body of a man, speech follows an evolution parallel to that of the growth of a human being: androgynous and confined to the brain and the clavicles of the fetus, it then differentiates into male and female and is conveyed by the blood through the internal organs along precise paths.

The victim of the mythical sacrifice, who has received "speech" during the fetal stage, will be charged after his resurrection with externalizing it and revealing it to mankind. The spoken word is, however, the verbal expression of the divine thought that presided over the creation of the universe and manifested itself in abstract signs inscribed on the placenta of the world in the process of formation. These signs foretell things to come, defining and situating them. They are classified into twenty-two basic categories. At this stage, "speech" is organization; it implies systems and structures including the social.

The joints of the resurrected body are the evidence of the categories. Each totem is connected with one of the categories: by belonging to a clan, a man is also intimately associated with them. The taboo of the *binu* is considered to be evidence of the cosmobiological correspondences between the parts of the resurrected body, the stellar system, the animal kingdom, and the plant kingdom. All these relationships are synthesized in it.

In a 1937 article describing and commenting on paintings that he calls *totemic coats of arms*, executed on the front of the shrines of the *binu* at the time of the festival of the sowing of seeds, Marcel Griaule was able to isolate the function of the "totem" in the ritual execution of the graphics, a fundamental expression of the creative "speech" of God.

More recent research has revealed that the depiction of figures on totemic shrines follows rigorous rules.

1. The set of signs of the category relevant to the totem must be depicted on the inside or the outside of each of the

Totemic shrine for the *binu* cult. Traces of millet ale mash that has been offered in sacrifice to the ancestors. Paris, Musée de l'Homme collection. Photo N'Diaye.

main shrines over a period of sixty years, sixty being the "count of the placenta," that is, the count associated with the creation of the universe.

2. The position of the graphics on the inside or the outside is a function of the mythical representations of which they are the object or the thing that they symbolize: (a) in the inside is depicted what was created in the beginning and formed in the still-closed womb of the creator God; (b) on the outside is depicted what was elaborated or what happened after the opening of the womb; (c) above the door, what took place in the sky; (d) below the door, what took place on earth; (e) on the jambs of the door, what took place in the space "between sky and earth," etc.

3. All the figures must be read according to a polyvalent symbolism. Thus the alternating black-and-white patchwork generally present on all the facades of the shrines signifies at least three things: the ark on which men came down from the sky to earth; the members of the clan; and the tilled soil, that is, the main functional fields, including that of the clan.

For the Dogon, all the drawings executed on all the shrines in the same year represent in mythical time "one day's work" by Amma. For the totems of the Dogon, all of the signs of Amma are depicted voluntarily in the course of sixty years, a period that signifies the "duration" of Amma's creation. "Each thing," say the Dogon, "each creature, came out of the womb of god with its name and its placenta—a placenta on which his sign had been engraved." The totemic coats of arms thus reproduce and repeat the "gestation" of the represented thing. This repetition is considered to be effective in perpetuating in time and space—and most particularly at the time of sowing seeds—the creature or the object of the universe that is represented.

Much like the Dogon, the populations located on the banks of the Niger River—the Malinke, the Bambara, the Bozo, the Soninke, and the Marka—have worked out a system of totemic classifications comparable to the one just described. For these populations, Faro, the resurrected body of the victim of the mythical sacrifice, is represented geographically by the course of the Niger, from its source in Guinea to Lake Debo. Here the river represents the body of Faro lying on his stomach in the water. Similarly, the river is marked by twenty-two spots known as *faro tyin*, situated

near water holes that symbolize the twenty-two joints of the resurrected body. Each of these designated spots on the river is associated with an animal from the bush that originally protected Faro's ritual field. Later these animals became the taboo animals (*ntana*) of the forty-four clans who still claim to have come from the Mande. They also became for each of them protectors of the "seeds" that had initially germinated in the *faro tyin* of the Niger after the sacrifice of Faro.

At the same time, when the Dogon fled the upper valley of the Niger in the twelfth and thirteenth centuries in order to avoid conversion to Islam, they inscribed their lost geography on their current territory, where the course of a winding and temporary river, the Gona, is marked out with standing stones that indicate and perpetuate the memory of the *faro tyin* on the Niger, i.e., the "count" of the joints of the sacrificed Nommo.

These designated spots are therefore also witness to one of the functions of totemism as it seems to be understood and experienced by the Dogon and the river dwellers along the Niger: revealing, maintaining, and perpetuating the "categories" that the clans bear witness to on the level of society, and the "correspondences" established among these categories, since each clan is connected with the others and yet distinct, like the "joints" or organs of any living body, in this case the body of the mythical progenitor of man, the microcosmic image of the universe.

G.D./g.h.

BIBLIOGRAPHY

G. DIETERLEN, "Les âmes des Dogon," *Travaux et mémoires de l'Institut d'ethnologie* 20 (Paris 1941); "Les correspondances cosmobiologiques chez les Soudanais," *Journal de psychologie normale et pathologique* (1950), 350–66; "Blasons et emblèmes totémiques des Dogon, République de Mali," in *Emblèmes, totems, blasons*, catalogue de l'exposition du musée Guimet (Paris, March/June 1964), 40–47. S. DE GANAY, "Le Binou Yébéné," *Miscellanea Africana* (Paris 1942). M. GRIAULE, "Blasons totémiques des Dogon," *Journ. Soc. Africanistes* 7 (1937): 69–78; *Dieu d'Eau* (Paris 1975), 19e journée, pp. 117–20. M. GRIAULE and G. DIETERLEN, "Le renard pâle," 1: "Le mythe cosmogonique," fasc. 1: "La Création du monde," *Travaux et mémoires de l'Institut d'ethnologie* 72 (Paris 1965).

YORUBA MYTHS AND RELIGION, AND THEIR AFRO-AMERICAN EXTENSIONS

The cults of the Orisha among the Nago-Yoruba of southwestern Nigeria and southeastern Benin, formerly Dahomey, may be defined as cults of deified distant ancestors who during their lifetimes were able to establish bonds with certain forces and phenomena of nature: thunder, winds, rains, watersheds, contagious diseases, the power of plant growth, and the fertility of woman.

Some authors[1] see these divinities as intermediaries between men and a supreme God,[2] Olorun (the sky) or Olodumaré, whose etymology is still disputed. The supreme God dwelt in the vault of heaven. *Orun* should, however, be taken to mean the beyond, what is outside the world, *ayé*. They are unanimous in describing him as occupying a distant and powerful position and in assigning him a fixed character

so insensitive to prayers that any worship of him would be to no avail. This is an instance of the belief in Power, the vital force, *ashè*, in its most absolute sense.

Only the Orisha are entreated by their devotees and receive offerings and sacrifices to maintain their strength and power. According to Bernard Maupoil,[3] "a bond of solidarity unites the Orisha and men. They complement one another. Through their prayers and sacrifices, men 'give strength' to the Orisha. The more numerous and sumptuous the offerings, the more powerful the divinities and the better their intentions. If the number of offerings decreases, the Orisha weaken. Man is restrained from the path of abandon by social constraint, fear of divine reprisals, and his confidence in the efficacy of an alliance with the unknowable. If one stopped honoring an Orisha altogether, his name would disappear."

Babalola Yai[4] defines faith in the Orisha as a religion in which there is no place for devils or hell. It does not sadden man's life with an original sin that he must cleanse himself

Alafin Oyo (and Shango). Photo Pierre Verger.

Ataoja of Oshogbo (and Oshun). Photo Pierre Verger.

of, but urges him to overcome his imperfections through his own efforts and the efforts of the community and through the Orisha. All in all, the Yoruba religious message stems neither from anxiety nor from "fear of the gods." Rather it is an attempt to respond to man's problems from within his physical and social environment.

The Orisha is therefore an alliance between an ancient and distant ancestor who founded the family lineage, and a force of nature. Although the force is eternal, the ancestor is mortal. To maintain the validity of the protective pact, the members of the family must not only evoke the memory of the departed ancestor but call his spirit back to earth, which they do during the ceremonies of worship of the Orisha by provoking trances in which the ancestor possesses one of his descendants. The initiation of an Orisha priest consists in inculcating in him the behavior of the deified ancestor. He thus becomes an *elegun*, one who is mounted, ridden, or possessed by the Orisha whose presence reactualizes the ancient pact of "ancestor power."

The descendants of the same distant ancestor engage in his particular cult and not the cult of all the Orisha. These are juxtaposed monotheisms rather than polytheism. Moreover, a perfect spirit of tolerance prevails between the various cults.

The importance and position of the Orisha in relation to one another varies markedly. Although Shango is supreme in Oyo, because he was the fourth king of that realm during his lifetime, he occupies only a secondary position in Oshogbo, where Oshun is in first place, and in the Ekiti region, where Ogun is in first place, and in Ifé, where first place is held by Oduduwa or Obatala.

This is because the dynasties of local kings are closely tied to the principal deities of each locality. Such ties could involve the cult of a royal ancestor such as Shango for the Alafin, the kings of Oyo, or Oduduwa for the Oni, the kings of Ifé; or a pact that united the founding ancestor of the dynasty with a deity already present in the locality where he settled long ago, such as the river Oshun for the Ataoja, the kings of Oshogbo. The cults of Shango and Oshun are virtually absent in Ifé, except for a few families who have come from elsewhere and practice the cults in private. Thus the Orisha do not form a pantheon, organized hierarchically and formed identically throughout the Yoruba land.

The transatlantic slave trade that supplied the Americas with forced labor had as an unexpected consequence the importation into the New World, along with teams of agricultural laborers, the influence of African culture, particularly the religion of the Yoruba Orisha, in Brazil and Cuba.[5]

At one time Catholicism was the only religion permitted in these countries. The cult of the Orisha managed nevertheless to survive in hiding, with each African god assimilated to a saint in the Catholic church. These comparisons were based on superficial resemblances between certain characteristic features of the gods and certain details on the images of the

141

saints. The assimilation was only apparent, and the syncretism was simply a mask, a cover behind which the worship of the African gods continued secretly. In time these cults became authorized and Creole blacks born in the New World and brought up respecting both religions equally came to regard the Afro-Catholic syncretism as a reality. For them, the saint and the Orisha were one; only the name changed, but depending on the place and time, it was appropriate to address him in Latin (before the aggiornamento) or in an African language.

I. Obatala or Orishanla

The gods of the lineage of Obatala are the only ones who have the right to be called Orisha. In stories known and told by the Babalawo, the Yoruba prophets, the word Orisha always designates Obatala (the king in the white loincloth), also known as Orishanla (the great Orisha), whose temple is at Ifé. The other Orisha of the lineage of the funfun Orisha (white Orisha) are Oshalufon (the Orisha owner of Ifon) at Ifon, Orishaguian at Ejigbo, Orisha Popo at Ogbomosho, and a few others whose names are not so well known.

Obatala or Orishanla is often called Oba Igbo (king of the Igbo), the name of the people who were living in Ifé before Oduduwa's arrival. Ulli Beier[6] notes that Obatala was said to be the deity whose ritual was performed by the Igbo before their defeat by the Yoruba.

Other sources[7] say that Obatala was deposed by Oduduwa and his crown (are) was seized by the victor. According to Akinjogbin,[8] the crown was preserved until now in the palace of Oni, king of Ifé, descendant of Oduduwa, and is now one of the objects used for the coronation of the new Oni. During the ceremonies for Obatala, the priests of this great Orisha, Orishanla, allude to the loss of the are crown. We may speculate that the ancient king of the Igbo was deified after he was stripped of his kingdom. It is also very likely that the story of the conquest of the kingdom of Obatala by Oduduwa, after passing from the profane to the sacred, was transformed into a part of the myth of the creation of the world in which Oduduwa takes the place of Obatala:

> Olodumaré, the supreme God, sent Obatala to create the world, aye, on the surface of the primordial waters. He was equipped for this task with the bag of existence, ape aye, which also means the bag of the earth. He set out but soon felt the need to quench his thirst, and after drinking an excessive amount of palm wine, he fell asleep. Olodumaré then sent Oduduwa to look for him. He found Obatala drunk, asleep on the roadside, and he took hold of the bag of existence, with which he created the earth by pouring the bag's contents over the surface of the waters. Greatly vexed, Obatala returned to the world beyond, where Olodumaré charged him with the responsibility of creating human beings. He fashioned the bodies with clay, and Olodumaré breathed life into them.

Obatala occasionally indulged his desire for palm wine, and on those days he would create imperfect bodies. Men would emerge from his hands deformed, hunchbacked,

Shango in Africa. Photo Pierre Verger.

Shango in Brazil. Photo Pierre Verger.

Ogun in Africa. Photo Pierre Verger.

lame, or one-armed, and through his unfortunate negligence, some of them were undercooked and came out sadly lacking in color. Their skin was white; they were albinos. That is why such people are consecrated to Orishanla. Three of the priestesses of Oshalufon Ifon are albinos. Hunchbacks and cripples are also consecrated to this great Orisha who was subject to unfortunate distractions.

Obatala is married to Yeye Mowo. Their statues stand side by side in their temple in Ifé, in the *ilesin*, the place of worship. They are represented sitting with their hands on their knees and surrounded by bags of cowry shells as evidence of their wealth.

Orishanla is regarded as an old man full of dignity but with a stubborn and undisciplined character which was the cause of his many misadventures.

The people who are devoted to him dress in white and wear necklaces of white beads and bracelets made of tin or ivory. He receives offerings of crushed yams, ground corn, goats, snails, hens that have had young, and karite butter. He has forbidden the use of palm wine (because of the troubles that he had as a result of abusing this intoxicating beverage), dogs, pigs, palm oil, salt, horses (to be neither eaten nor ridden). The high priest must eat alone, like a king, far from any onlookers, and his meal must be prepared in silence as a sign of respect.

Legends justify these prohibitions and obligations.

The ban on eating salt is explained by a story in which Obatala was supposed to make an offering of salt and a calabash to avoid shame on earth. He refused to fulfill this obligation. The consequence of his negligence was that Eshu attached to his back the calabash that he had refused to offer, thus making Orishanla a hunchback. The salt that he had refused to offer became one of his prohibitions.

Another legend, which involves palm oil, horses, and the silence imposed on Orishanla's followers, tells how Orishanla decided to journey outside his kingdom to pay a visit to his neighbor and friend Shango, the king of Oyo, against the advice of the soothsayers who had been consulted. On the way he was the victim of mistreatment by Eshu, who poured a container full of palm oil over him. Farther down the road, he came upon a runaway horse that belonged to

Shango. After stopping it by force, he was accused of stealing it by Shango's slaves who had been sent out to look for the animal. They beat him brutally with sticks, broke his arms and legs, and threw him in prison. Years of misfortune ensued in the kingdom of Shango until Orishanla was freed, and Shango's subjects, dressed in white and keeping a deep silence out of respect for Orishanla, went to fetch water three times to wash him.

A ceremony of purification called *agua de Oshala*, "the water of Orishanla," takes place every year to commemorate the legend in the temples built in Brazil by descendants of Nago Yoruba, who settled there.

In Brazil, particularly in Bahia, Oshala (Orishanla) has many followers. He is syncretized with O Senhor de Bomfim (Lord Jesus of the Good Final End). Friday is the day of the week consecrated to him. On that day the church of Bomfim receives a considerable number of devotees, generally dressed in white in honor of Orishanla. One of the most popular festivals in Bahia is the day of the Lavagem de Bomfim, the washing of the floor of the church of Bomfim, which for the followers of Orishanla is a Catholic replica of the ceremony of the water of Oshala. This god is known by two names in Bahia, Oshalufan, or old Orishanla, and Oshaguiyan, or young Orishanla. When Oshalufan is manifest in the body of one of his followers in a state of trance, he walks bent over like a very old man leaning on a *pashoro*, a kind of crook made of white metal. But Oshaguiyan moves around with energy and dynamism. He is also called Ajagunan, the warrior. When he dances, he carries in his hand his emblem, a pestle, the instrument used to grind yams. Certain legends in Africa explain his name Orishaguiyan by a play on words: *Orisha o gunyan*, "the Orisha grinds the yam."

Oshala receives offerings of food without salt or palm oil, but with karite butter. People greet him shouting: *Epa baba!*

In Cuba, Orishanla is syncretized with Nuestra Señora de la Merced, Our Lady of Mercy, probably because the habits of this Catholic religious order are white like those of the great Orisha.

Yoruba deities are generally called Orisha, but this term seems to be improper and is only applicable to the funfun Orisha who were established in Ifé before the arrival of the Yoruba. The other gods are called Shango, Ogun, Oshun, names by which the Ifa always refer to them in the traditional stories of divination, and not as Orisha Shango or Orisha Ogun. The term Orisha seems to be applied to them to define their divine nature comparable to Orishanla's and is only an expression of comparison and generalization. For this reason, we shall avoid using the term for any deity who is not of the lineage of the funfun Orisha.

II. Shango

Shango is the Yoruba god of thunder. He is virile and hardy, violent and just. He punishes liars, thieves, and lawbreakers. That is why death by thunder is ignominious. A house struck by lightning is marked by the wrath of Shango: the owner has to pay heavy fines to the priests of this god and make offerings to appease him. Moreover, the priests of Shango investigate the places where lightning has struck. They collect thunderstones or axes, *edun ara*, hurled onto this spot by Shango.

These *edun ara* (Neolithic axes) are placed on the altar of Shango, which is made of a carved wooden mortar, an allusion to the action of the thunderstones, brutal and

Oshun in Brazil. Photo Pierre Verger.

Yemanja in Africa. Photo Pierre Verger.

crushing, like the action of the pestle thrust inside a mortar. These *edun ara* support the *ashè* of Shango. The blood of animals sacrificed to him is poured on these stones in order to sustain their strength and vitality. The ram, the thrusts of whose head are as sudden as lightning, is the sacrificial animal that best suits him.

Shango's emblem is the stylized double ax, the *oshé*, which his *elegun Shango* priests (those mounted by Shango) hold in their hands when they are in a trance.

Shango dances to the beat of the bata drum. A rattle called *shèrè*, made of a stretched calabash, is specially reserved for him and is shaken to salute him and to accompany his songs of praise, *pipé* Shango.

The kings of Oyo claim Shango as their ancestor. He was the fourth king of the Yoruba, Alafin Oyo. During his lifetime he had the power to make lightning strike. He was also the owner of talismans that could make fire and flames come out of his mouth and nostrils. By terrifying his adversaries, he won many wars and annexed the territories next to his kingdom. He met a mysterious and controversial end. The first authors to deal with the problem, the Reverend T. J. F. Bowen[9] and Richard F. Burton,[10] tell how Shango was said to have been the king of Ikoso with the title of Oba Koso before he became Alafin Oyo. More recent authors, R. P. Baudin,[11] Pierre Bouche,[12] and A. B. Ellis[13] copying one another, have proposed an etymology based on the following legend:

> Shango was a despotic and cruel king in Oyo. His subjects tired of his tyranny and rebelled. Shango left his kingdom and hanged himself from a tree of the type called *ayan*. The next day his supporters learned of his death and looked for his body where he had hanged himself but did not find it. At the foot of the tree, they saw a hole with an iron chain protruding from it. Shango had become a god. They built a temple on the site, and priests established his cult there. Back in Oyo, they met Shango's enemies, who spread the news: "The king has hanged himself, *Oba so.*" His supporters retorted: "The king has not hanged himself, *Oba koso.*" Terrible storms unleashed by Shango destroyed the houses of his opponents, whom he finally killed with thunderstones. The people then declared unanimously, *Oba koso*, and gave that name of Ikoso to the site where the temple was built.

Thus there is an ambiguity in the interpretation of the title of Oba Koso.

Shango married three deities: Oya, who rules over storms and the Niger River, and Oshun and Oba, who became rivers with those same names.

In Brazil, Shango is syncretized with Saint Jerome. The only apparent link between the Yoruba god and the Catholic saint is the lion who escorts the saint on the paintings depicting him and is one of the symbols of kingship in Oyo. Wednesday is his holy day; his devotees wear the same red and white collars that they wear in Africa and greet him with shouts of *Kawo Kabiyèsilè* when he appears incarnate in the body of his *elegun*. During his dance, Shango brandishes his *oshé*, the double ax, with pride. Later the rhythm called *aluja* picks up speed, and he gestures as if filling an imaginary bag full of thunderstones and hurling them to earth. His dance then shows his libertine and bawdy character.

He is associated with the numbers 6 through 12.

In Cuba, despite his virile character, Shango is syncretized with Saint Barbara. This saint must have some connection with thundering things, for she is the patron saint of artillerymen, and on warships her name is given to depots of

Omolu in Brazil. Photo Pierre Verger.

Oshumaré in Africa. Photo Pierre Verger.

gunpowder and ammunition. The habits of her order are red and white, colors that are symbolic of Shango.

III. Ogun

Ogun is the god of blacksmiths and of all those who use iron: warriors, hunters, farmers, butchers, fishermen, and barbers, and for nearly a century, drivers of cars and trains, mechanics, and motorcycle repairmen.

Ogun is one, but he is given seven names because he is associated with the number seven, and he is complete when all seven parts are accounted for. He is represented by seven, fourteen, or twenty-one instruments cast in iron, threaded on an iron rod. He is also represented by frayed fringes of young palm leaves called *mariwo*. This was the garment once worn by Ogun, and the presence of these fringes above a door or across the entrance to a road is enough to evoke him and keep bad influences at bay. When placed closer to the ground, they forbid people to pass; to cross the line means to expose oneself to the wrath of the god. On the one hand, Ogun seals off the road from wicked outside forces, and on the other, he opens the road to the realization of all the actions that can be undertaken.

During sacrifices to other deities, praise is given him and offerings are made to him because without the knife made with his help, the sacrifices would not be possible. We shall see later the conflicts between him and certain other deities on this subject.

Ogun was the firstborn son of Oduduwa, and he commanded the armies in his father's place when his father was temporarily blinded. He took the city of Ire in Ekiti, but was entitled only to a small crown, *akoro*, which earned him the title of Ogun Alakoro Oniré, Ogun the bearer of the small crown, king of Ire.

He receives offerings of dogs, palm wine, and dishes prepared with beans.

In Brazil only his warlike features are retained; his other functions have disappeared. The slaves who once perpetuated his cult in the New World and worked in the fields had no interest in asking him to make the land they worked fertile, since its crops did not belong to them. Another god of the hunt, Oshosi, was already filling this role. Ogun's blacksmith's activities were evoked by metal instruments that looked exactly like those in Africa.

Tuesday is the holy day of Ogun in Brazil; his followers wear strings of deep blue beads, his dances mimic war, and he is greeted with shouts of *Ogun ye!* In Bahia he is syncretized with Saint Anthony, and in Rio de Janeiro, with Saint George. In Cuba he is compared with Santiago, Saint James the Greater.

IV. Oranyan

Oranyan, according to legend, was the son of two fathers, Oduduwa and Ogun, who slept successively with the same woman. That is why his body was half-black and half-white, Oduduwa's skin being light, and Odun's very dark.

Oranyan was the third king of Ifé. He was the father of Ajaka and Shango, who were the third and fourth kings of Oyo. Another of his sons became the king of Benin.

Oyo tradition regards Oranyan as the creator of the earth, over which he continued to rule, although he was the youngest of the seven princes who came from the world beyond all at the same time. He created the dry earth over the surface of the water and his brothers had to pay him tribute and rent for the right to dwell on it.

The myth of the creation of the world by Oranyan, which differs from the one in which Oduduwa plays the same role, reflects the rivalry that existed between Ifé, the spiritual center of the Yoruba, and Oyo, which was its actual capital. These two deified heroes were the founders of the ruling dynasties in these two places.

V. Dada or Banyani

Dada or Banyani is the name given to Ajaka, Shango's older brother, who ruled in Oyo before and after him as the third and fifth Alafin. He was a weak king who loved children, beauty, and decoration. After abdicating in favor of Shango, he was content to have a crown of cowrie shells. He was deified for his kindness, his elegance, and for having hair as curly as a wig.[14]

In Brazil songs in his honor are the same as those in Africa: Dada ma sokun mo (Don't cry, Dada), sung to console little children, for, as the story goes in Bahia, Shango's brother whined constantly. During the festivals celebrated in his honor, the priest of Dada appears before his devotees. He wears on his head the ade of Banyani, the crown of Banyani, made of thousands of cowries. After a short time, the crown is taken by the priest of Shango in remembrance of Ajaka's abdication in his favor, and after he has danced with the ade on his head, it is placed again on Dada's head, in commemoration of the second ascension to the throne of Shango's older brother. The ceremony seems to be a reenactment of very ancient historical facts.

According to other sources, Dada was Yamasse, Shango's mother, and the ade crown of Banyani which belonged to him is worn in a procession during a festival that ends the Shango cycle in another temple of Orisha in Bahia.

VI. Oya

After she was Ogun's wife, Oya became Shango's wife. She is said to have come from the Tapa or Nupe country, and when Shango entered the underground in Ikoso, she did the same in Ira, thus becoming the goddess of storms and of the Niger River.

Buffalo horns are placed on her altar. A legend known in both Africa and the New World explains their presence:

A hunter lying in wait saw a buffalo coming near. He was about to kill it when he saw the animal shed its skin and horns and transform itself into a beautiful woman. It was Oya. She hid her skin in a thicket and went to the market in the next town. The hunter seized the skin and hid it in his granary. Then he went to the market, met the beautiful woman, and asked her to marry him. She refused, but later, when she could not find her skin, she was compelled to accept his offer. She did, however, pose one condition: the hunter had to observe absolute discretion about her animal origin. Later the hunter's other wives became jealous of Oya. They succeeded in getting their husband drunk and made him reveal the secret. As they went about their household chores, they sang, "Ma je, ma mu, awo rè gbe l'aja ([Make yourself pretty], eat and drink, but [we know that] your skin is in the granary)." Forewarned by this, Oya was able to transform herself again into a buffalo and gored her former rivals to death with her horns. She then headed toward the fields with the intention of killing her former husband, but he was

able to calm her by offering her akara, bean fritters, her favorite dish. Oya then took off her horns and handed them to the hunter. Whenever he needed her help, she would come running to him as soon as he hit one against the other to call her.

Oya receives offerings of goats, yams, palm wine, and akara.

In Brazil she is more often called Yansan, a name by which she is also known in Africa and that may be an allusion to the nine arms of the Niger Delta. She is syncretized with Saint Barbara. Wednesday is her holy day, as it is for her husband Shango. Her followers wear strings of dark red beads. When she appears during public ceremonies, she is greeted with shouts of Epa hei Oya! Her dance is wild and frenzied. She brandishes a sword in one hand and a flyswatter in the other, or else she dances with her arms stretched out and her hands forward as if to keep at bay the Egun, the souls of the dead, for she is the only divinity that can cope with them and control them. In Cuba she is syncretized with the Virgen de la Candelaria, the Virgin of Candlemas, who bears elements of fire.

VII. Oshun

Oshun is the goddess of the Nigerian river that bears her name. She is Shango's second wife, which does not prevent her from having amorous involvements with Oshosi, the deity of hunters, according to some, and with Obatala, according to others. She has the reputation of being very coquettish and of loving jewels and ornaments of yellow copper (a precious metal at that period), of which she owns a large quantity. She bears the title of Iyalodé, she who leads all the women of the town. And she has the reputation of making wishes come true for those who want children. She goes by various names associated with the deep places, ibu, that are distributed along the course of the river from its source at Igede to Leke, where it empties into the lagoon. The ibu have the names of Ijumu, Iponda, Ipetu, Aboto, Apara, Ikare, etc. One of the most important Oshun is the Oshun of Oshogbo. Every year Ataoja, the local king, commemorates with great ceremonies the arrival of his ancestor Laro on the banks of the Oshun River, whose waters flow ceaselessly. Judging the spot favorable, he decided to settle there with his people. Laro's settlement on this site was marked by a series of supernatural events. One of his daughters vanished under the water as she was bathing in the river and reemerged a short time later superbly dressed. She announced that she had been received and treated admirably by the deity who resided in the water. Laro then made offerings of thanksgiving to the river. A large fish came swimming near the spot where he was standing and spurted water. Laro caught some of this water in a calabash and drank it, thus making a pact of alliance with the river. He then stretched out his hands and the large fish jumped in. He took the title of Ataoja, a contraction of the phrase Yoruba, a tèwo gba èja ("he who extends his hands and takes the fish"), and he declared Oshun gbo, Oshun is in a state of maturity, its water will always be abundant, which is why the city is called Oshogbo.

On the day of the annual festival of Oshun, Ataoja renews the ancient pact by approaching the river with great ceremony to throw in offerings of food which the fish come to fight over before his eyes.

In Brazil, and in Bahia in particular, Oshun is a very popular deity. She is known by the various names of the ibu listed earlier. Her dance imitates the gait of a coquettish and vain woman who goes to swim in the river, puts on necklaces and bracelets, shakes her arms to make them jingle, shows herself off gracefully, and looks at herself with satisfaction in a mirror. As in Africa, she is greeted with shouts of *Ore Yeye o!* She is symbolized on her altar by river pebbles on which yellow copper bracelets and fans are arranged. It is good to offer her a dish called *omuluku,* a mixture of onions, beans, salt, and shrimp. She also gladly receives *adun,* corn flour mixed with honey and sweet oil. She is syncretized with Our Lady of Candlemas, and Saturday is her holy day. Her followers wear necklaces of yellow beads and copper bracelets.

In Cuba her features are the same, but she is syncretized with the Virgen de la Caridad del Cobre, the Virgin of Charity of Copper.

VIII. Oba

Oba is Shango's third wife and the goddess of the river that bears her name. She is the heroine of a sad story that began with her rivalry with Oshun and her efforts to obtain the exclusive love of their common husband. Oshun played

a mean trick on her by claiming that she aroused Shango's love with certain of her culinary concoctions. Oba, eager to learn her secrets, surprised Oshun one day as she stood with a scarf wrapped around her head so that it hid her ears; she was engrossed in cooking a soup for Shango. Leaning over the pot, Oba saw mushrooms shaped like ears floating on the surface. Oshun pretended that she had cut off her ears and was cooking them in this soup that would delight Shango. When it came Oba's turn to do the cooking, she did not hesitate to cut off one of her ears in order to make the same soup. The result was catastrophic. Shango found it atrocious and was horrified at the sight of Oba with her ear cut off. Oshun then took off her scarf, revealing to Oba that she had played a trick on her. Oba became furious and attacked Oshun. Shango became angry. The two women fled and turned into rivers. When the two rivers meet, the waters are always very agitated in remembrance of this dispute.

In Brazil, when Oba appears during a ceremony, one of the ears of her "horse" is hidden to recall this legend, and if on the same day Oshun possesses one of her priestesses, the two deities, once again confronting each other, still want to fight, and care must be taken to keep them apart. In Bahia, Oba is syncretized with Saint Catherine.

Osanyin in Brazil. Photo Pierre Verger.

Eshu in Brazil. Photo Pierre Verger.

IX. Yemanja

Yemanja, the goddess of the Ogun River (which has nothing to do with the god of blacksmiths), is the daughter of Olokun, the sea, into which her waters empty in a constant flow. She had very large breasts, the symbol of happy motherhood, but she could not bear jokes about this, which caused frequent fights with her husband. She was the mother of many Yoruba gods. Her principal temple is located in Abeokuta in the Ibara district, where she receives offerings of rams, yams, and corn. Her importance comes from her power over the waters. At one time bodies of water were scarce in this country; when she slept and rolled over in her sleep, springs of water would gush forth.

In Brazil, Yemanja is a very popular deity. The mother of the waters is syncretized with Our Lady of the Immaculate Conception. Her followers wear strings of transparent crystal beads and greet her with shouts of *Odoya*. Major festivals take place in her honor every December 8 and February 2 (Candlemas, which is syncretized with Oshun, who is also associated with the waters). On that day a huge crowd gathers in Bahia on the beach of Rio Vermelho to offer a gift to Yemanja, the *Mae d'agua*, the mother of the waters. Gifts are stacked in large baskets—soaps, perfumes, pieces of fabric, necklaces, and bracelets. All of it, along with requests and letters, is tossed out to sea at the end of the day.

In Cuba, she is syncretized with the Virgin de Regla.

X. Shapannan, Omolu, and Obaluaye

Shapannan is the god of smallpox and contagious diseases, but it is better to avoid uttering this terrible name and to call him Omolu or Obaluaye, king of the earth. He is regarded as Shango's older brother, which probably means that he is an older god. Another sign of his greater age is the fact that animal sacrifices to him are made without the use of a knife. Tradition has it that people sing a certain canticle and the animal dies of its own accord. This detail is justified by a legend about an argument between Ogun and Omolu. Ogun claimed that no one could eat without his help, since his forge made the metal knife that was designed to kill and carve animals. Omolu proved to him that it was possible to kill without using iron. The same was true for Nana Buruku mentioned earlier. This dispute between deities may be interpreted as a superimposition of religions belonging to different cultural groups who successively settled in a given place, giving rise to a myth that substituted a rivalry between gods for a rivalry between the people who worshiped them. The quarrel that opposed Ogun to Omolu (or Nana Buruku) may express an opposition between the ritual instituted for the ancient god during the period when iron was still unknown and the new ritual that was established when the god of iron, Ogun, appeared. The attitude of the followers of Omolu or Nana Buruku was simply fidelity to the ancient ritual in which they could not slaughter with a metal knife because iron was still unknown. This may be further underscored by the traditions in Lower and Middle Benin that speak of successive migrations of people who came from Yoruba country. It would appear that the first waves left before the knowledge of iron and established the cults of Omolu and Nana Buruku, and that those who followed brought the other gods with them.

In Brazil, Omolu (or Obaluaye) is syncretized with Saint Lazarus or Saint Roch, because the bodies of these two Catholic saints are covered with wounds. Monday is his holy day. He is offered roasted popcorn and receives sacrifices of male goats. His followers wear necklaces of either red and black or white and black beads. People possessed by him cover their heads and bodies with fringes of straw and dance to a beat called *opanijé*, meaning "he kills someone and eats him." They mimic suffering, convulsions, itching, and the shivering of fever. He carries in his hand a broom called *shashara*, made of the central veins of palm leaves. He is greeted with shouts of *Atoto!* an expression of respect and submission.

In Cuba his characteristics are the same.

XI. Nana Buruku

Nana Buruku is a very ancient deity. Her cult is widely distributed, and it is not easy to determine its place of origin. Did it start in Ifé and move westward into the Adele region of modern Ghana and even beyond? Or did it begin in Adele and find followers to the east? The question remains unanswered. In certain places, she is considered the supreme god; elsewhere, she is not distinguished from Obaluaye. She is the deity of the primordial waters, of the muddy water containing the silt from which the world would later emerge. Like Obatala, she is an archaic deity older than all the others known among the Yoruba, and very little is known about her.

In Brazil, Nana Buruku is regarded as the mother of Omolu and as the oldest of the deities of the waters. She is syncretized with Saint Anne. Her followers wear strings of red, white, and blue beads. Saturday is her holy day, as it is for all the other deities of the waters. She dances with dignity, carrying a kind of curved broom called an *ebiri*. She is greeted with shouts of *Saluba!*

XII. Oshumaré

Oshumaré is represented in the form of a rainbow snake. He has multiple functions. He is the symbol of continuity, and he also represents vital strength, movement, and everything that stretches. He is both male and female. He holds up the earth and keeps it from disintegrating. He is wealth and fortune. He is thought to be one of Shango's servants, and his task is to take some of the water on the earth and bring it up to his palace in the clouds. His followers wear necklaces of shells strung to look like the scales of a snake. He holds in his hands an *ebiri,* a kind of curved broom similar to Nana Buruku's.

In Brazil, Oshumaré's followers wear necklaces of yellow and green beads. Tuesday is his holy day. When he dances, he points alternately to the sky and the earth with his index fingers. He is greeted with shouts of *Ao boboi!* He is syncretized with Saint Bartholomew. In Bahia he is celebrated in a village that bears his name, where, each year on August 24, crowds of his followers go swimming under a waterfall crowned by a mist that permanently reflects Oshumaré's rainbow.

XIII. Oshosi

Oshosi is the god of hunters and the brother of Ogun. He owes his importance among the Yoruba to several causes. The first is material, because it is Oshosi who makes a hunt successful and consequently ensures abundant food. The second is medical in nature, because the hunters in the forests frequently come into contact with Osanyin, the god of medicinal and liturgical leaves. The third cause is social, for again it is the hunter, *odè*, who, under Oshosi's protection during his pursuit of game, discovers a site suitable for a new farm or a future village where he will someday settle with his family. He will become the first occupant of the site and will rule over those who will come to live there after him. He also presides over law and order in towns and villages where once the only owners of firearms were the hunters. They made up the society of *olodè* responsible for the night watch over populated areas.

In Brazil he is syncretized with Saint George in Bahia and with Saint Sebastian in Rio de Janeiro. Thursday is his holy day. His followers wear necklaces of green beads. He is symbolized by a bow and arrow made of wrought iron. When he appears during a ceremony, he is greeted with shouts of *Oké!* His dance mimics the hunt, the pursuit of game, and the shooting of arrows. The same applies in Cuba. The cult of this god, so popular in Brazil and Cuba, has almost disappeared in Africa.

XIV. Erinlè, Ibualama, Logun Èdè

Oshosi is also known in Brazil and Cuba by the name of Inlè (Erinlè in Nigeria) or Ibualama. According to a legend, he was a hunter who was seduced by Oshun and lured by her into the river where she lived. His emblem is a flyswatter made of three leather straps which people use to whip themselves during a trance. His principal temple in Nigeria is in Ilobu, where the Erinlè River passes not far from where it joins the Oshun River. He is represented by river pebbles and an iron object topped by a bird.

Logun Èdè is known in Brazil as the son of Inlè and Oshun Yeyeponda. For six months of the year he is a man who lives in the brush and eats game, while for the other six months he is a woman who lives in the water and eats fish. His/her temple in Nigeria is in Ilèsha. In this city, he receives offerings of rams, roosters, kola nuts, and small bananas known as *ogèdè wèwè*.

XV. Osanyin

Osanyin presides over medicinal and liturgical leaves. His importance is primordial; no ceremony can take place without his cooperation. He is the keeper of the *ashè* (force, power), which the gods themselves cannot do without. Osanyin's symbol is an iron rod topped with seven points aimed upward like the spokes of an upside-down umbrella. The middle one bears the image of a bird.

Osanyin is the constant companion of Ifa the prophet. He is represented by a little wrought-iron bell tipped by a pointed rod stuck into a thick seed. The rod is planted in the ground next to the prophet's iron *osun* (the symbol of his ancestors). By his presence he brings the influence of the power of the plants to the processes of divination. Bernard Maupoil[15] records a legend which emphasizes the bonds between Ifa and Osanyin:

> When Ifa came into the world, he asked for a slave to till his field. A slave was bought for him at a market. Ifa sent him to the field to cut some herbs, but the slave, who was none other than Osanyin, realized as soon as he began his work that he was going to cut the herb that cures fever. He shouted, "Impossible to cut that one! It is too useful." The second herb that he noticed cured headaches. He also refused to destroy that one. The third cured stomachache. "Surely," he said, "I cannot dig up such vital herbs!" When Ifa found out about his slave's behavior, he asked him to show him these herbs and decided that Osanyin

would stay close to him to explain to him the virtues of these plants and that he would remain stationed next to him during the consultations.

Each deity has its own leaves. Each leaf is endowed with a certain virtue. There are leaves of fortune, happiness, glory, fertility, joy, luck, coolness, and courage, but there are also leaves of misery, indiscreet chatter, and others still more undesirable. While making the various preparations using these plants, one must utter incantations in order to awaken and activate their power, their *ashè*.

XVI. Eshu

Eshu, also known as Èlègbara, has multiple contradictory features that make it difficult to formulate a coherent definition of him.

Eshu is the messenger of the other Yoruba deities, and nothing can be done without him. He guards temples, houses, and towns. He shares the anger of the gods and of men, too. His character is touchy, violent, irascible, cunning, coarse, vain, and indecent. The first missionaries were so horrified by him that they assimilated him to the Devil and made him the symbol of all that is wicked and perverse, abject, hateful, and in opposition to goodness, purity, uplifting things, and the love of God. Eshu likes to cause accidents and public and private calamities, to arouse arguments, dissension, and misunderstandings. He is the hidden companion of people and impels them to do unreasonable things. He incites and stirs up bad inclinations. Nevertheless, he also has his good side, and in this Eshu shows that he is the most human of the gods, neither completely good nor completely bad. He works for good as well as for evil and is the faithful messenger of those who dispatch him and make offerings to him. He has the good qualities that go with his faults, being dynamic and jovial. It was he who revealed the art of divination to human beings.

Because of his function as messenger and the touchiness of his character, one must be careful during ceremonies always to make offerings to him first, before making them to other gods, so that the celebration of these festivals can proceed calmly and with dignity.

In Brazil he is familiarly called *compadre*. Monday is his holy day. His altar is made of a mound of earth in which iron tridents are planted. His devoted followers are few because of his alleged syncretism with the Devil. His necklaces are red and black, and he receives offerings of male goats and roosters, preferably black. He is greeted with shouts of *Laroyê!*

P.V./g.h.

NOTES

1. WILLIAM BOSMAN, *Voyage de Guinée* (Utrecht 1705), 148. R. P. GEOFFROY LOYER, *Voyage au royaume d'Issiny* (Paris 1774), 242. P. LABARTHE, *Voyage à la côte de Guinée* (Paris 1863), 183. REV. T. J. BOWEN, *A Grammar and Dictionary of the Yoruba Language* (Washington 1858), chap. 16. R. P. BAUDIN, *Fétichisme et féticheurs* (Lyons 1884), 6. ABBÉ PIERRE BOUCHE, *La côte des Esclaves et le Dahomey* (Paris 1885), 106. RICHARD F. BURTON, *A Mission to Gelele, King of Dahome* (London 1864), 2:88. A. B. ELLIS, *The Yoruba Speaking People* (London 1894), 35.

2. PIERRE VERGER, *The Yoruba High God*, in *Odu*, Ibadan, vol. 2, no. 2.

3. BERNARD MAUPOIL, *La géomancie à l'ancienne côte des Esclaves* (Paris 1943), 56. In our citation we replace the word *Vodun* with the equivalent term *Orisha*.

4. BABALOLA YAI, *Influence de l'Afrique sur la littérature au Brésil,* in *Cultura* (Brasilia 1977), special issue on the Second Festival of Black Arts.

5. The principal authors who have studied these questions:
For Brazil: NINA RODRIGUES, *Os Africanos do Brasil* (São Paulo 1945). ARTHUR RAMOS, *O Negro Brasileiro* (São Paulo 1940). EDISON CARNEIRO, *Candomblés da Bahia* (Bahia 1948). RENÉ RIBEIRO, *Cultos afro-brasileiros do Recife* (Recife 1952). DONALD PIERSON, *Brancos e Pretos na Bahia* (São Paulo 1971). ROGER BASTIDE, *Sociologie et psychanalyse* (Paris 1950); *Les religions africaines au Brésil* (Paris 1960). PIERRE VERGER, *Notes sur le culte des Orisha et Vodun . . . ,* Memoir no. 51 de l'IFAN (Dakar 1957).
For Cuba: FERNANDO ORTIZ, *La Africania de la Musica Folklorica de Cuba* (Havana 1950). LYDIA CABRERA, *El Monte* (Havana 1954).

6. ULLI BEIER, "Obatala Festival," in *Nigeria Magazine,* no. 52, p. 10.

7. I. A. AKINJOGBIN, "The Yoruba Culture Area," in *The Notions of Power in Traditional Africa,* UNESCO, forthcoming.

8. I. A. AKINJOGBIN, personal communication.

9. T. J. F. BOWEN, *A Grammar and Dictionary of the Yoruba Language* (Washington 1858), chap. 16.

10. RICHARD F. BURTON, *Abeokuta and the Camaroons* (London 1883), 1:187.

11. BAUDIN, *Fétichisme et féticheurs,* p. 18.

12. BOUCHE, *La côte des Esclaves et le Dahomey,* p. 115.

13. ELLIS, *The Yoruba Speaking People,* p. 46.

14. ONADELE EPEGA, *The Mystery of the Yoruba Gods* (Lagos 1931), chap. 12.

15. MAUPOIL, *La géomancie à l'ancienne côte des Esclaves,* p. 176.

THE RELIGION AND MYTHS OF BANTU SPEAKERS

I. The Unity of the Bantu-speaking Peoples from the Great Lakes to South Africa

The Bantu-speaking peoples cover, without interruption, the third of the surface of the African continent south of an east-west frontier formed by an extension of the coast of the Gulf of Guinea from the south of Nigeria to the south of Somalia. More than three hundred peoples, tribes, or nations can be distinguished in that group, whose definition as a group is founded only on a linguistic criterion, that is, on the fact that they all speak many very closely related languages. This fact has led to the hypothesis of a relatively recent expansion (two thousand years?) breaking out of a common primitive source. The totality of Bantu languages constitutes only a small subdivision at the heart of the much more differentiated great family of the languages of West Africa.

This linguistic uniformity spans an enormous diversity of physical types and cultural configurations, inextricably entangled by incessant currents in all directions and from diverse origins. Unlike the languages, the religion and myths of Bantu speakers have seldom been explored in comparative or synthesizing studies. Moreover, the information about these realms is insufficient or deficient, either because British ethnologists, excellent in other ways, have tended to regard such questions as subsidiary, or because missionaries, who have a special interest in them, have often pursued that interest in a biased manner and in a frame of mind that leads to distortion. That said, one can nevertheless define several broad lines in Bantu religious thought.

Bantu-speaking peoples recognize a supreme God, distant and hidden, whom they do not worship but who is an explanatory principle, the symbol of the preexistent. In certain more or less allegorical narratives he appears in an externally anthropomorphic form, but outside of this context he is conceived more abstractly as a principle of life, fertility, and chance, simultaneously Cause and Providence. It would be wrong, however, to insist on the specifically monotheistic character of these beliefs, to the extent that uniqueness itself is never stressed or highly valued. This God is unique inasmuch as he is an abstract principle, but he is divided concretely in certain circumstances.

The fundamental cult is of the spirits of ancestors, with a concern less to glorify them than to appease their rancor and bitterness, which can destroy the living, or to gain their benevolent protection against other malevolent forces. In this search for security and protection, divination plays an essential role and is conceived of as connected, in one way or another, with the principle personified by the distant God or his representative. The other entities that animate the cults fall into one of two classes: either spirits of nature or divinized heroes (kings, chiefs, founding ancestors, culture heroes, great hunters or warriors, prophets, mediums, exceptional women). The former are not opposed to the latter and tend to be intermixed with them. Bantu speakers seem to see social forces as a harmonious extension of natural forces rather than as a break from them. The sacred and even divine character of their kings and others who hold religious power springs from the fact that they are regarded as the equivalent, in the human world, of natural forces, or at least as special mediators between natural forces and society (in their role as rainmakers, catalysts of fertility, eliminators of monstrosities, etc.). In some Central African societies, the cult of nature spirits, often associated with water, excludes any kind of ritual relationship with the ancestors.

On the level of fundamental values, the Bantu-speaking peoples are remarkably constant in their belief that the blessings of life lie less in a hypothetical afterlife, generally depicted as a world of shadows with rather sad contours, than in numerous offspring who not only will preserve their memory in the framework of ancestor worship, but especially will maintain their physical and social existence in life on earth. This idea is sometimes symbolized by a sacred fire which, like the life of one's offspring, continues to burn with the same flame even when it changes fuel, so that, inversely, extinguished embers evoke the death of a man who left no offspring.

On the level of cultural configurations, the religious thought of Bantu speakers is not generally expressed in great cosmogonical or purely mythological constructions or by a regular succession of public rites and festivals punctuating the annual cycle. Rather, there are in each case choices of various ritual solutions for various circumstances and an interlacing of sects, of particular cults, and of interventions by quite diverse specialists. Even though the same symbolic principles are at work in all of these, it is often difficult to regard as mere elements of the same concrete "religion" (in the sense that we understand it) such factors as the rites of sacred kingship, ancestor worship, séances and trances, various types of initiation, and numerous therapeutic forms

1 Bantu speakers of the Great Lakes region
2 Central Bantu speakers
3 Bantu speakers of southern Africa

of magic. Nevertheless, this visible religious pragmatism is expressed in a marked taste for a concrete symbolism that is directly attached to things rather than to their signs. And within this pragmatism, recent research has revealed a coherent symbolic space at the interior of which different facets of religious practice are organized. Relationships that are stable but variable from one region to another are established between the individual, the society, and the universe; the ritual manipulations of materials and of diverse objects constitute rebuses in which things, directly combined among themselves like signs, speak.

But rituals are rarely presented as the direct translations of myths, which are often missing or, where they do exist, are ignored by most of the people who perform the rituals. The genuinely mythical material is rather to be sought among the historical narratives about the origins and development of the dynasties and clans or the life of heroes. Similarly, myths are found in poetic genres with complex structures, inscribed in various institutional, ritual, and other frameworks, or even in the exegeses and commentaries on the rituals themselves. When these oral data are connected with a comparative internal and external analysis, we can retrieve various "codes," which encompass the relationships of kinship, animals, plants, geography, the earth and the sky, the sun and the moon, Venus, lightning, etc. In this way it is also possible to mark general categories based, for example, on colors, heat and cold, light and its absence, and the image of the body. Yet it seems rash to affirm, as some have done, that these symbolic groups, which can be shared by very different cultures, make explicit everywhere a common philosophical content. If Bantu speakers had a common philosophy, bound to the semantic characteristics of the languages and to certain symbolic and religious constants, it could exist only in opposition to attitudes of thought manifested in other large

cultural groups, and the comparativist gaze of the ethnologist could then disclose equally well, according to other criteria, similar ruptures within the Bantu-speaking world itself.

Two things are certain: with no other peoples did the evangelism of missionaries during the colonial period encounter such incredible apparent success, and among no others were there so many new messianisms, prophetic movements, and diverse sects, which, often for the sake of political protest, mixed traditional elements with Christian or biblical elements.

II. Historical Differentiation and the Criteria of Classification

Once the basis of the unity of the Bantu-speakers' world is recognized—that is, language and its peculiar logical structures, geographical unity, common agricultural and metallurgical (iron) technology, and a number of very general religious conceptions—it must be said that in all other respects Bantu culture is crossed by the most diverse and contradictory historical currents, which are found not only in neighboring groups but also within the same society. One can distinguish certain characteristic culture areas within the Bantu-speaking group, but it would be difficult to define a body of criteria that could give them a precise order. Among the criteria often discussed, we will mention three: first, the principle of patrilineal or matrilineal descent; second, the presence or absence of a political organization, usually centralized in the form of a sacred kingship whose territorial foundation can be anything from the smallest principality to an empire; finally, the absence or presence and relative importance of the cow, the breeding of which is accompanied by a complex of cultural traits, some of which seem to be inherited from non-Bantu-speaking pastoral societies of East Africa. Some examples are the taste for warlike pageantry and exploits of elite warriors and the social and aesthetic prestige attached to cattle (a prestige that is surprising in relation to the agriculture that is generally prevalent).

Each of the eight possible combinations of these three criteria is represented by several societies among Bantu speakers. The Herero, for example, in the extreme southwest (Namibia), are pure cattle breeders whose customs and attitudes closely resemble those of the Bantu cattle breeders of the Great Lakes region, but the Herero give priority to the matrilineal principle and lack a centralized political organization. It is noteworthy, nevertheless, that the patrilineal societies are principally situated in the whole northern region of the Bantu-speaking area and in the southeast, while cattle are found in the entire southern region and to the northeast, where cattle breeding must have been introduced from outside. The societies in the north and south are completely separated from one another by a very wide belt, from the Atlantic coast to the Indian Ocean, consisting of predominantly matrilineal societies that have no large cattle. Remarkable national developments take place, on the one hand, in the patrilineal societies of the northeast (the region of the Great Lakes) and the southeast (South Africa), which are also the ones most strongly marked by the cattle complex and within which other striking correspondences are observed; and, on the other hand, at the heart of the zone of the central Bantu, in Zaire, Angola, and Zambia. These three groups are the most deeply marked by the historic dimension and the richest in oral traditions, and it is their mythological conceptions that are treated in two of the following

151

articles, "Cosmogonies of Bantu-speaking Societies" and "Sacred Kingship among the Bantu Speakers of Zaire and Southern Africa."

P.S./d.f.

BIBLIOGRAPHY

G. BALANDIER, *Sociologie actuelle de l'Afrique noire* (Paris 1955). H. BAUMANN and D. WESTERMANN, *Les peuples et les civilisations de l'Afrique* (Paris 1962). *Ethnographic Survey of Africa*, International African Institute, London (25 vols. on Bantu-speaking peoples). L. DE HEUSCH, *Pourquoi l'épouser? et autres essais* (Paris 1971). A. KAGAME, *La philosophie bantu comparée* (Paris 1976). G. P. MURDOCK, *Africa, Its Peoples and Their Culture History* (New York 1959). A. WERNER, *Myths and Legends of the Bantu* (London 1933).

COSMOGONIES OF BANTU-SPEAKING SOCIETIES

I. A Mythology of the Body and Its Anomalies (Kongo)

The important Kongo language group, situated to the north and south of the mouth of the Zaire River, came into contact with the first Portuguese colonizers at the end of the fifteenth century. The traditional symbolism of water (the preeminent domain of spirits) explains at least partially the relative success of these Christian baptizers who had come from the ocean and were assimilated to distant albino ancestors. The first missionaries nevertheless did not succeed in extirpating the rites and beliefs that their Belgian successors, at the beginning of the twentieth century, would describe even as they fought them. A comparative examination of fragmentary historical sources reveals that the cradle of the old Kongo culture should be sought to the north of the river, in the Mayombe region. It was from there that the conquerors would depart, shortly before the arrival of the Portuguese, to found in Angola a kingdom whose capital (Mbanza Mbata) would soon be christened San Salvador. The ancestral religion more or less held its own against the assaults of a vindictive Christianity which fought tooth and nail against revolutionary prophets in the twentieth century much as it had in the eighteenth. To the life imprisonment of Simon Kimbangu, who died in 1951 in a colonial jail for founding a black messianic church, we may compare the assassination in 1709 of a twenty-two-year-old black woman named Dona Beatrice, who died at the stake for preaching the restoration of the Kongo kingdom while attacking the European Church.

The mythology of this matrilineal society includes a mass of popular accounts that comment on the disappearance of an original humanity, who, although physically imperfect (half-men having only one arm, one leg, and one eye), were endowed with superior magical powers. These people, the Nzondo, plunged into the Congo (or Zaire) River, while from the shore sprang up the verdant ficus, the foundation tree of Kongo villages. A comparison of texts and an examination of rites leads to the conclusion that the Kongo drew a connection between the mythic Nzondo and dwarfs or others with congenital disabilities, who are exceptionally numerous in the region. Could these be a perpetuation of the memory of the pygmies (who have disappeared today)? In any case, the Nzondo are derived from mythic thought and not from

history, since they have a knowledge of metallurgy that could not be attributed to hunters and gatherers.

At Mayombe a complementary mythic cycle explains the appearance of the new humanity by a twin birth. Here we discover an African version of Orpheus's descent into hell. The hero Kivanga belongs to the world of primordial sacred monsters, but in this case through an excess rather than a lack of limbs: he has twenty-four fingers and a huge head. Abandoned by his divine parents, he goes to the netherworld to bring back his twin sister, who had been given in marriage to a cannibalistic Nzondo. He enters into this dangerous subterranean and frozen universe with eight companions who never stop singing. At the end of this somewhat shamanistic voyage, Kivanga enters the village of the Nzondo, whom he puts to sleep. Luckier than Orpheus, he flies off with his sister; the Nzondo pursue them in vain with their javelin thrusts. The hero founds with his sister the first entirely human village.

A pair of primordial twins, first separated and then reunited, are thus at the origin of matrilineal Kongo society. Before leaving the netherworld, Kivanga carries off all of the human masks that the Nzondo had borrowed from the master of the earth, Mbenza, in order to trick men. From this time on, the separation between these dangerous incomplete beings and modern mankind is definitive. But mysterious spirits curled up under pebbles, the *nkita*, continue at Mayombe to attack the integrity of the human body: they render men blind in one eye or paralyze their limbs, and their aggression necessitates the intervention of a priest of Mbenza. The water spirits (*simbi*), on the other hand, protect man from every sort of physical deformity.

There are many variations of myths about the origin of the human body. What is interesting about the Kivanga variant is that it has a cosmogonic dimension. It may be read as the transformation of a solar myth preserved in the Manyanga tradition. A sheet of water (Kalunga) separates the earth from the netherworld. When the sun sinks into the ocean in the west, it crosses this sheet to illuminate the netherworld (Mpemba), which is the world of the dead and a replica of the world above. The water that separates these two symmetrical worlds is qualified as a "door" or a "wall of the changing of the body." But when Kivanga ventures into the subterranean world, he finds himself before a closed door which he forces open with his magic. Besides this, the "wall of the changing of the body" clearly evokes that intermediate place where Mbenza keeps the faces of complete humans. Two Mayombe traditions clearly articulate this cosmogony in folktales about the first incomplete human race. According to the first tale, dwarfs stand at each end of the world, close to the iron pillars that hold up the sky. The second puts these creatures in the malevolent moon, which is associated with sorcery: like the Nzondo in the myth of Kivanga, they pursue the sun with their javelin thrusts. The story of Kivanga is thus also the account of the daily victory of the sun over the moon; the world without fire, where the hero searches for his sister, is the world of the cold night. Midnight corresponds to midday in the Manyanga cosmology, as west corresponds to east; and the initiatory sign of the cross, which is found in diverse rites, symbolizes this spatiotemporal schema. The intermediate water that the sun and the deceased sink into is the source of life. White clay, extracted from the bottoms of rivers, is used in the fabrication of numerous Kongo magic objects.

The figure of Mbenza, the master of the earth, merits further attention. In the ancient Yombe culture, the priest of Mbenza controlled the investiture of chiefs, who could not

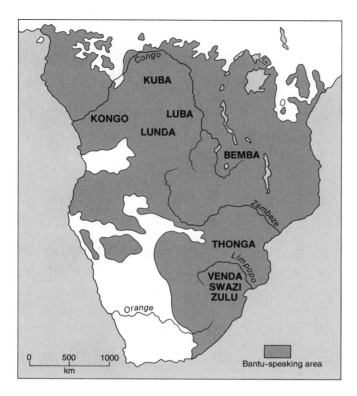

reign without the acceptance of the local genies. But the small political communities of Mayombe also worshiped a second chthonic deity, particularly associated with earthly waters, who was the serpent-rainbow Mbumba. The Yombe myth that recounts the quarrel between Mbumba and Pulu Bunzi, the master of tornadoes and floodwaters, also involves the alternation of seasons and the conflict between the sky (where lightning reigns) and the earth, the domain of Mbumba. Hero of the rain, Pulu Bunzi ends up playing the role of lightning: he decapitates the serpent-rainbow. According to a widespread belief in Central Africa, the serpent-rainbow keeps the rain from falling. Mbumba was once put at the center of an important group of rites. He presided over the great *nkhimba* initiation. This master of terrestrial waters, associated with sheatfish, thus regulates well-tempered fertility: while his rival Pulu Bunzi provokes twin births, Mbumba controls girls' puberty rites, as well as the sacred marriage that in former times insured the priests of the *lemba* cult a great and harmonious progeny. He is not unconnected with the original androgyne whose memory the esoteric Manyanga tradition has kept alive: the cutting of the body of Mahungu into two beings of different sexes was the origin of marriage. Then mankind, living together in one place, had its golden age, which brought an end to the tempestuous appearances of the genie Nzondo. This half-man had exceptional magical knowledge; he brought on the flood that was the origin of the Zaire River, into which he disappeared. Mankind came to know famine and was dispersed. In this tradition, the history of mankind is one of progressive degradation in which the invasion of an incomplete being with an excess of power inaugurates the present era with catastrophe.

The figure of Mbumba has ceased to dominate ritual life in recent Kongo culture, to the south of the river. But the Ntandu affirm that the rainbow contains the heaving mass of celestial waters (Mbu), the source of all animal life, which it pours into the ocean (Kalunga). Mbumba is also the generic name for the ensemble of magic talismans (*nkisi*), which still contain an element of aquatic origin.

At Mayombe, Mbenza and Mbumba are different chthonic powers, related to distinct cults. But there are structural articulations between the two. Dwarfs, who play an important ritual role in the religious *nkhimba* initiation (which is placed under the sign of Mbumba), are regarded as the owners of the sacred enclosure. And Mbenza oversees the dangerous chthonic *nkita* spirits who most notably give rise to paralysis in the limbs. Now, cripples are placed on the same plane as dwarfs in the *kimpasi* initiation, which is the equivalent of the *nkhimba* initiation to the south of the river (Ntandu). The function of this complex and little-known institution is to transform the initiates of both sexes (representing their lineages) into albino aquatic spirits. In the southern Kongo zone, these distant ancestors, who suffered a violent death, are called *nkita,* while dwarfs—like twins—belong to the other category of nature spirits, the indigenous *simbi.* The functions of the *simbi* and the *nkita* are subject to permutations in the Kongo universe, in the same way that the symbolic distribution of sacred monsters is subject to variations. But everywhere, dwarfs and deformed creatures are regarded as related, in one way or another, to the master of the earth. As an example of the coherence of the transformation system, the Ntandu attribute to the *simbi* the power of paralysis which the Yombe attribute to the *nkita,* while the Yombe assume that the *simbi* are horrified by all physical deformities. Through the mediation of *nkita* lineage cults (which involve spirit possession) the Ntandu regain contact with their historical ancestors, especially so that they will be warned of gynecological accidents; through the mediation of the *simbi,* who must not be disturbed, they maintain their ties with a more distant mythic past, with the ancient masters of the surface of the earth. Thus we understand how the *simbi,* represented by dwarfs, come to be associated with certain places, and the *nkita* with certain social groups, in this part of the Kongo world. There is another transformation among the Mbata and the Ndibu: these regard the aquatic *simbi* as the tragic ancestors of the beginning, of whom the *nkita* are emanations or messengers. The ficus, the sacred tree left behind by the first incomplete humanity in the old Yombe mythology, is for the Ndibu the witness to the dispersion of the clans and the place at which the *simbi* assemble to protect the village.

The ancient Kongo culture displays clear traces of a cosmogonic dualism that has been partially obscured today by the monotheism spread by the missionaries. The missionaries popularized the name of Nzambi, which had previously probably been only one of the terms applied to the transcendent power of the god of the sky and of the king. The Yombe always contrast a Nzambi of the Sky with a Nzambi of the Earth. The local spirits (*nkinda*), who are associated with political power, are no more than manifestations of this great chthonic power, which is represented as either Mbenza or Mbumba. But a third great figure appears in the north of the Kongo zone: Funza. Once regarded as the equal of the god of the sky, Funza now appears primarily as the creator of a counterorder: he is the source of all twisted forms of nature, which is why all abnormal births are attributed to him (including the birth of twins, who are the product of an excess of procreative power). But although Funza has the power to mutilate the embryo, he also collaborates with Mbumba in its development. Still further to the north, the Vili of Loango, along with certain Yombe groups, present

153

An initiation ceremony. The members of the *mungonge*, their bodies covered with kaolin and their leader wearing a headdress made of bamboo fibers, perform a kind of seated dance (not unlike certain Eastern performances) around the candidate. Tervuren. Musée royal de l'Afrique centrale. Photo A. Scohy.

The members of the *mungonge* crawl forward hidden from the initiation candidate: they are about to rise up, leaping and howling, thus putting the candidate to the first trial, the trial of fear. Tervuren, Musée royal de l'Afrique centrale. Photo A. Scohy.

A member of a *mungonge* photographed during an initiation trial. He appears to have an arrow driven through each of his cheeks. Each of these arrows divides into two parts; one part has a point which, after traveling through an opening previously made in the cheek, fits into a groove in the other half. Photo A. Scohy.

Funza, an aquatic and terrestrial power, as the wife of Mbumba. Even though the figure of Bunzi, master of rain and of the sky, has almost disappeared in this region as elsewhere, a certain number of elements suggest that he is directly associated with the sacred Loango royalty, just as Funza is associated with the complementary and antagonistic power of the indigenous clans.

II. The Luba-Lunda Region: A Royal Conquest of the Universe

Properly mythic utterances are as rare in Central Africa as in southern Africa. Bantu-speaking groups have, however, developed a cosmogonic viewpoint; but as it is dispersed through short folktales, or veiled behind rites that refer to it, it has rarely held the attention of researchers. The richest speculations are hidden away in a few great pseudohistorical texts whose explicit function is to account for the origin of the state among the Luba, Lunda, and Bemba. Such is at least the interpretation which we proposed in Le Roi ivre. Everywhere, sometimes under unexpected forms, the battle of the python-rainbow, the master of the dry season and the terrestrial waters, against the hero of lightning and rain, dominates the mythic stage upon which is played the advent of a dynasty that brings new cultural values. In the Luba scenario, the decapitation of a first rainbow king, Nkongolo, separates the sky from the earth and guarantees the rhythm of the seasons and fertility. This fundamental theme is associated, in numerous regions of Central Africa, with accounts which may be deciphered as so many African variants of the myth of the Tower of Babel: God brings about the separation of the sky and the earth by knocking down the enormous edifice that men had constructed to penetrate his secrets. Linguistic and cultural diversity as well as death result.

Without variants in its framework, the tale of the foundation of the state nevertheless undergoes numerous transformations from one kingdom to another. Nkongolo, the dangerous masculine rainbow of the Luba, elsewhere becomes a seductive feminine figure. In the Lunda tale, she is a sterile indigenous princess, Lueji; in the Bemba tale, a femme fatale. Here the fatal passion that Tshilimbulu arouses in a foreign prince, Tshitimukulu, who is assassinated by a jealous husband, is the direct cause of the establishment of the dry season; later the violent death of this tragic heroine in turn liberates the rainy season. The royal Bemba myth is a funerary hymn dedicated to the life of the cosmos. It is possible to show term-for-term correspondences between these transformations. As Nkongolo bears the name of the rainbow, the dysmenorrhea from which Lueji suffers is a sanguinary metaphor for this meteorological phenomenon. The corpse of Nkongolo, like that of Tshilimbulu, is mutilated and cut into two or more pieces, precisely to introduce a spatiotemporal discontinuity, the dialectic of the seasons. The desiccated skin of the Bemba heroine's stomach is the equivalent of the head of Nkongolo, buried in the dried earth of a termite mound; and his decapitated body, which is buried under a river, corresponds to the heroine's mortal remains, which are cut into pieces and thrown into an earthen water jar. This basic code undergoes an even greater transformation in southern Africa: in a Venda myth, the python is no longer associated with the rainbow and the dry season and sterility; while retaining his quality of master of terrestrial waters, he passes over to the side of the rains. The presence of the aquatic serpent among men connotes the wet season; his absence signifies drought. For the Venda the python is cold, while for the Luba he is burning hot. He smokes a pipe in the Venda myth; he abstains according to Luba beliefs. For the Zulu, the python is "the coldest animal in the world" but also the calmest and the most reflective; he is closely associated with the freshness of the rains which the lord of the sky dispenses when he is in a calm mood. By contrast, when he is angry, he heats up and the drought sets in. A rigorous acoustic ritual code corresponds to these transformations, since the Luba drive the python away by making a racket, while the Zulu pass silently before the animal, taking care not to disturb it. Kuba mythology holds other surprises. It is based entirely on an original excessive wetness which the benevolent sun brought to an end. Since that time, the dry season has been more highly valued than the rainy season.

This central cosmogonic theme must be completed by the representations of the world that are used in the many ritual practices that transform the status of human beings. Particularly rich is the coherent symbolism which, throughout the Lunda culture area, underlies the rituals that accompany the circumcision of the young men and their initiation into the *mungonge* ritual association. These set up a cosmogonic code which consists of a quest for sunlight (the source of life and abundance), which is placed under the sign of Venus.

The sun, moon, and Venus are eminently mobile signs in the symbolic sky of Bantu speakers. Luba beliefs place the moon, the masculine principle of fertility, under the same heading as the rain; the evening and morning stars are his wives. In the royal epic, the hunter Mbidi Kiluwe, master of the rain, is a lunar hero, while his hostile brother-in-law, Nkongolo, personifies both the rainbow and the sun. A short Luba account tells how the moon keeps the universe fresh and alive while the sun dries it up; the beginning of every lunar cycle is accompanied by intense ritual activity.

This system is reversed with the Lunda, although they share with the Luba the same concept of sacred royalty. Like his Luba homologue, the hero of the Lunda tale is a hunter who introduces fertility. But this time the founder of the new dynasty, Tshibinda Ilunga, is a solar hero, and the indigenous princess whom he marries (Lueji) is associated with the dry season, sterility, and the malevolent moon. The position of Venus is also modified. According to Lunda popular belief, in myths as well as rituals, Venus, the wife of the sun, takes over for her husband in the night sky. She is symbolized by the little black, white-bellied stork (*Sphenorhynchus abdimii*) who takes flight at dusk. She is also the torch, the promise of life, that an official who is mounted on stilts brandishes with arm extended just before dawn after the night of tests imposed upon the new initiates to the *mungonge* religious association among the Pende. The night before, "ancestors" brutally fall upon the bodies of the novices and hyena-men and beat them under the sign of the hostile moon. This initiatory ritual with a rare eloquence contrasts the sky and the earth, above and below, day and night, sun and moon, life and death, the abundance of food and alimentary deprivation or famine. After a symbolic death, the initiate is reborn as a solar creature, a being "with eyes of light," in contrast with the animals "with eyes of darkness" that the ancestors provide for their descendants at the time of the hunt. In the foundation myth of this institution among the Lunda proper, the little Venusian stork is also the mediator between the seasons: by flapping her wings in the company of another bird (Sirius?), she dries up a pond and introduces the female fishing season (the dry season). The solar hero of the royal tale inspires an abundance of game, and yet another hunter is regarded as the source of the

Kuba. Photo Luc de Heusch.

mungonge for the Pende: decked out in the feathers of the birds of death and darkness, he dances to combat a famine. On the dawn of the last day, the new members of this ritual association go on a ritual hen hunt, and this solar bird is consumed during a great final banquet. Venus and Sun, her husband, each mitigate a threat of death. And a female Venusian fire corresponds to a male solar fire in the Lunda rituals of circumcision.

On the sociological level, the tales of the foundation of the state also lend themselves to an overview of the two fundamental options in kinship systems (patrilineal and matrilineal), which are found side by side in Central Africa in the savanna that extends to the south of the great forest, a zone of vast and very ancient commercial exchanges. Cosmogonic codes and kinship codes correspond. It is not by chance that Kalala Ilunga, the Luba genie of lightning, is the maternal nephew of the rainbow Nkongolo, his rival, but is at the same time closely related to his father, the personification of the first beneficent rains. Here all relations that evoke the matrilineal configuration are given a negative value: not only does Kalala Ilunga decapitate his own uncle who had tried to catch him in a trap, but the uncle, in turn, does not hesitate to bury his own mother alive. On the other hand, the matrilineal Kuba mythologically interpret the patrilineal system as the original norm, which was abolished by an outraged primordial father. This pattern of themes is constant throughout Central Africa. At times there seems to be something like an echo of the myth invented by Freud in

Totem and Taboo. The myth captures the universe and dreams the society, in order better to justify that society's project. But the myth is the society's founding charter only at the price of a long dialectical detour which functionalist anthropology has too long neglected.

Nearly all of the societies discussed here developed strong political organizations in the savanna. The very diversified small communities that populate the equatorial forest of Zaire are also preoccupied—but apparently less often—with the symbolic structure of space. A primary horizontal opposition between the village and the forest, the place inhabited by animals and the dead in one case and nature spirits in the other, characterizes the cosmogony of the Komo and the Lele, two societies which are very distant from each other. The Lele entrust to a strange animal, the pangolin, a scaly anteater that has, like men, the property of being monoparous, the role of ritual mediator between the two domains. The Komo introduce a second vertical opposition between above and below. Most of these clans claim a celestial origin and are associated with the rain, the principle of fertility. Between the sky and the earth, the rainbow, the principle of desiccation identified with the dangerous horned viper, participates simultaneously in fire and water, that is, in the elements associated with the sun and the moon, respectively. An original anthropocosmogonic combination takes form in this way: all healing entails the symbolic passage from the lunar white to the solar red; in the same way, at the moment of conception, the woman passes from the influence of the moon into that of the sun, the source of life. The priority of the sky over the earth cannot be discussed without invoking the initiatory language of the Pende, although this does involve a radical inversion of color symbolism. The solar red, the purifier, participates in the higher world for the Komo, and the lunar white connotes the impurity of the imperfect world below. By contrast, the origin myth of the *mungonge* states that red is the color of death for the Pende, and white the color of life. The reversal is rendered all the more curious by the fact that the Pende, like the Komo, associate the lunar principle with a state of deficiency—which is characteristic of the earthly condition—and the solar principle with the saving light located above.

III. Points of Reference in Southern Africa

The linguistic, cultural, and religious diversity of the Bantu speakers of southern Africa—in some places characterized by a pastoral economy (unknown to the Kongo, Luba, Kuba, and Lunda agriculturalists)—is at least as great as it is in Central Africa. Within the very homogeneous group of the Nguni people, the differences between the symbolic thought of the Zulu and the Swazi are considerable. We shall examine under the heading of sacred kingship the deep influence of Swazi cosmogony in the great national ritual of the *incwala*. While for the Swazi it is a solar king and a lunar queen mother who rule together over the heavenly waters, among the Lovedu it is a masculinized queen who holds the secrets of rain medicine.

Two myths are widespread in southern Africa: that of the emergence of men from a reed or a reed swamp, and that of the origin of death. In the Thonga version, the original lord of the swamp sends a chameleon to bring the message of immortality to men. But the animal is delayed in his journey and the demiurge changes his mind in the meantime: he sends a great lizard who announces to men that they are condemned to rot in the earth. The Zulu version specifies that the chameleon while on his way climbed into a tree to enjoy the sun and fell asleep. Many rituals are founded on a pattern of heat: the excited state that is associated with fire and drought is contrasted with the calm and beneficent freshness of water. We have just mentioned Zulu beliefs about the python. By carefully analyzing the very rich descriptive materials of Junod, we find that the Thonga rites of passage implicitly develop an anthropocosmogony based on a kind of thermodynamics. As a combination of masculine water and feminine fire, and as the result of a successful intrauterine cooking, the development of the embryo is also the product of a moderated union of the sky and the earth. Pregnancy is conceived as a concentration of menstrual blood, which is burning and dangerous, in the womb: a symbolic association is established under the sign of dreadful fire between childbirth, infancy, and disease, which is itself the product of overheating. It is for this reason that the first rites of social integration set in motion a cooling-down procedure, and are placed under the sign of the refreshing moon. Three months after birth, the male infant is thrown in the direction of the moon and then placed on a pile of ashes before his father is permitted to take him in his arms. The action of the feminine moon is associated with growth in the social universe of the father, as the action of the masculine sun was associated with the natural development of the embryo in the womb of the mother. Every twin birth imperils both the sociological equilibrium and the alternation of the

seasons, since it results from a tempestuous displacement of the pregnant woman toward the sky. Albinos represent the other pole of the alternative: these monstrous creatures were burned by lightning in the womb of their mother.

But this thermodynamic equilibrium is reversed at the time of the collective rites of circumcision that mark the accession of young men to sexuality, which is regarded as a release of heat. The rites symbolize a solar quest. They begin, significantly, at the coldest time of the year, just before dawn, with the rising of the morning star. Each morning and each evening of their long initiation retreat, which is obligatory and involves numerous deprivations, the young men cautiously approach a ritual fire that burns in the enclosure, from which they are kept away in the night. This "fire of the elephant" has a symbolic connection with menstrual blood and the sexuality that is temporarily prohibited. The end of the ordeal is marked by the symbolic union of the earth and the sun that illuminates the encampment at the dawn of the last day. The novices then run toward the water, the source of life. They reappear in the village dancing the dance of the chameleon; thus they definitively separate themselves from their mothers and are thrown simultaneously into life and death.

L. de H./d.w.

Stool with a kneeling female caryatid. Berlin, Museum für Völkerkunde. Museum photo.

BIBLIOGRAPHY

1. General Studies

V. GÖRÖG, "Pour une méthode d'analyse de la littérature orale africaine: Introduction à une bibliographie analytique sélective," *Cahiers d'études africaines*, 30, 8, 2 (1968): 310–17; "Bibliographie analytique sélective sur la littérature orale de l'Afrique noire," Ibid., 21, 8, 3 (1968): 453–501; 36, 9, 4 (1969): 641–66; 40, 10, 4 (1969): 583–631. L. DE HEUSCH, *Le roi ivre ou l'Origine de l'État*, Mythes et rites bantous 1 (Paris 1972). A. WERNER, *Myths and Legends of the Bantu* (London 1933; 2d ed., 1968).

2. Kongo and Loango

K. M. BUAKASA TULU, *L'impensé du discours, Kindoki et nkisi en pays kongo du Zaïre* (Kinshasa and Brussels 1973). A. DOUTRELOUX, *L'ombre des fétiches, société et culture yombe* (Paris and Louvain 1967). A. FU-KIAU, *Le Mukongo et le monde qui l'entourait, cosmogonie kôngo* (Kinshasa 1969). F. HAGENBUCHER-SACRIPANTI, *Les fondements spirituels du pouvoir au royaume de Loango* (Paris 1973). LAMAN, *The Kongo*, 4 vols. (Stockholm 1953–68). W. G. L. RANDLES, *L'Ancien Royaume du Congo des origines à la fin du XIXᵉ siècle* (Paris and The Hague 1968). M. SINDA, *Le Messianisme congolais et ses incidences politiques*, introduction by R. Bastide (Paris 1972). J. VAN WING, *Études Bakongo, 2: Religion et magie* (Brussels 1938).

3. Other Societies of Central Africa

M.-L. BASTIN, *Art décoratif tshokwe* (Lisbon 1961). H. BAUMANN, *Lunda, bei Bauern und Jägern in Inner-Angola* (Berlin 1935). T. O. BEIDELMAN, "Right and Left among the Kaguru: A Note on Symbolic Classification," *Africa* 31 (1961): 250–57; *The Kaguru, a Matrilineal People of East Africa* (New York 1971). W. F. P. BURTON, *Luba Religion and Magic in Custom and Belief* (Tervuren 1961). M. DOUGLAS, *The Lele of the Kasai* (London, Ibadan, and Accra 1963); *Implicit Meaning: Essays in Anthropology* (London and Boston 1975). ED. LABRECQUE, "La Tribu des Babemba," 1: "Les origines," *Anthropos* 18, nos. 5–6: 633–48. W. DE MAHIEU, "Cosmologie et structuration de l'espace chez les Komo," *Africa* 45, nos. 2–3 (1975): 123–38 and 236–57. A. I. RICHARDS, *Chisungu: Girl's Initiation Ceremony among the Bemba of Northern Rhodesia* (London 1956). P. RIGBY, "Dual Classification among the Gogo of Central Tanzania," *Africa* 36 (1966): 1–17. L. DE SOUSBERGHE, *Les danses rituelles mungonge et kela des Ba-Pende (Congo belge)* (Brussels 1956). TH. THEEUWS, *De Luba mens* (Tervuren 1962); "Textes luba," *Bulletin du CEPSI* 27 (1954): 1–153. V. W. TURNER, *The Forest of Symbols: Aspects of Ndembu Ritual* (Ithaca, NY, 1967); *Lunda Rites and Ceremonies*, Occasional Papers, 10 (Livingstone 1953). J. VANSINA, "Initiation Rituals of the Bushong," *Africa* 25, no. 2: 138–53; "Les croyances religieuses des Kuba," *Zaïre* 10, no. 9: 899–926; *Le Royaume kuba* (Tervuren 1964); *Introduction à l'ethnographie du Congo* (Brussels 1966).

4. Southern Africa

H. CALLAWAY, *The Religious System of the Amazulu* (London 1870). A.-I. BERLUND, *Zulu Thought-Patterns and Symbolism* (London 1975). W. D. HAMMON-TOOKE, ed., *The Bantu-speaking Peoples of Southern Africa* (London and Boston 1974). H. A. JUNOD, *Mœurs et coutumes des Bantous: La vie d'une tribu sud-africaine*, 2 vols. (Paris 1936). E. J. and J. D. KRIGE, *The Realm of a Rain-Queen* (London, New York, and Toronto 1943). H. KUPER, *An African Aristocracy: Rank among the Swazi* (London, New York, and Toronto 1947). H. A. STAYT, *The Bavenda* (London 1931).

Note: The notation of Bantu terms has been simplified intentionally to facilitate reading; it does not indicate tones.

TWINS IN BANTU-SPEAKING SOCIETIES

Symbolic thought among the Kongo people is marked by a singular attention to sacred monsters: dwarfs, albinos, and twins all take part, according to the different modalities of one region or another, in the world of aquatic spirits. If we take into account the ancient mythological substratum, it appears that dwarfs (and cripples) are reminders of the first incomplete humanity, the Nzondos, while albinos are associated with the distant ancestors of the clan. In the ritual formulas of the Mbata and Ntandu, dwarfs and albinos, vigorously distinguished from one another, are compared to the two banks of the river. The Yombe myth of Kivanga clearly explains the position of the first twins: they are the mediators between the Nzondos and humanity as it exists today. Other stories expand upon this: the passage from one historic age to another takes place because of an excess of fertility after a period of want. Throughout the Kongo area the birth of twins is greeted with joy, but not without reservations. The Yombe attribute twin births to the genie of tornadoes, Pulu Bunzi. Among the Mbata, there is no connection between twins and rain, but the first twins establish a kind of mediation between the water at the bottom of deep ravines, the domain of the thunder, and the rivers, the realm of the ancestors: as aquatic spirits, they can emerge from either location, but in the first case they are more irascible. In any case, one must carefully avoid angering them. The Ntandu associate albinos with the first clan ancestors, the *nkita*, and dwarfs, who have a right to the title of chief, with the nature spirits, the *simbi*; twins themselves come from this second category, since on the day of their birth it is forbidden to draw water or collect firewood for fear of meeting aquatic or land *simbi*. The great *kimpasi* religious initiation gathers dwarfs and twins around a priestess who is certified as the mother of albinos: she must also be as hideous as possible and have given birth to only one stillborn child. The candidates, made up with rouge, are associated with albino ancestors to whom the initiating mother is supposed to have given birth. Symbolically the mother of albinos here serves a mediating function between the dwarfs (considered sterile) and the twins, products of a too-generous nature.

Twins in Central Africa are often marked by this excess. But the ambivalence of their status is generally more evident than among the Kongo tribes. In Loango twin births are attributed to the great female genie Funza, as are congenital deformations and gynecological accidents, for Funza is held responsible for all the twisted forms of creation. Ritual chants accuse a father of twins of having too great a harvest and thus of being at the source of the disorder; the disorder nonetheless is a sign of the economic prosperity of the clan. The Lele affirm that twin births put the village in danger. However, the parents of twins are called upon to become diviners: they are special mediators between the village and the forest, between men and animals, for animals live in close proximity with the spirits of nature who are responsible for fertility and the success of the hunt. Here too, twins are considered sacred monsters.

The "ritual of affliction" which the Ndembu require of mothers of twins is like the inverse of the ritual that mothers who miscarry must undergo. The second "remedies a deficiency," while the first corrects "another type of excess" (Turner). This ambivalent attitude becomes downright aversion among the Luba of Shaba (different in this from the Luba of the Kasai, where the father of twins is heeded as a chief). Twins are called "children of unhappiness"; they are associated with the moon, a powerful reservoir of fertility. The father must pay a fine and submit to obscene insults. The myth of origin among Luba royalty also takes a position against twin births: they stem, as does incest, from an earlier and less refined cultural order. The celestial hero Mbidi Kiluwe brought the principle of moderate fertility to the Luba. On earth, he entered into two hyperexogamic marriages: the first wife gave him a single son, Kalala Ilunga, the second, twins of different sexes. But the founder of the new dynasty was Kalala. Kisula, a stupid giant with his twin sister, Shimbi, at his side, was Kalala's rival. They met in single combat to fight for possession of the sacred kingdom. Kisula was on the verge of winning when Shimbi, who secretly loved Kalala, cried out and threw herself on her twin brother, forcing him to let his adversary go. Taking advantage of this diversion, Kalala had no trouble killing his opponent. This epilogue to a complex myth marked the end of the primordial era, the end of the insipid reign of twins devoted to incest.

In southern Africa, the devaluing of twins is clearer yet. The Thonga judge that the mother of twins is even more impure than a widow. In the past, one of the children was put to death, as among the Zulu, the Tswana, and the Kalanga. The Thonga interpreted twin births, a threat of drought, as the product of a dangerous and burning union between sky and earth: the mother is believed to have put the sky on the earth, or to have ascended into the sky during her pregnancy. This state is generally conceived of as a delicate operation of cooking, exposing the child to two opposite excesses: twins, "sons of the sky," have affinities with the heat of the sun, while albinos have been seared in their mother's womb by lightning. In times of great drought, the graves of twins are subjected to a special revitalizing treatment.

In the Bantu-speaking world, the human person generally has no reference to the ideal of twins. The mystery of twins is interpreted sometimes as a more or less monstrous projection of animal fertility into the human order, sometimes as a dangerous meeting of sky and earth, associated with an excess of rain (Yombe) or of drought (Thonga), except where it signifies the invasion of a counterorder (Loango). Some populations, however, see twins as the very incarnation of the spirits. Luba sacred kingship rejects this anomalous expression of the body, but the Swazi project the fantasies of royal incest onto it: the king and his mother, who rule together, inseparable and yet separated, are assimilated to twins.

L. de H./d.b.

BIBLIOGRAPHY

M. CARTRY, "Compte rendu des conférences," *Annuaire 1973–1974*, École pratique des hautes études, V[e] section, sciences religieuses, 82:17–38. M. DOUGLAS, *The Lele of the Kasai* (London, Ibadan, and Accra 1963). F. HAGENBUCHER-SACRIPANTI, *Les fondements spirituels du pouvoir au royaume de Loango* (Paris 1973). L. DE HEUSCH, "Le sorcier, le père Tempels et les jumeaux mal venus," in *La notion de personne en Afrique noire* (Paris 1973), 231–42. H. A. JUNOD, *Mœurs et coutumes des Bantous: La vie d'une tribu sud-africaine*, 2 vols. (Paris 1936). I. SCHAPERA, "Customs Relating to Twins in South Africa," *Journal of African Society* 26 (1927): 117–37. V. W. TURNER, *The Ritual Process: Structure and Anti-Structure* (London 1969).

SACRED KINGSHIP AMONG THE BANTU SPEAKERS OF ZAIRE AND SOUTHERN AFRICA

I. The King's Alliance with the Powers of the Sky and the Earth (Loango, Kongo)

A victorious splinter group of the Kongo people set up a sacred kingship in southern Zaire shortly before the arrival of the Portuguese. Their king, Nzinga Nkuwu, welcomed the Portugese enthusiastically, was baptized in 1491, and reigned thereafter as Jaõ I. The capital, Mbanza Mbata, became San Salvador. Later records, though incomplete, reveal that Catholic ceremony never completely broke through the skin of certain traditions that show uncanny affinities with those of the little kingdom of Loango to the north, which always remained pagan.

In Loango, the priest of the great celestial spirit Bunzi, the master of the rain and of farming, the Bunzi *nthomo*, directs the rites of enthronement and is thought to be permanently united with the sovereign through ceremonial exchanges that guarantee fertility. But the cult of the local spirits of the earth is entrusted to the matrilineal clan chiefs or to their representatives, who are chosen because of the peculiarity of their birth or because of a physical handicap. These "sacred monsters" are thought to be in direct contact with the great chthonic and aquatic deity, Funza, the wife of Mbumba, the rainbow python. The cosmogonic dualism described elsewhere is synchronized with the political order, and we can better understand the meanings of observations made in the seventeenth century: Dapper notes the presence of dwarfs around the sovereign, and Battell reports that albinos were presented at birth to the sovereign, who made them his official magicians. The king of Loango had to have a perfect physical constitution. The requirement that the sacred king

be physically intact (in contrast with the abnormalities of the priests of the earth, who are marked by a chthonic deity) occurs elsewhere in Africa.

The myth of origin of Loango kingship must be interpreted in this cosmogonic perspective. After a period of abuse, the first dynasty was overthrown. Consulted by the influential people, the priest of Bunzi decreed that the only way to resolve the crisis was to bring a particularly sacred creature to him. After considerable reflection, the clan chiefs decided to buy a Pygmy young woman from the back country. The priest of Bunzi deflowered her. She gave birth to a son and then to a daughter; they were the beginning of the new matrilineal dynastic lineage. The presence of dwarfs around the royal throne obviously preserves the memory of this remote hierogamy, which marks the agreement between the powers of the sky and the earth.

Let us now examine the traditions of the ancient kingdom of Kongo. Throughout its turbulent political history, the sovereign was always enthroned by a high dignitary, the Mani Vunda, who was the direct heir of the ancient priest of rain and agricultural fertility who exercised his ministry at Mbanza Mbata under the title of Mani Kabunga. This important person belonged to the clan of Nsaku Vunda, which claims to be descended from indigenous dwarf or Pygmy ancestors. The first ruler married one of his daughters.

All the elements of the Loango myth are found together in this historical account: the founding of a new dynasty is sealed by the magicoreligious alliance of the king and the daughter of the priest of the rain, whose distant ancestors are indigenous peoples of small size. For the Kongo associate dwarfs with the spirits of nature. A decisive union is asserted: in each province, the priests of the earth, the *kitomi*, had the mission of investing the functionaries designated by the king. The *kitomi* are evidently the counterparts of the *tshitomi*, the priests of the indigenous clans in Loango. The ancient Kongo kingship reproduces the symbolic pattern that is characteristic of sacral power in Loango: responsible for the enthronement, the Mani Vunda is the replica of the Bunzi priest of the god of the sky. The local priests of the earth ritually insult the envoys of the Kongo king during their investiture; in Loango, after a seven-year period of maturation, the sovereign must travel throughout the country in order to be accepted by the spirits of the earth, notably by playing the role of a sacred cripple.

But a second high dignitary, who belongs originally to the same indigenous Nsaku clan as the Mani Vunda, the "duke" of Mbata, also took part in the process of enthronement. He seems to have been connected with the ritual tools of the forge and the royal iron bracelet. As late as the beginning of the twentieth century, in the eastern Kongo districts that resulted from the disintegration of the central power, the blacksmith delivered new iron bracelets to the "crowned chief" after having him step up on the anvil stone. The chief-to-be had previously suffered a ritual death inside a hut whose entrance was extremely narrow, suggesting a uterus. Once inside he was identified with the spirits of the water by receiving a catfish in his mouth. After he was pulled out of this enclosed shelter by the smith, he was washed like a newborn child. South of the river, the sanctity of the power held by the indigenous Nsaku clan was probably based on the control of both rain and the forge, which explains why a blacksmith's emblem, evoking the hammer and anvil, was used for the capital of the kingdom.

The iron bracelet did not stop symbolizing the power of the chiefs of the Kongo clan after the collapse of the kingdom. But the Christian cross is the last avatar of the ancient sacred power of the kings of the Mbata nation. The elder of the district clan, whom we met in Mbanza Mbata in 1975, long after the sovereign power had been lost, held a brass crucifix that had once belonged to the "Kongo of the king"; whoever possesses this object has the power to perform the investiture of the elders of the other clans of the Mbata ethnic group in the shadow of a very ancient wooden cross on the top of a high plateau where a Portuguese cannon stands, the witness of tragic violence.

II. The Glamour of Hunting and War (Luba-Lunda)

Among both the Luba and the Lunda, a hunter who came from a distant country founded the sacred kingship. An analysis of the Luba epic shows that the wandering prince Mbidi Kiluwe, a celestial creature who brought fertility, was connected with the rain. This refined man made cautious contact with a violent and crude indigenous chief who was none other than the rainbow python Nkongolo. The two characters were to be contrasted at different levels. In every instance Nkongolo behaved too openly while the stranger's conduct was always controlled, notably his fastidious table manners. The stranger married his host's two sisters but soon left them to return to his native country, the mountains to the east. In his absence, one of the wives, Bulanda, brought a supernatural child into the world, Kalala Ilunga. This bouncing creature, a great warrior and clever gambler, provoked the jealousy of his mother's maternal uncle, who tried in vain to set a trap for him. Kalala Ilunga outsmarted him and fled to the east, where he joined his father. Nkongolo pursued him with his troops but failed to cross the Lomami River, which marked the boundary of his domain, i.e., the frontier between the sky and the earth. Kalala Ilunga soon returned with a powerful army and easily defeated his mother's brother: a great captain, he decapitated the rainbow, the master of the dry season.

As the founder of a new dynasty, Kalala Ilunga looked like the sole heir and master of the world. Like his successors (who eventually saw their empire collapse when the Belgians arrived at the end of the nineteenth century), he reaped complementary benefits from both a heavenly father, who taught him the culinary rites of sacred kingship (bulopwe), and a mother's brother, a rustic landowner who held the political power (bupfumu). The royal fire called for silence. He was the double mediator between the sky and the earth: he was introduced by the spirit of rain, and he was probably associated with Venus. Other aspects of cosmogony were projected into the great story of the founding of the state, the only mythical text of any importance that the Luba have preserved.

The royal epic of the Lunda, who founded an empire shortly after the Luba (perhaps in the early seventeenth century), is clearly derived from the preceding account. A wandering hunter, Tshibinda Ilunga, married a barren indigenous princess named Lueji. The dysmenorrhea with which she was afflicted was a symbolic transformation of the rainbow. Passionately in love with her husband, Lueji did not hesitate to give him a second wife who gave birth to the founder of the dynasty. This mythological charter probably legitimates, as in the case of the Luba, the seizure of power by a conquering group. The ritual of enthronement that is based on this charter depicts a solar king, the master of the thunderbolt. He penetrates the realm of the serpent (the primordial ancestor of Lueji) in the midst of the dry season, after lighting a ritual fire in the middle of the night. The

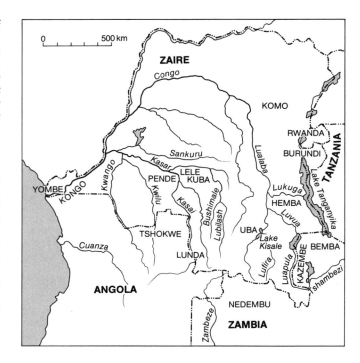

hyperexogamous union of Tshibinda and Lueji sets the pattern of hierogamy.

But from various perspectives, this marriage of the sky and the earth remained sterile: Lueji had no children, and the advent of the stranger, who received the royal bracelet, provoked the emigration of her brothers, who took a large number of people with them. Tshibinda was content to hunt: he considered himself essentially a provider of game. However, the symbolism of the hunt clearly reveals that this activity is a promise of fertility in the Lunda universe. Of particular interest is the nkula ritual practiced by the Ndembu to cure menstrual disorders, a ritual that was supposedly first used for Lueji. The patient, who is clothed in animal skins and equipped with a bow and arrows, identifies herself with the hunter. On this basis, Tshibinda Ilunga foretold future fertility. However, sacred kingship was not truly founded until the next generation, when the warrior son of the hunter took power. Naweji established the state on military values, and his successors were expected to inaugurate their reigns with new conquests. In Lunda symbolic thought, war and hunting are contrasted in more than one way. The royal myth complied with a code of blood that Victor Turner's wonderful analyses of the Ndembu make it possible to reconstitute.[1] Lueji's menstrual blood, the blood shed by Tshibinda in the hunt, and the blood of homicide assumed by Naweji are contrasted with one another through their specific symbolic properties. The three types of blood make up the framework of Lunda myth; they are evoked in Ndembu rituals by the color red. This color, however, is part of a wider symbolic system that is itself based on a threefold model: the "triangle" of colors also includes white (connoting purity, life, social harmony, etc.) and black (evoking contrasting values, notably witchcraft). It can be demonstrated that the red apex of this triangle connotes war as a positive value in the political ideology of the Lunda. In this semantic field, the blood that comes from hunting is situated precisely on the axis joining the red and the white, halfway between these two values, because blood in hunting (a promise of fertility, as seen above) is always ritually associated with white symbols. The same process leads the Ndembu to describe fertile sperm as whitened blood. On the other hand, menstrual blood ("blackened," impure) is situated on the axis joining the red and the black.

It should be noted that the symbolism of colors is far from stable among Bantu speakers. The Luba epic story pits Nkongolo the red against Kalala Ilunga the black. In southern Africa black is valued highly in the fertility rites of the Swazi kingship. The symbolic systems of the Komo and the Pende of Zaire reverse the properties of white and red.

III. Royal Incest

Nkongolo, the first chthonic ruler, was not aware of the great social law of matrimonial exchange. He had sexual relations with his two sisters before they were given in marriage to the foreign hero, Mbidi Kiluwe. This double hyperexogamous union abolished incest. But as successors to both Nkongolo and Mbidi, the Luba kings were expected to perform ritual incest with their mothers and sisters when they were enthroned, in a windowless and doorless hut known as the "house of ill fortune." In the eyes of the Luba, incestuous relationships are a source of calamity. Sacred kingship among the Luba thus integrates this accursed part of the power bequeathed by Nkongolo. Through this transgression, the sovereign is projected into a zone of absolute solitude, within and without the cultural order. He is outside the lineage, just as he is without a table companion (in his role as heir to Mbidi Kiluwe).

This theme is frequent in Africa, where it sometimes takes the form of total isolation. A chronicle from 1619 reveals that the Christian king of Kongo continued to have sexual relations with his older sister. Randles, who reports these facts, suggests not without reason that the labyrinthine form of the royal palace had the symbolic function of cutting off communications between the king and his people.

The symbolism of royal incest takes on a considerable breadth in Kuba mythology and rituals. Woot, a solar culture hero, had to leave his people after he slept with his sister Mweel, who in rituals is associated with the moon and the rainy season. The separation of the incestuous lovers is analogous to the separation of the sky and the earth: Woot's voluntary departure to the east, upriver, causes an eclipse. In sociological terms, the Kuba myth in a way asserts that a well-balanced matrilineal society implies the (chaste) social union of brother and sister. That is why, at the request of Mweel, Woot restores the solar light to his own people. The incestuous Woot never stopped being the ultimate source of all fertility. Unlike the Luba epic, which tells of the transition from a violent, drunk, and incestuous king to a moderate king, the bearer of a higher civilization, Kuba myths describe cultural history as a progressive degradation of primordial harmony and social unity. Drunkenness and incest are precisely the principal agents of this process. In an account that may be read as an African variant of the story of Noah, Woot creates the matrilineal system and the rites of initiation for young men in order to punish his sons who had mocked him as he was lying drunk and naked. He disinherited them in favor of his daughter, who modestly covered him up. Fleeing his own people, who miss him and set out to find him, Woot institutes linguistic diversity in order to place as many obstacles as possible between himself and his people.

He ends up by sinking into a lake (or by vanishing in a whirlwind) after he has also created geographical, zoological, and botanical diversity.

The quest for the vanished Woot is the symbolic framework for the initiation of young men. The initiation wall that separates their encampment from the village symbolizes the universe and refers back to the mythical story. The sacred king, the *nyim*, whose power is associated with the blacksmith's anvil, is the heir of the cursed and regretted culture hero, the source of all life. Shortly after his coronation, he must have sexual relations with one of his sisters; then he marries a grandniece, breaking all allegiance to his matrilineage. This transgression, which guarantees him additional power, also assimilates him to an evil sorcerer. Royal transcendence is expressed by the term *paam*, which connotes fire, the sun's rays, and the leopard's aggressiveness. At the ritual level, the sovereign governs the forces of the universe. He is comparable to the sun, and through the mediation of his sister (the replica of Mweel), he is connected with the moon. He has the power to bring rain. However, in political life he is only a special partner and could not reign without taking the advice of the counsels that represent the nation.

IV. The Annual Regeneration of Sacred Kingship (Swaziland)

Once a year, during a sumptuous national ritual, the representatives of all the Swazi clans gather around the ruler to regenerate the forces of sacred kingship at the winter solstice, which in southern Africa corresponds to the rainy season. This Frazerian theme, described by Hilda Kuper, has been the object of various interpretations. But neither the penetrating sociological commentary by Max Gluckman nor Beidelman's symbolic decipherment exhausts the complexity of a ritual that expresses the close correspondences between the sovereign, bound to his mother, and the universe. We offer here a new analysis in the light of our earlier research on the kingdoms of Central Africa.

The festival of water and vegetation, the *incwala*, also bears the strong imprint of the pastoral and military values characteristic of Swazi culture. A few days before the opening of the ceremonies, two separate processions led by national priests go to draw "the waters of the world" in the sea and the rivers, after sacrificing a black ox and using its skin to decorate two calabashes called "princesses." Each group carries one of them on a black shield.

The public ceremony begins with the new moon before the day when the sun of the southern winter solstice "rests in its house in the south." The priests of the water are welcomed in the capital by army veterans in military dress, who sing of their desire to follow into exile their ruler, who has become the object of popular hatred. Other regiments form a crescent moon in front of the queen mother, and princesses and common women are grouped around her. At the exact moment when the sun sets, the king goes inside the sacred hut while the warriors form a circle that suggests the full moon. The members of the royal clan, as well as the strangers, are suddenly chased away. Surrounded only by faithful subjects, the king then spits out the magic potions prepared by the priests of the water to strengthen the earth. A song of praise breaks out. That night the moon reappears. But the sun abandons the king, the lion; this is what the warriors shout to him when they awaken him shortly before dawn, while the moon still shines. The king goes inside the sacred hut for the second time at sunrise. He repeats the rite

performed the night before, spitting first toward the east and then toward the west, and the crowd shouts that he has "bitten for the year just past."

The second part of the ritual takes place two weeks later, on the eve of the full moon. Young men bring "pure and fresh" acacia branches into the capital, and the roof of the sacred hut is covered with them. The branches of another tree, robust and green, are used to rebuild the walls. The assembled regiments spread out again in the form of a crescent moon. A black ox is beaten to death by young men whose violent action is compared to that of the "waters of the world." The king helps them. The victim is finished off by the priests of the water who remove from its body various pieces that they later include in the royal magic potion. A second black ox is brought in. This one is not sacrificed as the first was but is identified with the regenerated king, who is stripped of all his clothing and seated on the animal, which is held on the ground. The king is then washed with holy water made foamy with particular plants: this strengthens the sexual prowess of the males of the herd and of the men. The king becomes the "bull of the nation."

The next day (the "great day") the king, wearing only a penile sheath made of ivory, walks through the crowd. The people chant songs of desertion; the women weep and wail. The king goes inside his hut, where he celebrates his first marriage with "the queen of the right hand," the first ritual wife. He spits out a magic concoction toward the east and the west to "awaken his people." Then he goes to the sacred enclosure, where he "bites" the firstfruits. The ceremony seems to be more in keeping with the general renewal of vegetation than with the labors of farming. The king spits out a mixture of green foods (which have been soaked in seawater) and ingredients from the sacrificed ox. In the afternoon he appears disguised as a spirit of vegetation, his body covered with foliage and his head completely wrapped in a cape of black feathers. He breaks into a crazed dance, resisting the calls of the princes who try to draw him away. The ritual war shields are brought before the regiments. The men in the front row hammer them with their fists while the singing evokes rolling thunder. The king approaches the warriors, holding a black stick in his right hand. They step back. The king moves back and forth in this way several times, from the sacred hut to the crowd. During his last approach, the king's right hand is empty. The princes and the foreigners are then asked to leave. Isolated from his lineage, facing alone the nation that he incarnates, the king, the spirit of vegetation, holds a gourd in his hand, still green although picked the year before. The shields are placed on the ground, and the king throws the gourd on one of them. The warriors salute the solemn act with a great uproar: they whistle and stamp their feet.

The king spends the rest of the "great day" in complete isolation, in "obscurity." Only the two ritual wives, the queen of the right hand and the queen of the left hand, may come near him. He must sleep with the first (or if not the first, with the second) that night, when sexual relations are forbidden for everyone. The image of the full moon is painted in black on his face. He is very closely associated with the distant queen mother, who is the object of a separate ritual treatment: a black ox is sacrificed for her, and its face is marked with the sign of the half-moon.

Statuette of hunter chief Tshibinda Ilunga (Angola). Berlin, Museum für Völkerkunde. Photo Hietzge-Salisch.

On the sixth and last day, a ritual of purification takes place. The king himself kindles the great pyre where the plant costume and ritual gourd that he handled are burned. The gourd is connected with the year gone by, and in the royal palace a fresh gourd is carefully preserved that will in turn be cast into the flames the following year. While he walks around the pyre in which his own "defilement" and that of his people are being consumed by the flames, the king washes his face. The drops that fall on the ground "activate" the celestial water. When the sun is at its zenith, the warriors and the women gather to dance and to intone the final chant of the *incwala*. They are sure that the rain will fall to put out the purifying fire. The queen mother and the king's wives offer the people a huge meal, and on the next day the warriors go to weed the main cornfield of the queen mother.

The symbolism enacted on the royal stage is extremely complex. We shall only point out its essential cosmogonic aspects, leaving aside the sociopolitical dialectic (the king is sometimes united with his clan, sometimes separated from it and closer to his people). Two major metaphorical configurations dominate the ritual. The king, the bull of the nation, the master of vegetation, is associated with the sun and the light of the full moon, while the queen mother is associated with the crescent moon. The king and the queen mother, assimilated to twins, reign together. But the contacts between them are reduced and ritually controlled. The queen mother has her own quarters in the royal enclosure; she can visit the king in the "white" part of the quarter reserved for her son, but she may not touch him. She is strictly forbidden to venture into the "black" part, where the young king receives his mistresses. Later, the king will normally live with his harem in a separate village, distinct from the capital. What is the meaning of the ritual union of the solar king and the lunar queen mother as instituted by the *incwala*? The first part of the ceremonial begins when the moon is "black." The moon is the wife of the sun and when the moon is absent, it means that her husband "covers" her. In effect, during that night the sun rests in her hut in the south. But at the winter solstice, the darkness of the sky also coincides with the threat of the disappearance of daylight (the sun abandoning the king). The sacrifice of the black ox is a symbolic execution of the solar king. The subsequent identification of the king with the "bull of the nation" is a resurrection. The double animal is associated with fire; it is forbidden to approach the sacred ox and all those who come in contact with it must wash after the rites. When it dies, its body is burned.

All of this suggests that kingship, in peril during the winter solstice, is regenerated by a double hierogamy that bears the marks of incest. During the little *incwala* the queen mother, the vanished moon, approaches a solar son from whom she is usually distant (as the day is distinct from the night). During the big *incwala*, the queen mother does not appear in public. While the full moon shines, the king regenerates nature in the hut where the first ritual spouse made him "come out of obscurity" on the day of his wedding. He is required to have relations with her on the next day. But the same "queen of the right hand" once solemnly mixed her blood with that of the king; "she is considered to be a part of him and he must treat her with the greatest respect" (Kuper); he addresses her by giving her the title of "mother." This substitute mother in fact represents the real mother, who in turn is symbolically considered to be her son's twin sister. The queen of the right hand is duplicated in the second ritual wife, the "queen of the left hand," who can substitute for the first.

What, then, do these two women stand for in the royal solar/lunar cosmogony? No explicit indication can be found in Hilda Kuper's description. But there is the striking fact that the ritual begins with the making of the two ritual calabashes referred to as princesses. They are ritually carried in procession, one toward the seawater, the other toward the rivers. These sacred objects are wrapped in leather straps made from the hide of the black ox first sacrificed. The clothing of the "princesses" is later burned in the final pyre, while the calabashes are carefully preserved until they spoil. All along their journey toward "the waters of the world" (which begins at sunset), the calabash princesses, each placed on a black shield, cannot touch the ground. All of this suggests that they are connected with a luminous celestial principle that triumphs over the dark of night (the moon is absent) and announces the return of the sun. The sun in turn completes its southward course and then rests in its house of the solstice. In the context of Bantu cosmogonic speculations as a whole, this could only refer to Venus, who doubles as an evening and morning star. The two calabashes are associated with light, for after the ritual they are placed in the white part of the royal palace, in a sacred storeroom situated behind the hut reserved for the two ritual queens. Across the way, in the other quarter, the ritual hut of the queen mother and her storeroom of accessories form a symmetrical group, south of the first quarter. This typography confirms the hypothesis that the solar king, at the southernmost point of his course, is supposed to realize during the little *incwala* an incestuous hierogamy with the lunar queen mother. The ritual hut, where the king then sleeps with the queen of the right hand, the substitute mother, during the big *incwala* opens onto the house of the queen mother. If we accept the notion that the two calabashes are only the plant symbols of the two ritual wives, it follows that the royal palace is a celestial space. Hilda Kuper connects the term for princesses (*incosatana*), which applies to such objects, with the name of an old celestial deity associated with both the rainbow and lightning. There are hints of this deity among the Zulu, where the name Incosazana designates the virgin daughter of the Lord of the Sky, the master of the rain (Berglund). It is more understandable that the two calabash princesses are directly associated with the quest for the "waters of the world" in the Swazi ritual. This also sheds light on the ritual role of the third ritual gourd, the one that the king throws on a shield while the crowd sings of thunder. The calabash princesses are associated with inland waters and the ocean, the third gourd with the celestial water that the *incwala* finally causes to fall, while the depleted forces of the past year are consumed on a solar pyre. The feminine principles of kingship are associated with water in all its forms and with the lights of the night sky (the moon, Venus). Since they are regenerated as the solar king is through the sacrifice of the black ox, the two calabash princesses, symbols of the queens of the right and left hand, correspond to the absent queen mother in the darkness of the new moon. They maintain the perpetuation of light, the source of life, until the full moon of the great *incwala*, which coincides with the season of heavy rains.[2]

The little *incwala* revives the vanished, "dead" moon through an initial hidden hierogamy that symbolically implies the incestuous union of the mother and the royal son; the great *incwala* regenerates the sun itself, in the brilliance of the full moon, through the avowed sexual relations of the king and the queen of the right hand, the substitute mother, in order to ensure the triumph of the rain through the mediation of the stars.

L. de H./g.h.

163

NOTES

1. We have freely reinterpreted here the facts furnished by this author.

2. Note, however, that Hilda Kuper explicitly rejects the idea that the two ritual marriages of the king might have an incestuous connotation. One might object that the king is also flanked by two masculine blood brothers (*tinsila*), who are charged with intercepting attacks of sorcery, and that these blood brothers are implicitly assimilated to the twins: indeed, just as one cannot lament the death of a twin brother, so there cannot be any manifestation of mourning for an *insula* who dies before the king.

BIBLIOGRAPHY

1. General Studies

L. DE HEUSCH, *Essais sur le symbolisme de l'inceste royal* (Brussels 1958); *Le roi ou l'origine de l'État: Mythes et rites bantous I* (Paris 1972). T. IRSTAM, *The King of Ganda: Studies in the Institution of Sacral Kingship in Africa* (Stockholm 1944). J. VANSINA, *Les Anciens Royaumes de la savane* (Kinshasa 1965).

2. Regional Monographs

T. O. BEIDELMAN, "Swazi Royal Ritual," *Africa* 36 (1966): 373–405. M. GLUCKMAN, *Rituals of Rebellion in South-East Africa* (Manchester 1954); *Order and Rebellion in Tribal Africa* (London and Glencoe, IL, 1963). F. HAGENBUCHER-SACRIPANTI, *Les fondements spirituels du pouvoir au royaume de Loango*, ORSTOM (Paris 1973). 1. DE HEUSCH, "Le roi., le forgeron et les premiers hommes dans l'ancienne société kongo," *Systèmes de pensée en Afrique noire*, École pratique des hautes études, Laboratoire associé no. 221 (Paris 1975), 165–79. H. KUPER, "A Ritual of Kingship among the Swazi," *Africa* 14 (1944): 230–56. W. G. L. RANDLES, *L'Ancien Royaume du Congo des origines à la fin du XIXᵉ siècle* (Paris and The Hague 1968). J. VANSINA, *Le Royaume kuba* (Tervuren 1964).

SACRED KINGSHIP AMONG THE BANTU SPEAKERS OF THE GREAT LAKES REGION

The sacred, or divine, king is not merely a strictly mythological figure installed at the top of a political hierarchy; he is also a pivot around which other essential mythical and religious representations are organized. Throughout the cultural area with which we are concerned here, the figure of the sacred king is additionally and characteristically marked by a historical consciousness that is, by contrast, lacking in several societies (like the Bakiga of southwest Uganda) that are wedged between kingdoms and that have resisted this model in order to maintain a political organization based on lineages alone, with the absence of centralization. This historical awareness cannot be reduced to the mere memory of certain important events, wars, or migrations; it implies a veritable philosophy of history conceived as the deployment and the embodiment of the links between the sky and the earth, nature and culture, the living and the dead.

In the region overall, the universal theater is conceived as a three-tiered structure. At the center is the earth, a large horizontal and circular platform that ends "where things stop," "where things fall off," with a hedge of plants and pillars on which the mineral dome of heaven rests. Above this stone dome and below the crust of the earth are two inhabited worlds similar to our own in many ways but not in all. The upper world knows nothing of death, nor of the difference between nature and culture. From it the earth

draws life and all that is needed to sustain it and make it flourish, especially rain and fertility. The Thunderbolt, or Thunderbolts, and the other celestial phenomena are great persons up above. To the Rwanda, for example, the Thunderbolt is "the king above," who holds the rain and thus also exercises his rule over the wild zones and wild animals of the earth, just as the earthly king rules over humans, domestic animals, and tilled lands. This heavenly king is conceived of as an animal, a ram or a gigantic rooster. The men who live in the country of the sky are depicted in different ways that distinguish them from the earthly condition. They are dazzlingly bright and shining (Bunyoro), like the celestial light. They have tails (Rwanda), for up above, nature and culture are not distinguished; and if they visit earth, one only has to cut off their tails to prevent them from returning and to turn them into terrestrial men no different from others. They have only one side, one eye, one arm, one leg, etc. (Nyamwezi), that is, they are exempt from the ambivalence that marks the earthly condition where the right is favorable and evokes all that promotes life, while the left is unfavorable and marks the pull of death. The lower world is the home of the dead and the shadow; the Bunyoro see it as a sun-scorched world: "The soil is strewn with burned grass and charcoal on which black skins are stretched out; everything from beds to kitchen utensils is covered with soot. The food is smoked." The king of this place is called Nyamiyonga, i.e., "Flakes-of-soot." In Rwanda, he is called Nyamuzinda, or "Lord-of-oblivion."

The earthly world is therefore an intermediate and ambiguous world, marked both by the forces of life that it takes from above and by the pull of death that consumes beings and sinks them into the underground shadow and oblivion. This situation intermediate in space is also intermediate in time, where human life, which is already marked by the important alternation of day and night, of waking and sleeping, and of the phases of the moon, goes from birth, which is a gift from the brilliant sky, to death, which "hides" beings forever.

On this stage where the lives of men take place, all is marked in one way or another by the relations maintained with the other two worlds. All accounts, mythical and historical alike, say so, and the rites underscore it. The mythical accounts are divided into two distinctly different genres: first, fables or allegorical narratives about the logical or symbolic origins of what is permanent in the human condition, and second, historical legends about kings and their entourage or their equivalents, from the time of the origins of the dynasties (which are confused with the origins of time), right up to the recént past, the strictly mythological character of these narratives decreasing as time goes by. However, since these narratives generally focus on creatures that are simultaneously human and divine, real and surreal, that is, the kings, history is never totally absent from the most distant end of that spectrum, any more than myth is absent from its nearest end.

The exercise of sacred kingship is inscribed within a context of rites, symbols, and extremely complex prescriptions by which the royal person is identified with the nation as a whole and plays on its behalf the role of a catalyst of natural and supernatural forces that are generally intermingled in the Bantu conception. If he is wounded or weakened, the entire country is afflicted. If he turns over in his sleep, the entire country becomes upside down. If he bends his knees, the whole country contracts. If he dies, all vital activities, agriculture, procreation, bodily care, stop. He is the active representative of the supreme God, remote and hidden, whose influence mankind recognizes in the manifestations of life, but who remains inaccessible and has no cult. This conception is clearly expressed in a famous Rwanda poem of the late eighteenth century, preserved by oral tradition. Some excerpts follow:

> The king cannot have any rival. He is unique! He therefore never establishes two hearths; he builds one and only one. Yet this hearth covers the whole country and anticipates the needs of generations to come. He who becomes king ceases to be a man! The king is the god, and he rules over humans! . . . I behold the god in the present house. I find in him the god accessible to our supplications. The other god, he knows him. We for our part can only see this defender! . . . The sovereign king present here drinks the milk drawn by the god, and we drink the milk that he draws in turn for us. The king is the only one truly in charge; he takes responsibility for the whole country and he manages, as only he can, to satisfy it!

Added to these mystical relationships between the king and his people, on the one hand, and the king and the natural and supernatural forces, on the other hand, are those that tie him to his predecessors, of whom we still have not only the regalia but also, in some cases, mummies, lower jaws, or as in Buganda, the umbilical cord conceived as the twin brother of the departed king. The rites of sacred kingship, by which the king honors the spirits of his predecessors, brings rain and fertility to the country, prepares or legitimizes conquests, etc., nevertheless remain his own concern and that of the various ritualists and functionaries who surround him. The people take part only occasionally, and most of the rituals are even deliberately kept secret and hidden, as in Rwanda.

The rites practiced by ordinary men are for the most part occasional rites that do not go beyond the context of lineage and neighborhood and that aim above all to assure the individual of his physical, mental, material, and social well-being, or to restore it to him. The blessing of fertility is the theme most emphasized. The starting point is generally a problem experienced or feared, and the diviner is often the first to be consulted to determine the identity of the agents who have malevolently caused it or who might give protection. The problem may be attributed to the purely human sphere: natural illnesses, evil spells cast by magicians, real or imagined poisoning due to witchcraft, etc.; people can therefore resort to various specialists to protect themselves. The problem may also stem from the realm of spirits who require people to resort to rituals. The first category of spirits, first in the sense that it is certainly the oldest in these cultures and also the closest to the individuals concerned, is the category of the spirits of ancestors, lineal and collateral, recently dead. Some of these spirits, instead of being permanently engulfed in the lower world of shadow and oblivion, can continue to roam for some time around the sites where they lived and around their relatives and to affect the lives of their relatives out of bitterness at not being alive anymore or because they hold a grudge for not having had a satisfying life, for example, if they died childless or violently or prematurely. They must then be remembered and offered whatever they want, cattle or spouses (whom people marry in their names or dedicate to them), all this to ensure their good will.

This cult is perfectly adapted to societies in which the ties of kinship and lineage constitute the ins and outs of social life. But just as the sacred king and his representatives came to transcend the lineage organization, and even to reduce or destroy it, depending on the case, in order to set up new and

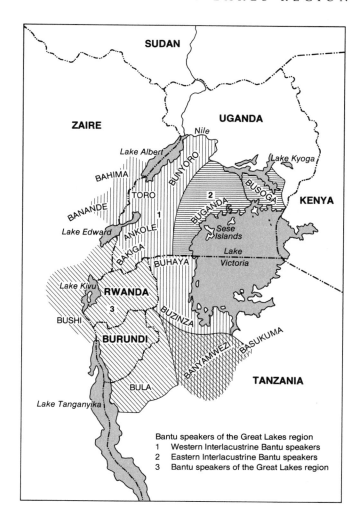

Bantu speakers of the Great Lakes region
1 Western Interlacustrine Bantu speakers
2 Eastern Interlacustrine Bantu speakers
3 Bantu speakers of the Great Lakes region

Bantu speakers of the Great Lakes region

more open relationships and new constraints tied to the existence of a national life, so too, new spirits, conceived as more powerful in their positive as well as their negative aspects, came to supplant the older ones. They ruled over the spirits of the dead just as the sacred king ruled over the bodies of the living. These spirits belong to uncommon historical persons, almost deified heroes, who are believed to have participated in some way in the actual sacred kingship, though always with some time lags. Like the king himself, such spirits are seen as both historical characters and representatives of natural forces. Their cult requires not only offerings and attention but membership by initiation and complex rites within the framework of sects. In place of the missing bond of kinship that still implies a certain distance, there is an even closer relationship, possession or its semblance. While the spirits of ancestors are usually simply consoled for their irreversible state by the attention given them by the living relatives, the spirits of deified heroes are reincarnated in rites in the persons of their adepts, who identify themselves with them and through whom they speak and act.

Such spirits, who make up veritable pantheons, tend to multiply, and in the various societies of the region many of them are honored in cults, although no stories are told about them. The principal ones among them, however, are always historically situated, and their legends can be regarded as mythological corpora. This cultural area may be divided into three subsets (see map). In the center, from northwest to southeast, are the people conventionally called the Western Interlacustrine Bantu speakers (Bunyoro, Toro, Ankole, Buhaya, etc.); in the northeast are the Eastern Interlacustrine Bantu speakers (Buganda, Busoga); in the southwest are the Southern Interlacustrine Bantu speakers (Rwanda, Burundi, Bushi, Buha, etc.); the cultural area of the Interlacustrine Bantu speakers is clearly defined by linguistic, political, and other criteria on all sides except in the regions located south of Lake Victoria, where influences from the first and third subset intermingle and then vanish. Subsets one and three are distinguished by the presence of a minority that is politically dominant, traditionally cattle breeders: the Bahima (Hima, Hema, Huma) in the west, and the Batutsi (Tutsi, Watutsi, Tusi) in the south. Of a racial origin that is clearly different from that of the peasant majority, they have tended to preserve their identity by means of an ideology of hierarchically organized castes. Finally, in the southern zone there is also a pariah cast, a small minority, of Batwa Pygmies who specialize in hunting, pottery making, and certain services to the court. The different groups share the same language and culture within each kingdom but with typically different attitudes. Each of them has contributed to the elaboration of cultural configurations peculiar to the region, which encompasses even more diversity than we can suggest in this study. We shall now focus our attention briefly and successively on the most characteristic mythical representations of the three kingdoms that, in each subset, have the richest and best-known oral traditions. What is said about each, especially about their mythical figures, is largely applicable to the other societies of the subset. In each case we shall situate the emergence of the deified heroes first in connection with pure mythology and second within the context of the national histories.

Bunyoro

Bunyoro traditions distinguish three dynasties. The source of the first, very obscure, dynasty is the supreme god called Ruhanga ("the One who creates, fashions, establishes"). The stories about him are allegorical. They tell how Ruhanga comes to separate the sky and the earth, retires forever into the sky, creates the conditions of life on earth, but fails to prevent the advent of evil and death, and finally establishes the unequal roles of the three social components: the king and his clan, the herdsmen, and the farmers. The instigating agent, unaccounted for in this distribution of roles, is called Kantu ("Little Thing"), and he is responsible for introducing evil and death into life on earth. The last king of this mythical dynasty, Isaza, is approached by the king of the netherworld, "Flakes-of-soot," who proposes a blood pact and seeks to take over entirely the earthly world that is held in equilibrium by the other two. A shrewd little servant maid who solves the puzzles that are proposed invites Isaza to thwart the plan by sending not his own blood but that of his servant, Moon. But "Flakes-of-soot," informed about this trick, decides to lure Isaza into the netherworld against his better judgment by first sending him his daughter Nyamata ("Milky"). This trick fails. He then sends him two beautiful cows who make him fall into the fatal abyss and finally make him a captive of the netherworld. But Nyamata bears him a son, Isimbwa, who later goes hunting on earth with his own son, Kyomya. On earth a usurper reigns, Bukuku, Isaza's

former porter, and the diviners foretell that the son who will be born of his daughter will kill him and succeed him. (We should note that throughout the region the intervention of the diviner usually marks the passage from allegorical myth to historical myth; oracles, omens, curses, and the other signs that predict the future intervene throughout the historical legends, a genre less preoccupied with exposing the broad permanent outlines of life on earth than with recounting the strategies devised to maintain and develop that life, a genre that therefore claims to reveal a meaning in history.)

In order to forestall his daughter's seduction, Bukuku shuts her up in an enclosure without doors and leaves her only one eye and one ear. The wandering Isimbwa finds her nevertheless and gives her a son, Ndahura, who is taken in by a potter; later he kills Bukuku and after a few more adventures becomes the first king of the supernatural dynasty of the Bacwezi, who originally came from the sky and from Ruhinda, but reemerged from the netherworld to reign on earth for the great happiness of mankind. Ndahura expands his dominion over a vast empire, the Kitara, which encompasses the whole western zone and beyond. He does not die but disappears and leaves his succession to his son Wamara, who brings the dynasty to a close. Wamara's brothers, uncles, and cousins rule with him over the different regions of the empire, but soon dissension appears, always over women. Dissension first affects relations among the Bacwezi themselves and later between themselves and their people. Diseases and noxious insects appear that were previously unknown. The people stop venerating the Bacwezi, and the women sow trouble and no longer respect anything.

The final episode stems from the passionate attachment of one of the Bacwezi, Mugenyi, to his ox, Bihogo. He had made a vow to kill himself if the ox died. When the day comes, the other Bacwezi do their utmost to keep him from killing himself and decide to have the animal's entrails examined by a haruspex. A foreign diviner from the Nilotic countries of the north presents himself and insists on making a blood pact with Mugenyi before giving his pronouncement, in order to avoid reprisals. The animal is opened up and there is nothing inside. The diviner then discovers the entrails in the head and in the hooves; a flake of soot comes to rest on them. He gives his verdict: "The empty body means that the country is empty and that the reign of the Bacwezi has come to an end; the entrails found in the head tell me that you will nonetheless continue to reign *in people's heads*; the entrails found in the hooves mean that you will wander forever on the surface of the earth; the flake of soot announces that a dark man, a barbarian from the north, will establish a new dynasty in the country." Mugenyi, bound by the blood pact, releases the diviner, who is in fact the diviner of the future rulers. Shortly after this, an old aunt of Mugenyi mocks him for having vowed to commit suicide but seeming to have forgotten about it. This time things have gone too far and all the Bacwezi gather around Wamara and leave the country for good. They vanish into the lakes contained inside the craters of extinct volcanoes. The dark barbarian from the north inaugurates the new Babito dynasty that rules to this day and that claims, through an unconvincing narrative twist, to be, in spite of everything, descended from the Bacwezi, who lived twenty-six generations ago.

The historical reality of the Bacwezi is not in doubt. Numerous strictly historical traditions refer to them, and huge earth fortifications, without equivalents in this part of Africa, are attributed to them. Historians place their ephemeral reign somewhere around the fourteenth and fifteenth centuries. The Bunyoro depict them as light-colored and bright men (like the celestial beings) who vanished as suddenly as they had appeared and who brought a superior political organization and culture, marked by the cattle complex. Various types of weapons and tools which now characterize the technology of the area are attributed to them as well. All the other kingdoms of this zone, located south of Bunyoro, trace their own history back to the time when the Bacwezi passed through and somewhat later vanished. But their historical reputation is greatly overshadowed by their religious importance, for they are the ones who reigned thereafter as spirits in the people's heads, just as the diviner had foretold, all over the interlacustrine culture area, even in distant countries where their historical role was completely unknown.

As many as nineteen Bacwezi are honored in Bunyoro. Specialized mediums let their wishes be known, but the spirits can possess other people, and possession induced by initiation is considered good therapy. Every Cwezi spirit has particular psychological features evoked in ritual manifestations, and is connected with certain natural forces and certain cultural activities: thunder, smallpox, yaws, hoof-and-mouth disease, fire, wild animals, sexuality, and fertility; hunting, animal husbandry, kingship, the state of servitude, etc. All of them, however, can be honored in order to obtain the same basic blessings: children, health, luck, etc. They form the college of the beneficial white *mbandwa* (spirits of possession, but also the possessed themselves), to which were later added the evil black *mbandwa*. The latter have recently included the spirits of Europeanism, tanks, airplanes, and even the spirit of "Polishness" as a result of the presence of a large Polish refugee camp in the area in 1942.

Buganda

The culture of Buganda is quite different from that of Bunyoro and of the other western kingdoms. The Hima herdsmen played no particular role in it, and the Baganda do not refer to the Bacwezi as such. The birth and development of the kingdom seem to have occurred less as an extension of the power of neighboring Bunyoro-Kitara than as a reaction to it. A long series of wars was to last into the nineteenth century, when Buganda, more populated and more efficiently organized, emerged as the indisputably preeminent power.

The supreme God of the Buganda is called Katonda ("embryo," "creator"). He is a somewhat faded figure who does not appear in narratives but is referred to as the father of the *balubale*, i.e., of the spirits worshiped in cults. There is no myth of creation here, but there is an allegorical account bearing simultaneously on the origin of the dynasty and the origin of death, the two fundamental antithetical poles of the earthly condition. Kintu, "Thing," meets the daughter of Gulu, "Sky," who falls in love with him. To make him prove himself, Gulu has Kintu's cow abducted to heaven. Kintu is warned by Nambi and goes up to get what is his sole means of existence. After putting him through all kinds of other tests, Gulu consents to let Kintu take Nambi to earth, but he advises them to leave secretly at dawn in order to avoid being accompanied by Nambi's brother, Death. They leave taking many precious things with them, among them the domestic animals and the banana tree that will later become the basic crop of Buganda. But halfway there, Nambi notices that she has forgotten the millet for her fowls, and despite Kintu's pleas, she goes back and then returns, this time accompanied by her brother. Gulu subsequently attempts to

have Death captured in order to eradicate him from the earth. But when Death is inadvertently helped by children and takes shelter in the netherworld, plans to eradicate him are abandoned. Woman is again responsible for the ambivalence of the human condition, just as she is responsible for the succession of generations that eclipse one another. This is also the oblivion, the eclipse of the spirit, that is echoed in the Ruwanda name of the king of the netherworld and of the dead, "Master of Oblivion."

Kintu is otherwise represented as a culture hero and as the founder of the only dynasty recognized by the Buganda (more than thirty successions to date). Numerous traditions of historical and clan foundings are connected with this symbolic name. His first successors are presented as contemporaries and kinsmen of the first Babito kings of Bunyoro. It is not until the eighth king that the heroes appear who are to become the principal national gods. They are thought to be descendants of a companion of Kintu who left to rule over the islands of Ssese located in the northwest part of Lake Victoria, and they all formed a group in which certain names of the Bacwezi honored by the Bunyoro appear again, notably Wamara, who in this case plays a minor role. Interrelated over three generations, they are thought to have died or vanished without leaving behind any other descendants before they became national spirits who speak through mediums in the various temples dedicated to them. The two principal ones are brothers, Kibuka and Mukasa. Kibuka is a purely Ganda hero, unknown elsewhere, and the only real god of war honored as such all over the culture area. Called to the rescue by the king of Buganda who is being threatened by the Bunyoro, he intervenes by hiding in the clouds and massacring the enemy army from there up above, without being seen. After a first victory, he yields to the charms of a Nyoro woman prisoner who learns his secret and reveals it to her people. At the next battle, the Bunyoro all point their arrows toward the clouds and kill Kibuka. His cult is apparently the only one to have required human sacrifice, a requirement commensurate with the violent nature of his death. Unlike his brother, Mukasa is present in all interlacustrine temples (Mugasa, Mugasha, Ngassa). He is above all a spirit of the water, especially of Lake Victoria. He controls the storms and appears as the supreme God among certain groups of fishermen around the lake. The Buganda view him as a kindly god to whom people turn for all needs except war, and notably for fertility. The Ganda kings are his "in-laws."

The other *balubale*, quite numerous, also include figures portrayed as later historical individuals not related to the princes of the Ssese Islands. Still others have no historical character whatsoever and are connected with animal species (crocodiles, leopards, etc.) that are present near certain shrines or else connected with natural wells, large rocks, caves, and venerated trees. Among the principal *balubale* who are presented as historical are gods of rain, of hoof-and-mouth disease, smallpox, lightning, earthquakes, drought, and hunting. The god of hunting, Dungu, is also present among the Nyoro Bacwezi (Irungu) and in Rwanda (Nyabirungu).

Rwanda

Rwanda developed independently of the historical currents that came from Bunyoro, whose influence is openly acknowledged in all the kingdoms located north and east of Rwanda. The genealogy of its dynasty, the Banyiginya, is at least as long as the genealogies of the kings of Bunyoro and

Buganda, but the spirits of the Bacwezi appear in the country only later, as foreign intruders who have no place in the local political history.

Here the supreme God, Imana, figures prominently in words and thoughts, although no one worships him. The stories that circulate about him, which are all allegorical, emphasize his various attributes and his modes of intervention, but they remain clearly separate from the historical tradition. The same goes for the various accounts of the origin of death and of other negative aspects of life, which delight in stressing that the negative aspects were essentially already written into the dark side of life. Imana is a more abstract figure than the Ruhanga of the Bunyoro; he is present throughout the universe and not just in the sky; he is depicted less as the original creator of the material world than as the perpetual source of life, fertility, and luck.

The origin of the dynasty is in the sky where Thunder reigns. With the help of divinatory ingredients mixed in with the saliva of Thunder and with milk, a barren woman concocts a wondrous child inside a pot. Since his father regards him as illegitimate, he is allowed to fall to earth along with his brother Mutusi, his sister who will become his wife, and a Twa Pygmy couple. He also brings certain domestic animals down to earth in couples, and he brings fire. Kigwa ("he who has fallen") is not himself a king. He is received by an indigenous petty king who belongs to one of the clans called the "found-on-earth." The numerous and astoundingly rich Rwanda legends tell how the various indigenous petty kings, magicians, and rainmakers fail in the end to maintain a positive link between the sky and the earth, and how the descendants of the heavenly Kigwa gradually constitute the great Rwanda at their expense. The founder of the dynasty as a political institution and not just a mystical bond is Gihanga, whose name is just a variant of the name of the supreme god of the Bunyoro. Under his successors, certain kings or certain heroes who are their allies sacrifice themselves voluntarily for the kingdom and are called "Saviors." Their memory is honored by the dynasty, but, unlike what was just seen for Buganda, they do not otherwise intervene in the cults.

After Gihanga, fifteen successive reigns (for most of which there are detailed historical traditions) passed before the emergence of Ryangombe, king of the Imandwa (see above, the *mbandwa* of the Bunyoro), who are sometimes also called Ibicwezi. This took place under the reign of Ruganzu Ndori, perhaps at the end of the sixteenth century. Ryangombe does not appear to be part of the Bunyoro pantheon, but he can be found, however dimly, in the pantheons of the other kingdoms within the Nyoro zone of influence. He is a brother of Wamara, who plays the principal role in the myths of these same kingdoms (his tragic disappearance is emphasized), though he is himself totally absent in Rwanda and the southern zone.

Ryangombe, honored in Burundi under the name of Kiranga, is a great hunter who proves to be rather impulsive and is too fond of women. He is in the process of losing his kingdom in a game of chance against a powerful magician who is a king and related to him, when suddenly his son Binego, born far away and soon endowed with Herculean strength, comes forth and kills the opponent. Subsequently, Ryangombe, despite the warnings of his mother and by transgressing the prohibition that she imposes on him (to wear his belt over his clothes), goes hunting and in the forest meets a young mother without breasts (a double prohibition). He yields to her charms, and she asks that he recognize his child by giving her the customary gift of a skin pouch to carry the baby. She then chooses for this a monstrous buffalo that gores Ryangombe and throws him onto a tree with fiery red blossoms, the erythrina, which then becomes the sacred tree of the cult. Binego rushes in and kills the buffalo, but Ryangombe's blood is spilled, and there is no longer any question of returning to Rwanda, for the effects of the mystical force of the blood of the "Saviors" must not be reversed. All the Imandwa therefore commit suicide over his body, or vanish with him in the crater of the extinct volcano, Karisimbi (4,500 meters high), where the spirits of those who are initiated into their mysteries will join them and drink with them after their deaths. So Ryangombe, his mother, his brothers, his children, his affinal relatives, his companions, and his servants, removed from the succession of the generations (which makes the dead forget), leave no descendants; instead they adopt the population of Rwanda as a whole, with no distinction between castes and ranks, and remain forever suspended between the sky and the earth, in direct communication with the netherworld through the crater. They reign thereafter over the spirits of the dead and serve as mediators between the heavenly and subterranean forces, on the one hand, and the living who are affiliated with them, on the other.

Several well-known Bacwezi are found in the Rwanda pantheon, notably two antagonistic characters, the refined Kagoro, who is associated with thunder and with pastoral values, and Mugasa, who is here thought to have come from Zaire, who is rough and foul-smelling (like the fish), and who demands the right to cross over all currents of water. This pantheon also includes Mashira, the most famous of the indigenous kings who were supplanted by the Rwanda dynasty, as well as the spirit of Mutwa (a Pygmy pariah) and various spirit animals.

Here there are no temples, no specialized mediums, no true trance. All the initiates play the roles of heroes by consciously simulating a kind of frenzy that makes them assume, in the name of the spirits that they incarnate, incongruous, obscene, and depraved attitudes and speech, in which all the essential values of social life can be temporarily forgotten and prohibitions violated, at least symbolically. It may be the absence of trance that here produces strange texts that sound to us somewhat like the products of trance when they are shouted during the ritual performance. These texts may also help us to penetrate the intimate mystical identification with the royal spirits that reign in the head. The following are some excerpts:

> Ryangombe says, "I am the Price, I am the Buyer, I am the sterile female of the leopard, and no one buys me. I sleep with the daughter and the mother to get both of their gifts. I disturb the current like a male hippopotamus. I am the one who killed I-know-it-all. I killed the Violator of secrets. I am the One-expected at the main entrance, and I suddenly appear from hidden doors. I am the Elbow-who-does-not-spend-the-night-without-a-Virgin. I am the Sword-that-does-not-spend-the-night-without-flesh. I am the one who escapes recognition, the one whom others weary. I look like a peasant, but I behave like the other kings! I am the One-who-ceaselessly-receives-supplications, the Savior, the One-who-carries-off-the-object-of-desires-by-dancing."

> Binego says,

> Ababab! I am the dismemberer. I strangle the bulls and the old cows die in heat. I am Urine-of-Thunder. I am the flaw that breaks the mother-cow's hoof. I have killed my

mother's brothers. I am Blood-of-the-viper. They brew me, but they do not drink me. I am Bitter-and-pungent Taste. I am the obscurity wherein no one ventures. I am a wandering prohibition. I am a runny nose. I am a bleeding anthrax. I am a foreign body in the eye. I hate the man who constantly smiles; let him smile with a stitch in his side!

We shall not attempt to analyze the important correspondences and variants that the reader will notice in comparing one kingdom with another. But note certain constant features: a passion for hunting or cattle; a tragic death or mysterious disappearance that leaves no physical descendants; the negative role of women, who are in essence responsible for this succession of generations so highly valued elsewhere, but also responsible for the death of individuals, a death transcended by the deified royal spirits; and a retreat into volcanoes and lakes, the favored sites for communication between the three worlds.

There is always a gap between deified heroes and the reigning kings. In Bunyoro the Bacwezi represent a golden age never again recovered. They shine upon history as the sun shines upon the earth; they are superkings. In Buganda, they stem from a parallel lineage attached to the islands of Lake Victoria and they come to the rescue of official kings; they are what might be called parakings. In Rwanda, Ryangombe has no ties to the dynasty, comes from abroad, and in historical legend is opposed to the most famous king of Rwanda, Ruganzu Ndori, the archetypal epic hero; Ryangombe is thus manifestly an antiking: he traps Ruganzu and his knights in a fog and retorts to their aristocratic and martial attitudes with incongruities and magic. Whatever it may be, this gap is surely necessary if everyone is to be able to claim within the ritual settings: "I too am king!" We can thus say that the inhabitants of these regions lived and thought with at least three figures of sacred kings in mind: first, the abstract and symbolic figure of the mythical sacred god, the principle of explanation, the mediator between the sky and the earth and between natural forces and society; second, the figure of the real, contemporary king who exercised total physical power over all of them; and finally, the imaginary

figure of the mystical king, the inverted and positive link between the living and the dead, with whom they could identify themselves by letting his spirit live within them.

Finally it should be noted that the fusion of myth and history and the fusion of gods and men may go even farther. For example, a female spirit of more recent origin, Nyabingi, who is manifest through true trance and through mediums, has invaded the entire zone north of Rwanda and in the southwesternmost part of Uganda, most often inciting uprisings against official authorities within these politically marginal regions. Nyabingi, the wife, daughter, or servant of the king, depending on quite contradictory versions, was a girl cursed to have a tragic fate. But the woman mediums who later practiced in her name and often had tragic fates themselves were in turn designated as the true Nyabingi whom they merely embodied in various regions. This is probably how the Bacwezi traveled and were adopted as national spirits in kingdoms far away from their original zone of political influence.

P.S./g.h.

BIBLIOGRAPHY

J. BEATTIE, *Bunyoro, an African Kingdom* (New York 1960); *The Nyoro State* (Oxford 1971). J. BEATTIE and J. MIDDLETON, *Spirit Mediumship and Society in Africa* (London 1969). A. COUPEZ and T. KAMANZI, *Récits historiques rwanda* (Tervuren 1962). R. B. FISHER, *Twilight Tales of the Black Baganda* (London 1911). J. GORJU, *Entre le Victoria, l'Albert et l'Edouard* (Rennes 1920). L. DE HEUSCH, *Le Rwanda et la civilisation interlacustre* (Brussels 1966). A. KAGAME, *La poésie dynastique au Rwanda* (Brussels 1951). A. KAGGWA, *The Kings of Buganda* (Nairobi 1971). L. DE LACGER, *Rwanda I: Le Rwanda ancien* (Namur 1939). L. MAIR, *An African People in the Twentieth Century* (London 1934). R. OLIVER and G. MATHEW, *History of East Africa* (Oxford 1963). C. PAGES, *Un royaume hamite au centre de l'Afrique* (Brussels 1933). M. PAUWELS, *Imana et le culte des mânes au Rwanda* (Brussels 1958). J. ROSCOE, *The Baganda* (Cambridge 1911); *The Northern Bantu* (Cambridge 1915); *The Bakitara* (Cambridge 1923); *The Banyankole* (Cambridge 1923). P. SMITH, *Le récit populaire au Rwanda* (Paris 1975). B. ZUURE, *Croyances et pratiques religieuses des Barundi* (Brussels 1929).

MYTHS OF COSMIC AND SOCIAL HARMONY AMONG THE DINKA, ANUAK, AND SHILLUK

The Nilotic peoples, who almost certainly have a common origin, are today distributed over various regions in the Upper Nile basin, from southern Sudan to Ethiopia, Zaire, Uganda, Kenya, and Tanzania. Their languages, mythologies, and religions, despite a large number of common features, differ enough to preclude a synthesis of all aspects of the problem in one brief overview. We shall therefore consider here only a few peoples, the Dinka, the Shilluk, and the Anuak of the southern Sudan. All three share a basic myth about the emergence of a chief from the heart of the river.

Their traditions depict the Nilotic peoples as eternal pastoralists, both nomadic and warlike, devoted to their herds to the point of obsession. Today the Dinka are closest to this

ancestral image, but they all have as their basic economy a mixture of agriculture, fishing, and cattle breeding in varying proportions. The Shilluk have fewer cattle than the Dinka, and the Anuak have even fewer, with correspondingly less interest in the values of pastoralism. Nonetheless, words, metaphors, and customs associated with herds permeate all of Nilotic culture, and sacrificing cattle to the gods is the highest form of religious ritual. The gods differ from group to group, and it is thought that new ones appear from time to time, normally when men and women are possessed by them. The gods have a spiritual nature and no perceptible form. They all merge into an encompassing experience of a transcendental sky god. Compared to any number of other African peoples, the Nilotes are striking for the absence of any imaged representation of the divine, either anthropomorphic or zoomorphic. Their holy places and sacred objects and their material culture in general are among the simplest found anywhere: small altars made of mud, specially arranged cattle sheds, forked branches and cattle goads to which sacrifices are offered, certain trees, certain rocks, and other natural objects, or hunting spears, stools, and pearls. Even effigies of the first "god kings" of the Shilluk are reduced to poles tipped with ostrich feathers. And in the myths, the absence of any elaborate symbolic content is in keeping with such visual austerity. Folkloric narratives are full of imagination and fantasy, but the myths that deal with social or religious questions of primary importance are not fixed in form or prosaic in style. They may be regarded largely as historical accounts (the local populations themselves do not hesitate to do so), for which the circumstances surrounding the birth of the oldest chiefs provide the clearest content.

The events of most of these myths are supposed to have taken place in a physical and social environment similar to today's. In order to understand them, one must imagine a flat savanna, subjected every year to seasonal floods from rainwater and rivers, or, on the other hand, to great droughts and dehydration. From the standpoint of the life of the group, the local effects from these seasonal variations are not predictable from one year to the next and can be catastrophic. The relationship between the earth, the river, and the sky is thus of prime importance for the very survival of mankind. This is metaphorically projected in myth.

The social context of myth is one of clans and descent lines divided and structured by exogamous patrilineages, the basis of political and moral life among the Nilotic people. From early childhood, this social universe is divided between the mother and the father, the mother's family and the father's family, and the mother's lineage and the father's lineage. In polygamous households, in particular, this means tensions and sometimes even conflicts of loyalty, since children related through the father may be separated through the mother. Thus, on both the social scale and the geographical scale, the world of the Nilotic peoples is made of clear-cut dichotomies and contradictory experiences, which the myths eventually incorporate and mediate under the rubric of harmony and order.

In keeping with the apparent historicity of many Nilotic myths, cosmogonic themes do not predominate. However, one can generally find the notion of a sky and earth, originally joined in one way or another, and the idea that the first humans had direct access to the sky or were closer to the sky god than they are today. The Dinka myth is the most complete and explicit on this particular point. The deity (nhialic, "in the world beyond") was close to earth, and sky and earth were joined by a rope that allowed men to reach their god at will. There was no death. God told the first man and the first woman to grind only one millet seed per day, and that would meet their needs. The woman wanted more, and brandishing a long wooden pestle like those still in use today, she began to grind the grain. She struck the god with the pestle, which prompted him to send a bird to cut the rope that united sky and earth. The god retreated into heaven where men could no longer reach him. This marked the appearance on earth of death and toil. Ever since, men have attempted to make the divinity accessible again by means of prayer and sacrifice, in the hope that he would come to their aid. As a result, the belief in a radical division of the world is represented in cosmic terms. Prayers to god ask him to help men like an absent father whose children have been separated because of the first mother's conduct. Among the Dinka, the prohibitions against relations between husband and wife until the weaning of the child signify and imply that during his first few years the child will see little of his father, since he will be raised and fed in his mother's hut. The mother's brother is thus emotionally closer to him and also

the principal adult male link between the child and the structurally opposed groups of the mother and the father. Similarly, Dinka priests (bany bith, "masters of the spear"), who bridge the gap between men and the sky god, are represented as the mother's brothers of the communities for which they intercede.

There are many versions of the Dinka myth that reveal the origins of the priestly clans from which the masters of the spear are descended, but the account is essentially as follows. An aging and childless widow has brought her husband's lineage to an end and laments her fate near the river. A river deity tells her to step into the water, lift her leather loincloth, and let the water ripple into her vagina. She complies, becomes pregnant, and brings a male child into the world. The child soon shows evidence of remarkable powers. For instance, he singlehandedly obtains a gourd of milk while he is still nursing, not unlike Kṛṣṇa stealing butter. A few years later he makes water pour out of an old stump during a great drought. At the beginning his mother's people reject him and he leaves. Then, for reasons that are unclear, a few members of the tribe decide to follow him and join him on the banks of a river he has just crossed. As they attempt to cross the river themselves, he strikes them on the head with a harpoon, from the other side of the river. But one of them affixes the sacrum of a cow to a fishing rod and pushes it forward. In most versions, the supernatural child, whose name is Aiwel Longar, harpoons the bone, and the man holding it emerges from the river, fights with Longar (who in some versions passes through several metamorphoses, like Proteus), and wins. After overcoming him in this way, the Dinka chief priest summons all the people together, distributes sacred harpoons, and demonstrates how to use them to invoke the gods and pray to them. The Dinka priestly clans are descended from this priest and his people. In this highly abridged form of the myth, the fact that the first priest has no father among men puts him outside the bounds of the conflicts and contradictions inherent in the agnatic lineages of his nearest relatives. His spirit father, the river god, gives him a kinship with the divine, and today the role of the priests is to reconcile the deity and man beyond the initial separation referred to above. But the powers that allow the priests to pray effectively for life and fertility can also spell danger for those who offend them. Similarly, the river from which they are descended or the sky and its phenomena, with which they are associated (the basic relationship being between the waters of the river and those of the sky), can be as much a danger to life as they are necessary to it. During the seasonal movements of herds and in the migrations of the past, rivers had to be crossed and people had to overcome the danger of crossing just as the original people finally triumphed over their first chief, who was born of the river, and lived instead of dying. Just as they provide the spiritual link between the earth, with its inhabitants, the river, and the sky, so the Dinka priests mediate the antagonisms in their society. As the Dinka aphorism states, they are "the mother's brothers" of the community, making every effort to harmonize the divergent interests that are constantly produced by the agnatic lineages that structure the social universe.

Some of the same themes apply to the Anuak, with one difference of meaning that reflects the idiosyncracies of their particular culture and political system. While the Dinka are basically pastoralists who value their cattle above all else, the Anuak are primarily farmers who value most highly certain ancient pearls that they use to pay "the price of the betrothed." The land that they live on guarantees them a more secure habitat from year to year, and although they refer to a transcendent sky god, explicitly contrasted with mankind and the world here below, this feature is much less pronounced than it is for the Dinka. They too, however, view the river in the myth as both a source of life and a danger of death. In one of their myths, the god (a sky god, though he then lived on earth) throws a stone into the river to indicate that men will have to die. A dog warns men, but they ridicule the dog when he asks them to help him retrieve the stone from the river. He manages by himself to recover a small part of it, which secures for men the limited life span that they now have. As in the Dinka myth, the river is the cause of death but also the source of life.

Unlike the Dinka, the Anuak do not have a class of sacrificial priests, but they do have nobles who are, like the Dinka priests, descendants of a river spirit. Their myth of origin tells of children going fishing. One of them catches the head of the fish, another catches its tail. The fish escapes. A river spirit in human form tells them that in the future the one who catches the fish by the head can claim it as his own (the best way to hold on to a fish is to hold it by the gills). They go back to the village and speak to the chief about the river spirit. The chief dispatches his men to mount guard. They capture the river spirit (sometimes depicted, like the first Dinka priest, as one who changes form during the struggle) and bring him back to the village, where he is invited to unite with the chief's daughter. She becomes pregnant, and the spirit returns to the river with his cattle, leaving the woman with a string of pearls for the child, who turns out to be a boy, the founder of an aristocratic clan. The string of pearls is the principal emblem of the Anuak, and the sons of aristocrats cannot aspire to nobility unless they have worn the necklace at some time in their lives. There is a saying among the Anuak that the spiritual founder of the noble clan impressed the people by showing that he could resolve a conflict, even if he did this by issuing an order rather than by mediating. The children who were fighting over the fish lost the fish because neither of them was willing to give in. They represent the self-destructive nature of lineage conflicts in village life, conflicts that today's nobles, more powerful than their predecessors, are supposed to be able to suspend if not bring to an end altogether. As the river flows across the boundaries of territory that is politically divided, so nobles who originated spiritually from the same river may by virtue of their progeny appear to belong to the entire country, while their mothers give to each a social locus in their villages. Just like the Dinka priests of the harpoon, Anuak nobles are regarded as people associated with celestial phenomena, although they do not make up a priestly caste in charge of sacrifice. There is good reason to believe that they took over the power in their villages progressively at the expense of the lineages of their mother's brothers, among whom they had been raised, like their first ancestors. The potential conflict that characterizes this situation is also reflected in a myth that tells how the mother's brother of the first noble was jealous and tried to kill him. The people finally decided to follow the noble nephew, and to this day it is the mother's brother who seats the aristocrat on the royal stool, although the aristocrat gets his nobility from the clan of his father.

While each Anuak noble rules in his own village, and there is no single king for the country as a whole, the Shilluk, to whom they are related, have a more extended and powerful royal clan, from which a king is chosen either by election or by combat among the princes. The Shilluk king incorporates some of the spiritual functions of the Dinka priests and the Anuak nobles. The Shilluk myths about the royal house

reflect this idiosyncracy. While the Dinka priests and Anuak nobles are related to the river and to the sky through the male line and to the earth and its subdivisions through the female line, Nyikango, the first Shilluk king, is of divine origin through both lines of descent. According to one account, he is a descendant of a man who came from the sky; according to another, he is a descendant of a cow created by the god in the river. His mother was a crocodile, though she had a human form. On assuming power, each Shilluk king becomes a reincarnation of Nyikango. Thus the king is both the sovereign and the high priest of the Shilluk nation, and at the same time he transcends the opposition between spirits and men that is set forth in Dinka and Anuak myths. In songs and elegies, the king is associated with the river and the sky. Like the river, he symbolically links all the political subdivisions of the Shilluk nation, and like the sky he transcends them all. In fact, custom demands that Shilluk princes be brought up far from the royal capital, which is situated in the middle of the long strip of territory occupied by their nation on the western shore of the White Nile. Such princes normally grow up in their mothers' villages and thereby have their particular local communities throughout the country. But when a prince becomes king, the rites of installation clearly establish that he has become the sovereign ruler of the entire nation, explicitly enacting the theme of the unification of what was once disunited, a theme that lies at the heart of Nilotic mythology. When a new king rises to power, the traditional division of the Shilluk nation into two halves is the first idea stressed in the ceremonies. Images of the first kings, symbolizing spiritual kingship, are carried to the capital by an army from the northern half. The new king, also escorted by an army, comes from the south. The two troops camp on the opposite banks of a watercourse just south of the capital. After a sacrifice, the king-elect crosses the water and engages his army in a mock battle with the army headed by an effigy of Nyikango, the first king. Nyikango defeats the king-elect, captures him, and identifies himself with him. The new king is thought to have brought his nation to life, and by ascending to power, to have restored its unity with the river and the sky. Thus he becomes manifest as the one who rescued his people from the depths of the river (symbolized by the watercourse) and brought them across it, and who, after engaging in combat with his divine ancestor, inherited his spiritual power and unified the divided earth.

Thus the role of the spiritual leader in Shilluk myth is again that of the initiator of an agreement, even if only a temporary one, between the different lineages and political factions. But the link between the royal clan and the mother's brothers is depicted as being somewhat different from the case of the priestly clans of the Dinka or the noble clan of the Anuak. Dak, the second Shilluk king, is, both in the tradition and in the ceremonies, a warrior king who represents the political supremacy of the sovereign, just as his father, Nyikango, represented the sovereign's spiritual prominence. In the myth, he kills the descendants of his grandmother, the crocodiles, thus asserting the king's full dominion over the lineage of his affines, a situation also reflected in the custom forbidding any marriage with the king's daughters. The myth shows how Dinka priests and Anuak nobles, who boast of divine origins on their father's side but are fully human on their mother's side, depend on the lineages of their affines, whom they simultaneously direct and serve. At least in this myth, the Shilluk kings appear to be free of this dependency.

Nilotic deities are immortal. The chiefs who are their

descendants die, of course, but they are supermortals who act as particular humans, and they participate in the deity's immortality. When their power begins to wane, eminent Dinka priests enter their own tombs while still alive, so that they are not seen dying like other men, and their death is an occasion not for mourning but rather for celebrating the renewal of the vitality of the community. It is said that the Shilluk king was killed when he became too old or too weak to embody the creative life spirit of Nyikango. The standard word meaning "to die" is not applied to the deaths of these chiefs, and during their lifetimes Anuak nobles and Shilluk kings are referred to as *jwok*, "spirits," and not as humans.

The cosmic and social harmony represented ideally in these myths is what the Nilotic people consciously strive for. This could be further demonstrated by other examples. The harmony is never achieved in reality, since in reality the problems of ecological adaptation, battles, and other dissension between the various lines of descent that make up the group, each of which is demanding and egocentric in its own way, remain obstinate facts. But the myths do show at the level of the imagination how to rise above the conflict, whether it is a conflict with the environment or with other people, and they establish the circumstances under which the original chiefs pointed the way to a higher cosmic and social order that their successors continue to represent symbolically.

G.L./g.h.

BIBLIOGRAPHY

Two difficulties arise in the study of Nilotic peoples. The first is that the concept "Nilotic" is partly linguistic, partly cultural and ethnological, and partly geographical. Some linguists have classified as Nilotic the languages of the Masai, the Bari, and the Nandi, which used to be called "Nilo-Hamitic"—see, for example, Joseph H. Greenberg,

"Studies in African Linguistic Classification" 5: "The Eastern Sudanic Family," *Southwestern Journal of Anthropology*, 6, 2 (1950). In the present article, the word "Nilotic" refers to a more limited group of peoples, of which the list and summary description are found in the collection of A. J. Butt, the first work in the bibliography below. The second difficulty lies in the rather unobjective estimation of their population. The most extensive groups certainly include hundreds of thousands of people, and Professor Evans-Pritchard estimated as early as 1952 that their population totaled "very approximately" 2.5 million. The Dinka may have about a million; the Shilluk may be over 120,000; the Anuak about 50,000.

Principal Titles

A. J. BUTT, "The Nilotes of the Anglo-Egyptian Sudan and Uganda," *Ethnographic Survey of Africa, East Central Africa*, part 4, 4 (1952), with bibliographic supplement (London 1964). J. P. CRAZZOLARA, *The Lwoo*, part 1: *Lwoo Migrations*; part 2: *Lwoo Traditions*; part 3: *Lwoo Clans*, Museum Combionianum (Verona 1950–54). F. M. DENG, *The Dinka and Their Songs* (Oxford 1973); "The Dinka of the Sudan," in *Case Studies in Cultural Anthropology* (New York 1972). E. E. EVANS-PRITCHARD, *The Political System of the Anuak* (London 1940); "Nilotic Studies," *Journal of the Royal Anthropological Institute of Great Britain and Ireland*, vol. 80 (1950); "The Divine Kingship of the Shilluk," in *Essays in Social Anthropology* (London 1962); *Nuer Religion* (Oxford 1956). W. HOFMAYR, "Die Schilluk, Geschichte, Religion und Leben eine Niloten-Stammes," *Anthropos*, 2, 5 (Vienna 1925). P. P. HOWELL and W. P. G. THOMSON, "The Death of Reth of the Shilluk and the Installation of His Successor," *Sudan Notes and Records*, vol. 27 (1946). R. GODFREY LIENHARDT, "The Shilluk of the Upper Nile," in *African Worlds*, D. Forde, ed. (London 1954); "Nilotic Kings and Their Mothers' Kin," *Africa*, vol. 25 (1955); *Divinity and Experience: The Religion of the Dinka* (Oxford 1961); "Getting Your Own Back: Themes in Nilotic Myth," in *Studies in Social Anthropology: Essays in Memory of Sir Edward Evans-Pritchard by His Former Oxford Colleagues*, J. H. M. Beattie and R. G. Lienhardt, eds. (Oxford 1975). B. A. OGOT, *History of the Southern Luo* 1: *Migration and Settlement* (Nairobi 1967). C. G. and B. Z. SELIGMAN, *Pagan Tribes of the Nilotic Sudan* (London 1932). D. WESTERMANN, *The Shilluk People, Their Language and Folklore* (Philadelphia 1912). A. SOUTHALL, *Alur Society* (London 1956).

THE MYTHOLOGY OF THE KABYLES OF THE MAGHREB

A lively form of present-day Islam is experienced deeply by almost all the inhabitants of the Maghreb and constitutes the major characteristic of Maghrebian culture. Yet this undeniable adherence to a monotheistic religion occasionally takes on particular colorations that stem from a very old pre-Islamic mythology that has its roots in ancient Mediterranean soil.

These vestiges persist especially within the culture of rural people, most particularly among women, for whom schooling in most regions is still problematic. One can still hear such people tell tales that sometimes sound like myths. They still know the sacred places, the terrifying or helpful characters; sometimes they perform rituals at variance with Muslim orthodoxy. In many cases there is a syncretism at the heart of a tolerant Islam which like many universal religions has integrated many traditions dear to local piety, thus maintaining the permanence of the sacred.

It is risky to attempt to reconstitute a mythology of which now, after eight centuries of Islam, only a few scattered remnants can be discerned. Moreover, these fragments survive at the very heart of popular culture, among beliefs practiced or neglected within rituals still commonly observed, or revealed through a rich oral literature that is now unfortunately threatened with rapid extinction. However, one can attempt to understand certain attitudes and contemporary social customs only by considering these elements of an ancient mythology, the study of which may reveal many of the terms in which fundamental problems are posed within specific social groups. Far from yielding merely arcane points of interest, far from indulging in a cult of archaism, the knowledge of the elements of this mythology, still an integral part of Maghrebian culture, often sheds light on the present.

The sources from which the elements are drawn are primarily popular tales, myths collected by ancient and modern authors, pieced together in contemporary personal research conducted for the most part among women speaking the Berber language, natives of Kabylia.

I. Characters

1. The First Mother of the World

One of the most interesting characters is a "First Mother of the World" (*yemma-t n dunnit*)—a woman who was ambivalent in her youth but in maturity developed a knack for evildoing; she was not unlike those embittered old women so frequently referred to by men as "old witches." She is the most important among them, the great *settut*. Here are some of her exploits. A bringer of bad omens, she experiences joy in doing evil, so that she brings misfortune especially to men. She is blamed for eclipses, which she created by catching hold of the sun and making it fall into a mirror of water. Since then, eclipses have recurred every five years.

Since "one bad turn deserves another," she instituted the sacrifice of a child, the only thing that could put an end to an eclipse. She created clouds out of the bubbles formed when she stirred her mirror of water. She is also said to have created the stars, which were only the teeth of a sickle she used for stirring the mirror. To this rather positive creation she is said to have added the creation of beneficent animals. She invented sheep, which she formed from dough made from flour ground in her hand mill. But she was unable to produce anything completely satisfactory; she retained traces of soot on her hands, and sheep have had black muzzles ever since.

The basic vocation of the *yemma-t n dunnit* was to dispense bad advice. She instituted eventual death for all men by counseling a young mother to ask for death for her child in the hope of seeing him again soon. Since she instituted death as man's fate, her evildoing can still be felt among the living, for she is responsible for the first dispute that created discord within the great house of humanity. As the dispute worsened, the language of men slowly became distorted so that it became incomprehensible to others. Thus, it is said, the first seven languages of the world were born, sanctioning the breakdown in communication that was instituted by the First Mother of the World.

Another piece of her bad advice resulted in the creation of the monkeys, whose ancestor is none other than a young boy that the great *settut* induced to soil a platter of couscous. Many animals bear the mark of her wickedness. The hedgehog was unable to rid itself of the teeth of a carding comb with which the First Mother of the World beat him. Similarly, the porcupine bears forever the wood splinters from the spindle of this *settut*, and the turtle is none other than a young bull at which she threw the two grinding stones from her hand mill, striking the animal on its back and chest.

Even old women who resemble her blame her for their misfortune. For, wicked and ill-tempered, she is said to have insulted the month of January as it came to a close, but January managed to obtain a few extra days from February and unleashed such severe weather that the First Mother of the World was petrified and frozen. From that time on, many old women have died at this time of year.

2. The Ant

Fortunately, the disastrous activities of the First Mother of the World may be offset by the intervention of a character benevolent toward human beings, namely, the ant.

The very opposite of the *yemma-t n dunnit*, the ant is a good counselor, and is credited with the role of initiator. The ant is said to have explained to men the use of created things. Thus, once the First Mother of the World created sheep, the ant told men how to use their meat for food and their wool for clothing and how to exchange both of these for the indispensable wheat. Finally, the ant is supposed to have instituted feast days and to have shown men how to sacrifice oxen or sheep on those occasions. The initiator of rituals and husbandry, the ant is said to have induced wild bulls to let themselves be domesticated by men. The ant also taught

Sacred olive tree. Note the outline of the stock of a swing plow entrusted to the care of an *āssas*. Algeria. Photo C. Lacoste-Dujardin.

men agriculture by showing them how a grain of wheat planted after the rains could produce many other grains of wheat. And it also taught the first couple how to make bread by crushing grain with a stone, making fire with two stones and dried weeds, and baking the dough.

3. Ogresses and Ogres

A whole universe peopled with more or less mythological characters still comes to life in these tales. For women, these characters remain objects of belief—or of doubt.

Ogresses, sterilizing agents, are fallen women. In the mythical times of the origins, in the era of the first men and women who are thought to have come to the surface of the earth from an underground world, women lived apart from men. Women are said to have initiated sexual contact and thus to have dominated men. But men assembled stones and built houses, where women then were kept and hence became dependent on men.

One woman and one man, however, preferred to lead a wild life without a house; this is how the woman became *teryel*, the cannibal ogress, and the man became the lion.

Kabyle mythology is peopled with more ogresses than ogres. The ogresses, known as *teryel/teryalin*, are savage, untamed, and dangerous women. Another myth credits one of them with being the mother of all ogres, whom she bore because she consumed the golden leaves of an extraordinary tree. Even more than ogres, who appear to be subordinate to them, ogresses are mistresses of wild space, where they behave totally at variance with all that takes place in the civilized world.

"Jema" of sidi Khaled, seacoast shrine. Algeria. Photo C. Lacoste-Dujardin.

4. Guardians

Unlike ogresses, who haunt mainly the wilderness, guardians are familiar and are present everywhere, especially in the world inhabited by men.

The most familiar of all is the guardian of the house, *āssas buxxam*, whose invisible presence controls all family life and whom everyone tries to satisfy. If there happens to be a stone ledge inside a house, that is where the guardian will establish his home, and the occupants will provide him with a lighted lamp on feast days. The guardians are also partial to cultivated fields; trees of unusual location, appearance, size, or fruit; certain caves, etc. It is necessary to greet them whenever it is appropriate, thus showing them the respect to which they are entitled, for they represent the Master of the World and are charged by God with watching over the actions of men.

On all of this property—land, fields, houses—man is only a tenant. "Everything belongs to God," and the guardians are God's sentinels who watch over the proper use of these earthly goods just as they watch over the good conduct of human beings. On the other hand, they can intercede with God on behalf of men.

5. Assembly

The guardians and other supernatural powers can assemble on the occasion of events important to men. Indeed, most of the decisions made by villagers in their assemblies have previously been debated by these powers.

The powers appear in the form of large birds—vultures and eagles—which gather on some high point when a serious decision has to be made concerning men. Most likely, these are especially pious men, holy men, "dervishes," madmen, or idiots, long dead or still alive. Their decision is almost always unanimous, and the sentences they pass may range from acquittal to some climatic disaster, such as hail, drought, or locusts.

"Tisira," a hollow sacred rock. Algeria. Photo C. Lacoste-Dujardin.

6. Mediators

Other intercessors between the supernatural and men are the counselors, wise old men who appear in tales under the name of *amgar azemni* and are equivalent to the Arabic *muddebar*. They guide the hero and show him the right path to follow to reach the end of his quests or accomplish his exploits. Sometimes the daughters of an ogress or a genie are mediators, who can use the power inherited from their parents on behalf of heroes and men in general. Finally there is the whole host of spirits who are integrated into Islam under the general rubric of good or wicked jinn, who appear frequently in the tales.

7. Mythological Animals

The world is also occasionally peopled by animals with extraordinary powers. Thus, the female dragon *talafsa*, a kind of seven-headed Hydra, haunts the forests and springs and holds back the water from an entire region, several villages, or a town unless a young maiden is sacrificed to her each year. This ancient, universal myth of the dragon-slaying hero is widespread in the Maghreb and is especially well known in Kabylia.

Most of the other animals seem to have mythical functions, probably because they are either guardians or spirits who disguise themselves in this form.

II. Cosmogonic Myths

Alongside these mythical, theogonic, and etiological elements, a few other traits help us to understand the mythical cosmogony.

The First Mother of the World, the first couple, and the first humans are said to have appeared on earth, on the visible surface of the earth, when they came out of another world, the netherworld, invisible but peopled, an obscure world of shadows, where sterility is the rule and everything is the reverse of the human, civilized world. The netherworld is the other side of the world where we live, the world of men that has been conquered by men, organized, and made fertile.

A number of things in the netherworld look very familiar: landscapes, forests, mountains, ravines, herding—but everything there is the antithesis of what exists in the human-world. Sheep are black, and so is goat's milk, for the goats there are forced to graze on cinders and coal. When an ogress tries to do something productive she actually indulges in a parody of the activity. The same is true of the hero sent down into the netherworld, who must act to denounce these "inversions": he induces the ogress to destroy her own bedding, throw out her cooking utensils, make a parody of kitchen gardening, and even to eat her own children.

In the netherworld, from which the first man and the first woman came, there are strange beings, spirits of all kinds, giants like the ogresses and the ogres, and dwarfs swarming everywhere like the ants with whom they may have some kinship. Between this "other world" and the world of men, a network of communications exists. Wells permit contact, as do caves and sometimes a door; an iron gate may close off the entrance. Mediators make use of such communications: heroes of tales, spirits, snakes, and also the dead while in contact with this world beyond are dedicated to the earth and can secure its fertility. The time when the netherworld threatens particularly to invade the world of men is at night, when the inhabitants from the other side of the world haunt human habitats. And at night, as in the other world, only the bravest and the most devout men can overcome the ominous forces of the supernatural.

One myth explains the succession of day and night by the roles assigned to two brothers unwinding two balls of string. One has white thread and is day; the other has black thread and is night.

III. An Eschatological Myth

Finally, an eschatological myth foretells the overturn of the civilized world by the other side of the world, the chthonic world. According to the myth, the end of the world will be preceded by such signs as total darkness, the confusion of the sky and the earth, the movement of mountains, and a deluge lasting seven days and seven nights. After this the world will turn upside down and a dwarf, a kind of a head with a single leg, arm, eye, and ear, without a trunk, rather like a cricket, will invade the whole universe by multiplying into a frenetic swarm like lice or ants and spreading disorder, drought, destruction, and sterility.

IV. Current Mythology

Despite certain characteristics peculiar to Kabyle culture, the last myth without a doubt borrows the very name, if not the features, of the Muslim *Dajjāl*, Islam's Antichrist, a giant of great beauty, a seducer of men, who will rule on this earth for forty days before being slain by the Mahdi or by Jesus, near Mecca or Medina, just before the Resurrection and the Last Judgment.

The adaptation to Islam and the Islamization of the mythology can be recognized in many other cases. The First Mother of the World, the initiator of death, meets the opposition of God himself, though he sanctions her actions or may even take her place in inspiring the reply of the young mother (in the myth of the origin of death). In certain versions of the same myths, she may be replaced by God himself, who performs her tasks, for example, in certain etiological myths. Islamization is even more strongly marked in the case of the guardians, who come to be referred to as *lmalayekkat*, or angels.

The continuity of the sacred is especially evident in cult sites. Certain caves and springs have been regularly frequented from prehistoric times to the present day. Traces of prehistoric, Roman, and pre-Islamic cults can be found near contemporary shrines built to the glory of some devout Muslim figure. The continuity of the sacred implies a permanence of the creation of myths and their frequent enactment.

History itself may sometimes be integrated with or stimulate mythological thought or mythogenesis. A tree with golden leaves arose out of the pool of blood shed by all the Spanish warriors killed by the Kabyles during the Spanish invasions. By eating from the tree, a *teryel* (ogress) became pregnant and gave birth to the first eighty ogres. From a branch of the same tree born of Spanish blood came the two fruit trees vital to the Kabyles: the fig tree and the olive tree.

Mythological creation tries to account for everything up to and including very modern inequities of colonization. Thus, God is said to have charged a young woman with the following mission: to distribute three bags, one containing money and meant for the Kabyles; the other two containing lice and meant for Arabs and Europeans. The young woman made a mistake, and the two bags of lice fell on the Arabs and the Kabyles, while the bag full of money went to the Europeans.

Recent events and phenomena deeply affecting the life of the Kabyles can still inspire the creation of myths. Some sacred trees have unique attributes. A certain mastic tree has become a "long-distance-call tree." Women climb up into its branches and call out to their husbands, brothers, or close relatives who have emigrated to France. The women never fail to obtain a quick response from the absent person, either a letter or, more frequently, the actual return of the emigrant.

Thus, the apparent permanence of mythology should not be interpreted as an index of stagnation, inflexibility, or archaism, for even today modern adaptations often slip into the mold of mythical form to bear witness to the dynamism of contemporary mythological creativity.

C.L.-D./g.h.

BIBLIOGRAPHY

L. VON FROBENIUS, *Volksmärchen der Kabylen* (3 vols., Jena 1922). R. MAUNIER, "Le culte domestique en Kabylie," *Rev. d'ethnographie et des traditions populaires* 23–24 (1925): 248–65. A. ABEL, "Al dadjdjál," in *Encyclopédie de l'Islam.* B.A.M., J.M.D.—Iâssassen, "Gardiens," 17.3.49, 24.3.49, *C.E.B.*, 866–992, 11 p. J.M.D., "Agraw l-lejwat," *F.D.B.*, 1.5.49, 20.3.49, 23.3.49, 866–992, 11 p. Assemblée des Puissances surnaturelles. J. M. DALLET, "Mystagogie kabyle. Iâssassen, agraw, 866–992," *F.D.B.* (mars–mai 1949), 12ᵉ année, 3ᵉ trim. 1959, no. 63, pp. 1–24 (reprint of three texts above with transcription normalized). B.A.M., J.M.D., "Lmalayekkat: Les Anges, notions traditionnelles," *C.E.B.*, (January 1951): 2009–22, notes 2034–37. A. S. TRITTON, *Islam: Belief and Practices* (London and New York 1951). STEPHAN and NANDY ROUART, *Concise Encyclopaedia of Arabic Civilisation* (Amsterdam 1899). "La mort, le deuil et les rites funèbres," *F.D.B.* (Fort National, Algeria, 1962). J. SERVIER, *Les portes de l'année* (Paris 1962); "Extraits du folklore lyrique: Vues sur l'au-delà," *F.D.B.*, no. 88 (Fort National, Algeria, 1965). H. GENEVOIS, "Superstition, recours des femmes kabyles," *F.D.B.* (1968), nos. 97 and 100. C. LACOSTE-DUJARDIN, *Le conte kabyle* (Paris 1970).

Celts, Norse, Slavs, Caucasians, and Their Neighbors

THE INDO-EUROPEANS

At the beginning of the nineteenth century it seemed that the solidarity of language and culture long recognized between the Greeks and the Latins could be extended to the peoples who, toward the end of the Neolithic, occupied northern India, Iran, the Russian steppes, the shores of the Baltic Sea, central and western Europe, and the British Isles. The Germans and Celts, the Persians and Scythians whom Rome had taken for barbarians were shown to be closely related to one another as well as to the Parthians, the Armenians, the Greeks and Romans themselves, and to other peoples whose very existence was unsuspected by the ancients. Recognition of this kinship was the accomplishment of linguists who, during and after the 1780s, had access, for the first time, to the sacred texts of India and Iran: the analysis of Sanskrit, then that of Avestan, revealed the close kinship of both of these languages with Latin and Greek. Very rapidly, with the aid of Old Germanic, Slavonic, Old Irish, etc., it became possible to construct a sort of grammatical norm of the archaic language from which, according to the evidence, the various languages derived.

This language was quite naturally given the name Indo-European, since the elements that served for its reconstruction were found across a geographical area stretching from Iceland to Bengal. Besides basic grammatical structures (the inflection of nouns, the conjugation system, sentence syntax), comparison revealed a considerable vocabulary made up of thousands of words which appeared to have a common etymology: names of animals and plants, sociological and religious terms, military and agricultural terms. As research progressively enlarged the field of knowledge, the outlines of an astonishingly rich and complex culture bearing a distinctive ideology appeared. The derivative languages attested both to the endurance of this ideology in widely separated locations and to its inevitable adaptations in contact with populations of different origins. This last trait explains how Indo-European culture in the strict sense could give birth to nations as diverse as Celtic Gaul, the Hittite Empire, or the Roman Republic. There is the supplementary fact of great distance: detaching itself from the central kernel, a given community inaugurates an autonomous mode of existence that causes it to evolve in a distinctive way, until it becomes unrecognizable to other communities that have undergone an analogous evolution. It would have astonished the Greeks to be told that the Scythians were their cousins. The Romans considered the Parthians to be as totally foreign as, say, the Egyptians, and never discovered their own linguistic and cultural solidarity with the Parthians, obvious to us today, which radically distinguished them from the Egyptians.

The religious domain, so important in this type of culture, is no exception: the peculiarities of Greek mythology result both from the Hellenes' contacts with the peoples of the Eastern Mediterranean and from the specific histories of cities devoted to maritime commerce. In such a context, it is not surprising that "oceanic" divinities should have played a dominant role in the religious consciousness of the Greeks. Inversely, we could hardly be surprised at the almost complete absence of a Poseidon in the mythology of the Indians and Iranians. Having arrived in Bactria and Kashmir after several centuries of wandering in Central Asia, these peoples were more interested in taming horses than in the art of navigation—and with good reason. But they had barely settled on the shores of the Indian Ocean before they rediscovered myths of the sea in their own tradition: the sovereign god Varuna became a lord of the waves, living in an undersea palace with his consort and his court of Tritons and Sirens.

Ultimately, the endurance of archaic values remains characteristic of the religious evolution of every sector of the vast Indo-European domain. We know that when Christian missionaries set out to evangelize Lithuania around the thirteenth century, they discovered that the Lithuanians worshiped Perkunas, the god of storm and rain, recognized by modern linguists as the exact homologue of the Vedic god Parjanya, who was also in charge of the fertilizing rain clouds. Such correspondences, thirty centuries and thousands of miles apart, suggest a visceral attachment to an astonishingly powerful tradition.

It is equally possible that fidelity to the original ideology was reinforced, or reactivated, by movements that affected the Indo-European domain throughout antiquity: in Italy, for example, there was first an Umbrian form of the Indo-European religion, then a Roman form; the Etruscan influence on the latter was soon corrected by the vogue of the *ritus graecus* (and the *interpretatio graeca*). Later, the diffusion of the Iranian Mithra in the Empire of the Mysteries revived a certain pagan sensibility at the very time when Christianity was beginning to assert itself. In fact, it was the implantation of the Church that really put an end to the Latin, Greek, Celtic, then Germanic, Baltic, and Slavic forms of the ancient religion, in a process that took more than ten centuries to complete, and that corresponds to the Islamization of Iran between the seventh and tenth centuries in the Middle East. In India, on the other hand, neither Buddhism nor Islam succeeded in eliminating Hinduism, which is a direct continuation (albeit with profound changes) of Vedic religion. Noting, in addition, that a small community of Zoroastrians (the Parsis) found refuge on Indian soil and has continued to exist there up to the present, we can say that India (with the island of Bali) plays the role of a sanctuary for Indo-European traditions: one can hear the Avesta and the Veda recited there, and observe ceremonies that have remained unchanged for more than four thousand years.

These ceremonies are, however, few in number: they primarily concern domestic ritual and the domain of sacraments (initiation, marriage, funerals); so they are not in themselves a sufficient source of information on the religion practiced by the Indo-Europeans. To get a global view of this religion, we must turn to documents provided by archaeology and textual studies, of which only the latter are truly convincing since it is in texts that we hear the voices of bygone peoples. The objects discovered by archaeologists allow us to verify the details of textual descriptions; but without such descriptions we would understand little or nothing of the actual use of these objects in religious ceremonies. For example, the Viking boats that have been discovered in Sweden attest to the veracity of Scandinavian epic tales, but without these tales how could we know that the boats were also used for the ritual cremation of chiefs? The objects found by archaeologists are rarely signed, and the attribution of a particular copper axe, statuette, or tumulus to the Indo-Europeans is often subject to lengthy debate. Finally, religious texts, while abundant, are extremely disparate. Certain hymns of the Ṛg Veda could have been composed around 1800 B.C., while on the other hand the *dainas* (Lithuanian and Latvian songs) were collected only in the nineteenth century. These are the two extreme cases (extreme also in nature: the Vedic hymns constitute a very sophisticated form of priestly literature, while the *dainas* are folk songs), but they show how heterogeneous the documents are: while nothing remains of the Latin ritual texts, we have enormous liturgical treatises from India; for the Celts we have only external descriptions and legendary tales written after their conversion to Christianity; in one place the literature is exclusively epic, in another it is purely secular, and so forth.

The scholars who have devoted their lives over the last hundred and fifty years to rediscovering Indo-European religion have had to go about their task like detectives, seizing on the smallest clue and comparing it systematically with all the others, with the support of other human sciences, particularly linguistics. Studies of Indo-European vocabulary, for instance, already marked by O. Schrader's *Real-Lexicon* (Berlin, 1917), culminated in E. Benveniste's *Indo-European Language and Society* (Paris, 1969); in the same way, studies of Indo-European religion led, after a long history, to the work of Georges Dumézil (*L'idéologie tripartite des Indo-Européens*, Brussels, 1958). But we must repeat, and emphasize, that the results of these efforts must, in the nature of things, remain partial. Their fragmentary state in itself leaves them open to question. Still, the general lines of Indo-European ideology are now well known, and we shall summarize them briefly.

Rituals

Let us state right at the start (and it is not at all self-evident) that the Indo-Europeans believed in another world (in Sanskrit *paradeśa*, in Iranian *para-daeza*, from which the biblical "Paradise" is derived). This mysterious universe is peopled with living beings superior to humans but resembling them to some degree, just as humans resemble animals yet are radically distinct from them. Thus there is a continuity between the humblest of creatures and the highest of gods. This does not mean that all of these beings are interchangeable or equal: on the contrary, they form clearly separated and hierarchized groups: it would be madness (Greek: *hybris*) for a man to want to turn into a god, or for a god to think of abandoning his rank. It can, of course, happen that certain gods (Zeus, Indra, Jupiter, etc.) impregnate mortal women or that certain humans (Sigurðr, Purūravas, Peleus, etc.) have love affairs with goddesses, but these are very exceptional, indeed rather "monstrous," events (such as Zeus taking the form of a swan to unite with Leda; Prince Arjuna uniting with a nymph who has the form of a snake; etc.). The norm is for each living being to assume his condition fully: what the Veda calls his *dhāman*, which is both his "status" and his "position," i.e. his place in the hierarchical scale of beings.

This hierarchy exists everywhere, even within the various groups: animals have greater or lesser "value" with respect to each other (hence the rich symbolism of the eagle, the wolf, the lion, the migrating bird, etc.); human beings are divided according to broad social functions; the gods have more or less importance depending on whether they live underground, on the earth (nymphs, satyrs, etc.), in the atmosphere, or in the sky. Yet here again the idea of hierarchy remains dominant: kingship over the world belongs by right to the gods of the sky (Zeus, Jupiter, Óðinn, Wotan, Ahura Mazdā, Varuṇa, Perkunos, etc.), never to divinities of the earth or sea—not even among seafaring peoples such as the Greeks or the Vikings.

Sacrifice

In every way, the Immortals, whoever they be, have the advantage over human beings of belonging to a superior category, and it is wise to propitiate them. Now, "those who know" (Brahmans, druids, flamens, etc.) teach that the gods, like all living beings, need food. There is no better way of gaining their favor than by inviting them to dine. The only object of the ritual is to specify the forms in which this invitation should be sent, how it should be organized, what food to serve, when and how, etc. The ceremony can become extremely complicated, as it did progressively in India, or it may be reduced to its simplest expression, as happened in Greece and Iran, but it remains fundamentally the same throughout the Indo-European domain. The first step is to call the gods; this function is sometimes performed by a special priest (the "invoker": Sanskrit *hotar*, Avestic *soatar*, Gaulish *gutuater*, Germanic *gudja*) when the liturgy is highly elaborate; otherwise it is simply the first act of the person who is to offer the sacrifice (*hotar* also means "offerer of the oblation"). The call is sometimes as short as a few syllables (such as: "This offering for Mitra!") and sometimes amplified into a solemn hymn. In this case it is best to remind the being to whom the words are dedicated (the guest) of his exact titles and how he acquired them. If need be, the officiant can use the occasion to mention his own merits and to express the wishes that really motivate the ceremony (for nothing is ever free in this kind of religion: to sing someone's praises, or to thank him for benefits received, necessarily implies that this someone will surpass himself for the worshiper and grant new favors). Speech is one kind of offering, as is the preparation for the ceremony—the choice and preparation of the site (or decoration of the temple) and of the officiants (purification rites, special clothing, etc.).

Yet the true offering, it is said, consists of food. It can be either vegetable or animal in origin, but it must always be cooked, or at least have been in contact with fire. This is why almost everywhere we find the gods being offered breads, porridges, roast flesh (and fat). If we look a little closer we see two different procedures here: cooking, strictly speaking, gains its value from the effort that has been made to transform raw material into a new product bearing the distinctive sign of human skill; contact with fire is quite different, since it brings about the destruction of what is burned. In India the Brahman theologians explain that the gods eat the offering "through the mouth of Agni" (the god of fire, the *ignis* of the Latins, the *ogen* of the Slavs, the *ugnis* of the Lithuanians, etc.), or that the god takes the offering "in his arms" and carries it to the Immortals, and so forth. This concept was probably shared by all the Indo-Europeans, though we cannot confirm it since the priestly literature has disappeared almost everywhere outside India. What is important is that here the notion of sacrifice appears in its specificity: man sets aside a portion of his inherited goods and offers it to the gods.

The gift, of course, is effective only when it does not return—in this case, when the designated portion disappears (is destroyed). That is why, for example, wild animals cannot be sacrificed: only a domestic animal taken from a householder's stock can provide a victim worthy of being offered. It follows that prisoners of war (future slaves) can be killed sacrificially, and even, though very exceptionally, objects can be destroyed (there is the case of the Tectisagic Celts who threw the booty from the sack of Delphi into the lake so that the gods would cure an epidemic that was decimating them). When we reach the point of throwing coins into fountains, as the Gauls of the Roman period did, we are on the verge of passing from religion to superstition; yet even this act still retains something of the sacrificial spirit.

The notion of the destruction of the offering does not mean that the offering should be completely burned: the meal offered to the gods is shared with men, as is the custom in secular banquets. When the animal has been immolated, only a piece of it is detached and thrown into the hearth (in practice, a little fat), while the rest is cooked and eaten by the priests and the worshipers. And we know that in Rome and Greece the sacrifices of the first century A.D. were nothing more than a kind of ritual slaughtering (which led to the question the first Christians asked Saint Paul: When we go to the butcher, may we buy meat that has been "offered" to the pagan gods?). Sacrifice is thus a communal rite, an occasion for men to "feast with the gods" as they will do after death, if they obtain the grace of going to heaven. There are some exceptions: not only the (somewhat "heretical") one of the destruction of material wealth, but also the case of certain ceremonies that are dedicated to the gods "below." In Greece, the victim chosen for the chthonic deities was slaughtered in a pit dug for the purpose: the animal's blood flowed as a libation, and the bloodless corpse was totally burned "in a holocaust." The human victims sacrificed by the Celts were treated similarly, which means that they were not sacrificed in the strict sense of the word (the heads of certain victims, for instance, were preserved, while by definition nothing that has been offered to the gods should remain).

One special type of ceremony involves the preparation and consumption of a "drink of immortality" (in Greek *ambrosia*, in Sanskrit *amṛta*, "non-dead"), which, for reasons of secrecy, is often called only "juice" (Sanskrit *soma*, Iranian *haoma*). It is stated that the gods above (the Olympians, the Ādityas, the Sovereigns) regularly drink this nectar, which assures them of eternal life. There is evidence that in certain circles it was believed that only the consumption of ambrosia allowed the gods not to die. The "Twilight of the Gods" will begin, they said, when men cease to offer the "sacred juice" to the Immortals (in India it is still believed that the world will come to an end once the last Brahman has performed the last sacrifice). It is thus a pious duty for men to prepare this drink for the gods, and at the same time it is the guarantee that those who offer (and drink) it will go to heaven after they die ("We have drunk the nectar, we have become gods!").

All the evidence suggests that this kind of "magic potion" was not accessible to just anyone: the Veda says explicitly that it is the appanage of warriors and Brahmans, but afterward it was also granted to people of the third function, and thus to the whole body of *āryas* (but to the exclusion, naturally, of all others: servants, foreigners, etc.). In Greece it would have been said that it was for citizens, but not for resident foreigners and slaves. But in Greece the "soma" sacrifice seems to have disappeared by the classical period. We must stress the uncertainty still, since at a certain period ceremonies using ambrosia fell into marked disfavor. In Iran, for example, Zoroaster absolutely forbade their performance (along with that of blood sacrifices) around the seventh century B.C. In historical times, soma also disappears from India and seems to be maintained only in a rather veiled form among the Celts, Teutons, and Slavs. This fall from favor is probably due to the fact that the consumption of the drink of immortality produced a specific type of intoxication whose effects made a strong impression on nonparticipants. The drinker "went out of himself" and, for a time, "visited the gods." Hymns of the Ṛg Veda celebrate the soma which allows the drinker to go up to the sky, the place of eternal light, joyous with dance, music, and song. In the image of the god of battles, a great lover of nectar, warriors forget their fear, believe themselves invincible, and perform extraordinary feats. We know that when they were first permitted to drink the sacred liquid, the young warriors went through the cities in wild bands and committed all kinds of excesses. What is more, the cult of the "nectar" seems to have been linked with some of the bloodiest rites of Indo-European religion. All these things express the latent opposition between the third social class and the first two, and certainly contributed to the disappearance of this type of sacrifice.

We should add that there is still debate about the exact nature of the plant which, at the earliest period, provided the sacred "juice." According to one recent theory (which appears to be the most convincing), soma was a preparation made from the pulp of a hallucinogenic mushroom of the northern temperate zone, the *Amanita muscaria* (the "fly agaric"), a parasite of the roots of beech trees. It continued to be consumed in Russia and Siberia at least up to the seventeenth century, if we can believe the reports of the evangelists who sought to wipe out "paganism" in these regions. Quite early, when the soma sacrifice became obsolete (or was forbidden), it was replaced by the drinking of alcohol (*surā* in India; *oinos*, "wine," in Greece) or fermented drinks (beer, mead) on the occasion of festivals—all of which, at this period, were religious in character. In certain sectors of the Indo-European domain (notably in India and Iran), soma sacrifices continued to be performed, but with the help of substitutes (explicitly presented as such) for the sacred plant: today's Zoroastrians (the Parsi community of Bombay and the Ghebers of Iran), for example, use only a few drops of the anodyne *ephedra* (in the same way that throwing a little animal fat in the fire replaces the ancient blood sacrifice). It is interesting to note, however, that even in Iran, where Zoroaster's preaching was particularly virulent against Haoma and the killing of animal victims, the ritualists could not help reinserting these two elements into the ceremony—proof of their importance.

Domestic Rituals

We must remember that the great sacrifices were not the only means of putting oneself under the protection of the gods. On the contrary, it was the domestic rituals that constituted the basis of Indo-European religion. They alone were obligatory: one could not be an *ārya* (a citizen, a Roman, etc.) without having undergone the ritual initiation of adolescents (Vedic *upanayana*, Iranian *naojote*, the Roman *toga praetexta*, etc.). This status was lost if one failed to perform domestic worship; it was quite possible, on the other hand, to live one's whole life without ever offering a "great sacrifice." Moreover, the domestic ritual was not complicated: it consisted essentially of maintaining the household fire and using it regularly for oblations to the fire god himself and to the family divinities (the gods of the pantheon who were particularly linked with one clan or another).

As an example, let us describe the Vedic *agnihotra* ("oblation in the fire"): just before dawn (when the east begins to brighten but before the sun appears), the head of the family (*gṛha-pati*, "master of the house") revives the "householder's" fire (*gārhapatya*, derived from the preceding word), then milks his cow (or has the cow milked and the milk brought to him); he takes a spoonful of the milk and presents it to Agni (the god of fire), then pours it into the fire as a sacrificial offering, dedicated to the divinities of his choice (in the right order: Agni, then the sun god, the goddesses Night and Dawn, the Aśvins/Dioscuri. . .). It is explicitly stated that this morning sacrifice has the double object of making the sun rise and of guaranteeing the prosperity of the family. In a patriarchal society like that of the Indo-Europeans, the paterfamilias officiates for the good of all the members of the extended family. His wife assists him silently (in the Veda it is prescribed that she be behind her husband and hold onto his clothing to mark her participation in the common work). When the sun is up, a prayer of thanksgiving is recited and the milk that has been consecrated by the rite is drunk.

The *agnihotra* must have been done primarily by people of the third class (pastoralists, farmers, artisans, merchants) and additionally by Brahmans "who have a cow." Warriors also profited from the *agnihotra* by associating themselves with it "in thought" (recitation of a morning prayer) or by sending gifts to the sacrificers. The rustic nature of this rite, its simplicity, but at the same time its perfect fit with the "great" sacrifice are proof of its archaism, that is, of its Indo-European character. We should note in passing that the *gārhapatya* hearth was round, as was the temple of Vesta in Rome, where the sacred fire was maintained. The "guarding of the fire" appeared to foreign observers to be one of the typical characteristics of each of the Indo-European peoples, to the extent that the "establishment of the fire" often symbolically marked the annexation of a conquered territory:

this was an absolute rule in Iran (still in force in the Sassanid period, the third century A.D.), in India in the earliest period, and probably in other parts of the domain as well. The marriage ritual also provides evidence of the family's identification with the hearth: the first part of the ceremony takes place at the girl's home, where her father solemnly gives the bride to her suitor (or to his representatives) in the presence both of the god who watches over the sacred fire of his clan and of the other divinities of the family altar, the Lares and Penates. The second part of the ceremony takes place in the groom's house, where the new bride is solemnly presented at the hearth of her parents-in-law: the fire and the family divinities adopt her, in the strong sense of the word, so that her children will have the right to bear her husband's name.

It is easy to understand that the central place accorded to the ritual fire in the administration of the sacred should have led the Indo-Europeans to valorize the cremation of their dead. We suppose, on the basis of a great deal of evidence—notably archaeological data: tumuli (*Kurgan*) erected in the Ukraine, then in Central Europe between the fifth and third millennia B.C.—that burial (or exposure of the body) was the initial practice. It was after this that burning the dead came to appear as a final sacrifice in which the head of the family offered himself as sacrificial victim. An impressive ceremony took place, in the course of which the wives of the dead man were burned along with him, as were the instruments of his power—his chariot, his boat, his weapons, etc.—as well as "samples" of his wealth—slaves, cattle, jewels, clothing, etc. There are many reports of this kind of ritual, the most recent in date being the funeral of a Viking on the banks of the Volga, recorded in 922 by the Arab diplomat Ibn Fadhlan (cf. J. Broensted, *The Vikings*, London, 1965, p. 301). The Veda presents a more "toned-down" version of the same rites: the son goes up onto the funeral pyre, takes his father's bow, and invites his mother to come down from the pyre before he lights the fire; but we know that in India the sacrifice of widows at their husbands' funerals continued up to the nineteenth century. The privilege of cremation extended progressively to wider strata of the population (this happened in Rome, India, and Greece), but it could be combined with the practice of burial (for example: the burial of an urn containing the ashes of the dead) and with the custom of raising funerary monuments (tumuli, mausoleums, tombs).

Myths

We can assume—in the absence of decisive proof—that the different types of funerals corresponded to specific beliefs about eschatology. Such beliefs are very complex, to the point of appearing contradictory at first. Nevertheless, if we reduce the many mythological stories to their central theme (or their structure), coherence reappears.

Eschatology

According to one type of eschatological promise, life after death—conditioned by the merits and demerits of the individual—begins with a journey. The soul separates from the body at the moment of death and goes forward, sometimes guided by a psychopomp, until it reaches an obstacle: a river or a chasm. To get over this, the soul must obtain the services of a ferryman, and, depending on whether it can get these services, it enjoys the delights of paradise or suffers in hell. The most developed form of this myth is found in the Avesta, where the test is a Bridge of Selection (Chinvat): here the soul is met by its own conscience (*daēnā*) which either brings it across the bridge or else hurls it into the freezing darkness of hell. In one variant of this theme (Greece, India, etc.), the obstacle consists of a judgment rendered by various judges (one of whom is often the first man): the moral value of the person's acts is gauged (often weighed) and the sentence is without appeal. The tribunal nearly always sits in an underground chamber (and so can be reached through caverns that lead to shadowy underground passages); fierce guardians, notably dogs, stand watch at the entrance. This early type of belief appears to be closely tied to ritual, for the Greeks, the Latins, and to a lesser degree the Indians believed that not celebrating the funerary rites was enough to exclude the deceased from the Elysian Fields, whatever his virtues may have been. Even after arriving in this abode of delights, the souls of the good (which have become Manes) remain dependent on the living: they must be offered sacrifices (libations, gifts of food), for just as the gods subsist by virtue of ambrosia, the fathers survive on the oblations dedicated to them.

A second type of eschatological narrative portrays direct access to the world of the gods. The best model is that of the warrior who falls valiantly on the field of battle; psychopomps (Germanic Valkyries, Indian Apsarases, etc.) seize his soul and carry it off to the feasting place of the gods: the Veda and the Norse epics enthusiastically describe the greeting of the heroes by those who went before and by the "daughters of heaven" who will henceforth be their consorts. This road, which the Indians called "solar" (since the world of the gods is "beyond the sun," where eternal light shines), is open to all in the community who have done their duty—even their peaceful duty—with particular zeal. Thus the criterion here is an ethical and no longer a strictly ritual one, even though, in a culture like that of the ancient Indo-Europeans, communal service cannot be dissociated from "piety." It is also sometimes said in the same context that the supreme psychopomp is the fire god: when the body is cremated, he takes the soul of the deceased in his arms, just as he takes the offerings thrown into the hearth, and carries it to the gods. This is a a mythical justification for ritual cremation, which, as we have seen, was understood as a sacrifice with the dead person as the offering.

On the other hand, the Indo-Europeans certainly believed in reincarnation. The belief is evident among the Celts and the Indians, but there are also veiled traces of it throughout the domain (numerous stories of "returns" to earthly life). It is likely that the dead were initially believed to come back to life in their own family upon the birth of a child, perhaps to use up the potentialities of their being through progressive realization; once these had been fully realized, reincarnation was no longer necessary and the soul could "rest" in death. This belief was, however, in conflict with the other two: it took the dialectical genius of the Brahman theologians, alone in the entire domain, to harmonize these diverse eschatologies. For the Brahmans, the holy go to heaven and dwell there with the gods until the end of time; the wicked suffer in hell, depending upon the extent of their crimes; the people in between (the immense majority!) first become Manes, then return to earth to live other lives in conditions determined by the weight of their acts (karman). But it should be noted that this synthesis was worked out in India only after the end of the Vedic period, and so at a time when the religion was moving away from the ancient Indo-European model.

All these views of the afterlife are complicated by the belief in fate, a mysterious force that rules all beings, including the gods. Mention is made, for instance, of three women "weaving the fate" of each individual (Moirai, Parcae, Norns, Laimos, etc.: all the Indo-European peoples speak of them, and all describe them in identical terms). But if all our actions are in the hands of these women, what happens to our merits, and how can we understand our punishment or reward? What good is it to pray to the gods when they, too, are subject to this blind force? We see that the problem of predestination and grace is not only a Christian one. The Indo-Europeans seem to have held that fate is really the expression of the necessary interlinking of our actions (the law of causality); from this point on, my will (or that of a god who intervenes in the course of things) appears as a "materialization" of my fate; I can be a hero if I want to; and if I become a hero (if my will has been strong enough, if the gods haven't been against me, etc.), we can justifiably say that such was my fate. This is obviously valid for all living beings, including gods; but the gods, since they are superior to us, have wills of almost unlimited force: thus fate can be called "divine," i.e. "of the gods," as it is in the Veda (daivam).

The Organization of the Pantheon

Fate (or, more precisely, the government of the world) is not in the hands of just any god: it is allotted to those gods whom the Greeks called Olympians. The gods of the underworld, while awesome, dangerous, hard to propitiate, still play a subordinate role in the organization of the pantheon. Hades the Invisible, the Infernal Judges, administer an important province (the domain of the dead, the subterranean fire), but one that is only a part of the universe. As much could be said for the innumerable "spirits" (for they are scarcely gods) who inhabit springs, rivers, trees, caves, cliffs; those, too, who circulate in the lower atmosphere: winds, various meteorological phenomena, shooting stars. All of these spirits appear more or less as servants, and, in certain cases, their position is not an enviable one (there are many legends of characters condemned to play these kinds of roles, who can be freed from their condition by a hero or a god). All the Indo-European peoples tended to multiply these "godlings" indefinitely (there is the famous passage in which Saint Augustine mocks pagan beliefs about them), but no Indo-European people ever questioned the sovereignty of the gods above, who were called the "celestials" or the "shining ones" (Sanskrit deva, Lithuanian dievas, Germanic teiwa, Latin deus, Iranian daeva, Irish dia, etc; all derive from a root meaning "luminous sky").

This does not mean that the relations between the great gods are easy to decipher. Here too, in fact, we find ourselves facing a multitude (three thousand, three hundred and three gods, says the Veda) that is riven with disputes about precedence and composed of individuals with attributes that are disconcerting at first glance—disconcerting since they are contradictory, at least to our eyes. Still, we must not forget that the worshipers themselves knew perfectly well what they were doing, knew which god to ask for what, and when, and how. The confusion is thus only apparent, and is a result of our ignorance. It is because the Indo-Europeans never ceased to affirm the majesty and harmony of the pantheon that historians of religions have tried so hard to put some order into our information on the organization of the divine. Besides the naturalistic interpretation (solar mythology, gods of the storm and rain, etc.) and the interpretation that highlights moral values (gods of truth or of oaths, gods who punish or reward), and without discussing references, today abandoned, to a questionable "primitivism" (mana, totem, taboo), there now exists a "sociological" presentation of the Indo-European pantheon. Developed since 1934 in the works of Georges Dumézil, this theory has gradually won over the majority of researchers working on the religious forms of the different sectors of the Indo-European domain.

Schematically, Dumézil's reasoning is as follows: the Indo-Europeans believed that divine society was organized in a way similar to that of human society (or: the latter reflected that of the gods, its model), with, consequently, a harmonious division of labor under the authority of equally specialized sovereigns. Now the social organization of the Indo-Europeans was based on the division of the community of free men (*ārya* in Sanskrit, *airya* in Iranian, etc.) into three great functions covering the administration of the sacred ("spiritual" power, "magico-religious" sovereignty), the exercise of physical force ("temporal" power, the "warrior" function, the nobility) and the production of wealth (pastoralists, farmers, artisans, merchants, etc.). Below this elite, a mass of servants (or slaves) formed a fourth class excluded from all forms of autonomous power. Following one of the constants of Indo-European ideology, these functions were hierarchized: the maintenance of cosmic order depended above all on the stability of the relations among these various "classes," and any imbalance (for example, the second function trying to take the place of the first) must ineluctably lead to a breakdown of this fragile order (in which case the sky, said the Gauls, would fall to the earth). Projected into the divine world, this vision of society led to a division of the gods into three broad groups. In India, for example, the sovereigns were Mitra and Varuṇa (assisted by Aryaman and Bhaga); the warriors were Indra and Vāyu (assisted by the Maruts and Viṣṇu); the third function was represented by the two Aśvins (assisted by Pūṣan and several others). In Rome there were Jupiter (and Dius Fidus), Mars, and, in the third position, Quirinus (Vofionus). Among the Teutons, Óðinn (Wotan) and Týr in the first position, followed by Þórr the warrior, then Freyr and Njörðr.

The similarities in these domains are striking: Indra and Þórr both wield throwing weapons; both are great lovers of intoxicating drinks (soma, beer, mead); both are possessed of a mysterious power ("furor") which drives them to do heroic acts; both are capable of sins that must be expiated, etc. Such similarities cannot be fortuitous, especially since they are not isolated but are defined in relation to the roles played by the other gods. The first function, for example, includes a jurist (calm, serene, overseeing, etc.) and a "frowning" chief (as the Greeks called Zeus), who "storms," punishes, rewards, and keeps the secrets of wisdom. Óðinn and Varuṇa represent this latter type of sovereign to perfection, while Mitra, Týr, and Dius Fidus are good examples of the former type. In this way we can understand that the warlike attributes of Varuṇa, Óðinn, or Zeus do not in themselves make them gods of war. A Roman would know perfectly well that war was the preserve of Mars (for a Greek, Ares; for a Norseman, Thor; for an Indian, Indra; etc.). After all, while the gods of the second function actually fight, those of the first intervene only on the level of magic: they "confound" the wicked (or drive them "mad") and so leave them at the mercy of the good. They would never be neutral (since any war involves the cosmic order), but neither would they take the place of the combatants.

Another example: Jupiter and Zeus are masters of the thunderbolt and the rain. Does this mean that they are "agrarian" or "natural" divinities? Not at all. But the major atmospheric phenomena (the stars in their courses, storms, control of time and weather) belong exclusively to the first function because they are the concrete expression of the governance of the world: it is the great gods, and they alone, who laid down the path the sun must follow, it is their "decrees" that fixed the length of the sun's journey, the alternation of the seasons, the distribution of beings and things on the earth's surface, and so forth. Thus it is both right and necessary to give thanks to Zeus if it has been a good year, in agriculture, among other things (or in the increase of family wealth), but this does not prevent anyone from worshiping Ceres for making the wheat sprout (inversely, it would not occur to a Greek to give thanks to Ceres for the administration of the universe). Similarly, the gods of the second function could be thanked for having gotten the community "good pasturelands," not because they are "agrarian" gods but because war was a way of seizing fertile lands. Thus neither the Roman Mars nor the Iranian Mithra (who inherited the attributes of the warrior god whose worship had been forbidden by Zoroaster) presides over germination: they are gods of conquest, "breakers of resistance" (Verethraghna in Iran, Indra Vṛtrahan in India). Even when a furrow is traced in their honor, it is as the symbolic marker of the "Aryan" control over the land through the use of violence (for the plow tears the soil like a sword).

The Dumézilian explanation also has the advantage of allowing us to understand the ambiguous status of the gods of the third level. Thanks to the Veda, we know that they had a hard time getting admitted into the community made up of the gods of the first two functions. It was for these gods, not for the Aśvins, that the soma was pressed, and many legends explain how the Aśvins finally obtained their share in the sacrifice. This rivalry illuminates, among the Germanic tribes, the rivalry between the Aesir (sovereigns and warriors) and the Vanir (Freyr, Njörðr). It may parallel (but this is less clear) one opposition between Asuras and Devas in India and Iran—as well as that between gods and Titans in Greece, but this last is even more questionable. These tensions in the world of the gods probably correspond to confrontations that could have occurred in Indo-European societies: in Greece, for example, the priestly class was progressively eliminated, as was the aristocracy; among the Germanic peoples, the military function held the foremost place at the time they entered history; in India, the Brahmans clericalized the society as a whole; only the Celts seem to have maintained a balance among the three functions, according to the descriptions of their nations by Greek and Latin authors. But we must not forget that the documents concerning the various peoples of this domain date from very different periods: the imbalance among the functions may have occurred only recently (first millennium B.C.). It does, however, affect the mythology and probably accounts for the disappearance of certain gods in certain provinces of the domain.

This is not, however, to say that everything in Indo-European mythology is clear—far from it. The works of Georges Dumézil, himself heir to earlier scholars, have opened a path on which work has barely begun. But problems remain, starting with that of the sun god (and the correlated problem of the moon god): his preponderance in the Indo-European religious universe cannot be denied (think of the importance of Apollo for the Greeks, Mithra for the Iranians, Saule for the Balts, etc.), but his place is not clearly determined in the balance of the three functions (especially when there are traces throughout the domain of a legend recounting a battle waged against the sun god, whose chariot was damaged not by the demons but by other gods). Another problem involves female divinities. The pantheon is no less patriarchal than was the society of the times; goddesses, therefore, have subordinate status. Yet they are present at all levels, since it is understood that every god has his consort. There are, however, autonomous goddesses, including some of great prestige: Athena, Minerva, Anāhitā, Freyja, Uṣas, Epona. Some of these visibly belong to the third function (such as Freyja, Anāhitā). Others seem polyvalent; according to Dumézil, Minerva is among these, her attributes being the bird of wisdom (first function), the spear (second function), and the olive branch (third function). The question of the mother goddess is still disputed: the Indo-Europeans do not seem to have had such a figure in their pantheon: neither Juno, nor Hera, nor the relatively undefined wives of Óðinn or Varuṇa play this role. The other goddesses are all unmarried women (Athena, Artemis, Anāhitā, Saule, Sūryā, Uṣas), either virgins or sexual partners. They may have children, but they are not "mothers" in the symbolic sense of the term (there is no image of Juno nursing a child).

The catalog of our uncertainties could go on indefinitely, but this would be of interest only to whet the appetites of potential researchers. The important thing, the main fact, is that as a whole, in its major lines, in its fundamental structure, Indo-European mythology has now been illuminated. It took a hundred and fifty years to reach this result; surely the coming decades will bring their own contribution to an undertaking which, all in all, has only just begun.

J.V./j.l.

BIBLIOGRAPHY

P. BOSCH-GIMPERA, *Les Indo-Européens* (Paris 1961). J. HAUDRY, *Les Indo-Européens* (Paris 1979). G. DEVOTO, *Origini Indo-Europee* (Florence 1962). W. KOPPERS et al., *Die Indo-Germanen* (Leipzig 1936). A. SCHERER et al., *Die Urheimat der Indo-Germanen* (Darmstadt 1968). E. BENVENISTE, *Vocabulaire des institutions indo-européennes*, 2 vols. (Paris 1969). H. LOMMEL, *Die alten Arier* (Frankfurt 1935), also in French. G. DUMÉZIL, *Les dieux des Indo-Européens* (Paris 1952). C. SCOTT-LITTLETON, *The New Comparative Mythology* (Berkeley 1966). J. PUHVEL et al., *Myth and Law among the Indo-Europeans* (Berkeley 1970). S. WIKANDER, *Der arische Männerbund* (Lund 1938).

THE MYTHS AND NARRATIVES OF THE CELTS OF THE ISLANDS

Pioneer research in the second half of the nineteenth century and the beginning of the twentieth led to the first bold theories in the study of Celtic mythology. Most of these efforts concerned the etymology of names of gods and of heroes and heroines and the interpretation of stories as allegories of natural phenomena, particularly of day and night, the sun, the moon, dawn, thunder, etc. Later, when such speculations were rejected, the subject itself fell into disfavor. Textual and linguistic studies of the sources continued, however, and there was still interest in separating the mythological from the historical. A great number of oral traditions were carefully collected and some attempts were made to retrace individual stories through their successive stages. An overall study which was widely accepted as a guide by some specialists in the Celtic world was *The Growth of Literature*, by H. M. and N. K. Chadwick, 1932–40, in which the ancient literature of the British Isles appeared as one of the elements of a broad attempt to discover the general principles behind the whole history of the literature based on oral traditions. The authors noted the "parallel developments resulting from similar social and political conditions" and gave a fundamental importance to the concept of a heroic age. Still more easily acceptable were the classifying and indexing of traditional stories and their component elements according to rules developed by Scandinavian and American scholars and the study of the diffusion of types and motifs. Medieval legends which previous generations had supposed to be Celtic myths now appeared to be examples of international folktales which were judged to have deteriorated or been confused if, in the light of the common sense of today, they were less easy to understand than their modern-day parallels.

During the 1930s and 1940s, other types of analyses were applied to the nature and meaning of traditional narratives. Besides various psychoanalytic interpretations, there was the work of Vladimir Propp, whose careful examination of a major (and perhaps even central) category of folktales led him to the "totally heretical" conclusion that they merited the "ancient and today rejected name of mythical narrative." Then came the theories and studies of the "myth and ritual" school, among which was Lord Raglan's analysis of the lives of mythical heroes. And finally, Benveniste and Hocart also discovered connections between the four-caste system so basic to ancient India and the ideologies and social organization of other peoples. During this period, however, no new analysis of Celtic mythology was published along any of these various lines of thought (but see Rees 1936). The mythology described in Thomas F. O'Rahilly's very detailed book, *Early Irish History and Mythology* (1946), could for the most part be reduced to the struggle between a hero and a "god of the other world" (a god of "many functions and many aspects"), with prominence given to sun gods and weapons flashing like lightning and much recourse to the etymology of proper nouns.

The concise and lucid book by Marie-Louise Sjoestedt, *Dieux et héros des Celtes* (1940), opened up a new approach, and in the few years that followed, Georges Dumézil was already including the interpretations of the Irish narrative about the Second Battle of Magh Tuiredh in several of the comparative analyses through which he had begun to retrace the ramifications of the ideology of the "three functions": (1) connections with the sacred, sovereignty, knowledge; (2) the use of force, the role of the warrior and king; (3) the attainment of riches, health, beauty, harmony, abundance, "quantity." This ideology was often discovered in the study of various mythologies, both by him and by other specialists. Recently it was even suggested that the three states of medieval Europe derived principally from the Celtic tradition. Thus even though it was still standard among specialists in the Celtic world to disdain "the murky depths of comparative mythology," and even though it was still maintained that "the insular mythology . . . is anarchical and shows nothing that resembles a system as other mythologies do," some dissident voices began to be heard. Françoise Le Roux-Guyonvarc'h, for example, stated unequivocally: "As far as we are concerned, we have studied Celtic tradition only in order to restore its importance as an area of study" (*Ogam*, 19 [1967], p. 344n). Other researchers also felt that the myths were a trail, a world of symbols and meanings which were lived as such and which could live on in man's imagination and continue to shape his very existence even after people had stopped believing them.

Narratives of which the characters, situations, and themes are as far removed as possible from the teachings of the Scriptures and ecclesiastic tradition are found in manuscripts dating back to eleventh-century Ireland and thirteenth-century Wales, and the study of their characteristics, linguistic and other, show that certain of these traits had already been observed several centuries earlier. The oldest of these texts were written in monasteries, and nothing directly proves that any of the narratives existed during the pagan era. But aside from the fact that it would seem strange that the first Christians "devoted themselves with such energy to giving Ireland (and Wales) a fine pagan literature which they would otherwise have lacked," comparative analysis verifies that many of these legendary narratives belong to ancient traditions.

Learning the traditional narratives, among which many survived, was of primary importance in the long and difficult apprenticeship of poets, who enjoyed considerable power and social status. In Ireland, these scholarly guardians of tradition were equal to kings before the law; the poets enthroned the kings, supported them with panegyrics, and, when necessary, destroyed them with their satires. They were the genealogists and historians of royalty, the authorities in matters of royal duties and prerogatives. They prepared incantations and devoted themselves to divination and prophecies. It is also said that in one period, they were judges: some parts of the oldest legal texts are in fact written in the form of archaic poetry. According to some admittedly scanty evidence, the traditional narratives were recited during winter evenings and regular provincial assemblies and also at other solemn occasions such as weddings, taking possession of a new house, the night before a battle, taking possession of an inheritance or patrimony, the feast held for a prince, the departure on a voyage or hunt, and the beginning of a judiciary session. Since the narratives were classified under the rubrics of the genre, such as "Battles," "Voyages," "Feasts," "Cattle Raids," "Marriage Quests," "Births," etc., it is reasonable to assume that the subject of the narrative was related to the event in question, so that past battles were evoked on the eve of new ones, as is indicated in one or two stories, and "sad stories of the death of kings" were integrated into the ritual accompanying such deaths. Those who listened to these narratives with the reverence they deserved were assured of safety, victory, success, and prosperity; a legend from Irish folklore, faithful to tradition, shows the Devil absolutely incapable of entering a house where stories of the life of a hero are being recited.

Although these narratives were transmitted and elaborated for centuries by Christians who may not have understood them very clearly, it has become more and more apparent that they contained a symbolism as coherent as it was complex, and that everything that they included—such as dates, places, actions, kinship connections, the qualities and deeds of this or that character, directions, colors, animals, etc.—might be significant in a way that would require the most patient examination and a certain amount of intuition in order to be fully understood.

It is also evident that the ideology of the three "functions" not only appears sporadically in the narratives, but structures the entire tradition. Thus, Irish narratives encompass, first, the *Mythological Cycle*, the principal characters of which belong to the people of the goddess Danann, the Tuatha Dé Danann, magicians, about whom it is recorded that their men of art were gods (*dée*) and their farmers were *andée* (non-gods? giant-gods?); second, the *Heroic Cycle*, which deals with the imperial noble warriors of Ulaidh (Ulster); and third, the *Ossianic Cycle*, narratives about the *Fiana*, the bands of young vagabonds, hunters, and fighters who lived in the forests and wild regions. The *Historic Cycle* includes narratives of various types about kings and royalty.

The eleven Welsh narratives known today by the name of *Mabinogi* include, first, *The Four Branches of the Mabinogi* and *The Story of Lludd and Llefelys*, two cases where the three functions appear prominently, but where the first is supreme and the third subordinate; second, the three Arthurian novels, *Peredur, Owain,* and *Gereint*, which have essentially the same structure as three of the narrative poems of Chrétien de Troyes, *Perceval, Yvain,* and *Erec*, of which each represents one of the three functions; and finally, three other narratives with no explicit connection between them: *The Dream of Macsen*, which one can view as the story of a quest for sovereignty; *The Dream of Rhonabwy* which deals exclusively with military matters; and the story of *Culhwch and Olwen*, which can be related to the third function.

An Irish narrative for which we have a text dating from the end of the Middle Ages tells of a dispute which arose under the reign of Diarmaid mac Cerbhaill (in the sixth century A.D.) regarding the boundaries of the royal kingdom of Temhair (anglicized to Tara). It explains how the scholars, nobles, and elders of the kingdom wanted the house of Temhair to be reorganized as it had been before their day and as it must remain forever. Fintan mac Bóchra, who had observed the entire history of Ireland since before the Flood, was called upon to give his opinion. He spoke of another, earlier judgment. On the day of Christ's Crucifixion, a person of divine nature appeared before the king of Ireland and his court. He was the one responsible for the rising and setting of the sun, and he remained among them for forty days. When in answer to his questions about the chronicles of deeds and heroic exploits in Ireland he learned that the Irish had no historians to whom this task could be assigned, he said, "You will have this thanks to me, and I will establish for you the succession of histories and chronicles of the house of Temhair with the four quarters of Ireland gathered around, for I am the truthful and wise witness who explains to all men that which they do not know." The seven wisest men from each "quarter" of Ireland, as well as the historians of the king of Temhair, were called before him, "for it is only just . . . that each one take his part in the chronicles of Temhair." And he asked Fintan how Ireland had been divided, "and where things were located." "It's very simple," Fintan replied, "knowledge to the west, combat to the north, prosperity to the east, music to the south, and royalty in the center." The august visitor then confirmed this arrangement, according to which each of the five provinces, Connachta (Connaught), Ulaidh (Ulster), Laighin (Leinster), Mumu (Munster), and Midhe (the "middle," Meath), received their appropriate part of the traditional legendry of Ireland.

It will appear clearly in our different headings that the distribution of these things among the different provinces mentioned by this legend is not an isolated imaginary trait but a true representation of "where things were located" in the realm of the narrative tradition. A similar arrangement is encountered in Welsh tradition, although the report that we have of it is less precise than the Irish narrative. In Wales, Gwynedd, which includes the island of Anglesey to the northwest, is regarded as the traditional province of great plans, boastful words, high births, wise men, and relics;

Powys, to the northeast, is the province of martial arts, where one had to be first in the line of battle and last to retreat. Glamorgan, in the southeast, like Laigin in Ireland, was credited with riches, generosity, courtesy, and high spirits, while Dyfed, to the southwest, similar to Mumu, was considered the place of mystery and paradox. This arrangement plays a part in the symbolism of the *Mabinogi*.

It has been shown that this qualitative arrangement of provinces has its parallel in the arrangement of the royal fortresses of the ancient Indian tradition, an order according to which priests had their place to the north, warrior-nobles to the east, farmers to the south, serfs to the west, and the gods and the king in the middle. An Indian structure for the gods—Varuṇa, the sovereign-magician in the west, Indra, the warrior in the north, Kubera, the lord of riches, in the east, and Yama, lord of the kingdom of death in the south—presents an even closer analogy to the Irish tradition. In a perhaps more unexpected way, among the Zuñis, the association of priests with the west, warriors with the north, dancers with the east, and doctors and farmers with the south, requires only the reversal of the two last "quarters" to be similar in structure to the Irish kingdom (see Rees, *Celtic Heritage*, 118–39, 173–85; Dumézil, *Mythe et épopée*, 2.253–54).

Two final remarks. First, the Gaelic (or Irish) language was introduced into Scotland from Ireland in such a way that all during the Middle Ages the two countries had the same culture. The little that remains of the literature of the end of the Middle Ages in Cornish and Breton, languages which are very close to Welsh, is almost entirely Christian and didactic. Second, the distance between the language of the oldest prose narrations and the current literary language is much greater in Irish than in Welsh. In their commentaries, most Irish scholars therefore retain the ancient spelling of proper nouns, while Welsh scholars generally make the slight changes which allow them to write medieval names according to modern usage. Certain contradictions in our accounts will result from this practice.

B.R./d.b.

BIBLIOGRAPHY

Points of departure for bibliographic research: R. I. BEST, *Bibliography of Irish Philology and of Printed Irish Literature* (Dublin 1913); *Bibliography of Irish Philology and Manuscript Literature* (Dublin 1942). *Bulletin bibliographique de la Société internationale arthurienne* (Paris 1949–).

Principal Texts

1. In Official Editions

R. I. BEST and O. BERGIN, *Lebor na huidre* (Dublin 1929). R. I. BEST, O. BERGIN, and M. A. O'BRIEN, *The Book of Leinster*, 1 (Dublin 1954). R. I. BEST and M. A. O'BRIEN, *The Book of Leinster*, 2–4 (Dublin 1956–67). J. GWENOGVRYN EVANS, *The White Book Mabinogion* (Pwllheli 1907); reprinted as *Llyfr Gwyn Rhydderch*, introduction by R. M. Jones (Caerdydd 1973). J. RHYS and J. GWENOGVRYN EVANS, *The Text of the Mabinogion and Other Welsh Tales from the Red Book of Hergest* (Oxford 1887).

2. Other Editions

a) Without Translations

Ireland: F. SHAW, *THE DREAM OF OENGUS* (Dublin 1934). M. DILLON, *Serglige Con Culainn* (Dublin 1953). E. KNOTT, *Togail Bruidne Da Derga* (Dublin 1936). W. MEID, *Die Romanz von Froech und Findabair* (Innsbruck 1970). B. Ó CUÍV, *Cath Muighe Tuireadh* (Dublin 1945). C. O'RAHILLY, *Cath Finntrágha* (Dublin 1962). R. THURNEYSEN, *Scéla Mucce Meic Dathó* (Dublin 1935). J. C. WATSON, *Mesca Ulad* (Dublin 1941). O. J. BERGIN et al., *Anecdota from Irish Manuscripts* (Halle 1907–13). D. GREENE, *Fingal Rónáin* (Dublin 1955). A. G. VAN HAMEL, *Immrama* (Dublin 1941); *Compert Con Culainn* (Dublin 1933). W. STOKES, "Acallamh na Senórach," *Irische Texte*, 4 (1900).

Wales: M. RICHARDS, *Breudwyt Ronabwy* (Caerdydd 1948). B. F. ROBERTS, *Cyfranc Lludd a Llefelys* (Dublin 1975). D. S. THOMSON, *Branwen uerch Lyr* (Dublin 1961). R. L. THOMSON, *Pwyll Pendeuic Dyuet* (Dublin 1957); *Owein* (Dublin 1968). I. WILLIAMS, *Breudwyt Maxen* (Bangor 1928); *Pedeir Keinc y Mabinogi* (Caerdydd 1930). G. W. GOETINCK, *Historia Peredur vab Efrawc* (Caerdydd 1976).

b) With Translations

Ireland: O. BERGIN and R. I. BEST, *Tochmarc Étaíne* (Dublin 1938). R. I. BEST, "The Settling of the Manor of Tara," *Ériu*, 4 (1910). E. GWYNN, *The Metrical Dindsenchas* (1903–35). G. HENDERSON, *Fled Bricrend* (London 1899). V. HULL, *Longes Mac n-Uislenn* (New York 1949). R. A. S. MACALISTER, *Lebor Gabála Érenn* (Dublin 1938–56). C. O'RAHILLY, *Táin Bó Cúalnge* (Dublin 1967). H. P. A. OSKAMP, *The Voyage of Máel Dúin* (Groningen 1970). W. STOKES, "The Second Battle of Moytura," *Revue celtique* 12 (1891): 52–130; "The Prose Tales in the Rennes Dindsenchas," *Revue celtique* 15 (1894–95); "The Bodleian Dinnshenchas," *Folk-lore*, 3 (1892); "The Edinburgh Dinnshenchas," *Folk-lore*, 4 (1893); "Cóir Anmann," *Irische Texte*, 3 (1897). E. WINDISCH, *Die altirische Heldensage Táin Bó Cúalnge* (Leipzig 1905). K. MEYER, *Fianaigecht* (Dublin 1910). S. H. O'GRADY, *Silva Gadelica* (London 1892). N. NÍ SHÉAGHDHA, *Tóraidheacht Dhiarmada agus Ghráinne* (Dublin 1967).

Wales: R. BROMWICH, *Trioedd Ynys Prydein* (Cardiff 1961). T. JONES, *The Black Book of Carmarthen, "Stanzas of the Graves"* (London 1969).

Translations

Ireland: CHRISTIAN-J. GUYONVARC'H, "La razzia des vaches de Cooley," *Ogam*, 15–16 (1963–64); "La mort de Cúchulainn," *Ogam*, 13 (1961); "La conception des deux porchers," "L'ivresse des Ulates," *Ogam*, 12 (1960); "La navigation de Bran, fils de Febal," "La mort du fils unique d'Aífe," *Ogam*, 9 (1957); "La maladie de Cúchulainn," *Ogam*, 10 (1958); "La courtise d'Emer," "Les exploits d'enfance de Cúchulainn," *Ogam*, 11 (1959); "Le rêve d'Oengus," *Ogam*, 18 (1966); "La mort tragique des enfants de Tuireann," *Ogam*, 16–17 (1964–65). "La nourriture de la maison des deux gobelets," *Celticum*, 18 (1969); "La courtise d'Etain," *Celticum*, 15 (1966), with commentary by F. Le Roux. T. KINSELLA, *The Táin* (Dublin 1969). T. P. CROSS and C. H. SLOVER, *Ancient Irish Tales* (London 1936). H. D'ARBOIS DE JUBAINVILLE, *L'épopée celtique* (Paris 1892). E. HULL, *The Cuchullin Saga* (London 1898).

Wales: J. LOTH, *Les Mabinogion* (Paris 1913). G. JONES and T. JONES, *The Mabinogion* (London 1948, 1974).

Studies

F. J. BYRNE, *Irish Kings and High-Kings* (London 1973). C. Z. CZARNOWSKI, *Le culte des héros et ses conditions sociales* (Paris 1919). H. D'ARBOIS DE JUBAINVILLE, *Le cycle mythologique irlandais* (Paris 1884). J. H. DELARGY, *The Gaelic Story-Teller* (London 1946). J. DE VRIES, *Keltische Religion* (Stuttgart 1961). M. DILLON, *The Archaism of Irish Tradition* (London 1949); *Early Irish Literature* (Chicago 1948); *The Cycles of the Kings* (London 1946). D. DUBUISSON, "L'Irlande et la théorie médiévale des trois ordres," *Revue de l'histoire des religions*, 1975, 35–63. G. DUMÉZIL, *Jupiter, Mars, Quirinus* (Paris 1941); *Servius et la fortune* (Paris 1943); *Mythe et épopée*, 3 vols. (Paris 1968, 1971, 1973). E. HULL, *Folklore of the British Isles* (London 1928). K. H. JACKSON, *The International Popular Tale and Early Welsh Tradition* (Cardiff 1961). T. GWYNN JONES, *Welsh Folklore and Folk-Custom* (London 1930). E. KNOTT and G. MURPHY, Introduction by James Carney, *Early Irish Literature* (London 1966). F. LE ROUX, *Les Druides* (Paris 1961); "Études sur le festiaire celtique," *Ogam*, 13–15 (1960–63). R. S. LOOMIS, *Wales and the Arthurian Legend* (Cardiff 1956). R. S. LOOMIS, ed., *Arthurian Literature in the Middle Ages* (Oxford 1959). P. MAC CANA, *Celtic Mythology* (Feltham 1970). J. A. MACCULLOCH, *The Religion of the Ancient Celts* (Edinburgh 1911); *Celtic Mythology* (Boston 1918). M. MACNEILL, *The Festival of Lughnasa* (Oxford 1962). K. MEYER and A. NUTT, *The Voyage of Bran, Son of Febal* (London 1895). G. MURPHY, *Duanaire Finn III* (Dublin 1953). T. F. O'RAHILLY, *Early Irish History and Mythology* (Dublin 1946). T. M. OWEN, *Welsh Folk Customs* (Cardiff 1959). A. D. REES, "The Divine Hero in Celtic Hagiology," *Folk-lore* 47 (1936): 30–41; "Modern Evaluations of Celtic Narrative Tradition,"

Proceedings of the Second International Congress of Celtic Studies (Cardiff 1966), 29–61. A. REES and B. REES, *Celtic Heritage* (London 1961). B. REES, *Ceinciau'r Mabinogi* (Bangor 1975). J. RHYS, *Lectures on the Origin and Growth of Religion as Illustrated by Celtic Heathendom* (London 1898); *Celtic Folklore* (Oxford 1901). A. ROSS, *Pagan Celtic Britain* (London 1967). M.-L. SJOESTEDT, *Dieux et héros des Celtes* (Paris 1940). R. THURNEYSEN, *Die irische Helden- und Königsage* (Halle 1921). A. G. VAN HAMEL, *Aspects of Celtic Mythology* (London 1935). M. DILLON, *Celts and Aryans* (Simla 1975).

THE RELIGION AND MYTHS OF THE CONTINENTAL CELTS OF GAUL

I. The Continental Celts

The cradle of the Celts appears to have been a region from the Rhine to Bohemia (inclusive). Their presence has been identified by the archaeology of the Second Iron Age (the last five centuries B.C.) or the era of La Tène (the station by that name on Lake Neufchatel in Switzerland). They spoke an Indo-European language, related to Latin, German, and Greek, from which the Gaelic of Ireland and Scotland and the Breton of Wales and Brittany are derived.

Beginning in the fifth century B.C., the Celts began a remarkable expansion through conquest (aided by their excellent iron weapons), raids, and mercenary armies. They occupied Spain, Gaul, northern Italy, Austria, Slovakia, Hungary, Rumania, and northern Yugoslavia. They crossed the rest of Yugoslavia, overran Greece and Bulgaria, and reached Asia Minor, where they founded the kingdom of Galatia and implanted the Celtic language. They took Rome in about 385, but gradually the Romans in revenge took over most of their territories, until they were left with only the British Isles. They began to settle there in the fourth century (perhaps earlier) in successive waves. They left regional names almost everywhere: Paris, Leiden, Milan, Coimbra, Vienna, Mainz, Bohemia, and many others are of Celtic origin.

In spite of the great diversity due to the variety of countries occupied and native cultures assimilated, Celtic culture had a strong unity which was expressed through Celtic language, art, coinage, and religion. The art of the Celts was imaginative and decorative, based on the play of curved lines and the fineness of reliefs, in direct opposition to the classical Greco-Roman order. Their religion, with its class of Druids, unique in antiquity, was original. Since the Celts did not commonly use writing before adopting the Latin alphabet, the records are most numerous during the Roman period.

The Celts never formed a nation or an empire. They lived as different peoples, having a kind of preurbanism, organized into tribes and groups of tribes. There is nevertheless a Celtic substratum in the history of ancient Europe.

II. The Gallic Clergy

Essentially disappearing shortly after the Romanization of Gaul, the Gallic clergy is known to us only through inadequate texts that sometimes contradict each other.

Druids are attested only in Gaul and Great Britain (as well as in Ireland, as we know only by their continued survival there today). The Celtic name "Druid" has two possible translations: "the very wise" and "those (priests?) of the oak tree." The Druids were the highest class of the clergy: they were organized into a kind of confraternity with judiciary powers and played a very important civil role. They were responsible in particular for the education of the sons of the aristocracy; custodians of scientific secrets and probably of the calendar, counselors of kings and then of oligarchs, they appear to have had, through their traditional bonds with their insular confreres, an influence or role in other Celtic countries, to which they also served as ambassadors. In Gaul they presided over human sacrifices.

Below and next to the Druids (though it is not possible to determine an exact hierarchy), we know of three other categories of people having something to do with religious matters. The *vātes* (a Gallic word related to the Latin word) were responsible for divination, and therefore had great power—especially since some writers even give them the same religious attributes as the Druids and the same knowledge of "physics." The bards were the official poets, authors, and singers and reciters of hymns and epic texts; they were particularly knowledgeable about genealogies and were probably responsible for keeping them up to date. Druids also had their bards, as did princes and war chiefs. More directly responsible for officiating over the cult, if their name is a reliable indication, were the *antistes templi* among the Boïens of Italy or the *gutuater*, "father of prayer," who was one of the clerics (the only one we know) of the Gallic and Gallo-Roman clergy.

Finally, there were types of witches or fanatic priestesses, particularly on an island in the Loire and on the island in the Seine. Under the Roman Empire, Druidesses would survive as tellers of good and bad fortune.

III. Sacrifices

1. Greek and Latin texts, as well as monuments and carved objects, tell us something about sacrifices practiced in pre-Roman Gaul. These were almost always human sacrifices, for which the Romans violently reproached the Gauls and which Tiberius (A.D.14–37) officially forbade. Such sacrifices were also attested in Britain in the second half of the first century (Tacitus, *Annales*, 14.29–30; Dion Cassius, 62.9 and 11).

Caesar described the following sacrifices: to Mars the Gauls "pledged, at the beginning of a battle, all that they would take; once they were victorious, they set fire to the living booty and piled the rest in one place" (*Bellum Gallicum* [*B.G.*], 6.17).

Among the Gauls, "one sees those who suffer from serious illnesses, or live in combat or in other dangers, sacrifice or vow to sacrifice human beings as victims. To arrange such sacrifices, they appeal to the Druid ministry. They believe that only by buying the life of one man with the life of another will the immortal gods be appeased, and there are sacrifices of this type which are a public institution. Some people have huge mannequins made of braided willow that they fill with living men. They set fire to these structures and the men perish in the flames" (*B.G.*, 6.16).

Lucan, under Nero (*Pharsale* 1.444–46), speaks of "those (among the peoples of Gaul) who appease with detestable blood the ferocious Teutates, the hideous Esus at his cruel hearth, and Taranis at altars no less inhuman than that of Scythian Diana." This is a reference to three of the greatest gods of Gaul, chosen also for their bloodthirsty habits.

A Latin commentary, known from a tenth-century manuscript, whose text dates back in some parts to the fourth, and in others to the seventh or ninth centuries, describes the types of sacrifices offered to these three Celtic gods assimilated, according to various sources, to various Roman gods:

Teutates-Mercury: "A man is plunged on his head into a filled half-cask in order to asphyxiate him." A scene of this type may be illustrated on a plaque of the Gundestrup basin (Denmark), a piece in gold and gilded silver, probably made in the "istro-pontic" region (Lower Danube and Black Sea) toward the beginning of the first century B.C. To the left of a file of warriors is a figure twice as large as the man he is holding upside-down and plunging into an object. The object is clumsily carved, but may be interpreted as a half-cask, circled and bound with horizontal and vertical metal bands. The narrow form of this receptacle, half of a lengthened barrel, may have been chosen so that the victim, whose shoulders were bound all around by the wall of the vessel, would not be able to move. The executioner, given his size, would here be the god of war himself, Teutates (the assimilation with Mercury made by the commentator does not seem substantiated), performing a sacrifice to himself in front of the warriors.

Esus-Mars: "A man is hung in a tree until his limbs go slack from the outpouring of his blood." The reason for suspending the victim must have been to allow the effects of the bloodletting to be verified more clearly than if he were on the ground, tied to a column or tree trunk. No relationship can

Gallic coin with a figure sitting cross-legged, perhaps a divinity.

be presumed between this sacrifice to Esus and the only two representations we have of the god (in Paris on the Nautes pillar and in Trèves on a stela dedicated to Mercury), where he is depicted cutting down a tree with a woodcutter's tool. Nothing indicates that trees, whether in a forest or at a place of worship, were particularly consecrated to Esus.

Taranis-Dis Pater: "In a wooden vat [or a mannequin? *alveus ligneus* designates a wooden 'container'], a certain number of men are burned." This sacrifice is so close to the one described by Caesar that one may assume that Caesar's text formed the basis of this commentary, after some details were changed.

Taranis-Jupiter: "Accustomed to being appeased with human heads in times past, he must now be content with heads of livestock." For the commentator, "times past" (*olim*) referred to the pre-Roman period, "now" (*nunc*) to the Imperial era. It thus appears that the free Gauls must have offered severed heads to Taranis, the Celtic equivalent of Jupiter, but also, according to the commentary, a "master of war." In this case the heads were probably those of enemies, although there may have been other victims as well.

The habit of cutting off the heads of dead adversaries is attested by a text of Posidonius, who witnessed it in southern Gaul toward the beginning of the first century (cited by Strabo, 4.4.5), though no sacrifice was involved. Elsewhere, pre-Roman fragments of porticos and lintels hollowed out

with cavities holding skulls (at Roquepertuse, Glanum, and Saint-Blaise) show that in the Bouches-du-Rhône region, human skulls were displayed in this fashion. Though it is impossible to determine whether the heads belonged to enemies that had been killed, executed prisoners, or victims executed in the course of a sacrifice or simply in order to be displayed, the ritual nature of such a custom does not seem to be in question.

According to Strabo (4.25), the Gauls "beat victims to death with arrows or impaled them in the temples; or, after constructing a giant of wood and straw, they pushed in livestock, wild animals of all kinds, and human beings and offered the whole lot in a holocaust."

2. During the Imperial era, the use of substitutes for human sacrificial victims was attested not only by the commentary of Lucan, cited earlier, but also by a text of Pomponius Mela (under Claudius), according to whom light wounds were inflicted instead of death blows (*De Chorographia*, 3.2).

Two types of offerings continued to be made to the deities: animals and food or drink. These were Roman rites, not limited to Gaul: the instruments of sacrifice were represented in various hierarchical patterns on votive monuments, and altars had the traditional arrangements for libations. All the cults, official or not, had their sacrifices, usually attested in regions other than the Celto-Roman provinces. At the most, one can point to the remarkable popularity in Gallo-Roman areas of the taurobolium: the sacrifice of a bull, whose blood pours down on an initiate, in the cults of Cybele and Mithras. Various factors may explain its success: the importance of Gallic mother goddesses, which could only have facilitated the acceptance of the Great Mother imported by the Greeks and Romans; the presence of legions on the Rhine, who popularized the Mithraic religion (whose consolations and promises for the afterlife ensured its diffusion); and the existence of a flourishing herd, providing valuable animals to sacrifice.

IV. The Myths

The continental Celtic myths attested by Greek and Latin texts and by carved monuments or objects are few and are limited mostly to Gaul, where they survive on Gallic coins and Gallo-Roman monuments. One object of great value, the gilded silver basin found at Gundestrup (Denmark), is practically the only work of art showing allegorical scenes: made in the first half of the first century B.C., probably in the Black Sea region, it proves the antiquity of certain mythic elements across Celtic Europe and the areas influenced by the Celts.

Greek and Latin texts do not attribute anything properly called Celtic to Gaul, but they do include this country (or Spain) in Mediterranean legends, such as that of the return of Heracles from Iberia to Greece across southern Gaul, mentioning cities that he founded (Alesia) and battles that he won (in the Crau). There has been no success to date in identifying indigenous legends retold in the Greek or even Latin fashion in these stories, which are especially about the founding of cities, particularly Lugdunum (Lyons).

Before the Roman epoch, Gallic coins illustrated, without naming them, scenes or subjects which can only be related to legends we do not know. The naked female warriors and the horsewoman whose head has horns are probably mythological beings. The transformation of the harnessed chariot on Macedonian coins into a single flying horse driven by a fantastic being derived from a coachman evidently belongs in

Gilded silver basin discovered at Gundestrup. Copenhagen, Nationalmuseet.

the realm of legend, particularly when the animal has a human head that sometimes even wears a helmet. When instead of a driver there is a naked acrobat soaring above the horse, this may be a memory of the "salmon leap" that the hero in Irish epics performed on the shaft of his chariot, above his mount. The head, which seems to have a spoke coming out of it and is surrounded by four small severed heads attached by cords of pearls, may recall the hero Cú Chulainn who throughout the insular literature has a stream of blood spurting from his head like a mast and is surrounded by the "skulls of Bodb" that flutter about his head. Other images on coins evoke metamorphoses which could have been familiar to continental as well as insular Celts and may date back to their common past: the boar with a human head, the bull under a bird, the horse driven by a large bird of prey. Finally, coins show not only the serpent with horns, or more precisely, with a ram's head, but this monster under a horse or eagle, as if they were engaged in battle—scenes of combat and violence which must have had their history in contemporary folklore.

The compositions on the Gundestrup basin are more precisely mythological, because figures of gods and goddesses are shown: four gods, arms raised, holding in turn two men offering them two boars, two monsters of the sea-horse genre, and two large stags with heads lowered; the fourth is simply flanked by two figures and a small horseman. Of the three goddesses, one is accompanied by a dancer and a man fighting with a lion; another, with her hair being dressed by a servant, holds a bird while two birds of prey and a wolf frame her, and a person and a wolf are shown upside down, presumably following a deadly struggle. Thus, on these seven plaques, where there is action it is violent action, to the death. Combat and carnage are implied by the images. Of the five other, larger plaques, two are much more crowded and detailed, since scenes with several figures are depicted. The most striking is that of a parade of soldiers in two files, separated by a large fallen tree (the Tree of the World?): musicians and infantry below and horsemen above seem to be led by a serpent with the head of a ram who appears to be opening the march. To the left a huge figure accompanied by a god plunges a man head downward into a barrel; this act, apparently performed by a god, gives the whole scene a supernatural feeling. Another plaque shows the god with the antlers of a stag, seated cross-legged,

holding in one hand the horned serpent and in the other a wreath. He is surrounded by animals: stags, bulls, wolves, lions, and a dolphin ridden by a small figure. The god here is the master of wild animals, livestock, fish, and the monstrous serpent. Another scene portrays a known myth: next to a bearded god with arm raised, a figure wearing a helmet with horns holds a large wheel with many spokes. A soldier, a bearded god in the prime of life, and a wheel: Taranis, master of thunder and battles, would not be portrayed any differently. He is here also the master of wild beasts and monsters, wolves, griffins, and the snake with a ram's head. Without venturing beyond safe territory, this is as far as the interpretation of such mythological monuments and carved objects can go.

On the other hand, some elements of Gallic mythology are reported by writers: the Gauls regarded themselves as descended from a god of the subterranean and nocturnal world (Caesar); they had a mythical tyrant named the Taurin (Tauriscus) who had once ruled the land (Ammianus Marcellinus, 15.9); they worshiped the god Ogmios, a kind of Hercules and patron of eloquence (Lucian); Plutarch (*De facie in orbe lunae*, 26) calls Kronos a Celtic god of death who lives on an island in the Atlantic afterworld.

Carved monuments show some scenes from legends. The Nautae Parisiaci pillar has two: the god Smertrios beating a serpent to death and the god Esus cutting down a tree in the forest where the Bull with Three Cranes is hiding.

As for what is called "French mythology," legends written since the Middle Ages as well as folklore, these legends contain nothing that indisputably dates back to the Celtic and Gallo-Roman times; they teach us nothing about the mythology of these eras, unlike the insular literature, so rich in survivals from pagan times.

V. The Cult of the Dead: Funeral Rites and Rites of the Funeral Cult

Like many other peoples, the ancient Celts practiced both burial and cremation, either in different eras or simultaneously. There was burial beneath funeral mounds during the first period of La Tène and burial in flat tombs or graves later. Cremation was less frequent in the same periods, in terra cotta urns in flat tombs, and the urns were sometimes then reused in the funeral mounds. Cremation dominated during the last period of independence, perhaps with much less emphasis on equipment; cremation dominated again during the High Roman Empire and in the Middle Empire in graves marked with stelae, possibly in wells, and under mausoleums, until the introduction of Christianity, which imposed burial in open ground, in a coffin of wood or lead, between stones or tiles, or in a sarcophagus placed in an aedicule above the ground or in a burial vault. It would be a great mistake to attribute these two rites to distinct peoples or distinct periods. Their choice depended on various factors: the habits of seminomads or settled peoples, the amount of space in the burial ground, the security or insecurity of visible or invisible tombs, hygiene more or less observed, the type of soil, and one's rank in the social hierarchy. The difficulty of studying these funeral rites is increased by many factors. In the pre-Roman era, it is exceptionally rare to discover the necropolis of a given habitat (sometimes one has the necropolis alone, sometimes the habitat alone); it is no less rare to be able to explore a necropolis that is entirely intact and thus to be able to set up a sequence. In the Roman era, the ravages of the third, fourth, and fifth centuries

Gallic coins: a nude warrior, probably divine; a head encircled with small "cut-off heads"; transformations of a charioteer.

generally destroyed the cemeteries, and the reuse of stelae and sarcophagi in the foundations of fortifications broke the connections that existed between these monuments and their locations. During both eras the burial places of the poorest segments of the population, particularly the servant classes, are almost totally unknown to us; and finally, as Franz Cumont has shown (*Lux perpetua*, 1948), conservatism with regard to the material of funeral rites led to contradictory practices (food was placed near the ashes of a corpse destroyed by fire, etc.).

1. The pre-Roman era. The "chariot tombs" of La Tène I and II are well known: the warrior with his weapons, the parts of a two-wheeled chariot, occasionally the bones of a horse, arrangements more or less constant but not necessarily explicable for a particular group of objects. For less elaborate burials, some problems are now being studied: the existence of a winding sheet or a fabric cover for certain objects, the presence of vases made expressly for the tomb or only of reused receptacles, the use of "andirons" not usable at the hearth, the apparently random arrangement of a portion of the fibulae, the significance of the bending of swords, of the ceramic decorations, and of the selection of

buried jewelry, to mention only some practices. The study of the La Tène funeral rites has only begun.

The existing texts tell us little. However, Caesar reports some customs which touch on the afterlife. In Aquitaine the chiefs had totally devoted companions or servants, the *soldurii*, who voluntarily accompanied them to their death (*Bellum Gallicum*, 3.22). The Gauls believed so strongly in an afterlife that they threw letters addressed to the dead man into his funeral pyre (Diodorus, 5.28). After a battle the winning chief sacrificed live booty to the Celtic "Mars," the Gallic war god (*Bellum Gallicum* [*B.G.*], 6.17). "In relation to the level of civilization of the Gauls, funerals are magnificent and sumptuous" (evidently referring to a chief or important personnage). "Everything which the deceased is thought to have loved in his life is carried to the fire, even animals. Not long ago, a man's complete funeral ceremony required burning with him the slaves and clients he valued most highly" (*B.G.*, 6.19).

According to Nicander of Colophon (second century A.D.), one Celtic funeral practice was to spend the night next to the tomb in order to receive oracles. This is presumed to have been an incubation rite; it may not have been exactly that, but the role of the wake is a common point. In the south, the Entremont statuary (Bouches-du-Rhône) seems to be connected with a cult of a dead chief (warriors, their heads with eyes closed, with one hand holding the hair, a series of heads in bas-relief or in sculpture in the round) which corresponds to the process of heroization that is elsewhere, in Greece and Ireland, idealized in the epics. Albert Grenier and Fernand Benoît have done studies of the "cult of heroes," which is, however, concretely attested only in southern Gaul.

2. The Roman Era. Some rites or elements of rites seem limited to the Celto-Roman world. The symbol of the *ascia*, an adz-hammer (cooper's adz), is depicted on funeral stelae, cippi, altars, and sarcophagi, in Gaul much more than anywhere else, and sometimes accompanied by a still enigmatic formula of the *sub ascia dedicavit* type, which also often appears without the carved instrument. In Limousin, during the second and third centuries, near the stone chest containing a glass funeral urn there was an iron ascia; placed all around like spokes were large nails (the indestructible remains of a cremation in a coffin that the adz was used to build?). Lead sarcophagi decorated with symbols were particularly frequent in Gaul. Vases in pairs or in larger even numbers have also been found. As for the objects contained in the tomb, what is called funeral "furniture" for lack of a better word, we now realize that this consists of fragments of objects broken up before the cremation and thrown on the pyre and of offerings made to the dead man for his eternal life—these offerings being intact. Coins are also frequently found, and not only near the mouth of the deceased.

The organization of the tomb and the homage paid by the mourners are known in Gaul through the many inscriptions which reveal either Celtic practices or Roman customs known elsewhere—the funeral or anniversary meal, for example, and the vine and garden intended to provide food. An epitaph called "the testament of Lingon" is particularly detailed (for rites to be followed at the cremation of the master and his belongings, as well as at the anniversary meal); another, from Géligneux (Ain), stipulates that on the fourteenth day of months having thirty days a dinner should be held at the tomb.

Finally, all the subtleties of Roman law were called into play to insure the proper maintenance of the tomb and to decide which heirs would be allowed to use it.

VI. Ceremonial Rites of the Cults of the Gods

Some rites in independent Gaul are known through texts. The Gauls, said Posidonius (in *Athena*, 4.36), pray prostrate before their gods, turning toward the right. Pliny the Elder describes the gathering of mistletoe from oak as practiced by the Druids (before they were suppressed by Tiberius): "They prepare a religious feast according to the rites at the foot of the tree, leading forth two white bulls whose horns are then tied for the first time. A priest, all in white, climbs the tree, cuts the mistletoe with a golden knife, and catches it on a white tunic. He then kills the victims" (Pliny, *Natural History*, 16.95.250–51).

He also notes the precautions to take in the gathering of *selago* and *samolus*: the one is to be picked with the right hand through the left opening of the tunic; the other should be picked with the left hand and only on an empty stomach.

The Gallic calendar as we know it is inscribed in bronze on the Coligny table (Ain) that is dated at the middle of the first century A.D. at the earliest. It was lunisolar: lunar (and the Celts counted time by nights, not by days, according to Caesar), but adjusted to the solar cycle by intercalations. It did not include sacred names, but did have notations which may have referred to seasonal feasts: one feast, probably at the beginning of November, involved three successive nights connected with a feast of the dead, a communication with the afterlife; the other, which may have been connected with divination, was the "throwing of the sticks."

Divination is known to have existed among the Gauls: they got information from the flight of birds and the entrails of sacrificial victims, as other people did, but also from the way the victim fell in human sacrifices, the nature of his convulsions, and the way his blood flowed (Diodorus, 5.31.3, and Strabo, 4.4).

Cult sites were still often in the open air during the period of Gallic independence.

Lucan, a century after the conquest, gives certain a posteriori information about the sacred clearings. Near Marseilles there was "a sacred wood never profaned since ancient times, that hems in with its woven branches a gloomy air and chilling shadows, never reached by the sun . . . Altars are raised on sinister mounds and all the trees have been purified by human blood . . . Floods of water fall from black springs, and sad statues of the gods, shapeless and crude, stand on the cut trunks . . . The people do not come near this place to practice their cult; they have yielded it to the gods. This forest remains very thick, in the middle of cleared hills" (*Pharsale*, 3.399–428).

Archaeology cannot tell us anything about these open-air sanctuaries; furnished with statues probably made of wood, they were eminently perishable establishments. It is notable that the people found not only wood to carve, but also springs (according to Lucan). The same association can be found at the height of the Gallo-Roman period at the sanctuary of the sources of the Seine, where hundreds of wooden ex-voto offerings (and not statues of gods) have been discovered since 1963. In 1968 thousands of objects of this type were uncovered near a spring at Chamalières (Puy-de-Dôme). Apparently in both cases these were sanctuaries of healing gods dating back to Celtic times, but we know nothing of their material equipment.

Among the Celts of Gaul, Germany, Bohemia, Great Britain, and Hungary, two types of archaeological remains indicate Celtic and Celto-Roman cult sites. Quadrangular walls, averaging 80 by 80 meters, formed trenches with their slopes and enclosed, at least in one case (at Holzhausen in

Bavaria), an aedicule which was certainly used in a cult, since it was accompanied by sacrificial wells: again apparently an open-air cult. At Libenice in Bohemia, an 80-by-20-meter enclosure with a trench and embankment enclosed at one end a sacrificial area and a large formless stela. In the same country, at Mšecké Žehrovice, there is also a quadrangular structure which yielded a man's head, carved in stone, of pronounced La Tène style dating from the first century B.C.

From the Gallic era there are some remains of a small temple, recognizable from the holes in its columns as the first stage of a somewhat more imposing building, the masonry *fanum* of the Roman era. This type of building, known from southern Great Britain to Hungary, was alternately circular, quadrangular almost to the point of being square, a regular or irregular polygon, or cruciform; it faced east and was built on a height or a high subfoundation; most often it was surrounded by a fairly wide gallery made for people to walk around (priests, worshipers, or both together in procession?—it is not certain that worshipers were allowed access to the sanctuary) and place their offerings. Did this gallery exist before Roman times? It is difficult to believe that this type of temple, the only example of its genre in Western antiquity, would be built in the Celto-Roman period without having had a precedent among the rites indigenous to the area. Nor does it appear, regardless of what has been said recently, that this construction was part of a funeral cult: the mortuary chamber of a funeral mound or hypogeum is different from the *cella* consecrated to the cult of a god; heroization follows from the existence of divinities and not the reverse.

VII. Interpretation of Divine Entities

When one people conquers another, either they impose some of their gods on the vanquished people, who assimilate them to their own gods to some degree, or they are satisfied with giving the gods of the conquered people the names of their own closest counterpart. This phenomenon is universal among pagan countries. Tacitus, referring to the Teutons, called it *interpretatio Romana* (*Germania*, 43.4): "among the *Naharvales*, . . . the gods after Roman interpretation would be Castor and Pollux; such is the nature of their divinity and their name is *Alci*; they are worshiped as two brothers, two young men."

Caesar gave the model for this practice when he wrote about the Gauls: "At the head of the gods they worship Mercury; he is portrayed most often, he is considered the inventor of all the arts, the god of roads and voyages, the great master of profits and commerce. Then come Apollo, Mars, Jupiter, and Minerva. These they think of much as other peoples do . . . All the Gauls claim to be descended from *Dis pater*" (*Bellum Gallicum*, 6.17). It is likely that this way of presenting the Gauls not only was convenient for the historian but also served a purpose in its own time: it was a way to reassure Roman families about the reportedly bloodthirsty requirements of the Gallic gods, a program to assimilate the two pantheisms that would be in contact from then on.

J.-J. Hatt and F. Benoit have noted that one can also refer to an *interpretatio Celtica*; Roman gods were frequently given a Celtic surname. This phenomenon was in fact complex, for it concerned the relative weight of the gods in question: either the dominant god was Celtic and was given a Roman interpretation with the name, or he was Roman and was given a Celtic interpretation with the name. P. MacCana

Sacrifice by immersion and procession of warriors. Plaque from the gilded silver basin discovered at Gundestrup. Copenhagen, Nationalmuseet.

points out that *Mars Vesontius* could mean (1) the Roman Mars honored in Besançon; (2) an important local god, identified with Mars in this city; or (3) a local god assimilated to his Roman counterpart. This raises the whole question of surnames for deities, slightly different from the interpretation issue, but closely related; as in the case of French local

Goddess with a torque and ritual headdress. Plaque from the gilded silver basin discovered at Gundestrup. Copenhagen, Nationalmuseet.

saints (Notre-Dame de Lorette), the indigenous surname of a Mars or a Mercury may be geographical, but it may also express a quality for which the assimilated local god is named: Apollo Vindonnus, "white, shining, sparkling."

VIII. Local Gods and Surnames

An important aspect of the Gallo-Roman pantheon is the fact that most of the divinities (several hundred) that have Celtic names are known only by one, two, or perhaps three inscriptions, either alone or attached to the name of a well-known Roman god. This happened also with Greek religion, particularly in areas conquered by Hellenism: Asia Minor, for example. The nature of the surname is variable and often difficult to determine. Many are topical, that is, attached to the site of a cult or derived from one: *Sequana,* at the sources of the Seine, *Borvo,* at the source of Mount Dore. It is also possible that the site, spring, or river in question may have been named for the deity, as is probable for *Divona,* "the divine" (Cahors), or *Matrona,* "the (great) mother" (the Marne). Other surnames express superhuman qualities: *Camulus,* "Powerful." Still others remain unexplained and may someday furnish definitions for other categories. It would not be legitimate in any case to report systematically the multiplicity of names from the Gallic era that the Latin writing system allowed to be recorded and passed on to us: these divine entities were able to take on flesh at a time when Roman customs were giving them a density that their own diffuse personalities had not yet acquired; and how many places have been deified by the Romans just by lending them a Latinized Gallic name! Many of the nature cults must have grown and been perpetuated in this way, from prehistoric times—cults of rocks, springs, trees, heights, and animals which did not yet bear Indo-European names. These were tenacious cults, judging by the prohibitions pronounced against them by the first councils and until well into the sixth century.

IX. The Deities of Gaul and the Indo-European "Three Functions"

The works of Georges Dumézil have brought to light the characteristic aspect of the personality of the deities in relation to a functional tripartite division of Indo-European society. This scholar analyzed certain gods of the ancient Celts in this light, according to their survival in the medieval insular literature, and showed parallels with Germanic, Roman, and Indian gods. He pointed out the absence among the independent Gauls of the third function, essentially that of agricultural work, because this was the work of women and slaves ("those that watched over milk and grain were doubtless demons or minor genies, enslaved and held at the mercy" of the great gods). The horn of plenty and the basket filled with fruits still appeared just as frequently as attributes of the Gallo-Roman gods—but there was no laborer god among them analogous to that of the Gauls (Amaethon). On the other hand, the ruling function (*Taranis*-Jupiter, perhaps *Lugh*(?)-Mercury) and the warrior function (*Teutates*-Mars) were clearly represented.

P.-M.D./d.b.

BIBLIOGRAPHY

Sources

Knowledge of the divinities, myths, and rites of the ancient pagan Celts, especially in Gaul where the documents are the most abundant, notably for the Roman era, comes from sources of many kinds: written, pictorial, and on monuments.

Greek and Latin texts, and scholia, or commentaries: J. ZWICKER, comp., *Fontes historiae religionis Celticae, 3 vols., Fontes historiae religionum . . .* , vol. 5, by C. Clemen (Berlin 1934–36); descriptions and summaries by P.-M. DUVAL, *La Gaule jusqu'au milieu du Vᵉ siècle*, vol. 1 of *Sources de l'histoire de France des origines à la fin du XVᵉ siècle*, by A. MOLINIER, 2 vols. (Paris 1971). The most important texts are those of Posidonius, Caesar, Diodorur, Strabo, Lucan (and commentary), Pliny the Elder; the *Acts* of the councils of the fourth to seventh centuries: citations in A. BERTRAND, *La religion des Gaulois: Les druides et le druidisme*, vol. 4 of *Les origines* (Paris 1897); some *Lives of Saints*, especially the older ones.

For the Irish and Welsh sources, see the brief bibliography in M.-L. SJOESTEDT-JONVAL, *Dieux et héros des Celtes, Mythes et religions*, vol. 7 (Paris 1940).

Inscriptions.—Gallic: J. WHATMOUGH, *The Dialects of Ancient Gaul* (Cambridge, MA, 1970). —Latin: *Corpus Inscriptionum Latinarum*, 12–13 (1888–1943), and various supplements by Espérandieu, Finke and Nesselhauf, Wuilleumier; other volumes and supplements for the other areas of Celtic settlement.

Sculptures: E. ESPÉRANDIEU, later R. LANTIER, *Recueil des Bas-reliefs, statues et bustes de la Gaule romaine*, 1–15 (1907–66); E. ESPÉRANDIEU, *Recueil . . . de la Germanie romaine* (1931). F. BENOÎT, *L'art primitif méditerranéen dans la vallée du Rhône. Sculpture* (2d ed., 1955). Various collections of bronzes, bibliography in: H. ROLLAND, *Bronzes antiques de Haute-Provence: Basses-Alpes, Vaucluse* (1965), supplement 17 to *Gallia*.

Terra-cotta: F. OSWALD, *Index of Figure-Types on Terra Sigillata* (Margidunum 1936–37). M. ROUVIER-JEANLIN, *Les figurines gallo-romaines en terre cuite au Musée des antiquités nationales* (1972), supplement 27 to *Gallia*.

Gallic coinage: H. DE LA TOUR, *Atlas de monnaies gauloises* (Paris 1892). L. LENGYEL, *L'art gaulois dans les médailles* (Paris 1954); *Le secret des Celtes* (Morel 1969).

Books and Articles

A systematic bibliography concerning the divinities is given in: P.-M. DUVAL, *Les dieux de la Gaule* (2d ed., Paris 1976), 129–34. The essential synthetic works are grouped below in alphabetical order with some others concerning religion. See the bibliographies of particular articles for works on a particular divinity.

A. BAYET, *La morale des Gaulois* (Paris 1930). F. BENOÎT, *Art et dieux de la Gaule* (Paris 1969); *Mars et Mercure: Nouvelles recherches sur l'interprétation gauloise des divinités romaines* (Aix-en-Provence 1959); *Les mythes de l'outre-tombe: Le cavalier à l'anguipède et l'écuyère Epona* (Paris 1950); *L'héroïsation équestre* (Aix-en-Provence 1954); *Le symbolisme dans les sanctuaires de la Gaule* (Paris 1970). F. BERGE, "Tableau du Calendrier folklorique," in Gorce and Mortier, *Histoire générale des religions*, 5 (Paris 1952). J.-M. BLAZQUEZ, *Diccionario de las religiones prerromanas de Hispania* (Madrid 1975). G. BLOCH, "La religion des Gaulois," *Revue internationale de l'Enseignement*, 29–30 (1895). D. BRETZ-MAHLER, *La civilisation de La Tène I en Champagne: Le faciès marnien* (Paris 1971), supplement 23 to *Gallia*. M. CLAVEL, "Le syncrétisme gallo-romain: Structures et finalités," *Praelectiones Patavianae* (Rome 1972). C. CLEMEN, *Die Kelten*, vol. 1 of his *Religionsgeschichte Europas* (Heidelberg 1926). F. CUMONT, *Recherches sur le symbolisme funéraire des Romains* (Paris 1942). J. DÉCHELETTE, *Manuel d'archéologie préhistorique, celtique et gallo-romaine*, 4 (2d ed., Paris 1928). J. DE VRIES, *Keltische Religion*, vol. 18 of Schröder, *Die Religionen der Menschheit* (Stuttgart 1961); *Altgermanische Religionsgeschichte* (2d ed., Berlin 1956–57). G. DUMÉZIL, *Mythes et dieux des Germains* (Paris 1939); *Jupiter, Mars, Quirinus* (Paris 1941); *Naissance de Rome* (Paris 1944) = *J.M.Q.* 2; *Les dieux des Indo-Européens* (Paris 1952). P.-M. DUVAL, *Les dieux de la Gaule* (2d ed., Paris 1976); "Les Celtes continentaux," *Mythologie des montagnes, des forêts et des îles* (Paris 1963); "Les religions des Celtes," *Histoire des religions*, 5 (Paris 1956); "L'originalité de l'architecture gallo-romaine," *Le rayonnement des civilisations grecque et romaine sur les cultures périphériques* (Paris 1965). A. GRENIER, *Les Gaulois* (3d ed., Paris 1970); *Manuel d'archéologie gallo-romaine*, part 3, "L'architecture," 1 (Paris 1958); part 4, "Les monuments des eaux," 2 (1960). J.J. HATT, *La tombe gallo-romaine* (Paris 1951); "Essai sur l'évolution de la religion gauloise," *Revue des Etudes anciennes*, 67 (1965). C. JULLIAN, *Histoire de la Gaule*, 2 (Paris 1908) and 6 (Paris 1920). O. KLINDT-JENSEN, *Gundestrupkedelen* (Copenhagen 1961). W. KRAUSE, *Religion der Kelten*, Bilderatlas zur Religionsgeschichte, 17 (1933). P. LAMBRECHTS, *Contributions à l'étude des divinités celtiques* (Bruges 1942); *L'exaltation de la tête dans la pensée et l'art des Celtes*, Dissertationes Archaeologicae Gandenses, 2 (Bruges 1954). R. LANTIER, "La religion celtique," in Gorce and Mortier, *Histoire générale des religions*, 1 (Paris 1947); "Keltische Mythologie," in H.-W. Haussig, *Wörterbuch der Mythologie* (Stuttgart 1963). P. MACCANA, *Celtic Mythology* (London 1970). E. MÂLE, *La fin du paganisme en Gaule et les premières basiliques chrétiennes* (2d ed., Paris 1962). A. ROSS, *Pagan Celtic Britain: Studies in Iconography and Tradition* (New York 1967); *Everyday Life of the Pagan Celts* (London and New York 1970). M.-L. SJOESTEDT-JONVAL, *Dieux et héros des Celtes* (Paris 1940); "Légendes épiques et monnaies gauloises: Recherches sur la constitution de la légende de Cuchulainn," *Études celtiques*, 1 (1936). E. THEVENOT, *Divinités et sanctuaires de la Gaule* (Paris 1968); *Sur les traces des Mars celtiques (entre Loire et Mont-Blanc)*, Dissertationes Archaeologicae Gandenses, 3 (Bruges 1955). J. TOUTAIN, *Les cultes païens dans l'Empire romain (provinces latines)*, 3: *Les cultes indigènes et nationaux* (Paris 1917–20). A. VARAGNAC and E. DEROLEZ, "Les Celtes et les Germains," in *Religions du monde* (Paris 1965), 5–60. J. LEITE DE VASCONCELLOS, *Religiões da Lusitania nã porte que principalmente se refere a Portugal*, 2 vols. (Lisbon 1897–1905). J. VENDRYES, *La religion des Celtes*, collection "Mana," 2, vol. 3 (Paris 1948).

Specific Bibliographies

1. Sacrifice

P.-M. DUVAL, "Notes sur la civilisation gallo-romaine," 4: "Teutates, Esus, Taranis," *Etudes celtiques*, 8, 1 (1958). A.-J. REINACH, "Les têtes coupées et les trophées en Gaule," *Revue celtique*, 34 (1913). P. LAMBRECHTS, *L'exaltation de la tête dans la pensée et l'art des Celtes* (Bruges 1954). F. BENOÎT, *L'art primitif méditerranéen* (2d ed., Aix-en-Provence 1955); *Mars et Mercure: Nouvelles recherches sur l'interprétation gauloise des divinités romaines* (Aix-en-Provence 1959). H. GRAILLOT, *Le culte de Cybèle, Mère des dieux, à Rome et dans l'Empire romain* (Paris 1912),

445–75. R. TURCAN, *Les religions de l'Asie dans la vallée du Rhône* (Leiden 1972).

2. Myths

C. JULLIAN, *Histoire de la Gaule* (1908), 2:380–84. P.-M. DUVAL, *Les dieux de la Gaule* (2d ed., Paris 1976), 94–98; *Les Celtes* (Paris 1977). O. KLINDT-JENSEN, *Gundestrupkedelen* (Copenhagen 1961). M. MAINJONET, "Les animaux imaginaires des monnaies gauloises," in the catalog of the Hôtel des Monnaies exposition, *Le bestiaire des monnaies, des sceaux et des médailles* (Paris 1974).

3. The Cult of the Dead

J. DÉCHELETTE, *Manuel d'archéologie préhistorique, celtique et gallo-romaine*, 4 (2d ed., Paris 1928). P. SANKOT, "Le rite funéraire des nécropoles laténiennes en Champagne," *Etudes celtiques*, 15, 1 (1977). J.-J. HATT, *La tombe gallo-romaine* (Paris 1951). C. MENNESSIER, "Tombes gallo-romaines du Limousin: Traitement graphique de l'information," in P.-M. Duval et al., *Recherches d'archéologie celtique et gallo-romaine* (Paris 1973). J.-Y. AUTEXIER, "Cinq sépultures en coffre cinéraire provenant de la région d'Auzances (Creuse)," *Revue archéologique du Centre*, 15 (1976). R. REENE, ed., *Burial in the Roman World*, Council for British Archeology, report 22 (1977).

4. Ceremonial Rites

A. GRENIER, *Manuel d'archéologie gallo-romaine*, part 3, "L'architecture," 1 (Paris 1958); part 4, "Les monuments des eaux," 2 (1960). P.-M. DUVAL, "L'originalité de l'architecture gallo-romaine," *Le rayonnement des civilisations grecque et romaine sur les cultures périphériques* (Paris 1965). G. ANTIER, "La galerie du fanum gallo-romain," *L'information d'histoire de l'art*, 20 (1975). J. WALDHAUSER, "Die keltischen Viereckschanzen in Böhmen," in *The Celts in Central Europe* (Székesfehérvár, Hungary, 1974) = *Alba Regia*, 14 (1975).

5. Interpretation

G. WISSOWA, "Interpretatio Romana," *Archiv für Religionswissenschaft*, 19 (1916–19). F. RICHTER, *De deorum barbarorum interpretatione Romana quaestiones selectae* (Halle 1906). P.-M. DUVAL, *Les dieux de la Gaule* (2d ed., Paris 1976), 67, 69, 86. P. MACCANA, *Celtic Mythology* (London 1970), 13–14. F. BENOÎT, *Mars et Mercure: Nouvelles recherches sur l'interprétation gauloise des divinités romaines* (Aix-en-Provence 1959), chap. 4.

6. Local Gods and Surnames

Lists of divine names or surnames are covered in: J. TOUTAIN, *Les cultes païens dans l'Empire romain (provinces latines)*, 3 (1917–20); the tables of the *Corpus Inscriptionum Latinarum*, 12 (1888), 13 (1943), and various supplements; J. VENDRYES, *La religion des Celtes*, collection "Mana" (1948). F. BENOÎT, *Mars et Mercure: Nouvelles recherches sur l'interprétation gauloise des divinités romaines* (Aix-en-Provence 1959), chap. 4. P.-M. DUVAL, *Les dieux de la Gaule* (2d ed., Paris 1976), 59–62 and 117–22.

7. The Gods of the Gauls and the "Three Functions" of the Indo-Europeans

G. DUMÉZIL, *Mythes et dieux des Germains* (Paris 1939); *Jupiter, Mars, Quirinus* (1941); *Naissance de Rome* (1944), Introduction; *Les dieux des Indo-Européens* (Paris 1952). P.-M. DUVAL, *Les dieux de la Gaule* (2d ed., Paris 1976), 26, 91.

THE RELIGIONS OF THE CONTINENTAL CELTS OF SPAIN, GREAT BRITAIN, AND THE DANUBE

I. The Iberian Celts and Roman Spain

The Celts mixed with the Iberians so much that, since ancient times, the term Iberian Celts has been used to designate the populations of two-thirds of the Iberian peninsula and there was a language, Iberian Celtic (attested by inscriptions), different from its two components but fairly close to continental Celtic. Texts, numerous Latin inscriptions, and carved monuments and objects allow us to place the Celtic religion among those of Spain and Portugal, before and especially after the Roman conquest.

As in Gaul, there were many gods. Among them were the god with stag horns on a painted vase from Numance, Sucellus with his mallet in statuettes in bronze, and Epona in bas-relief. Various inscriptions mention Matres (Aufaniae, Brigeaecae, Gallaicae, Monitucinae, Tendeiterae, Useae), Ataecina, Anderon, Bormanicus, the Lugoves, Candamius, Dercetius, and Suttunius. Cults of the bull, the snake, and the sun horse have been verified. Endovellicus, a warrior god, also had a Celtic name.

As in Gaul, naturist cults (water, trees, rocks), which date back to the pre-Celtic period, survived the advent of Christianity.

II. Celto-Roman Great Britain

Although in Ireland our evidence is limited to memories of pagan religions recorded in the written literature of the Christian era, dating back to the sixth century at the earliest, the Roman occupation of Great Britain left inscriptions and carved monuments which provide information on religious matters, as in Gaul. In addition, some works of art and pre-Roman coins provide rare information about an aspect of the local customs that Caesar, Tacitus, and Dion Cassius failed to discuss: the last two authors merely indicated the existence of the Druids and their magic practices.

As in Gaul, naturist cults have been attested, dating back to before the Celtic period: deified rivers, lakes, and wells to which offerings were made, aquatic birds perhaps connected with a cult of springs, and the sacred character of the swan, the crow, and the crane, as well as the eagle, the owl, and the goose. Monstrous beings, part animal, were worshiped as on the Continent: the god with stag horns and the horned serpent which was often carved in the form of a bracelet. Also archaic were the collective divinities known from dedicatory inscriptions and allegorical carvings of the Roman era: the three mother goddesses, for example, though less frequent and widespread than in Gaul or the Rhineland.

Deities known on the Continent were also known overseas: Mars, with numerous surnames, such as Toutatis (Teutates), Olloudios, Lenus, Segomo, Leucetios (Lucetios), Camulos; Epona and Nemetona, although there were fewer goddesses than in Gaul. There was a column of Jupiter with the snake foot and one of Jupiter at the wheel.

No less Celtic, but part of the insular pantheon, were the gods Nodons, Mogons, Maponus, Belatucadros, Rigisamus, and Mars Cociduis, Condatis, and Vitiris, as well as the goddesses Andrasta, Arnemetia, Brigantia, Coventina, and Sulis, a kind of Minerva of the waters whose temple was at Bath.

The same Celto-Roman temple, of circular or quadrangular design with a gallery, existed in Great Britain as on the Continent.

III. Celts and Celto-Romans of the Danube

Dedicatory inscriptions from the Roman period give us information about some Celtic gods of the Danube region, which were also honored elsewhere in the Celto-Roman world, in Gaul, and in Great Britain. The goddesses were Epona, Sirona, the Triviae and Quadriviae of the crossroads, and Sula and the Suleviae (Sentona and Noreia belong properly to the Danube countries). The gods Apollo Grannus, Belinus, Mars Toutatis, Mars Latobius, Bindus Neptunus, Jupiter Bussumarus, and Jupiter Cernenus (if the last was indeed different, as seems likely, from Cernunnos) were known only in these regions.

Evidence of temples of Celto-Roman design is given by substructures found in Aquincum (Budapest) and in Linz and Bregenz in Austria.

P.-M.D./d.b.

BIBLIOGRAPHY

Vols. 2, 3, and 7 of *Corpus Inscriptionum Latinarum*.

1. Iberian Celts

J.-M. BLÁQUEZ, *Diccionario de las Religiones prerromanas de Hispania* (Madrid 1975). J. LEITE DE VASCONCELLOS, *Religiões da Lusitania . . .* , 2 vols. (Lisbon 1897–1905).

2. Great Britain

J. TOUTAIN, *Les cultes paëns dans l'Empire romain (provinces latines)*, 3 vols. (Paris 1905–20). A. ROSS, *Celtic Pagan Britain* (London and New York 1967); *Everyday Life of the Pagan Celts* (London and New York 1970), chap. 6.

3. The Danube

J. TOUTAIN, *Les cultes païens dans l'Empire romain (province latines)*, 3 vols. (Paris 1905–20). G. ALFÖLDY, "Zur keltischen Religion in Pannonien," *Germania*, 42 (1964).

DRUID AND POET: THE IRISH *FILIDH* AND THE WELSH *BARDD*

The ordinary word for "poet" in Irish is *filidh,* which is related to the Welsh word *gweld,* "to see"; in Welsh the word for poet is *bardd.* The highest rank of *filidh,* the *ollamh,* seems to correspond to the Welsh *pencerdd,* "master of song, or of art." The *filidh* of ancient Ireland was much more than a poet in the modern sense. He was a learned genealogist and the keeper of a tradition with the force of law and at the same time a prophet who practiced rites of divination, of which we know some details. The Irish *bard,* on the other hand, was not considered a man of knowledge, and his rank was a good deal lower. At the beginning of modern times we see him at least sometimes playing the harp and reciting poems composed by a *filidh.* In the hall of a Welsh king the *pencerdd* sat in the highest part of the room, with the king and chief dignitaries; the *bardd teulu* ("bard of the warrior band") sat in the lower part of the room, next to the captain of the warriors. When the king wished to hear a poem, first the *pencerdd* sang two songs, a song of God and a song of kings, and then the *bardd teulu* sang a third one. The latter also sang for the queen in her chamber, and he intoned "The Monarchy of Britain" when the troops went off to battle or returned with booty.

In ancient Irish law the status of the druid (*druí*) was that of a subject without special privileges, probably because he was identified with the pagan past. In Irish tales his function and role are similar to those of the *filidh,* except that he does not seem to tell stories; he had, it is said, the privilege of speaking before the king spoke. The *druí* acts as arbitrator and peacemaker.

The evidence provided by Greek and Roman authors about the educated classes in the Celtic world, while somewhat repetitive, is still not without contradictions. It does, however, seem reasonable to think that the druids, whose name refers to the idea of knowledge, enjoyed the highest rank. Besides being scholars who taught and arbitrators who could put an end to conflicts even between battling armies, it was they who, by means of their knowledge of the divine and their understanding of divine language, presided over sacrifices. The *vātes,* or seers, were also men of knowledge, who told the future through auguries and the sacrifice of victims. The presence of a druid was necessary for this sacrifice. The name *vātes* is related to words meaning prophecy, inspiration, and poetry. The bards were singers of praise poems which accompanied the music of their string instruments and, probably less often, of satires. It is generally held that the first meaning of *bard* is "singer of praise." It seems reasonable to see in the druid a figure of the first function, that closest to God or the gods, and to divine law; to see in the *vātis,* the *filidh,* and the *pencerdd,* who are concerned with what are and will be the powers and acts of the temporal sovereign, figures of the second function (recall the association of the warriors Conchobar, Mars, and Indra with the calendar); and to see in the bard of Gaul and Ireland, the *bardd teulu,* as well as the *teuluwr* ("member of the warrior band, of the guard") of Wales, a figure of the third function. The role of the *teuluwr* was to entertain the company—it was generosity and courtly supplication. The hostel keeper, in the story of Cú Chulainn's childhood, considers himself not only the one who greets and plays host to the men of Ireland; he also defends them when they are slandered and engaged in battles for honor, which seems to indicate that he is a provider of praise. The fact that the Irish bard gets his poems from the *filidh,* his superior, for recitation, may be compared with the free peasant's acceptance of a "fief" of cattle from his lord and with the inability of the *vātis* to perform a sacrifice except in the presence of the druid.

The three figures that we have been considering should probably be compared with the roles the three main priests required for a Vedic sacrifice, first of all the *brahman,* the most important, who by his presence ensures communication between the visible and the invisible, the latter being identified with the sacred; then the *adhvaryu,* the most active, who is in charge of a large number of activities (and whose name is derived from a verb meaning "to perform the sacrifice," a verb which itself is derived from a root denoting the "liturgy" considered as a "path"); and finally the *hotar,* a reciter of hymns. Georges Dumézil has connected the first two of these with the *flamen dialis* and the *pontifex* of ancient Rome.

B.R./j.l.

BIBLIOGRAPHY

G. DUMÉZIL, *Servius et la fortune* (Paris 1943), 64, 89; *Idées romaines* (Paris 1969), 79. A. D. REES and B. REES, *Celtic Heritage* (London 1961), 124–25, 140–41, 181–82. J. E. C. WILLIAMS, *The Court Poet in Medieval Ireland* (London 1973). F. LE ROUX, *Les Druides* (Paris 1961). M. DILLON, *Celts and Aryans* (1975).

MOTHER GODDESSES AND COLLECTIVE DEITIES IN THE CELTIC AND CELTO-ROMAN WORLD

Mother goddesses are an important part of the ancient Celtic and Celto-Roman pantheon. Two characteristics distinguish divinized maternity there: the goddess holds or suckles an infant, and she has one or two companions (sometimes all three of them cuddle their infants together). This is thus clearly the preeminent mother, and one should beware of seeing here a goddess of "mother earth," or more vaguely of prosperity: maternity and prosperity symbolized by the cornucopia, for example, are two related matters. The mothers are called *matres* in Latin, *matrae* or *matronae* in Gallic. They often, but not always, have a surname that characterizes them precisely: Namausicae (at Nîmes), Glanicae (at Glanum), Vacallinehae (in Germany), Dervorunae (in Cisalpine Gaul), Aufaniae (in Spain). Occasionally the goddess has a male companion, but the anonymous woman that one bas-relief shows at the side of a god is not necessarily a mother. The uncertainty is therefore great about many representations of the goddesses, especially when they are alone or married, because in twos or threes and without attributes to characterize them, they are or can be women, mothers, whose number magnifies fecundity by "intensive repetition." The collective character of these divinities, especially when they have only one generic name without personalization (here "mothers"), is, for ancient Celtic and Celto-Roman religion, an archaic trait, as is the frequency of divine animals or monsters, which were no longer extant, nor had they been for a long time, in Greece or Rome.

The ancient collective goddesses were perpetuated in Christian Ireland (the Mórrighans, Brighids, Machas), where fairies reigned. If the cult of the mothers, which also existed in Northern Italy, had so much success in Gaul, it was the celebrated fecundity of the women of that country that was thus honored there. This benefit probably explains why under the Roman Empire the cult of Cybele, the Great Mother of Ida, had a remarkable success in the Gallic countries. Other collective goddesses, Proxumae, "very near," Fatae, "fairies," or Suleviae were also called Iunones, which is the feminine equivalent of genies: familiar spirits, "guardian angels of paganism," J. Toutain has called them. More adapted to a special role were the guardianesses of crossroads of two, three, and four branches, the Biviae, Triviae, and Quadruviae, who are seen represented in twos, threes, and fours with their serpent familiar on Gallo-Roman vases ornamented with reliefs.

P.-M.D./b.f.

The goddesses of crossroads with two, three, and four branches. Gallo-Roman sigillated vase.

The mother goddesses of Vertault, Côte-d'Or. Musée de Châtillon-sur-Seine. Photo Lauros-Giraudon.

BIBLIOGRAPHY

F. HEICHELHEIM, "Matres," in Pauly-Wissowa, *Real-Encyclopädie*, vol. 14 (1930); "Muttergottheiten der Gallorömer," in ibid., vol. 16 (1933–35). J. DE VRIES, *Altgermanische Religionsgeschichte* (2d ed., 1950), 1, map. P.-M. DUVAL, *Les dieux de la Gaule* (2d ed., Paris 1976), 55–57.

SOME RELIGIOUS ASPECTS OF CELTIC ART

I. Seated, Cross-Legged Pose

Among the ancient Celts and in Roman Gaul, the seated, cross-legged pose appears to have been reserved for gods and goddesses, if one is to believe the illustrations found on the Gundestrup (Denmark) basin and in Gallo-Roman sculpture. It is sometimes called a "Buddhist" or "squatting" pose, but these are less accurate terms given, the position of the legs, which are simply bent or crossed in front of the body. Cernunnos, for example, is always shown in this position, but it is also used for goddesses, for gods whose names we do not know, and even for Mercury (bronze statuette from Puy-du-Touge, Haute Garonne). This means that there was no "god of this pose," but rather that the posture was used for several deities, perhaps in the image of man, since several writers have stated that the Gauls took their meals seated on the ground in this fashion. J. Vendryés noted a dedicatory inscription in Gallic (from Autun, Saône-et-Loire) in which the word *canecosedlon*, object of the offerings designated a cushion or padded chair: this may have

197

Unidentified god with three faces and with horns or winglets. Appliqué from a vase from northern Gaul. Paris, Bibliothèque nationale, Cabinet des Médailles.

God from Bournay-sur-Juine (Essonne). Statuette in sheet bronze. Early first century. Saint-Germain-en-Laye, Musée des Antiquités nationales.

Small statuette of a three-headed, antlered god suckling two ram-headed serpents. From Autun. Saint-Germain-en-Laye, Musée des Antiquités nationales.

been the type of chair on which the gods preferred to be depicted, since they were often shown seated on a cushion. In any event, the pose alone is not sufficient to prove divinity: it is not certain that the pre-Roman statues of Roquepertuse and Glanum (Bouches-du-Rhône) are statues of gods; they may be heroes or even priests. On the other hand, the figure that appears on Gallic coins from the end of the independent period is certainly a deity.

II. Intensive Repetition

Multiplying one or more elements of a divine being or symbol to increase its power is called "intensive repetition." Among the Celts, the use of triple faces or three heads is the most striking example of this, shown by Mercury, Cernunnos, and several unidentified gods and goddesses. The tricephalus has the notable advantage of allowing the god to see in three directions: an important quality for Mercury, the god of voyages. There is even a Gallo-Roman statue in bronze showing Mercury with four faces.

III. Magic

Magical protection is used to ward off the "evil eye," to repel threats, and to petrify enemies: this apotropaic value is the only one that can be ascribed to certain ornaments, often symbolic as well, included in the extensive repertory of motifs of ancient Celtic art. Dynamic symbols include the swastika, sign of "good luck," carved on a buckle and the triskelion, with its gyratory motion, adorning coins, jewelry and scabbards, among other things. On vases, scabbards, and coins, the eye, which uncovers danger, is depicted. Everywhere in Celtic art is the human mask, smiling or not, which sees and prevents danger. Finally, there is the strange impression produced by transformations in progress, a plant motif on an animal subject and vice versa: metamorphosis—beginning, advanced, or completed—participates to a variable degree in the supernatural, which was eminently dear to the Celts.

The action of magic is often dual: by warding off evil, it allows good to assert itself. This action also takes place in certain ex-voto offerings representing the afflicted parts of the body for which a cure is sought, by substituting the symbol for the living body: this type of offering, in wood, stone, or metal, is found frequently in the temples of Roman Gaul, particularly in sanctuaries at springs. Other procedures were hostile: lead tablets are said to have been used for curses or for conjuring. Examples of these have been found written in Gallic, Latin, or Greek on sheets of lead.

P.-M.D./d.b.

BIBLIOGRAPHY

P. PRAY BOBER, "Cernunnos: Origin and Transformation of a Celtic Divinity," *American Journal of Archaeology* 45 (1951). P.-M. DUVAL, *Les Celtes* (Paris 1977). A. AUDOLLENT, *Defixionum tabellae* (Paris 1904).

UNIDENTIFIED FIGURES OF CELTIC DEITIES

An extensive Celtic and Celto-Roman iconography (the latter frequently separated from the inscriptions which would have accompanied and identified them) has left us with figures of gods unlike any others and consequently not yet identified. In many cases, identification can be made on the basis of the principal characteristics and attributes: a god or goddess of the hunt, a goddess of abundance, a mother goddess, a warrior god or goddess, a god with birds, a divine couple, etc. But the unknown element remains much stronger when no particular attribute offers any clear association.

It is not known whether the seated cross-legged pre-Roman figures from Roquepertuse and Glanum (Bouches-du-Rhône) are gods or priests, or who the god is, also sitting cross-legged, that is made of bronze sheeting and is found at Bouray (Essonne). And we do not know the identity of the

Unidentified hunter-god from Mount Donon (Lower Rhine). Strasbourg, Musée archéologique.

two naked gods, one three-headed, who accompany Pan on a stela from Beaune (Côte-d'Or); or the bearded deity seated cross-legged, a human face on his knees, at Bouriège (Aude); or the goddess shown in a pharmacist's dispensary (or so it appears), with many details, at Grand (Vosges); or the portraits of gods on the Gundestrup basin. Many other gods of Gaul, Great Britain, Spain, and the countries of the Danube are known to us only by their images and would merit careful comparative analysis. So would the supernat-

Back of a stone statue of a seated goddess covered with representations of animals. Le Coutarel, Poulan-Pouzols (Tarn). France, Musée d'Albi. Photo Groc.

ural beings, divine or simply sacred, depicted on Celtic coins, such as the androcephalous horse or boar, the birds of prey alone, in combat, or driving a horse, and the series of monsters so common in these scenes.

P.-M.D./d.b.

BIBLIOGRAPHY

E. ESPÉRANDIEU, after R. LANTIER, *Recueil général des bas-reliefs, statues et bustes de la Gaule romaine*, 15 vols. (1907–66); E. ESPÉRANDIEU, *Recueil . . . de la Germanie romaine* (1931). F. BENOÎT, *L'art primitif méditerranéen dans la vallée du Rhône* (2d ed., 1955), pre-Roman sculptures; to be supplemented by the bronze statuettes and appliqués, coinage, intaglios, mosaics, ceramic seals, and terra cotta figurines. M. MAINJONET, "Les animaux imaginaires des monnaies gauloises," in the catalog of the Hôtel des Monnaies exposition, *Le bestiaire des monnaies, des sceaux et des médailles* (Paris 1974).

GALLO-ROMAN DEITIES

"Gallo-Roman deities" means Gallic gods assimilated to their Roman parallels, or Roman gods assimilated to their Gallic parallels, by means of Roman interpretation or Celtic interpretation. Some major examples of such fusion resulted in divinities who were apparently aspects of great Roman gods who were only to be found in Celtic countries, and most particularly in Gaul, though a Celtic substratum alone was not necessarily the cause of this fusion: it is possible that a mutation took place in Gaul alone, but through a convergence of factors in which the indigenous element was not the only one. For example, the presence of foreign troops in Italy and Gaul in the armies of the Rhine could have produced, through their contact with the Gallic substratum, an effect which a mere contact between Gauls and Romans would not have provoked. The part played by Greek influences, which were either directly felt through the south of France, which had long been impregnated with Hellenism, or less directly through various elements imported under the Roman domination (by soldiers, merchants), is not to be underestimated.

I. Jupiter, master of combats, a rider mounted upon a giant snake-footed creature while holding a wheel alone or with a thunderbolt and perched on a column or pillar, sometimes with a horse or a small companion, belongs to Gaul, where he is present nearly everywhere. He is the result of a complex mixture.

II. Mercury, the patron not only of travel and commerce but of crafts, like the Irish Lug Samildánach ("the polytechnician"), of whom he may be the continental expression, is always bearded, clothed, seated cross-legged in the Gallic style, and even has three faces like other Celtic divinities. As the hammer bearer he is grouped together with Minerva and Vulcan. He is characterized in these ways in Gaul and nowhere else, and he is, according to Caesar's testimony, the greatest god in the country. There alone he is depicted as offering his purse in his open hand, as a divine provider.

III. Minerva is, in Gaul as in Greece, the worker who watches over the arts and crafts and over women's work in particular. She may have an Irish parallel in Brighid, who was honored by doctors and smiths, diviners and poets; and a Gallic goddess named *Bricta* or *Brixta* may correspond to her. As late as the fifth century, Salvian wrote that Minerva was honored in the gymnasia; in the seventh century, Saint Eligius prohibited women from "invoking her . . . either for spinning, for dyeing, or for doing any other chores."

IV. Vulcan very likely overlaid a Celtic god of the forge whose name is found in Ireland (Goibhniu) and in Wales (Gofannon). His remarkable popularity in Gaul under the Roman empire—a popularity which was exceptional in comparison with the other provinces—suggests this. He appears on a base composed of four gods, discovered in Vienne-en-Val (Loiret), with his foot on the prow of a ship: this is proof of the role his cult played among boat builders in this country so rich in rivers, iron, and wood.

Jupiter. Bronze statuette discovered at Châtelet, near Saint-Dizier. Saint-Germain-en-Laye, Musée des antiquités nationales. Photo Giraudon.

Mercury, from Puy-de-dôme. Clermont-Ferrand, Musée Bargoin. Photo Giraudon.

V. Sylvanus was closely assimilated to Sucellus, the god with the mallet, which throws more light on the nature of Sucellus as master of chthonic forces than it does on Sylvanus. This mixture of aspects and of attributes is nonetheless a Gallo-Roman original.

VI. The Dioscuri. Two sources, a Greek text and a Gallo-Roman inscription, may be invoked in support of a Gallic cult of two brothers, parallel to the Greco-Roman Gemini. In the third century B.C., Timeus wrote: "The Celts who dwell along the ocean venerate the Dioscuri [i.e., "gods who resemble our Dioscuri"] above any of the gods, since they have a tradition handed down from ancient times that these gods came among them from the ocean. Moreover, there are on the ocean shore, they say, many names which are derived from the Argonauts and the Dioscuri" (cited by Diodorus of Sicily, 4.56.4, in the first century B.C.). Elsewhere, a dedication found in Hérault associates with the name *Martes* two Gallic gods who were the young warrior chiefs *Divanno* and *Dinomogetimarus*, but warriors are not necessarily Dioscuri. Finally, it should be recalled that among the Germans, who were so close to the Celts in the beginning at least, the *Naharvales*, according to Tacitus, honored two divine young brothers named *Alci* (*Germania*, 43.4–5). These references

may be interpreted as support of the existence of Celtic "Dioscuri," since Gallo-Roman dedications to Castor and Pollux are more numerous in Gaul than in other parts of the Roman empire.

VII. Gallo-Roman Gods of the Week. Among the Romans—as among the Egyptians—luminaries, planets, and satellites, seven in number, came to designate—under the name of "planets"—the seven days of a week which has become that of the Romance peoples, though the days were at that time marked only by letters or numbers; their names came later. The first day (Saturday) is that of Saturn, while the last (Sunday) is that of the sun. Ausonius attests to the common use of the planetary week in the fourth century. Inscriptions, monuments, and ornamented objects (notably the columns dedicated to the Gallic Latinized Jupiter) demonstrate the success of the "planetary" week in Gaul in the Roman period. It existed neither among the Babylonians nor among the Hebrews or Greeks, but the Alexandrines used it and it was instituted in the West probably under their influence. Thirty-seven monuments or objects represent (standing or as busts) the seven divinities of the planets (Saturnus, Sol, Luna, Mars, Mercurius, Jupiter, Venus): three of these are "on weekly duty," with a hole meant to receive

Vulcan at the prow of a ship. From a frieze with four gods discovered at Vienne-en-Val (Loiret).

a slip for each day. The calendar of Coligny (Ain), engraved in bronze in Gallic in the second half of the first century, counts the days by fifteens, and distinguishes them only by numbers: it would thus appear that the use of the planets was not Celtic, although it might have been especially widespread in Roman Gaul. It is impossible to see in the so-called Belgian "planetary" vases—which are ornamented with a variable number of divine busts—representations of the gods of the week; these perpetuate the very ancient tradition of vases inlaid with busts or faces, of which there were often only two.

P.-M.D./d.w.

BIBLIOGRAPHY

P.-M. DUVAL, "Les dieux de la semaine," *Gallia*, 11 (1953); *Les dieux de la Gaule* (2d ed., Paris 1976): Jupiter, 29, 73–76, 110–11; Mercury, 26–28, 69–71, 110; Minerva, 32–33, 82–84, 120; Vulcan, 33–34, 84–85, 111; Sylvanus, 78–79, 111–12; Dioscuri, 18, 87.

CELTIC SACRED MONSTERS

I. The Three-Horned Bull

No one is certain whether the three-horned bull, known only in Gaul through bronze statuettes and a life-sized bronze statue (located in the Zurich Museum), was a sacred animal of the pre-Roman Celtic period. Its frontal horn may have evolved from the bird or from the crescent that was affixed with a pin to the head of the bronze bulls of Italy. But in Gallic thinking, when this accessory became transformed into a third horn it magnified the power of the bull monstrously (by virtue of "intensive repetition") and turned him into a supernatural, if not divine, animal. We know this bull only from monuments decorated with figures, especially in east central Gaul.

II. The Monstrous Boar

In both independent and Roman Gaul, the monstrous boar was a devastating and terrible inhabitant of the forests that symbolized aggression, combative strength, and endurance. It participated in the supernatural world in two ways. First, as shown on coins of central Gaul, it bore an impressive human head instead of the head of a boar. Second, on a bronze statuette the boar has three short horns (or perhaps three tusks?) implanted on its head (statuette found in Burgundy currently in the Medals Room of the Bibliothèque nationale). This is another case of "intensive repetition." The tusk of the boar, his natural protection, was a talisman often used as a pendant or a piece of a necklace, as were the strongest teeth of certain carnivores.

III. The Sacred Serpent with the Head of a Ram

In the Celtic divine bestiary the sacred serpent with the head of a ram appears anonymously alone or as the companion of a god. When its head is that of a ram, it combines with the fighting power of this quadruped leader of the herd the magic qualities of a reptile. It lives in constant contact with the ground, slides sinuously through swamps and waters, and sheds its skin every year as the hart regrows its antlers. It draws its strength from its venom, its coils, its silent cunning, and from the mesmerizing glance it casts on fascinated prey with eyes that gleam through transparent lids. Finally, it has the virtue of being tamable. When its head is that of a serpent with horns, the composite animal has the same combination of qualities, although the ram cannot be identified.

This sacred monster accompanies the god with antlers as early as the fourth century B.C. on rock drawings of the Camonica Valley (Italian Alps) and in the first half of the first century B.C. on the bowl from Gundestrup (Denmark), probably made near the Black Sea. This ancient and durable alliance is therefore well attested in the outer reaches of Gaul and perhaps all the way to the easternmost reaches of Celtic culture. On the Gundestrup bowl, the horned snake also appears alone, at the head of a parade of warriors; he has the necessary mythical qualities to lead knights and foot soldiers (in this role he has been seen as a funereal symbol, which is not certain). On Gallic coins (among the Sequani of Togirix), he appears underneath a horse, perhaps in a battle scene. On other coins such as those of the Boii of Bohemia, who had come down the Danube as far as Bratislava by the first century B.C., there is a kind of horned snake with a body that is stouter in relation to its short length than is the body of a reptile, and with a head more reminiscent of an imaginary quadruped such as a dragon, occasionally with an outline of twisted horns.

Three-horned bull. Besançon, Musée des Beaux-Arts. Photo Giraudon.

During the Roman era the monstrous reptile accompanies a god and a goddess of war on the pillar of Mavilly (Côte-d'Or) and appears on an altar dedicated to Mercury at Beauvais (Oise) in France. On votive reliefs Cernunnos holds the monster and feeds him. Bracelets and armlets coiled like serpents, with ram's heads at both ends, have been found in the British Isles. An open tubular torque with two elk heads rather than horse heads (but without antlers), dating back to the second century B.C., was found in Vieille-Toulouse (Haute-Garonne). It is clear that the composite creature, made of a snake's body with the head of a quadruped and especially with horns, was a familiar sacred monster from one end of Celtic Europe to the other, particularly in Gaul where it survived the Roman conquest.

P.-M.D./g.h.

BIBLIOGRAPHY

A. COLOMBET and P. LEBEL, "Mythologie gallo-romaine: Les taureaux à trois cornes," *Revue archéologique de l'Est et du Centre-Est*, vol. 4 (1953). P.-M. DUVAL, *Les dieux de la Gaule* (2d ed., Paris 1976), 10, 47. Three-horned wild boar: E. BABELON and A. BLANCHET, *Catalogue des bronzes antiques de la Bibliothèque nationale* (Paris 1895), no. 798. Horned serpent: P.-M. DUVAL, *Les dieux de la Gaule*, 17, 21, 38–39. C. KASTELIN, "Das böhmische Rolltierstater und die süddeutschen Regenbogenschüsselchen," *Jahrbuch für Numismatik und Geldgeschichte*, 14, 1964.

THE MYTHIC ORIGINS AND SUCCESSIVE POPULATIONS OF IRELAND

In the *Leabhar Gabhála Eireann*, "the book of the taking of Ireland," the history of the Irish people is traced from Adam to Noah as far as the Bible permits; after this, descendants of Japheth that they are, the Irish have an extrabiblical history parallel to that of the descendants of Shem. The *Leabhar Gabhála Eireann* recounts the story of the expedition of the sons of Míl from Spain all the way to Ireland, where they settled; but first it tells of the five races that had successively occupied Ireland before them; the five races are clearly the complex prototype of Irish society, but also a symbolization of the cosmos, as is the case for the five related figures in the *Rg Veda*, who also came from a place beyond the seas. These five races were those of Cesair, Partholón, Nemhedh, followed by the Fir Bholg and the Tuatha Dé Danann. Almost all of them had to battle the dark race of the Fomhoire.

Let us begin with a few remarks on the Fomhoire. A monstrous race associated with the sea and its islands, the Fomhoire, sometimes represented as having descended from Cain or Ham, were the antagonists of the successive populations that occupied Ireland. At the time of occupation by the race of Partholón, they were believed to be a society in which the women outnumbered the men. And even though she had only one arm and one leg, the most imposing figure among them was the enormous deformed mother of their male leader, a woman who alone had the strength of her entire tribe. The people of the race of Nemhedh were obliged each year to give them two-thirds of their grain, their milk, and their progeny. As strange as it may seem, the marvelous Tuatha Dé Danann before coming to Ireland were allies of the Fomhoire. And it was by the marriage of Cian, son of Dian Cécht (the god of health) and Ethniu, daughter of Balar (the one-eyed Fomhoirian king of the islands), that Lugh was born, he who would deliver the Tuatha from the oppression of Bres the Fomhoire. Eochaidh Bres ("Eochaidh the Beautiful") was the son of Elatha ("skill"), a king of the Fomhoire, and of Ériu, a queen of the Tuatha Dé Danann. It was the women of the Tuatha who instantly asked that Eochaidh Bres be made king. His reign, marked by the greatest miserliness, ended in the second battle of Magh Tuiredh between the Tuatha and the Fomhoire who were assembled by Bres and led by three kings: Balar the champion, Indech mac Dé Domhnann, and Elatha ("skill"). Defeated, Bres saved his life by teaching the men of Ireland how to work the fields, to sow, and to reap. After this it was said that he met his end while trying to take the milk from the cows of the people of Mumu (Munster).

The Fomhoire thus appear as the adversaries of the established order, who sometimes had at least the support of the women of Ireland, but who were interested in farm work. When the Tuatha were defeated by the Sons of Míl, they also retreated into the magic dwelling places of the hills, the islands, and the undersea regions. They provided women for the new rulers of Ireland and had the power to destroy or to preserve their grain and milk for them. The difference between the Tuatha and the Fomhoire was thus rendered less obvious.

It seems that in order to have women, to protect their progeny and their livestock, and to take advantage of the fruits of the land, the rulers of Ireland had to triumph over hostility and obtain the cooperation of neighbors whose ways of life were different from their own.

I. Cesair

Refused a place on Noah's ark, which was not intended as "a boat for bandits, a den of thieves," Cesair ("thin"), the daughter of Bith, himself the son of Noah (but not according to the Bible), and her companions became worshipers of an idol. Then, in order to escape the Flood, they left for Ireland and landed in Corco Duibne in western Mumu, which was the place of arrival for various waves of invaders. This group, the first of the "five races" that came to Ireland before the "Sons of Míl," comprised fifty women and three men: Fintan, son of Bóchra ("the ocean"), Cesair's husband; Bith ("world"), her father; and Ladra, the pilot. In Ireland these three divided up the women among themselves, the first two taking seventeen each, which left Ladra very unhappy with his mere sixteen. Ladra left for the south and was the first to die (from having too many women, according to one version). The women were then once again divided up, and upon the death of Bith, who had gone to the north, the original three groups were reassembled at "the confluence of the three waters." Faced with all these women, Fintan took to his heels. The women died and Fintan hid for one year in a cave on the Hill of the Wave and thus survived the Flood. Taking on the form first of a salmon, then of an eagle, and then of a falcon, he was afterwards witness to all the invasions that followed.

In Celtic tradition, the waves of the sea are considered to be sheep. Cesair was the first to introduce sheep in Ireland. After the Flood, Ireland remained without inhabitants for three hundred years. When the next group arrived, that of Partholón, it had to deal with the opposition of the accursed Fomhoire, once again a predominantly female group which was associated with the sea, and which had been there hunting birds and fishing for two hundred years. During the time of the race of Nemhedh, the Fomhoire made Ireland a land of sheep.

According to an ancient version of this traditional tale, the woman who came before the Flood was named Banbha, an eponymous form of Banbha of the Women, or Ireland. She declared to the sons of Míl that she was older than Noah: "Look at that hilltop from here (the Hill of the Wave): the waves of the flood reached all the way up to here."

Some of those who have recorded this tradition challenge the inclusion of Cesair's group among the five races. Similarly, there was disagreement about the inclusion of a second province of Mumu as one of the "five provinces" (to the exclusion of Midhe, the central province).

II. Partholón

Partholón, the leader of the second of the five races that occupied Ireland before the Sons of Míl (and of the first to come after the Flood), was, like Cesair, someone who was fleeing punishment, for he was guilty of the murder of his own father and sovereign. But in the end he perished along with all his people in a plague, which spared only Tuan, whose story repeated that of Fintan of Cesair's group. Like Fintan, like Mug Ruith, Eochaidh mac Luchta and other figures of the province of Mumu, Partholón had only one eye. The names of his four sons recurred, as did the names of the four sons of Ébher (at the time of the Sons of Míl) who were in power in Mumu. Like the Fomhoire, the race of Partholón hunted and fished, and when the two groups confronted each other, their rather strange and ominous battle was fought by people with only one leg, one arm, and one eye. Not one man was killed. Their occupation of Irish land was marked by the formation of lakes. They also cleared four plains. These people were clearly farm laborers, for among them are seven agricultural workers, two plow drivers, two plowshares and four oxen. They also practiced useful skills, such as churning, milling (with a millstone), cooking meat, brewing beer, building a guest house (foreseeing the arrival of superiors?), and Partholón is described as the "master of all skills." The oldest of his captains was the son of Senboth ("serf"), and names beginning with Sen- ("old") are usually the names of persons from the province of Mumu, that of the "Fourth Estate." Partholón was also the first cuckold in Irish history, and his wife and the serf she seduced were the first adulterers.

III. Nemhedh

Nemhedh and his people were the third of the five races that occupied Ireland before the Sons of Míl. Unlike the delinquent fugitives who had preceded them, Nemhedh (which means "privilege," "holiness") and his people embarked on their boats for no specified reason. They were free men who were not characterized in any special way. Laigne Lethan-glas, the father of Liath who represents them in a text, is the eponym of the Laigin and of their province which signifies prosperity. It was Liath who cleared the entangled woods of Tara, so that "its grain was rich grain." The race of Nemhedh sustained a prolonged war against the Fomhoire and battled them in each of the three "upper" provinces— Connacht (Connaught), Ulaidh (Ulster), and Laigin (Leinster)—but when Nemhedh died (of the plague, like Partholón, who was likewise a farmer), he had to give them two-thirds of his grain, his milk, and his progeny. People no longer dared to allow smoke to be seen above any house in Ireland. After a renewed attempt to defeat their oppressors, this time in a naval battle, Nemhedh's people were able to save only one of their vessels. The survivors split up into three groups. One of them settled on foreign ground and disappeared from the tale. The descendants of the other two groups ultimately returned: first the Fir Bholg, and second the Tuatha Dé Danann. These two races had kings. Their ancestors, the people of Nemhedh, had built two royal fortresses, apparently destined for them, and while the race of Partholón had cleared four plains, the race of Nemhedh cleared twelve—perhaps four for them and four for each of the two groups of descendants for whose arrival they had prepared.

IV. The Fir Bholg

The fourth of the five races that occupied Ireland before the arrival of the Sons of Míl were the Fir Bholg. They descended from their immediate predecessors, the race of Nemhedh, and came to Ireland in search of liberty. They landed in three groups: the Fir Domnann in Connacht, the Gailioin in Laigin, and the Fir Bholg proper in Ulaidh, the warring province; or according to another version, in Mumu, through which the Ulaidh passed in order to reach their destination. The entire race was governed by five brothers who instituted the political division of Ireland into five provinces, this division being considered "the oldest and the best attested of the deeds in Irish history." Also, the Irish word for province is cóiced, "a fifth," which indicates the antiquity of the concept of a united Ireland. The kings of the Fir Bholg were the most ancient of Ireland, and one of them, Eochaidh, son of Erc, an exemplary king, rendered justice there for the first time. He was also the first king to be killed by a weapon; it was said of one of his predecessors that it was in his time that weapons were first equipped with points. When the Tuatha Dé Danann came to Ireland they spoke the same language as the Fir Bholg, to whom they were related, and the two races met each other with respect. The weapons of the Fir Bholg earned the praise of their adversaries.

V. Tuatha Dé Danann: "The Peoples of the Goddess Danann"

The last of the five races that occupied Ireland before the arrival of the Sons of Míl, the Tuatha Dé Danann came from the islands in the north of the world, where they had acquired their esoteric knowledge. They were believed to be the ancestors of educated men in Ireland. They came through the air in black clouds and landed on a mountain in Connacht, the province of knowledge. Their two famous battles also took place in Connacht, at Magh Tuiredh; the first was against the Fir Bholg, their predecessors, and the second against the Fomhoire. And Mider, the diviner in one of the most beautiful mythological tales, was the lord of the *sídh* of Bri Leith, again in the same province. The Tuatha Dé Danann appear to be a race versed in all the arts, masters of sorcery and marvels, and great magicians. Danann (or Danu, as it is written in some old texts) is a parallel to *Dôn* of Welsh tradition. Like Anu, she is believed to be the mother of the gods of Ireland. In the Middle Ages Irish writers were still conscious of the fact that the Tuatha had once been objects of a cult. One text states that their artists were gods (*dee*), and their farm laborers *andee* ("giant gods"? "non-gods"?). Among the artists, Lugh appears as the master of all artistic roles, including that of warrior, champion, poet, sorcerer, doctor, blacksmith, and carpenter. His Welsh counterpart is Lleu Llaw Gyffes, "Lleu of the ready (or able) hand." On the Continent his name can also be compared to those of the divine Lugoves, and he seems to be thus commemorated in place names such as Laon, Leiden, and Lyons (Lugudunum), to which one should add Carlisle (Luguvalium). It was he who instituted horse racing, ball games, and meetings (which were to become fairs). It is believed that he was the god whom Caesar said the Celts adored more than any other; he was their Mercury, the inventor of all arts, their guide in voyages, and the greatest power in commercial affairs. Caesar mentioned four other gods in addition to this one, giving them all Roman names: There was Apollo, who protected against sickness; Mars, who presided over wars; Jupiter, the lord of the skies; and Minerva, who told them the first principles of professions and skills. These figures have been compared to the leaders of the Tuatha with whom Lugh conferred before the second battle of Magh Tuiredh: first the Daghdha, the god of Druidism, the Lord of the Great Science; and Oghma, the champion, the strong. Joining them next was Dian Cécht, the god of health, and Goibhniu, the artisan. The four of them combined to ensure all the functions. Oghma is certainly the same god as the Herculean Ogmios represented by Lucian in a way that is strangely confirmed by a similar description of one of the men of Ulaidh in *Táin Bó Cuailnge*. The powers of eloquence are emphasized here. This god is also credited with the invention of ogham writing. Other divinities mentioned in Irish sources are Neit, the god of war; Manannán mac Lir, the Irish and Welsh god of the sea—he is associated with Inis Manann (the Isle of Man) and with Emhain Abhlach in the estuary of Clyde—and Brighid, the daughter of the Daghdha and the companion of the miserly Fomhoire king Eochaidh Bres. Brighid was revered by poets, and she had two sisters, her homonyms, goddesses of the arts of smithery and of medicine. Many of the legends about Saint Brighid, who rivals Saint Patrick in importance in Irish folklore, probably derive from those about the goddess, whose name also appears in Ireland, Wales, and England as the name of rivers. The name is also related to *Brigantes*, the name of several Celtic tribes. It probably meant "liberty" or "privilege," and it is significant that devotion to Saint Brighid was centered in Kildare in Laigin, the province most specifically associated with free men (of the Third Estate).

When the Tuatha Dé Dannan arrived in Ireland, which was at that time still occupied by the Fir Bholg, their king was Nuadhu (whose name is related to that of Nodons or Nodens), a god commemorated in dedications and symbols found in a Celto-Roman temple in Lydney in Gloucestershire. According to one version of the story of the first battle of Magh Tuiredh, the battle ended in a pact of peace and friendship. According to another, the Fir Bholg were beaten and retreated to the neighboring islands. In any case Nuadhu lost an arm in the battle, a handicap that made it impossible for him to remain king. Whence the reign of Bres, son of Ériu by a king of the Fomhoire. But Dian Cécht provided Nuadhu with a silver arm, giving him the name of Nuadhu airgedlámh, "Nuadhu of the silver arm" (this is the Lludd Llaw Ereint mentioned in the Welsh tale, *Culhwch and Olwen*). His original arm was, however, returned to him later and he resumed his royal function after Bres became the victim of the first satire ever carried out in Ireland. Nuadhu was presiding over a great feast at Tara when the handsome and charming Lugh arrived. First calling himself a carpenter, he in fact quickly revealed himself to be an incomparable master of all sorts of skills. He played the game of *fidchell*, and when he had won all the stakes, he took the seat of the sage. Next he accepted the challenge of the powerful Oghma in a rock-throwing contest; then, challenged to play the harp, he played magic chords which caused the entire audience to fall fast asleep; next he made them weep, and then made them rejoice. Thus victorious from the point of view of each of the three functions, Lugh acceded to the royal throne, given up to him by Nuadhu for thirteen days. Afterwards, in the second battle of Magh Tuiredh, Lugh walked around the army on one foot, singing and using only one arm and one eye. He found himself in front of his maternal grandfather, the terrible Balar, who had already killed Nuadhu. Balar had an evil eye which he never opened except on the battlefield, where he would render armies powerless. With a slingshot, Lugh threw a rock which made Balar's eye move through the back of his head and exercise its destructive power on the Fomhoire camp. The victory fell to the Tuatha. The life of Loch Lethglas, the Fomhoire poet, was spared when he granted Lugh three wishes, one of which was that up until the final Judgment he would divert all of the plundering activity of the Fomhoire. Bres's life was also spared, in exchange for instructions about the time of farm labor, sowing, and harvesting. Then all the livestock of Ireland was brought back and began to graze once again.

This battle, which took place during Samhain, the chaotic time between summer and winter, has been compared to the battle of the Norse gods, the Aesir against the Vanir, these latter being gods of the third function, and also to the conflict between the Indian Devas and Asuras, "the fundamental theme of the Vedic tradition." All these battles were between allied groups, on the one side the highest of gods, and on the other the adversaries who incorporated the indispensable feminine principle.

VI. The Sons of Míl

Last in the line of Japheth, son of Noah, the sons of Míl reached Spain where their relative, Ith, caught sight of Ireland and left to explore that country. On the island the Tuatha Dé Danann, suspicious of his intentions, killed him, and the Sons of Míl came to Ireland to avenge his death. Among them were Donn, the king, Amhairghin, the poet and judge, Éremhon, who led the expedition, and Ébher.

Upon landing, Amhairghin had the principal role. Placing his right foot on the ground, at the feast of Beltene, the calends of summer, he chanted a poem, a series of "I am . . . " which revealed that he was in himself all that was—declarations similar to those uttered by Krsna in the *Bhagavad-Gītā* and to those of Visnu himself in his sleep between the dissolution and the recreation of the Universe. In three different places he held what was essentially the same conversation with the three queens whose names were to become those of Ireland: Banbha, Fódla, and Ériu. At Tara the three kings, Mac Cuill, Mac Cécht, and Mac Greíne, begged the queens to leave them in peace for three days and asked Amhairghin to make an equitable judgment, at the risk of being put to death. He ruled that they should retreat beyond the ninth wave. The spells sung by the druids and the poets of the Tuatha caused the sons of Míl to be carried out to sea. But Amhairghin counterattacked with a more powerful poem which invoked the land of Ireland, "the high vessel of Ériu." The invaders landed again, defeated the Tuatha, and took possession of the country. Georges Dumézil has noted that Amhairghin's role during the preliminary landing was the counterpart of what the *pater patratus* did in Rome in a rite that secured a basis for protests against fines on foreign territory or demands for a just war on the other hand; and it was also the counterpart of Visnu's role when he took three steps to open a field of action for Indra.

Amhairghin assigned the defeated Tuatha the secret Ireland of magic dwelling places (*sídh*). As the invaders were approaching the shore, the eldest brother, Donn, offended the Tuatha. His boat was sunk, and he was prevented from taking part in the occupation of the country. His body was placed on an elevated rock and Amhairghin declared that his people should come there to the house of Donn (*Tech Duinn*) off the coast of Mumu. There are other ancient references to this meeting place of the dead ("To me, to my house, you will all come after you are dead"), and Donn maintained his place in popular beliefs until only recently. In some ways he reminds one of Yama, the first man to die, the assembler of humanity.

When a dispute erupted between Éremhon and Ébher about the kingship, Amhairghin decided that Donn's inheritance should go to Éremhon and after him to Ébher. The latter, however, insisted that a division be made, and Éremhon acceded to kingship in the north, and Ébher to that in the south (unless one believes another version, that Éremhon obtained both the north and royal sovereignty, while Ébher took the south; there are indeed other indications of the primacy of the north). The two brothers drew lots to see who would have the poet and the harpist (among musicians, ancient laws stated that only the harpist could, insofar as he accompanied the nobility, accede to the status of a free man). The poet, "a knowledgeable man and of great power," went to Éremhon, and the harpist to Ébher. Thus

dignity and knowledge were assured in the north, and "the sweet music of strings" in the south. "May it be thus until the final Judgment!" (One should note that in the *Rg Veda* the Gandharva musicians are opposed to the Brahmans, and that in the *Śatapatha Brāhmana* words and songs were linked, respectively, to the earth and the sky). Finally Ébher rebelled and was killed by Éremhon; this hostility persisted among their descendants. According to a poem attributed to a ninth-century author, Éremhon took the north as the inheritance of his race, with its legendary tradition, its unique qualities, and its laws, as well as its fortresses and its fierce armed bands, its violent confrontations, and its animals. Ébher took the south, with its harmony, its excellence, its humility and hospitality, its vivacity, its festive spirit, its purity—the same division that appears in the tale, *The Establishment of the House of Tara* (see the article "The Myths and Narratives of the Celts of the Islands," above).

B.R./t.l.f.

BIBLIOGRAPHY

R. A. S. MACALISTER, *Le bor Gabála Érenn* (Dublin 1938–56). G. DUMÉZIL, *Mitra et Varuna*, 1948; *Jupiter, Mars, Quirinus* (Paris 1941); *Servius et la fortune* (Paris 1943); *Le troisième souverain* (Paris 1949), 167–86; *L'idéologie tripartie* (Brussels 1959), 94; *Idées romaines* (Paris 1969), 75–78, 304. F. LE ROUX, "Le dieu druide et le druide divin," "Le dieu celtique aux liens," *Ogam*, 12; "Notennoù . . . diwar-ben an doue Manannán," *Ogam*, 17–18; "Le Dieu-Roi Nodons," *Celticum*, 6. C. STERCKX, "Une formule païenne dans des textes chrétiens de l'Irlande ancienne," *Études Celtiques* 14 (1974): 229–33. T. M. CHARLES-EDWARDS, "Native Political Organization . . . and the Origin of MW brenhin," *Antiquitates Indogermanicae* (Innsbruck 1974), 35–45. On the general view given above: A. D. REES and B. REES, *Celtic Heritage* (London 1961), 95–117 (and 28–41, 131, 137).

MYTHS OF SOVEREIGNTY FROM WALES (THE *MABINOGI*)

A. The Four Branches of the "Mabinogi"

I. Pwyll and Pryderi

The four branches, or sections, of the Welsh *Mabinogi* contain stories about three families that appear at the beginning of the first, second, and fourth sections (the third section opens with events that reunite characters already present in one or both of the first two sections, but it is essentially only a prolongation of the first; these two sections concern the lords of Dyfed, in southwest Wales). The first word of the first section is the name of Pwyll ("prudent—or wise—slowness"), prince (*pendeuic*) and lord of the seven cantons ("cantreds") of Dyfed. A common Irish noun is associated with his name, but with a depreciatory prefix, *doichlech*, or "serf." The Celtic god Sucellus (whose name is also quite possibly related to Pwyll's, but this time with a favorable prefix) is generally considered to be a distributor of riches and prosperity: "his worshipers are above all the common people" (Jan de Vries).

The second section of the *Mabinogi* opens with the name of Bendigeidfran, son of Llŷr, the king of the Island of the Mighty. The first part of his name, which is sometimes missing, is an adjective that means "blessed"; the resulting name is Bran. The common noun *bran* usually means "raven," but the combined form *cynfran* also means "warrior" or (like the Irish *bran*) "leader." Bran received the crown of London, but place names associate him with Powys in northeast Wales. The fourth section opens with the name of Math, son of Mathonwy, the lord sorcerer of Gwynedd in northwest Wales. Characters of the same name in Irish tradition are Mathu—who is mentioned with Nuadhu and Goibhniu as one of the three pagan "prophets"—and Matha, the druid who opposed Saint Patrick. These three initial names—Pwyll, Bran, and Math—respectively indicate the nature of these three families.

Pryderi ("trouble"), son of Pwyll, is named first among the seven survivors of the army of Bran in the second section. In the third he offers his mother, Rhiannon, in marriage to Manawydan, Bran's brother, and in the fourth he is defeated and killed by Gwydion, Math's nephew. The family of the south thus forms a link between the two families of the north, just as the people of Nemhedh, in Irish tradition, were the ancestors of both the Fir Bholg and the Tuatha Dé Danann.

In the course of these stories the lords of Dyfed, when they visit their land, remark that they have never seen a more agreeable country to live in, one more suitable for hunting or richer in honey and fish. Welsh laws specified that only villeins had to provide the masters with honey and fish. Almost all the hunts that take place in Wales in the *Mabinogi* occur in the south, just as most of the adventures of the Fenian hunters take place in southern Ireland. Earlier in the *Mabinogi*, when Manawydan sows the wheat, he grows "the best in the world"; "no one had seen more beautiful wheat," which reminds one of the remark about the free men of the land of Nemhedh: "their grain was rich grain." Manawydan, son of Llŷr, is doubtless the Manannán mac Lir of Irish tradition, of whom it was said that he was the god of the sea for the Irish and the Welsh. For the Greeks, Poseidon was likewise the god of farmers as much as he was god of the sea. The "southern" sections of the *Mabinogi* seem to deal as much with villeins as with free men.

Pwyll and Pryderi had something unique among the rulers mentioned in the *Mabinogi*: Their realm was counted in *cantrefi* or *cantreds* (*cantref*: can, hundred, and *tref*, dwelling), which reappears only in the case of the young Lleu, who is given power over a *cantred*. What is also remarkable in their story is the exceptional frequency of the words *cyfoeth* ("realm," "riches") and *cyfannedd* ("dwelling," "social pleasure," deriving from *anned*, "residence," "dwelling place"). It may be noted that (1) the *viś* of the *Ṛg Veda*, the principle of the third class, is defined as "peasantry," "organized habitat," and in the plural, "the totality of the people in their social and local groupings" (G. Dumézil); (2) in the oldest Irish society, the head of a hospice (who didn't belong to the nobility) was described as *cétach* (man "of hundreds"), his wealth being calculated in "hundreds"; (3) in Roman tradition it was Servius, whose name derives from *servus*, a king closely bound to the *servi* and to freedmen, who reorganized the political assembly using the *centuria* as a foundation.

In the first section of the *Mabinogi*, Pwyll offended Arawn, king of Annwn ("underground world" or "great world"?) by his failure to recognize Arawn's right to the stag brought down by his dogs. He was reprimanded for his *anwybot* and his *ansyberwyt*, that is, for his discourtesy (words which by their components in fact denote a lack of knowledge and nobility). But he didn't seem to notice, and in order to win Arawn's friendship (and to avoid the defamatory remarks

with which he was threatened) he agreed to substitute himself for Arawn for one year in order to confront Arawn's steadfast enemy, Hafgan ("whiteness of summer"), who could easily be defeated with a single blow, but never if there were to be a second blow. Arawn carried out the exchange of physical appearances, and Pwyll was instructed to learn the manners of Arawn's court, which was marvelous in its aristocratic perfection and the urbanity of its customs. Pwyll enjoyed the company and the conversation of the queen, the most charming woman he had ever seen, and at night chastely shared her bed. He then defeated Hafgan, thus unifying Annwn in a single kingdom. Upon his return to Dyfed, he declared that during the past year his subjects had found their prince to be more courteous, kind, generous, and just than ever before, and that it was therefore expected of him that he maintain this excellence. Annwn and Dyfed were then also united by the friendship of their two rulers and by their generous exchange of gifts. Pwyll would henceforth be known as the Head of Annwn and not as the Prince of Dyfed. In a poem, *Is-dwfn* ("underground world") seems to refer to Dyfed, exactly as *the house of Donn* (island of the dead) appears in relation to the province of Mumu (Munster) or its dynasty.

Three series of events take place afterwards, each one beginning at the magic mound which was near the court of Narberth in Dyfed. The first marvel Pwyll witnesses is the apparition of Rhiannon: After the swiftest horses have failed to catch up with her white horse, which was just ambling along, she reveals that out of love for Pwyll she has refused to marry the suitor who has been chosen for her. During the celebration of his wedding a year later, Pwyll demonstrates a great and naive carelessness in guarding what is his and is forced to give his bride to the rejected suitor, Gwawl ("light"). Rhiannon reproaches him but gives him a magic leather bag which allows him, at Gwawl's wedding, to capture his rival, to mock him by calling him a "badger in the bag," and to retrieve his wife (similarly, the rival to the throne of the king of Mumu [Munster], the defeated rival, is called the "badger of Mumu"). They wait long for the birth of a son, after which the child disappears; this event is connected with the yearly loss, on the first day of May, of the colt regularly born to the mare of Teyrnon ("lord"), lord of a territory in southeast Wales. Teyrnon succeeds in cutting off the claws of the thief—a badger?—and when he finds Rhiannon's child on his doorstep, he and his wife raise him as their son and later take him back to his parents. Teyrnon is considered "the best man on earth." It should be noted that in Welsh tales, "the best man" and also the "good man" are expressions that are reserved for free men, gentlemen of the third estate, as "the best horses," etc., are expressions attributed to their possessions. The hope that Pryderi ("trouble") will reveal himself to be a true gentleman often arises. Many years later Pwyll dies.

In the third section, Pryderi, who has conquered seven more "cantreds," entrusts Dyfed to Manawydan when Manawydan takes Rhiannon as his wife. The two lords and their wives visit the magic mound, but then a magic transformation takes place. Not a sign or a trace of habitation (*cyfannedd*) or riches is any longer visible on the deserted land. Later they have to compete against the leather workers in Lloegyr (England), "villains and rogues." The impetuous Pryderi is restrained by the patient Manawydan, but in the end he stupidly allows himself to be lured into a magic fortress where his mother, like him, is held in captivity. Manawydan sows the wheat and prepares to trap one of the countless mice that are depriving him of his harvest. He goes to the magic mound, readies himself to hang this "thief," and, obstinately refusing to release him, forces his enemy, the magician Llwyd ("grey"), Gwawl's avenger, to unveil himself, to reestablish life on his land with all its riches, its inhabitants, and its princes, as they were "at their best," and to promise that Dyfed will never again be the object of such extortion. After this Pryderi becomes the lord of a third group of seven cantreds, including the land of Teyrnon, "the best man in the world."

It should be noted (1) that the rulers of Dyfed do not make use of any magical powers; (2) that Pwyll and Pryderi are twins by name, appearance, and behavior—behavior which in the beginning belies their name. Their relationship reminds one of that of the father and son Njörðr and Freyr, Norse gods of the "third function," and also perhaps of Elatha and his son Bres; and of Laigne Lethan-Glas and his son Liath, of Irish tradition. (3) As for the destinies of Pwyll and Pryderi, they are recurrently linked to horses. One may reasonably compare the Aśvins and the Dioscuri; and in Rhiannon, Henri Hubert and other scholars have seen the Celtic goddess Epona. (4) The hunts, the feasts, and the interest in the art of leatherworking and cultivating wheat which appear in the tales, as well as the care Pryderi takes with the pigs of Annwn (in the *Triads* he is the swineherd of Pendaran Dyfed) and the song of Rhiannon's magic birds (in the second section), which is comparable to the music of southern Ireland—all this confirms the "third function" character of these southern princes. Their adversaries have characteristics of one or another of the three functions: Hafgan the indefatigable combatant, Gwawl the "badger," who tries to steal both the wife and the feast, and Llwyd the magician. All three, who are also connected by their names, are defeated by nocturnal vigilance and restraint, by one single blow, by the food necessary to fill a little bag, and by what could be given in exchange for a mouse ready to be killed. Beyond that, Pryderi becomes lord of seven cantreds through the fortune of his birth; he gains seven more from conquest, and the final seven seem to fall to him only after the magician has been defeated. The same three aspects are probably also to be seen in the shields, saddles, and shoes made by Manawydan and Pryderi, as well as in the shields, horses, and greyhounds that Pryderi accepted from Gwydion.

The *Mabinogi* begins in southwest Wales with the story of the deficiencies of Pwyll and Pryderi in the courtesy and moderation that would enable them to achieve their aristocratic destiny. It devotes itself for a time to Teyrnon, "the best man in the world," at that time in the southeast, then moves on to the families of the north, first to the family of the warrior-king Bran, the destroyer and protector commemorated in place names of the northeast, and then to the family of Don in the northwest, a family of magicians whose knowledge was used as much for slander as for exaggerations. It ends with the accession to sovereignty of Lleu, whose name, "light"—as the narrator understands it, and whatever its origin might be—is similar to those of the mysterious adversaries of Pwyll the careless and of Pryderi the imprudent: Hafgan, Gwawl, and Llwyd.

II. The Family of Llŷr

In the second section of the *Mabinogi*, Bran is the king of the Island of the Mighty, and the crown of London is granted to him. The story deals with the marriage of his sister Branwen to Matholwch, king of Ireland. Bran holds court in northwest Wales, although medieval tradition as well as

place names seem to connect him with the northeast, just as the seven guards to whom he entrusts his kingdom when he sends his army through Ireland are in Powys, the northeast province.

Branwen's marriage had been arranged so that the two kingdoms could be united and consequently strengthened. But as a result of the malevolent jealousy of Bran's halfbrother, Evnissyen, and Matholwch's weakness, which made him the victim of bad advice, the people meet with disaster, and the country is devastated. Bran rejects Matholwch's terms of surrender, the Irish are disloyal, Evnissyen ceaselessly foments disputes, and Branwen's attempt to save her country from destruction is in vain. Her son Gwern is thrown into a fire, Bran is mortally wounded, Evnissyen breaks his heart in a late attempt to save his people, and Branwen's heart is broken too when she sees the destruction she has caused throughout the two kingdoms. Caradawg, the son of Bran, also dies of a broken heart when he sees his men, the guards left on the Island of the Mighty, perish under the blows of the swords of an invisible enemy (his relative Caswallawn). This is a tale of war and misfortunes, marked by the most violent and cruel acts. But there are interludes of timeless celebration during the sad voyage that the seven lone survivors of the army of the Island of the Mighty make to London to bury the head of Bran, which will afterwards protect them from all invasions. The five sons who are born to the five pregnant women who were left alive in a cave in Ireland govern the country and divide it into five provinces, thus establishing the political order.

As in the magical family of Dôn, Llŷr's family preserves traces of the three functions. The colossal Bran and his magician successor Caswallawn represent the two aspects of a warrior, similarly represented in other Indo-European traditions. Manawydan, whose name is similar to that of the Irish Manannán, although not entirely its equivalent, is the wise adviser who in the third section of the *Mabinogi* defeats the sorcerer Llwyd. And in addition to their sister Branwen, they have two half-brothers, Nissyen, "a good young man," who reestablishes peace in disputes, and Evnissyen, who sows strife. These two half-brothers seem to be the equivalent of Sencha and Bricriu in the Irish tales of wars and warriors.

Concerning the name of Gwern, "alder," one may add that *Pengwern*, "the top of the alder," appears in the oldest poetry as the name of the court of the province of Powys; and that Gweirnion, "the people of Gwern," was the name of one of the families of Powys. A twelfth-century poem claims for Powys the right to carry out the first assault, in front of the armies, while in another poem about a battle of trees, the alders (*gwern*) are in front, the first to attack. A parallel to this identification may be seen in the tale of the oak—the tree that Pliny mentions in connection with druidic rites—in which Lleu appeared in Gwynedd (cf. the remarks on Dôn); and the presence of the yew (?) is notable in the name of Dinefwr, the royal fortress of southwest Wales, the yew also being the tree of the kings of Mumu in Irish tradition.

III. The Family of Dôn

In the fourth section of the *Mabinogi*, Math, son of Mathonwy, lord of Gwynedd (in northwest Wales), cannot live if he does not have his feet in a virgin's lap, unless the turmoil of war makes this impossible. His nephew Gilfaethwy, son of Dôn, is in love with this foot-holder, the maiden Goewin, and in order to enable him to approach her, his brother Gwydion the magician provokes a war between

Gwynedd and the south. Pryderi of Dyfed, duped by Gwydion, accepts his gift of horses, greyhounds, and shields, and despite the agreement that he has made with his people, gives him the swine that has been received from Annwn. After this he sets out in pursuit of the northerners. A great slaughter follows, and Pryderi is killed in single combat with Gwydion through the effect of Gwydion's magical powers (his fate is exactly the same as that of Ébher and of Mug Nuadhu in Irish tradition). During that time the two brothers come to their end. Goewin has been raped, but Math makes her his wife and bestows upon her the power over a kingdom of her own. And he punishes his disloyal nephews by having them mate as the male and the female of three different species successively, making them have a litter and a change of sex each year. The offspring, three "warriors," are designated the sons of Gilfaethwy. When Aranrhod, the daughter of Dôn, is taken to Math to take her turn at holding his feet, he asks her to straddle his magic rod, upon which she drops a beautiful child at his feet, as well as another small thing. The child is called Dylan, "the sea," and he immediately departs for the sea, takes on its nature, and swims as well as a fish. The other small thing is hidden by Gwydion; it will later reappear as the fabulous child that is eventually named Lleu Llaw Gyffes, or Lleu (which seems to mean "light") of the able hand. Aranrhod casts three spells on him: first that he will have no name before she gives him one; next that he will be unable to obtain weapons before she arms him; and finally that he will not take a wife from among the women of the race that is then on earth. Gwydion manages to have her name him and arm him without realizing it, and Math and he create a wife for him, Blodeuwedd ("flowers"), out of the flowers of the oak, the broom, and the meadowsweet. In Lleu's absence Blodeuwedd falls in love with Gronw, lord of Penllyn (in Powys), and agrees to strip Lleu of the specific conditions that protect his life. He cannot be killed in a house or out of doors, on horseback or on foot, and judging from his situation when he is finally struck down, neither can it be when he is dressed or when he is not. In addition, the spear that will strike him has to have been made in the course of a year, but only during the timeless moment of the Sunday Mass. Lleu is lured and induced to assume the only position that will avoid the above-mentioned alternatives, upon which, hit by Gronw's spear, he escapes, flying swiftly in the form of an eagle. While looking for him and pursuing an errant sow, Gwydion succeeds in finding him at the top of an oak tree on the plain of a hilltop ("the rain doesn't dampen him, the heat doesn't melt him"), where his rotting flesh, fallen to earth, is devoured by the sow. Gwydion then returns him to his human form and the good doctors of Gwynedd minister to him. Blodeuwedd is transformed into an owl, hated by all other birds. Gronw suffers from Lleu's hand the same death that Blodeuwedd had wanted for Lleu, and Lleu later becomes lord of Gwynedd.

This is a story of magic, of supernatural knowledge. It is also a story of treachery, of the abuse of knowledge, and of a violation of oaths. As Georges Dumézil has stressed, the three functions all appear in the family of Dôn: Gwydion the magician; Gilfaethwy, who achieves his ends through war and whose sons are warriors; Gofannon, whose name comes from *gof*, "the blacksmith"; and Amaethon (*amaeth*, "plowman, farmer"), who appears in the story of Culhwch and Olwen. His very marked absence from the *Mabinogi* is equivalent to the very brief reference to Nissyen the peacemaker in the "warrior" section (*Llŷr*) and to the minor role given to Teyrnon in the *Mabinogi* taken as a whole. The functions are also exemplified in the three sons of Gilfaethwy (a buck, a boar, and a wolf), in the three spells cast on Lleu concerning his name, his weapons, and his wife, and also apparently in the shields, the horses, and the greyhounds accepted by Pryderi.

The means of avoiding the alternatives that rendered Lleu vulnerable have been compared to the way in which Indra succeeded in killing Vṛtra, the enemy of the gods—but also the Sacrifice—in archaic Indian tradition, a myth charged with a deep meaning and already mentioned in the *Ṛg Veda*. Lleu's appearance in the form of an eagle in the oak tree, after he is hit by Gronw's spear, recalls the death of Óðinn, god of magic powers in Norse tradition. Stabbed by a spear and hung for nine nights from a tree, Óðinn sacrifices himself. Between the moment of the stabbing and the moment of the hanging of the men sacrificed to Óðinn, an "eagle of blood" had been slashed upon their backs: thus they had been symbolically transformed into eagles. And the way in which Lleu was induced to assume the required position (a ritual position perhaps?) is similar to that which King Vikar had to assume for a sacrifice (which was, incidentally, ostensibly fictive), which permitted him to be truly consecrated to Óðinn. Óðinn, who is sometimes referred to as an eagle, came back to life after having obtained mystical runes. In north and central Asia, it was believed that the first shaman had been the offspring or the disciple of an eagle, the bird of the sun, and "in his initiatory dreams the shaman is carried to the Cosmic Tree in whose top is the Lord of the World. Sometimes the Supreme Being is represented in the form of an eagle" (Mircea Eliade, *Shamanism*, New York 1964, p. 70). After his own restoration, Lleu becomes lord of the province ruled by the magicians of the family of Dôn and the successor of Math, who got wind of every word spoken.

Lleu's name is related to that of Lugh, the supreme figure among the Tuatha Dé Danann in Irish tradition. And Gofannon's name is derived from the same root as that of Goibhniu, their blacksmith. The name of Dôn is apparently related to that of Danu (or Donu, as some texts say), who, like Anu, is said to be the mother of the gods of Ireland. In one or two texts one finds *Dono* instead of the usual form, *Dôn*. *Dono* could well be a variant of *Donwy*, which in the compound form *Dyfrd*(d)*onwy* (*Dyfr* means "water") appears as the name of a river in Wales, as well as that of one of the "three sources of the ocean," the two others being the tide and the falling of rain through the atmosphere. This word is probably also related to *Danuvius*, the Latinized Celtic name for the Danube, and to other names of rivers—the Don, the Dnieper, and the Dniester—as well as to that of the Vedic goddess Dānu, mother of Vṛtra and wife of the ruling gods Mitra-Varuṇa. The Vedic *dānu* means "flow," "waters of the heavens."

B. Lludd and Llefelys

Lludd, son of Beli, whose name is probably a variant of *Nudd* and related to the Irish *Nuadhu*, was the king of the Isle of Britain and was renowned for his constructions, his generosity, and his prowess in war. When his kingdom suffered under three forms of oppression, he sought the advice of his brother, the wise Llefelys, king of France, whose instructions made it possible for him to rid himself of the afflictions. The island had fallen prey to a people who could not be prevented from hearing all that was said or even whispered in the country; there was also the terrifying cry of a dragon that every May Eve would battle the dragon of an alien people; and there was a thief with magical powers who surreptitiously made off with all the food and drink from the royal courts, with the exception of what was consumed on the first evening.

Georges Dumézil has stressed the structural character of these three "evils" and has found parallels to them in the archaic traditions of Indo-European cultures. In other respects the two brothers—the wise man and the warrior—who conspired to rid themselves of the people who hear everything, have their counterpart in the figures of Gwydion and Gilfaethwy in their relationship to that of Math, as it appears in the magic section of the *Mabinogi*. The references to the bewilderment caused by an unseen enemy and the protection guaranteed to the island by the dragons that were buried there have their counterpart in the warrior section (that of Llŷr). The thief's basket and his songs and games are reminiscent of Pwyll's bag and of Rhiannon's conversation and the song of her birds, while the promise that he makes to save his life recalls that of Llwyd to Manawydan, that of the earl at the hedge of mist to Gereint, and that of Loch, the poet of the Fomhoire, to Lugh, after the second battle of Magh Tuiredh, all antagonists in contests of the third function.

C. Three Arthurian Romances

(See the article "Arthur and the Arthurian Heroes in Wales," below.)

D. Culhwch and Olwen

When one has seen that the ideology of the three functions gives both form and substance to the four sections of the *Mabinogi*, to the story of Lludd and Llefelys, and to the three Welsh Arthurian romances, there still remain three other stories of the *Mabinogi* to consider, stories that are not specifically connected to one another. One of them, *Culhwch and Olwen*, is generally believed to have been written down by around 1100, and much of the story bears the mark of great antiquity. *The Dream of Rhonabwy*, on the other hand, begins with a deed attributed to a twelfth-century lord of Powys. It remains nevertheless remarkable that the two "dreams"—*The Dream of Macsen* and *The Dream of Rhonabwy*—take place in north Wales, the former in Gwynedd and the latter in Powys, while in *Culhwch and Olwen* the court of Arthur is in Cornwall; that the hunt of Twrch Trwyth, one of the great exploits of the story, is carried out from Dyfed in southwest Wales to the Severn in the southeast; and that several other adventures still are situated in southern Wales, whereas nothing takes place in the north of Wales.

Moreover, *The Dream of Macsen* is the tale of the discovery of an empress in Gwynedd and the reconquest of Rome thanks to the wisdom of the empress's two brothers, "the wisest young men in the world." Before going into action, they drink to gain courage, and afterwards they return the city to the emperor.

Rhonabwy of Powys had his dream when he departed to look for the brother of the prince of Powys, a jealous man who began to destroy everything after having rejected the prince's offer to give him the title of captain of his troups, a title equal in rank to his own, and horses, weapons, and honors of all kinds. In Rhonabwy's dream his guide was Iddawc, who was named the Agitator of (Great) Britain,

because in his furious need to fight he incited the battle of Camlan by sowing dissent between Arthur and his nephew Medrawd, an act that cost him seven years of penitence before he obtained a pardon. They went to see the emperor Arthur and observed a great gathering of armed troops in Powys. Caradawg of the Strong Arms, son of Llŷr, urged the emperor to leave for the battle of Badon. While Arthur and Owain, son of Urien (the captain of Arthur's troops, who was the hero of one of the three romances), were occupied at their game table, news arrived of a quarrel that opposed Owain's "Ravens" against Arthur's soldiers (with the sons of the gentlemen of the island). The first three messengers came out of tents whose tops were decorated with a black snake, a red lion, and a golden eagle (very appropriate symbols of the three functions). On the helmets of the next three were images of a leopard, a lion, and a griffin, which have the same functional meaning. When Arthur's council assembled they turned to Rhun, son of Maelgwn Gwynedd, whose authority was so great that each of them always asked him what he should do. All of the characters of this tale of war were men, which recalls certain privileges claimed for Powys: first, exemption from having to receive the women of the royal court while traveling; then "a portion (of an inheritance of lands) for the sister—which cannot be obtained from Powys." The narrator takes pleasure in describing the weapons and accoutrements of the combatants.

In its structure *Culhwch and Olwen* is a typical folkloric tale of the type studied by Propp and based on the quest for a bride. The hero's stepmother magically sets his destiny in motion: he will have no other wife than Olwen, the daughter of the giant Yspaddaden. He goes to the court of Arthur, his cousin, to have his head shaved (a theme that comes from initiation rites), and asks for the help of warriors from the king's army. With their help, sorcerers and giants are massacred, and magical boars are hunted. The help of animals and of great mythical characters is obtained (for example, Gwynn ap Nudd, described elsewhere as the King of Annwn), and as a result all the conditions for the marriage which had been laid down by the giant are met.

Culhwch, from his place of birth as much as from his name, is associated with pigs. He is the son of Cilydd, whose name is related to the Irish word *cele* ("client or dependent of a nobleman"). In Welsh the word for "client," as well as for "son-in-law," is *dawf*, related perhaps to the Greek *demos*, and throughout the entire tale Culhwch is, in effect, the predestined *dawf* of Yspaddaden. In Sanskrit, *viśpati* means both lord of the *viś* (the third function) and son-in-law. In the four sections of the *Mabinogi*, where, however, several marriages are mentioned, only Pwyll appears in his relationship with his father-in-law; and in the Arthurian romances, only Gereint (apart from Peredur's relationship with the father of the virgin who represents the third function). In the three tales that have been considered, except for the silent picture of the empress's father who appears in *The Dream of Macsen*, it is only for the folkloric hero of the third function that the role of son-in-law is charged with meaning. Furthermore, the woman who is offered to Culhwch is said to be worthy "of whichever gentleman it may be." Arthur is proud of the good and noble manners of his men and of his own manners. As for Culhwch, he was as ready to celebrate Arthur as to tell of his infamy (that was the function of the bard). The giant's head was cut off by Goreu (the "best"), the son of Custennin and "the best of men" (cf. above, "Pwyll and Pryderi," and below, "Arthur and the Arthurian Heroes in Wales").

B.R./d.b.

BIBLIOGRAPHY

A. The Four Branches of the Mabinogi

Pwyll and Pryderi

H. HUBERT, "Le mythe d'Epona," *Mélanges linguistiques*, offerts à M. J. Vendryes (Paris 1925). W. J. GRUFFYDD, *Rhiannon* (Cardiff 1953). J. GRICOURT, "Epona-Rhiannon-Macha," *Ogam*, 6 (1954).

The Family of Llŷr

G. DUMÉZIL, *Loki* (Paris 1948), 258–66. P. MAC CANA, *Branwen, Daughter of Llŷr* (Cardiff 1958).

The Family of Dôn

W. J. GRUFFYDD, *Math vab Mathonwy* (Cardiff 1928). G. DUMÉZIL, *Heur et malheur du guerrier* (Paris 1969), 130–33. On the general view given above: A. D. REES and B. REES, *Celtic Heritage* (London 1961), 41–53, 175–80, 183–84, and A. D. REES, *Ceinciau'r Mabinogi* (Bangor 1975).

B. Lludd and Llefelys

G. DUMÉZIL, *Mythe et épopée* (Paris 1968), 613–23. A. D. REES, *Ceinciau'r Mabinogi* (Bangor 1975), 15–16, 52.

D. Culhwch and Olwen

R. S. LOOMIS, *Arthurian Literature in the Middle Ages* (Oxford 1959), 31–43. G. W. BREWER and B. L. JONES, "Popular Tale Motifs and Historical Tradition in *Breudwyt Maxen*," *Medium Aevum* 44 (1974): 23–30. J. LAYARD, *A Celtic Quest* (Zurich 1975). J. A. CARSON, "The Structure and Meaning of the Dream of Rhonabwy," *Philological Quarterly* 53 (1974): 289–303. A. D. REES, *Ceinciau'r Mabinogi* (Bangor 1975), 58–60; A. D. REES and B. REES, *Celtic Heritage* (London 1961), 262–71.

ARTHUR AND THE ARTHURIAN HEROES IN WALES

There are allusions to a paradigmatic Arthur in two old Welsh poems (dating to perhaps 600 and 635). At the beginning of the ninth century, in the *Historia* "of Nennius," Arthur is said to have fought with the Celtic kings of the Isle of Britain in the time of Octha, son of Hengist: he was the *dux bellorum* ("commander of the armies"?). Twelve of his victories are mentioned, among which is the victory of Mount Badon (apparently the victory of *mons* Badonicus cited by Gildas, who wrote some three centuries later) and another in which Arthur himself killed 960 men in a single day. The Mirabilia of the *Historia* cite two wonders associated with the name of Arthur, both in southeastern Wales: the tomb of Amr, his son, and a stone bearing the paw print of Arthur's dog, Cabal, left during the hunt for the Troit boar—the Twrch Trwyth that plays such an important role in the story of Culhwch and Olwen. The *Annales Cambriae*, which date back to the tenth century, tell of the battle of Camlann "during which Arthur and Medrawd fell." In the *Lives of the Saints,* from the eleventh century and the beginning of the twelfth, Arthur usually appears as an initially hostile ruler whose aid was finally enlisted as a consequence of a miracle. In the *Vita Gildae* he is reunited with his wife Gwenhwyfar who had been kidnapped by Melwas, the king of the Summer Country (*aestiva regio*); this tale reappears in the work of Chrétien de Troyes (and in a Welsh poem). In an old Welsh poem which refers to Pwyll and Pryderi and the cauldron of the Chief of Annwn, Arthur and his men sail three full ships to Caer Siddi, a stronghold in the kingdom of the world beyond (in Irish: *sídh*); only seven men return. In yet another poem, a dialogue between Arthur and his gatekeeper Glewlwyd, Cai and, to a lesser degree, Bedwyr have the highest rank among Arthur's companions, who are considered "the best men on earth" (among them, Manawydan, son of Llŷr, and Mabon, son of Modron, names which are equivalent to the *Maponus* and *Matrona* found in Celtic inscriptions). Their exploits consisted of killing witches of all sorts, as well as monsters who ravaged the countryside. In still another poem, Arthur is called "the emperor," and in the story of Culhwch and Olwen, the gatekeeper Glewlwyd—of Arthur's court, which had been founded in Cornwall—says that he was there when Arthur conquered the lands from Greece to the Orient. He had been in India and Africa and the islands of Corsica. It should be added that in the twelfth century, in Wales as well as in Cornwall and Brittany, it was widely believed that Arthur was still alive and would return.

The texts just mentioned depict the Arthur of the first Welsh tradition, predating the works of Geoffrey of Monmouth, Wace, Layamon, and Chrétien de Troyes, the great Arthurian authors in Europe. But there are some indications which lead us to believe that even before the appearance of Geoffrey's *Historia* in approximately 1136, stories about Arthur had already found a wide audience in much of the Christian world.

As a warrior, hunter of magic boars, killer of giants and witches and monsters, and leader of a band of heroes whose exploits lead them into a world of marvels and mysteries, the Welsh Arthur has much in common with the Irish Fionn. Both are central figures in a powerful and lasting folkloric tradition which educated men knew and occasionally referred to but did not consider to be of the greatest importance. Both cycles took final form in the twelfth century. In the stories of the *Fian*, the adventures are mostly situated in southern Ireland. Fionn is attached genealogically to the ancestors of Laigin (Leinster) and also, even though this is contradictory, to the Érainn, the ancestors of Mumu (Munster); he is the lord of Almu in Laigin. In Wales, Arthur is placed in the south, according to the *Mirabilia* of Nennius, *Culhwch and Olwen,* and other texts. Pwyll and Pryderi are mentioned in connection with him, and they are the central figures of the southern sections of the *Mabinogi* (in addition to Alun Dyfed and Gwynn ap Nudd, king of Annwn).

From the family of Llŷr, there is also Manawydan who receives Dyfed at his marriage to Rhiannon, and from the family of Dôn, Amaethon and Gofannon, the laborer and the blacksmith. Arthur's court is either in Cornwall or in southeastern Wales. Even the Arthurian knight, the young gentleman (a "knight" and not a "lord") who sets out to prove his courage, protect women, and go adventuring in forests, wildernesses, and mysterious realms of the beyond, has certain affinities with the young warrior of the Fian.

Of Fionn it is said that if the autumn leaves were made of gold, and the foam of the sea of silver, he would give them to anyone who asked. Generosity, "openness," the essential virtue of the third function, is also the highest virtue in Arthurian literature.

The three Welsh stories about Peredur, Owain, and Gereint are similar in their themes, settings, and ethics. In addition, each is connected with one of Chrétien de Troyes' narrative poems, *Perceval* (or the *Story of the Grail*), *Yvain* (or the *Knight of the Lion*), and *Erec*. The exact relationship which associates these texts in pairs is still a matter of dispute, but it is clear that while the basic material is largely of Celtic origin, the three Welsh stories bear marks of French influence. Whatever the differences between the two series of texts, the following remarks apply equally to the poems of Chrétien de Troyes and to the Welsh narratives.

In each of the narratives, Arthur's knights choose the most perilous path, accepting all challenges wholeheartedly and coming to the rescue of every maiden or lady in distress. In the final analysis, this is how a knight proves himself to be as valorous as he claims to be and wins the heart of the woman he loves. If, from time to time, one hears talk of bad relations between the hero and his lady, it should nevertheless be noted that there is never any mention of children being born. Each of the three heroes is guilty of a serious mistake which causes the needless suffering of others and for which he is publicly reprimanded. After the hero has lived through a number of marvelous adventures in strange lands, he is discovered by Arthur and his knights. Cai the cantankerous senechal and Gwalchmai (Gauvain in French) the courteous captain attempt, each in turn, to bring the new man before Arthur. Cai is overpowered by the young man, but Gwalchmai recognizes the skills of his companion, and the respect is mutual. At last the young hero understands what his duty is, and the narrative ends with an exploit of which he is once again the agent. While generosity appears to be the supreme virtue in these three narratives without distinction, the narratives demonstrate three different aspects of what a knight may be.

Of these three heroes, two come from the north and one from the south. Peredur is the son of Efrog, the count of the North; Owain is the son of Urien (the king of Rheged, in the Solway estuary region); and Gereint is the son of Erbin, king of Cornwall. In Wales, Peredur is associated with Gwynedd, Owain with Powys, and according to Chrétien, Erec's county is called "Destregalles" (Southern Wales? Strathclyde?), and the story ends with his coronation at Nantes, in southern Brittany. His name, and the name of Enid as well, have been identified as two names from the kingdom of southeast Brittany. Finally, each of the three narratives is connected with one of the virtues and failings which are characteristic of the three Indo-European functions:

(1) *Knowledge.* In the story of Peredur, oaths, prophecies, and destinies play a decisive role. The hero leaves Arthur's court vowing never to return until he has righted the wrong done by Cai to a dwarf and his lady. Later in the narrative, he swears never to speak to another Christian soul until he has won the heart of Angharad with the golden hand, and still later he swears that he will not sleep until he has discovered the meaning of the bleeding lance and other wonders which he has seen in his uncle's court. His error, ill-fated and having disastrous consequences, is that he failed to ask the significance and the cause of the strange wonders when they appeared before him. As a consequence of this mistake, he is unable to avenge the murder of his cousin and the crippling of his uncle. Had he asked the question, his uncle would have been cured and peace restored in the land. Instead, battles are waged, knights die, ladies remain widows, and maidens are left without protection.

Peredur successively wins the hearts of three ladies, each apparently symbolizing one of the three functions: first the beautiful girl in need, with skin as white as snow, hair as black as a crow's wing, and cheeks as red as blood; then Angharad, whom he meets in the court of the knights; and

finally the Empress, who offers him three cups of wine—the drinking of which meant that one claimed supremacy (cf. *Medhbh,* in the Irish tradition). It is with the Empress that Peredur establishes himself and begins his reign.

Peredur is an object of respect for Gwalchmai because he finds him lost in noble reverie.

The story ends when Peredur learns the meaning of the wonders he has seen. His final exploit is to kill the Witches of Caerloyw as he was predestined to do. His "muses" of the second function provide him with a horse and weapons and instruct him in their use.

(2) *Combat.* Owain's task is to conquer and guard "with sword and shield" the Lady of the Fountain whose husband he has killed. Like Peredur, Owain is loved and aided by a humble maiden (who is made rich by her mistress, however), and with her help he wins the hand of the Lady of the Fountain. When he comes to her for the first time, the fastenings of his boots are in the shape of golden lions. Later he saves a lion who is being held captive by a serpent. The lion becomes his faithful companion and bodyguard. The sin Owain commits is to stay three years in Arthur's court when he has his lady's permission only for a three-month visit: the company of the knights makes him forget the woman who married him so that he would protect her property "on horseback, with weapons, and with all his might." His final exploit is to defeat the black tyrant, a false Hospitaler knight who is then forced to play that role in reality, faithful to the ideal of the third function.

The story ends with an indication that Owain was the captain of the troops at Arthur's court until the day when he took possession of his own property: the Three Hundred Swords of the Race of Cynfarch and the Flock of Crows. "And everywhere that Owain went and they with him, he carried the victory."

The resemblances between the story of Owain and two narratives about Cú Chulainn (*The Bed of Suffering of Cú Chulainn,* and *The Courtship of Emher*) have been pointed out. The adventures of Cú Chulainn are, however, adventures in magical countries, reached by crossing water. They are not the highest exploits of the great hero of the warrior function.

(3) *Wealth.* Like the story of Pwyll, the story of Gereint begins with a hunt (which takes place here in southeastern Wales; in Chrétien's poem, it begins in Caradigan in the southwest). Here also the hero is separated from the hunt, but at the end of the story his beloved will receive the head of the white stag that was being hunted. In the meantime, Gereint, wishing to avenge an insult, like Pwyll in Annwn, has proved his courage by conquering Edern, the son of Nudd, and settling an old quarrel between a certain Yniwl and his nephew, each of whom claimed title to the other's land. The names Yniwl ("fog") and Nudd ("light mist") are antonyms of Hafgan and Gwawl in the story of Pwyll, and Yniwl's poverty is in opposition to the flawless possessions of Arawn. Gereint, who has received the hand of the beautiful Enid, asks that she remain a maiden until they return to Arthur's court (Enid does not appear before Gereint on a majestic white horse, like Rhiannon when she comes to Pwyll: she comes to care for his horse instead). Three years after the celebration of their marriage with festivals, songs, games, and the distribution of gifts, Gereint gets permission to leave the court to manage his estate in the place of his aging father, Erbin, son of Custennin, and to protect his borders. Gereint and Enid are escorted by gentlemen, and on the other side of the Severn they are met by the gentlemen of Cornwall and the ladies of the court, who welcome them joyfully. The Welsh words for gentleman, homage, estate,

gift giving, and joy occupy an important place in this whole part of the narrative. Gereint enriches his court with better horses, better weapons, and the greatest and most famous treasures. But he also begins to love his pleasures, his wife, and the peaceful life of his court, filled with songs and amusements. He is so fond of the intimate company of his wife in his bedroom that he no longer takes pleasure in anything else, and for this reason he begins to lose the affection of his knights just as he loses his taste for the pleasures of the hunt. His court grumbles and the people mock him behind his back because he has neglected them too often for the love of a woman. In order to prove his courage once again, he leaves his estate and all his pleasures and sets out for Lloegr (England). Keeping his wife at a distance and forbidding her to speak a word to him, he chooses the most dangerous route, where it is probable that he will be met by robbers, brigands, and wild animals.

The resemblance between this episode and the story of Pryderi, Manawydan, and their wives in the *Mabinogi* is significant. In the *Mabinogi*, when the two couples have taken pleasure in festivals and their leisure and have enjoyed each other's company so much that they can no longer be separated night or day, they abandon all this comfort and all that society has to offer and also set out for Lloegr, where they must face the hostility of "robbers." Rhiannon, famous for her conversation, is deprived of speech, and the two husbands are separated from their wives. In the Arthurian narrative, however, it is the wife and not the husband who demonstrates patience and solicitude.

The two stories also end in the same way. Gereint's last exploit is to rid himself forever of the hedge of mist and the magical illusions which accompany it. Then all find one another again in a general reconciliation. In Chrétien's poem, this exploit, called the "Joy of the Court," is made necessary by the exclusive (and isolating) love between Mabonagrain and his lady, who are guilty of the same impoverishing abandon that Gereint himself has been accused of. The general rejoicing and the festivals which later take place at Nantes are equal to the joy and abundance which reigns in the house of Buchet in Laigin, the Irish province of prosperity. In the *Mabinogi*, the narratives from the south speak of the pleasures of society, great festivals, and joy; in other texts the spirit of festivity and generosity and the taste for lusty songs is attributed to Glamorgan in the southeast.

It is noteworthy that by obeying the instructions of his lame uncle and not asking the reason for the wonders which no one has the courtesy to explain to him, Peredur is deprived of the knowledge that he wishes to acquire; by taking pleasure in the company of other knights, Owain is prevented from protecting his lady and his estate; and by abandoning himself to the pleasures and company of his wife, Gereint loses the affection and company of the gentlemen of his court.

As we have seen earlier, the kidnapping of Arthur's wife by Méléagant was a story that was told in Wales before Chrétien de Troyes had written *Le Chevalier à la Charette* (*The Knight in the Cart*); but Chrétien's poem has no parallel in Welsh literature. The theme of love outside of marriage, the "excess" that characterizes the behavior of the two lovers, the sin of Lancelot, who agreed to ride in the ignominious cart—an act described by Gauvain as "vile"—all suggest that the work was planned both to complete *Erec and Enid* and to stand in opposition to it. Erec's excess leads to joyous reconciliation in both conjugal love and courtly society.

B.R./d.b.

BIBLIOGRAPHY

(See also the bibliography for ''The Myths and Narratives of the Celts of the Islands.'')

R. S. LOOMIS, *Arthurian Tradition and Chrétien de Troyes* (New York 1949); *Arthurian Literature in the Middle Ages* (Oxford 1959), 1–19, 31–39, 52–71. G. GOETINCK, *Peredur* (Cardiff 1975). D. D. R. OWEN, ed., *Arthurian Romance* (Edinburgh 1970), 24–36. On the interpretation given above: A. D. REES and B. REES, *Celtic Heritage* (London 1961), 70–72, 178; A. D. REES, *Ceinciau'r Mabinogi* (Bangor 1975), 52–58.

CELTIC "APOLLOS"

There are three or four Celtic Apollos whose Gallic names are coupled with that of the great Roman god and express the qualities that are appropriate to him: light and warmth, beneficence and healing. Gods of the sun, of its dazzling brilliance, of white or flaming light: *Belenos* bright as fire, *Grannos* luminous and salutary (*Aquae Granni*: Aix-la-Chapelle); gods of the bubbling spring: *Borvo, Bormo,* and *Bormanus,* ancestors of all the Bourbons. Thus, when Caesar places in the second rank of the five great Gallic gods an "Apollo" who "drives away illness," his implication is too synthetic: there were many indigenous personifications of the beneficent sun or healing springs, and in Romanized Gaul they are all assimilated to Apollo. In addition, Belenos was honored outside of Gaul, for example, in Cisalpine Gaul, in the region of Aquilia. Other Gallic parallels are even more assimilated to Apollo: *Moritasgus* in Alesia and *Vindonnus* in Essarois (Côte d'Or), and elsewhere he is called *Virotutis,* "Benefactor, protector (or healer) of men." The sun everywhere visible, the thermal waters so rich in Gaul—all of this was Apollo for their worshipers, and it was only in this country that he took on the aspect of master of healing waters.

P.-M.D./m.s.

BIBLIOGRAPHY

P.-M. DUVAL, *Les Dieux de la Gaule* (2d ed., Paris 1976), 76–78. J. GOURVEST, ''Le culte de Bélénos en Provence occidentale et en Gaule,'' *Ogam, Tradition celtique,* 6 (1954).

Cernunnos, the God with the Horns of a Stag

Cernunnos is a Gallic god, undoubtedly Celtic in a more general sense, whose name is known thanks to a panel of a pillar dedicated to Jupiter by the Nautae Parisiaci, the mariners of the town of the Parisii of Lutèce, under Tiberius (14–37). The inscription consists of nothing but the name, above a bas-relief which represents the upper part of the god, the block bearing the rest having disappeared. By comparison with other representations of the same god and with the other panels of the pillar on which the god is depicted, it can be seen that he could only have been seated cross-legged here. He is dressed in a sleeveless tunic which reveals the right shoulder and wears a beaded torque around his neck. His head, which is quite large and apparently bald with a wrinkled brow, has the ears and antlers of a stag, along with human ears. A small beaded torque is suspended on each antler.

The name, missing its first letter because of a very early breakage, is placed on the molding in such a way that it could be lacking only one letter if one assumes that the word was centered, as were the names of the other gods on all other such panels. From the time of the discovery of the block, which had been put to new use in a very old wall beneath the chancel of Notre-Dame of Paris, in 1711, the reading Cernunnos was proposed, because the first part of the word seemed to be close to the Latin word for "horn," and because the appearance of the god suggested such a connection. In fact, these are "antlers," not horns, and it is only as a matter of convenience that one calls them horns. Nevertheless, the restoration of the initial c is justified by the Irish, which uses the word cern- to designate the forehead of young caprines and bovines when these swell with the first growth of antlers and horns. "Having a forehead coiffed with antlers" is thus the translation of cernunnos, a word whose form is not completely restricted to Gallic regions. In fact, there is in Roman Dacia a (Jupiter) Cernenus, but this may be a case of a topical surname (its place of origin, Verespatak, is close to Korna), with the bulging evoking no more than a swelling of the ground on which it is found, since there is no reason to attribute to the master of the sky the same peculiarity as that of the Celtic god, whose nature is essentially earthly. There is also a French waterway called the Sanon (an affluent of the Meurthe), a name whose ancient forms were Cernune, Cernone, Kernone (in the seventh and eighth centuries). We also know that in antiquity the river gods were represented as having horns. Finally, Les Cerny and Cernay come from Cerniacum.

Some representations may be grouped under the name Cernunnos by reason of the characteristics that they share with the representation in Paris. The oldest predate the Roman period and attest to the antiquity of the god in the Celtic context: in the Italian Alps, often crossed by the Celts, at Val Camonica, a cave engraving which may be dated to the fourth century B.C. represents a great personage who is ithyphallic, has antlers, and is accompanied by a small man; on his right arm he wears a torque, on the left, apparently a horned serpent. In Spain, in the lands of the Iberian Celts, a ceramic potsherd found at Numancia and dated to the middle of the second century B.C. has painted on it the upper body of a man with the same antlers. Following this, dating from the first half of the first century B.C., there was the gilded silver basin found at Gundestrup (Denmark), of which an interior panel shows the god in a slightly more relaxed pose than his cross-legged one. He wears a torque around his neck, he holds another in his right hand, and he squeezes a ram-headed serpent very tightly in his left hand. To his right is a great stag and around him two bulls, two lions, two wolves (apparently) as well as a small man seated upon a dolphin. The god is thus presented as the lord of the forest, of wild animals, of cattle, and even of marine fauna; he has as his attendant an imaginary composite being which is particularly chthonic: a powerful serpent that also has the horns of a ram. The somewhat Oriental character of the rich iconography of the basin, whose origin may be sought in the region of the Black Sea, explains the presence of the lions.

In Gaul, representations from Roman times confirm this role of the god of the forests of inland Europe, the master of quadrupeds and of livestock (although not of horses). He sometimes (as at Autun) bears two horned serpents which he appears to feed, sometimes (as at Reims) a great sack out of which falls a flood of coins (or sometimes coarse grains), with a stag and a bull on either side, while on the front of the stela a rat appears; sometimes there is a basket of food or a cake on the knees of the god. The god may at the same time be represented as having three faces, which serve to further increase the power of this master of earthly treasure, who is rich in heavy torques—obviously of gold—which he wears around his neck, in his antlers, or in his hands.

From the stag he derives strength in combat, sexual power, acute hearing, speed, the annual and seemingly perpetual renewal of his antlers, which are natural weapons, and finally, the power of longevity.

He has companions. Besides the ram-headed serpent, there are the little man with upraised arms of Val Camonica and the various divinities alongside of whom he is enthroned on votive bas-reliefs: the goddess with the horn of plenty, for example. He has no traditional consort, and none of his companions have titles. Cernunnos is also associated with two other divinities (though this does not make a triad of them) at Bolards, near Nuits-Saint-George (Côte d'Or). These are two goddesses with the horn of plenty, of which one has a male sexual organ. Below, here and there in a tree, a bull, a dog, a pig or boar, a stag, and perhaps a hedgehog may be seen. The cattle, the god's companions, and the king of the forest are all of terrifying appearance but all could nevertheless be tamed.

This monstrous god has no parallel, classical or barbarian, in antiquity. However, this master of wild animals—from whom he borrowed the renascent power of his antlers—and of the most powerful of domesticated animals (the bull), already existed, long before the Christian era, in the Indus Valley: a seal from the fourth or third millennium depicts a horned god with an apelike face, seated in a cross-legged pose; on either side of him are wild animals: a lion, an elephant, a rhinoceros, and a bovine with immense horns; below him are quadrupeds. Nevertheless, the exact equivalent of Cernunnos is found only among the Celts, in whose realm one may also evoke, in connection with the two horned serpents that circle his body in order to eat on his knees, the terrible reptile of the Irish epic who slips into the girdle of the hero Conall without harming him in the least.

Certain characteristics of the god nevertheless do not belong to him alone. The antlers are worn by a goddess seated cross-legged and holding a horn of plenty, represented in two bronze statuettes. As for the three faces, Mercury and gods and goddesses whose names are unknown to us also had these. The ram-headed serpent also accompanies Mercury and a Gallo-Roman "Mars." Finally,

The antlered god and the ram-headed serpent. Plaque from a gilded silver basin discovered at Gundestrup. Copenhagen, Nationalmuseet.

The antlered god with three faces (far right). Stela showing three deities, discovered at Les Bolards, Nuits-Saint-Georges (Côte-d'Or).

Cernunnos flanked by Apollo and Mercury. Votive stela. Reims. Photo Giraudon.

the cross-legged pose is also found on pre-Roman stone images from Narbonensis and on images of unidentified Gallo-Roman gods and goddesses, as well as on Mercury. In other words, there is no "tricephalic god," "cross-legged god," "antlered god," or still less a "horned god": there is rather an aspect, a pose, one or several attributes (with a distinction to be made between the horns of a bull or ram and the antlers of the cervines) which different divinities may present. The pose, moreover, may well be a characteristic of Celtic customs: "The Celts," said Strabo (4.4.3), "eat while seated, even upon the ground strewn with branches."

If the Gundestrup basin belongs, as scholars now believe, to "Istro-Pontic" works of the Lower Danube from the first half of the first century B.C., then this is the only certain representation of Cernunnos known outside of Gaul, more particularly, among the eastern Celts. Neither the bronze plaque of Popeştil (Romania) nor the statuette of the same metal from Łukaszewka (Moldavia, USSR), which depicts a person seated in a cross-legged pose wearing a torque, are definitely representations of him. If the dedication to Jupiter Cernenus does in fact concern the same god, this would be the only known case of the existence of his name outside of Gaul. His cult could nevertheless have been extremely widespread in the continental Celtic world. It is neither clear nor impossible that the Gallic Cernunnos may have left some traces in French place names: the name of Sanon, as noted,

had Cernune as its earliest form; Cernon-sur-Colle (Marne) may have the same origin. It would be more hazardous to see in the god or spirit named Herne, who has the antlers of a stag Herne and lives in the forests (and whom Shakespeare evokes in the last act of *The Merry Wives of Windsor*), a descendant of Cernunnos: the name and perhaps the character as well probably belong to the Anglo-Saxon period. On the other hand, the antlers which crown the Devil on some monuments of Irish sculpture (Ahenny and Clonmacnoise) and Roman sculpture (the cathedral of Parma), as well as on illuminated manuscripts (the Book of Bobbio, the Stuttgart Psalter) may well be derived from Cernunnos, who had become for the Christians an old demon of a dying paganism.

P.-M.D./d.w.

BIBLIOGRAPHY

Article "Cernunnos," in Pauly/Wissowa, *Real-Encyclopädie*, vol. 6, 3 (1899). P. PRAY BOBER, "Cernunnos: Origin and Transformation of a Celtic Divinity," *American Journal of Archaeology*, 45 (1951). On the stag in Occidental art: J. BAYET, "Le symbolisme du cerf et du centaure à la Porte Rouge de Notre-Dame de Paris," *Revue archéologique*, 44 (1954). P.-M. DUVAL, *Les dieux de la Gaule* (2d ed., Paris 1976), 21, 37–38, 47–48, 121.

Cú Chulainn and Conchobar: The Warrior Hero in Irish Mythology

I. Cú Chulainn is the supreme warrior hero of Ulaidh (Ulster). He was the son of Deichtine, sister or daughter of king Conchobar, and of Sualtaim (or Sualtach Sídech), who, like his son, appeared to be immune to the evil spell that was brought on by Macha (a typical figure of the Indo-European third function, who gave her name to Emhain Mhacha). This spell confined the king of Ulaidh and all his warriors in Emhain for three months so that they could not come to the defense of their province, a delay which finds parallels elsewhere. Cú Chulainn is also the son of the god Lugh (king of the Tuatha Dé Danann during their great battle), who supports him during his most difficult battles and takes his place for three days in one of them. As an infant Cú Chulainn is given to his aunt Findchoem to be fostered, but four warriors contest with her for this honor and affirm their rights. One is Sencha, the always calm, the *ollamh* (the noble), wise and learned, the judge, who addresses the people in the presence of the king and also adjudicates battles in his presence. Another is Blaí, the hospitable, who assembles the men of Ireland, entertains them for a week, supports their voyages and their pillages, and also supports them when they are defamed or when their honor is at stake. Another is Fergus, who boasts of his valor and his prowess, a champion who offers his protection against all evils. And finally there is the poet Amhairgin, who gains esteem through his wisdom, his success, his age, and his eloquence. They all take part in the education of the child in such a way that he excels from the point of view of each function. While still a child, he routs the army of young boys of Emhain Mhacha. With his bare hands he destroys the wild dog of

Culann the smith and takes his place as guard, whence his name, the dog of Culann. In his seventh year, hearing Cathbhadh the druid predict that the life of the young man who should take up arms that day would be brief but eternally glorious, he immediately demands arms from the king, accepting only the king's arms and war chariot. Boldly he enters a foreign land and challenges in combat the three terrible sons of Nechta Scéne who have killed half the warriors of Ulaidh. He massacres all three: the crafty one who can never be brought down by the blows of a weapon, the champion who, if he is not struck with the first blow, can never be struck, and the youngest, who moves over the water like a swallow or a swan. They also clearly symbolize the three functions. For the speed of the third, see the article "Fionn and the Fian," below. Cú Chulainn returns to Emhain Mhacha intoxicated with combat, threatening friend and foe alike. Naked women are sent out to meet him, and he is plunged into three tanks of cold water, which calms him, after which he is clothed in fresh garments and given his place near the king.

His courtship of Emher, the daughter of Forgall the nephew of Tethra, king of the Fomhoire, leads him into other equally extraordinary adventures and a harsh training in military exploits at Alba. For instructors he has Domnall the Bellicose and later the warrior Scáthach ("shade"). The daughter of the latter, Uathach ("terrible"), and her adversary Aífe ("beautiful"?) become his mistresses in turn, and Conlaí, his son by Aífe, will come later to Ulaidh but only to be killed by his father in single combat: a story which has parallels in the stories of the warrior heroes of the Germans and the Persians.

During the epic quest of Donn Cuailnge, Cú Chulainn alone, through a long series of battles, stops the advance of the army of Medhbh, which numbers in its ranks several exiles from Ulaidh (among them Fergus mac Roich) and contingents that have come from other provinces in Ireland. Juvenile and inoffensive in appearance, Cú Chulainn is transformed when he is taken over by the fury of combat. His body trembles from head to foot like a reed in a cross-current. He puts his body into such convulsions that his heels, calves, and thighs seem to be in front, his feet and knees behind. He draws one of his eyes far into his head, the other spurts out onto his cheek, and his mouth is so contorted that the whole head of a man could easily fit into it. Sparks of blazing fire are seen in the clouds above his head, his hair bristles wildly, like the red hawthorne, the light of the champion beams forth from his forehead like a whetstone, and from the crown of his head ascends a thick column of black blood that is like the mast of a great ship.

During the festival of Bricriu, the troublemaker Bricriu (whose character is the opposite of that of Sencha) sets up a joust between Cú Chulainn, the supreme warrior, and two of his comrades in war. The first is Conall Cernach, his cousin and foster brother, the son of Amhairghin the *poet* and the grandson of Cathbad the *druid*. The bad relations between him and the people of his mother, the *Connachta*, are often noted, although his mother was the sister of Conchobar and Deichtine. In the story of the pig of Mac Dathó it is said that for three hundred years before the birth of Christ there was war between Connachta and Ulaidh (between Connaught and Ulster). In this account, of which the most dramatic moment is a verbal jousting match, Cú Chulainn does not appear, but Conall routs his maternal uncle, Cet de Connacht. It should be noted that just as in the *Tain* the first exploit of Cú Chulainn (which was to trim a young oak from top to bottom in one fell swoop, using only a foot, a hand, and an eye) recalls the singular "rite" of Lugh at Magh Tuiredh, so what is said of Conall in the two stories recalls Nuadhu Airgedlámh: entering into combat with an adversary who had lost a hand in a previous battle, Conall, differing in this from the adversary of Nuadhu, agrees to have one of his hands bound to his side. In still another account the arm that holds the sword is hacked by blows, since it lacks the protection of the buckler which is held in the other hand, the wounded hand; this trait alone marks the intensity of the combat. The third claimant in the festival of Bricriu is Loeghaire Buadhach, son-in-law of Conchobar. Loeghaire means "freeman-of-calf," just as *bó-aire* means "freeman-of-cow": the terms are thus practically synonymous. The name appears as the name of the most striking ancestor of the Osraige in the area of Laigin (Leinster) and of Mumu (Munster) (Loeghaire Bern Buadhach), of an ancestor of the kings of Laigin, of the ancestor of the southern branch of the royal family of Ui Néill, and of a prince of Connacht who renounces the kingdom of his father in order to live in a delightful magic country (*síd*). The prize fought for in the combat includes a full vat of wine, in which one recognizes the first function, a bull (second function), and a wild boar and one hundred round wheaten loaves cooked in honey (third function). The judgment on the comparative value of the heroes is handed down in turn in Connacht, Mumu, and Ulaidh. Medhbh of Connacht cuts each one in turn, the difference in the cuts marking the rank of the one who receives it. In Ulaidh the rivals are challenged to a joust in which someone's head must fall. In Mumu, the exploit that Cú Chulainn alone can perform is to compel a mysterious assailant, at night, on pain of death, to concede to the hero three vows pronounced with one breath: sovereignty over the warriors of Ulaidh, the role of champion, and the precedence of his wife. This promise made by a vanquished enemy resembles the promise made by Loch to Lugh at the

end of the battle of Magh Tuiredh, the promise made by the thieving giant to Lludd, the promise of Llwyd to Manawydan, and the promise of the count of the hedge of mist to Gereint—all of whom are persons of the third function. The three functions thus appear in the components of the Role of Victor, in the three rivals, in the provinces where the judgment is handed down, in the character of the exploit required in each province, and in the triple supremacy which appears in the end.

Of the three cousins, sons of three sisters, Cú Chulainn, Conall, and Naoise, it is Naoise the son of Uisliu (who fled with Deirdre, whom Conchobar wished to make his wife) who has the characteristics of the third function: beauty, fleet-footedness, and a melodious war cry which is pleasing to all those who hear it and makes cows increase their production of milk by two-thirds. The life of Deirdre and the three sons of Uisliu in the woods and in solitude and the poems chanted in honor of this existence are very similar to the life and poems of the *Fian*, and their entire history in many ways echoes that of Diarmaid and Gráinne and the even more famous Gallic legend of Trystan and Esyllt (Tristan and Isolde). When a distinguished scholar characterizes the tragic history of Deirdre as "the most beautiful of all the histories of Ulaidh," one may well think that his judgment diverges indeed from the tradition of Emhain Mhacha—unless beauty be recognized as a trait of the third function.

II. Conchobar was the king of the warrior province, Ulaidh, and he ruled at Emhain Mhacha. He was the son of Cathbad the druid. But he was also reputed to be the son of Fachtna Fathach, the king of Ulaidh. People sometimes speak of him as one would speak of a god of the earth, and his sister Deichtine, the mother of Cú Chulainn, is also called a goddess. Like Mars and Indra, he is associated especially with the festivals of the new year and the calendar. He obtained for the first time the royalty of the husband of his mother Ness, Ferghus mac Roich, for a period of one year. There were 365 men in his cottage, each providing food and drink for one night. Conchobar himself made provision for the festival of Samhain at the calends of winter.

He is called the bull of the province, and his people are also compared to bulls. It should be noted that in the ancient traditions of India and Rome, the bull symbolizes the power of the combatant. Although the "Third Estate" is traditionally that of cattle breeders, the *bó-aire* of Ireland, a typical independent proprietor, would usually receive from his lord a fief in the form of cattle, for which he would pay rent. Similarly, although the province of the combatant king, Conchobar, was Ulaidh, Medhbh, who was the incarnation of sovereignty, was king of Connacht. It was the Fir Bholg who gave to Ireland its first kings, but it was the Tuatha Dé Danann who brought Fal, the stone which reveals the true king. Thus, although these two royal peoples descended from the kingless people of Nemhedh, it is clear that each function derives its principle from the function that is above it in the social hierarchy.

B. R./m.s.

BIBLIOGRAPHY

R. THURNEYSEN, *Die Irische Helden = und Königsage* (Halle 1921). G. DUMÉZIL, *Horace et les Curiaces* (Paris 1942); *Loki* (Paris 1948), 258–66; *The Destiny of the Warrior* (Chicago 1970); *Mythe et épopée* 1 (Paris 1968), 602–12. J. DE VRIES, "Aided Óenfir Aífe," *Ogam* 9 (1957): 122–35. A. D. REES and B. REES, *Celtic Heritage* (London 1961), 53–62, 124, 152–54, 241; A. D. REES, *Ceinciau'r Mabinogi* (Bangor 1975), 42, 57–58.

EPONA

Epona is the Celtic name of a Gallic, and more broadly, Celtic goddess. She is the only Celtic divinity to enjoy widespread dissemination, as attested by literary, epigraphic, and decorative sources from the Roman era. The name, which has no variants, consists of the radical *epo-*, the Celtic equivalent of the Latin *equo-* and the Greek *hippo-*, "horse," or "mare," and the suffix *-ona*, which means merely "connected with." (Attempts are sometimes made to connect it with the gloss *onno* = *flumen* from the Vienna Glossary and to view it as a suffix evoking water, particularly since the name of the sacred fountain at Bordeaux mentioned by Ausonius is *Divona*. But this word means "divine," and nothing more.) "Horsewoman," "equine," "equestrian," "connected with horses," or "connected with Equidae" are various translations of *Epona*. On the other hand, "mare" would be a mistranslation, as would "connected with mares"—there is absolutely no proof that Epona began as a zoomorphic deity, a mare goddess, or even a sacred mare. Our only knowledge of her is in human form, in the Roman imperial era, under the name meaning "the one who is concerned with the Equidae." The importance of the goddess in Gaul was connected with the importance of the horse, horse breeding, and the cavalry.

The name was used to form the names of people and places, such as Eponicus, Eponine, Eponius, *Epona (Epône? Yvelines).

Dedicatory inscriptions and decorative representations of Epona were numerous and came from Gaul (the eastern region particularly), Italy, Spain, Great Britain, and especially the Danubian provinces. This widespread diffusion is partially accounted for by the role of horsemen in the armies. Epona's name appears on a Roman calendar (her festival is on 18 December). Apuleius's *Golden Ass* attests that her image adorned the stables of the military in Rome. While the goddess never has a male companion, a little girl sometimes appears at her side.

Epona is not only the patron of all equids (horses and brood mares, mules, and asses), all horsemen, civilian and military, and all grooms and drivers; she also protects travelers and, mythically, the voyage to the hereafter; for this reason she appears on funeral stelae. She is also, as a woman, a goddess of fertility, appearing with a horn of plenty, a basket of fruit, and a patera (dish); and with a child, or foal, at her side. Without her mount, she would resemble the mother goddesses, but she is distinguished from them by having no companion. She has been considered the protectress of the house, since in one bas-relief she is shown holding an object which looks like a large key. It is less certain that she has any connection with springs; and she does not appear to have had the character of a healing divinity.

Certain pagan vestiges in the Irish epic can be evoked in connection with Epona: the mare queen Rhiannon, the three Macha whose legend involves horses and mares. This does not mean, however, that Epona is necessarily connected with all myths in which a woman or goddess appears together with horses.

P.-M.D./d.b.

BIBLIOGRAPHY

KEUNE, "Epona," in Pauly/Wissowa, *Real-Encyclopädie*, vol. 6, 1 (1907), and supplement 3 (1918). P.-M. DUVAL, *Les dieux de la Gaule* (2d ed., Paris 1976), 49–51. R. MAGNEN and E. THEVENOT, *Epona, déesse gauloise des chevaux, protectrice des cavaliers* (Bordeaux 1953) (a collection of documents). H. HUBERT, "Le mythe d'Epona," in *Mélanges offerts à M. Vendryes* (Paris 1925). G. DUMÉZIL, *Le problème des Centaures* (Paris 1929), chap. 5; "Le trio des Macha," *Revue de l'histoire des religions*, 146 (1954). F. BENOÎT, *Les mythes de l'outre-tombe: Le cavalier à l'anguipède et l'écuyère Epona* (Brussels 1950).

The goddess Epona. Gannat (Allier). Saint-Germain-en-Laye, Musée des Antiquités nationales. Photo Lauros-Giraudon.

ESUS

Esus is a Gallic god whose name is inscribed and whose image is sculptured in bas-relief on one of the blocks of a pillar dedicated to Jupiter by the Nautae Parisiaci, the mariners of the city of the Parisii, Lutèce, in the reign of Tiberius (14–37). The god, in the short garment of a laborer, is chopping down a tree with a wide-bladed billhook; a large branch, already nearly detached from the trunk, hangs toward the ground. The next panel represents Tarvos Trigaranus, the Bull with Three Cranes, carrying the three birds, behind a large tree. This is the same subject as is shown in a Gallo-Roman stela from Trèves in which the two episodes are combined into one: the god, who is not named in this case, is dressed like the one depicted at Paris, and he chops at the trunk of a large tree with a long-bladed ax; the head of a bull and three large birds appear in the branches.

Esus (at left), and the bull with three cranes (at right). Base of a column from Nantes. Paris, Musée de Cluny. Photo Jean Albert.

The name of Esus, Celtic and not Latinized, is of uncertain etymology. It may be related to an Indo-European noun for the divine, *eisar,* and it may mean "god." Or it may be related to the Latin *herus,* "master, good master." The root was widespread, in any case, in western Celtic names, both ethnic and toponymic: the Esuvii are a people of western Gaul, according to Caesar; *aesica* is a stand of limes in great Britain; the Esubiani are a people of the Maritime Alps region. It is found in the proper names Esumagius, Esumopas, Esuccus, Esugenus, Esunertos, and Esuvius (the surname of the Gallic emperor Tetricus). A Hesus figures among the characters of Petronius's *Satyricon.*

Lucan cites Esus "of savage altars" among three Gallic gods thirsty for human blood. (This is a case of three great gods and not of a "triad" of masculine gods, as they have too often been characterized.) A medieval commentator, drawing on diverse sources, assimilates Esus to both Mars and Mercury (statements which cancel each other out and are undoubtedly of little value). On the other hand, he describes in great detail the kind of human sacrifice offered to the god: "A man was hung from a tree until, through loss of blood, his limbs went limp." It is highly improbable that human sacrifices were ever offered to Mercury; the identification of Esus with this god and with Mars is thus due to the ignorance of the medieval commentator, who, although he informed himself about Gallic sacrificial rites, he did not inform himself about the personalities of their gods. As in the *Lives of the Saints* and the *Acta Concilii,* the same gods are always used to represent the survival of paganism: especially Jupiter, Mars, Mercury, Minerva, and Diana.

There is no other Gallo-Roman inscription that definitely cites Esus. We thus know this god, whom Lucan apparently places at the same level as Teutates and Taranis (i.e., among the greatest gods), only in the particular form that he takes in the myth of the pursuit of the Bull with Three Cranes, after his Gallo-Roman representation which is a survival of the Gallic period. It is not without significance that the tree is an element common to both the representations of Esus and the genre of sacrifice that was offered to him.

We may recall the ordeal which Óðinn, the Germanic god, imposed upon himself: he hanged himself, wounded by a lance, from a tree blowing in the wind, for nine days, "consecrating himself to himself."

P.-M.D./d.w.

BIBLIOGRAPHY

"Esus," in Pauly/Wissowa, *Real-Encyclopädie,* vol. 6 (1909). P.-M. DUVAL, *Les dieux de la Gaule* (2d ed., Paris 1976), 26–27, 34–35; "Teutates, Esus, Taranis," *Études celtiques,* 8, 1 (1958); "Esus und seine Werkzeuge auf Denkmälern in Trier und Paris," *Trierer Zeitschrift,* 36 (1973). E. THEVENOT, "La pendaison sanglante des victimes offertes à Esus-Mars," *Latomus,* 28 (1957). S. CZARNOWSKI, "L'arbre d'Esus, le taureau aux trois grues et le culte des voies fluviales," *Revue celtique,* 42 (1925).

FIONN AND THE FIAN

Fionn mac Cumaill is the central figure of that branch of Irish tradition—comprising both prose and poems—known by the name of *Fianaigheacht,* the tale of the *fian,* a *fian* being a roving band of young fighters and hunters (the Fenians). This branch of the literature is also named the Fenian (fian) or Ossianic cycle, Ossian being the Scottish form of the name of Fionn's son, Oisín, the poet to whom most of the poems are attributed: his poems generally tell of the happiness which one feels at the sight of the wild and uncultivated regions of the land, as well as of its rocky coasts.

It is said that when Feradhach Fechtnach, the king of Ireland, died, his two sons, Tuathal and Fiachna, divided Ireland between them. The first received its abundance and

wealth, its herds and forts; the second its cliffs and estuaries, its acorn crops and fruits of the sea, its salmon and game. Learning of this division, the nobles of Christian Ireland had to see it as extremely unjust. When Oisín asked them which of the two portions they would have chosen, they answered, "Its banquets and dwellings and all that is good in it." At which Cáilte, the leader of the *Fian,* remarked that the portion that they had judged the worse was the one that "we ourselves would prefer." Tuathal became king. Fiachna, who had chosen the rivers, the fallow lands, the wildernesses, the woods, the precipices, and the estuaries, joined his fate with that of the *Fian.* Nevertheless, upon his brother's death he succeeded him upon the throne.

The *Fian* society was an institution recognized in the laws of ancient Ireland. The conditions of membership appear in detail in the narratives. If their pledges were violated, the members of the *Fian* were to accept no material recompense.

They were not to refuse either food or anything of value to any person. When alone they were not supposed to flee even in the face of nine adversaries: these are conditions which reflect the three functions. Renouncing the protection of his relations and his people, who would not be responsible for his deeds and misdeeds, the candidate for a *Fian* must first be a poet familiar with the twelve books of poetry (first function); next, sunk into a hole up to his belt, he must defend himself with a shield and a small hazel staff (without being injured) against nine warriors who attack at the same time with nine javelins (second function); and third, pursued across the woods of Ireland by those who would wound him, and with nothing more between him and them at the beginning than the bough of a tree in the forest, he must not be caught, his weapons must not tremble in his hand, his carefully arranged hair must not be disheveled, nor a dead branch crack under his foot; he must leap over a hedge as high as his forehead and pass under one as low as his knee, and he must be able to pull a thorn out of his foot without slowing down (third function). The *Fian* was thus an "elite corps made up of fair young men." According to Céitinn (Keating), who wrote in the seventeenth century, they were expected to keep order in the country, and in addition, no daughter could be given in marriage without having first been offered to one of these men.

In a part of the *Táin Bó Cuailnge* there is a story of druid harpists who are transformed into deer—a form often taken by Brahman seers. The name of the poet Oisín and perhaps that of his son Oscar derive from *os*, "stag"; and besides being a warrior (second function) and a hunter (third function), Fionn is a magician with double sight (first function). The Fenian heroes—whose mothers, it is said, are the Tuatha Dé Danann—constantly appear in a hostile or friendly relationship with the inhabitants of the magical dwellings (*síde*) of heights and promontories. Fionn was the grandson or great-grandson of Nuadhu, which would seem to relate him closely to the Gwynn ap Nudd (Gwynn son of Nudd) of Welsh tradition. Gwynn ap Nudd is a "warrior-hunter-seer" and the king of Annwn, a domain similar to the *síd* of Irish tradition. The division of Ireland by the sons of King Feradhach recalls the division made by the sons of Milid and the Tuatha Dé Danann, as well as the division made by Éremhón and Ébher. The adventures of the *Fian* take place most often in the southern half of Ireland; the stronghold of Fionn is at Almu in Laigin (Leinster), and his rival Goll is the chief of the *Fian* of Connacht (Connaught: it was to protect himself from his enemies that Fionn learned the art of poetry). Fionn is said to have been the captain of the soldiers of King Cormac mac Airt and also captain of his guard, of his mercenaries, and of his huntsmen; this recalls the place occupied by the captain of the guard in the lower portion of the hall of the Welsh king. In contrast with the warriors of Ulaidh (Ulster), the *Fian* fought not in chariots but on foot, and the joyous camaraderie which one finds in these stories is quite different from the harsh and incessant rivalries that characterized the northern heroes. Similarly, Fionn's power of divination and the illumination that comes to him when he nibbles on his thumb are of a much lower and more human level than the magic of the Tuatha Dé Danann. It is in this branch of the tradition that one finds the most heated human feelings, as well as a tender nostalgia for bygone days and for the active life that passes so happily in the company of others of the same spirit. And there is great emphasis on Fionn's unlimited generosity—the essential virtue of the third function.

Although we know that certain of the stories of the *Fian* already existed by the eighth century, they played a limited role in the repertory of scholarly poets as the manuscripts describe them. It is only toward the end of the twelfth century that the extended text of the *Accalam na Senórach* ("The Colloquy of the Ancients") is attested and that this aspect of the traditional heritage appears on the highest level. This was also the period of the diffusion of the Arthurian literature in Europe, and there are certainly many relationships between the legend of Fionn and that of Arthur. Perhaps the best known of the stories of the *Fian* is that of the flight of Diarmaid and Gráinne, which recalls the story of Tristan and Isolde in the Arthurian tradition. Although this story is identical in essence to that of Naoise and Deirdre in the tradition of Ulaidh, it is the narrative of the *Fian* that came to occupy the foremost place in the popular imagination.

B.R./d.w.

BIBLIOGRAPHY

M. DILLON, *Early Irish Literature* (Chicago 1948), 32–50. G. MURPHY, *Duanaire Finn* (Dublin 1953), 3. J. WEISWEILER, "Vorindo-germanische Schichten der irischen Heldensage," *Zeitschrift für Celtische Philologie*, 24 (1954). M.-L. SJOESTEDT, *Dieux et héros des Celtes* (Paris 1940), 81–91.

NEHALENNIA

A Celtic or Celto-Germanic goddess worshiped in the province of lower Germania at Domburg (Netherlands), Nehalennia had a temple on the coastline that is submerged today.

The name, apparently more Germanic than Celtic, has yet to be explained. Numerous votive monuments discovered at various times depict the goddess with attributes of abundance and show her with a dog at her side, sitting in state in the company of Neptune, because she was sometimes invoked, like him, to request a safe crossing or to give thanks for one.

P.-M.D./g.h.

BIBLIOGRAPHY

Article "Nehalennia" in the *Real-Encyclopädie* of PAULY and WISSOWA, 2d ser., vol. 16, part 2, 1935 (F. HEICHELHEIM). P.-M. DUVAL, *Les dieux de la Gaule* (2d ed., Paris 1976), 58. A. HONDIUS-CRONE, *The Temple of Nehalennia at Domburg* (Amsterdam 1955).

OGMIOS

A Gallic god and in a broader sense a Celtic god, Ogmios is known through a text by the philosopher Lucian of Samosata, who wrote in the third century and traveled in the West, in Italy, and probably on the coasts of Gaul, perhaps staying in Marseille. In a work entitled *Dialogi Mortuorum*, he tells of a conversation he had with a Celt. (He uses this word rather than Galatian, which he reserves for the Celts of Galatia in Asia Minor. Thus the scene takes place in the West and not, as has been suggested, in Galatia.) The Celt describes for him a mythological painting representing an old man with tanned skin, equipped as was Heracles (with lion's skin, club, bow and quiver), who "attracts a considerable crowd of men, all tied by their ears with golden and amber chains," the other ends of which are then attached to the hero's pierced tongue, and in this way he leads the procession. The Celt tells him that the painting symbolizes proven eloquence assured of its means. This Gallic Heracles, this charmer, whom authors in the French Renaissance revived with enthusiasm in their writings, is thus a symbol, almost an allegory.

Ogmios was originally a Gallic name. It is cited on two tablets containing incantations (found at Bregenz in Austria). The Irish turned it into *Ogma*, "the strong [god], the champion," and the inventor of the Ogham alphabet, similarly an alliance of physical strength and culture.

There is no reason to identify this god with the figure on Armorican coins, where a man's beardless head is surrounded by little "cut-off heads" attached together but not attached to his tongue. However, Greek writers refer to parallel legends. According to Eunapius, Porphyry had a chain "like that of Hermes" to tie his listeners together by means of magic; Lucian himself in his *Damis* says that in order to oppose the gods, Hermes dragged men who were attached by the ears. So the magic chain in the ears of charmed individuals exists in places other than the story about Heracles, but it is described most completely there.

P.-M.D./g.h.

BIBLIOGRAPHY

The article "Ogmios," in PAULY/WISSOWA, *Real-Encyclopädie*, vol. 17 (1936) (F. HEICHELHEIM). KOEPP, "Ogmios," *Bonner Jahrbücher*, 1919, 125–26. P.-M. DUVAL, *Les dieux de la Gaule* (2d ed., Paris 1976), 79–82.

RITONA

Ritona is a Gallic goddess whose Celtic name is known through several inscriptions and whose image is known from a stela with inscriptions and pictures found at Pachten in the Sarre: a clothed woman with a dog at her feet. The name, in its ancient form of *Pritona*, is also depicted in that form on some dedicatory inscriptions that read *Ritona Pritona*. It contains the word for a gateway or ford, *(p)riton* (related to the Latin *portus*). The importance of all places or means of crossing or transition, whether natural or artificial, was great in ancient beliefs. Ritona must have been a frequently invoked deity. The name may have also been given to a river, known today as Rieu, which flows in the Gard region of France.

P.-M.D./g.h.

BIBLIOGRAPHY

The articles "Pritona," by HEICHELHEIM, in Pauly/Wissowa, *Real-Encyclopädie*, vol. 23, 1 (1957), and "Ritona," by HAUG, 2d ser., 1 (1914). P.-M. DUVAL, *Les dieux de la Gaule* (2d ed., Paris 1976), 58. S. LOESCHCKE, *Der Tempelbezirk im Albachthal zu Trier*, 1 (1938). J. MOREAU, in *Bulletin de la Société nationale des antiquaires de France*, 1957.

ROSMERTA

Rosmerta is the Celtic name of a Gallic goddess, formerly *[P]rosmerta*, made up of an emphatic prefix and the root *smert-*, "provision, foresight, providence." Rosmerta was the "great provider," whom one invoked in order to lack nothing and to have much more. One logical, though unattested, parallel would be the Romans' Abundantia.

Numerous inscriptions testify to the vitality of her cult and her association with Mercury, the god of prosperous barters, voyages, and commerce. Some rare Gallo-Roman monuments that bear both a dedicatory inscription in her name and her likeness in bas-relief suggest her appearance and attributes. She was portrayed as a woman clothed, draped, and standing and holding a horn of plenty or purse and a libation saucer. Other monuments that have lost the dedicatory inscription depict a goddess of similar appearance who has often been taken for Rosmerta, by analogy but without any solid proof. There may well have been several provider deities among the Celts, who also venerated mother goddesses characterized by similar features but bearing different names.

Rosmerta's companion is Mercury according to dedicatory inscriptions and some decorated monuments. The couple is well matched, since they are both devoted to the making and distributing of material profits. People have also seen Rosmerta, perhaps too hastily, in the anonymous goddess who often accompanies Mercury. In any case, as far as we know he is her only known companion.

In one case, on a pillar found in Paris, in a panel next to one occupied by Mercury, a goddess is shown carrying a caduceus, just as he does. She is not necessarily Rosmerta.

P.-M.D./g.h.

BIBLIOGRAPHY

The article "Rosmerta," by KEUNE, in Pauly/Wissowa, *Real-Encyclopädie*, 2d ser., vol. 1 (1914). P.-M. DUVAL, *Les dieux de la Gaule* (2d ed., Paris 1976), 57. C. BÉMONT, "A propos d'un nouveau monument de Rosmerta," *Gallia* 27 (1969).

SIRONA

Sirona is a Gallic goddess whose Celtic name appears in several inscriptions. It was written with a Greek *theta* (or two), with a Latin crossed *D* (or two), with *ST, TS, SD,* or *DS, DD,* or *SS,* to render a sound existing only in Celtic, though it approximates *tst* so much that we find in *stirona* an Indo-European root of the English word for star (French *astre*, German *stern*). Moreover, in eastern Gaul the goddess was associated with Apollo, the god of the sun, and with his parallel god *Grannus*. On stelae she looks altogether commonplace, but she appears once wearing a crescent on her head, indicating that she is surely a goddess of stars and perhaps even the Moon.

P.-M.D./g.h.

BIBLIOGRAPHY

Article "Sirona," by Kees, in Pauly/Wissowa, *Real-Encyclopädie*, 2d ser., vol. 3, 1 (1927). P.-M. DUVAL, *Les dieux de la Gaule* (2d ed., Paris 1976), 58.

SMERTRIOS

Smertrios, a Gallic and more broadly Celtic god, is known in Paris from a panel on the pillar of the Nautae Parisiaci that bears his image and his partially spelled-out name; the name must be completed as *Smert[rios]* after a dedicatory inscription *Marti Smertrio* found among the Trevires. All that remains is the upper part of the god, who holds a short mace over a snake that has risen up in front of his head. The weapon reminds one of Hercules, but the animal is neither the Lernaean Hydra nor the dragon of the Hesperides, and the name is that of a Gallic god: a Celtic parallel of the Greek hero, assimilated on Gallo-Roman dedicatory inscriptions sometimes to Mars and sometimes to Hercules (under the name of Mertronnus, which has the same root *[s])mer-*, "foresight, provision, providence"). This god has in common with the two Roman gods a superhuman physical strength that respects adversaries of all kinds but ensures the maintenance of prosperity in peace.

The four inscriptions come from Gaul and from Noricum (Mertronnus in northern Italy). The root has supplied various anthroponyms in Gaul, Great Britain, and Galatia (Asia Minor). A name recognized by everyone under various widespread forms distinguishes this Gallic champion of protective physical force.

P.-M.D./g.h.

BIBLIOGRAPHY

P.-M. DUVAL, "Le dieu *Smertrios* et ses avatars gallo-romains," *Études celtiques* 6, 2 (1953–54); *Les dieux de la Gaule* (2d ed., Paris 1976), 39–40.

SUCELLUS, THE GOD WITH A HAMMER

Likenesses of Sucellus appeared often and exclusively in Roman Gaul, on bas-reliefs, bronze statuettes, and even pottery. The "god with the hammer" has been definitely identified with Sucellus (to whom six Gallo-Roman inscriptions were also dedicated), thanks to one monument and one object that bear his name and likeness: the stela of Sarrebourg, on which he is depicted with the goddess *Nantosuelta*, and the ornamental medallion on a Rhone Valley vase. The name may go back to pre-Roman Celtic times, because it is not Latin and may mean in Gallic "he who strikes well,"

which does not mean that the hammer is a deadly weapon. One could use a hammer to open a gate, to overturn an obstacle, or to build. Moreover, in various representations of the god, the head of the hammer forms the upper part of a long staff which he holds with his raised arm like a scepter that he leans on. Otherwise it is shorter, but not as short as an ordinary mallet (on some reliefs) and is resting upright next to him, so it is probably only a substitute for the staff-scepter to suit the requirements of the smaller image. Naked, with a wolf skin on his head or dressed in Gallic clothing, the god strikes a majestic pose reminiscent of Jupiter, whose physical features he shares: bearded and in the prime of life or somewhat older. His other principal attribute is a pot of the *olla* type which he holds flat in the palm of his right hand and seems to offer as a symbol of the wealth generously dispensed by a landowner. With his hammerhead scepter and his pot filled with food, he looks like a powerful and wealthy god. When he has a dog at his side, the animal is his familiar protector. When he has a wolf skin on his head, back, or arm, like the Hades painted on the wall of an Etruscan tomb (known as "dell-Orco," in Tarquinia), he looks somewhat infernal and calls to mind Dis Pater. According to Tertullian (*Ad Nationes* 1.10), Dis Pater came equipped with a hammer when he escorted the corpses that were being dragged out of the arena (at least a bit player was costumed in this way). When he goes by the name of Pluto (Dis Pater never seems to have been represented under his own name), this infernal brother of Jupiter sits on his throne in majesty and has by his side a three-headed dog—who sometimes appears as the companion of the god with the hammer. In pre-Roman Gaul, coins from the west central region minted during the second century B.C. have on the back a short-handled hammer and a cauldron with a suspending chain, above and below a horse ridden by a rather strange figure holding a sword. It is not clear if there was a connection between the short-handled hammer and the cauldron, the scepter-mallet, and the bulging pot, over the span of centuries. If there is a parallel between Sucellus and Dis Pater, it must be that Caesar applied the latter name not only to the brother of Jupiter and the divine father of the Gallic race, but also to a very great Celtic god who bore such a striking resemblance to the infernal brother of Jupiter that the conqueror of Gaul called the god by that name, *ad usum Romanorum*. Sucellus, who was very often represented in Gaul, must have eclipsed his Roman counterpart. Neither Dis Pater nor even Pluto was visibly present in the Romanized sections of Gaul, where their cults were almost nonexistent. Moreover, Pluto's fortune comes from the wealth of the dead rather than from the fruits of the earth tilled by the living.

Given the way it was presented, it is not clear how the hammer was used. With its long leaning staff, a sign of sovereign power, it is a key symbol, almost a talisman, and not a real, deadly instrument as it would be in the hands of Charun, the infernal demon of the Etruscans.

The bulging pot contains a beverage, a product of the tilled earth. This beneficent feature of the god is certainly very important, for therein lies the identification with Silvanus, who in southern Gaul exchanged features with Sucellus: the quasi nudity, animal skin, laurel crown, billhook, hunting knife, syrinx, fruits, and tree are borrowed by Sucellus; the hammers on an altar are borrowed by Silvanus. The feeding pot thus seems more chthonic than infernal; it corresponds to the fruits that Silvanus carries in the folds of his short cloak. Sucellus is a god who dispenses beverages. Moreover,

Sucellus dressed as Sylvanus. Bronze statuette from Orpierre (Hautes-Alpes), France.

he was depicted more than once in the Gallic style with one or several kegs, and sometimes even with an amphora at his feet. This is a benefactor who has reserves.

Other attributes which might be considered secondary are sometimes found on votive bas-reliefs and sometimes on bronze statuettes: crosses and circles, probably astral in nature and conceivably suggesting the heavenly dwelling place of souls. These details are scattered over his garment. There is also a nail affixed to his belt (which has not been explained) and in one instance a club, which is probably connected with Heracles.

Unlike Hercules and Silvanus, Sucellus is often seen with a female consort, though he does not appear beside a divine companion. It is typical for Celtic gods to be married, and iconographically speaking, at least, it is peculiarly Gallic. The best example is a Sarrebourg stela that shows the couple Sucellus and Nantosvelta, named by a dedicatory inscription. The god, warmly dressed in the Gallic style, holds the staff-scepter with the hammerhead and the feeding bowl; the goddess, dressed in the Roman style, holds a libation saucer above a small altar and a staff-scepter on top of which is a small building that some see as a house, others as a hive, and still others as a temple or *fanum.* The name of the goddess, which might have resolved the issue, has not been deciphered. Her look is majestic, imperious, and worthy of her companion. Not unlike Juno, she has the presence of a *regina.* Below the couple on the the stela is a large raven, the flying oraculum in the cult of Apollo, whose presence in this context is rather enigmatic. Other depictions are less precise and less detailed. An anonymous goddess seated next to the

Gallic god with a hammer, with pipes. Stela. Avignon, Musée lapidaire. Photo Giraudon.

god holds a cornucopia, and when Sucellus leans on a barrel (notably at Alesia and in Burgundy), it is obvious that this is primarily a godly couple watching over the prosperity of the landowner.

We may find a parallel in one of the principal gods of pagan Ireland, namely, Daghdha, also known as Ollathair, the "good god," "Father of All." There are resemblances and differences. Daghdha is omnipotent, omniscient, Herculean, boorish, and bawdy, and is dressed in a short tunic, a hood, and leather boots. He pulls a huge club mounted on wheels (which Sucellus does not have), which kills with one end and revives with the other. He has an enormous cauldron always full and ready to refresh anyone who approaches. Finally, he periodically mates with the goddesses of the earth. The points in common are notable: a god of imposing size, complete with a bowl full of food that he dispenses; a god who willingly mates since he is the father of the race, like the Gallic Dis Pater according to Caesar. We cannot overlook these concordances; but the hammer, a deadly weapon associated with the Germanic Thor and the Etruscan Charun, belongs to another register.

P.-M.D./g.h.

BIBLIOGRAPHY

Article "Sucellus," by KEUNE, in Pauly/Wissowa, *Real-Encyclopädie*, 2d ser., vol. 4 (1932). P. LAMBRECHTS, *Contributions à l'étude des divinités celtiques* (Bruges 1942), chap. 6. A. GRENIER, "Le dieu au maillet gaulois et Charun," *Studi Etruschi* 24 (1955–56). J. DE VRIES, *La religion des Celtes* (1963), pp. 99–105. P.-M. DUVAL, *Les dieux de la Gaule* (2d ed., Paris 1976), pp. 62–64, figs. 45–46. S. BOUCHER, "Sucellus = Dispater? Remarques sur la typologie et les fonctions du dieu gaulois," *Revue belge de philologie et d'histoire* 54 (1976). M. F. HEICHELHEIM and J.-E. HOUSMAN, "Sucellus and Nantosuelta in mediaeval Celtic mythology," *L'Antiquité classique* 17 (1948).

TARANIS

Taranis was a Gallic god who was in a broader sense a Celtic god; his name contains the word for thunder, *taran-*. He was thus the god of the thundering sky, of the sky at its most terrifying and sublime, but also by virtue of the storm he was the rainmaker. To him were attributed the deafening rolls and claps of thunder, the coming and going of the threatening cataclysm, the blinding bolts of lightning before they struck high points or crashed onto the ground, the oppressive mugginess in the air and the torrential downpour, the rainbow and its enchanting light, light and sound that terrified crowds or individuals, the strongest cosmic menace in countries that did not have earthquakes or tidal waves, fire that destroyed and killed, and flooding from rain that ravaged and drowned but also fertilized. Such irresistible power made Jupiter the master of the gods in the classical pantheon. It is not known whether this was also true of the Celts, but it is probable that such primacy was established among them during Roman times, since Taranis was assimilated to Jupiter in various ways. Along with the gods Esus and Teutates, he was one of the three important Gallic gods who thirsted for human blood, according to Lucan; but the three gods did not constitute a triad.

Only Lucan knew the name Taranis (nominative or genitive), but it appeared in other forms in dedicatory inscriptions in Greek letters (*Taran(o)ous*) and especially in Latin letters: *Taranucnus*, i.e., son of Taranus; *Tanarus*, perhaps instead of *Taranus*; and the epithet Taranucus (applied to Jupiter), i.e., "pertaining to Taranus." These inscriptions come from France, Germany, Hungary, Yugoslavia, and Great Britain, which suggests that the cult of Taranis was widespread during Roman times throughout the ancient Celtic world. Like thunder itself, the god was ubiquitous and feared everywhere. His name is still associated with the town of Martigny in the Valais region of the French Alps, where a shrine to Jupiter once stood.

A medieval commentator on Lucan assimilated Taranis sometimes to Jupiter and sometimes to Dis Pater, his underworld brother. He confirmed the cruel nature of the god by attributing to him the following mode of sacrifice. For Taranis–Dis Pater some men are burned in a wooden vat (or small hamper, *alveus ligneus*). To Taranis-Jupiter (Jupiter being considered the master of war) went an offering of severed human heads. The first of the two sacrifices recalls one that Caesar described without naming the deity: human victims were burned alive, packed inside a wicker mannequin. Inscriptions dating from Roman times associate the two names by giving Jupiter a variant of Taranis as a surname and thus confirm the assimilation. Nevertheless, Taranis had to rest content with the name, for he inherited only one of the characteristics of Jupiter, namely, control of thunder and lightning. Moreover, there are no known decorated monuments that include dedicatory inscriptions bearing the name Taranis or one of its variants. On the other hand, some depictions show a god who looks like Jupiter and has features which might be illustrations of Taranis.

One such feature is the wheel. An individual holds a wheel next to a bearded god depicted on a plaque on the Gundestrup bowl from Denmark, probably made near the shores of the Black Sea during the first half of the first century B.C. During the Gallo-Roman period, Jupiter the Very Kind, Jupiter the Very Great, on horseback or standing, held in his hand either the thunderbolt or the wheel or both. The wheel may very well symbolize lightning or evoke the roll of thunder. The wheel also appears on Gallo-Roman altars dedicated to Jupiter.

Another feature is *s* shapes. A bronze statuette found at Le Chatelet (Haute-Marne) in France depicts Jupiter holding a large wheel, the thunderbolt, and spirals that may symbolize the sinuous lines of lightning.

Yet another partly non-Roman version of Jupiter is the Gallo-Roman god on horseback, perched atop a column and subduing a giant who has the tails of a snake or fish, as the sky arches over the earth. Sometimes the god stands erect with the monster at his feet. Often he holds the wheel. Surely it must be Taranis dressed like a Roman (at times in armor) and turned knight. He is the omnipotent master of the universe. Pillars and columns abound along the Rhine, as well as in other parts of Gaul. They have a complex iconography, including various gods and goddesses on pedestals, octogonal drums with planetary deities on top, and capitals depicting the seasons supporting the group at the top. These figures may well have originated in Greco-Roman images: Zeus's victory over the giants and the knight with his horse above a human bust that seems to carry it. What is Celtic within this Gallo-Roman complex is the name of the god and the wheel.

There is no god of thunder in Ireland.

P.-M.D./g.h.

BIBLIOGRAPHY

Article "Taranis," by F. HEICHELHEIM, in Pauly/Wissowa, *Real-Encyclopädie*, 2d ser., vol. 4 (1932). P.-M. DUVAL, *Les dieux de la Gaule* (2d ed., Paris 1976), 27, 29, 73–76. J.-J. HATT, *Rota cum flammis circumsepta; "A propos du symbole de la roue dans la religion gauloise,"* *Revue archéologique de l'Est et du Centre-Est* 2 (1951). P. LAMBRECHTS, *Contributions à l'étude des divinités celtiques* (Bruges 1942), chap. 4.

TARVOS TRIGARANUS

The bull with three cranes is a sacred or divine Gallic animal, perhaps more broadly Celtic. Its Gallic and non-Latinized name is inscribed on one of the three blocks of the pillar dedicated to Jupiter by the Nautae Parisiaci, the boatmen from Lutetia, the city of the Parisii, in the reign of Tiberius (A.D. 14–37). Depicted in bas-relief on the same block, a bull stands in front of a tree, with three long-legged birds on its back, specifically cranes (*garan* in Gallic). And on the side face of a votive stela from Trier dedicated to Mercury, the head of a bull with three birds appears through the foliage of a tree. On the pillar in Paris, the next panel shows the god with his Gallic name *Esus* pruning a tree with a billhook. The joining of the two scenes into one myth is attested by the fact that in Trier the birds are perched on the tree itself, which a man dressed in a short garment like that worn by the Esus in Paris is felling with an ax.

There have been vain attempts to explain *trigaranus* as a deformation of Latinized Greek words, one of which is said to have meant "three-headed" (*trikarènos*), another "three-horned" (*trikératios*). The Indo-European noun for crane (Old English *crane*, French *grue*, Greek *geranos*, Latin *grus*, and Celtic *garan*) is more clear here in that the epithet "with three cranes" is found, *trigéranon* (variant, *trygéranon*), in an Attic comedy written ca. 279, shortly after the Celts went to Greece. It designates a present which Athens had to send to the Seleucid king—to whom the Celts had just dealt a crushing defeat—in exchange for the tiger that the king had sent to Athens. The sacred animal "with three cranes," was thus known in Athens as typically Celtic, exotic, and alien.

On the islands, an epic legend belonging to the old sources of Celtic mythology contains elements parallel to what is understood by the name and depiction of the bull. The Irish hero Cú Chulainn, in search of the Cows of Cooley in Ulster, pursues a divine bull who is taking shelter in a forest. Three birds in succession warn the bull of the impending danger: when Cú Chulainn proves his strength by felling a tree, goddesses who assume the appearance of crows warn the bull of the hero's approach.

Finally, a Gallic coin attributed to the Carnutes bears on its back a bull with a bird on its back, the kindly cowbird that eats parasites, a rather curious, though realistic subject for a coin. It may in fact be a memory of the old legendary bull.

One inscription in Gallic, one verse from a Greek comedy, and two decorated monuments connected with a myth about Esus—these sources reveal a cult and a myth represented in Gaul and brought as far as Greece by the Celts. Georges Dumézil has pointed out parallel mythical elements at the other end of the Indo-European spectrum: in Iran and in India, there is a myth about a carpenter who decapitates a

Tarvos Trigaranus. Boatmen's monument. First century A.D. Found under the Cathedral of Notre-Dame, Paris, in 1711. Photo Jean Suquet.

monster whose three heads, hollow like boxes, contain a grouse, a sparrow, and a partridge.

P.-M.D./g.h.

BIBLIOGRAPHY

Article "Tarvos Trigaranus," by F. HEICHELHEIM, in Pauly/Wissowa, *Real-Encyclopädie*, vol. 4 (1932). P.-M. DUVAL, *Les dieux de la Gaule* (2d ed., Paris 1976), pp. 35–37, 45; "Le groupe de bas-reliefs des *Nautae Parisiaci*," *Monuments . . . Piot*, 48, 2 (1956). J. VENDRYES, "Sur un passage du comique Philémon: Le Tarvos Trigaranos en Grèce," *Revue celtique* 27 (1906). H. D'ARBOIS DE JUBAINVILLE, "L'enlèvement des Vaches de Cooley," *Revue celtique* 28 (1907); 32 (1911). G. DUMÉZIL, *Horace et les Curiaces* (Paris 1942), 133.

TEUTATES, TOUTATIS

The name of Teutates is based on the word for "tribe" (*teuta, touta, tota*). It may be a common noun, "tribal god." Lucan cites "the cruel Teutates" along with two other important Gallic gods who thirst for human blood. Four Latin inscriptions found in Great Britain and in the Danube country mention *Mars Toutatis*. Another dedicatory inscription made

by a veteran in Rome links the two names of *Toutates* (or *Toutatis*) and *Meduris*, the latter most likely being the equivalent of the Irish god Mider, also a war god. Although the medieval commentary on Lucan assimilated Teutates variously to Mars and Mercury and did so on the basis of different sources, the evidence of the inscriptions supports the first identification, which is not contradicted by the kind of sacrifice described by the commentator. He tells us that the victim was plunged headfirst into a vat until death came. On the gilded silver bowl found in Gundestrup (Denmark), a work believed to date from the first half of the first century A.D. and decorated with mythological scenes and deities (at least two of which, the god with antlers and the snake with the ram's head, are typically Celtic), we can see, in front of a line of foot soldiers and horsemen armed in the Gallic style, a huge figure plunging a man headfirst into a deep vat. This may be the sacrifice in question, performed by a divine being, which would serve to reinforce the argument that Teutates was indeed the tribal war god identified with Mars. Another explanation sees in the scene on the bowl not a sacrifice but an immersion designed to bring about immortality; in this case we might conclude that the war god himself thus opened to each of the heroes the gates to the beyond. We might also recognize a Celtic war god, if not Teutates himself, on a bas-relief of the pillar in Mavilly (Côte-d'Or) in France, dating from the later Gallo-Roman period. Armed in the Roman style, he has near him the erect snake with the ram's head (that appears on the Gundestrup bowl) and a goddess escorting him. She too is armed, but her left breast is exposed. This is a divine warrior couple, obviously indigenous.

Teutates is therefore known from texts in Gaul; from Latin inscriptions in Britain, on the Danube, and even in Rome; and from the Gundestrup bowl, which may have its place of origin in the Black Sea area. He was a great Celtic and then Celto-Roman god, probably worshiped among all the "tribes," whose warriors he probably protected, and by Celtic soldiers in the Roman armies.

There are approximate insular Irish equivalents of the tribal god. There is an oath in the Ulster Cycle "to the god to whom my tribe swears allegiance." The mythical use of immersion appears in place of the sacrifice: two kings are drowned in liquor as they attempt to escape a fire, and the hero Cú Chulainn is plunged into three cold vats, which as a result of his ardor become boiling hot and thus capable of curing him.

P.-M.D./g.h.

BIBLIOGRAPHY

Article "Teutates," by GRÖBER, in Pauly/Wissowa, *Real-Encyclopädie*, 2d ser., vol. 4 (1932); article "Mars (keltisch-germanisch)," by F. HEICHELHEIM, ibid., 14, 2 (1930). P.-M. DUVAL, *Les dieux de la Gaule* (2d ed., Paris 1976), 26–27, 29–31, 71–73; "Teutates, Esus, Taranis," *Études celtiques* 8, 1 (1958). J. GRICOURT, "Sur une plaque du chaudron de Gundestrup," *Latomus* 13 (1954). J. CARCOPINO, "Inscription à Teutates," *Revue des études anciennes* 9 (1907). J.-F. HIMLY, "*Medros*, dieu gaulois de la guerre en Basse-Alsace, *Teutates Meduris* et le dieu irlandais Mider," *Cahiers d'archéologie et d'histoire d'Alsace* 38 (1947).

ELEMENTS OF THE SACRED AMONG THE GERMANIC AND NORSE PEOPLES

The study of Germanic and Norse mythologies immediately presents serious difficulties, largely because of the documents available to us: these documents are either archaeological and therefore rarely authorize definitive statements; or else they are literary in nature (runes, Eddic and Skaldic poems, reports of non-Germanic observers, later the Icelandic sagas), and so present major problems of interpretation or decipherment. To give only a few examples, the runic inscriptions are early and appear toward the third century A.D., but specialists are still trying to work out what they mean; our two principal sources, the *Poetic Edda* and the *Edda* of Snorri Sturluson, were put together, in the form in which we now know them, in the thirteenth century by literate people raised on Christian culture, who often no longer understood (and in any case no longer lived) what they were talking about, even though some of the texts they passed on seem to date back to a much earlier period. As for the notes left by observers from Rome (Tacitus), Byzantium (Constantine Porphyrogenetus), Arabia (Ibn Fadhlan), etc., these must be passed through a double interpretive grid, first concerning the author and then the matter he is dealing with.

Beyond this, there is nothing less certain than the very notion of "German," "Germanic." Without dwelling on the point here, we may simply say that these terms were not used by the people themselves. The historical data on these religions show a fundamental instability which makes analysis extremely difficult. While these religions certainly belong to an Indo-European culture, their originality definitely derives from various indigenous substrata which were conquered by invaders and about which we know very little, despite the efforts of philology (particularly toponymy and onomastics), other than that they belong to a very old tradition, as is evident from the many stone engravings going back to the Norse Bronze Age (1500 to 400 B.C.) found throughout Scandinavia. But since that period, the distinctive traits of Germanic culture seem to have been an extraordinary capacity for adaptation and intellectual curiosity, and intimate contact with the Greek and Latin, Celtic, Slavic, Finno-European, and finally Christian worlds, which all, to different degrees, left their mark on Germanic culture. The Norns resemble the Fates; Týr and Mars, Óðinn and Mercury go together; Loki resembles Lug, even in his name; Fjörgyn and Perkun are probably the same word; and the *Völuspá* could have been written by Hildegarde of Bingen!

The foregoing has two consequences: any synchronic view of these mythologies is necessarily risky (and yet this is the error that is usually made, without seeing the danger that lies in wanting to base a firm conclusion on documents that are disparate in age, in provenance, and, one presumes, in immediate purpose), but diachronic perspectives, the only admissible ones, also reveal the complexity of an evolution in which the gods keep taking one another's functions, and myths dissolve or deviate from their initial meaning, while new additions, only half understood, produce new confusions. This is to say that a strictly Dumézilian interpretation of these mythologies is possible only with reservations. The Germano-Nordic world probably could have conformed to the old tripartite scheme of society: an Eddic poem like the *Rígsþula* could verify this, were it not completely saturated with Celtic influence and, above all, if it did not present sociological traits that are difficult to verify (the "class" of slaves). But in our present state of knowledge, the situation is too fluid to authorize definitive claims: Who is the god of war? Óðinn, Týr, Thor, or even Freyr? Who is responsible for magic? The Vanir alone seem clearly situated in the tripartite scheme.

We find nothing more definite if we turn to the kinds of historical theories so popular in earlier centuries: the fact that some of the gods are called Aesir is not enough to make us see them as Asiatic imports; inversely, we could easily see Óðinn as Oriental if he did not appear, with his spear, on a Bronze Age petroglyph. The present Germanic area saw one or more invasions, probably around 2000 B.C.: prudence prevents us from being too quick to confer on the newcomers traits which may have already existed before their arrival. Interpretations of a symbolic nature come to grief in a similar way: while a myth like the one retold in the *Skírnismál* is admirably suited to a naturalistic explanation, the mythology as a whole is so composite that any effort at rational global organization is doomed to failure. We must not forget that most of our information comes from the writings of Snorri Sturluson (beginning of the thirteenth century), a great reader of the *Etymologia* of Isidore of Seville; Snorri Sturluson was a great abstractor of the quintessential and above all a rationalistic pedagogue. This is why our first impression when we face our mass of heterogeneous documents is one of confusion: here are religions that have no term that quite means "religion" (only terms for "practice" or "custom": *siðr*), nor for "faith" or "belief," "worship" or "prayer"; religions that have no dogmas, probably no castes of priest-sacrificers; perhaps not even any real temples in the form of specific buildings.

This is why on the one hand we should probably abandon explanatory systems that are overly subtle or complex and return, in conformity with a tendency exemplified by Mircea Eliade or Folke Ström, to a few simple and flexible orienting principles; on the other hand, it is why it is more valuable to see these religions from a diachronic point of view, without excessive rigor. With the "vertical" axis provided by these principles and the successive "horizontal" axes provided by a simple periodization (Prehistory, Bronze Age 1500 to 400 B.C., Iron Age 400 B.C. to about A.D. 800, Viking age from 800 to about 1100)—both periods and principles being envisaged here as working hypotheses, not as certainties—we obtain a grid on which we can at least inscribe the myths and gods in a fairly satisfactory way.

We will start from an obvious point: the Germanic and Nordic countries are, more than others, subject to a constraining natural substratum which has never in the past made human existence easy, and does not now. The soil is generally unyielding, rocky, arid, worked by frost, and polished by glaciers; the winter nights are long and lend themselves to all kinds of terrors; water (of seas, lakes, rivers, swamps), ever-present and hostile, imposes its perils and complicates all distances; finally, the sun, indispensable but miserly with its benefits, has all the properties of the preeminent power. Rock, water, sun: these are the principles which have an incontestable obviousness and an unavoidable existence.

The Germanic people have conceived one of the most beautiful fabulations or formulations of this natural theme ever invented in a mythology. This is the ash tree (or better, perhaps, the yew) Yggdrasill, a cosmic creation of immediate beauty and the source of intense poetry. All of our sources, from Tacitus to Adam of Bremen or Thietmar of Merseburg, from the petroglyphs to the sacred glades of Sweden, attest the fervor with which these tribes worshiped trees, the Tree. Born of the earth, fed with water, stretching toward the sun, Yggdrasill, holding the earth in place, justifies the order of the earth; an erect trunk (or beam, Mímameiðr, Mímir's beam—and it is surely not irrelevant that one of the possible etymologies of the word *áss* leads back to the theme *ansu*-,

meaning "beam"), sprung from the rock, it stands to its roots in primeval and fertile white clay water *(aurr)*, shooting its arrow toward the summit of the world. In continental Germany, it is also called Irminsul (the Pillar of Irmin; this can only evoke the element *jörmun*- of Jörmungandr, another name for the great Miðgarð serpent, himself equally responsible for the placement and maintenance of the universe). The rainbow, or Bifrost, watched over by the enigmatic Heimdallr, whose name, too, can mean Pillar of the World, connects Yggdrasill with the world of the gods. Yggdrasill is the source of all life, as the profuse rustling of its leaves and branches attests, ceaselessly stirred as they are by a whole symbolic fauna. It is the guardian or depository of all knowledge, since the world's memory is at its base in the person of Mímir, who agreed to share his wisdom with Óðinn in exchange for Óðinn's eye: after all, Yggdrasill specifically signifies the horse of Óðinn, a shamanistic trait. Finally, Yggdrasill presides over all destinies, those of the living and that of the universe, since the Norns watch at its base near the spring Urðr. With all the confusion and ambiguity of the great cosmogonic myths, Yggdrasill implies a series of equations (rock–earth mother–vegetation–life; water–magic–knowledge–memory; sun–eternal return–transcendence–destiny) which thus allows us to add more intellectual harmonics to our natural (or telluric or chthonic) principles, on condition of freezing nothing into rigid precepts. It is not by chance, after all, that in another myth with Promethean resonances the first human couple is born from trees (Askr, the first man, the ash tree; Embla, the first woman, the elm or vine branch).

We must next insist on the importance of the rock etchings mentioned above, which cover cliffs all over Scandinavia and on the southern shore of the Baltic. They are of interest in several ways: they are distributed about equally through the whole area just described and show an astonishing uniformity of themes, motifs, and even traits. They may represent our earliest source of information on these mythologies, since it is agreed that they go back as far as 1500 B.C. Above all, and even though their interpretation is necessarily conjectural, they authorize certain directions of "reading"— directions which are particularly thought-provoking since it seems neither excessive nor even difficult to see in these rock carvings the three vertical axes introduced above. They offer evidence for a solar cult of the processional type (confirmed by the discoveries of the chariot in Trundholm in Denmark, from around 1200 B.C., or the chariot in Dejberg, also in Denmark, from around 400 B.C.), illustrated by their innumerable disks, cupules, swastikas, and heliophoric figures or objects. We can read in them the preeminence of two heliophores or theophores which should be envisaged in alternation: the horse (as on the Trundholm chariot), who would be the diurnal or springtime theophore, and the curious "comb boat," which carries the sun at night or during the winter. This alternation is not fortuitous: its two terms are certainly the sources of the pair of divine twins (Skaldic poetry would make the horse boat one of its most common *kenningar*) who haunt this mythology in so many ways: Tacitus's Alci, the pairs Óðr-Óðinn, Ullr-Ullinn, Hengist-Horsa (in which the word for horse [Icelandic *hross*] can be read clearly), Vili(r)-Vé, Guðr-Gunnr, etc., without going into the *aesir* gods (singular *áss*) who may derive their name from the Vedic twins, the Aśvins.

If not, that is if we insist on an individualization, the solar or celestial cult could refer to a definitely fundamental god Týr (Tiw, Tyg, Ziu), whose name itself signifies "god" (*Tiwaz, Dyaus, Ju[Piter], Zeus, the French word *dieu*) and whose attribute is the magic ax. In any case, the petroglyphs repeatedly present this sun ax figure whose instrument would one day become Thor's hammer, which serves to bless as much as, if not more than, to destroy.

The rock carvings also portray a sort of giant with a spear. It is impossible to see this as anyone other than the prototype of Óðinn, god of the magic that is itself intimately connected with the liquid element (in the *Grímnismál* of the *Poetic Edda*, for example). Toponymy and evidence of all kinds confirm the role played in this paganism by springs, waterfalls, sacrificial mires, or *keldur*, in which sacred drownings were practiced, for the propitiation or consultation of augurs: this, it seems, is the case of the Tollund man who was found preserved intact in the blue clay of Denmark. The petroglyphs are rich in depictions that can only be magical in character: sacred weapons, ritual scenes that are hard to understand today, even if a vague memory of them is preserved in folklore, masks, disguises which reappear in the Middle Ages in the Icelandic *dansar*, and the giant hands of a sacrificer offered for the worship of the people, if these are not theophanies like the innumerable footprints.

Finally, the cult of the earth mother or of fertility-fecundity is amply attested, first of all by the multitude of male figures, always ithyphallic, that cover these rock faces (and are later found on certain standing stones—if, indeed, the fact that texts of all kinds were inscribed on standing stones or *batausteinar* is not in itself evidence for this cult); second, by the presence of a phallic-sword god connected with the boar, who must surely be identified with Freyr or his prototype; third, by the frequent representation of the *hieros gamos* or the very numerous symbolic depictions (ocular or, more probably, vaginal) of the earth mother herself. These documents thus verify the regular presence throughout this area of a uniform culture and an indigenous substratum which not only were able to assimilate and adapt different and later ethnic and cultural contributions, but also coincide to a remarkable degree with much more recent texts and documents about these religions. These petroglyphs also have another trait that is perfectly representative of what would in the historic period be Germano-Nordic cultures, a trait belonging to the history of art as much as to that of religions: the design, the style, and the organization of the whole group of tableaux indicate an advanced sense of symbolism which has been tempered or tamed and a proper balance between an abstraction without excess and an animal naturalism, both of which will become more and more developed in later periods.

Armed with these pieces of evidence on the one hand, and with texts of the Middle Ages on the other, it may not be too venturesome to attempt a reconstruction of the prehistoric stage of this religion. Here again the most striking thing is the importance of the worship of natural forces, which is shown incontestably from Caesar to the *Book of the Colonization* (*Landnámabók*) of Iceland. The various reconstitutions, of which Snorri Sturluson's is the most important, place the creation of giants and dwarfs at the dawn of time. The former evidently represent the sun, both by reason of the solar kinship that popular tale-telling attributes to them and because of the patent solar traits that encumber their mythic history; when they are not divinized as such, they will give birth to the gods, by virtue of the principle of alliterative genealogy so dear to the Germanic tribes; and they will give rise as well to the preeminent solar heroes, the Norse Daedalus Völundr-Weland, or the archetype that will be individualized one day in the heroic complex of Helgi-Sigurðr-Sîfrît-Siegfried. Yet even so, the giants remain

tied to all the great telluric forces; their names and myths also refer to the chthonic element (such as Ymir who corresponds to the fundamental Sanskrit hybrid Yama, or Aurgelmir, from *aurr*, "primeval slime") or the liquid element (Hymir-/Gymir, and Bergelmir, the Norse version of Noah). When human imagination takes pleasure in diversifying and portraying them, the giants are always given names that suggest the ideas of violence, instinctive force, and natural overflow (Hraesvelgr, Hrymir, Skrýmnir, Hrungnir, Øjazi). The dwarfs, who inhabit and support the world, are more tied to the earth mother and to the dead that she shelters and restores. They are cave dwellers, enemies of the light and guardians of the world beyond (some are called Nár, "cadaver," or Nýi, "the new moon," a symbol of death—note that in Old Norse the moon is masculine and the sun is feminine).

Two details merit attention: giants and dwarfs are intimately and variously associated with magic, particularly with ritual and esoteric operations typical of hunter-gatherer or agricultural tribes. In this, they are constitutive of the primeval world (the famous prefix *ur-* which evokes the farthest bounds of memory) *and* holders of the most secret knowledge—most secret because it is, literally, fundamental. Before their deliberate degradation by the Church and their relegation to folklore, giants and dwarfs were benevolent, clever, technically skilled powers, and in particular bearers of the secrets of poetry and the runes, all traits which Óðinn would inherit from them. Above all, they are ethically neutral, i.e., they realize a proper balance between order and disorder, two notions which seem to be of capital importance and appear to arise out of what is deepest in the Germano-Nordic mentality. This essentially active, dynamic, agonistic universe, whose major coloration is called energy, lives on tension, not on rest or meditation, certainly not on ecstasy; it expresses itself in action, not in lyricism or speculation. When one day near the end of the thirteenth century a group of Icelandic chroniclers, or *sagnamenn*, undertook a retelling of the history of the last two centuries of their island in terms of controlled antagonisms between great families (in the *Sturlunga Saga*), they reproduced exactly, probably without knowing it, this perfectly organic dialectical movement of the mentality of their very distant ancestors.

Starting from around 400 B.C. and continuing to about A.D. 800 (what in the north is called the Iron Age, with its three stages: Celtic, Roman, and then Germanic), we enter into a new age, the general characteristics of which are fairly clear. In this period Celtic influence seems to be the determinant one (cf. the famous sacrificial cauldron from Gundestrup). It is also in this period that, perhaps under Christian influence, the notion of a trinity, or at least of a triad, takes shape. There are many versions of this notion, all of which have an interesting point in common: Óðinn almost always figures in them. This suggests that he is already moving toward his place as the major god who, much later and under the clear influence of Christian thought, will become the Supreme Father (Alföðr) and probably that almighty Lord of the Aesir (*Áss hin almáttki*) whose exact identity has always been problematical. It was during the Iron Age, moreover, that the characterizations of the gods as individuals became current. A noteworthy fact—and one that confirms the essentially natural or naturalistic inspiration at the origin of this paganism. The gods seem to have been largely undifferentiated for a long time and continued in spite of many changes to be conceived of in the collective neuter under a great prodigality of names referring to their beneficent (*guð, goð*), active (*regin, rögn*), or "binding" virtues, a clear allusion to their magical

Rock engraving representing a boat. Photo Hasen. Hamlyn Group archives.

Chariot of the sun from Trundholm. Copenhagen, Nationalmuseet. Museum photo. Hamlyn Group archives.

Amulet representing Freyr. Bronze. Stockholm, Historiska Museet. Museum photo. Hamlyn Group archives.

Head of a man discovered at Oseberg. Oslo, Universitetets Oldsak-samling. Museum photo. Hamlyn Group archives.

powers (*höpt, bönd*, which literally means "bonds"). Moreover, Germano-Nordic mythology would continue to know many divinities or divine collectives in the plural: *álfar, dísir, vaettir, landvaettir, nornir, valkyrjor*, etc.

But it now seems plausible to make a prudent attempt at a coherent organization of this pantheon. And it requires no effort to find once again the three cosmic principles already mentioned several times. Óðinn is connected with the solar theme that leads to Völundr by a typically North Germanic alliterative genealogy: the series Wachilt-Wade-Woden/Óðinn-Widia (or Wittich)-Völundr. This theme can be easily connected with the cult of the dead—who, in fact, do not disappear completely: they haunt the other world, preside over fertility and infertility, and inform, in all the senses of the word, the world of the living; they preserve the above-mentioned idea of the nocturnal or hibernal boat of the sun, which is strikingly demonstrated both by the boat tombs in which important men had themselves buried (that of Oseberg, for example, with all its equipment, or the funeral on the banks of the Volga in 822 which is described in the extraordinary report of the Arab diplomat Ibn Fadhlan) and by the boat-shaped alignments of the standing stones (*skibsaetninger* in Danish) which dot the ground all over Scandinavia. The liquid theme is closely implied in this idea of the boat and continues to preside over magic, still under Óðinn's aegis, in particular in the form of a secret knowledge carried in the runes of which Óðinn claims to have been the "inventor," in the medieval sense of the term, in a number of texts such as the *Hávamál*. Probably of Italo-Celtic origin, the runes made their appearance around the third century A.D. While their magical nature has been sharply debated for several decades (A. Baeksted, L. Musset), it seems difficult not to see them, at least before the Viking period, as a means to esoteric power, since, as we shall see, in the beginning they were closely and constantly connected with divination. As to the chthonic theme, it gains from another Italo-Celtic contribution: the cult of the mothers (matres, matronae, matrae), evidently tutelary goddesses of fertility-fecundity, who are ordinarily cited in the collective or in triads which will be picked up again in devotions to the medieval three Marys, but are sometimes individualized, as in the case of Nehalennia. At this point of evolution, there is a curious sexual confusion in the mythology: beginning with Tacitus, who presents as a goddess Nerthus, a figure who etymologically can only be the god Njörðr (and what the Latin author tells us about Nerthus and the processional cult that culminates in an immersion in a sacred lake finds a surprising confirmation more than a millennium later in an Icelandic "telling," the *Ögmundar þáttr dytts*), this paganism shows a distinct taste for androgynes, among the first of which we must place Fjörgyn(n) (male or female depending on whether we give him/her one or two *n*s), not to mention the couple Freyr-Freyja. This tendency must be an extremely profound one, since it has never disappeared from the Nordic view of the world, from Swedenborg (Seraphitus-Seraphita) to the doublings of the ego in the theater of Strindberg, by way of C. J. L. Almqvist (Tintomara).

For this period, there is one trait that allows us to make a synthesis of the three themes we have been discussing, a point that thus forms the most eloquent illustration of this paganism: this is the theme of sacred kingship. The king, although he is elected from among a certain number of privileged families, finds himself, once he is made king, invested with discretionary powers and with genealogies preserved in the long poems that also form the earliest literary documents (like the *Ynglingatal* of Þjóðólfr of Hvín):

through these, the kings are provided with lines of descent from the solar principle. The king becomes both object and judge of these poems, the artistic secret of which was perhaps more or less sacred at first: the Skaldic poetry, the most immediate and confusing characteristic of which is the avoidance of the use of proper terms for things, replacing them with synonyms or *heiti* (some of these are gathered in the *Alvíssmál* of the *Poetic Edda*) and complex metaphors or *kenningar*. This avoidance of certain terms is probably due to the taboo nature of an entire vocabulary. It is possible that, like the Irish filidh, the skalds first formed a sort of caste dedicated to the service and glorification of the prince and having an esoteric knowledge of which the sovereign was reputed to be the beneficiary. Considerable work remains to be done on this point. But above all—and this is a point that cannot be overemphasized—the specific responsibility of the king is not necessarily to guarantee victory in particular cases but rather to promote fertility-fecundity. He is king *til árs ok friðar*: to assure fruitful years and peace; and nothing is more instructive than reading the statement of the very Christian Icelander Sturla Þórðarson in his biography of the Norwegian king Hákon Hákonarson (d. 1265), written at the end of the thirteenth century, that the best sign of the excellence of this long-reigning king was that in the year of his enthronement the birds laid twice and the trees gave superabundant fruit. If, on the other hand, the king did not bring material prosperity with him, he was pitilessly sacrificed. What must be stressed here is that his possible virtues as a warrior were only ranked second: he was expected to be *ársaell* and *friðsaell* (propitious for good seasons and for peace) much more than *sigrsaell* (victorious). In sum, he incarnated in his person a sedentary, agrarian, and, one might say, magico-intellectual ideal which suggests nothing of the clichés and romantic commonplaces about the ancient Germanic peoples.

The situation evolved in a more martial direction during the following period, the last one we will be looking at, which is generally called the Viking period (ca. 800 to ca. 1150). Because of the incessant and deep contacts that the Germanic peoples then had with the rest of the known world (whose boundaries they pushed back in both the east and the west), that is, because of the intense Christian penetration that they underwent, especially around the year 1000, which marks their general Christianization, their mythologies took on a much clearer shape, while in their main principles they remained faithful to a distant past. But they came to be structured along lines which for once correspond much more clearly to the great Dumézilian functions; their cosmogony and theogony, as presented in the great myths as they are now elaborated, attest solid Classical, southern or Oriental influences (the latter generally via the Bible or one of its innumerable commentators or glossers). In spite of these outside influences, the Germanic peoples must still be given credit for the foundation of the myths, once we have identified the imported additions, elaborations, or morals. To give only one example, while Snorri Sturluson indulged in applied euhemerism in his *Edda* and his *Ynglinga Saga*, a detailed comparative study proves that the actual substance of the myths he rationalized was based on an ancient tradition: this is the case for the mysterious battle between the Aesir and the Vanir, for the pact made between the Fenrir wolf and the god Týr, who leaves the wolf his right hand, and for Thor's battle against Hrungnir, to mention only these few.

Above all there appears, with a clarity that continues to increase in the eyes of modern researchers, the presence of what we could call the soul of this mythology, the real

Supreme God of the Germanic north: Fate with its innumerable names and forms. A power that is neither blind nor strictly speaking moral or immoral but undeniably original, both in its manifestations and its omnipotence and in the extremely interesting dialectic in which it engages the human being. Noting that Fate rules equally over the history of the gods and over that of the cosmos and of men, we will give here a very brief outline of this purely agonistic dialectic, which we suggest is the most remarkable trait of the religious universe of the ancient Germanic peoples. At birth the child was laid on the earth, then raised (toward the sun), and finally sprinkled with water: in this way he was explicitly consecrated to the Powers—later partially individualized under the collective term the *dísir* (which is directly related to the Sanskrit *dhisana*), kinds of hypostases of the Norns, in any case divinities of fate—that is, the child was expressly given by these powers a specific coloration to his fate, which is called *máttr ok megin*: capacity and possibility of success (or victory). The child was thus connected with the divine; the gods and he had made a kind of pact such that for the rest of his life he would worship them in signifying gestures, each constituting a return to his resources; he would bestow a sort of affection on them (the Nordic called his god *vinr, ástvinr*: "friend, dear friend") and would consider them as "patrons," in the Christian sense of the word: *fulltrúi*, in whom he has full confidence. This feeling of belonging to the sacred, the certainty of this destined endowment, he would call his "honor," and would put all his pride into justifying it, making it known or recognized. From which came, on both the ethical and the metaphysical levels, his peculiar type of behavior, expressed in three verbs: to know oneself, to accept oneself, and to manifest the nature that has been thus conferred. For to attack someone's dignity means to attack the sacred that has been present in him since the beginnings of his existence; to go against one's destiny would be to do harm to the Powers; the willing accomplishment of this destiny amounts to a communion with the sacred. It follows from this that few universes have been as attentive to the decrees of fate, while at the same time few have been less oppressed by an anonymous or grim fatality, once fate is accepted and its aspects manifested in acts. Furthermore, chance—for which the language has no special term—does not exist, and the same word is used for luck and for happiness.

This provides a sort of fixed theoretical frame on which to construct the structural system that we have defined: in a universe which denies chance, instinctively aligns itself with the great elementary drives, and knows itself and defines itself through its acts, a working hypothesis can be suggested of an ideal axis of order-force-dynamism, all notions which play an ample role in the history of the Germanic nations, and onto which it is easy to graft the three themes which we have been following from the beginning.

We thus propose, first, a "solar" variant: force of right or force of war. Right and war were indissolubly linked among the Germanic peoples, and their "oldest" god, Týr, was called, precisely, Mars Þingsus (Mars of the Þing, the seasonal assembly of free men in which common legislative and judicial decisions were made) by the Roman legions stationed in Friesland. This category is roughly represented by a party of gods called Aesir. We will present this variant through a dichotomy which, although a bit simplistic, is fairly well adapted to the Germanic mental universe in which friends and enemies, strength and slackness, and order and disorder are strongly opposed. This world is thought of as a perpetually threatened balance between order and disorder,

the latter essentially caused by the giants, who from now on will be seen almost exclusively as powers of evil. It is they who gave birth to the god of evil, Loki (or Loptr, literally "air, atmosphere"), and his infernal progeny. Loki poses insoluble problems if we try to envisage him only from an ethical point of view. On the other hand, in the perspective we have adopted here, and whatever the multiplicity of his faces, he is above all the fomenter of disorder: each of his interventions has the effect of shattering an equilibrium. Disorder and destruction are equally associated with the giant or spirit Surtr (whose name means "black"), who—the only mention of the fact in this mythology—is the incarnation of devastating fire, and who will consume the world at Ragnarök; they are also associated with the god Höðr, who may well represent a Manichaean influence and who is clearly conceived as the antithesis of Baldr the Good, whom he puts to death.

This last god brings us to the "solar" powers of order. We will enumerate three of these powers, to whom we will add the heroes (Völundr, Sigurðr) mentioned above. We know that in the first place comes Týr (Tiw, Saxnot, Saxneat?) who is *the* god par excellence. Just as Óðinn is one-eyed, Týr is one-handed, for the reasons stated above and by virtue of the sort of structural principle illuminated by Georges Dumézil. At the period we are discussing, Týr had almost become a *deus otiosus*, most of his attributes having been taken on by other divinities, but there is no doubt that he represents what is most fundamental in the Germano-Nordic mentality: the exercise of sovereignty, founded, by right, upon force. Nevertheless the great god of the Viking period, everywhere present in toponymy, onomastics, and popular devotion, even promoted to the title of official adversary of Christ at the time of the evangelization of the north, is Thor (Donar, Thunor), who combines in his person most of the attributes of divinity: he is, etymologically, thunder, and his hammer, Mjöllnir (Crusher), represents lightning. He thus incarnates force and war, but also fertility, since the storm brings the fertilizing rain, especially since Thor was made the son of Jörð/Erde, the Earth. And furthermore: his hammer is a magical instrument with which he resuscitates goats that have been sacrificed (in the highly elaborated myth of his voyage to see Loki of Útgarðr) and blesses or consecrates marriages and other ceremonies—something that is attested in the Bronze Age petroglyphs. Defender of Order par excellence, his first function is to battle the wicked giants in his frequent expeditions "to the east." His boorish brutality is opposed to the unquestioned rectitude of Týr, as well as to the shadowy subtlety of Óðinn. But we find on closer study that he is something quite different from a cheerfully truculent personification of muscle. As for Baldr/Balder, his character perhaps strikes a rather discordant note in this universe of tension and violence. He very strongly evokes a whole Oriental complex (his name recalls that of Baal, his character that of Tammuz or Adonis), and obviously solar, he is beautiful, good, and inactive. His unlucky death at the innocent hand of his blind brother Höðr will be the only inexpiable evil the world will know, but it is he who will preside at the universal regeneration and at the rebirth of men. Like that of Freyr, his name signifies "lord." One is tempted to see in him either some fundamental archetype overshadowed for millennia by more virile ethnic elements or else, along the contradictory dialectic that we have been sketching, the expression of a concept of perfect rest or quietude indispensable for the vivid perception of the idea of violence so clearly exemplified by the other Aesir.

Before leaving the theme of order/disorder, which is nowhere better represented than in this solar variant, we will look at the cosmogony and mythical history of the Germano-Nordic world, since it, too, admirably illustrates this theme. Snorri's subject matter, confirmed by other sources, is the way in which the universe emerged from primeval chaos, the gulf of Ginnungagap (the Gaping Void), to which it will return one day; how from the antithetical confrontation between the World of Shadows and Cold (Niflheimr) in the north and the World of Fire (Múspellsheimr) in the south was born the hybrid Ymir who engendered the giants, while the primeval cow Auðumla created the ancestors of Óðinn and his brothers out of a stone that she licked. As their first labor, these beings slew Ymir and created the world out of the various parts of his body. After this they hastened to weigh it, count it, and divide it, establishing one domain, Ásgarðr, for the gods, another, Miðgarðr, for men, and a third, Útgarr, for the giants. There followed the creation of men proper, while the gods divided up their own territory and built themselves palaces. It remained to create the sun, moon, and stars; to assign a dwelling place for the dead; to inscribe the whole in a vast mandorla whose organizing function as well as unifying principle is the ash Yggdrasill, which ties together the nine worlds thus created and assures constant circulation from one to the other. In spite of this last image, nothing is frozen or static in this view of the world: the sacred rivers flow without ceasing, wolves tirelessly pursue the sun and moon in the hope of swallowing them, the wind stirred up by the eagle perched on top of Yggdrasill continually moves the branches of the tree, the gods are constantly in movement in imitation of Thor, life springs forth without respite for human or divine beings, and the dead themselves interrupt neither this circulation nor this activity: they are marching toward the world of Hel, daughter of Loki and guardian of the netherworld, or Helheimr, by the Bifrost bridge which resounds under their steps, to reach Valhöll (Walhalla), where their second life will be spent in never-ending battle, since every evening they will rise from their wounds to feast. Given the necessary distance, we cannot help comparing this Weltanschauung to an enormous active anthill in which, under the appearance of a disorderly and tireless swarming, some fearful time, frozen and minutely structured, is constantly realizing itself: as in stroboscopic vision, here too vertiginous movement takes on the appearance of an illusory stillness.

This universe is subject to a history dominated to a remarkable degree by fate; all are familiar with it from the beginning, and in a sense most of the great texts of the *Edda* have no function but to recapitulate what is going to come. It is here, indeed, that we find the full expression of the ethico-metaphysical balance that we have been stressing, which makes the equilibrium of order and disorder the condition sine qua non for running the world. A rupture will appear in this status quo, provoked in every case, whether directly or not, by Loki; the immediate motive for this rupture varies with the half-dozen different traditions that obscurely report the fact. It can be called avarice, or lust, or ambition—this does not matter in the end—but its deep cause is in all cases a false oath on the part of the gods. This is true even when one would be inclined to stress the ethnological or "historical" incidences of the fact (the famous battle between the Aesir and the Vanir). The only thing obvious is that the gods have broken their word. If we admit the interpretation of the destiny-honor-revenge dialectic proposed above, with its permanent, obligatory, and constraining reference to the sacred, we can understand that in this universe this is the only inexpiable deed: the gods have broken their word, and by that very fact they are doomed,

they and the universe that they have put in order.

Not quite all of them, in fact: in this mental complex which seems to have no place for radical nihilism, in which life, the life force, matters above all else, to the point where nothingness, nonlife, seems inconceivable, it could not happen that everything should be finished once and for all. This is why, parallel with the gods' false oath, there took place another event, the death of Baldr, which preserved Baldr's innocence by dissociating him in advance from the sin in question. This does not change the irrevocability of the world's doom. This will be Ragnarök or Fate of the Powers (a reading infinitely preferable to Ragnarøkkr or Twilight of the Powers) as it is described in the *Völuspá*, the jewel of the *Poetic Edda*, in Dantesque passages of an unforgettable wild beauty. Is it the triumph of the forces of disorder, and will primeval chaos come back into its own? We have already answered no. In fact, Ragnarök has all the qualities of a catharsis. It makes us think, on a gigantic scale, of the initiatory trials that abounded in this religion so deeply marked with shamanistic traits. Nothing is finished once and for all, everything starts over again, but raised a tone, in a sort of spiral progression. Out of this new chaos spring the green plains where Líf and Líf Þrasir (Life and He Who Holds Fast to Life), the new human couple, transfigured, miraculously spared at the foot of Yggdrasill, begin again a magnified human history in the rays of an invincible sun, while Baldr, intact, Höðr, innocent as Baldr, and the sons of the former great Aesir return again and find in the tall grass the golden tables, a piece of luck symbolic of their immortal collusion with Fate:

This is where the faithful Troops will dwell	And for all eternity Dwell in happiness (*Völuspá*, strophe 64).

There is thus no need to weep for the old gods: they have returned, and with them the ideal order, the order of imperishable life.

But if we privilege the second variant, the "water of magic" variant which we will inscribe on the axis of a "force of science" or "force of poetry" (the distinction would seem specious), we find, differently elaborated, the same constants. Science and poetry are associated with the adjectives *vitr* or *fróðr*, whose semantic fields are fluid: here again, it is not a question of speculative knowledge but of life force. The runes, like the Greek epigram, have the power to destroy (especially in the grossly satiric form of *nið*), to constrain, and also to cure, to edify; Skaldic verses can enchant, in the strong sense: they can bless or curse. Both of these and, in a more general sense, magic serve to maintain an order of things as much as to deal with particular problems. The second variant is represented by the rest of the family of the Aesir, with the intrusion of Freyja, a goddess of the Vanir, insofar as she is the high priestess of *seiðr*, the preeminent magical operation.

Here the leading role falls to Óðinn/Wotanaz/Wodan, who is certainly the strangest figure of this pantheon: ugly, one-eyed, deceitful, cruel, misogynous, and cynical, he has, unlike Thor, Ullr, Freyr, left very few traces in toponymy and absolutely none in onomastics (other than having given his name to Wednesday, like Týr to Tuesday, Thor to Thursday, and Freyr to Friday). His name indicates that he has the sacred madness, *óðr*, which comes from mystical drunkenness or primordial knowledge. In Dumézilian terms, he is the preeminent god-king-priest-sacrificer, master and arbiter of *blót*, or, which comes to the same thing, the supreme sorcerer. His knowledge is his power. He is great because he is the master of all trickery, which opposes him to Thor, who generally conquers straightforwardly, by force; all seduction, unlike Freyr or Baldr, who conquer by their goodness, their beauty, or the imperious evidence of their desire; all dialectical argumentation and casuistic word twisting—in opposition, therefore, to Týr, who represents imprescriptible righteousness and justice. He learns nothing; he does not teach, but confuses and ridicules. If he presides over combat and war, he does not do so directly: he is content to throw his spear Gungnir over a warrior, dooming him to death; his involvement in battle is first of all through his beast-warriors or *berserkir* and then through his messengers or Valkyries. The former realize on the human level what Óðinn is on the divine level: dressed in the skins of bears (whence their name, which means "bear shirts") or wolves (they are also called *úlfheðnar*, "wolf-mantles"), they go into states of sacred madness which increase their strength tenfold, making them capable of the most extraordinary feats. It is possible that they constituted a sort of caste grouped around chiefs and kings--their bodyguards.

The Valkyries have a different nature, which is indicated in their very name: they are the ones, delegated by Óðinn, who choose (the verb *kjósa*, which gives *-kyrja*) the dead on the field of battle (the substantive *valr*). In this way they represent Óðinn as master of individual fates. Valkyrjur or Alaisiagae, they bear eloquent names which, symptomatically, fall into two semantically distinct areas: some are purely martial, like Gunnr-Guðr (Battle), Hildr (Combat), Hrist (Shaker of Weapons), Baudihillie (Rule-Battle); others, perhaps the more interesting, are clearly magical: Göndul ("handling the *gandr* or magic wand"), Göll and Hlökk (the idea of terrifying screaming), Mist (English *mist*, "torpor"), not to mention Herfjöturr, a name evoking the bonds (*fjöturr*) that fall on a warrior or an army (*herr*) and paralyze them, leaving them at the mercy of their enemies. These are divinities who have nothing really fearful about them, as is indicated in yet another of their names, Friagabi (Give-Freedom), for the warriors who are mowed down on the field of battle are not doomed to a grim death: they are promoted to the rank of *einherjar*, awaited in Valhöll (or the Hall of the Fallen). It is not certain that this myth is authentically Germano-Nordic, but its Odinic principle is certainly deeply rooted. Their forces, like their power of choosing, should not be taken as military virtues in the strict sense, but rather as magical gifts.

In the end, everything that involves Óðinn is marked in this way to the extent that he has often been seen as a sort of shaman-god to whom sacrifices are made by hanging—and nothing, absolutely nothing in his affairs has the clarity of rational phenomena. His marriages with Fjörgyn, the earth mother, the fruit of which is Thor, then with Frigg/Frija, who may be nothing but a hypostasis of the former, connect him quite clearly with fertility-fecundity, whereas his union with the giantess Rindr, with whom he will have three sons, Viðarr, Vāli, and Hermoðr, introduces a martial theme (Hermoðr means "eager in combat"). And the fact that he presides, with the otherwise little-known Hoenir and Lóðurr, over the creation of man also gives him the status of a founding god.

In fact, our certainties about Óðinn are few and unclear, outside of the fact that he is magical in essence and that he is always linked to some liquid element, waters of divination, sacrificial blood, the drink of poetic ecstasy, or sexual humor. This is why there is unanimity about him only on one point, although an essential one, in the Germano-Nordic mental complex: he presides over poetry, which is a divine and royal art, charged with the learned transmission of a profound science and served, to this end, by a sort of (at first) highly

esoteric caste, the skalds. This is an eminently aristocratic art, and its epithet applies perfectly, on the whole, to this god. In this connection, the *Prose Edda* records a learnedly elaborated and well-explicated myth, the myth of the origin of all poetry. It tells how the nectar of poetry, made of the saliva of the Aesir and the Vanir, was transformed into a man named Kvasir (whose Slavic consonance is worth noting) supposed to be supremely wise, who was killed and whose blood was kept in two containers jealously guarded by a giant, Suttungr. At the price of a series of animal metamorphoses, Óðinn managed to swallow this liquid in order to return it to Ásgarðr. This role of "savior" or, more exactly, of inventor of poetic inspiration, seems primeval if we do not forget that poetry is a matter of penetrating the arcana of wisdom or, once again, of controlling furor, in this case poetic furor, the creative power of speech, its ability to found the world. It seems that we are here at the heart of an extremely important complex in which the magical shout and the measured and sonorous cry are expressions of the supreme force, dynamic manifestations of a profound life. For in the end, as Amphion built Thebes to the harmonics of his lyre, the force of magical speech composes the world. It must be acknowledged that nothing is less "barbaric" or primitive than the complex of ideas, images, and feelings that underlie both this myth and this figure. Here, in giving the word all its primary force, speech is a spell. One may think further of the incredibly elaborate ornamentation of Viking jewels, of the *knörr* or door frames of the stave churches (*stavkirker*) of Norway: here complexity and refinement are not mannerisms but the suggestion of a power which departs from nature to organize it, recreate it, and finally grant it a higher meaning.

We will return to more basic considerations when we finally examine the third and last variant which we are proposing, the earthly one: that in which force belongs to fecundity, order here being explicitly life and disorder being all that tends to mutilate or deny life.

This theme is the most important, the deepest, and finally the only truly constant and determining one of the Germano-Nordic mental world. It has appeared often in the preceding pages. If the warrior theme hardly ever appears in the pure state, if the magic-wisdom motif always remains so impure that it often allows a great many contradictory interpretations, the principle of fertility-fecundity shows an impressive omnipresence and is always ready to encompass all the others. The king is expected above all to assure good harvests, the magician to drive off famine, and the priest or *goði* to assure the perpetuation of life. Thor, who unleashes the thunder, also ipso facto brings the fertilizing rain. Óðinn, who strikes people with terror and paralysis, also has strange powers to make beer "succeed," to make women have children, etc.

This is why it is appropriate to make a special place for the bisexual archetype, Fjörgyn(n), whose name means "the one who favors (gives) life," and who is Jörð, the earth mother. It is she who disposes of the essential force or capacity for success (*jarðarmegin*) and from the Eddic poems to the Conjurations of Merseburg, she alone is the object of the very rare real prayers we find in the documents. As wife of Óðinn and mother of Thor, she brings together the three themes or principles (or functions) that we have tried to isolate. She is what man inhabits and prepares and makes fruitful, connotations carried in the verb *búa*, from which comes the noun *búandi*, *bóndi*, which in the Viking period designated the man par excellence, the free man, pillar and soul of this society.

The fertility/fecundity force is the well-differentiated attribute of the divine family of the Vanir, fairly openly conceived sometimes as the antithesis of the Aesir, even though through the course of history their mutual interferences, encroachments, and cross-cuttings ("marriages") keep increasing, to the point where Freyr is sometimes assimilated to the man of war (Sigurðar vinr) and, inversely, as already discussed, Thor to the master peasant. Strictly speaking, there are only three Vanir: Njörðr, his son Freyr, and the latter's female counterpart, Freyja.

Njörðr/Nerthus, a hermaphrodite like Fjörgyn(n), is clearly the moist and germinating earth near the water, since he lives at Nöatün (Ships' Haven). Perhaps we should see another of his figurations in Aegir-Gymir, the god of the seas. It must have been by virtue of this that he married Rán, the goddess of the seas, whose name means plunder and who has a net with which she catches sailors destined to die. The lovely myths about the Vanir are always susceptible, without undue distortions, to interesting naturalistic explanations. Thus Njörðr is supposed to have married Skaði, who is the frozen, snow-covered earth of the north and thus mistress of the ski (whose invention goes back a long way). Since the two spouses are unable to live together for meteorological reasons, Njörðr because he hates the mountains and the howling of the wolves, Skaði because of the screaming of the gulls, they return to their respective domains for a part of the year.

They have two children, Freyr and Freyja. Freyr/Fro is, with Thor, certainly the most popular of the Germano-Nordic gods. He presides over love, wealth, and orgies, and his weapon, the sword, is a transformation of the *phallus impudicus* which we have already evoked in speaking of the standing stones. Through the good offices of his messenger Skírnir (the Sparkling One), he had a tryst with a giantess, Gerðr, who represented the earth and who gave herself to him after some delay, in the spring: hence fertile fields and seed. The poem that retells this myth, the *Skírnismál* of the *Poetic Edda*, manages to give an almost physical impression of overpowering desire. And it is from the same point of view that we should see Freyja, also called Gefn/Gefjún (a name into which the idea of the gift enters), who must not be confused with Frigg/Frija, the wife of Óðinn, even though certain similarities between the two are confusing: for instance, Freyja married Óðr (literally, "sacred madness"), who forms an alliterative pair with Óðinn. Freyja is unchained, lascivious sexual love, as evidenced by the orgiastic cult devoted to her, her chariot drawn by cats, and her single ornament, the great necklace Brisingamen, which suggests a simple psychoanalytic explanation. But Freyja also presides over magic, probably black magic—which is why an obscure couplet makes her the tutelary divinity of the dead—and she must have had her own caste of priestesses. All of these are traits, however, that do not make the relatively well defined family of the Vanir susceptible to a great diversity of interpretations.

Natural forces, life forces, forces of struggle and combat, a universe in which the verb "become" ends up being half-divinized (in the form of the Norn Urðr): we can clearly see what could give rise to such a world view if we retain only this outline of movement, tension, and progress, especially if we relate it to the illusive and little-known Vikings. And it is incontestable that this religion was made for and by them, men of action privileging the values of action, men of an exceptional destiny and for this very reason exceptionally conscious of their destiny. Seen in terms of the murky glamor

of Wagnerian music, rudely illuminated in the light of a primitive dawn, this image glows most brightly in periods, like our own, burdened with existential anxiety, decadence, and a taste for nihilism. But, as we hope this short study has shown, this is too limited a view. Here, despite appearances, the right of the (muscularly) strongest is not the best right, force does not dominate over what is right, wishing does not make one able to do something. We would even say that the exact opposite is true. For this force, in its beginning and even in its abundance, is always dominated, measured, controlled: transcended—at least in two ways which are surely only the two sides of a single reality--by poetry and by magic.

If the Germano-Nordic supernatural world is an onrushing force, it is not one that rushes on blindly, nor one that finds its fulfillment in its pure exercise. Rhythm balances and stylizes magical speech, magic duplicates and deepens speech, the world is put in place, justified, magnified, and thus loved, through the effect of action: once again, nothing is left to chance. The men who thus projected their desires and their dreams on a sacred with which they were able to communicate were certainly not arrogant brutes. They were poets and magicians.

R.B./j.l.

BIBLIOGRAPHY

a) General works: (1) Sources: W. BAETKE, *Die Religion der Germanen in Quellenzeugnissen* (Frankfurt-am-Main 1938). C. CLEMEN, *Fontes historiae religionis germanicae*, Fontes historiae religionum 3 (Berlin 1928). (2) Sources and studies: R. BOYER and E. LOT-FALCK, *Les religions de l'Europe du Nord* (Paris 1974). (3) Studies: J. DE VRIES, *Altgermanische Religionsgeschichte*, 2 vols. (2d ed., 1956–57). G. DUMÉZIL, *Mythes et dieux des Germains* (Paris 1939). F. STRÖM, *Nordisk hedendom: Tro och sed i förkristen tid* (Göteborg 1961).

b) Specialized studies (supplementing those that are given in the individual articles): A. ARNTZ, *Handbuch der Runenkunde*, 2 vols. (Halle and Saale 1935–44). H. BÄCHTOLD-STÄUBLI, *Handwörterbuch des deutschen Aberglaubens* (Berlin 1927–42). W. BAETKE, *Das Heilige im Germanischen* (Tübingen 1942); *Die Götterlehre der Snorra-Edda* (Berlin 1952). H. C. BROHOLM, *Danmarks Bronzealder* (Copenhagen 1943–49). J. BRØNDSTED, *Bronzealderens Soldyrkelse* (Copenhagen 1938). M. CAHEN, *La libation: Etudes sur le vocabulaire religieux du vieux scandinave* (Paris 1921). B. COLLINDER, "The Name Germani," *Arkiv. f. nordisk filologi* 59 (1949): 19–39. G. DUMÉZIL, *Gods of the Ancient Northmen* (Berkeley 1973). K. A. ECKHARDT, *Der Wanenkrieg*, Germanenstudien 3 (Bonn 1940). E. ELGQVIST, *Studier rörande njordkultens spridning bland de nordiska folken* (Lund 1952). H. R. ELLIS, *The Road to Hel: A Study of the Conception of the Dead in Old Norse Literature* (Cambridge 1943). H. R. ELLIS DAVIDSON, *Scandinavian Mythology* (London 1969). J. G. FRAZER, "Balder the Beautiful," in *The Golden Bough*, part 8 (3d ed., London 1911–15). W. GEHL, *Der germanische Schicksalsglaube* (Berlin 1939). G. HALLSTRÖM, *Monumental Art of Northern Sweden from the Stone Age* (1960). A. G. VAN HAMEL, "Odinn Hanging on the Tree," *Acta phil. Scand.* 7 (1932): 260–88. K. HELM, *Wodan: Ausbreitung und Wanderung seines Kultes* (Giessen 1946). O. HÖFLER, *Germanisches Sakralkönigtum* (Münster 1952). H. KUHN, "Das nordgermanische Heidentum in den ersten christlichen Jahrhunderten," *Zeitschf. f. deut. Altertum* 79 (1942): 133–66. K. A. LARSEN, *Solvogn og solkult* (Kuml 1955). S. LINKQVIST, *Gotlands Bildsteine* (Stockholm 1941–42). H. LJUNGBERG, *Tor: Undersökningar i indo-europeisk och nordisk religions-historia* (Uppsala 1947). G. NECKEL, *Walhall: Studien über germanischen Jenseitsglauben* (Dortmund 1931). S. NORDAL, *Völuspá* (Reykjavík 1927). A. OHLMARKS, *Gravskeppet: Studier i förhistorisk nordisk religionshistoria* (Stockholm 1946). TH. PALM, *Trädkult* (Lund 1948). F. STRÖM, *Diser, nornor, valkyrjor* (Göteborg 1954); *Den egna kraftens män: En studie i forntida irreligiositet* (Göteborg 1948).

SACRIFICE IN GERMANO-NORSE PAGANISM

The word *blót* in ancient Germanic and Norse religions means "sacrifice" or rather all the operations, rites, and acts that marked the critical time when these religions became real. Devoid of any dogma, with little inclination for meditation and prayer, this paganism appears to have consisted essentially of meaningful deeds performed when the community, local or familial, gathered and realized that it was open to the sacred. To quote Folke Ström, in this religion "faith is expressed in the cultic act" almost exclusively. In other words, despite the attempt at rational presentation that Snorri Sturluson made in the *Edda* in the thirteenth century, despite attempts at structuring that are being made even now, even a cursory study of its cult may well explain the essence of Germanic and Norse paganism. Though it is slightly forced, the distinction between public and private cult remains useful.

The public cult was celebrated in a precise location, near the Þing. All ancient evidence, including archaeology, shows that the site was a natural one in the open air and might be marked by an altar, but apparently there was no actual building, except in continental Germania where there might have been *hofs,* which correspond more or less to our notion of a temple. But whether they were *hörgr, haugr* (also a funerary mound), or *vé,* these were still natural sites with rocky mounds nearby, small groves (*lundr*), forests, springs, rocks, isolated trees, etc. As late as the thirteenth century, texts concerning Icelandic colonization attest to the custom of "devoting oneself to a cult," or offering sacrifices at a copse, cascade, rock, etc. We cannot rule out the possibility that the *hörgr* was reserved for the cult of the Vanir, performed by women, and that the *vé* (and later the *hof*) was for the possibly less ancient cult of the Aesir, performed by men. But these are merely conjectures.

Toward the eighth century, when the *hof* as an edifice became the rule, it consisted of a rectangular building flanked by a small, also quadrilateral structure, according to our best source, the *Eyrbyggja Saga.* The first building was the common room where the sacrificial banquet was given with libations for all; the second was the sanctuary where the actual *blót* was performed. It had a raised level, an altar of sorts, called *stalli* or *stallr,* on which animal victims were sacrificed. Their blood (*hlaut*) was collected in a round receptacle (*hlautbolli*) before it was sprinkled over the participants by means of bundles of sticks (*hlautteinar*). The *stalli* was also the location of the sacred ring (*stallahringr*) which one had to hold with the right hand in order to make a vow. It is not known whether the *hof* also contained representations of deities in wood or stone. These probably circulated in the form of amulets (see *Vatnsdoela Saga* for more details). Because of very probable Christian, or more precisely biblical, influences, the very existence of the *hof* has been questioned by more than one scholar. A famous passage from the *Austfararvísur* by the skald Sighvatr Þóðarson (beginning of the eleventh century) suggests that any room could be transformed into a *hof* according to need.

Conversely, Germania seems to have practiced sacred hanging, characteristic of Odinism, or the drowning of human victims in springs or quagmires (*blótkelda*) as evidenced by the surprisingly well preserved remains of the Tollund man found in the blue clay of Denmark. Similarly, probably in the event of war, there must have been a custom of throwing into wells, ditches, or quagmires designated

The Tollund man. Copenhagen, Nationalmuseet. Museum photo.

offerings (*blótgröf*): the weapons of the vanquished, money, precious objects, etc., as an act of atonement or of thanksgiving. The well of Budsene (island of Møn, Denmark) offers a striking example.

In any event, nature was the normal framework for Norse cultic activities. Furthermore, it was the necessary element basic to a worship focused on the great cosmic forces.

Even the dates of the great sacrifices followed the laws of nature and corresponded to whatever we know of the cult of fertility and fecundity: midwinter sacrifices or *dísablót* in February; midautumn sacrifices or *haustblót* (*vetrnaetr* in Iceland) in October; the great sacrifices of the winter solstice, *jól* or *miðvetrarblót* or *álfablót,* later blended into Christmas; and the summer solstice, *sumarblót,* around midsummer day. The last was one of a kind, and may have been more oriented than the others toward warfare, not a convenient activity in that part of the world during the winter. All the evidence shows that these ceremonies gave way to ritual processions which ended with drowning (of victims, offerings, and even of the idol if there was one).

Blót is from the transitive verb *blóta.* One does not sacrifice to the gods in this universe; rather the saying goes, *blóta guð,* which shows that the operation has an aspect of direct communion. Although the sources are meager and imprecise on this subject, we shall attempt to reconstitute the *blót* by giving what was probably the order of its four rites.

(1) The actual sacrifice of animals and probably sometimes of humans as well. Human sacrifice took place most often by

hanging, as shown by the great illustrated rocks of Gotland (off the east coast of Sweden). The human victims may have been volunteers, if we can believe the strange account given by the Arab diplomat Ibn Fadhlan concerning the burial of a "Rus," i.e., Swedish, chieftain at the beginning of the ninth century. When animals were involved, they must have been birds and pigs, and especially oxen and horses, animals associated with the cult of Freyr in particular. The *Flateyjarbók* has preserved a very curious text in which an entire family worships the embalmed penis of a horse (*Völsa þáttr*).

(2) It seems that every sacrifice required the consultation of the oracles, which is not surprising when one realizes how thoroughly Germanic and Norse paganism was immersed in such an atmosphere of prophecy that Fate rose to the rank of the unnamed but supreme god of this pantheon. Liquids played a major role in the series of oracular performances which Tacitus had already pointed out as among the major characteristics of this religion (*Germania* 10.1). A sacrifice was performed in order to consult the sacred oracles (*ganga til fréttar*) regarding anything of consequence to the community or any one of its members. This function may have devolved particularly upon women. Snorri Sturluson considered it demeaning for men to engage in it, and the *völva*, or prophetess, who is described in *Eríks saga rauða* and speaks in the *Völuspá* of the poetic *Edda*, confirms it.

(3) After this ritual came the solemn banquet or *blótveizla*, *blótdrykkja*, which may well have been the high point of the *blót*. By consuming the meat of the sacrificed animal, the congregation felt that it was demonstrating its internal communion and its connection with the Powers it worshiped. At the same time, the congregation drank a beer especially brewed for the occasion, the required libations, which, normally followed by drunkenness, clearly had a sacred character. The libations were accompanied by toasts to the gods and then to deceased relatives, another reference to fertility and fecundity by means of the cult of the ancestors.

(4) The final item was probably the pledging of oaths or *heistrengning*, which could be seen as a proof of obedience and fidelity. The sacrifice of victims, the eating of their flesh, the ritual libations, and the solemn oaths were all meaningful actions intended to strengthen the bonds of the double community of the living and the dead and of the human and the divine worlds.

As for the celebrant of these ceremonies (to the extent that one can say that he existed), it is not certain that the Norse had a specialized caste of priests. The *goði* and the *gyðja* may only have been occasional sacrificers. It was not until much later that their function became specialized (*hofgoði*), while at the same time it took over juridical and administrative duties reaching far outside the religious sphere. It would be safer to say that the office of priest-sacrificer normally reverted to the king, the prince, or the head of the family, an idea in line with both the notion of sacred kingship and the prime importance of the family in the global conception of their society that these people had.

Moving away from the head of the family, we can make a kind of logical transition to the *private cult*, which does not appear to have differed much from the public cult in spirit or in practice. The private cult may have, as is usual, placed slightly greater emphasis on more or less magical practices connected with the worship of the ancestors. But the same practices and, more important, the worship of the forces of nature, particularly the tree and the meadow, occur in both cults. The *tún*, an enclosed meadow in front of each farm, even today is clearly a vestige of this practice. Important dates on the family calendar were occasions for special sacrifices: births, marriages, funerals. Much is known about the sacrifices associated with funerals and their importance, especially for the passing on of the indivisible inheritance, or *óðal*, and the investiture of the official successor to the deceased man. The character of continuity between the world of the living and the realm of the dead, as illustrated by the rites, is striking. The deceased leader was laid in a tomb boat with his favorite weapons, supplies, jewels, slaves, concubines, and animals. He was thus simply off on a journey, and the funeral mound which was to cover the entire retinue just described, situated on the ancestral grounds, was the object of its own cult. The dead continued to inform the world of the living, and when needed appeared to them in the quasi-physical form of ghosts, *draugar*, or in dreams. What mattered was the unbroken link between one world and the other, in other words, the unfailing continuity of life, even if that life had taken on a different form.

The general impression left by even a cursory study of ritual in Norse religion is that it was very important, certainly more important than the entire mythological, theogonic, and cosmogonic apparatus, which does not seem to have taken coherent form until relatively late. These religions were heavily laden with symbolic acts directed to supernatural powers that were barely anthropomorphic. Paganism ended when cult practices were abandoned, not when dogmas or beliefs were rejected. How true it is that, in this context, there were no true values other than actions.

R.B./g.h.

The offering well at Budsene. Copenhagen, Nationalmuseet. Museum photo.

BIBLIOGRAPHY

H. BIRKELI, *Fedrekult*, 1943; *Huskult og hinsidighetstro*, 1943. R. BOYER, *Le culte dans la religion nordique ancienne*, Inter-Nord 13/14 (1974): 223–43. H. CELANDER, *Förkristen jul enligt norröna källor*, 1955. TH. PALM, *Uppsalalunden och Uppsalatemplet*, 1941. M. OLSEN, *Aettegaard og hellingdom*, 1926.

THE AESIR AND THE VANIR

The two "families" of gods that people the Germano-Norse pantheon are called Aesir and Vanir. The origin of each group is obscure and has already given rise to a great many theories, but since the efforts of rationalization attempted in the thirteenth century by Snorri Sturluson in his *Edda* are partially supported by various much older myths, the dichotomy must be looked upon as authentic, probably in history if not in sociology. The trouble is, one realizes, that we know very little for certain about the ancient Germans and that at the very interior of the Germanic complex, the differences between the two families are great.

These differences may be connected with the fact that the Germanic invaders had to conceal an indigenous foundation, the exact identity of which would probably give us the interpretation of a primitive mentality and culture for which archaeology by itself can now risk proposing only very conjectural interpretations. But it seems that the indigenous foundation was constituted from a peasant society with pronounced material interests: their gods then are said to have been the Vanir—a word for which no satisfactory etymology has been proposed—who are certainly typical divinities of fertility-fecundity, hence of the cult of the dead. Few of them are enumerated: Njörðr, whom Tacitus saw as female and who is called Nerthus; her children Freyr and Freyja, to whom it is sometimes proposed to add Hoenir, about whom not much is known. Their sexual ambivalence is curious and corresponds to a state of mind that has continued to our times in Scandinavian culture and folklore; the insistence on their sexual character is clear: they are certainly gods connected with the phallic cult manifested in rock engravings from the Norse Bronze Age, amulets, the uniformly attested use of menhirs, and more recently the support of runic inscriptions. Joined to the representations of the *hieros gamos,* to the cult of erect staves (*stafr, stafgarðr*) and of the horse's penis (*Völsa þáttr*), these representations, with implications that are nearly always magical, are naturally associated with the liquid element and with boats, determining an agrarian complex in which the dead play the principal role. The Vanir are in reality gods of funerary mounds and of boats (Freyr is thought to have a magical ship, Skiðblaðnir, which has the property of folding itself in order to enter the god's pocket after use, an amusing representation of a collapsible processional boat such as was still known in the last century in the part of Finland that retained the strongest Scandinavian influence). And Freyja is given as the supreme mistress of magic, especially of practices which have been called *seiðr.* It follows from all this that they presided over a mass of essentially vitalist and perhaps North Asian beliefs and devotions, in which the cult of life and the cult of the dead—the world of the germinating earth and the spiritual universe—were not separated. The best example of this is furnished by the poem *Skírnismál* (in the *Poetic Edda*), which symbolizes the union of the male fecundating principle and the female earth in order to assure the perpetuation of life. In any case, love and profuse life are the natural climate in which the Vanir evolved.

When the area called Germania suffered the invasion of martial tribes armed with battle-axes, probably about 2000 B.C., it is possible that the newcomers imposed upon their new territory their mentality, their customs, and their gods. From them the Aesir are supposed to have come; afterwards, all the other great Norse divinities belong to them: Óðinn,

Týr, Thor, Heimdallr, Frigg, etc., and their numerous hypostases. Whether the word "*aes*" (*áss*) corresponds to an ancient *ansur* and is the result of the divinization of a primitive hero whom Jordanes calls Anses, Anser, or whether this name must be derived from the common Germanic **ansu-,* "beam," because the Aesir were supposed to have had the novel characteristic of being represented in the form of wooden idols, or even whether (a more tempting solution) the word is to be connected to an Indo-European theme **ansu* (Gothic *us-anan,* Sanskrit *asu*), with a meaning connected with the Latin *anima,* and therefore with the idea of life, of active existence, of vitality—all of this leaves intact the problem of the origin of the Aesir and of the Vanir. One soon discovers that the distinction is often specious because of the many displacements, overlaps, and substitutions that have occurred over time, and that, for example, the kind of order Vanir-Aesir thus suggested clearly cannot be authentic; for Týr, who ought to have something fundamental and original and who is represented on some of the oldest evidence, does not have the characteristics of a Vanir god. The same is the case for another Aesir god, Ullr, who is little

Bronze statuette. Reykjavik, National Museum. Hamlyn archives.

Phallic rock. Esselte Studium collection. Akademiförlaget, Göteborg. Hamlyn archives.

known but who had his hour of celebrity nevertheless, as is confirmed by toponymy. For, in sum, the Aesir can scarcely be credited with attributes that are absolutely incompatible with those of the Vanir; and the confusion is so serious that, for instance, a distribution according to the three Dumézilian functions simply does not occur except at isolated points. In a sense, Aesir or Vanir, all the Germano-Norse gods preside over sacred sovereignty (even if Óðinn excels in this), over war (especially Thor or Týr), and over fecundity (over which the Vanir alone are supposed to rule). And paronymic confusions (between Freyja and Frigg, among others) permit every infringement.

Nevertheless, a solid tradition, conveyed by half a dozen different testimonies, emerges as the echo of a very violent confrontation between the Aesir and Vanir, the probable historical support for which it is difficult to call into question. This struggle could not have come to a decisive end, in favor of one of the two sides: they would have had to make and exchange guarantees in order to end by living on good terms. This point may lead us on another path. The Aesir have a mentality that is different from the mentality of the Vanir, who are plebeians and materialists: they are willful aristocrats, cynical, misogynous, and scornful of the vulgar. One might then assert—and this would be to accede in part to the euhemeristic theories of Snorri Sturluson—that the Aesir may have represented an aristocracy, an invading elite forced to compromise with the indigenous people before becoming assimilated to them. This phenomenon is not unique in the history of the world; it is found again in the colonization of what is now White Russia by the Swedes called Varangians. The theory is tempting in that it accounts for a double mentality that was very much alive in the ancient north and clearly visible, for instance, in the Icelandic sagas, where, set against a "noble" text that is full of arrogance (such as the *Vatnsdoela Saga*), there is another text that is rather sordid and at a commonplace level (such as the *Hoensa-Þóris Saga*).

An explanation of a such a historical type requires reservations. Action, the inclination to action, seems clearly always to have been the principal component of the Germanic world from the beginning, and the feeling of belonging to an elite can be inferred, independently of any foreign interference, from the cult of the family, which no one doubts was the deepest constituent trait of the mentality of this people.

But it is better not to try too hard to personalize these divinities, as our modern anthropomorphic passion tends to do more or less unconsciously. Aesir or Vanir, they are after all only "relative" gods, since they are, like men, subject to a destiny that they can do nothing to change. And what the Germano-Norse world appears to have understood much better than such individualized divine entities are the assemblages of collective powers, powers that accord admirably with the other basic characteristic of that world's mentality: its reverence for natural forces.

R.B./b.f.

BIBLIOGRAPHY

E. BRATE, *Vanerna* (1914). K. A. ECKARDT, *Der Wanenkrieg* (1940). G. DUMÉZIL, *Jupiter, Mars, Quirinus* (1940); *Tarpeia* (1947); *The Gods of the Ancient Northmen* (Berkeley 1973), 2d ed. trans. F. R. SCHRÖDER; *Ingunar Freyr* (1941). E. O. G. TURVILLE-PETRE, *The Cult of Frey in the Evening of Paganism* (1935).

NORSE MAGIC

In the Norse religious world, contrary to general belief on this subject, it was not warfare, combat, or physical strength that was most highly valued, but magic. Runic inscriptions, large stones with illustrations difficult to interpret, esoteric poems, and amulets of all kinds, all prove that magic played a preeminent role. It begins with the very history of the gods, who never ceased to metamorphose, to split in two, and to cast their spells and powerful charms. Thor himself, seemingly so incompatible with this order of ideas, "blessed," exorcised, and brought back to life. And it was not by chance that in the *Gylfaginning* (its eloquent title means "Fascination of Gylfi") Snorri Sturluson ascribes to Thor, in the land which is indeed one of magic, an entire series of half-symbolic and half-epic adventures that in the final analysis can only be explained as a function of magic: his visit with Loki-of-the-Outer-Walls.

Written at the height of the literary era, the sagas of families and other people cannot be understood without an elaborate arsenal of highly occult practices. A poem such as the *Völundarkviða* is nothing but a catalog of rituals of the same genre, and the tradition offers us an impressive number of incantations, sorcery, evil spells, levitations, etc. After all, Óðinn is the preeminent god of magic. Our purpose is not to dismiss completely the controversy that has sought to make him, within the Norse pantheon, an upstart of clearly shamanic origin from northern Asia. It is, however, incontestable that all his power comes to him from black magic, as is expressly stated in the last part of the *Hávamál* or in the *Grímnismál* as a whole (both of these titles are part of the *Poetic Edda*). We see migrations of souls, constant passages

The great illustrated stone of Lärbro (Gotland). Stockholm, Antikvarisk Topografiska Arkivet. Hamlyn archives.

from the natural to the supernatural world, sacred terrors and screams, knowledge of the secrets of the past or the future, beneficent or malevolent objects with extraordinary properties, trances, lethargies, reincarnations of all shapes and sizes—and all of it acquired at the cost of trials of initiation reported in minute detail. All the sources substantiate the reality of a double world in constant cross-communication. Indeed, very few religious realms are so thoroughly dominated by oneiric practices, to such a degree that all that we can know about how these peoples conceived

of the soul amounts to a strange notion of an inner or double principle, or a "form" (*hamr*), prone to escape from its material framework in defiance of the imperatives of space and time, in order to go to haunt other worlds and return again with sacred news. We shall not here inquire into the possible origins of this view of the world; but a whole array of indices seems to point in the direction of the Sames (the "Finns" of the Icelandic sagas). In fact, almost everything known about this religion probably depends on an explanation on the basis of magic. Since this point has rarely been brought to light, it seems appropriate to insist on it, especially since it is self-evident that magic and the knowledge of Fate go hand in hand, and that modern research discovers more and more the prominent role played here by Fate in its many characters.

Whether magic combines forces with Fate or defends itself against the enemy or the obstacle of the moment, its purpose is always to free occult forces held back by the Powers. Our sources have preserved the traces of a certain number of such detailed performances as the *níð*, or defamation designed to brand someone in order to destroy him or chase him away, or the rituals which ridicule a man by accusing him of homosexuality (*ergi*). But the most interesting and evolved example is the *seiðr*, which various texts describe—the word itself implies the power to bind, another power attributed to Óðinn.

The *seiðr*, too, may have been either divinatory or malevolent, and probably was in league with the Vanir. He used a very complex apparatus, was occupied as much with incantation as with ecstasy, and depended sometimes on simple sorcery, sometimes on pure magic, and eventually on black magic. Furthermore, in this context shamanistic characteristics (levitation, migration of souls, use of a magic drum with Cabalistic signs engraved on it) are numerous. With her bizarre accoutrements (magic wand or *stafr* or *gandr*, catskins adorned with brass and pearls), the magician-woman or *völva* cut a very primitive figure. In any case, more than one text gives evidence for the violently paralyzing or devastating effects that the maleficent *seiðr* had upon the psyche of the intended victim. Óðinn was able, moreover, to control the elements and unleash tempests and storms. The *Hávamál* records eighteen of the spells offered to the power of Óðinn. One can easily surmise that these are facilities attributed to the *seiðr*.

In conclusion, the sum of the magical practices in Norse paganism confirms not only the important role played by the spiritual and the other world but, more importantly, the kind of ongoing osmosis established between the two realms.

R.B./g.h.

BIBLIOGRAPHY

S. AGRELL, *Runornas talmystik och dess antika förebild*, 1927. A. BAEKSTED, *Målruner og troldruner*, 1952. S. BUGGE, *Der Runenstein von Rök*, 1910. N. LID, "Magiske fyrestellingar og bruk," in *Nordisk Kultur*, vol. 19 (1935). I. LINDQUIST, *Galdrar*, 1923. I. REICHBORN-KJENNERUD, *Vår gamle trolldomsmedisin*, vols. 1–5 (1927–47). D. STRÖMBÄCK, *Sejd* (Stockholm 1935).

HEIMDALLR

Heimdallr is only one of the Aesir gods of Germano-Norse mythology. But his personality, which has been much discussed, has given rise to various theories which give us a good view of the mythology as a whole.

The sources provide very few references to him: he has left no traces in toponymy, and although there once existed a poem dedicated to him, the *Heimdalargaldr*, all that is left is one verse, in which he is called "the son of nine mothers." He lives at Himinbjörg (Sky Mountain), and he is called "the White Ás" (which suggests "White Christ"), "the most brilliant of the gods." He watches over Ásgardr: he never closes his eyes and his sharp ears hear the growing of the grass in the fields and the growing of the wool on the backs of the sheep; because of this quality, he serves as guardian of the security of the gods. Besides this, the *Rígsþula* (in the *Poetic Edda*) makes him the founder of the human race, instituting the division of humanity into the classes of slaves, free men, and jarls (which includes kings). His name, which can be written with one or two *ls*, draws upon the idea of support, of the pillar of the world. A skaldic *kenning* calls the blade of a sword or a spear "Heimdallr's head." In the end, it is his eschatological role that is determinant: it is Heimdallr who, on the day of the Fate of the Powers (Ragnarök), will call the gods together for the final combat at the sound of his horn.

Some of these traits would tend to make him a god of the sea, because of his nine mothers (three times three waves); or a solar god (his "whiteness," his dwelling place on "Sky Mountain"), or a lunar god (the wakeful), all points which could connect him, depending on the case, with Janus, Mithra, or Varuna.

Yet there is a constant idea throughout the conceptual complex concerning him: that of origin, of support, of guardianship. This is why (and the mental process that guides the interpretation should be stressed, since it corresponds perfectly with everything known about the mentality of these people) he came to personify, probably at a fairly late date, the ash or yew Yggdrasill, which is generally recognized as the most striking, eloquent, and magnificent conception of this universe.

For Yggdrasill is also a unifying and tutelary original principle. It brings together the nine existing worlds, from its roots to its top; in it are concentrated all life (because of the dazzling white clay, *aurr*, that spatters its roots); all knowledge, since at its foot flows the fountain guarded by Mímir-Memory, the giant who watches over all science; and all fate, since the three Norns sit next to a second fountain, Urðorbrunnr, at its base.

On the other hand, there are striking similarities between Yggdrasill, which supports the world, and the great serpent of Miðgarðr, who holds it in place in the coils of its body. When Miðgarðsormr unwinds (when Yggdrasill falls), the world will come to an end. Now Miðgarðsormr is also called Jörmungandr: literally, the "gigantic magic wand." And Mímir's drinking horn is called Gjallarhorn, just like Heimdallr's horn. As for the image: iron spear = head of Heimdallr, we can specify: = head of (the) serpent.

We thus obtain a series going from Yggdrasill (or Jörmungandr-Miðgarðsormr) to Heimdallr, which certainly looks like an equivalent. In addition, one explanation, a shamanistic one, proposes that through generalization and extension we see in Yggdrasill (whose name literally means "horse of Óðinn") the centerpost of the yurt, symbolizing the center of the world, to which the shaman attaches the "horse" he will ride on his voyages to the netherworld.

Nothing more is needed to make Heimdallr a perfectly convincing representation of the Germano-Nordic mental world. Here, for reasons that are apparent, the struggle for life and the cult of energy are realities which need no commentary. If the divine world is really the projection of human dreams and passions into the absolute, we can find no better symbol for a Norse Weltanschauung than the splendid trees of Sweden, Norway, and the Baltic coasts, which are vibrant with intense life, defying the long winters and severe weather, and whose falling has indeed something of the apocalyptic about it.

R.B./j.l.

BIBLIOGRAPHY

B. PERING, *Heimdall*, 1941. J. DE VRIES, "Heimdallr, dieu énigmatique," in *Études germaniques*, 1956.

LOKI

One of the most baffling figures in Norse mythology is Loki, a god of evil (or at least so-called). Any analysis of this character is wrought with tremendous difficulties, first because Norse culture was subject to so many successive influences that it is troublesome indeed to disentangle his authentic profile; and second, because in order to get a firm hold on him, we would need to be very familiar with a way of thinking about which we can only conjecture. Notwithstanding all the risks associated with such an operation, it seems that an attempt to reconstitute Loki's portrait diachronically might shed some light on an altogether vexing area of inquiry, namely, what this mythology made of the concept of evil—though of course no concept is more difficult

to delineate than evil, particularly since it must take into account time, people, and places.

Originally Loki must have been one of the giants who inhabited the primitive world (scores of whom were known to the Norse), at least according to one text which places him in this genealogical context. This accounts for Loki's claim that he is the sworn brother of Óðinn, himself descended from the giants. We might further assimilate him to Loki-of-the-Outer-Walls, the master magician who ridicules Thor himself in the *Edda* of Snorri Sturluson. Through the mediation of this latter god, who had become the most popular of all among the Vikings, the giants seem rather quickly to have come to be regarded as evil powers. And therefore Loki, whose name, according to one of the possible etymologies, may imply closure, end, and consequently destruction, supposedly became the incarnation of evil. However, like all the primitive giants, he is entrusted with knowledge, and like all the archaic deities in this pantheon, he excels in magic. Furthermore, by his association with Óðinn and with a virtually unknown god named Hoenir, he takes part in the creation of the first human couple, to whom he gives human "color" and "shape"; he thus brings to mind Prometheus, who himself serves as a foil to Zeus, structurally speaking, in the same way that Loki serves as a foil to Óðinn. What is more, at this stage he is called by the name Lóðurr, a word which may have some relation to the idea of fire, and, this time under the name of Loptr ("air"), in one text he is depicted in the act of burning one of his own inventions, the net. Or one might prefer a purely naturalistic explanation which would make him into a deification of the spider, again because of the net. And as a spirit of air and fire, renowned for his marvelous beauty, in the Christian era he probably took on the attributes of Luki-fer, which may further explain the fact that Sirius bears his name.

But all these suggestions do not allow a sustained line of interpretation. A more strictly metaphysical and ethical point of view would undoubtedly be more satisfactory but would risk excessive oversimplification. In fact, Loki's most striking characteristic is the extreme multiplicity of his faces, as well as their ambiguity. He is rarely totally evil, and in some myths he even turns out to be useful, indeed helpful. The scope of his actions is impressive. Sometimes he is a malicious little devil addicted to crude clowning (to cheer up the goddess Skaði, for example) and not above indulging in coarse jokes (as when he disguises Thor as a woman). Sometimes he resembles the biblical conception of Satan as the foremost slanderer. In the only poem of the *Edda* that deals with him, the *Lokasenna* ("Gibing of Loki"), he appears as the true expression of the bad conscience that prevents the world from enjoying indispensable self-satisfaction. He can be thoroughly amoral and can represent the Norse version of the trickster known in all folklores. Thus, without rhyme or reason, he steals the golden hair of the goddess Sif and the apples of youth of the goddess Iðunn, and he "sabotages" the technical marvels that the industrious dwarfs forged for the gods. If Thor's hammer has a handle that is too short, it is likely to be Loki's doing. In addition he may owe to the Vanir a curious propensity for the libidinous and a strange sexual ambiguity in which magic intervenes in full force. He thus mates with a horse in order to give birth to Óðinn's wondrous eight-legged war-horse, Sleipnir. Conversely, with heterosexual abandon he begets with the giantess Angrboða three monstrous children: Hel, goddess of hell;

Miðgarðsormr, the Norse Leviathan; and the dog (or wolf) Fenrir (or Garmr)—these two being among his own hypostases, since yet another etymology of his name yields the term "wolf." This last myth could actually come out of a reading of Isidore of Seville. It does not alter the fact that the aforementioned monsters are directly responsible for the Fate-of-the-Powers or Ragnarök. And the figure of Loki takes on the colossal dimensions of Satan Trismegistus, double-dealing and sadistic, the inexpiable fomenter of the downfall of the world. We are back again to Prometheus, all the more so because the gods inflicted on Loki a terrible punishment that evokes the atrocious tortures of the great Titan.

It should be stressed that what is evil in Loki is that he steals, insults, and perjures himself or leads others to perjure themselves. And the Norse world deemed these three sins the only inexpiable ones. Death by execution without judgment or condemnation was reserved for thieves alone. Insult, that is to say, an affront to honor, to human dignity, and thus to the feeling of belonging to the sacred that the Norse nourished, demanded immediate bloody vengeance. As for perjury, it was worse yet: it was the conscious and voluntary disregard of the guilty party's honor; it was in a sense his desacralization. In other words, in all of these instances, there is irreparable infringement of sacred law, a notion that can surely be viewed as the most basic in their world. The sacred, honor, and law—these are the virtually exclusive foundations of the Norse social order. And Loki is the foremost instigator of disorder, from insignificant farce to the Machiavellian scheming that ultimately leads to chaos.

As a last resort, we would like to propose for this disconcerting creature an interpretation that also happens to take into account another tendency characteristic of this mental universe that is so addicted to simple dichotomies and the opposition of dual powers. The sacred, honor, and law are, as we said, intimately connected, forming the attributes of the archetypal Norse god, Týr (whose name means "god"). In this sense, one could regard Loki as the "anti-Týr" or anti-god.

R.B./g.h.

BIBLIOGRAPHY

G. DUMÉZIL, *Loki* (1948). F. STRÖM, *Loki* (1956). J. DE VRIES, "The Problem of Loki," *Folklore Fellows Communications* 110 (1933).

SLAVIC MYTHS, RITES, AND GODS

The major difficulty presented by the study of Slavic paganism stems from the paucity of available sources. Not only are there precious few in any particular area of concern, but it is also often difficult to be certain that they actually deal with Slavic reality, because for centuries history gave such uncertain contours to these peoples and to their culture. Suffice it to say that we have no eyewitness accounts recorded by the parties involved nor any accounts that go back far enough in time to apply to early Slavic religion as it may have been practiced. We should also note that non-Slavic observers may

indeed have said something about the subject, but these witnesses either refused to see things as they were or forced on the subject matter criteria that were either extremely inappropriate (Arabs) or hostile (Christians). Finally, historical accident has constantly put the Slavs in contact with other cultures, thus favoring a loss of character or distinguishing features and confusion to the point where it is often difficult to tell whether certain archaeological evidence or certain customs are Slavic or Germanic or Celtic in origin.

Furthermore, the extant written accounts are relatively late. The oldest is the *De Bello Gothico* 3.4 of Procopius of Caesarea (ca. 550), which at best comments only on the southern Slavs and that only in passing. The situation is comparable in many ways to the state of scholarship on

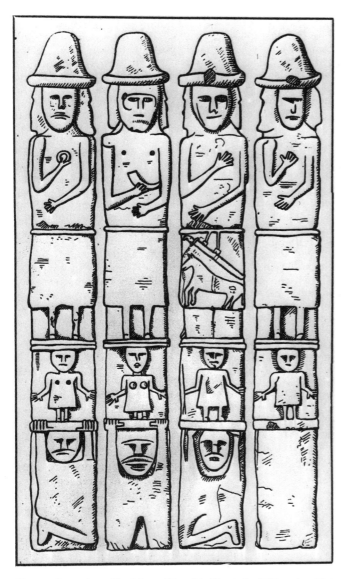

Stone column from Husiatyn. Albrecht, *Slawische Bildwerke*, Mainzer Zeitschrift. From Quillet, *Histoire des religions*.

The best information is thus on Russian and Baltic Slavs. Our texts on the Russians belong to two main categories. One includes the so-called *Primary Chronicle*, or *Chronicle of Nestor*, which was composed in the twelfth century but which comes to us only in a manuscript written two hundred years later. It is interesting because it tells about the paganism practiced by the old Russian Prince Vladimir (Valdimarr) (918–1015) and his people, though it calls for more restraint than scholars are usually willing to use; it is not clear to what extent this text discusses matters actually Slavic rather than Norse. The same problem applies to the other kind of texts still extant, namely, the various travel literature by Arab diplomats, generally dating from the ninth or tenth century and containing descriptions of the customs of the people they visited. Only two other types of sources are left. The first are Christian texts, generally polemical, homilies and prayers of penitence from the eleventh century at the earliest; they castigate pagan survivals, thus implicitly exposing them. The second are travel journals, much more recent (from the sixteenth century), which provide an occasional valuable detail. But on the whole the sources are meager.

The same applies to the written documents concerning the Baltic Slavs at that time. One must carefully sift through the *Gesta Danorum* of Saxo Grammaticus, a Danish monk who wrote at the end of the twelfth century (about the fall of Arcona, among other things); the Norse *Knytinga Saga*, a work from the end of the thirteenth century that tells of the same events and probably uses the same source; or the *Gesta Hammaburgensis* of Adam of Bremen (ca. 1075). None of these authors, first-class observers as far as Germania and Scandinavia are concerned, were really interested in the Slavs. They speak of them only when there happens to be overlap, as did Thietmar of Merseburg in his *Chronicle* (ca. 1015). What is left is the *Chronicon Slavorum* of Helmold, a cleric who lived in the region of Lübeck around 1170, and three biographies (written by three different monks, of whom the best known was one Herbord) of Otto, the bishop of Bamberg, who died in 1139. This bishop was remarkable for having gone on two missions (in 1124–25 and 1128) to western Pomerania. These *Lives* appeared around 1160.

More could certainly be learned from folkloric sources, which are both numerous and highly picturesque, but their interpretation raises thorny questions, typical of this kind of document. Moreover, the oldest among them were recorded only a little more than one hundred years ago, and it is likely that many popular songs, for example, go back no farther than the Christian era in Slavic countries.

Here as elsewhere, archaeology ought to unravel some of the mystery, but in this case it does not play the primary role that it has in other areas. Archaeologists have excavated a few shrines, in particular at Rügen and at Ptuj in Slovenia, and they have uncovered a few idols at Husiatyn in Galicia (a four-faced head perched on top of a square column about eight feet high), but in each case questions have been raised as to whether or not these remains are authentically Slavic.

Finally, as in so many other older religious systems, we should be on guard against the troublesome dichotomy of diachrony-synchrony. By the accidents of history, invaders came, who grafted onto the popular Slavic stem a more autocratic character, about which we know, paradoxically, more than we do about the indigenous plant. Examples include the Scandinavians in Russia and perhaps the Veneti (though it is not clear what reality is captured by that designation) in Mecklenburg and in Pomerania. We must consequently bear in mind a distinction between an ancient

ancient Germany, only much worse. When we are briefly told about Slavic paganism, it is often seen either as moribund or as dead and buried. The authors are in most cases Christian converts who tediously tell us about matters that they abhor and willfully distort. Furthermore, most of what they have to say focuses on the Slavs of what is now Russia or on those who settled on the Baltic coast, or in other words, on those who lived in the farthest reaches of the Slavic domain. As for the central Slavs, who were certainly far more numerous and undoubtedly more interesting to study because they were less contaminated by contacts with neighboring peoples, we have only two Czech sources, the *Chronica Boemorum* of Cosmas of Prague (died 1125) and the *Homiliary* of Opatovice. They are both of little value. The situation is even more deplorable for the Poles, for whom we have no text extant before the fifteenth century, i.e., long after Christianization.

and very primitive religion practiced by the local population and a much more evolved religion reserved for the elite.

In other words, we cannot overemphasize the historical problems, which are very important here; their solution would undoubtedly shed some much-needed light on the subject.

Unfortunately, we know very little except that the Slavs indeed stem from the Indo-European group. Their first settlement must have centered between the Vistula River, the Carpathian Mountains, the middle Dnieper River, and the marshlands of the Pripet River. In any case, beginning around the first century A.D. and more and more after the fifth century, these peoples began a vast and obscure expansion that can only be approximately dated about the ninth century. At that time, Slavic tribes covered all of central Europe between the Baltic Sea and the Carpathian Mountains (Veneti), between the Elbe River and the Oka River (the Antes to the east), and between Lake Ladoga and Greece, where they were subdued by the Sarmatians. This differentiation among southern, western, and eastern Slavs is important for two reasons. First, the dates of conversion to Christianity varied depending on the region; and second, the Slavs were receptive to foreign influences. They came into contact with Byzantium, Rome, and the Frankish Empire, and reacted differently in each case. But this does not explain the elusive personality of the Slavs. Thus, the very name of the Veneti, or Wends, seems to be of Germanic origin, and the people in question probably did not apply it to themselves. There are relationships among Germanic, Slavic, and Celtic cultures to the extent that it is often very hard to distinguish between them. A few examples may help to illustrate this point. It is well attested that the rooster plays a major symbolic, prophetic, and tutelary role in all three cultures, but it is not known in which culture this role originated. It is not known why Mokoš, one of their deities, is so strongly reminiscent of the Scythian Great Goddess. As for the bird-god Simurgh, he was undoubtedly borrowed from the Iranian bestiary by way of the Sarmatians, but what are we to make of a whole complex of shamanistic representations? We should not underestimate the role played by evangelism, which in this part of the world began in the eighth century for the Slovenes and the Croatians, and in the ninth century for the Bulgarians, the Moravians, and the Serbs. For reasons more political than sentimental, the first group converted to the Roman Church, the second to the Byzantine Church. The Poles and Russians did the same in the tenth century. That left the Baltic Slavs, between the Elbe and the Oder, for whom conversion meant coming under the control of the German Empire. They put up a stiff resistance until the twelfth century, when it ended either in extermination or in Germanization. Given such geographical and historical diversification, even assuming that there is a basis for Slavic unity, we should still distinguish between Baltic Slavs, on the one hand, and eastern and southern Slavs, on the other.

It should be noted that the term "Slav" appears for the first time only in the sixth century in the works of Procopius of Caesarea. Its meaning remains obscure. We must reject outright the absurd etymology of Slav-slave. It is more tempting to connect the word with the Common Slavic word *sLowo* meaning "spoken word," on the premise that the Slavs were regarded as people who spoke a comprehensible language, but this explanation is flimsy at best.

In any event, two important and perhaps surprising assertions can be made about the ancient Slavs.

The first is that they were sedentary and fundamentally peace-loving farmers, as all observers have recognized. It is hard to find any military or even distinctly political structures among them. Whenever these appear, they are sure to be foreign imports, notably Scandinavian. Even their lawmaking was reduced to a rather elementary application of the law of "an eye for an eye." There was, as far as we know, nothing of genuinely high culture. The Slavs remained at the archaic stage of fertility-fecundity.

This is supported by their second characteristic: the basic social unit is the family or tribe, the clan limited in number to the members of an extended family (*rod*, plural *rody*). This is the point on which the ancient Slavs were perhaps most like the ancient Germans. The family was the basic unit from all points of view, including the perspective of religion.

I

We are thus able to disentangle a deep archaic structure which places ancient Slavic religion under the rubric of the family (*rod*), that is, by way of the cult of ancestors and the dead, the rubric of fertility-fecundity.

On this point, a Russian text probably dating from the end of the eleventh century is clear. Known as *The Story of How Pagans Honored Their Idols*, it states that the eastern Slavs "first" offered sacrifice to the *rody* and to the *rožanicy* (assimilated to the deities of the ancestors), "then" to Perun, "their god," whereas "before that time" they were devoted to a cult of vampires and *beregyni* (nature spirits). This provides a kind of diachronic skeleton that will guide this account. The first section will deal with ancestors, the second section with the forces of nature, and the third section with the anthropomorphization and individualization of deities. This is in keeping with what Procopius said: "They recognize only one god, the maker of lightning, as the lord of the world; they sacrifice oxen and other animals to him . . . They also worship rivers, nymphs, and other spirits and make offerings to all."

Like all other Indo-Europeans, they believed in life after death. This has been attested archaeologically: tombs were exhumed in which the deceased was provided with all the goods necessary for his other existence. The soul was accordingly a kind of living corpse (*lebende Leiche*, as Klare put it) more or less attached to its bodily remains and interacting secretly with the living, whose prosperity it might promote. It is conceivable that the Slavs believed in reincarnation, given this well-known mental complex, and that the continuity of the clan was ensured by the eternal return of the departed.

Eventually individualization made its mark on the *rody* (Rod became a male deity), and in part on the *rožanicy*, who remained feminine plural but acquired a capital "R." Both were offered a feast during the winter solstice. A fifteenth-century manuscript depicts Rod "seated in mid-air" and throwing to the ground little heaps from which children are born, a clear way of saying that he presides over the perpetuation of the species. Another text, this one from the sixteenth century, complements the earlier one: when the child has reached the age when he is allowed to be officially initiated into the clan, his hair is cut, and the women prepare a special porridge "for the Rožanicy," with whom the initiated is supposed to be placed in symbiosis. Philologists affirm that one of the meanings of *rod* is "origin," "birth"; another is "family," "kinship"; but *rožanica* means simultaneously "mother," "motherhood," "genealogy," and "fortune." For this reason, many have turned Rod into the tutelary deity of the clan and Rožanica into his consort. The plural of the feminine may be related to the polygyny that was common in these societies during this phase of their history. Initially, there was probably no difference between these entities and the departed ancestors. It is not necessary to look for the Slavic version of the Indo-European theme "young god–mother-goddess" in the Rod-Rožanicy couple (in the feminine singular). F. Vyncke has made such a claim; the couple per se is not attested. The family, and especially the extended family (*zadruga*), has always been the prescribed framework of life for the Slavs, and the cult of the ancestors, or *domovoï* (protectors), remains central in a mentality that, for all intents and purposes, has hardly changed on that point, even to this day.

The fertility cult expressed by the cult of the ancestors may explain why the Slavs practiced cremation before adopting burial (they probably adopted burial in response to foreign pressure).

Finally, the fact that this cult must go back to a very remote antiquity would explain its long persistence, under degraded but well-attested forms, until the present time. Vampires became *beregyni*, female spirits who dwell locally on precipices and on shorelines, as the etymology of the word indicates: Old Russian *beregŭ* (shore) or Old Church Slavic *brĕgŭ*; and then they become *rusalkí*, the "souls of the dead," a more recent specialized version that tends toward the "souls of the dead who died a violent death." The werewolves that haunt more recent texts may be based on the same ideology, if they are not the result of shamanistic or Scandinavian influences (or the one via the other). On this point, Herodotus, speaking of the Neuri, most likely a Slavic tribe, is clear (in his *History* 4.105): "Once a year every Neurus becomes a wolf for a few days and then returns to his original form."

Clearly magic played a vital role in beliefs so intimately tied to the world of the beyond and to the supernatural. This universe evolved perpetually in a dual ambiance, as just described with reference to vampires and werewolves, which constituted an isolated feature of a vast demonology. Everything has its correspondent in the other world, even corn or cattle, which even in the nineteenth century had their common tutelary spirit or *spor*.

II

A Russian homily relates that the sacrificial victims offered to the ancestors were later often drowned in lakes or rivers. There was thus probably a connection between the cult of the ancestors and what may have been the second phase of this religion, unless it is more correct to speak of simultaneous development. Rather than saying that the development was from manism to animism, it may be that the two states coexisted, the latter gradually taking precedence over the former in the course of centuries.

Many texts bear witness to the cult that the Slavs devoted to rocks, mountains, stones, springs, rivers, lakes, forests, isolated trees, and fire. Helmold von Bosan (in Holstein) pointed out in his *Chronicon Slavorum* that they swore by stones. The *Homiliary* of Opatovice confirms that they worshiped fire, air, i.e., the winds, water, and especially trees, particularly the oak (see below), the walnut, and the elder. In some places cutting down these trees was forbidden, and there were sacred woods that no one was allowed to enter, such as the woods of Zutibure, near Lützen. As for animals, snakes seem to have inspired special respect, as did the horse.

As early as 1700 B.C., symbols that are found on the Lusatian ceramics attest to a cult of the sun and fire that would long persist. The Russians worshiped Mother Earth, perhaps using as intermediaries the oxen and bulls they depicted so freely. The Slavs were well ensconced within the realm of fertility-fecundity, where they would essentially remain, and the other two functions were so seldom and so poorly represented that they raise questions as to their authenticity whenever they do appear. According to Herbord, in an admittedly late text, the typical Slavic idol says this to his devotee: "I am your god. It is I who cover the fields with grass and the woods with foliage. The fruits of the fields and the trees, the fecundity of cattle, and all that is of value to men are within my power" (*Vita Ottonis* 3.4).

We are tempted to conclude that many divine personifications ultimately refer to these natural forces. Thus the sun may have given birth to Jarilo (in his brilliant aspect); to Ivan Kupalo (as he disappears on the horizon at sea only to return); to Svarog (who is fire in the strict sense of the term); to Perun (associated with thunder); as well as to Simurgh, already mentioned. Water, rain, and moist soil were recognized behind Mokoš. The wind was thought to have breathed life into Sventovit with his four faces. As for Volos, the guardian of the herds, he was more clearly chthonic, but the process of deification of celestial bodies and great natural phenomena was indeed evident. This did not prevent the eventual emergence of a thoroughly Indo-European supreme god, one so fearsome that it was forbidden to pronounce his name. He was often symbolized by a sword, and he lived in the sky like the ancient *tiwaz*. At least that is what Helmold claims around 1150: "Among the different deities to whom they dedicate the fields and the woods and to whom they attribute their joys and pains, they say that there is only one god in the sky; this god rules over the others." If this is the case, it may be that this *deus otiosus* finally manifested himself under the name Svarog, from which the form Svarožic is derived.

The same ideas are behind the creations of the secondary order that are found in folklore and the popular forms of religion: spirits of the house (*domovoï*), of the farmyard (*dvorniki*), of housewives (*kikimora*), sylvan spirits (*lešiï*), naiads (*vodjanoï*), water spirits (*rusalkí*), etc. It was to these undifferentiated entities that sacrifices were offered. Until the nineteenth century, they remained the objects of superstitions and popular rites.

Bronze fibula. Valanke, near Vilnus. Librairie Larousse archives.

For like the religion of the ancient Germans, Slavic religion probably came to be known through cultic practices, especially rituals. Few prayers or dogmatic texts have been preserved. Rather, what we know refers to symbolic actions: sacrifices for the spring equinox, which is a symbol of resurrection, and for the summer solstice, which is an assurance of creation. By chance the harvest feast was described by the Dane Saxo: "The people having assembled before the gates of the temple, the priest removed the vessel from the idol's hand and examined it to see if the amount of liquid had diminished. If it had, he would forecast a famine for the following year; if it had not, he would forecast abundance. After having honored the statue by gesturing as if to offer it something to drink, in a solemn invocation he asked him for all kinds of benefits for himself and for the country, and for wealth and glory for the people. He then saluted the crowd in the name of the idol, enjoined the crowd to persevere in its devotions and sacrifices, and promised them the certain reward of victories on land and at sea." One could not hope to find a more fitting example of the emphasis placed upon the vegetative function. Later, when individualized idols proliferated, the offerings made to them would be weapons and the booty of war, in case of need, but especially vessels and precious objects, fruit, food, and victims, animals certainly but perhaps also humans. The type of relationship that the Slavs established with their god was also remarkable for its lack of terror or incomprehension. They spoke to him with affection, in a childlike tone of voice, called him by his diminutive, and flattered him freely.

The long and interesting quotation from Saxo has the merit of implicitly stressing the role of fate in this type of religion. Other sources attest that the Slavs practiced divination assiduously. They threw wooden tablets on the ground and would then interpret their arrangement, or they carefully observed the behavior of a sacred horse in a particular situation. Herbord depicts this ritual in detail: wooden sticks were placed on the ground and the horse would be brought to that area. They walked the horse back and forth three times. If the animal walked over the sticks without touching a single one with his hooves, that was a good omen. It is not known whether a special caste of priests existed to perform all of these rites, with the possible exception of the western Slavs, who had such a caste.

Such deep devotion to the forces of nature explains why even after Christianization, Russian Slavs continued to be faithful to their past, notably in the areas of superstition and folklore, which is why they were accused of long remaining of "mixed faith." All the demonology just mentioned serves as tangible proof of this: witchcraft and popular magic, divination, vampires, and other forms of reincarnation of the souls of the departed, and friendly and familiar little devils, the Polish *uboze* or *topielce* to whom chickens were still being sacrificed in the nineteenth century, reflect this intimate collusion with natural powers, a collusion that cannot be overemphasized.

Wooden model idol of Novgorod the Great. Librairie Larousse archives.

III

The final phase—the systematization and individualization of these forces—is certainly quite recent, so recent that some modern commentators place it no further back than the Middle Ages. It is not absolutely necessary to ascribe it all to Sarmatian influences. The tendency is widely attested, and if one has to speak of influences, it would be simpler to point to Celtic or Roman ones rather than speaking yet again of Germanic influences. Furthermore, Slavic family communities of the patriarchal type referred to above had a tendency to wither away slowly during the early Middle Ages, the net effect of which could only have been the gradual dethroning of the *rod* and *rožanicy*. It would seem that the slide toward anthropomorphism was accomplished by the ninth century. Starting with the eleventh century, in any case, our eyewitness accounts describe pantheons in the classical sense of the term.

And starting from this period it becomes possible to make some necessary distinctions. Against a common background, there appear to be growing divergences between eastern Slavs (i.e., Russians) and Baltic Slavs, differences which justify separate treatments.

A. Only three divine persons seem to have been recognized by all the Slavs: Svarog, Svarožic, and Dažbog, although some tribes probably specialized in the cult of one of them to the exclusion of the other two. According to Thietmar of Merseburg (6.17), Svarožic was regarded as the primary god of the Veletes at the beginning of the eleventh century. He was said to have had a temple at Radogoszcz (Rethra); by an amusing error the name of the place was later taken by Adam of Bremen (2.21) for that of the deity Radogost, who was thus equated with Svarožic.

One of these gods must be the last avatar of the supreme *deus otiosus* mentioned earlier, but all evidence indicates that Svarog filled that role, since Svarožic was only a derivative form, and Dažbog was probably only a subsequently personified epithet. Svarog may thus have prolonged the archaic solar cult.

Archaeologists have shown that the temples whose remains they uncovered were dedicated to individualized idols. These discoveries have usually been further substantiated by literary sources. We know, for example, that temples existed at Rethra, as noted (the exact site has yet to be identified), at Stettin, Wollin, Wolgast (at the mouth of the Oder), Gützkow (west of the Oder), Malchow (in Mecklenburg), Kessin (near Rostock), Plön (in the area of Kiel), and especially Arcona and Garz (both on the island of Rügen). Generally such a temple was a small square building with a red roof and wooden walls, erected inside those fortified towns that served as refuges (German *Zufluchtsort*) exclusively in times of war but remained unoccupied in times of peace. They housed ornate and sometimes gigantic idols made of polychromatic wood. The Sventovit idol at Arcona measured some twenty-five feet in height.

B. The *Chronicle of Nestor* gives much information about the eastern Slavs. Despite the real historical obscurities and the confusion between Slavs and Scandinavians, which have inspired heated debates, it has been established that the Great Prince of Kiev-Koenugardr, Vladimir-Valdimarr, unquestionably of Swedish origin, tried to set up a national religion in 980 to offset Christianity, which was making threatening inroads. Here is what the *Chronicle* says about that religion: "Vladimir set out to rule alone over Kiev and built idols on the hill outside the palace. There was Perun made of wood with a silver head and a golden mustache, and Chors and Dažbog and Stribog and Simurgh and Mokoš. The people offered sacrifices to them and called them gods; they brought their sons and daughters to them and offered them in sacrifice to these demons, defiling the earth with these sacrifices. The Russian soil and the hill were defiled with blood." Vladimir's efforts soon proved to have been in vain, for he had himself baptized in 988, but this text is a precious source because of its list of names, the most important of which we will now discuss.

The first name, Perun-Perkun, raises several problems. The name goes back to the Lithuanian Perkunas, who was the supreme sky god and god of thunder; the name is etymologically related to the Latin *quercus* (oak), a tree reputed particularly to attract lightning. The name may also bring to mind the modern Polish word *piorun* (thunder). The name relates to a complex of ideas about the sky and lightning. Perun may have been the supreme god of the eastern Slavs. In any case, the Sviatoslav Vareg princes swore

by him when they signed treaties: Oleg-Helgi in 907, Igor-Ingvarr in 945, and Sviatoslav in 971. Perun controlled the seasons, dispensing rain and thereby fertility. He is thought to have had a statue in Novgorod and in Kiev, the two cities in Russia founded by Swedes. Near Novgorod-the-Great, on the shores of Lake Ilmen, in the Peryń area (which bears his name), some twenty-five years ago the ruins were discovered of an imposing building containing the remains of a colossal statue probably depicting Perun.

This brings up two very interesting observations. First, the homilies do not distinguish between Perun and Rod. Second, and more important, linguists have easily established exact parallels between the word *perun* and several others: in addition to the Lithuanian *Perkunas*, there are the Old Norse *Fjörgyn(n)* and the Sanskrit *Parjanya*, as well as the Greek named Phorkys, the father of the Pleiades. All these names refer to a supreme sky god who manifests himself primarily through storms and who promotes life. The problem is in knowing if this is really a Slavic equivalent of the various deities listed above or if the Vareg input is responsible for the god's existence. Indeed, Perun-Perkun, by way of Fjörgyn(n), might be a Slavicized version of the Scandinavian god Thor, relayed through the name of Thor's mother, Fjörgyn. Thor, armed with his thunderbolt hammer, is the god of thunder and as such sends down the rains after the storm. He also rules over fecundity. However, nowhere in Norse sources is Thor clearly taken to be the supreme god. This role belongs to Týr, who is without a doubt the supreme Indo-European god. It is possible that Fjörgyn(n), whose role is obscure in the available Old Norse sources, in fact occupied a far more important position in the Norse religious universe—or at least in the Swedish one—as this faint Slavic trace or correspondence would have us believe. In any case, Perun raises one of the most serious problems of Slavic mythology, namely, its relation to Norse mythology.

In second place comes Svarog, whom the *Chronicle of Nestor* identifies with Hephaestus, turning him into the father of the sun, called Dažbog (from Slavic *bog*- "wealth," and the verb *dati* "give") or "dispenser of all wealth." Dažbog is almost always referred to in connection with Svarog, from which some have concluded that he might be nothing but a facet of Svarog. In fact, the sources attest Svarog quite differently, as the great legislator and restorer of monogamy. His name may be based on the Indo-European root *suer*- "to tie," which would be appropriate both to his qualities as a supernatural metalsmith (he "ties" or welds with fire) and to his solar properties, as well as to his talents as a judge and his magic knowledge. He was the center of a mental complex that was certainly more intellectual than that of Perkun. This does not, however, diminish his characteristics of the third function, which was by far the most important one for the ancient Slavs. In this sense, like Dažbog, the Stribog of the *Chronicle* may very well have been merely another representation of Svarog, since his name has approximately the same meaning as Dažbog (from Common Slavic *sterti*, etc., "to spread forth").

As for Chors, speculation remains wide open, with the only acceptable suggestions leading to the Ossetic *xorz*, "good." The Alans also had a god named Xorz, famous for his goodness.

With Mokoš, the only Slavic goddess we know of, and especially with Volos (or Veles), who is not mentioned in the *Chronicle of Nestor* but is invoked twice as a "god of cattle" in treaties dated 907 and 971, we stand on somewhat firmer ground. Volos was also known by the Czechs. He was in charge of commerce or property; on the basis of the stem *veleti,* "to will, decide, legislate," he was the god that regulated exchange activities and managed things. In testimony whereof, he presided over commercial transactions, watched over their integrity, and made certain that promises were kept. Significantly, following Christianization he was more or less incorporated, probably through paronymy, into the image of Saint Blaise, the bishop of Sebaste in Cappadocia; Saint Blaise was worshiped throughout Christendom as the patron saint of wild animals. Between him and Volos there was probably a kind of reciprocal changing of places back and forth.

C. The situation is somewhat more confused among the Slavs living on the Baltic shores. They were more directly in contact with the ancient Germans and ultimately more influenced by the Germans' dynamic view of the world and of life. Their supreme god was Sventovit, a sun god, to whom a temple of Arcona was dedicated on the island of Rügen, which he protected. He seems to have been a version of Svarog, also well known by the Baltic Slavs under the patronymic name of Svarožic. He was usually seen as a god of fire, benevolent and useful. This brings us to the marvelous metalsmith.

Sventovit (or Svantevit) as a name has an aristocratic element unknown among the Russian Slavs: the suffix *-vit,* "lord," which is part of the names of several other Slavic

Bronze figure from Schwedt. Albrecht, *Slawische Bildwerke.* From Quillet, *Histoire des religions.*

deities (Iarovit, based on *-jar:* "strong, furious"; Porevit, based on *por-:* "power"; Rujevit, based on *ruj-:* "rut"). For the rest, *svent-* conveys the idea of energy and thus takes us into a realm of ideas in which power, strength, and energy play an important role. Though these terms should not be taken in too martial a sense, they are not so clearly in the domain of the third function as the terms discussed earlier. Saxo (14.29) depicts Sventovit as the great deity of Rügen (Rana in Slavic; the inhabitants, "Ranes," may have supplied the caste of priests referred to above). Saxo's story is most interesting. The cultic performance that he reports—a consultation of the soothsayers to find out if the coming year would be good or bad—brings us back to fertility-fecundity, and in the same context of prophecy that has already been emphasized. Svantevit had a horse that he was said to ride at night and that was believed to foretell the future; these traits are familiar to anyone acquainted with ancient Norse religion, as well as the fact that the horse—which was exalted in the temple of Sventovit and, being sacred, could not be ridden by anyone but the guardian priest of the temple—is remarkably like the untouchable Freyfaxi in the Icelandic saga of Hrafnkell, the priest of Freyr. Beyond this, Svantevit was regarded as the god of war, probably because of his dynamic powers. In any case, he had the broad shoulders of a supreme god.

At Arcona he was depicted with four faces, apparently to symbolize his multiple nature, whether he was thought to embody in his power all four worlds—the sky, the earth, the netherworld, and the realm of the spirits—or to gather together in this way the four elements over which he presided.

One of the curious traits of the Slavs was their marked predilection for this kind of representation. Not only were there idols with four or five faces (Porevit) or even seven (Rujevit), but the Pomeranian god Triglav was true to his name—from Common Slavic *tri(je)* "three" and **golva* (e.g., Polish gŁowa) "head." This brings us back to a realm of ideas that we have touched upon several times already. It is difficult to distinguish between Svarog/Svarožic and Dažbog/Stribog; and we have just listed the series Sventovit-Jarovit-Porevit-Rujevit. Whenever the sources note the names of Slavic idols, they bombard us with names. Now the Slavs of historical times remained faithful first to the manistic and then to the animistic orientations that we have emphasized in discussing probable origins. It is possible that they continued to visualize their deities in a pluralized form (as was the case with the *rožanicy*), expressed by the many heads or rather the many faces of the gods and by the lack of clear boundaries between the attributes of the various deities in the age of anthropomorphism.

Syncretism seems to be the natural climate in which these representations evolved. This interpretation seems more solid than one that would make of all these entities (we have not exhausted the list) tutelary deities of noble clans and consequently of particular places. It makes more sense to see this multitude of individualized names as local, even clanic, specializations of certain divinized forces or ideas. This would also explain why after Christianization inexpugnable paganism reappeared in folklore in the guise of quantities of genies, goblins, and other spirits.

The Old Norse *Knytlinga Saga* includes two more names of idols of Rügen, namely, Pizamar and Tjarnaglofi (in Norse writing). The latter if spelled in the Slavic manner would yield (in modern Polish) *czarna głowa,* i.e., "black head," which suggests a whole chain of associations. There happens to be a Czerneboch, i.e., *černo bog (czarny bog),* which clearly means "black god"; a Siva (based on the Old Slavonic *sivŭ*, "black"), the tutelary god of the Polabians; and a Pripegala, cited in a letter of Archbishop Adelgot of Magdeburg in 1108 (based on the Slavic term *pĭkŭlŭ*, "tar, pitch," with the prefix *pri-(przy)*, "to"). Blackness may of course suggest ideas of malice and wickedness and may then indicate the influence of Christian demonology. It does not seem, however, that this idea was prevalent in the ancient Slavic world, where the notion of evil did not have the resonances that are associated with it today, anymore than it did with the Germanic people. It is therefore more convincing to see in this "blackness" a return to the chthonic theme that so definitely constitutes the basis of our understanding of this religious realm.

Let us turn briefly to Proven, the tutelary deity of Oldenburg, who closely duplicated Sventovit's role as a lawmaker. Helmbold portrays him as the patron of a sacred site where the local people gathered each week to hear justice rendered by the prince and a priest, a reference curiously reminiscent of the Norse Þing. F. Vyncke points out that the name Proven must be connected with the Slavic word *pravo*, "right, legal."

In the Slavic world there were also deities, among those already named, who can be seen to take on purely military or warlike features. Ebbon identifies Jarovit as a war god and compares him to Mars. But this evolution seems to have been only relatively recently sketched out. On the whole, even if the observers who described the temples clearly note the presence of arms and shields among the offerings, they rightly emphasize the cornucopias, the magnificently decorated drinking cups, and other such objects that they saw.

Finally we should devote a few words to the Baltic peoples, in the strict sense of the term, the Old Prussians, Lithuanians, and Latvians, who lived in close association with the Scandinavians and then with the Slavs. Since the Baltic religious world differs very little from that of the Slavs, it seems that the north as a whole had a largely homogeneous religious mentality. Indeed, virtually all the components that we have just listed appear among the Baltic peoples. First, cults of nature are attested by various accounts, among which that of Peter of Dusburg (dating from the beginning of the fourteenth century) in particular mentions the cult of the sun and of fire, while stressing the fact that the word for sun (*saule*) is feminine in the Baltic languages, as it is in Old Norse, and that the cult of fire included oracles and divination. The fertility-fecundity cult was practiced everywhere, culminating in Perkunas, particularly among the Old Prussians and the Lithuanians. Among the Latvians this cult gave rise to many very specialized deities whose names are built on the word *mate*, "mother, woman": Jurasmat (mother of the ocean), Laukamat (mother of the fields), etc. The most

interesting creation by far is the Lithuanian heavenly smith Telavel, who "made" the sun, very much like Ilmarinen in Finnish mythology. According to Jerome of Prague, a fifteenth-century missionary, the Lithuanians worshiped a huge hammer, the very one used by Telavel to make the sun. The connection with the Svarog-Svarožic-Dažbog complex, or with Thor, is obviously suggestive.

The last word belongs to history. Throughout the centuries, it must have been difficult to be a Slav: Scythians, Sarmatians, Huns, Alans, Goths, Avars, and finally Swedes all attempted to annex these tribes who, like their idols, had to become multifaced in order to survive. In their nature they were profoundly peace loving; in their culture they showed an abiding respect for the family and for their ancestors. All of this may help to explain an amalgam of rather elusive religious beliefs, fairly difficult to pin down—but its very haziness is in and of itself instructive.

R.B./g.h.

BIBLIOGRAPHY

Sources

1. In the original languages: C. H. MEYER, *Fontes historiae religionis slavicae*, in *Fontes historiae religionum* (Berlin 1931). This also contains the *Knytlinga Saga* in Norse and in Latin, and the Arabic texts in Arabic and in German. V. I. MANSIKKA, *Die Religion der Ostslaven*. vol. 1, *Quellen* (Helsinki 1922).

2. In translation: A. BRÜCKNER, *Die Slaven*, Religionsgeschichtliches Lesebuch, 3 (2d ed., Tübingen 1926).

History

T. ARNE, *La Suède et l'Orient* (Uppsala 1914). F. DVORNIK, *The Slavs* (Boston 1956). L. NIEDERLE, *Manuel de l'Antiquité slave*, 2 vols. (Paris 1923–26). R. PORTAL, *Les Slaves* (Paris 1965). G. V. VERNADSKY, *The Origins of Russia* (Oxford 1959).

Religion

1. General works: B. O. UNBEGAUN, "La religion des anciens Slaves, in Mana, *Introduction à l'histoire des religions*, 2, 3 (Paris 1948): 389–445. N. REITER, "Mythologie der alten Slaven," in *Wörterbuch der Mythologie* 1, 6 (Stuttgart 1964): 167–71. P. PASCAL, "La religion des anciens Slaves," in M. Brillant and R. Aigrain, *Histoire des Religions* 5 (Paris 1956). F. VINCKE, "The Religion of the Slavs," in C. J. Bleeker and G. Widengren, *Historica Religionum*, 2 vols. (Leiden 1969), 1:648–66. F. VINCKE, "La religion des Slaves," in *Histoire des religions* under the direction of H. C. Puech, Encyclopédie de la Pléiade,, vol. 1 (Paris 1970), 695–719.

2. Some particularly interesting studies: A. STENDER-PETERSEN, "Russian Paganism," in *Russian Studies, Acta Jutlandica* 28, 2 (1956): 44–53. T. PALM, *Wendische Kultstätten* (Lund 1937). E. WIENECKE, *Untersuchungen zur Religion der Westslaven* (Leipzig 1940).

THE KINSHIP OF SLAVIC AND NORSE MYTHOLOGIES: THE PROBLEM OF PERUN-PERKUN-PERKUNAS-FJÖRGYN(N)

One of the most fascinating and burning issues in Slavic mythology is its relationship, if not its collusion, with Germano-Norse mythology. Rather than analyzing influences, we propose to study in greater depth what appear to be identical natures and structures so thoroughly intermingled that anyone investigating this matter systematically may

be tempted to draw bold conclusions. Of course both of these mythologies are Indo-European and thus share basic features within a Dumézilian frame of reference. But the same could be said of Greek or Celtic mythology. In this case, however, the parallels are of a very different nature.

We shall start with the preeminently Germanic and Norse personage of Thor, whose "mother" was Fjörgyn ("one who gives and promotes life," thus a primordial deity of fecundity and fertility). But Fjörgynn also exists in the masculine gender, with two *n*'s, in keeping with the sexual ambivalence that is one of the most curious characteristics of Nordic mythology (see Njörðr-Nerthus, Freyr-Freyja, etc.). The cult of this god must have been brought by the Swedish Varangians when they settled in Novgorod-Holmgarðr, Kiev-Koenugarðr, and Staraia Ladoga-Aldeigjuborg, and Vladimir-Valdimarr sought to impose it in counteracting Christianity in 980.

The Swedes do not seem to have devoted to Thor a cult comparable to that of the Norwegians, for example. Rather the Swedes chose Freyr, a deity of fecundity and fertility, as their principal god. Since this function was also attributed to Thor, the god of storms and thunder, and by extension the god of the fertilizing rain that follows the storm, the two gods can thus be connected, except that especially during the period being discussed here, the martial and warlike features of Thor are an obstacle. On the other hand, his "mother" Fjörgyn never participates in the second function and would therefore lend herself admirably to adoption by the Slavs.

Moreover, it is very likely that the Swedish Varangians were the *rus* or *rhōs* to whom Arab or Byzantine observers referred (probably because the Varangians came mostly from the Swedish province of Ros-lagen) and who thus gave the Russians their name. Imposing their beliefs was merely the next step. The paucity of sources before the tenth century combined with the inconsistencies in what has come to be called "Slavic" before the Middle Ages makes such a conclusion plausible. Without going into the details of a quarrel that has put Scandinavian and Russian specialists at odds with one another over the last seventy-five years, let us merely say that it is possible that the Varangians imposed their religion on the Eastern Slavs, and there are several reasons to support this belief. The indigenous populations were poorly organized and divided among themselves; they were, furthermore, not inclined to warfare and were therefore incapable of uniting against an eventual determined adversary. The name of the Varangians is *vaeringjar* in Old Norse, *varjagi* in Russian, and *Baraggoi* in Greek. In these forms the word has not the narrow meaning that it was to acquire later, as the designation of the bodyguard of the *basileus*, but the general meaning, the eastern equivalent of *víkíngr*. The Varangians were a kind of semimilitary, semimercantile brotherhood, depending on whether one chooses to explain their name by the Old Norse word *vara*, "merchandise," or *várar*, "binding agreement." (The two meanings are not mutually exclusive, since there were during the Middle Ages countless guilds of merchants who were compelled to practice their crafts with weapons in hand.) They came to bring a management, an aristocracy, and a government; and they simultaneously imposed their religion, with the necessary adaptations.

This does more than explain the philological and semantic identity of Perkun and Fjörgyn. This argument can shed light on the problem that individualized gods seem to have appeared only relatively late among the Slavs. Following a manistic phase and then an animistic phase (the order is not to be taken too literally because the two phases may well have existed simultaneously), the Slavs may finally have come to know anthropomorphic and clearly distinct deities because the Scandinavians planted the idea in their minds and brought them one or more supernatural characters. I say one or more because, although no one challenges the equivalence of Perkun-Fjörgynn, there may be other names that lend themselves to a similar interpretation; thus Volos may well correspond to the rather enigmatic Swedish god Ullr—if we assume an etymology that would show him to be the Gothic *ŭulþus*. Ullr is well attested in the parts of Sweden from which the Varangians primarily came. In other words, the undifferentiated cult of the *rody* and *rožanicy,* as well as the cult of the forces of nature, would thus go back to the

Slavic idol from Holsgerlinchen (eastern Prussia). Ninth to tenth century. Photo X.

Slavs proper. The cult of individualized gods may be credited to the peaceful Scandinavian conquerors.

This theory is still not fully satisfactory, and we might feel compelled to push this line of argument further. The only Slavs about whom we have any substantial information are those who have long lived in close contact with the Scandinavians, namely, the Russians and the Slavs of the Baltic Coast. The situation might be different if we had better documentation about the central or western Slavs, who were probably the most numerous.

There are analogies of all sorts which bring together what is known about the ancient Norse and about the Slavs. Sociologically speaking, there were great similarities. In Germania and Slav country alike, the family (*aett* in the north, *zadruga* [really Serbian] among the Slavs) played a predominant role and was the basic nucleus both of religion and of everything else. *Rod* or *rožanica* and the Norse *hamingja* or *fylgja* were very much alike. Similarly, a concern for legislation is shared by the two domains, and Proven, in his role as the guardian and protector of the public assemblies where decisions affecting the common interest were made, was strongly evocative of Týr, *Mars þingsus* as a Frisian inscription calls him, the god of the *þing*. Finally, there is an acknowledged homology between Perkun and Thor, via the latter's "relatives" as go-betweens, and by virtue of the fact that both of them were the privileged deities of the free man, the Scandinavian *bóndi* or Slavic peasant. In other words, law, family, and free man—these three foundations of Norse society were also found on the opposite shores of the Baltic Sea.

The cult of nature and of the forces of nature was common to both cultures. By way of example, the sun and fire were enjoyed with equal fervor, were equally deified, and became equally incarnate in solar heroes and deities. Here and there, there were one or more marvelous smiths, and one or more heroes responsible for perpetuating what must have been an absolutely primordial devotion to the dispenser of all heat in cold countries where winters are long, dark, and gloomy. Nevertheless, from the Icelandic *Landnámabók* to the homilies of public admonition directed at the Slavs, there were the same sacrificial practices and the same offerings made to rocks, waterfalls, lakes, rivers, groves, and other natural sites. Furthermore, the ancient Germans are known to have devoted a special cult to trees, to the point of conceiving several eloquent deifications such as Irminsul or Yggdrasill. It is striking to note that the Slavs worshiped wooden idols, some of which, insofar as archaeologists have recovered them, are enormous tree trunks barely trimmed. In fact, one of the etymologies suggested for the Scandinavian word *ase*, "god," relates it to **ansuR*, "wooden beam."

A major role was played in Slavic paganism by animals, notably the snake and the horse. Hardly any runic inscription mentions the Norse serpent ritual without referring to such a grandiose creation as Miðgarðsormr, and the importance of the horse in Germanic ritual is clear, particularly in defamatory magic, or *níð*. And Sventovit's horse is strongly reminiscent of Óðinn's Sleipnir; they may both betray the same shamanistic influence.

As for shamanism, the text by Herodotus about the Neuri—assuming they were Slavs—would not surprise anyone familiar with Icelandic sagas. The Neuri could turn into werewolves and were thus in Old Norse terms *hamrammr* (in the singular form), i.e., they could change form so as to defy spatial and temporal categories. The trace here is so strong that one is tempted to see a pure and simple borrowing. More generally, magic seems to have played an equally important role, indeed a primordial role, in both mythologies.

To justify these resemblances on various levels would in the final analysis require a functional or structural interpretation.

These are mythologies perfectly circumscribed within the Indo-European thematic scheme as defined by Georges Dumézil. If in some cases one function seems to have been eclipsed by another, it is often because of our ignorance, particularly in diachronic matters. Sometimes a deity may have changed so much that his original attributes are forgotten, or another god may have usurped the functions of his predecessor, etc. But the overall scheme remains clear: everywhere a supreme, heavenly, and tabu god ordered all things and presided over a pantheon in which the three

functions are correctly attested, or have been attested at some point in history. However—and this is the first point where resemblances become truly troublesome—these functions, contrary to some unverifiable but generally accepted ideas, have an unexpected hierarchy: the warrior function is much lower than the sovereign-magic function, which in turn is lower than the fertility-fecundity function. This last function was clearly predominant, as much among the ancient Germans (however surprising this may sound) as among the Slavs.

In sum, the vegetative function, tied at all times and in all places to the cult of the ancestors, which in turn resulted from the importance of the clan, won out over all the others. This predominance extended all around the Baltic coast and for reasons that make good sense: these were countries with poor soil and a harsh climate; they were dependent on good weather and more than other countries they were victims of the elements. Although there is no need systematically to rewrite Montesquieu, it is clear that the soil and climate must have played a more significant role at these latitudes than elsewhere, if only in compelling men to live in close interdependence. This led the way to all kinds of collectivism, a road that the Slavs followed farther than the Germans did, as can be seen in modern history in what may be a logical resurgence of ageless sociocultural archetypes. Whether we stand on the shores of the Mälaren or the banks of the Dnieper, from the ancient mounds to the folklore of yesterday, the same ambience and spirit prevail.

Furthermore, in both areas, Slav and Norse, dogma, theology, and even ethics give way almost entirely to ritual. These are religions that became aware of themselves through significant actions and became real at the privileged moment of sacrifice. This has been proved as far as the ancient Germans are concerned, but it still remains to be proved for the Slavs. Although such a proof would go beyond the scope of the present article, we believe that the evidence would be the same: sacrifices of animals or human beings, banquets with libations, and the consultation of oracles, along with some practices in common, such as the immersion of victims after the offering (reminiscent of the immersion of the "goddess" Nerthus, as reported by Tacitus about the ancient Germans); the building of square temples in which wooden idols were enthroned, painted, and dressed; the hypothetical existence of an ill-defined corpus of sacrificer-priests performing half-religious, half-administrative functions, etc. It is quite disquieting to find the same detail (a sacred horse dedicated to a god and untouchable except by the priest or the guardian of the temple) in a Slavic version in which the horse is consecrated to Sventovit and in an Icelandic version, the *Saga of Hrafnkell, Priest of Freyr*, in which the horse Freyfaxi, "Mane-of-Freyr," is dedicated to Freyr, a god of fertility and fecundity. Finally, the role of fate was as primordial among the Slavs as it was among the ancient Germans, and one can find strict identities even in the principal way of consulting the oracles: the Slavs threw on the ground wooden "tablets," whose arrangement was interpreted by the priests; the ancient Germans did the same thing with "sticks" (*teinar*) dipped in sacrificial blood and thrown on either the bare ground or a piece of cloth.

Nevertheless, indecision often grips us when we read some of the sources. It is not known about whom Saxo Grammaticus is talking when he focuses on Rügen. And when Adam of Bremen mentions the ambassadors from the Caliphate sailing along the banks of Russian rivers, we do not know whether he means Slavs or ancient Germans. And we do not know why the same accusation, formulated in exactly similar terms, was brought against both Russian Slavs after Christianization and Norwegian-Celtic colonizers when they arrived in northern Iceland toward the end of the ninth century—the accusation that they were "of mixed faith," and that they sometimes invoked their ancient pagan idols and sometimes the God of the Christians, depending on need or circumstances. Surely the situation is identical in each case, at least during the period when the first witnesses are dated: on an indigenous base, of which precious little is known, the same import was grafted almost uniformly from the Black Sea to the Arctic Circle. It can be concluded that the very notion of "Slavic" remains nearly as hazy and enigmatic as that of "ancient German," at least when it comes to religion.

R.B./g.h.

BIBLIOGRAPHY

R. BOYER, "Le culte dans la religion nordique ancienne," in *Inter-Nord* nos. 13–14 (December 1974): 223–43. S. H. CROSS, *Slav Culture through the Ages* (Cambridge, MA, 1946). E. D. LIPSIC, *Byzanz und die Slaven* (Weimar 1951). E. V. ANIČKOV, *Jazyčestvo i drevnjaja Rus* (Saint Petersburg 1914). Z. R. DITTRICH, "Zur religiösen Ur- und Frühgeschichte der Slaven," *Jahrbücher für Geschichte Osteuropas* N.F. 9 (Wiesbaden 1961). V. V. IVANOV, "K etimologii baltijskogo i slavjanskogo nazvanii boga groma," *Voprosy slavjanskogo jazykoznanija* 3 (Moscow 1958). S. ROŽNIECKI, "Perun und Thor," *Archiv f. slav. Philologie* 23 (1901): 462–520. R. JAKOBSON, "The Slavic God Veles and his Indo-European Cognates," in *Studii linguistici in onore di V. Pisani* (Brescia 1962), 579–99. F. VYNCKE, "La divination chez les Slaves," in *La divination*, studies collected by A. Caquot and M. Leibovici, 2 vols. (Paris 1968), 1:303–31.

BALTIC MYTHS AND RELIGIOUS CATEGORIES

There is a certain mystery about the Baltic peoples, the group of tribes that settled quite early—certainly before the first millennium B.C.—on the southeast shores of the Baltic Sea. They are incontestably Indo-European. The fact that they formed a "block" between the Finno-Ugric, Germanic, and Slavic communities (although with the latter there may have been initial semi-identification) may indicate that they had to retreat, that they evolved more slowly and therefore remained much closer to their distant origins. On the other hand, the fact that they had such diverse neighbors could have caused the many interferences and confusions which have to be taken into account.

It is customary to distinguish between the Latvians, settled to the north of the Dvina, the Lithuanians, to the south of the Dvina up to the Niemen, and the Old Prussians, settled in Prussia (today Belorussia) at the mouth of the Vistula. Unfortunately, we have very few documents that might acquaint us with them, and such evidence as we have must be used with caution: we must disentangle opinions from the study of popular folklore, from reports of obviously misinformed foreign observers, and especially from reports or homilies composed by resolutely hostile clergymen. Moreover, from the thirteenth century, the Teutonic Knights enslaved the Baltic peoples, depriving them of all autonomy, and in the sixteenth century the Reformation succeeded in eliminating what remained of their originality. The Baltic peoples were nevertheless active and open tribes, and archaeology has revealed that they maintained enduring and substantial trade with the Swedes.

The general characteristics which we can extract from the rare sources on Baltic paganism are of two kinds. In the first place it appears that we are dealing with an ancient foundation, very close to Indo-European, where, in a Dumézilian perspective, the first two functions tend to be eclipsed by the third.

The Baltic peoples were dedicated to a cult of natural forces just as they are or, finally, as they are personified, emphasizing most those which restore fertility. Being agricultural tribes, they primarily revered trees, forests, fields, lakes, and rivers that their demons and their gods "inhabited." No temples were built for them: sacred forests or *alcas* took their

place. Special powers were conferred on all sorts of quadrupeds, and even on toads and snakes, in which the spirits of the domestic hearth were reputed to be incarnate. Thus a kind of tutelary animism reigned in their mental universe; *velè*, *kaukis* (dwarfs), and *laume* (feminine) were incarnate in everything which protects and gives life. As late as 1606, the Jesuit Stribing relates the Livonians made offerings "to certain trees and to certain woods. These trees are reputed to be sacred."

Among the Latvians, for example, the cult of the dead was celebrated in the sacred forests. Stribing reports a propitiatory formula addressed to the dead which says essentially, "Remember us," because, as the author specifies, the Latvians think that "souls take the form either of wolves and of bears or of gods." Thus, through the oblique line of the reincarnation or transmigration of souls in the beliefs of Baltic peoples, the veneration of natural forces is closely allied with the cult of ancestors. Either offerings were made to the dead, who were generally cremated in cemeteries according to a precise ritual, or vegetation and fields served as a kind of relay station for votive and propitiatory rites. In this way a constant circulation was established, which justified the great contempt for death that the Baltic peoples were said to have professed. So, too, since natural forces or manes were envisaged as a group, one can understand the absence of individualization which seemed to mark this paganism at an initial stage: it has a great number of collective deities, such as, among the Old Prussians, the *deïvaï*, the *kaukaï*, and the *aitvaraï*, who can be assimilated to werewolves, witches, and other demons whom the Lithuanians call the *lauma*, *deiva*, *ragana*. The constancy of incontestably Indo-European etymological themes, as in *deïvaï*, should be noted.

It is not that the first function is absent: the sun, moon, and stars were equally revered. The Old Prussians and especially the Lithuanians seem to have particularly venerated fire: they knew a variant of the famous celestial smith in the person of the Lithuanian god Telavel, who made the sun and whose giant hammer had its own cult, a detail which cannot fail to evoke the Mjöllnir of the Scandinavian Thor. Similarly, Diviriks, the rainbow, was considered divine and diverse testimony establishes that fire was the object of a very widespread cult. Fire was, moreover, closely related to some divinatory practices that were much esteemed by the Baltic peoples, practices for which there may have been a specialized caste of priests/sorcerers/diviners. The domestic hearth, already evoked and haunted by the preeminent creatures of fire, the serpent-dragons, is an aspect of the same mentality.

But it is incontestably the fertility cult that had first place in the religious preoccupations of the Baltic peoples, in the primitive form of the cult of mother goddesses, the "Mothers," *mate*, which surely goes back to a primordial earth mother goddess, indeed a sun goddess, since in these languages, as in Old Norse, the sun is feminine, its name, *saule*, also meaning "little mother." The Latvians developed a whole pantheon whose names are expressive in this regard: Laukamat (mother of the fields), Mezamat (mother of the woods), Lopemat (mother of cattle), Jurasmat (mother of the sea), Darzamat (mother of gardens), Vejamat (mother of the wind).

In summary, Baltic religion can first help us to understand what may be an Indo-European complex probably at an archaic and popular stage before the martial function was isolated and when the process of intellectualization and the emergence of an aristocracy were still only in gestation.

It is striking that at a later time, when some clear individualizations began to appear, it was still a rather vitalist domain, at an entirely vegetative stage. This is true of the only great god known to all the Baltic peoples, Perkunas, the god of the sky, especially of thunder and consequently of war, who must be a Baltic avatar of the supreme Indo-European god. His name is etymologically identical to the Sanskrit Parjanyah, Old Norse Fjörgynn, Slavic Perun or Perkun, and Greek Phorcys, all of which convey the idea of "propitious, favorable to life"; if this type of analysis is pushed to the extreme, one can establish a relationship of the same kind with Latin *quercus*, "oak." Perkunas would be the anthropomorphization of the tree which incarnates profuse and fertile life, and in this way a fundamental cult. Such would appear to be the Baltic peoples' idea of the supreme divinity. Next to Perkunas, the few other individualized divinities whose names are known to us can be seen as simple specializations of the same class of ideas: one is Zempat, who is master of the earth among the Old Prussians and whose name may indicate a Slavic influence; another is Laukosargas, guardian of the fields and protector of wheat. He should probably also be identified with the Kurke cited in a thirteenth-century source, who traditionally received the last reaped sheaf (a custom also familiar to the ancient Scandinavians), and both of them are eventually to be identified with the Lithuanian Nonadeï. It is nevertheless striking that we in no case do we get away from a fundamentally agrarian mental complex. This being so, the previously proposed idea of "forming a block" would apply to stage which is certainly far back in prehistory.

The second point to be emphasized requires less commentary and seems logically necessary. Baltic religion reveals, apparently for historical and geographical reasons, great similarity to North Germanic and Slavic paganism; several aspects of this have already been discussed.

Keeping the individualized deities in mind, we note that the Baltic people, especially the Lithuanians, recognized a strange hare god who haunted the forests, Meiden, who may be Slavic, as well as (or even more than) the Lithuanian goddess Zvoruna: the bitch. Under these circumstances one may think of totemism, as did F. Vyncke. But why not see instead, beginning with the theme of transmigration of souls discussed above, a fixation at the animal stage of a cult that was initially entirely natural and that was subject to foreign influence—Slavic in this instance? On the other hand, the preeminence which the cult seems to have had in Baltic paganism is related more clearly to the Northern Germanic world: we have already suggested various illustrations of this. Perhaps, as among the old Scandinavians, Baltic religion simply developed from a combination of rites and cultic acts which were charged with meaning in harmony with a vision of a world which was not very intellectual and not very anthropomorphic. Three powerful moments can be distinguished in this cult: the sacrifice or offering of goats, sows, oxen, horses (preferably black among the Old Prussians), and even human beings; divination (involving fire as well as water), which seems to appear more in inclement latitudes than elsewhere, in a precarious historical and geographical framework where the future—of the tribe, clan, crops—is more uncertain, more in danger than elsewhere; and the feast, or *snike*, whose function was to restrain the soul of the community when it was warmed by mead and which was the occasion for games and dances which were undoubtedly orgiastic and, later, energetically forbidden by Christianity.

As in all places where a primitive mentality reigned, and especially where the circumstances of time and place compelled immediate action, Fate had, among the Baltic peoples as among the North Germans, considerable importance in the religious universe. The very vocabulary established in the beginning a quasi-genetic relationship between the *laume* of the Old Prussians, tutelary entities attached to water and to forests, the Lithuanian *laima*, more clearly charged with watching over the destinies of the individual and the clan, and the Latvian goddess Laima, "that is, Fortune or the goddess of happiness," as P. Einhorn says. It is remarkable that the Lithuanian word *laima* signifies both happiness and Fate, like the Slavic *rozanica* and the Old Norse *hamingja* or *gaefa*. Such coincidences cannot be fortuitous.

Thus Baltic religion, although little known, nevertheless presents a double interest: it carries us back in time to an Indo-European stage that is not much developed, and it manifests interesting phenomena of a union of North Germanic and Slavic mentalities. Essentially, it brings to light a religious attitude which is clearly archaic in spirit, a religious attitude in which Fate, conjured or revealed by means of communal demonstrations, shapes a cult of nature and of the dead: life, still rough and primitive here, is, as it were, worshiped in a raw state. It has not yet been made into law, order, or science.

R.B./d.f.

BIBLIOGRAPHY

J. ANTONIEWICZ, "Prusowie we wczasnym średniowieczu i zarys ich kultury materialno," in *Pomorze wczesnośredniowieczne* (Warsaw 1958), 121–59. A. BRÜCKNER, "Litauische Religion," in *Die Religion in Geschichte und Gegenwart*, 3 (Berlin 1929). P. SCHMIDT, "Die Mythologie der Letten," in *Die Letten* (Riga 1930), 205ff.

THE MYTHOLOGY OF ALBANIA

Although Albanian mythology has not yet been the subject of a monograph, it has been treated in many essays and articles on linguistics, folklore, and ethnology. This mythology can be considered part of the Balkan pagan tradition. The monotheistic religions which were superimposed on it—Roman Catholic in the North, Orthodox in the South, Islamic in the country as a whole—had little effect on its nature. The history of the Albanians, whose origins date back to the first Indo-European migrations into the Balkans, is of a succession of invasions by the people around them: Romans in ancient times, Slavs, Greeks, and Italians during the Middle Ages, Turks at the beginning of the modern era. One would therefore expect Albanian mythology to be fairly syncretic. Foreign layers can be identified along an easily recognizable axis: the cult of the spirit of the tribe.

The divinities of this mythology are almost all pagan. There are oreads (*nuset e malit*, literally, the "nymphs of the mountains") and naiads (*këshetë*), as well as sylphs (*shtojza-valle*), and fairies (*zanë*). There are baleful giants (*baloz, katallā*), but also gnomes who delight in teasing people (*thopç*). One also encounters werewolves (*karkanxhol*) and a variation on Tom Thumb (*kacilmic*). Monsters (*përbindsh*) abound: ogres (*gogol*), Hydras (*kuçedër*), chimeras (*lubi*). Metamorphoses are common: men are transformed into stags, bears, and owls; women into weasels, cuckoos, and turtledoves. Divinities of the home may have human form (*nana e votrës*, "the mother of the hearth") or animal form (*vitore*, a type of serpent). Animals were sacrificed (women in earlier times) on the foundations of a building; charms were used (for example, to make a man impotent). There were chants for exorcism and others for rain. It was the custom to shoot at the eclipsed moon to scare away the wolves that were attacking it. Magical objects—mirrors, amulets, rings—played an important role. The Albanians believed in the Evil Eye (*syni i keq*), premonitory dreams, the power of stones and herbs, but especially in the power of heroes.

The cult of heroes, attested by a long national tradition reflected in the popular epic as well as in common law, has retained its mythic character in certain cantons of northern Albania. Protected by steep mountains, their inhabitants were able to resist Roman and Slavic colonizations and even kept a certain autonomy during the Turkish domination. These northern shepherds, mostly Catholic, continue to call themselves *Uk*, "wolf," *Dash*, "sheep," *Shpend*, "bird," and *Sokol*, "falcon"; they worship fire (to spit in the fire is taboo); swear "by the Sky and the Earth"; mourn their dead by scratching their faces according to a ritual which is part of a dance; and believe in genies of localities, and in spirits, demons, witches, and vampires. Totemism and animism mingle with classical myths and medieval legends. Odysseus and Perseus have their equivalents. The Albanian Polyphemus is called *katallā*, in memory of the atrocities of the Catalan mercenaries in the fourteenth century. The *zanë*, the patroness of heroes, is even etymologically close to Diana (the Roman goddess is accompanied by a doe, the Albanian goddess by a female wild goat), while her powers are similar to those of the Slavic fairy, the *vila*. Even the name *shtojzavalle* is a case of pagan-Christian syncretism: "Shotj, Zo(t), vallet" can be translated as: "Multiply, God, their choirs."

Many of the pagan beliefs also occur among other Balkan peoples, and some are of Latin or perhaps Celtic origin. In what sense does Albanian mythology show its own physiognomy, its own distinctive characteristics?

This mythology has no gods. Its divinities are secondary and have no names of their own, or only a collective name. People made oaths by heaven and earth, and the sun and the moon are invoked. But these are only personifications of elements or physical objects, not of beings. Among the elements, the earth is dominant. The highest accolade of a hero or heroine is *burri i dheut*, "brave man of the earth," or *e bukura e dheut*, "beautiful woman of the earth." An "oath on the stone," *beja më gur*, is a solemn oath (Gjeçov §534). A person who swears on a stone will be petrified if he breaks his oath (the *zana* had the power to petrify with a glance). Piles of stones (*muranë*) are found where someone has been killed in a vendetta (Çabej 360). And stones are thrown to ease fatigue (*me lanë pritesen*).

Another distinctive trait is the absence of an afterlife. The sky is not at all celestial, and there is no hell. Belief in ghosts (*kukuth, lugat, vurkollak*) is widespread, but the ghost is a soul in pain, rejected by the earth because of some serious misdeed. The soul is a shadow (*hie*), or a specter (*abe*), a corporal husk with a remnant of materiality (it can lift a weight).

Albanian mythology, filled with fairies and demons but without gods and without eschatology, and with a purely negative conception of the soul, is thus completely terrestrial. It is organized around an ethical bipolarity of good and evil. On one side there is the monster, the Hydra (*kulshedër* or *kuçedër, mamadragë*), represented as a serpent with seven heads, who dries up the waters and poisons the air. On the other side is the mythical hero who faces the monster in its lair and kills it. In the South, where the power of the sultan came to replace that of the Byzantine emperor, the champion is often noble ("the king's son"), whereas in the North he is the son of the people, born a *drangue* (from "dragon"). The dragon-man has wings under his arms and can fly. One can recognize here the myth of Hercules fighting the Hydra, which then becomes the myth of Saint George and the dragon. Saint George is very popular in Albania, and his feast coincides with the arrival of spring. George ("Gjergj") is also the name of the hero who frees his country from a "black monster from the sea" in what is perhaps the most beautiful Albanian rhapsody (KK 5).

The monument of Albanian mythology is the cycle of the rhapsodies of the North, which exalts a strongly ethnic conception of heroic life. The main heroes of this cycle, Muj and Halil, have Muslim names borrowed from Bosnian epic poems, from which they also borrowed their meter (rhapsodies are sung to the sound of the *lahutë*, the Albanian *gusla*). But the foreign elements do not affect the indigenous undertone of these mythical songs. Muj is a shepherd to whom the fairies of the mountain, in exchange for a service he performed for them, gave superhuman strength—he can uproot oak trees (KK 7). Another rhapsody attributes this power to his talent as a hunter: he was able to capture the three goats with golden horns in which the powers of the fairies were hidden (KK 1). Muj slays his enemies, the Slavs, but not without suffering misfortunes. One rhapsody shows him seriously wounded, accompanied by his guardian spirit, the *orë*, between a serpent who takes care of him and a wolf who guards him (KK 23). When he dies, the enemy comes to challenge him in his tomb. He awakes, and with a bird as intermediary, he appeals for help to Halil, who kills the Slav and exhumes his brother (KK 32). Muj returns to life. One day, he tests the quality of his gunpowder on his own hand.

When he sees his pierced hand, he knows that his time has come. He disappears from the earth, like Oedipus at Colonus, to await patiently the return of the age of heroes on earth (KK preface).

Vico conceived of the history of humanity as a cyclic process moving through three phases: theological, heroic, and human. The Albanian mythic mentality touched lightly on the first in order to revel in the second, from which it refused to emerge. Muj is far from being the only representative of this mentality. Another example is the national hero himself, Georges (Gjergj) Castrioti, called Scanderbeg (1405–68). The Albanian humanist Marinus Barletius, who wrote the first romanticized history of this hero (around 1510), tells that his mother thought she was pregnant with a dragon whose body would recover all of Albania and whose mouth would devour the Turks. The people elaborated on this myth, making Scanderbeg into a titan who could embrace "fifty people" and whose mustache measured "four hands" across. He threw rocks "as big as houses" at his enemies and stopped the waters of the river "with a kick" to prevent the Turks from crossing. He was invulnerable, having been born "covered," that is, "wrapped in the placenta" (*lē me kēmishë*). His horse flew from rock to rock, leaving, when he landed, the marks of his shoes—still visible today. And when Scan-

derbeg died, the people disinterred him to make talismans from his bones (Sca 113; 116.113; 24; 25; 127; 206).

A.P./d.b.

BIBLIOGRAPHY

J. G. VON HAHN, *Albanesiche Studien* 1–3 (Jena 1854); *Griechische und albanische Märchen* 1–2 (Leipzig 1864). HOLGER PEDERSEN, *Zur albanesischen Volkskunde* (Copenhagen 1898). MAXIMILIAN LAMBERTZ, *Albanische Märchen und andere Texte zur albanischen Volkskunde* (Vienna 1922). NORBERT JOKL, *Linguistisch-kulturhistorische Untersuchungen aus dem Bereiche des Albanischen* (Berlin and Leipzig 1923). B. PALAJ and D. KURTI, "Le trésor de la nation," 2: "Chants épiques et légendes," in *Visaret e Kombit* 2: *Kangë kreshnikësh e legenda* (Tiranë 1937); abbrev. KK. SHTJEFËN GJEÇOV, *Codice di Lek Dukagjini ossia diritto consuetudinario delle montagne d'Albania*, P. Dodaj, trans. (Rome 1941). EQREM ÇABEJ, "Albanische Volkskunde," *Südost-Forschungen* 25 (1966): 333–87 (contains an almost complete list of divinities and monsters). Authors Q. HAXHIHASANI and Z. SAKO, "Contes et chants populaires sur Scanderbeg," in *Tregime dhe këngë popullore për Skenderbeun* (Tiranë 1967); abbrev. *Sca*. A. PIPA, *Rusha* (Munich 1968) (an epic poem containing mythic elements). M. CAMAJ, *Legjenda* (Rome 1964) (lyric poems based on legends and myths).

THE RELIGION AND MYTHS OF THE GEORGIANS OF THE MOUNTAINS

The plains of Georgia were evangelized in the fifth century, but the Georgians living in the high valleys of the Caucasus chain were converted to Christianity only ten centuries later, and in a superficial way. The paganism of the Christian kingdom is very little known to us, through brief texts in the classics and in national chronicles. It survived into the modern period but only in a fragmented state, without unity, heavily influenced by Christianity, or else in the form of beliefs and practices that are simply folkloric.

The mountain Georgians, on the other hand, preserved a rich and well-organized religious system to the beginning of the twentieth century, with differentiated cults and a mythology that continued to be productive. This conservatism can certainly be explained by geographic and historical conditions, but above all by the existence for more than two thousand years of a priestly class with an orally transmitted body of knowledge. Even today it is possible to meet old men on the mountain slopes of the Caucasus who were sacrificers in their youth, before the First World War, at a time when the essential power was in the hands of the pagan priests. This eminent position of the priestly function is not new: it was noted by Strabo in the first century B.C. in Iberia, present-day central and eastern Georgia. In the social hierarchy of the ancient Iberians, priests occupied the second place, immediately after the king (Strabo 11.3).

It is therefore essentially the religion of the mountain Georgians that we will be studying here.

I. Cosmology and Basic Concepts

1. *Morige, supreme god of the Georgian pantheon.* The structure of the Georgian pantheon is simple: at the top, the

creator god; lower down, local or specialized divinities; between the two, an intermediate god, K'viria.

Despite his preeminence, and probably because of it, the supreme god has little place in the popular imagination. He figures in only a single myth, a very important one, since it is about the creation of the world. This is how a Georgian mountaineer told it at the end of the nineteenth century:

> God and the demon were originally brother and sister. The sister made God unhappy; that is why the brother cursed the sister and left her. The sister turned into a demon, tried to cause obstacles for God, and succeeded. God created the sky out of a net; the demon, to irritate God, created mice, and made them gnaw holes in the net: God created cats to eat the mice. He also created the vine. This lovely creation of God displeased the demon, and he created the goat and made it eat the vine. Challenge followed challenge. To eat the goats, God created wolves, and so forth. Woman was also created by the demon. This is why mountaineers think it is undignified to show respect for women; and husband and wife sleep separately and only meet in secret.
>
> The other divinities were created by God. In the beginning they were men without sin. They were all massacred by the demons, and that is why God turned them into celestial divinities. (Cited in Charachidzé 1968, p. 279)

This indigenous text expresses two major ideological elements of Georgian religion and mythology. (1) The universe is divided into two antagonistic series, one wild and demonic, the other social and divine; every being in creation, however humble, belongs to one or the other. (2) In the mythic order, Georgian religion can conceive of no foundation that does not entail a sibling couple.

After creating the world, Morige (whose name means "the ordainer") does not govern it directly. He is only the guarantor of its functioning. Seated on a golden throne in the highest heaven, he ensures the continuance of the order that

Pagan temple in the mountains of Georgia, still in use at the beginning of the twentieth century. Architecture of this type has been known since antiquity.

he has instituted. Without intervening himself, he manifests his will in the smallest details of human activity through intermediary divinities. For example, at the beginning of each year he divides "golden sheaves" among the local divinities. These sheaves constitute a sort of heavenly pledge for the "fleshly ones" (men) in exchange for the year's harvest.

2. *Georgian cosmology.* In Georgian cosmology, the universe consists of three superposed worlds, or spaces. They are, from high to low: (1) the space above the earth (the celestial world); (2) the earthly space (the surface of the earth); (3) the space below the earth (the netherworld). On the highest level are the gods; on the lowest, the demons and dragons; between the two, in the middle world, men, animals, plants, etc. There are two bodies of water: celestial water on level 1, subterranean water on level 3. The same is true for fire, which is divided into two opposed (often antagonistic) substances: the fire above, on the celestial level, manifested to men in the form of lightning; the fire below, on the subterranean level, perceptible in seismic phenomena.

The only entities or substances that have an ontological status are those belonging either to the superior level (heaven) or the inferior level (the netherworld). Between these two extremes, the space familiar to human beings, the surface of the earth, can only be a place of passage, of mediation, or of meeting. Thus the beings who people the middle world have no essence in themselves; they are nothing but emanations from above or below, or else their unions. This principle applies to all the provinces of existence.

Thus the water used by men, the hydrosphere, results either from a leveling of the underground body of water or from a spillover from the celestial water. In the same way the fire that humans use, the hearth, simply embodies the mediation between the two extreme levels.

Humanity is no exception to this mechanism. According to a variant of the myth of creation, in the beginning the gods lived alone on earth with the demons, whom they continually fought. Exhausted, they went up to heaven, leaving in their place men (*viri*, males), who could not resist the demons. The gods therefore hunted the demons down, forcing them to flee underground. The demons in turn left women behind them. Thus men and women are only emanations of, or substitutes for, the gods above and the demons below, respectively.

The existence of the human species and its perpetuation through marriage are due to the union of the celestial and the subterranean. The terrestrial fire is exactly the same: conditioned by its double origin, both divine and demonic, it too only survives because of the hearth, which occupies a position and function identical to those of marriage. This equivalence is made manifest in the extremely rich marriage rites, as well as in a multitude of specific actions expressing the link between man and the fire above, and woman and the fire below.

The sun makes its voyage between the two extreme worlds, the celestial and the subterranean, between the water above and the water below. Night results from the sun's fall into the underground body of water, from which it emerges at dawn and rises up to the "lakes of heaven." This is why only the otter can withstand the thrice-repeated shock of the rays of the sun at twilight, when the water of rivers and lakes is covered with gold (a human eye could not stand it); and if at this precise moment one plunges an otter skin into the sea, it is sure to come out spangled with gold.

The moon makes the same journey as the sun, but in the opposite direction and rhythm. Its nocturnal emergence out of the subterranean water is expressed in the following belief: the trout sees the first moon, the frog the second, and man the third.

The moon and the sun are, respectively, brother and sister.

The light of dawn is independent of the sun's light. It is produced by the morning star, conceived of as a personified entity, an auxiliary spirit who controls summer and winter but is himself subject to the goddess Tamar, who holds him captive.

3. *Possession.* Georgian paganism is a revealed religion. But unlike other, better-known systems, its revelation does not take place at the beginning of historical time by means of speech that is preserved orally or in writing. It is continually taking place, through the course of general or daily human history, depending on human needs or divine will. The means for this repeated revelation is the possession of a human being by a god. Following a complex process, a divinity, a Hat'i, takes possession of the soul of a human being (usually a man, but for certain Hat'i a woman), who from that time on will be a *Kadag*, a permanent, officially possessed person, a sort of shaman. When the *Kadag* goes into a trance, on the occasion of a religious ritual or an event marking individual or collective life, he speaks, and it is then the god who is speaking through his mouth. This is why a number of sacred texts or texts with a strong religious weight are formulated in the first person; it is the god who is speaking. He tells his own adventures, resolves problems that are brought before him, or foretells the immediate future.

This prophesying takes place, not in everyday language,

but in a secret language, "the language of the Hat'i." (The "Hat'i language" is also mentioned in a different context, that of Ossetian mythology. Scholars, quick to respond with enthusiasm, immediately took this for a historical survival of the Hatti, i.e., Hittite, language.) It is then necessary to translate the god's message. For example, the ram is called *rkazhangiani*, "rusty-horned"; the sun, *mzekali*, "the sun woman." Man is called *verchlis burtvi*, "the ball of gold"; the fields of the sanctuary are *korokroni*, "the sheaves of gold." If the god declares, "Morige" (the supreme god) "has entrusted me with the horned head of a mountain sheep," he is predicting the death of a man of the clan. If he says, "The sun woman has draped my sheaves of gold," there will be a great drought. But if the sentence is changed to "Sun woman the magnificent has sat on high, she has draped my sheaves of gold," it foretells the destruction of the harvests by heat. The imminent blindness of a member of the clan is announced by the words, "The veiled eyes of a sieve of gold."

The phenomenon of possession plays a decisive role in the religious, social, and political life of the human group. Indeed, the priest-sacrificer himself, a different person from the shaman, is also chosen by divine election, his choice being made manifest through possession. His role is not limited to the performance of religious rites; he is at the same time the political and military chief of the community.

4. *Sacrifice.* Sacrifice (as opposed to possession) is the most common and the least dramatic way of communicating with the world of the gods. The sacrifices which the community must perform, from the humblest to the most spectacular, are extremely numerous and costly. They monopolize a considerable portion of the goods produced by these generally quite poor societies. They consist partly of candles, grain in the form of large flat loaves of bread, and beer in impressive quantities. Beer is offered to the gods, while distilled grain spirits are exclusively reserved for the dead (in plains Georgia, beer is replaced by wine).

But the most important part of the sacrifice is the blood offerings. As part of the performance of the ritual, victims of all kinds—roosters, lambs, sheep, kids, goats, young and mature bulls—were formerly (until the end of the nineteenth century and perhaps even more recently) slaughtered in profusion. It was important that blood flow abundantly. Here is what was said, three-quarters of a century ago, by a mountain Georgian:

> It is obligatory to offer a blood sacrifice of cattle. To satisfy the Hat'i, the blood of the victim must flow abundantly. As soon as the blood gushes forth, it should flow into the cups and onto the ritual objects. The priest purifies his hands and arms with the blood, sprinkling his forehead with fresh blood. (Cited in Charachidzé 1968, p. 290)

Those present, the worshipers, try to get their bodies as bloody as possible. At the sanctuary of Lashari, for example, pits lined with stones are filled with blood, and the worshipers soak their clothes in the blood and put them back on afterwards. We should note that, contrary to the practice in many religions, here it is the still-quivering and bleeding victim that is dedicated and consecrated to the gods, and not the cooked meat.

This blood intoxication, inseparable from Georgian rituals, is not a recent phenomenon. It is already attested in the earliest chronicles recording the religious practices current before the conversion of the kingdom to Christianity, i.e., before the fourth century. We can read, in the "Conversion of Georgia":

> The mountains of impiety are now destroyed and the water of the rivers is now calmed; the blood of children sacrificed to the demons has ceased to flow.

And the first Christian king, Mirian, declares at the moment of his official conversion:

> To horrible idols our fathers immolated their children and the innocent population of this country. And some of our fathers mowed down their children like hay to please the idols. And especially on these two mountains of Armaz and Zaden, whose stones are still soaked with the blood of little children!

It can be seen that blood sacrifices are not new in Georgian religion; indeed, in the beginning they were human sacrifices. This is confirmed in other passages of the chronicle:

> King Rev (before the conversion), during his reign, permitted no one to sacrifice boys; for before him boys were sacrificed in honor of the idols. Once he was king, no one sacrificed boys to the idols; for this he substituted the sacrifice of sheep and cows.

5. *Ritual incest.* After possession and blood sacrifice, ritual incest is the third indispensable phenomenon for an understanding of Georgian religion, of which it is one of the ideological foundations. As is shown in the creation myth (cf. § I.1), Georgian thought divides the universe into two antagonistic series, one divine and the other demonic. Man belongs to the first series, woman to the second. Their union as a couple thus involves insurmountable difficulties; this is the reason for the disharmony of the conjugal couple. The fraternal couple, however, escapes this curse. For, in conformity with the myth of creation, the brother (God) and the sister (the future demon) live in harmony and on the same celestial level until the sister separates from her brother. The same is the case in daily life: as a sister, before leaving her brother to marry, woman is not yet demonic. The only thinkable couple is thus a brother and sister. But this is not a viable couple, and at any rate it remains precarious.

This is the source of the following beautiful and tragic custom, which no Georgian mountaineer can avoid. It consists in the circumvention of both the conceptual impossibility of a conjugal couple and the practical impossibility of a fraternal couple. It plays a considerable role in ancient Georgian culture, for it is manifested at the same time on the levels of society, ritual, and myth.

A young man and a girl (who are usually barely adolescent) fall in love. They are, from this time on and until their marriage, "brother-husband" and "sister-wife." These are official statuses, sanctioned by the society. Their love then develops during nocturnal meetings. They meet at the stable or in the mountains, and sleep together under the same shepherd's cloak. But these relations, based on sincere passion—unlike marriage, which excludes love—are doomed to tragedy: since they belong to the same community, these young people may never marry and must sooner or later separate forever. It is, indeed, this precariousness which makes the couple provisionally acceptable to the community and, through it, to Georgian religious thought.

This sociological incest is repeated on the level of myth: a number of divine couples (Lashari and Tamar, Giorgi and Samdzimari, for example) are conceived according to this model, or, on the other hand, since there is no historical preeminence in this domain, they remain inseparably united. It is the gods, at least some of them, who are supposed to have founded the custom. This is why there is also a corresponding ritual: a number of religious ceremonies (those of K'op'ala and of the Hat'i, cited above) require the unmarried worshipers to perform their "incestuous" practices within the sanctuary itself, during the night when the sacred rites are performed. While this cultural obligation has been likened to the hetairism of Oriental religions, this is a false comparison: the Georgian phenomenon is fundamentally different, since it is not sacred prostitution but artificial incest.

The custom, along with the conceptions on which it is founded, has exercised a powerful hold on the literary and popular production of the Georgian imagination. In the epic literature of the twelfth century, it left its mark on the structure of the great poem "The Man in the Tiger Skin," in which the four main characters form two couples, "incestuous" couples according to the social norms of the epoch. It is on the basis of the same model that the popular imagination represents the relations among a number of the great names of Georgian history, in particular Queen Tamar and her son Lasha Giorgi, thought of as "sister-wife" and "brother-husband."

II. The Main Divine Figures

1. *K'viria, administrator of the "dry."* K'viria, whose name is Christian in origin, is not involved in any mythical adventures, probably because of his universal vocation. He represents "the power of God," which he actualizes on the human level. He is also called "administrator of the dry," that is, of the earth in opposition to the celestial world. Alone of all the Georgian divinities, he has the privilege of "pitching his tent in the divine enclosure"; this is why he is also called *mek'arve*, "he who has a tent." The tent symbolizes the building where justice is rendered, for K'viria is the god of justice, whether for the benefit of men or to their detriment. In the latter case, if a human group has displeased God, K'viria falls upon them at the head of a detachment of Iessaul (a term of Cossack origin, the chief of a detachment suggesting the idea of repression in the Caucasus). The Iessaul are celestial wolves who bring sickness and devastation with them. If their howling is heard on the horizon, everyone bows to the earth and prays fervently.

2. *The Hat'i, local and specialized divinities.* On the lower level teems the crowd of gods or spirits who are directly connected with human communities of all sizes: tribe, clan, lineage, village, and community. These divinities, who numbered several hundred at the beginning of the twentieth century, are named either Dzhuar, "Cross," Saghmto, "Divinity," or, most often, Hat'i. This term properly signifies "that which is traced" and "that which represents something," that is, "sign." The sign is applied indifferently to the divinity itself, to its concrete manifestation which is perceptible to human beings, i.e., its symbol (image, object, real or imaginary animal), and finally to the place where it is worshiped, its sanctuary.

The Hat'i maintain two types of relations with humans: unmediated relations, through possession, and mediated relations, through sacrificial rites.

3. *Givargi, the Saint George of the mountains.* Givargi, despite the similarity of name and of several traits, differs profoundly from the Saint George of the Georgian plains. Enjoying great favor—his sanctuaries number in the dozens—he is striking for his multiple and polymorphic character. This quantitative and qualitative particularity does not result from external historical circumstances, but forms a part of his profound nature. His function implies that he is coextensive and congruent with all the wild spaces outside society, outside tamed and socialized territory (homes, cultivated fields, human creations). Nevertheless, he is not a god of the wilds, of the *Wildnis*, like Rudra in India, for example. His role is to put wild spaces at the disposition of man, protecting individuals or groups which go into this domain foreign to culture and therefore full of dangers (wild beasts, physical cataclysms, demons, and monsters).

From this are derived his multiplicity and his polymorphy (characteristics specific to the space of the wild), as well as his affinities with nature, with high mountains, running waters, alpine pastures, lonely trails. His vocation is also specified by the particular services which men expect from him: the protection of shepherds (though without any intervention in the activities of breeding), of travelers, of bandits and robbers (highly honorable professions in the Caucasus, where we find, for example, a Cherkess tribe that calls itself "the cattle thieves," Bjedougues).

Givargi is the incarnation of the use of wild nature by society. It is in this respect that he is the patron of two animal societies that wander freely through natural space, bees and wolves. Protector of beekeepers, who go into the forest to gather honey or swarms of bees, and of bees, whose social and nomadic character is obvious, he is also master of the wolves, which mountain Georgians regard not as a zoological species, but as the animal replica of human society (cf. § III).

Patron of travelers, Givargi is conceived of as a traveler himself. He is often addressed as "traveling angel." On the level of myth, this characteristic is transposed in the form of "stranger."

Givargi comes from a foreign, distant, and usually hostile land (Persia, Armenia, Tartary . . .). He keeps his foreign, even hostile, aspect even in his epiphanies: when he manifests himself to humans, he usually does so in the guise (or at least the clothes) of a Chechen warrior. Now the Chechen are fierce bandits and have always been the archenemies of the mountain Georgians.

In western Georgia (Svanetia), the god's affinities with the wild spaces are made manifest in the ritual itself. This takes place in the high mountains, far from all buildings, and its sacrificial victims come not from the cattle of the sanctuary, but from nomadic herds.

4. *Saint George of the Georgian plains.* Saint George (a pagan spirit under a Christian name, as is often the case in the Caucasus) is the only divinity whose worship has been more or less preserved in plains Georgia. There he holds an eminent place next to Christ, god of the dead, and Saint Elias, the spirit of the lightning (like *Watsilla* in Ossetia). Possession plays an important part in his rituals, but here, unlike in the mountains (cf. § I.3), the possessed are, by preference, women. The god seizes their souls, not, as in the mountains, in order to enter into communication with humans, but to punish them for an individual or collective sin.

The cult is marked above all by a ritual sequence which had its counterpart two thousand years earlier, in a Caucasian practice reported by Strabo. He tells us that on the borders of Iberia there was a temple to the moon that had a large number of hierodules (slaves of the god), "many of whom are possessed by the gods and prophesy. The most strongly possessed among them wanders alone in the forests; the priest captures him, binds him with sacred chains, and feeds him abundantly for one year. After this, offered as a sacrifice to the god, he is killed with other victims. The sacrifice takes place as follows: holding the sacred spear which, according to the rule, is used for human sacrifice, a man emerges from the crowd and pierces his side to the heart, with an expert thrust. The way the body falls reveals certain omens, which are publicly proclaimed. The body is then taken to a preordained place, and all those who are in need of purification tread on it" (Strabo 11.4.7).

Less than a century ago the following ritual, in honor of Saint George, was still being practiced in eastern Georgia (the former Iberia). Two women possessed by Saint George crawl around the church on their knees, with heavy sacred chains, which belong to the sanctuary, hanging from their necks. During the night, one of the possessed women, "the slave of Saint George," lies down in front of the western door of the church, her head to the north, her feet to the south, blocking the entrance. The priest and the worshipers must pass over the possessed woman, treading heavily on her, and she must keep silent. Priest and worshipers then perform rites to purify themselves of their past misdeeds and to free themselves from their slavery.

There is a striking similarity in the gestures, elements, and final aims of the cult: possessed people in chains, trampling, purification. All that is missing in the Georgian case is the killing. But the possessed person, inert and silent under the

The chain worn around the necks of Georgians possessed during their religious rituals. The practice has not changed for two thousand years, as witnessed by Strabo.

feet of the worshipers, strongly suggests the trampled corpse described by Strabo. We know, moreover, that human sacrifices were still being practiced in Georgia during the first centuries A.D.: the modern ritual probably represents this in an attenuated and symbolic form. This is confirmed by the fact that in another sanctuary of Saint George the possessed woman is struck with a sacred banner (a spear with pieces of cloth attached to its shaft) by a man who specializes in this function, but who is not the priest, exactly as in the practice described by Strabo, in which the possessed victim is chained and struck by a person expert in this, but different from the priest.

It is thus likely that the present-day cult of Saint George at least partly represents the survival of rites practiced two thousand years earlier. It is possible that we are dealing with an ancient moon god, but if this is so, the theological content has been lost. Only the ritual forms remain, a common phenomenon in the process of religious erosion.

5. *K'op'ala, the lightning god.* K'op'ala, the lightning god, like storm spirits all over the world, is also a mighty warrior and a demon killer (like the Indian Indra, or the Ossetic Batraz). This triple vocation assures K'op'ala of great popularity among the mountain Georgians. It is he who—aided by the god Iahsar, who represents one of his hypostases—drove away from the surface of the earth the demons who were exterminating humanity (cf. § I). Like the Vedic Indra, he is armed with a mace to which he is bound in close solidarity, to the point that he and his mace are often confused and one is invoked for the other. When the mace is manifested to human perception, its action is accompanied by tempests and the crashing of rocks. K'op'ala also has an iron bow made especially for him by the blacksmith god P'irkusha. In physical vigor he is the strongest of all the Hat'i, triumphing in the gods' sports in the divine enclosure in the skies.

K'op'ala plays a role of the first importance in the phenomena of possession, through a normal extension of his service as slayer of demons: he alone has the power to drive off the most stubborn demons when they have seized the soul of a human. The central part of his worship involves the curing of "diseases of the soul," especially of various forms of madness. He is also in charge of "freeing" the souls of those who have been hanged, drowned, or buried in avalanches, since these souls are materially trapped in the corpse and are easy prey for demons.

During the nocturnal vigil that marks the ceremony celebrated in honor of K'op'ala, the young men and women divide up into "brother-husband" and "sister-wife" couples. During this night they are expected to indulge in amorous activities. Couples who avoided this activity would be heavily punished by the mace of K'op'ala (cf. § I.5).

It is, moreover, to a couple of this kind that the myth attributes the founding of the sanctuary. The boy and the girl argue over the god, who has appeared to them in the form of a flying image connected to the sky by a thread that breaks. The boy gets the thread, the girl the winged image. She hides, pursued by the people of the village, who want to kill her. In the end she founds the sanctuary and establishes the rites and religious rules, but she does not officiate herself; she holds only the function of shaman, which is distinct from that of priest. After her death, the worshipers cannot carry her body away, even with the help of all their oxen, and they bury her on the spot; this constitutes a double sacrilege: no dead bodies and no women are allowed in the holy enclosure!

This mythical inversion of the social and religious values

that operate in reality should be understood in connection with one of the principal functions of K'op'ala: people bring him women with serious psychological problems; he cures them by taking possession of their souls. This practice, too, represents the contrary, if not of the rule, at least of the norm: in general, women are possessed by goddesses and men by gods.

6. *Lashari and Tamar.* The god Lashari and the goddess Tamar, who have distinct but connected sanctuaries, are thought of as an incestuous fraternal couple. They are credited with instituting the human custom of the brother-husband, which they themselves practice on the celestial level.

Lashari's name, which is of Abkhazian origin, means "the bright one" (from Abkhazian *a-lashara*, "light"). But he is above all a warrior, and he intervenes in all the great tribal wars carried on by the mountain Georgians. As a warrior, he spends most of his time traveling around in the world, both in his divine form and in the material form of a concrete symbol, the great banner of the sanctuary in which he is incarnate, and which special priests carry into battle. On the other hand, the god's continued presence in his sanctuary is marked by a sacred oak, the site of Lashari's mystical habitation and the visible sign of his presence.

In earlier days a huge oak grew inside the sacred enclosure, an oak whose top was bound to heaven by a golden cable or chain, which served for the comings and goings of the gods between the earth and the celestial world. But one day a foreign prince captured the sanctuary and succeeded in toppling the magic tree, not without difficulty: at each blow of the ax, the wood chips went back to where they were cut from the tree. Finally the prince had the trunk sprinkled with the blood of a black cat, and after this it was possible to cut it down. But the falling tree did not bring the golden cable down with it; the cable "sprang forth humming" (or "hissing like a serpent") "toward the sky." This is why Lashari has the epithet "Angel of the Tree."

During the last century, Lashari's sanctuary was known throughout Georgia for its rich treasury and the magnificence of its sacrifices. His priests sacrificed hundreds of oxen there. At the beginning of the twentieth century, dozens of victims were still being slaughtered, in such numbers that the sacrificers had to work in relays to rest their tired hands. The blood flowed into a large pit dug for this purpose. Worshipers "guilty of a sin" and the mentally ill soaked their clothing in the blood-filled pit to purify themselves.

The goddess Tamar, unlike her brother-husband Lashari, is noteworthy for her distant, almost inaccessible, character. Storks and nightingales brought the rocks and sand needed to build her palace on an unknown peak, so high that no one has ever seen it. This distancing into the highest regions of the sky is explained by Tamar's affinities with the sun, expressed throughout the mythology. She rides on a serpent with a golden saddle, a golden bit, and a golden bridle. We should note that in the Caucasus the serpent is a Uranian, rather than a chthonic, animal, despite its crawling and its habitat: the Cherkess, for instance, have a celestial serpent-horse (Shyble) for their storm god. Tamar keeps Morning Star, the master of winter, as her slave: "Morning Star, the creator of the summer and winter, was the prisoner of Tamar, who kept him in chains. This is why winter was unknown during her reign" (citation in Charachidzé 1968, p. 685). But one day Morning Star escaped and flew away to the sky. The sky immediately opened up and snow began to fall.

Tamar subdued the sea, in a way typical of solar myths: "She ordered the wind to strew the sea with straw and hay,

she poured gasoline on the sea and lit it. The sea was in terrible pain and made a great movement, shaking from the depths to the heights. And the sea surrendered" (citation in Charachidzé 1968, p. 682). Even Tamar's "loves" have an evident solar connotation. She was an eternal virgin and lived hidden from the light in her inaccessible palace. One day a sunbeam came through a crack and struck her. She became pregnant. A year later a boy was born, whom she abandoned in the forest in order to "avoid shame." He was fed by a doe and became a king or an angel.

Tamar's mode of action does not differ from that of the sun: when her human worshipers displease her, she punishes them "by setting fire to the sheaves of the barley fields, the horns of the cattle, and the branches of trees."

7. *The Giorgi-Samdzimari couple.* The sanctuary of Hahmat'i is consecrated to a divine couple, the god Giorgi (another Saint George, but distinct from the others) and the demidemon Samdzimari.

Giorgi, as befits a divinity who may retain the memory of Saint George the horseman, is the patron of stallions and watches over the birth of colts. Similarly, but without affecting fertility in the strict sense, he decides the sex of the human embryo and thus determines the birth of boys. But he owes his fame chiefly to the myth of the foundation of his sanctuary, for the mountain people see in this story the history and the justification of the origins of the society as it exists, with its coherence and its tensions, its rules and its excesses. In particular, they see in it the creation and explanation of marriage, an institution which is certainly indispensable for survival, but one which this culture, which privileges the incestuous couple, finds very difficult to conceive and accept.

Giorgi decides to go to ravage the underground kingdom of the Kadzhi, who are ferocious demon blacksmiths. Their whole country is merely an enormous smithy. He gets his blood brothers, the most warlike of the gods, to go with him, as well as a human helper with shamanic powers, notably the power of disincarnation; his soul abandons his body, which rots in a cleft in the rocks. The only way for Giorgi to pass through the "evil flame" that guards the way to the Kadzhi country is by having himself sewn inside the skin of a dead horse. Once inside the Kadzhi country, he massacres all of the Kadzhi, sparing only one woman, Samdzimari, whom he brings back as a captive, and a cow with one horn. To this booty he adds the anvil, the principal tools, and objects made of worked silver.

When he returns to his sanctuary, Giorgi takes the demoness Samdzimari as his sister-wife and turns her into a goddess. He transforms all the forged objects into implements of worship and directs that the horn of a cow be used as the measure for beer, the sacred drink.

Even though she is promoted to the rank of a goddess, Samdzimari still bears the marks of her wild and demonic nature; she abandons her form as a seductive and bejeweled woman (her name means "the lady with a necklace") to take on repulsive or monstrous animal forms. She grants her favors to many humans, especially priests and shamans, whom she visits at night in the forms of their wives or sweethearts. At the last moment, "just as the semen is discharged," she turns into a beast or disappears. She brags about her conquests in little songs in verse which she sings herself, through the mouths of those whom she possesses.

More than any other divinity, she is involved in the phenomena of possession, which she has made her specialty. Her basic function consists in intervening between the shaman and his god when the contact is broken. Always

259

available, she takes possession of the abandoned shaman's soul and reestablishes the link with the departed god.

She is a patroness of marriage, which she founded with the god Giorgi, and watches over normal pregnancy and childbirth. Parallel to this—just as the god Giorgi presides over the births of both colts and boys—she guarantees the fertility and productivity of dairy cows, the preeminent feminine domain (at least in this culture).

These two divine couples—Lashari-Tamar and Giorgi-Samdzimari—dominate the Georgian pantheon and organize the religious thought that underlies it. The system of their differences fits the dichotomy expressed, in its own way, by the myth of creation (cf. § I.1): man is a divine creature and woman a demonic creature. And yet in social life the two must be united in marriage. The couple Giorgi-Samdzimari submit to this contradictory necessity: whence the disturbing origin of this couple and the half-wild character of its feminine component.

The couple Lashari-Tamar, on the other hand, reproduces the state of things that existed before the separation of the primeval brother and sister into God and demon. Their incestuous union, like that of God and his sister in the beginning, and like that of the fraternal couple in social and ritual life, is located *on this side of marriage,* thus escaping the curse that marriage brings. From this comes the harmony of the divine couple of Lashari and the inaccessible purity of its feminine component, Tamar, in contrast with the savage character of Samdzimari.

III. Divinities and Myths of the Hunt

1. *Gods of the hunt in Georgia.* In western Georgia, in Svanetia, on the southern slopes of the Elburz range, hunting has been preserved almost intact as an economic, social, and conceptual system, with the highly specialized theology that accompanies it. In particular, to this day the Svanetians still maintain in a living and active form a classification of wild species that corresponds to a division of tasks among clearly differentiated gods. We can glimpse traces of such classificatory systems among the other Caucasians, though the principle behind these can no longer be understood. But it has remained quite clear in the minds of the Svanetians.

The gods of the hunt are organized into a small pantheon. At its head is *Ber shishvlish,* "the lord of the bald mountain," who lives on the highest peaks of the Caucasus. He is responsible for all the wild species of creation (all that are hunted). He is assisted by four divinities, among whom all game is divided.

(a) *Tshekish angelwez,* "the angel of the forest," is in charge of all carnivorous beasts of the forest: the fox, the jackal, the bear, and the Caucasian panther, which is rare nowadays (the wolf is not included in this category).

(b) The goddess Dali is patroness of "horned beasts of the mountain": deer, roebuck, wild sheep, chamois. She is the most important divinity of the hunt on the practical level, since her wild herds are composed of the most sought-after species, the sources of food. This is probably why she is the object of rich and precise representations. She lives in an inaccessible cavern on the side of a glacier. Her hair is solid gold, worn in long braids. Sometimes she seduces a human hunter, to his greater luck or greater misfortune (cf. § III.4). These unions often bear fruit, resulting in the birth of exceptional beings, demigods (cf. § III.5). Her action also extends to meteorological phenomena, especially to rain (cf. § III.4).

(c) The god Apsat watches exclusively over river trout and high-flying birds. This unexpected proximity of a fish and a bird within the same class can be explained if we see it in the context of the ancient Georgian cosmological system: the eagle is just as closely related to water as to the sky (cf. § III.3 and § I.2).

(d) The wolf constitutes a class of game in itself. A creature of the supreme god, not of the demon, and thus not belonging to savagery, the wolf is not thought of as an animal. Wolves form a society with the same structure as that of human beings, subject to the same rules and practices. Like men, they are given to feuding; this is why every "murder" of a wolf must be expiated exactly like that of a human. The hunter wears mourning, as do all in his clan, and the animal is wept over as passionately as if it had been a man.

This is why the patron of wolves is a god of human beings, Giorgi, and not a spirit who specializes in the hunt, as is the case for other species of game (cf. § II.3).

2. *The celestial dogs.* A number of Georgian divinities, notably the warrior Hat'i of Arhot'i (to the north of the Caucasian range), have "hounds," Mts'evar, in their service. These dogs accompany them on their expeditions and often, on the order of the god, fight in invisible form on the side of human beings, guaranteeing them victory. They are imagined as enormous multicolored dogs—white, red, blue—their claws perpetually dripping blood, their throats encircled by gold chains.

They run to the aid of warriors in trouble, or attack men who have committed some sin against the gods.

The celestial dogs receive regular worship like the other divinities, in the form of offerings and prayers: "Hounds with bloody claws, with golden chains. . . ." They live—mystically, at least—within the sanctuary enclosure, in piles of rocks which are the "tombs of the hounds." These "tombs" serve as altar and temple.

The tombs of the hounds must be distant relics of real burial practices, as is attested by the canine bones found in human tombs in the eastern Caucasus (Iberia and Albania). The existence of warrior dogs among the Caucasians and the fact of their burial were well known to the authors of antiquity (Strabo 11.4.5; Solinus 15.6). The poet Valerius Flaccus takes pleasure in describing the onslaught of troops of black Caucasian dogs fighting alongside Caspian warriors, and reports that they received their share of funerary honors; they were buried in human tombs (Argonautica 6.106–13).

The hound cult thus represents an extremely ancient phenomenon: reality or fiction, its essential elements have been known since antiquity. Just as the warriors of the ancient Caucasus had their supernatural guardians in the form of anthropomorphic gods, it is likely that their war dogs also had their celestial counterparts in the form of canine divinities, who were equally involved in the usual network of myths and religious practices. The real war gods have left the stage of history, but the mythic and ritual system has survived to the present day.

3. *The mythical birds of prey.* The mythical ornithology of the Georgians opposes three great birds of prey (one fantastic, two real) on the basis of the three relationships of fire and water, heaven and earth, and degeneration and regeneration.

(a) "The phoenix (Piniksi)," they say, "is the name of a bird who, when he grows old, gathers wood, sits on it, and blows on it until it bursts into flame and burns him up. But in these ashes there is something that, under the effects of the sun's heat, becomes a larva, grows, and regenerates the same bird."

This distant echo of Greek mythology offers an interesting variant on the technique of lighting the fire: the Georgian phoenix uses its own breath to light the pyre, while ancient authors mention only the spontaneous action of the sun or else the percussion or friction of the wings of the phoenix.

The Georgian phoenix regenerates thanks to the heat of a fire of celestial origin.

(b) The vulture. The inverse of the phoenix, the giant vulture (*Aegipius monachus L.*, sometimes confused with the *Gypaetus*) degenerates through contact with or absorption of terrestrial water. This is why Georgian shepherds make sure that the method used for exterminating vultures is appropriate to their hydrophobic physiology. They salt a cadaver or carrion of a lamb and leave it to the voracity of a vulture. When the vulture has eaten its fill, it is so thirsty that it drinks excessive amounts of water. Unable to take flight, it can be beaten to death with a stick.

(c) The eagle stands in opposition to both of these birds of prey, which are also opposed to one another: the eagle regenerates through contact with terrestrial water: "In its five-hundredth year, the eagle rejuvenates by falling from the highest part of the air and regenerates by its fall into the depths of the waters" (Saba Oreliani, 31).

The eagle's affinity for terrestrial and subterranean water is expressed in a mythic sequence known throughout Georgia. The eagle—which dwells in the underworld—is threatened with his own disappearance and that of his descendants because his access to the body of underground water (cf. § I.2) is blocked by a black dragon, the same one who swallows the sun and so is responsible for eclipses.

4. *The hunter hanging head down.* The myth of the hunter hanging head down, found throughout Georgia, is connected with a ritual for making rain. Its hero is the hunter Betkil (the name varies from region to region) and his dog Q'ursha, "Black Ear," a supernatural animal. He is the child of an eagle who, when she saw his deformity, threw him out of the nest. When he fell to earth, he was taken in and raised by hunters. He has the wings of an eagle, lips of gold, and eyes as big as sieves. His barking sounds like thunder. He can catch the mountain sheep or the chamois with a single leap.

The hunter was beloved of the goddess Dali, who made him infallible. But he was unfaithful to her, and the goddess took a cruel revenge. One winter night the hunter set out with his dog in pursuit of a white deer that led him to the top of a steep mountain. He got ready to shoot an arrow at the deer; suddenly the mountain crumbled under his feet. He fell into the abyss and remained hanging there, stuck to a branch by the sole of his moccasin. He remained there for several days, hanging head down, growing steadily hungrier and thirstier. His dog, who had stayed near him on a small rock spur, said, "Kill me and use me for food!" The hunter, death in his soul, said goodbye to Q'ursha and slaughtered, skinned, and roasted him; he used his bow and arrows to make a fire. But he could not bring himself to eat his companion.

In the end the villagers came to his aid. But the longer the ropes were that they threw him, the higher the mountain grew. At dawn, exhausted, the hunter let himself fall into the void and died on a rock at the bottom of the mountain.

It is on this rock that the rainmaking ritual is still performed today; the officiants sing a lament consisting of the myth I have just summarized, one of the most beautiful, from a literary point of view, of the Georgian repertoire. The lament even reproduces the song of the suspended hunter weeping for the dog he has killed but cannot bring himself to eat.

Curiously, we find in North America a mythico-ritual ensemble which, in its setting and its general thrust, recalls the story of the Georgian hunter. An Indian hunter (a Makah of Cape Flattery) remains trapped on the side of a mountain, which grows abnormally. The ropes thrown up by the hunter's family cannot reach him. He jumps into the void and dies. To make it rain, the Indians chant an incantation that reproduces the song that the hunter sang before he jumped into the abyss (Lévi-Strauss, *L'homme nu*, 137–38).

5. *Amirani, the Caucasian Prometheus.* Most of the Caucasian peoples—Georgians, Abkhazians, Cherkess, Ossets—have many songs about the adventures of a remarkable character, a supernatural hero, giant, or demigod, whom the Creator chained on a Caucasian peak as punishment for his excesses. Since this epic cycle was most widespread in Georgia, where it is still alive and has some two hundred variants, it is the Georgian version that we will concentrate on here:

Amirani is the fruit of the secret love between a hunter and the goddess Dali. The goddess is surprised by her lover's wife and has to leave this world. She orders the hunter to open up her womb. He takes out a premature child whose gestation is completed first in the belly of a young bull and then in the belly of a heifer.

The child, who is left lying close to a spring, is baptized by an old man who is none other than God. Then a peasant takes him in and raises him with his own sons. His overly vigorous childhood recalls that of Batraz and uses themes from the epic of the Narts. As an adolescent, he travels the world with his two adoptive brothers, taking on a series of more and more perilous exploits, massacring demons, giants, and dragons without respite, until the day when he meets a kind of resistant mass which he cannot overcome. He prays, and God grants him additional strength. He then leaves his brothers, who are too human for him, and continues on his murderous travels. He finally learns that he has wiped out all the adversaries worthy of him: no one and nothing is left to battle.

He thus quite naturally reaches the point of challenging God himself. God refuses to fight, but gives him a kind of sporting test, as a result of which Amirani finds himself chained to a metal stake whose roots plunge to the bottom of the earth. According to many variants, more simply, God has him chained to the stake by his celestial helpers as punishment for his excesses.

After this, God shakes the mountains, and Amirani is covered with a dome-shaped heap of rocks which completely cuts him off from the world. His companion in captivity, appearing from we know not where, is the winged dog Q'ursha, the abandoned child of an eagle (cf. § III.4). Day and night for a year, Q'ursha licks one of the links in the chain. At dawn on Easter Monday, at the very instant when the chain is about to give way and Amirani is about to be freed, "the blacksmiths of all humanity" go into their forges and, observing the strictest silence, strike the anvil three times, or else make a small symbolic object. Amirani's chains are immediately restored to solidity, the hero remains captive, and the winged dog takes up his work again for another year.

G.C./j.l.

BIBLIOGRAPHY

V. BARDAVELIDZE, *Opyt sociologičeskogo izučenija xevsurskix verovanii* (Tbilisi 1932); *Kartvelta udzvelesi sarc'munoebis ist'oriidan* (Tbilisi 1941); *Drevnejšie religioznye verovanija i obrjadovoe grafičeskoe iskusstvo gruzinskix plemen* (Tbilisi 1957). A. BYHAN, *La civilisation caucasienne* (Paris 1936). G. CHARACHIDZÉ, *Le système religieux de la Géorgie païenne* (Paris 1968). *Chroniques géorgiennes:* see Q'aux-çishvili. M. ÇIKOVANI, *Kartuli polk'lori* (Tbilisi 1946); *Midzhaç'uli Amirani* (Tbilisi 1947); *Nardonyj gruzinskij êpos o prikovannom Amirani* (Moscow 1966). P. DRAGOMANOV, *Notes on the Slavic Religio-Ethical Legends* (Bloomington 1961). I. DZHAVAXISHVILI, *Kartveli eris ist'oria*, 1 (Tbilisi 1928). E.

GABLIANI, *Dzveli da axali svaneti* (Tbilisi 1925). K'OT' and V. ISHVILI, *Xalxuri p'oezia* (Kutaïs 1934). S. MAK'ALATIA, *Pshavi* (Tbilisi 1934); *Xevi* (Tbilisi 1934); *Xevsureti* (Tbilisi 1935). *Masalebi Sakartvelos etnograpii-satvis*, 1–11 (Tbilisi 1938–59). I. MEGRELIDZE, *Rustaveli i fol'klor* (Tbilisi 1960). T. OÇIAURI, *Kartvelta udzvelesi sarc'munoebis ist'oriidan* (Tbilisi 1954). S. Q'AUXÇISHVILI, *Kartlis cxovreba*, Chroniques géorgiennes, 1–2 (Tbilisi 1955–59). G. RADDE, *Die Chewssuren und ihr Land* (Cassel 1878). SABA (ORBELIANI), *Sit'q'vis K'ona*, Iordanishvili, ed. (Tbilisi 1949). A. SHANIDZE, *Kartuli xalxuri p'oezia*, 1 (Tbilisi 1931). G. TEDORADZE, *Xut'i c'eli pshav-xevsuretshi* (Tbilisi 1930). VAZHA PSHAVELA, *Txzulebani*, 5, 7 (Tbilisi 1936, 1956). E. VIRSALADZE, *Kartvel mtielta zep'irsit'q'viereba* (Tbilisi 1958); *Kartuli samonadiro ep'osi* (Tbilisi 1964).

THE RELIGION AND MYTHS OF THE OSSETS

An islet of Indo-Europeans sheltered in the middle of the mountain chain of the Caucasus, the Ossets are the distant descendants and last representatives of the northern Iranians whom the ancients called Scythians and Sarmatians and who, at the dawn of the Middle Ages, under the name of the Alani and Roxolani, made Europe quake with fear. For many centuries their culture was subjected to a strong Caucasian influence in all areas, but it has nevertheless preserved several Indo-European characteristics that are manifest especially in religion and epic. The Ossetic gods and their cults clearly belong essentially to the Caucasus and differ only slightly from what can be observed among such neighbors of the Ossets as the Circassians, the Abkhazians, and the Georgians. Under other, sometimes Indo-European names, one can find specialized Caucasian deities with virtually identical cultural traits, deeply marked by a Christian imprint, as in Georgia.

The supreme god, Khutsauty Khutsau ("god of gods"), or simply Khutsau, like Anc°a among the Abkhazians or Morige among the Georgians, does not intervene directly in human affairs but delegates his powers to minor deities, specialized spirits divided, at least nominally, into two classes: the *izäd* and the *dzwars*, both Iranian terms.

The *izäd*—an Indo-Iranian word designating an object of sacrifice in general—seem to have a more universal vocation, less specialized than that of their associates, the *dzwars*, who are more exclusively engaged in the limited functions over which they preside. But for a long time the distinction has tended to become blurred, and the Ossets most often refer to the totality of their deities by the compound term *izäd-dzwars* (G. Dumézil, *The Book of Heroes*, introduction).

I. Deities

Watsilla and the Storm

Watsilla is the Ossetic transposition of Saint Elias, the storm spirit of the Georgians of the plain (a function held in the mountain by K'op'ala). *Watsilla* contains the name of the Christian prophet (*-illa*) preceded by an Ossetic prefix *wat-*, whose primary meaning remains obscure. If Watsilla should strike a man with his thunderbolt without killing him, he must receive a sacrifice consisting of a lamb and a kid, whose heads are fastened on two young trees planted on the spot where Watsilla struck, a custom that represents a modified version of Circassian and Abkhazian practice. The trees are replaced every year on the same date. If the victim of the thunderbolt dies, he is buried on the spot.

Like most spirits of lightning, Watsilla plays a role in the success of agriculture. Before they go to make hay, the Ossets sacrifice a specially fattened bull to Watsilla. The participants eat only the head, the feet, and the entrails; they consecrate the best meat to the god and put it on skewers. In return, the god watches over the harvest that begins with haymaking.

Aspects of Ossetic storm mythology that have no connection with Watsilla may have survived in the Nart legends about Batraz.

Wastyrdzhi, the Saint George of the Ossets

Wastyrdzhi is the Ossetic copy of Saint George, with the same prefix (*was*) as that of Watsilla and a transformation of Georgian *Giorgi*, or *Givargi*. Like the latter, he is the patron saint of men and travelers, and by extension he watches over stallions and colts. He also presides over oaths. All of this fits the description of the Saint George of the Caucasians, particularly of the Georgian mountain people.

In November a one-year-old bullock is sacrificed to him. To indicate clearly that the victim belongs to the god, its right horn is cut off long before, which forbids the herdsman to swear at it or even to give it an angry look.

Kurdalägon

Kurdalägon, a blacksmith spirit, appears especially in the myths that can be identified throughout the Nart epic. Like the Circassian god Tlepsch, he builds marvelous weapons for heroes, and he "tempers" in his forge Batraz, the demigod of thunder.

Tutyr and Fälvära

With opposite functions, Tutyr and Fälvära complement each other. Tutyr watches over wolves, and Fälvära watches over sheep. They both have names of Christian origin, difficult to recognize in their Ossetic contractions.

Tutyr (Saint Theodore of Tyre, whose feet the wolves came to lick) is worshiped preventively by shepherds all day on Easter Monday. The worship consists basically of a rigorous fast that is meant to persuade Tutyr to impose the same temperance on his wolves. If he wants to do this, he forces the beasts to fast by "stuffing their mouths with stones." Then the sheep can graze free of danger. If the god gets angry with his human dependents, he sends his pack of carnivores to their flocks under the command of a giant wolf named "Gray."

Sheep are put under the protection of Fälvära, a contraction of Saint Flora and Saint Laura. She is distinguished by her good heart and her endless patience. Although each family sacrifices one sheep to her in the month of August, her favorite offering remains the *dzykka*, a mixture of flour, butter, and milk.

Donbyttyr, the Spirit of the Waters

The name of Donbyttyr, the spirit of the waters, contains the old Scythian word for water, *don*, which the rivers of central Europe still preserve: Don, Danube, Dnieper, etc. The second part of the compound term, *byttr*, is the Ossetic alteration of the Christian Saint Peter. He is therefore "Peter of the Waters."

Living in the sea or in rivers, he pulls lingering swimmers down to the bottom of the water by means of a long chain. But he can also be kind to men, whom he benefits through the many uses of water in farming and in all of daily existence. He has many daughters, all very beautiful, naiads of a sort, who assist him in distributing his blessings to mankind, notably fertility and the steady supply of water sources. Donbyttyr's daughters are the object of a ritual performed by young girls on the Saturday following Easter.

Safa and the Hearth

Safa is the creator and master of the human hearth. He is incarnate in the great chain that hangs permanently over the hearth. This spirit and his concrete expression, the chain, play an important role during numerous practices, notably during the oaths of marriage and of vendettas, which were widespread until the turn of the century. As with all Caucasians, any attempt to break or steal the hearth chain constitutes the supreme insult and triggers the worst vengeance.

Minor Spirits

The Ossets have a host of local or highly specialized spirits. The following are just a few examples.

Gydyrty-kom, literally, "mouth of the lock," is the master of hail. His power exceeds that of Watsilla, the storm god. His upper jaw touches the sky, and his lower jaw touches the ground. If he is in a bad mood, he swallows with a single thrust of his giant jaw the thunderbolt that Watsilla hurls at demons. On the other hand, during one of his better moods, he was seen to trap a gigantic snake in a dense fog when the snake was about to devour all of creation.

Sau-dzwar, the "black spirit," lives deep in the forests (the "black" forests), which he protects against fires and deforestation.

Barastyr rules over the world of the dead; he judges the dead when they arrive in the world beyond; he punishes them if they have sinned and welcomes them if they are innocent of all sins. In this task, he is assisted by Aminon, who guards the gates of hell.

Apsat is the spirit of the hunt. (See "Gods and Myths of the Abkhaz.")

II. The Narts and Ossetic Mythology

The vast epic cycle of the Narts is fascinating in several respects: in the richness and beauty of its narrative content and in its uniqueness. It is the last great European epic still alive and flourishing today. In addition, it has preserved entire sections of an otherwise lost mythology. Finally, it encompasses many figures that give us a glimpse into the heritage of the distant Indo-European past that may still be identified by the historian, although it is largely unknown to the lay reader.

The Narts are heroes of the past, simultaneously earthly and miraculous, who are distinguished by supernatural qualities (steel body, magic power, superhuman strength, etc.) but who lead the same daily lives as Caucasian warriors with their houses, customs, and passions. Like them, they love to talk and fight, and divide their time among feasts, raids, and war, the very image of the northern Caucasus before the Russian conquest. The Nart epic is as richly represented among the Circassians and the Abkhazians as it is among the Ossets; it can be seen as the final result of an ancient collaboration among these cultures, a sort of reciprocal contamination. But its Ossetic, even Indo-European, origin is beyond doubt.

The Narts split up into three villages or sections of villages on different levels along a mountain slope: at the top are the Äxsärtägkats, halfway down are the Alägats, and below are the Boriats. Each of these three families is characterized by a dominant feature, all of which have been formulated by the Ossets themselves:

> The Boriats were wealthy herdsmen; the Alägats were exceptionally intelligent; the Äxsärtägkats excelled in heroism and vigor.

One recognizes here the old Indo-European pattern of an ideal society, as described by G. Dumézil, distributed in three complementary functions: magic and religious sovereignty; martial power; and fertility and material prosperity. Indeed, the Alägats are the specialists in great religious drinking (throughout the Caucasus, feasts have a sacred dimension) and the keepers of the Nart magic cup, the *nartamongä*; the most feared warriors, the fiercest fighters, are all Äxsärtägkats; and the Boriats are above all rich, *very* rich.

The incessant quarrels among the Narts are dominated by the great war between the rich, the Boriats, and the mighty, the Äxsärtägkats, a struggle with no beginning or end, and with no winners or losers. This fundamental but nonexterminating hostility between the two components of the society has been compared to the founding war of social groups as it is represented in Indo-European myths: between the Romans and the Sabines in Rome and between the Aesir and the Vanir in Scandinavia (see Georges Dumézil, *Mythe et épopée*, vol. 1, part 3).

The Nart epic offers inexhaustible material for the imagination of popular storytellers and includes many characters and episodes that originate in the chanson de geste and folklore. Among them certain great figures with clearly mythological origins stand out: these alone will be discussed below.

Batraz and the Lightning

The birth of Batraz is hardly ordinary. His heredity, conception, gestation, birth, and first steps all come from mythology. His father Hämyts, one of the greatest of Nart heroes, had a little frog-woman for a wife, whom he carried in his pocket because, since she was of divine origin, if anyone happened to see her she would have to return to her aquatic home. As the result of some treacherous maneuvers by Syrdon, the evil spirit of the Narts, the little wife lost her outer sheath and was doomed to disappear. Before she left, she told her husband that she was pregnant; she spit up the embryo, which landed between his shoulders, where it dug in like an abcess. At the end of the gestation period, the curiously pregnant father climbed to the top of a seven-story tower at the bottom of which were seven caldrons of cold water.

The abcess was lanced, and a child made entirely of molten steel jumped out. He jumped into the seven caldrons of water. Then, finally cooled off, or in reality properly "tempered," he took his place next to the fireplace.

After a turbulent and marvelous childhood, somewhat reminiscent of that of Heracles, he went to heaven, where he lived from that time on, never leaving except to "fall" (literally) onto earth, in the manner of lightning, sometimes to save his fellow Narts when they were in danger, but sometimes to decimate them cruelly and blindly, without any clear motive. Each of these "descents" is described in terms and images that express his lightning nature. Leaping to the rescue of the Narts when they were threatened by the evil giant Mukara, he sank into the ground up to his groin. The "thunder of his cry" was enough to rout the giant. In hot pursuit, Batraz's steel body heated up and he had to dive into the sea, smoking.

He rested on the peak of a mountain, leaning his head on a glacier "in order to cool off his steel." When he landed on earth, the Narts recognized him by the crashing sound of falling metal.

Later, seized by an incessant murderous rage, he terrorized the Nart countryside, slaughtering his own people and submitting them to more and more atrocious tortures. Finally, weary of life, he decided to die and ordered the Narts to build a huge pyre made of one hundred cartloads of calcined trees, with six pairs of bellows at each corner. He climbed onto the blazing fire, and when his steel body got white-hot, he danced and twirled his sword, cutting off the heads and arms of the Narts who were working the twenty-four bellows.

But he stayed alive, because he could not die until his sword fell into the sea. He laid it down on the fire, and the Narts had it dragged away to the Black Sea by a team of two hundred horses. They pushed it into the water, and Batraz finally died in the midst of a great storm. "The sword is still in the sea, the Ossets think, and when they see lightning in the western sky, they attribute the flash to Batraz's sword leaping from the sea toward the sky" (quoted by G. Dumézil, *Mythe et épopée*, vol. 1, p. 573).

This old myth of the storm can be compared with the cult of Ares among the Scythians as described by Herodotus:

> In each of the districts of the governmental divisions, there is a shrine established to Ares. Bundles of faggots are heaped up for three furlongs in width and length . . . Each year they pile one hundred and fifty wagons' worth of firewood upon this, for each year some of it gradually wastes away, from the winter seasons. On this pile is set an ancient iron sword for each of the peoples sacrificing, and this is the image of Ares. To this sword they bring yearly sacrifices of smaller cattle and of horses; indeed, they offer to these images more victims than to the other gods. Of such of their enemies as they take alive, they sacrifice one out of every hundred. (Herodotus 4.62; trans. David Grene; Chicago: University of Chicago Press, 1987)

> The case of Batraz proves therefore that the conservatism of the Ossets preserved in its framework and in several themes of Nart legends, not only the structure of trifunctional thought, but also and more concretely, mythical scenes and types. (G. Dumézil, *Mythe et épopée*, vol. 1, p. 575)

Soslan (or Sozryko)

Along with Batraz, Soslan (or Sozryko; Sawsyryq°e for the Circassians, Sawsyrqwa for the Abkhazians) is the most terrifying of the Nart warriors.

His character includes several traits of the solar type, but his interdependence with the heavenly body is not quite as close as that of Batraz and lightning. Like Mithra, he was born of a stone. At the sight of the beautiful Satana washing clothes on the riverbank, a shepherd across the river poured out his semen on a stone from which, nine months later, the child Soslan came forth. When he had grown up, he demanded to be "tempered" in the milk of a she-wolf, a treatment destined to make him invulnerable. The divine smith Kurdalägon dropped him into a trough containing one hundred goatskins of milk, but since the trough was too short, Soslan had to bend his knees, which consequently were not tempered and thus remained vulnerable.

After a long existence devoted to war exploits, mostly miraculous, Soslan insulted the daughter of Balsäg, a kind of celestial spirit, who took his vengeance by discharging at Soslan a living steel wheel that he controlled. The hero was hit by the wheel on all parts of his body successively and threw it back without being injured until, on the advice of the treacherous Syrdon, the wheel hit him on the knees and smashed them to pieces. According to an eastern Circassian variant, Soslan indulged in a game during which the Narts, again at Syrdon's instigation, threw a wheel made of serrated steel at him from the top of a hill. It hit the distracted Soslan in the knees.

As the hero lost all his blood, all the creatures of the world came to weep over him, all except one, who was none other than Syrdon in disguise. Since the mourning was not unanimous, Soslan had to die. He was buried in a tomb in which, at his request, three windows were installed. A Circassian song suggests that one day he will come to life again, and the earth will bloom.

As Georges Dumézil has shown (*Loki*, 1959), this account represents the remote traces of the Scythian version of the Indo-European myth of which the murder of Baldr provides the Scandinavian version.

Syrdon, the Ossetic Loki

Since the study of Loki by G. Dumézil (1947, revised German edition 1959), the curious character of Syrdon can be better understood when he is contrasted with his Scandinavian counterpart. Like Loki, Syrdon is endowed with magical powers and uses his corrupt intelligence to do evil all around him throughout his career. Committed to a permanent and gratuitous evil-mindedness truly natural to him, he dedicates his career to playing nasty tricks, sometimes without serious consequences but sometimes ending in death or misery. Just like Loki's, his baneful zest has nothing but negative effects on his people, the Narts.

Yet, on many occasions, his perverse intelligence, free of all constraints, allows him to succeed in areas where other more conformist Narts have failed, thus saving them from many tight spots. So despite his tricks and sometimes his crimes, "the Narts like him."

Like Loki, who knows no bounds and unleashes a veritable cosmic drama by bringing about the death of the god Baldr, Syrdon organizes the mutilation of the great Nart, Soslan, and finally prevents him from surviving his wound. This is the greatest of his crimes.

Unlike Loki, whose scheming intelligence is not creative

and is of no benefit to mankind, Syrdon is the inventor of the *fändyr*, the stringed instrument used throughout the Caucasus, which he builds with the veins of his own sons when they have been slaughtered by the victim of one of his nasty tricks. As soon as the musical instrument is in his hands, Syrdon quite naturally invents singing. Amazed by this invention, the Narts forgive the crimes of the one they call "the scourge of the Narts."

The creative function is well within the scope of the character; to mark human history with the gift of the poetic word is appropriate for one whom all recognize as a specialist in effective speech and whose power lies in the force of words. It is this power of the word that the Narts feared and that forced them to tolerate their "scourge"; they spared his life repeatedly because they were afraid of his "tongue." All of this confirms the parallel with Loki, who survives and often triumphs thanks to the fear that his verbal excesses inspire in the other Scandinavian gods and the precision with which he aims them. The great Óðinn himself yields to Loki, "for fear that he may utter injurious words to us in Aegir's hall" (*Lokasenna*, 10).

The End of the Narts

The race of Narts disappeared from the surface of the earth, as they themselves wanted to. By the natural inclination typical of all Caucasian warriors (Circassian and Georgian too; see Amirani), the Nart heroes, weary of adversaries too easily defeated, go in search of "someone stronger than them." When they have exhausted the resources of creation, all that is left for them is to challenge the author of creation, God himself. They do this by abstaining from all religious practice and by raising the level of the top of the doors to their houses, thus avoiding bowing their heads, which God might interpret as a sign of respect.

God worries about this behavior and sends them a messenger, the swallow, to ask about their grievances. The Narts proudly answer, "We have long served God, and he never deigned to reveal himself to us. Let him now come and we shall compare forces." God replies that the Narts have to choose between the total annihilation of their race and the guarantee of a poor line of descendants. They choose to be destroyed, saying "Why do we need to live forever? What we need is not eternal life, but eternal glory!"

God uses several means to subdue them by famine; the Narts thwart them all in a series of desperate struggles. Finally, weary of combat, weary of too long an existence, "each one of them dug his own grave and lay down in it. Thus perished the illustrious Narts" (G. Dumézil, *Le livre des héros*, pp. 259–60).

G.C./g.h.

BIBLIOGRAPHY

V. I. ABAIEV, *Osetinskij jazyk i fol'klor*, 1 (Moscow and Leningrad 1949); *Istoriko-etimologičeskij slovar' osetinskogo jazyka* (Moscow and Leningrad 1958). E. BENVENISTE, *Études sur la langue ossète* (Paris 1959). G. DUMÉZIL, *Légendes sur les Nartes* (Paris 1930); *Loki* (Paris 1947; German ed., 1959); *Mythes et dieux des Germains*, chap. 3 (Paris 1959); *Le livre des héros* (Paris 1965); *Mythe et épopée*, vol. 1, part 3, "Trois familles" (Paris 1968); *Romans de Scythie et d'alentour* (Paris 1978). B. GATIEV, *Sueverija i predzazsudki Osetin, Sbornik svedenij o Kavkazskix gorcev*, 9, 3 (1876). M. KOVALESWSKY, *Coutume contemporaine et loi ancienne* (Paris 1893). V. MILLER, *Osetinskie êtjudy*, 3 vols. (Moscow 1881–87).

THE RELIGION AND MYTHS OF ARMENIA

The paganism of the ancient Armenians is almost entirely inaccessible to us. We know of it only through the historians and chroniclers of the late Middle Ages, in a form influenced by the Iranians; it is a sort of local version of Zoroastrianism. At the other historical extreme, folklorists present a strongly Christianized picture of Armenian paganism, in which it is difficult, even more difficult than in Georgia, to find the ancient beliefs beneath their Christian trappings. Despite the early conversion of the Armenians to Christianity (fourth century), it is mostly Zoroastrian beliefs that can still be surmised. Religious thought appears to have been dominated by the pairs of opposing concepts important to the doctrine of Zoroaster: good Light confronting evil Darkness, served, respectively, by Angels and Demons, in relation to Life, the Day, and Happiness for Light, and Death, Night, and Sickness for Darkness. The figure of the Christian God remains without substance, hidden behind the activity of the multiple entities closer to man and calling to mind both the Yazata of Zoroastrian Iran and the Hat'i of Georgian paganism: angels, archangels, saints, Christ (quite distinct from God, as in Georgia), the Virgin.

Before the conversion to Christianity, the place of the supreme God devolved upon an entity called Aramazd, in which can be recognized the Armenian contraction of Ahura Mazdā. Aramazd had a temple at Ani, the great citadel of classical Armenia. Like his Iranian prototype, Aramazd was "the greatest and best of the gods, creator of heaven and earth." Unlike Ahura Mazdā, however, he was said to be "father of all the gods."

All of this serves to confirm Strabo's conclusion in the first century B.C.: "The Armenians worship what the Persians worship." However, the Armenian version of Zoroastrianism retains its originality, first because of the syncretism to which it was subjected, and second because it appears that the Iranian influence was not strictly Avestan in origin but also contained foreign religious elements, probably more popular elements.

I. The Gods

Anahit

Anahit was part of the great triad that dominated the Armenian pantheon: Aramazd, Anahit, and Vahagn (Agathange, chap. 12). She is partly identified with the Iranian goddess Anāhitā, whose name means "without stain, the immaculate," mistress of the waters and of fertility.

Armenians describe Anahit as a young girl of great beauty and pleasing plumpness, weighed down with golden necklaces and crowned with stars. She was referred to by the epithet Oskrhat, "made of gold," and a golden statue was raised to her. Priests and priestesses sacrificed white heifers to her in great quantity. According to Strabo, the daughters of great Armenian families were not permitted to marry unless they had previously been prostitutes for a period of time in the sanctuary of Anahit. This rule may be compared to the Georgian obligation to perform amorous acts within the sacred enclosure.

The Armenian goddess retained many of the functions of her Iranian counterpart, but she also annexed a much greater realm of influence than Anāhitā, greatly surpassing her in rank and popularity. She was a dispenser of life and fertility and was also the patron of healing, which indicates that she was a goddess of the third function. But she is also always invoked as "the queen," unlike the Anāhitā of Zoroastrianism. King Trdat defined her as follows: "The great queen Anahit, glory of our race and dispenser of life, whom all kings adore, even the king of Greece. She is the mother of all chastity, the benefactor of humankind, and the birth of the great Aramazd" (Agathange, chap. 4).

The "birth of the great Aramazd" (*cnund mecin Aramazday*) indicates that she was the daughter of the supreme god, although certain commentators claim that she is his mother. The most recent sources make her the wife of Aramazd. Comparison with her Iranian counterpart leaves no doubt in the matter: Anāhitā was definitely the daughter of Ahura Mazdā.

Vahagn

The third member of the great triad, Vahagn, is a warrior and a famous dragon slayer in whom we can see the Armenian equivalent of the Iranian Verethraghna and the Indian Indra Vṛtrahan. His title is the same: "dragon slayer" (Višapaklal). Aside from this exploit, seen in his name and his place in the triad, we know little about him and his cult. But the story of his birth is recounted in a versified myth that is reported by Moses of Khorene, the earliest historian of Armenia: "The sky and the earth were in labor; the purple sea labored also; the labor seized a small red reed in the sea; From the stem of the reed, smoke rose; And from the flame, a young man sprang forth; He had hair of fire; And his little eyes were suns" (Moses of Khorene, 1.31).

This strange birth from fire and water is remarkable on two counts. First, because it is the only mythological Armenian text to survive to the present day. Second, because the scenario corresponds to one of the misadventures of the Indian Indra, also a dragon slayer. But the Indian myth is about not a birth, but a rebirth. Exhausted by his exploit, Indra loses his legendary power and begins to shrink in an alarming manner. He regains his shape and his original powers through a second birth that duplicates exactly the scene described by Moses of Khorene (Dumézil, *The Destiny of the Warrior*).

Armenian mythology thus retained Indo-Iranian characters and patterns that originated before the Zoroastrian reform and reflected an earlier state of Indo-European religion.

This is true of the great triad Aramazd, Anahit, and Vahagn. It conforms to the tripartite ideology of the Indo-Europeans: a sovereign god (Aramazd), a warrior god (Vahagn), and a divinity of life and fertility (Anahit). This grouping is clearly Indo-European in heritage, but it is organized—and this makes it even more interesting—according to Iranian Zoroastrianism, which arranged the original pattern in other, much more complex, articulations. Here also, Armenia is a valuable witness to a pre-Zoroastrian state.

As a popular god who was absorbed by historicized legend, Vahagn must have been the object of a mythological work independent of the Zoroastrian tradition. Thus, he is regarded as the husband of the star goddess Astlik. He is also credited with the origin of the Milky Way, which the Armenians call *yardgol*, "thief of straw." One winter night, Vahagn had no more straw for his horse. He stole some from the god Baršamin and fled across the sky, leaving behind him a trail of wisps of straw that can still be seen in the firmament: the Milky Way.

This representation is not unique to the Armenians. It can be found in Iran and Turkey. In Osmanli Turkish, for example, the Milky Way is called *saman-oghrusu*, "the thief of straw."

Haurot and Maurot, Plants of Immortality

Haurot and Maurot is an old Indo-European representation, which survived in Armenia as a spring festival but retained the ancient names. In the final analysis, these names refer to the paired gods of the third function, the Nāsatya twins in India, and Haurvatāt and Amyrytāt, "Health" and "Nondeath," respectively, in Iranian Zoroastrianism, patrons of the waters and edible plants.

During the Armenian festival, held until recent times, young women went up onto the mountain to cut Haurot and Maurot flowers (varieties of hyacinth?) in great secrecy. In the meantime, others, who were hiding from the first group, drew water from seven springs or rivers. In the evening, the flowers and the water were poured together into a basin called Hagvir. The liquor which resulted was a potion for happiness. This was probably a country version of an ancient ritual to obtain health and possibly immortality, of which the sacred books of Iran retain only the theological aspect and basis.

The Sun

The Armenians must have had a cult, if not of the sun itself, at least of a solar divinity. Xenophon reports that they adored the sun and sacrificed sacred horses to it. This was confirmed by the historian Moses of Khorene in the seventh century A.D.: the mythical king Valaršak erected statues representing the sun.

The solar cult continued for a long time, as is attested by the existence of a sun-worshiping sect whose members called themselves Arevordi: "sons of the sun." They transmitted orally a tradition taught by the magus Zradasht.

Besides sacrifices of sheep and calves, Armenian rites included prostrations regulated by the course of the sun. Twice a year, men and women gathered in a dark pit to celebrate the cult there. They also held sacred, and used in their rituals, certain plants that "turned toward the sun": the aspen, the lily, cotton, salsify, chamomile, and chicory. There is a little poem about this: "Salsify, chamomile, chicory, amenable to the cult of the Arevordi, grow in separate bunches, following the sun's course each day."

II. Armenian Legends and Myths

Ara the Beautiful and the Licking Dogs

Aray (or Ara), a king in mythical times, was famous for his great beauty. News of it reached all the way to Semiramis, the queen of Babylon. She fell in love with him without ever seeing him, simply on hearsay. She sent him extravagant presents, asking him to join her in Assyria. But the Armenian king, faithful to the wife he loved passionately, refused her request, sending back the messengers with her gifts. In a rage, Semiramis assembled an army and invaded Armenia. A great battle ensued, and the Armenians were conquered and their king killed in combat.

Semiramis had his body carried to her palace in Babylon and exposed it high on a terrace. She then ordered the "licking gods" of her country to come to lick the wounds of the dead king to bring him back to life. In vain; the body began to decompose, and Semiramis had it secretly buried in an underground vault. She then commanded one of her favorites to put on the clothes and ornaments of the king and passed him off as Aray, brought back to life by the licking gods, and she kept him near her hidden from all eyes.

This legend doubtless contains the memory of an old myth. It evokes a scenario familiar to the historian: that of the dying and resurrected god, famous examples of which can be found in many Eastern religions: Atis, Osiris, and many others. From this it has been concluded, too hastily, that the legendary king Aray was an ancient god whose cult and mythology conformed earlier to this famous pattern. The story has also been interpreted as a local variation of the myth of Er the Armenian, which Plato records in a famous passage of the *Republic*. All of this is possible, but not demonstrable.

On the other hand, it is certain that the licking gods invoked by Semiramis corresponded to specific Armenian beliefs whose antiquity is attested by certain allusions of the apologist Eznik, who wrote in the middle of the fifth century. These supernatural beings were celestial dogs, who came to lick the wounds of warriors fallen in combat, healing them in this way. They were called Aralēz or Arlēz, a name which can be interpreted as the simple juxtaposition of two imperatives: "Take! Lick!" The Arlēz would thus be the "Take-licks." The ancient historian Faust of Byzantium tells how, after the death of Mamikomian, the commander-in-chief, the Aralēz were called upon in vain to resuscitate him:

> When his body was brought home to his family, they could not accept his death, even though his head had been separated from his body. In hope of reviving him, they tried to sew his head to his trunk. They said: He was a valiant man, and so the Arlēz will descend and bring him back to life. Thus they waited, hoping for his resurrection. But his body began to decompose. Then they brought it down from the tower, mourned it, and buried it according to custom. (5.36)

These two legends, at least in their last part, follow the same scenario: the corpse is carried to a terrace or tower where the licking gods can come to perform their services. The body decomposes and is buried. This conformity suggests a possible ritual memory.

The belief in canine gods licking the wounds of warriors is not limited to the Caucasus. It is also found among the Abkhaz, applied to the Alyshk'yntyr, who are supernatural dogs in the service of the god Ajtyr; one legend says that they licked the wounds of a hero for three days and three nights, finally bringing him back to life.

Mher Entombed

The legend of Mher, collected at the beginning of the twentieth century, is certainly connected with the highly productive cycle of the chained Caucasian giants, such as Amirani in Georgia, Abrskil among the Abkhaz, and Artawazd in Armenia.

The daughter of a king, rebelling against a marriage she does not want, runs away to the mountain to die. She enters a sort of cavern and there drinks of the water that flows from the vault above her. Then she leaves, but she becomes pregnant from having absorbed the mysterious water. She gives birth to a son who, from earliest childhood, is able to perform the feats of a man and champion. His name is revealed to him by an invisible voice: "You are Mher!" He pursues the career of a legendary warrior. According to several variants, one day he meets an aged horseman accompanied by a young girl. Mher challenges him, fights him, and brings him down. But the unknown warrior is none other than his father. He curses him for eternity; from that time on, Mher is unable to die; shut away in a cave, he will remain until the day of the Last Judgment and will then come out to destroy the world.

According to other variants, the great Mher is accompanied and assisted by two "other selves," Davit and the "little Mher." During a hunt, little Mher wounds a crow with his arrow, and on horseback chases it deep into a cave. But the cave closes up forever behind the horseman and his mount.

Not far from Van, there is a steep rock wall, called "Mher's Door." Black water seeps from it: this is the urine of Mher's horse. Behind the wall, the wheel of fortune turns continually, and Mher, who is entombed there, watches it night and day. When the wheel stops, Mher will be freed and will come out to destroy the world. On the night of the Ascension, Mher's Door opens and closes quickly. Inside, piles of gold can be seen; men have tried to take some of it, but in their greed, they forgot the time limit and are now entombed with Mher.

Artawazd Chained

The theme of the hero chained in a hollow on the mountain has been familiar in the Caucasus at least since the fifth century A.D., as is attested by two Armenian witnesses. One is the seventh-century historian Moses of Khorene, who reports this legend from Armenia's heroic age:

When the mythical king Artashēs died, he was buried on a golden bier, draped with a cloak of gold. An immense treasure was buried with him. All his wives followed him to the grave, as well as huge crowds of his subjects, who immolated themselves spontaneously or were sacrificed in obedience to orders. This excessive holocaust incensed his son, King Artawazd, who was outraged at having to rule a country that was like a desert; he reproached his dead father in the following way: "Now that you are gone, taking the entire country with you, how can I rule over these ruins?" From the world beyond, the dead king grew angry and cursed his son in these terms: "On horseback you will go and hunt on the Azat, at the top of the Masis; the Kadzh (demons) will seize you and carry you to the summit of the Masis; there you will stay and never again see the light."

"The ancients tell us," continued Moses, "that he was shackled in a grotto and bound with iron chains; that two dogs licked his chains ceaselessly, and that he tried to escape to bring about the end of the world; but at the sound of the smiths' hammers upon their anvils, his chains, they say, were strengthened. This is why even today many smiths, conforming to the legend, strike their anvils three or four times on Sunday in order to reinforce the chains of Artawazd" (Moses of Khorene, *History of Armenia*, 2.61).

The other testimony, even older, comes from the lively pen of the Armenian bishop Eznik, who wrote in the middle of the fifth century. The text is very brief, but suffices to prove that the legend and its hero were already the object of beliefs deeply rooted in Armenia, since the Christian apologist took the trouble to argue against them:

> The demons' art of seduction tricked the worshipers of false gods amongst the Armenians, making them believe that a certain Artawazd, shackled by demons, still lives to this day and will come forth and take possession of this world. (Eznik, *De Deo*, 136)

G.C./d.b.

BIBLIOGRAPHY

M. ABEGHIAN, *Der armenische Volksglaube* (Leipzig 1899). AGAT' ANGEŁOS, (Agathange), *Patmut'iwn* (Venice 1930). L. AŁISAN, *Hin havatk' kam het' anosakan Kronk' Hayoc'* (Venice 1895). A. CARRIÉRE, *Les huit sanctuaires de l'Arménie païenne* (Paris 1899). G. DUMÉZIL, *Le Festin d'immortalité* (Paris 1924); *The Destiny of the Warrior* (Chicago 1970). N. O. EMIN, *Očerk religii i verovanij jazyčeskix armjan* (Moscow 1864). EZNIK DE KOŁB, *De Deo* ("*Contre les hérésies*"), L. Mariès, ed. (Paris 1959). F. FEYDIT, *David de Sassoun* (Paris 1964). J. KARST, *Mythologie arméno-caucasienne* (Strasbourg and Zurich 1948). V. LANGLOIS, *Collections des historiens anciens et modernes de l'Arménie*, 2 vols. (Paris 1867–69). G. ŁAP'ANC'YAN, *Ara gełic'iki pastamunk'* (YEREVAN 1944). MOVSÊS XORENAC'I (Moses of Khorene), *Patmut' iwn Hayoc'* (Venice 1955). I. A. ORBELI, *Armjanskij geroičeskij êpos* (Yerevan 1956). G. XALAT JANC, *Armjanskij êpos v Istorii Armenii* (Moscow 1896), vols. 1–2.

Index

Numbers in italic type indicate pages on which illustrations appear.